Recht und Verfassung in Afrika – Law and Constitution in Africa

Band/Volume 41

Oliver C. Ruppel | Harald Ginzky (eds.)

African Soil Protection Law

Mapping out options for a model legislation for improved sustainable soil management in Africa – a comparative legal analysis from Kenya, Cameroon and Zambia

Nomos

In cooperation of:

The underlying project and the publication were financed by the Deutsche Gesellschaft für internationale Zusammenarbeit (GIZ) on behalf of the German Federal Ministry for Economic Cooperation and Development (BMZ).

Disclaimer:
The contents of the chapters, including any errors or omissions are solely the responsibility of the authors. Opinions expressed by the different authors, do not necessarily reflect those of the editors. The editors did their best to acknowledge the usage of copyright protected material. In case any copyright violation should be detected, please contact the editors and any such error or omission will be rectified in a reprint or 2nd edition.

The Deutsche Nationalbibliothek lists this publication in the Deutsche Nationalbibliografie; detailed bibliographic data are available on the Internet at http://dnb.d-nb.de
ISBN 978-3-8487-6693-2 (Print)
978-3-7489-0804-3 (ePDF)

British Library Cataloguing-in-Publication Data
A catalogue record for this book is available from the British Library.
ISBN 978-3-8487-6693-2 (Print)
978-3-7489-0804-3 (ePDF)

Library of Congress Cataloging-in-Publication Data
Ruppel, Oliver C. / Ginzky, Harald
African Soil Protection Law
Mapping out options for a model legislation for
improved sustainable soil management in Africa –
a comparative legal analysis from Kenya, Cameroon and Zambia
Oliver C. Ruppel | Harald Ginzky (eds.)
528 pp.
Includes bibliographic references.
ISBN 978-3-8487-6693-2 (Print)
978-3-7489-0804-3 (ePDF)

1st Edition 2021

Published by
Nomos Verlagsgesellschaft mbH & Co. KG
Waldseestraße 3–5 | 76530 Baden-Baden
www.nomos.de

Production of the printed version:
Nomos Verlagsgesellschaft mbH & Co. KG
Waldseestraße 3–5 | 76530 Baden-Baden

ISBN 978-3-8487-6693-2 (Print)
ISBN 978-3-7489-0804-3 (ePDF)
DOI https://doi.org/10.5771/9783748908043

Onlineversion
Nomos eLibrary

Table of contents

Foreword

It is with great pleasure that I write the Foreword for this eminent publication. The protection and sustainable management of soils are preconditions for sustainable development, the fulfilment of the Sustainable Development Goals (SDGs), and ultimately the survival of humankind. Without sufficient tracts of fertile soils, there is no food security and no chance to mitigate climate change. Degraded soils result in hunger, famine, migration and, under certain circumstances, even wars.

SDG 15 stipulates that we protect, restore and promote sustainable use of terrestrial ecosystems, manage forests sustainably, combat desertification, stop and reverse land degradation and halt biodiversity loss. It is important to underline that land preservation, and thus the sustainable management of soils, is required to achieve most of the SDGs.

It is clear that the African people depend heavily on fertile soils to earn a livelihood for themselves and their children. Thus, it is the Pan-African Parliament as the representative of the African people – and particularly its newly established SDG Alliance – which has to play a vital role in protecting the soils of Africa more effectively in the interest of present and future generations.

Core instruments to achieve sustainable soil management are effective soil protection legislation and governance. The drafting of model legislation on sustainable soil management for Africa to serve as a blueprint – approved by the Pan-African Parliament – for all members of the African Union would be a significant step forward. Article 17 of the African Union Constitutive Act requires that the Pan-African Parliament enlist "the full participation of African peoples in the development and economic integration of the continent". Moreover, the Pan-African Parliament is invited to recommend model legislation to the members of the African Union in the interest of the people.

This publication presents the results of the project comprising three country studies on current soil protection legislation in Cameroon, Kenya and Zambia. The results have been analysed and condensed into general recommendations for more effective soil protection regulations and provide an instructive and instrumental baseline for the development of such model legislation in the near future.

On 10 October 2019, an important cooperation agreement was signed between the Pan-African Parliament, Stellenbosch University (through its Development and Rule of Law Programme), and the German Environment Agency (Umweltbundesamt). As signatory of this memorandum of understanding (MoU), Stellenbosch University entered the realm of academic diplomacy and policy development.

On behalf of the Pan-African Parliament, the MoU was signed by its President, the Rt Hon. Roger Nkodo Dang. On behalf of Stellenbosch University, the MoU was signed by Professor Eugene Cloete (Vice-Rector: Research, Innovation and Postgraduate Studies) and Professor Oliver Ruppel (Director: Development and Rule of Law Programme). Professor Ruppel and the Pan-African Parliament have already gone a long way in cooperating on the issue of climate justice for Africa. On behalf of the German Environment Agency (UBA), which is Germany's central federal authority for environmental matters under the supervision of the German Federal Ministry for the Environment, Nature Conservation and Nuclear Safety, the MoU was signed by (then) UBA President Maria Krautzberger. Dr Harald Ginzky from UBA was a strong proponent of the MoU between the three parties.

The main objective of the partnership is to implement the Sustainable Development Goals of the United Nations 2030 sustainability agenda effectively. As a first project, the partners teamed up on the issue of land degradation neutrality (SDG target 15.3) and sustainable soil management on the continent. The project was supported financially by the German Ministry for Development Cooperation, through the Deutsche Gesellschaft für Internationale Zusammenarbeit. Its aim was to develop model legislation for sustainable soil management in Africa.

On 6 March 2020, the Pan-African Parliament SDG Alliance discussed the results of the aforementioned project and pledged its support for the development of model legislation as a crucial instrument to achieve sustainability in the interest of the African people. The plenum of the Pan-African Parliament has endorsed this support.

The results are set out in this publication, taking into account, first, the practical knowledge of policymakers; second, in-depth insights of natural scientists of the African Soil Partnership and further African scientific institutions; and, third, the inputs of representatives of civil society organisations. This methodological approach has grounded the results in real life, while simultaneously gaining the consent of the relevant actors.

For the development of a specific 'model law', this kind of involvement of all still needs to be intensified, by first reaching out to all the regions of sub-Saharan Africa, to national and regional policymakers, to responsible people in the villages (local chiefs), to natural scientists and to civil society organisations. Broad awareness of the importance of sustainable soil management and comprehensive support for strengthened legislation and governance are the key ingredients which could render such model legislation effective and successful.

The SDG Alliance will be working with all the permanent committees of the Pan-African Parliament, as SDGs apply to all of them. On behalf of the SDG Alliance, I would like to thank our partners and congratulate the editors and authors of this publication, which will guide us on the way forward.

Jacquiline Amongin
Member of Parliament of the Republic of Uganda
Chairperson of the Parliamentary Forum on Water, Sanitation and Hygiene
Member of the African Union Pan-African Parliament
Chairperson of the Pan-African Parliament Alliance on SDGs

Kampala, Uganda, December 2020

Preface

One World – No Hunger: Sustainable soil management in and for Africa

Through the One World – No Hunger initiative, the German Government has committed itself to doing its utmost to eradicate hunger all over the world using a joint and collaborative approach. The initiative One World – No Hunger which was launched in 2014, and which has never been more pertinent, addresses its main objective, fighting hunger and malnutrition, by combining measures from the areas of food security, rural development and the promotion of agriculture. We need to acknowledge that degradation of soil and land is constantly accelerating. We are losing ground, every year a plot the size of Italy, when ground is so urgently needed to produce food, to fight climate change, to host biodiversity and to provide people with a living – and thus to avoid societal, political and, especially, military tensions.

The non-discriminating nature of the Covid-19 pandemic has left us with no doubt that we are all in the same boat; that we all live in the same world. Owing to our close economic interrelationships and interdependence, on one hand, and our high mobility, on the other hand, the virus has reached almost every corner of the world. Governments have been forced to shut down social life as well as economic activities. The effects have been dramatic all over the world, but the countries of the Global South are likely to be hit hardest. For the first time in years, the number of hungry people around the globe has increased over the last few months.

Africa, home of about 1.2 billion people, with its abundant nature, culture, history and arts, has been hit severely by the Covid-19 pandemic. The reasons are diverse and multifactorial. Insufficient financial resources, weak health and welfare systems, poverty throughout many societies, insufficient digitalisation, poor law enforcement, and political or military tensions are all contributing to a less positive outcome. However, it cannot be denied that external effects, such as reduced income due to diminished exports of raw material, flight of capital at levels never encountered before and illegal or illegitimate land acquisition have impaired the situation in many African countries.

Thus, African states are looking for ways and means to deal with the Covid-19 crisis, to improve living conditions in general, and to flatten its way to sustainability. Certainly, sustainable soil management is one way forward. "Soils are the bedrock of all ecological functions" is an expression adopted by project team members who are committing themselves to work in and for Africa. All of these ecological functions coalesce in the fertility of soils, which is a precondition for the eradication of poverty, the alleviation of hunger and malnutrition and the halting of climate change. Thus, the maintenance and enhancement of the fertility of soils are essential to prepare African societies for sustainability, to render living conditions acceptable for all and to provide a long-term perspective for the youth and future generations.

The project "Mapping out options for model legislation for sustainable soil management in Africa" has been innovative, encouraging and forward-looking. It is somewhat like a spark in the darkness of the pandemic crisis – mainly for the following four reasons. First, the project seems to be the first one to approach the issue of promoting sustainable soil management from a legal and governmental perspective. Thus, it focuses on one of the core steering tools of societal development, which often has been somewhat disregarded.

Secondly, the bottom-up approach has allowed for the convincing recommendations of the project. On one hand, the main drivers of the project have been the African experts who have written the country studies for Kenya, Cameroon and Zambia. On the other hand, the involvement of local stakeholders has certainly enriched the analysis and has rendered the legal recommendations realistic and up to date.

Thirdly, through close cooperation with the Pan-African Parliament, and in particular its Alliance for Sustainable Development, an effective link to the policy world has been established. Therefore, it could well be envisaged that the instructive recommendations will soon be placed on the political agenda in various African parliaments. In addition, it needs to be stressed that the Pan-African Parliament has committed itself to work towards a model law for sustainable soil management and aims – as a starting point – to present this model to all national parliaments. In this pursuit, the Pan-African Parliament has requested the project team to assist with the implementation of this objective.

Fourthly and finally, this project has demonstrated sufficient quality and experience to serve as a best practice example for other regions in the world. A workshop held in 2019 in New Delhi, India, where project team members presented initial findings, was just a first step towards a global exchange of views, approaches and concepts to improve regulatory instruments for sustainable soil management.

The results and in particular the recommendations of the project are now summarised in this book by the NOMOS Publishing House – which will fortunately be open access and therefore publicly available. We wholeheartedly thank the editors of the publication and partnering project leaders, Prof Dr Oliver Ruppel of the Development and Rule of Law Programme (DROP), Stellenbosch University, South Africa, and Dr Harald Ginzky, German Environment Agency (UBA), Germany. The idea of the project was actually born on African soil in Nairobi, Kenya, in 2018. After a joint workshop on African soil law, the partners decided to branch out further on the topic. Ever since, the project leaders have developed and managed this project with their reliable, enthusiastic and inspiring leadership, and we thank them for their groundbreaking efforts.

Furthermore, we would like to congratulate all the team members, and in particular the academic lead authors, Prof Dr Patricia Mbote, Kenya; Prof Dr Christopher F. Tamasang, Cameroon; and Dr Pamela Towela Sambo, Zambia, for their engagement and excellent contributions. The same applies to the expert advisors Mr James Yatich from the Kenyan Ministry of Agriculture, Livestock, Fisheries and Irrigation; Mr Laurent Effala from the Cameroonian Ministry of Environment, Nature Protection and Sustainable Development; and Mr Andrew Nkunika from the Zambian Ministry of Justice. Thanks also go to all the additional supporters –from the academic or administrative world – for making this project a success.

The "Mapping out options for model legislation for sustainable soil management in Africa" has been instrumental in getting a step closer to this objective, which is essential for human beings all over the world and in particular in Africa. We certainly look forward to a second project phase by the partners in supporting the Pan-African Parliament to develop a model law on sustainable soil management – drafted in close cooperation with African and European experts – expressing the core idea of the underlying initiative, One World – No Hunger.

Martin Jäger
State Secretary, Federal Ministry for Economic Cooperation and Development, Germany

Prof Dr Dirk Messner
President, Federal Environment Agency, Germany
December 2020

Acknowledgements

It was August 2018 when we, the Editors of this book, were sitting with Walter Engelberg of the Gesellschaft für Internationale Zusammenarbeit on the beautiful terrace of the Windsor Golf and Country Club Hotel in Nairobi, Kenya, having lunch during an international workshop. It was already the second day of the workshop titled *Implementing land degradation neutrality in Africa: Means, legal instruments and institutional challenges?* This lunch meeting sparked the underlying idea that eventually led to the project which spawned this publication.

With about 40 legal and governance experts, mostly from Africa, the Nairobi workshop was already the second of its kind. The first one took place in Kampala, Uganda, in 2017. Both workshops had been co-organised by the German Environment Agency (UBA) and the Climate Policy and Energy Security Programme for sub-Saharan Africa of the Konrad-Adenauer-Stiftung (KAS).

During our discussions, Walter Engelberg and we agreed – deeply affected as we were by our marvellous view over the subtle green plains of that land – that it was time to take the next step and initiate a project to analyse the existing legislation on soil protection in Africa, to synthetise it and to come up with options for a model law on sustainable soil management.

More than two years later, we can now present the result of this second step with the publication of this book. The project *Mapping out options for model legislation for sustainable soil management in Africa* – which was funded by the GIZ on behalf of the German Federal Ministry of Economic Cooperation and Development (BMZ) – kicked off at the end of 2018 and was concluded in April 2020. This period constituted a fruitful learning experience for the two of us, enriching our perspective on soil in the wider African context, for which we are most grateful. We were enlightened about existing legislation, knowledge of processes and actors, implementation issues, and cultural and societal backgrounds and variations. It was also a period of making new friends and of meeting many experts and committed people. All in all, we worked in, with and for Africa.

A project such as this one, with a multi-authored publication as outcome is an enormous team effort. With many partners from different countries, our thanks go first and foremost to all the distinguished coordinating lead authors, Prof Dr Patricia Kameri-Mbote (Kenya); Prof Dr Christopher Funwie Tamasang (Cameroon); and Dr Pamela Towela Sambo (Zambia).

Moreover, we are very grateful to the project's expert advisors, Mr James Yatich, Director of the Department of Land Reclamation, Kenyan Ministry of Agriculture, Livestock, Fisheries and Irrigation; Mr Laurant Effala, Head of the Legal Unit,

Cameroonian Ministry of Environment, Nature Protection and Sustainable Development; and Mr Andrew Nkunika, Permanent Secretary of Legislative Drafting, Zambian Ministry of Justice.

All of the aforementioned persons were capably supported by the research team, consisting of Ms Irene Kamunge (Kenya); Mr Tassah Ivo Tawe (Cameroon); and Ms Nelly Zulu (Zambia).

We are indeed very appreciative to Prof Dr Dirk Messner, President of the German Environment Agency (UBA) for 'blessing our publication' with a Foreword together with Mr Martin Jäger, State Secretary of the Federal Ministry of Economic Cooperation and Development.

Our special thanks go to our funding project partners from Deutsche Gesellschaft für Internationale Zusammenarbeit (GIZ): Mr Walter Engelberg, Member of the Projects Steering Committee and Teamleader, Sector Project Soil Protection, Combating Desertification, and Sustainable Land Management; Ms Stefanie Preusser, Project Controller, Sector Project Soil Protection, Combating Desertification, and Sustainable Land Management; and Ms Juliane Wiesenhuetter, Teamleader (successor of Walter Engelberg), Sector Project Soil Protection, Combating Desertification, and Sustainable Land Management.

We are indeed grateful for the partnership with the Pan-African Parliament and humbled by the meaningful engagement with this esteemed body. Our sincere thanks go to all the members of the Pan-African Parliament Sustainable Development Goal Alliance and, of course, to H.E. Roger Nkodo Dang, President of the Pan-African Parliament; the Honourable Jacquiline Amongin, Member of the Pan-African Parliament and Chairperson of the Pan-African Parliament Alliance on SDGs; the Honourable Kone Dognan, Member of the Pan-African Parliament and Chairperson of the Committee on Agriculture; and Mr Galal Ari, Committee Clerk of the Pan-African Parliament. We look forward very much to the continued partnership between the Pan-African Parliament, DROP and UBA under the memorandum of understanding (MoU) between the three partners.

It is important to mention the constant and strong support for the project by the UBA leadership, namely the former President Maria Krautzberger; the current President Prof Dr Dirk Messner; as well as Dr Wolfgang Seidel, Head of the Presidential Division; Dr Lilian Busse, Head of Division II – Environmental Health and Protection of Ecosystems; Dr Christoph Schulte, Head of Department II 2 – Water and Soil; and Dr Jörg Rechenberg, Head of Section II 2.1 – General Aspects of Water and Soil. Special thanks further go to many colleagues who have contributed substantially, namely Ms Kirstin Marx; Ms Anne Klatt; and Mr Frank Glante.

For their continual support we thank the Stellenbosch University leadership and the Development and Rule of Law Programme (DROP) team involved with this project, namely: Prof Dr Eugene Cloete, Vice-Rector: Research, Innovation and Postgraduate Studies, Stellenbosch University; Prof Dr Gideon Wolfaardt, Professor and ERWAT

Chair: Department of Microbiology and Director: Stellenbosch University Water Institute, Faculty of Science, Stellenbosch University; Prof Dr Nicola Smit, Dean of the Faculty of Law, Stellenbosch University; Dr Katharina Ruppel-Schlichting, Project Coordinator, Development and Rule of Law Programme (DROP) and Research Fellow, Stellenbosch University Water Institute, Stellenbosch University; Ms Tania van der Merwe, Finance Manager, Development and Rule of Law Programme (DROP) and Stellenbosch University Water Institute, Faculty of Science, Stellenbosch University; and Ms Larissa-Jane Houston, Mr Georg Junger, and Ms Nicola Taljaard, all being Research Assistants at the Development and Rule of Law Programme (DROP), Stellenbosch University.

For various activities that were part of the underlying project, we need explicitly to thank Dr Francis Marthy Tetteh, President, Soil Science Society of Ghana, CSIR Soil Research Institute, Kumasi, Ghana; and Ms Audrey M. S-Darko, Sabon Sake LLC, Ghana, for the organisation of the workshop held in Ghana in February 2020. We thank Mr Alexander Müller, Managing Director, Töpfer, Müller, Gaßner GmbH, ThinkTank for Sustainability, Berlin, Germany, for the cooperation around the Global / African Soil Week in Nairobi, Kenya, in May 2019.

We also thank Ms Julie Streicher of Red Trumpet Language, Communication and Design Services, Johannesburg, South Africa, as well as NOMOS Law Publishers, Baden-Baden, Germany, and particularly Dr Peter Schmidt for his professional support and the distinguished Editors of the NOMOS Legal Publication Series Law and Constitution in Africa for accepting our manuscript for publication therein.

The Editors:
Prof Dr Oliver C. Ruppel, South Africa
Dr Harald Ginzky, Germany
January 2021

Lead authors

Dr Harald GINZKY
Legal Advisor, German Environment Agency, Germany; Editor in Chief, International Yearbook on Soil Law and Policy; and Senior Fellow, Development and Rule of Law Programme (DROP), Stellenbosch University, South Africa.

Prof Dr Patricia KAMERI-MBOTE
Professor of Law, former Dean, School of Law, University of Nairobi, Kenya; Chair: Association of Environmental Law Lecturers in African Universities (ASSELLAU).

Prof Dr Oliver C. RUPPEL
Professor of Law and Director, Development and Rule of Law Programme (DROP), Faculty of Law, Stellenbosch University, South Africa. Professor for Climate Law, Institute for Public Law and Political Science, University of Graz, Austria and Co-Director, Research Centre for Climate Law (ClimLaw: Graz). Professor Extraordinaire University of Central Africa (UCAC), Yaoundé, Cameroon; Strathmore Law School, Nairobi, Kenya; China-Africa Institute for Business and Law, Xiangtan University, China; and European Faculty of Law, Nova University, Slovenia. Founding Director, Climate Policy and Energy Security Programme for sub-Saharan Africa, Konrad-Adenauer-Stiftung, Germany; founding WTO Chair-holder, World Trade Organisation (WTO) and University of Namibia.

Dr Pamela Towela SAMBO
Law Lecturer; immediate past Head of Department, Private Law; past Assistant Dean (Undergraduate), School of Law, University of Zambia.

Prof Dr Christopher Funwie TAMASANG
Associate Professor and Vice-Dean in charge of Research and Cooperation, Faculty of Laws and Political Science, University of Yaoundé II, Cameroon; Coordinator of thee Masters of Laws programme in English; Former Sub-Director for Environmental Legislation in the Ministry of Environment, Protection of Nature and Sustainable Development, Cameroon; Member: IUCN Academy of Environmental Law; Member: World Commission on Environmental Law; Vice Chair: ASSELLAU in charge of the Central African Region.

Contributing authors

Mr Laurent Cyrille Aimé EFFALA
Head of Legal Unit, Ministry of Environment, Protection of Nature and Sustainable Development, Cameroon.

Ms Larissa HOUSTON
Project Assistant at Research Centre for Climate Law (ClimLaw: Graz). PhD Candidate at University of Graz, Austria. 2020 Research Assistant at the Development and Rule of Law Programme (DROP), Stellenbosch University, South Africa. She holds a BCom LLB degree from Rhodes University and an LLM degree from Stellenbosch University, both in South Africa.

Ms Irene KAMUNGE
Director Legal Services at the National Environment Management Authority, Kenya. She holds a Master of Law in Environment and Natural Resources, a Bachelor of Law of the University of Nairobi, and a Diploma in Law from Kenya School of Law and is an advocate of the High Court.

Dr Yvonne NANA AFUA
Senior Lecturer in Law, Gimpa Law School, Greenhill, Accra, Ghana. She holds a BA in Law and French from the University of Ghana, an LLM in the Law of International Trade from the University of Cape Town, and a PhD in International Environmental Law and the Law of International Trade from the University of Cape Town, South Africa.

Mr Andrew NKUNIKA
Permanent Secretary Legislative Drafting at the Ministry of Justice, Zambia.

Dr Katharina RUPPEL-SCHLICHTING
Attorney, international legal consultant, researcher and project manager. Senior Fellow at the Stellenbosch University Water Institute (SUWI), South Africa.

Mr Ivo T. TASSAH
Researcher at the Department of Economics and Environmental Sciences, Ministry of Scientific Research and Innovation, Cameroon.

Mr James Kipkerebulit YATICH
Director at the Department of Land Reclamation, Ministry of Agriculture, Livestock and Irrigation, Kenya.

Ms Nelly ZULU
Researcher at the School of Law, University of Zambia.

Executive summary

Harald Ginzky & Oliver C. Ruppel

1 The project

The project *Sustainable soil management in Africa – Mapping out options for model legislation* aimed to make proposals for improving legal provisions for sustainable soil management in Africa.

1.1 Preparatory work

The project was based on numerous preliminary studies by the DROP Institute (Development and Rule of Law Programme) at Stellenbosch University in South Africa and the German Federal Environment Agency (UBA). These included various workshops on soil protection governance in Africa and India, which UBA organised with local partners, of which two were the Konrad Adenauer Foundation[1] and Gesellschaft für Internationale Zusammenarbeit (GIZ). The workshops took place in Kampala, Uganda, in 2017;[2] Nairobi, Kenya, in 2018;[3] and New Delhi, India, in 2019.

Furthermore, UBA had already introduced the *International yearbook of soil law and policy 2015* (IYSLP).[4] So far, that is until mid-2020, three volumes of IYSLP have been published by Springer;[5] Volume 4 is forthcoming in March 2021 and Volume 5 is already in preparation. IYSLP has created a platform for discussions on soil protection issues at national, regional and international level. At the same time, networking with numerous experts worldwide has been made possible. In the run-up to the project discussed here, UBA also commissioned numerous research projects on legal issues relating to the implementation of the Sustainability Development Goal of land degradation neutrality, and another on updating of international soil protection governance.

---

1 For a summarising report of the workshop see https://bit.ly/3qZQUnT, accessed 28 January 2021.
2 See https://bit.ly/36ldijI, accessed 28 January 2021.
3 See https://bit.ly/36kAdf7, accessed 28 January 2021.
4 See https://www.umweltbundesamt.de/en/topics/international-yearbook-of-soil-law-policy, accessed 28 January 2021.
5 See https://www.springer.com/series/15378.

1.2 Project design

The project *Mapping out options for model legislation for sustainable soil management in Africa*, financed by the German Federal Ministry for Economic Cooperation and Development (BMZ) through GIZ, aimed at developing options for a model law for soil protection in Africa – which can and should then be taken up for further consideration by individual member states of the African Union, depending on their needs and taking into account the existing legal situation.

The project was carried out by the DROP Institute at Stellenbosch University, South Africa, from December 2018 to the end of April 2020 with the support of UBA. DROP and UBA successfully teamed up as project partners.

The project followed the approach that both the essential foundations and the political initiative should be contributed by African actors (bottom-up, integrated and inclusive). Firstly, African experts were therefore asked to prepare three country studies – in Cameroon, Kenya and Zambia (see the three chapters) on their respective applicable legislation, taking into account the main drivers of land degradation.

For each of these countries, a team of experts was formed, consisting of a lead author with an academic background, supported by a contributing author from the administration to ensure a practical view, and a research assistant for each of the teams. The lead authors were:

- Prof Dr Patricia Kameri-Mbote, Professor of Law; Former Dean, School of Law, University of Nairobi, Kenya.
- Dr Pamela Towela Sambo, Head of Department, Private Law; immediate past Assistant Dean (Undergraduate), School of Law, University of Zambia.
- Prof Dr Christopher Funwie Tamasang, Associate Professor; Vice-Dean in charge of Research and Cooperation, Faculty of Laws and Political Science, University of Yaoundé II, Cameroon.

On the basis of the results of the three country studies and taking into account findings from other scientific publications, including the *International yearbook of soil law and policy*, options were compiled for establishing an effective legal regime for sustainable soil management in Africa. The detailed set of options can be found in the chapter *Mapping out options for model legislation for sustainable soil management in Africa* by Patricia Kameri-Mbote, Christopher F. Tamasang, Pamela Sambo, Harald Ginzky and Oliver C. Ruppel in this volume.

1.3 Selection of project countries

The selection of the three project countries was based on the following criteria, among others: Geographical representation; different levels of economic development; several key drivers of soil degradation; anglo- and francophone official languages and legal tradition; available legal expertise; and project implementation (resources – project management).

1.4 Processing method

The project followed a bottom-up, interdisciplinary and participatory approach. The aim was that the findings and recommendations were mainly elaborated upon by African experts with different expertise, experience and perspectives, and with the wider participation of civil society. The main findings and recommendations were to be generated on the basis of scientific studies by African experts (country studies). The involvement of representatives from various national ministries also directly linked the project to political actors.

In the course of the project phase, the writing team met at four different locations across the continent: in March 2019 in Johannesburg, South Africa; in May 2019 in Nairobi, Kenya; in September 2019 in Lusaka, Zambia; and in February 2020 in Accra, Ghana. This meant that the majority of the sub-Saharan African regions of the Pan-African Parliament were represented – namely Southern, Eastern, Western and Central Africa. All these writing team meetings were held with representatives from academia, administration, business, politics, and civil society. Apart from the core writing exercise, the purpose of the events was to consultatively inform about the project, to raise awareness of the importance of soil protection, and to receive feedback on the results and proposals. The events were always well attended. The urgency of sustainable soil management was emphasised again and again. Many important and helpful practical tips came from the participants.

1.5 Cooperation with the Pan-African Parliament

The Pan-African Parliament, a politically influential African Union institution, has agreed to take on political ownership of the project to ensure that the project and its results are perceived and taken into account at the political level. In March 2019 the project was first presented to the newly established Pan-African Parliament Alliance on the Sustainable Development Goals. The Committee immediately expressed interest in the project and pledged its support.

Against the background that African national parliaments are playing an increasingly crucial role not only in domesticating Sustainable Development Goals (SDGs) in their respective countries, but also in ensuring that these goals are implemented in an inclusive, accountable, citizen-oriented and sustainable manner. Already in the pre-planning phase of the project, the Pan-African Parliament and some of its members discussed the specific roles and mandates of African parliaments in the

SDG process. One recommended course of action was to ensure harmonisation with the African Union (AU) Agenda 2063 to ensure optimal integration with the SDG indicators. African parliamentarians have a role to play here, in particular with regard to legislative tasks in the implementation of Agenda 2030 and to raise voters' awareness of this. They also play an important role in facilitating the mobilisation of resources; in setting and monitoring resource allocations to implement and achieve sustainable development goals; in aligning with national planning targets; and in domesticating SDGs by enacting and reviewing legislation to facilitate implementation at local, national, regional and continental levels.

With regard to the Pan-African Parliament's tasks and scope of action, a memorandum of understanding (MoU) was concluded on 9 October 2019 between the Pan-African Parliament, the DROP Institute and UBA. The cooperation anchored in the MoU refers to possible projects of future implementation of SDGs.[6]

The first project explicitly mentioned in the MoU was the ongoing project for the development of a model law on soil protection in Africa. From now on, the MoU allows for cooperation between the three partners the Pan-African Parliament, DROP and UBA on all issues relating to the implementation of Sustainable Development Goals in Africa.

The results and recommendations of the first project were presented to the Pan-African Parliament SDG Alliance on 6 March 2020. All members of the Alliance stressed the importance of sustainable land management in Africa and fully supported the project recommendations. The Pan-African Parliament SDG-Alliance recommended the consultative development of a concrete model law.[7]

In terms of its mandate, the Pan-African Parliament is entitled to draft model laws on all relevant issues and to recommend them to the national parliaments in the more than 50 African member states of the AU. With regard to soil, this could perhaps be achieved in one or more follow-up projects, where, among other things, model legislation on soil protection could be prepared in consultation, which could then be adopted by the Pan-African Parliament as model legislation, submitted to the national parliaments and recommended for implementation. The planned resolution of the Pan-African Parliament as a plenary body is still pending and has not yet been adopted owing to the corona pandemic.

6 See press release by Stellenbosch University at https://bit.ly/2Yms5Gr, accessed 28 January 2021.

7 Siehe Pressemitteilung des PAP, http://cosmoafrica.co.za/index.php/news-and-events/181-pap-maps-firststeps-for-model-legislation-on-sustainable-soil-management-in-africa.

2 Project results

In the following sections, the overall project results are presented, focusing on options to improve legislation on sustainable soil management.

2.1 Setting the scene

Africa is situated east of South America, south of Europe and west of the Oceania. The continent is flanked by the Atlantic Ocean on the west and the Indian Ocean on the east. The size of Africa is 30 million square kilometres, which makes it the world's second largest continent. The continent's population was estimated to be 1.2 billion in 2016. The major economic activity in Africa is agriculture and that is why soil protection is a pertinent issue on this continent. Other economic activities include mining, energy generation and investments. Africa has a range of climates, such as an equatorial climate, tropical climate, arid and semi-arid conditions and subtropical conditions in the highlands. The vegetation in Africa mirrors the climate but, generally, the continent is covered by vegetation.[8]

The economies of the more than 50 African states have developed differently. In some countries, industrialisation is already well established. But several conditions prevail in most, if not all, African states:

- Large portions of the population make their living from agriculture and the GDP of countries is largely based on agricultural activities. Most farmers practise on a small scale and are thus extremely vulnerable to external shocks due to climate or economic changes.
- National income often depends on the export of natural resources. The level of processing is usually low.
- Foreign investment in land, agriculture and extraction of natural resources is an important economic factor.
- African states often face a high or very high level of debt, which strongly hinders the ability to invigorate economic development by stimulus programmes.

The following factors constitute potential soil degradation drivers and present challenges to soil health: Agriculture; mining; industrialisation; urbanisation; weather and climate change; topographical constraints; poverty; poor law implementation and enforcement; and illegal or illegitimate foreign investment in land.

8 Detailed information is to be found in the three country studies in this publication.

2.2 Proposed options

The following solutions have been identified and proposed:

2.2.1 Framework legislation

Overarching provisions legally declaring soil as a critical natural resource and stressing its ecological functions would be beneficial for mainly three reasons: First, the costs of rehabilitation or restoration by far exceed the costs of sustainable management. Second, owing to the nexus of climate crisis, natural resources, poverty and development options, sustainable soil management is a required ingredient – along with, among others, avoidance of societal tensions and political and military conflicts, birth control, and fair trade – to achieve an improvement in the economic conditions in African countries and to achieve sustainable development. Third, as climate change is high on the international political agenda, considerable international funds are available for climate mitigation and adaptation projects.

Sustainable soil management and land degradation neutrality (LDN) implementation could be addressed by constitutional provisions or by an overarching framework of law. It seems to be reasonable to emphasise legally that soil is a natural resource which provides essential ecological functions which are linked to most relevant social and societal implications as outlined above. In particular, the link between sustainable soil management and climate change should be explicitly mentioned.

With regard to the control mechanism, the framing act should establish a permission regime for activities with severe risks for soils. The activities for which an *ex-ante* permission is required needs to be undoubtably determined in order to avoid any misunderstanding. In order to achieve LDN and to implement this objective, planning instruments to calculate the ongoing degradation and the envisaged restoration also need to be established. It would be beneficial if the framing legislation determines – at least roughly – the roles, competencies and responsibilities of the various governmental entities with regard to LDN management; the determination of environmental quality standards; the emission limit values and technical standards; the setting of regional standards which fit the regional specificities; and the permission regime.

Comprehensive and coherent soil policies are a further option to promote sustainable soil management in African countries. The advantage of soil policies is that they fill the gap between the legal norms and subsidiary standards and indicators. They could address how to get the 'soil engine' established and continuously running. Along with all these planning and prior control instruments, it is also reasonable to consider incentives for compliance. From a legal perspective, incentives could primarily be sanctions in all legal forms: fines, civil rights obligation to restore land/soil degradation, and even criminal sanctions such as penalties.

2.2.2 Climate change, land and soil

Climate change and soil/land management are interlinked. Sustainable soil management could be both a mitigation and adaptation measure. Climate change could cause significant negative effects on soils owing to, for example, higher temperatures or droughts. More research is required to understand the complex interconnections of land, soil, climate, water, society, sustainability and food, especially in Africa. In terms of technical and legal principles on adapting to climate change from the point of view of soil protection, the need for further action on how to implement climate protection in soil protection law becomes apparent.

The aims of climate-related soil protection should be introduced in accordance with other protected natural resources and political objectives, while the measures should be introduced into an assessment framework. In this light and also in support of the Nationally Determined Contributions (NDCs), a legal framework should be established to offer effective instruments in order to implement climate ambitions in Africa. Significant gaps in the NDCs and contained commitments need to be bridged and national governments might consider (re-)evaluating national, regional and transformative response options and policy instruments. More inclusive forms of socially just and more equitable governance processes and institutions should also be considered.

2.2.3 Agriculture

To improve legal provisions for sustainable soil management, agriculture needs to be addressed in respect of crop growing and livestock. Generally, it is to be recommended that national governments implement regulations on soil pollution and limit the accumulation of contaminants beyond established levels in order to guarantee human health and well-being, a healthy environment, and safe food. In addition, the lack of awareness about the significance of soil is an obstacle against achieving sustainable soil management (SSM). There is a need to increase awareness and understanding of the profound importance of soil for human life, and to educate the public about the crucial role soil plays in food security, climate change adaptation and mitigation, essential ecosystem services, poverty alleviation and sustainable development.

This can be effected through agricultural legislation addressing the following: The practices that may compromise and restore soil health and sustainability; standards on good practices, also regarding the impacts, monitoring, effectiveness and implementation; some of the unsustainable practices such as the use of chemical fertilizers and pesticides and 'slash and burn' are *strictu sensu* illegal in terms of already existing legislation in the three countries.

It is recommended that prohibitions on such unsustainable practices should be provided first. Secondly, there is a need to establish adequate mechanisms to ensure enforcement of such prohibitions: The Stockholm and Rotterdam Conventions on the control of pesticides and chemical fertilizers should be implemented in national provisions. Thereby, adequate standards for fertilizers and pesticides could be set. The inclusion of adequate sanctions in legal regulations such as fines or imprisonment is recommended. There is a need for qualitative and quantitative communication on what soil is, and how soil relates to sustainability, crop production and economic development, as well as other sciences. Lack of communication presents a limitation to the consideration of soil in the context of its role as an answer to sustainable economic development. Extension services are appropriate for these kinds of communications challenges. In addition, these services could cover physical soil health, agricultural practices and information dissemination. Information derived from soil research must be made available to the scientific community and to soil users, namely farmers, agronomists, foresters, civil engineers and society, thereby transferring and sharing knowledge with stakeholders, decision makers, land-use planners, politicians and others.

Traditional knowledge could be an important source for both setting adequate standards and to ensure the needed respect for cultural perceptions of land. Thus, there is a need to systematically collect and synthetise traditional knowledge in order to both preserve cultural heritage and to balance modern and traditional attitudes and approaches. The soil–science discourse must continue to expand beyond its traditional identification with agriculture as it becomes a partner in the earth, ecological and environmental sciences.[9] Adequate institutional settings are required for law implementation and enforcement. It is within this context that recommendations in the respective subsections should be considered. Among others, continuous monitoring is needed. Soil testing on a regular basis would be one option. As unsustainable practices are often the consequence of poverty and insecure living conditions, a system of soil stewardship payments or other economic incentives should be considered.

2.2.4 Livestock

The following is recommended: First, environmentally unsound practices should, at best, be prohibited. In this context, negative effects on forests and effects which may risk increased desertification should be taken into account. As far as possible, environmentally sound practices with regard to the protection of soils should be determined and approved as legally binding standards. Extension services need to be strengthened in order to better inform and consult with farmers concerning legal standards and acceptable practices. In order to also establish clear incentives, sanctions such as fines and imprisonment should be part of the whole regulatory concept. As provisions are

9 Usman & Kundiri (2016: 66).

senseless without implementation, an appropriate institutional setting is required. The science–policy interface is important in this context as well. Finally, as settlements, such as villages and cities, will sprawl over the next years, a zoning concept needs to be established and enforced in the context of spatial planning on a regional level and for town planning.

2.2.5 Industrial facilities

Industry is a potential further driver of soil degradation. The magnitude and the quality of the potentially negative effects depend on the level of industrialisation in a particular country and on the regulatory approach to deal with the effects.

In order to determine the potential options for good soil governance with regard to industrial facilities, it is helpful to arrive at conclusions on the major soil threats involved with industrial activities. Industrial facilities may primarily cause contamination via the emission of hazardous substances through air, water or other means. In addition, physical soil threats like land take, sealing and compaction may be caused by the establishment and operation of industrial facilities. The establishment of industrial facilities may also have detrimental effects on particularly valuable compartments of soils – taking into account the particular fertility of soils, the level of soil carbon and biodiversity – e.g., swamps.

It is recommended that a regulatory regime should first address soil degradation, in particular by contaminants, which has already been caused by existing facilities, and secondly avoid future negative effects by both existing and new facilities. In order to set clear requirements with regard to contamination, soil quality standards for the most crucial parameters such as lead, cadmium, mercury, benzopyrene and others, should be adopted.

In the case of contamination which has already occurred, the regulatory regime should require the restoration of the contaminated areas. Usually, the operator should be held responsible and should bear the costs of the rehabilitation measures, according to the 'polluter pays' principle. In addition, it seems to be reasonable to institute a soil restoration fund, to which all operators of industrial installations should contribute financially.

In order to avoid or at least reduce future soil contamination by industrial facilities, it is essential to establish a regulatory regime, whereby industrial facilities may not be established or operated without prior written authorisation. For the sake of clarity, it is recommended that the categories of industrial installations for which an authorisation is required should be listed in a subordinate legal instrument such as an ordinance.

Environmental impact assessments, including environmental impact studies, should be used as a baseline to decide whether an industrial activity is permitted or not. Furthermore, the operator should be committed to continually monitoring whether the requirements which are included in the authorisation are complied with. The monitoring should be at the expense of the operator.

Additionally, a regulatory instrument could be established which clearly sets economic incentives for the operators of new industrial installations to avoid negative effects on soils. In order to maintain soil functions, the operator could be required – before production starts – to examine and to document the status of soils beneath the industrial site in a so-called 'baseline report'. The baseline report should be one of the documents required for the application for a prior-written authorisation. Furthermore, it should be regulated that after the closure of the site, the operator has to rehabilitate the site to its original soil and groundwater status, if significant negative effects have been caused.

2.2.6 Mining

Mining has had a major impact on soil, water and biota since ancient times,[10] and documented examples from around the world abound of heavily contaminated soils associated with mining activities. The challenges with regard to the implementation of environmentally sound mining are diverse. First of all, mining activities by foreign investors certainly need to be treated differently from national enterprises and small-scale mining. With regard to mining operations by foreign investors, the recommendations concerning tenure rights and control by foreign investors have to be considered and applied. More generally, some further recommendations could be made. All recommendations which have been submitted with regard to industrial installations are equally valid for mining operations, for example: Restoration obligation for soil contamination which has already occurred; the equirement of a written prior authorisation based on an environmental impact assessment and the involvement of the public; and the establishment of an effective monitoring system.

A specific challenge is the regulation and control of small-scale mining. It is hardly possible to allocate sufficient resources so that an effective enforcement of 'good provisions' is doable and whereby such small-scale mining can be controlled. Three measures seem to be more promising: First, security of land tenure could work to avoid wild and uncontrolled mining as people have a clear concept of their possession and would hinder negative effects on their property. Second, awareness raising may cause people to look for other opportunities to make their living. Third, if the carrot does not provide sufficient incentive, the stick might work. In other words, severe penalties in cases of law infringements around mining operations may create a public perception that illegal small-scale mining is risky and unattractive owing to potential penalties.

10 FAO & ITPS (2015).

2.2.7 Infrastructure

It is recommended that the measures suggested to control foreign investors need to be implemented in the context of infrastructure construction. The recommendations with respect to industrial installation also apply for a better protection of soils on construction of infrastructure. The effective protection of soil quality needs to be a crucial criterion, either through an environmental impact assessment or as one of legal requirements of a permission procedure.

Along with these governance-related recommendations, it seems to be advisable that African governments consider investing in other forms of transport such as railways to reduce CO_2 emissions and negative effects on soils. Finally, increased internet connectivity is important, among others, to develop a basis for gathering, synthetising and publishing data on soil quality and status. This will assist in increasing awareness.

2.2.8 Urbanisation

Africa is an exceptionally biodiverse continent, but it is urbanising rapidly, to the detriment of its natural resources. The continent has "seven megacities, that is cities with populations over 10 million: Cairo, Kinshasa, Lagos, Accra, Johannesburg–Pretoria, Khartoum and Nairobi. In 15 years, Luanda and Dar es Salaam will be added to this list."[11] Although urbanisation is a necessary condition for modernisation, there is an increasing need to account for its direct and indirect impacts on the continent. With soil being the lifeline of biological diversity and ecosystem services, it is clear that there is an urgent need for sustainable urbanisation in Africa.

In order to manage the effects of urbanisation processes in African states, a routine, well-coordinated town-mapping process needs to be put in place. In order to come up with effective town planning, the required information on natural resources (soil) and human population needs to be available and to be taken into account.

Legal instruments such as mandatory town planning can only be effective if such planning is applied reasonably with a long-term development perspective – where sufficient information can become available to support decisions and where town planning is accepted as motivation for the subsequent authorisation of buildings and infrastructure. In addition, it should be obligatory to base town planning decisions on environmental impact assessments, which necessarily include soil quality. In order to achieve sustainable soil management, enhanced digital soil mapping tools could provide a cost-effective means of determining soil geographical distributions.

11 Güneralp et al. (2017).

2.2.9 Clarity of land tenure

Land tenure types and policies strongly influence land-use practices and hence affect the quality of soils in Africa. Land tenure in Africa – both statutory and customary – is characterised by insecurity, constituting a potential underlying driver of soil degradation in general, and specifically in Cameroon, Kenya and Zambia. There is a variety of land tenure types, giving rise to conflict and unsustainable land and soil management in these countries – which may arguably be a reflection of what occurs on the entire continent. There is, for instance, ample evidence where customary rules prescribe acceptable claims to lands among members of communities, but such claims are contradicted or nullified by national legislation. Communally 'owned' lands, in particular, in Cameroon and Zambia are insecure. Consequently, such lands are easily converted into national lands for development purposes. This conflict between the land tenure systems, both statutory and customary, leads to rising land tenure conflicts.

One reason for the insecurity of owned land is the high economic value presently placed on land and its appurtenant resources. This has invariably increased the tendency of the most powerful to engage in land-grabbing and dispossession in Africa. This is to the detriment of the vulnerable groups that are increasingly being displaced from their lands, which leads to heated disputes and conflicts. In fact, customary land tenure systems offer weak security, and the modern land law provides huge opportunities for land-grabbing.

In addition, all three countries have weak governments and a problem with corruption. Soil management systems in all three countries are linked to corruption, which contributes to the inefficiency of the law. Furthermore, the various pieces of land legislation in Cameroon and Zambia are completely void of soil protection provisions. That means, in particular, that the land tenure systems of Cameroon and Zambia are silent regarding the question of the environmental landowners' and users' responsibilities.

With the exception of Kenya, one does not find a strong anchor point for soil protection when perusing the countries' legislation on land tenure. None of the scattered pieces of legislation in Cameroon and Zambia make any direct or implicit reference to the need to protect soils. Also, despite Kenya's rich land law that lends support to sustainable soil management and protection, the various statutes have not been effective in the management of land and, by extension, have not enhanced the protection of soil in Kenya.

The main challenges of planning, corruption, political patronage, weak institutions and institutional conflicts have been disregarded. It is these shortcomings that have prompted the following recommendations: The multiplicity of legal instruments and requirements on access to land should be reduced by means of harmonisation and consolidation of the fragmented and dispersed pieces of legislation on land tenure be formed into a single and comprehensive and overarching land act. New legislation in some countries should recognise customary laws relating to land tenure or at least should ensure that procedures for access to land are comprehensible and accessible to all social groups. Preferably, land acts that harmonise and consolidate the segregated and scattered pieces of legislation on land tenure should be enacted in these countries and place customary and statutory land tenure on an equal footing in terms of their status. Alternatively, such land acts should recognise and accord customary land rights legal protection and consider such rights as a category of private property existing alongside national lands and state-owned lands. This may be accommodated within ongoing land tenure reform processes.

The responsibility to protect the environment, especially soils in the harmonised and consolidated legislation on land tenure, should be specifically mainstreamed. Appropriate and clear vertical as well as horizontal institutional arrangements should be crafted that make for a win-win situation in order to curb or completely put an end to institutional conflicts, as these are negative precursors to sustainable soil management initiatives. Measures to fight corruption and enhance institutional capacity in land administration matters should be put in place.

2.2.10 Control of foreign investors

Foreign investors constitute one of the main groups of actors responsible for soil degradation in many African countries such as Cameroon, Kenya and Zambia, necessitating their effective control. The increased role of foreign investors across many economic activities in these countries can possibly lead to spiral effects of land and soil degradation. Their role as main actors of soil degradation in these countries is much felt in the mining and agricultural sectors. Therefore, foreign investors constitute some of the actors to be considered in the process of developing model legislation for soil protection in these countries and the whole of Africa. The role of foreign investors in the mining sector is significant.

Improving the legal control of foreign investors is critical to guarantee the effective protection of soils. Such control is crucial in order to ensure that land-use investments are sustainable and that the laws of the countries are being observed. This can be done through the following measures:

Laws should be enacted that impose environmental degradation taxation, such for pollution or soil contamination, to be paid by all (foreign and domestic) investors who partake in activities that constitute a potential threat to the quality of soil. Certification schemes for commodities production susceptible to cause soil degradation should be legalised. Land reforms should be promoted that limit the amount of land that can be acquired by foreign investors or that specify sizes of land depending on the activity to be carried out.

Commitment of foreign investors to corporate, social and environmental responsibility or business/corporate citizenship should be fostered so as to avoid social conflicts with communities. This is a self-regulating paradigm that can help foreign corporate investors to be socially accountable to the public and thereby avoid activities that are likely to degrade the soils on which the public depends. Corporate social responsibility (CSR) should result in foreign investors increasingly respecting the environment and promoting sustainable development practices. In the era of globalisation, different approaches to this practice will also allow more effective protection of soils. In this light, CSR must go beyond legal obligations, but at the same time cannot be reduced to the expression of charitable compassion. It must penetrate all foreign investment practices in Africa, placing the peculiarities of the continent in relation to the benefit of any undertaking.[12]

Mobilising investment for sustainable development in Africa requires political commitment to overcome substantial barriers at various levels. To enable new markets for sustainable development requires adequate regulatory frameworks (international, regional and national) in order to give investors, the necessary confidence. The national state has to balance the interest of attracting (and securing) international investment while promoting peace and security for its population. The most appropriate approach for achieving both of the aforementioned is adherence to and promotion of the rule of law, while creating incentive structures for investors to act sustainably and to respect national social development goals, empowerment policies, labour standards and human rights.[13]

3 Institutional arrangements

The focus of the following section is on the implementation, the control, the monitoring and the enforcement of the substantial provisions. Good governance depends on both good regulation and effective implementation. In other words, without effective implementation the law in itself is useless, or – to put it more straightforwardly, it is not worth the paper it is written on. Insufficient or even lack of law enforcement is often a core issue in developing countries, in particular in counties of sub-Saharan Africa.[14] Thus the following section is of tremendous importance.

In order to be effective, several management tasks have to be implemented by the governmental bodies (or private institutions have to be managed by the governmental bodies in order to fulfil the specific tasks). An appropriate arrangement of institutional

12 Ruppel & Tchuente (2018: 13).

13 Ruppel & Shifotoka (2017: 56).

14 Cf. for example: Kameri-Mbote et al. (2019); Ruppel & Kam Yogo (2018); Ruppel & Dix (2017); Ruppel et al. (2017); Ruppel & Ruppel-Schlichting (2016).

roles and competencies requires that these tasks are clearly and undisputedly attributed to specific entities. First of all, information on soil conditions and soil quality, on ongoing activities which might affect soils and on technological options need to be gathered and disseminated among at least the competent authorities. Secondly, the management task involves standard setting: again, this is a complex, demanding and time- and resource-intensive task. Standards are important as they enable competent authorities to implement the, quite vague, legal provisions (for example: protection of soils). Standards should in particular be established for soil quality with regard to soil health as well as to physical parameters (e.g., for soil carbon, biodiversity, organic matter). These quality standards are particularly important as they define what level of interference is tolerable. Thirdly, soil authorities need to be involved in prior permission regimes for activities which might have negative effects on soils such as industrial installations, the use of pesticides, and the construction of roads, highways and railways. Moreover, monitoring of soils is an additional task. Finally, competent authorities need to control the compliance with substantial provisions for operators, in particular, and citizens, in general, to enforce compliance. Chiefs of local communities usually hold quite a strong position in African countries. It would be beneficial if their roles, responsibilities and oversight were clearly regulated and would dovetail with the existing arrangements of other governmental powers.

Sustainable soil management must be achieved taking into account the local specificities. From this perspective, it seems to be reasonable to strengthen the decentralised entities, at least at the level of regions and, to a certain extent, at the level of municipalities or local communities.

To re-arrange institutional processes and to clearly define the competencies and roles of the various entities – and further to decide which entities are superior and have a control function over others – all in all makes up a highly disputable process, as such clarity also means that responsibility may not be allocated to certain aspects with the consequent loss of power over them.

Advantages and benefits form the political buy-in which is needed to be successful. The potential advantages and benefits can be highlighted as follows: Clarity concerning the procedures should foster trust in the process. People tend to regard a decision as legitimate if it is taken on the basis of already established procedure; and clarity concerning the procedures enables good governance. If the procedure is clearly and appropriately defined, it seems likely that the decisions have been taken on a reasonable basis as the required information and expertise have been considered. Clarity concerning the procedures allows for accountability, reliability and transparency – all of which are ingredients of a modern and well-established civil society. The reputation of states could be increased – even at international level. Clarity would establish a level playing field for all – including foreign investors. Thereby, a positive regulatory environment for fair and responsible investors should be formed, in order to expel detrimental foreign investments.

Workable arrangements for institutions and procedures would ensure that the respective states would probably be in a better position to deal with future challenges, such as the effects of climate crisis or poverty and hunger. The detailed determination of the specific roles, competencies and responsibilities of the various governmental entities is important to enable the implementation of the substantial provisions effectively. It needs to be stressed that the determination of the specific roles, competencies and responsibilities is a demanding issue. It needs to be legally stipulated which ministry is responsible for which driver and for which task.

A further point to be considered is whether and to what extent competencies and responsibilities should be attributed to decentralised governmental entities. In general, decentralised competencies seem to be more effective as the regional specificities can be better assessed and taken into account by a competent authority which is familiar with the regional conditions. Local chiefs hold a strong position in most African countries with regard to the living conditions in the local communities. Cases have been reported where local chiefs have misused their powers to either neglect the requirements of environmental protection or to make short-term and unjustified earnings – sometimes to the disadvantage of the local communities which they represent. First, it seems to be reasonable that local chiefs receive more support and advice from soil scientists. Second, local chiefs must be seen as part of the whole soil-related administrative structure. Third, decisions by local chiefs must be taken via a transparent and inclusive procedure. Fourth, similar procedural rights of citizens and the general public should apply with regard to decisions by local chiefs, such as in respect to access to justice.

Water is an issue in most African countries. Thus, in most, if not all, African countries there are water ministries and a complex administrative setting of competent authorities. A simple and perhaps promising approach might be to add the responsibility for sustainable soil management to the water-related entities.

The aforementioned recommendation must be adapted on a case-by-case basis, owing to differing national preconditions. There is no single blueprint which fits all systems. However, they are options which should be considered seriously.

4 Procedures and procedural rights

Effective procedures which allow for a thorough assessment of all relevant aspects before taking decisions and procedural rights of concerned citizens are generally regarded as essential in order to achieve good protection performance. Procedural requirements and procedural rights can only be effective if implemented in practice – a challenge which is addressed in the following subsection. In the following subsection four aspects are discussed: environmental impact assessment, access to information, public participation and access to justice.

It needs to be stated, that the four instruments should be part of the legal system in order to ensure that environmental effects are assessed systematically and comprehensively and that citizens have the opportunity to access information, to participate in permission procedure on activities which are of concern to them, and to have access to justice. Moreover, it must be ensured that these instruments are effectively implemented. These are some of the proposals that may help to reduce the challenges that affect procedural rights: Environmental Impact Assessments (EIAs), access to information, public participation and access to justice. The recommendations that pertain to the strengthening of these rights and in particular to ensure effective soil protection include:

Environmental impact assessmentss should be mandatory by law for all activities which might have significant effects on soils; access to information on soil quality needs to be guaranteed; legislation should be enacted that defines the scope and structure of public participation in soil protection decision-making; resources should be invested in infrastructure that supports access to justice and other procedural rights in matters pertaining to soil protection; specialised courts on environment and land seem to be one option to strengthen the expertise of judges on soil and land topics both from a scientific and a legal point of view; programmes should be developed to raise awareness among the population of their right of access to courts, their right to public participation, and their right of access to information and any initiatives that can facilitate the protection of soil; marginalised people, indigenous groups, minorities, women, youth and people with disabilities should be particularly educated and encouraged in the attainment of procedural rights such as EIAs, access to information, public participation and access to justice

Moreover, the ministries of justice could be obliged to monitor the implementation of the procedural rights and to provide reports with regard to this implementation on a regular basis. A further option would be legislation that consolidates and harmonises soil rights in the African legal systems. This would create uniformity and cooperation in the advancement of soil protection in Africa. The African Union could play a specific role in this regard.

5 The role of science

Soil science can raise awareness about organic matter as a key attribute of soils and to illustrate its importance for soil functions and ecosystem services. Soil science can improve the transfer of knowledge about soils; contribute to educational programmes; facilitate communication with policymakers by framing research in terms that resonate with politicians on issues like the policy cycle or by considering drivers, pressures and responses affecting land-use change; and help to reach the United Nations Sustainable Development Goals (SDGs) in the most effective manner.[15]

The science and society interface is key in shaping effective laws and policies. Science must also inform the discourse on soil protection in Africa, which in turn must inspire new laws, policies and procedures that can deal with the state of crisis and elucidate a system that ensures that we 'leave no one behind' in the transformation towards more soil sustainability, resilience, equity, and justice. In this light, science can help to develop indicators and standards that can guide us towards more sustainable practices. LDN interventions must be informed by science–policy interaction as a basis for responsible land governance and soil management. Effective cooperation between scientific institutions can contribute to an advancement of understanding and commitments through greater scientific engagement with stakeholders.

While universities form actors and institutions for academic and scientific diplomacy, the African Academy of Sciences and its various country chapters, the Council for Scientific and Industrial Research in South Africa, the Ghana Soil Information Service, the Cameroonian National Observatory for Climate Change and the Global Alliance of Universities on Climate are examples of such emerging cooperative networks which can inform and promote research, policy development and implementation, technological innovation and entrepreneurship, creation of jobs and relevant knowledge and skills, and development of education and exchange programmes. Ultimately, the independence of scientists from governmental influence and political agendas must be preserved, so as to avoid the perception that they are working towards preconceived political goals or agendas. Responsible decision-making processes also need to integrate traditional knowledge systems and citizen science.

6 Global, continental and regional cooperation

Knowledge systems and infrastructure, citizen engagement and international cooperation gain increasing importance in the protection of ecosystems, mitigating natural disasters, halting biodiversity loss caused by changes in land use, direct exploitation of natural resources, and also climate change. In this light, a green transition and energy access can foster partnerships within Africa and contribute to building a low-carbon, climate resilient future, while fostering sustainable development.

While improving soil law and governance under the structures of the AU and regional economic communities (RECs), new legislative frameworks need to be developed to strengthen national strategies and policies and fill existing gaps in terms of implementation, among other things. For this matter, channels for finance and other support are needed to enhance the capacity on the ground. Improving African soil

15 Keesstra et al. (2016).

governance must also address options for enhancing coordination and coherence between the national policymakers, RECs, parliamentary forums and the AU structures at large.

The African Continental Free Trade Area (AfCFTA) agreement will create the largest free trade area in the world, measured by the number of countries participating. The pact will connect 1.3 billion people across 55 countries with a combined gross domestic product (GDP) valued at US$3.4 trillion. It has the potential to lift 30 million people out of extreme poverty but achieving its full potential will depend on putting in place significant policy reforms and trade facilitation measures.[16]

Enabling free trade goes hand-in-hand with actions at both the supranational and national levels. Potential negative externalities of trade on soils should not be neglected. Moreover, regional communities can provide framework potential for reform, for example, by bringing together regulators to define harmonised standards or to agree on mutual protection interests. In this light, the African Union and particularly its Pan-African Parliament and its members can play a role in ensuring harmonisation with Agenda 2063 "through integration" of the SDG indicators.[17]

In the United Nations Framework Convention on Climate Change (UNFCCC) process, input by the African Group of Negotiators should strengthen the views on soil protection, also using the findings of this project. With a view to fulfilling obligations related to the Paris Agreement, NDC cooperation opportunities may contribute to fostering long-term climate action and mobilising means for implementation – finance, capacity-building, and technology development and transfer on the continent. While all 54 countries have signed the Paris Agreement and submitted NDCs, many have also ratified them. However, in numerous instances, NDCs were drafted hastily, not fully taking all related interests into consideration.

Lastly, for African and existing REC courts to contribute successfully to dispute settlement (which could also become relevant in the context of soil protection and management), there lies great opportunity and potential for the future. Until now, however, frequent failures often prevented the attainment thereof.[18]

7 The way forward

In terms of a way forward, the task of a follow-up project could be to develop model legislation on sustainable soil management in Africa, to be adopted by the Pan-African Parliament and sent as a proposal to all national parliaments of the African Union.

16 World Bank (2020).

17 Also see chapter on the Pan-African Parliament of the African Union: Composition, mandate, partnerships and its quest for sustainable development in this volume.

18 Cf. Ruppel (2012).

Such a follow-up project should, among other things, comprise the following work packages: Elaboration of concrete proposals for legislative and sub-legislative changes in legislation on sustainable soil management in selected African countries representing all the regions of sub-Saharan Africa. Systematisation of the results in order to be able to develop different model legal modules (according to the principle of 'mapping out options') for Africa. Extensive consultations and adoption of the model law by the Pan-African Parliament would take into account the procedural requirements of the Pan-African Parliament and the African Union. A bottom-up approach would here again be necessary. The elaboration of the results should essentially be carried out by African experts with the involvement of stakeholders, representatives of governments, scientists and local traditional leaders. The follow-up project could make a substantial contribution to improved soil protection in Africa. The Pan-African Parliament SDG-Alliance has already called on the two project partners (DROP and UBA) of the initial project to work on this in a follow-up project.

References

FAO / Food and Agriculture Organization & ITPS / Intergovernmental Technical Panel on Soils, 2015, *Main report: Food and Agriculture Organization of the United Nations and Intergovernmental Technical Panel on Soils, Status of the World's Soil Resources (SWSR)*, at http://www.fao.org/3/a-bc590e.pdf, accessed 14 September 2020.

Güneralp, B., S. Lwasa, H. Masundire, S. Parnell & K.C. Seto, 2017, "Urbanisation in Africa: Challenges and opportunities for conservation". *Environmental Research Letters* 13 (1), 1.

Kameri-Mbote, P., A. Paterson, O.C. Ruppel, B.B. Orubebe & E.D. Kam Yogo (eds), 2019, *Law | Environment | Africa*. Law and Constitution in Africa, No. 38, Baden-Baden: Nomos.

Keesstra, S.D., J. Bouma, J. Wallinga, P. Tittonell, P. Smith, A. Cerdà, L. Montanarella, J.N. Quinton, Y. Pachepsky, W.H. van der Putten, R.D. Bardgett, S. Moolenaar, G. Mol, B. Jansen & L.O. Fresco, 2016, "The significance of soils and soil science towards realization of the United Nations Sustainable Development Goals". *Soil Journal* 2 (2), 111.

Ruppel, O.C., 2012, "SADC land issues before the SADC Tribunal – A case for human rights?". In: Chigara, B. (ed.), 2012, *Southern Africa Development Community land issues. A new, sustainable land relations policy*. London: Routledge, 89.

Ruppel, O.C. & H. Dix (eds), 2017, *Roadmap for sustainable biofuels in southern Africa. Regulatory frameworks for improved development*. Law and Constitution in Africa, No. 30, Baden-Baden: Nomos.

Ruppel, O.C. & E.D. Kam Yogo (eds), 2018, *Environmental law and policy in Cameroon: Towards making Africa the tree of life*. Law and Constitution in Africa, No. 37, Baden-Baden: Nomos.

Ruppel, O.C. & K. Ruppel-Schlichting (eds), 2016, Environmental law and policy in Namibia: Towards making Africa the tree of life. 3rd edition, Windhoek: Hanns-Seidel-Stiftung.

Ruppel, O.C., K.M. Scherr & A.D. Berndt (eds), 2017, *Assessing progress in the implementation of Zimbabwe's new Constitution. National, regional and global perspectives*. Law and Constitution in Africa, No. 32, Baden-Baden: Nomos.

Ruppel, O.C. & F. Shifotoka, 2017, "Foreign direct investment protection in Africa – Contemporary legal aspects between BITS and BRICS". *African Yearbook of International Law* 21 (1), 5.

Ruppel, O.C. & M.S. Tchuente, 2018, "Responsabilité sociétale et environnementale des entreprises: Normes et Régulations - perspective Africaine, cas du Cameroun". In: Kinhoun, E. & O.C. Ruppel (eds), *La question de la responsabilité sociale et environnementale de l'entreprise - perspective Africaine, cas du Cameroun.* Yaoundé: UCAC Presses, 13.

Usman, S. & A.M. Kundiri, 2016, "Role of soil science: An answer to sustainable crop production for economic development in Sub-saharan Africa". *International Journal of Soil Science* (11), 61.

World Bank, 2020, *The African Continental Free Trade Area: Economic and distributional effects.* Washington, DC: World Bank.

Country report for Cameroon

Christopher F. Tamasang (lead author), Cyril Effala (contributing author) & Ivo T. Tassah (contributing author)

1 Country information

Often referred to as 'Africa in miniature' because of its geographical and cultural diversity, the Republic of Cameroon is one of the countries that make up the Central African Subregion, which is a political and economic unit.

1.1 Geography and climatic conditions

The Republic of Cameroon is geographically located within Central Africa. The country stretches from latitude 2°N to 13°N of the equator and 9°E and 16°E of the Greenwich Meridian.[1] This location situates the country at the extreme north-eastern end of the Gulf of Guinea. It is bordered by the Federal Republic of Nigeria in the west, the Republic of Chad in the north, the Central African Republic in the east, and the Republic of Congo, Equatorial Guinea and Gabon in the south.[2] Important boundary landmarks are Lake Chad in the north and the Atlantic Ocean in the south-west. Cameroon is strategically located in the Gulf of Guinea[3] in the Central African Subregion and occupies a central position in the Economic and Monetary Community of Central African States (CEMAC). This geostrategic relevance of the country, coupled with the fact that it opens up to the Atlantic Ocean in the south-west, attracts many foreign investors for the exploitation of natural resources in particular, and trade in general. The country equally serves as a passageway for the landlocked countries of Chad, the Central African Republic and Congo Brazzaville for the importation and exportation of goods. As the meeting point of West and Central Africa at the heart of the Gulf of Guinea, Cameroon is the gateway to the economy of a part of Central Africa and a trade route between the economies of West and Central Africa.[4] The region's only deepwater ports of Douala and Kribi play a decisive role in its economy.

---

1 Neba (1987: 2).
2 Yahmed et al. (2007: 18).
3 Ngoh (1996: 3).
4 Tajoche (2008: 12).

Cameroon has a total surface area of 475,442 km^2, which is divided into 472,710 km^2 of total landmass and 2,730 km^2 of water bodies. According to Neba,[5] the country has the shape of a carelessly drawn triangle with a broad base measuring 888 km in the south and a narrow top in the north.[6] The distance from the south to the north is about 1,221 km.

Cameroon is located in the tropics where temperatures are generally high throughout the year for most parts of the country.[7] Rainfall is heavy in the southern part of the country, especially around the coast of the Atlantic Ocean and the Western Highlands, and decreases from the south towards the northern part of the country. Two main seasons, namely the wet season and the dry season, are experienced in the country. Cameroon has two main climates: the equatorial climate and the tropical climate.[8] The equatorial climatic type is experienced in the Equatorial Rainforest region in the southern part of the country between latitudes 2° and 6° north of the equator. It is felt mainly in the Coastal Lowland and the Southern Low Plateau which covers the Southwest, Littoral, Centre, South, and East Regions of the country.[9] The equatorial climate is made up of two sub-types: the Cameroon type and the Guinean type.[10] The Guinean type is experienced from the coast of Kribi to the Southern Low Plateau and is characterised by four seasons – two rainy seasons (in September and March–April) and two dry seasons (in December–January and July–August).[11] The Cameroon type, induced by both maritime and relief, is experienced along the south-western coast around Mount Cameroon extending to the mouth of the River Sanaga and the limits of the Western Highlands.[12] This sub-type has two main seasons – the rainy season and the dry season.[13]

The tropical climate is the second major type of climate in Cameroon and can be divided into two main sub-types: the humid tropical climate or the Sudan climate and the dry tropical climate or the Sahel climate. The humid tropical climate is common in the Western Highlands and Adamawa Plateau. The dry tropical climate is experienced in the Northern Lowlands which cover the North and Far North Regions of Cameroon.[14]

---

5 Neba (1987: 8).
6 Ibid.: 4.
7 Ayonghe (1999: 19).
8 Ibid.
9 Ibid.
10 Dobgima (2008: 238).
11 Ibid.
12 Mbu (2014: 12).
13 Ibid.
14 Ibid.

1.2 Economy

Cameroon is primarily an agro-based economy. Almost 70% of the population is engaged in agriculture and related activities.[15] The economy is dominated by a primary sector involved in the exploitation of primary commodities destined for exportation with little or no processing. The industrial base that drives the secondary sector is highly limited. However, the service sector is increasing considerably especially in the face of rapid urbanisation in the country. It should be noted that the country's economy was one of the fastest growing economies in Africa for a quarter of the 20th century after Cameroon gained independence in 1961.[16] However, a combination of factors such as a drop in the prices of export commodities such as petrol, coffee, cocoa and cotton alongside an overvalued currency and mismanagement led to an economic meltdown, giving rise to hardship and growing poverty.[17] However, after the completion of the heavily indebted poor country initiative of the International Monetary Fund and based on the country's Growth and Employment Strategy Paper (GESP), there are hopes for the economy to bounce back onto a growth track, everything being equal. Cameroon's gross national product (GNP) for 2018 was estimated at US$36.37 billion, a 10.66% increase from 2017.[18] The country's GNP for 2017 was estimated at US$32.87 billion, a 0.68% decline from 2016.[19]

Regarding its national debt over the first three months of 2019, Cameroon's public debt reached CFA F7,494 billion (i.e. franc of the African Financial Community[20]) (about 35% of gross domestic product (GDP)), according to MINFI.[21] In 2018, outstanding debt was CFA F7,318 billion (34.4% of GDP) against CFA F6,255 billion (30.8% of GDP) in late 2017.[22] However, the Autonomous Sinking Fund (Caisse Autonome d'Amortisement) – the organ in charge of public debt management in Cameroon – estimated the 2018 debt of Cameroon at CFA F6,527 billion.[23] The debt increase is motivated by acceleration in big infrastructure projects.[24]

Foreign direct investments (FDI) inflow to Cameroon is usually low compared to the potential of its economy. FDI reached US$672 million in 2017 and was stable compared to the previous year, according to the World Investment Report 2018 of the

15 Tassah (2018: 3).
16 Ngoh (2019: 2).
17 Mbu (2014: 21).
18 See macrotrends website on Cameroon GNP 1967-2019, at https://www.macrotrends.net/countries/CMR/cameroon/gnp-gross-national-product, accessed 3 October 2019.
19 Ibid.
20 *Communauté Financière Africaine Franc.*
21 See https://www.businessincameroon.com/finance/0705-9098-cameroon-public-debt-reached-xaf7-494bln-in-q1-2019-35-of-gdp, accessed 19 July 2019.
22 Ibid.
23 See Business in Cameroon website, at https://www.businessincameroon.com/economy/0507-8173-cameroon-s-debt-rose-to-cfa6-527-billion-by-may-31-2018, accessed 3 June 2019.
24 Ibid.

United Nations Conference on Trade and Development. In 2018, FDI stocks were estimated to represent 21.9% of GDP (US$6.4 billion; it was 19.8% in 2016). Most of the FDI came from the European Union, particularly France and Germany, and targeted the mining industry, including oil extraction. However, China has become a major investor in the country, carrying on large infrastructure projects. China has been investing steadily in Cameroon (with the total Chinese direct and indirect investments amounting to US$2.43 billion in 2016, according to the Cameroonian Ministry of Economy), allowing the construction of Kribi Port and Industrial Complex, Memve'ele Hydroelectric Dam, and new football stadiums.[25]

Cameroon's economy has the potential to become one of the most prosperous and best placed to receive FDI in Africa,[26] which is why the country continues to seek foreign investment to improve its inadequate infrastructure, create jobs, and improve its economic footprint. However, its unfavourable business environment remains a significant deterrent to foreign investment.[27] In addition to endemic corruption, lack of infrastructure, a risk of high political tension, and one of the highest tax burdens on the private sector in the world, Cameroon has a complicated business environment, as evidenced by its 163rd place out of 190 in the Doing Business ranking of 2018.[28]

1.3 Society

Available data on the total population of Cameroon and its distributions is contradictory. Different data are provided by different sources. According to one source, Cameroon has a total population of 24 million inhabitants with a population density of approximately 50.5 inhabitants per km^2.[29] According to another source, the population is unevenly distributed over a surface area of 475,442 km^2, giving an average population density of 40.8 inhabitants per km^2.[30] This is, of course, not a depiction of the true distribution of the population in Cameroon, because some areas are densely populated, some are moderately populated, and some are sparsely populated, while other areas are uninhabited. The areas of high population density in Cameroon include the Western Highlands, part of the Coastal Lowland around Douala and the extensive plantation zone along the coast, the Mandara Mountain region in the north, and the western part of the Southern Low Plateau around Yaoundé. The average population density in these

25 See Banco Santander, S.A website, at https://en.portal.santandertrade.com/establish-overseas/cameroon/investing, accessed 23 May 2019.

26 Ibid.

27 See IndexMundi website, at https://www.indexmundi.com/Cameroon/economy_profile.html, accessed 28 January 2021.

28 See Banco Santander, S.A website, at https://bit.ly/3vOIXoW, accessed 23 May 2019.

29 National population census data, 2005.

30 BUCREP (2010: 19).

areas ranges between 100 and 200 inhabitants per km^2.[31] The highest population concentrations are registered in the main urban centres of Douala, Bafoussam, Foumban, Bamenda, Limbe, Yaoundé and Mokolo in the Mandara Mountain region. The main factors responsible for the high population densities are the fertile volcanic soil in the Coastal Lowland and the Western Highlands, the gentle topography in the Coastal Lowland, the concentration of industries in the Coastal Lowland, and dense transport network. The level of education in Cameroon is more than average.[32] In 2015, the adult literacy rate was 75%.[33] This adult literacy rate increased from 41.2% in 1976 to 75% in 2015, growing at an average annual rate of 18.84%.[34] The current educational level of Cameroon is contained in the Strategy Paper of the Education and Training Sector, 2013–2020[35] – the education plan of Cameroon, whose primary objective is the achievement of quality universal primary education. This objective aligns with the national strategy for growth and employment goal of providing the production system with human capital capable of supporting economic growth. From 2006, the enrolment growth has been strong at all levels except at the primary level where it has been more modest: Pre-school +56%; Primary +14%; Secondary General +58%; Technical Secondary +75%; and Superior +85%.[36]

There is freedom of religion in Cameroon. The Preamble of the Constitution of Cameroon proclaims the freedom of religion, and the government respects this right by allowing for free practice of religion. Thus, the country is generally characterised by a high degree of religious tolerance. However, for a religious group (apart from African traditional religions) to be legally functional, it has to be registered as per Law No. 90/053 of 19 December 1990 on Freedom of Association. There are three predominant religions in Cameroon consisting of Christianity, Islam and traditionalist. Christian churches and Muslim centres of various denominations operate freely throughout the country, while the traditionalists operate in their shrines and temples. Although there is religious diversity and freedom in Cameroon, the most common religious belief is Christianity, which is adhered to by approximately two-thirds of the country's population.[37] Islam is the second most practised religion in Cameroon by roughly one-fifth of the population. A few others practise African Folk Religion and other religions, while some claim to have no religious belief.[38]

The Roman Catholic Church is the most dominant Christian faith group in Cameroon constituting about 39.2% of the total population, followed by the Protestants with

31 Ibid.: 1.
32 See https://bit.ly/3s9dtau, accessed 19 July 2019.
33 Ibid.
34 Ibid.
35 Republic of Cameroon (2013).
36 Ibid.: 28.
37 See Spain Exchange country guide website, at https://www.studycountry.com/guide/CM-religion.htm, accessed 19 July 2019.
38 Ibid.

about 28.1% of the population; Islam constitutes about 19.5% of the population; about 4.3% of the population, mainly in rural areas, still retain their indigenous religious practices referred to as African Folk Religion involving practices such as rituals in the form of animal sacrifices, and ancestor and spirit worship.[39] Other religious groups in the country include atheists and agnostics, estimated at 4.6%, and Hinduism estimated at 2.1%.[40] All these religious groups have an impact on the cultural and national life. For instance, most religious holidays are declared as national holidays, while the religions dictate and influence cultural practices such as food, dress, and moral conduct.[41] An important objective of various religious groups is the quest for land to spread their confessional beliefs. In this regard, the Catholics and Protestants have acquired large expanses of land across the country, both in the rural areas and urban areas.

1.4 Information on the organisational structure of Cameroon

Cameroon has three main powers of the state, namely the Bicameral Legislative, the Judiciary, and the Executive. Although it is said that Cameroon operates as a democratic system of government, it has had a strong centralised system of government dominated by the President since 1972. Cameroon, which was once a federal system, is now a decentralised unitary state as per Article 1(2) of the Constitution. It is made up of a central government and 10 regions.[42]

1.4.1 Legal system and legal tradition

Cameroon is a bilingual and bi-jurial country with two systems of law operating side by side. The legal system, like most in Africa, is a relic of the colonial era.[43] However, it is unique in that it consists of two distinct and often conflicting legal systems, the English common law and the French civil law, operating in some sort of tenuous co-existence.[44] However, it would be correct to say that Cameroon operates a mixed legal system of English common law, French civil law, and customary law. It must be noted

39 See Worldatlas website, at https://www.worldatlas.com/articles/religious-beliefs-in-cameroon.html, accessed 28 January 2021.

40 Ibid.

41 Ibid.

42 See Article 1(2) of the Constitution instituted by Law No. 96/06 of 18 January 1996 to amend the Constitution of 2 June 1972, amended and supplemented by Law No. 2008/001 of 14 April 2008.

43 See Hauser Global Law School program website, at https://www.nyulawglobal.org/globalex/Cameroon1.html#_The_Cameroonian_Legal, accessed 23 May 2019.

44 Ibid.

that the country is fully engaged in the harmonisation of laws from the two legal systems representing two major world cultures – English and French.

1.4.2 Competence of legislation

In Cameroon, the initiative of elaboration of legal acts belongs to the legislative power and the executive power.[45] The Cameroonian Constitution distinguishes between parliamentary power to legislate in Article 26 and the governmental power to issue rules and regulations in implementation of Parliamentary legislation in Article 27. Article 26 is the principal provision in the Constitution that specifies the scope of the Cameroon Parliament's legislative competence. This article, in broad terms, identifies the areas that fall within the reserved legislative domain. The parliamentary power to legislate is complemented by governmental power to issue regulations in implementation of such legislation. This is so because legislative texts are incomplete without their enabling instruments issued by the executive branch of the government, detailing and completing the legislative texts. Express governmental intervention in the legislative domain under the Cameroonian Constitution is provided for on two different occasions. The first is provided for by Article 27, which states that "matters not reserved to the legislative power shall come under the jurisdiction of the authority empowered to issue rules and regulations." This has the effect of giving the government the right to enact "laws" by way of "rules and regulations" in all matters not reserved for Parliament under Article 26. The President of the Republic (Article 8 (5)), the Prime Minister (Article 12 (3), and a host of other government officials share this general power to issue rules and regulations. The second instance of governmental intervention is provided for in Article 28 of the Constitution. According to this provision, Parliament may, on matters falling within its reserved legislative domain, "empower the President of the Republic to legislate by way of ordinance for a limited period and for given purposes." To be valid, such ordinances must be tabled before the bureau of the National Assembly and the Senate for purposes of ratification within the time limit laid down by the enabling law.

The legislative power deliberates and adopts bills, and the President of the Republic promulgates them into law. Regarding regulatory acts, the executive power and its down-the-line organs have exclusive authority to legislate.

45 See Article 14(1), 8(8), 26, and 28 of the Constitution.

1.4.3 Competence of law enforcement

The enforcement of legal acts is incumbent on the Executive and the Judiciary, which act through law enforcement officials usually referred to as judicial police or judicial authorities. The national police and the gendarmerie have primary responsibility for law enforcement with the aid of other judicial police officers, such as the bailiffs and the military.

Law enforcement in Cameroon is weak and difficult to navigate owing to endemic corruption and significant delays in court procedures. Bribery, nepotism, and corruption are rife in almost all sectors of the Cameroonian Government and economy but is particularly prevalent in the judiciary and finance services.[46] There is ample evidence of weak governance systems and lack of independence in the Judiciary.

The Executive arm of government is in charge of executing or implementing the law at the various levels of administration, be it central or decentralised, with the help of the agents of law enforcement. This involves, from a centralised perspective, government departments and, from a decentralised angle, regional entities, local councils and traditional authorities. This is covered respectively by the Constitution,[47] the law creating regions,[48] the local council law[49] and the chieftaincy law.[50]

1.4.4 The Constitution, statutory and customary law: Role of traditional entities

Although the Constitution does not expressly articulate on the role of traditional entities with regard to customary law, Article 1(2) stipulates that the Republic of Cameroon recognises and protects traditional values that conform with democratic principles, human rights and the law. Traditional values here can be interpreted to mean customary law which is guarded and enforced by traditional entities. The role of traditional entities is also recognised in laws relating to Judicial Organization Ordinances of 2011 and the law on Traditional Chieftaincies of 1977.

---

46 See Business Anti-Corruption Portal website, Cameroon corruption report, at https://www.business-anti-corruption.com/country-profiles/cameroon/, accessed 23 May 2019.

47 Article 57(2).

48 Law No. 2004/019 of 22 July 2004 fixing the rules applicable to regions.

49 Law No. 2004/018 of 22 July 2004 fixing the rules applicable to councils.

50 Decree No. 77/245 of 15 July 1977 to organize Chiefdoms. See Articles 19, 20(1) and (2) and 21.

2 Soil degradation

2.1 The state of the environment

The environment is the basis for the survival of many Cameroonians because of the extractive activities it provides for them. These activities are dominated by agriculture, grazing, timber and non-timber forest exploitation, mining, and fishing. Cameroon's diverse climatic conditions have fashioned an environment that is not uniform throughout the country. Generally, the state of environmental degradation in Cameroon remains relatively low though with significant variations in different parts of the country. Large-scale environmental degradation is most common in the northern Sahel zone and the Western Highlands of the country, owing to constant use of the land with inadequate or no fallow periods.[51]

2.2 Different types of soil and their vulnerability in terms of degradation

The soil types in Cameroon vary from place to place because of topography, amount of rainfall and natural occurrences. According to Ndzeidze, soils in Cameroon are classified into zonal and azonal soils found in different parts of the country.[52] The zonal soils are made principally of ferralitic and ferruginous soils, while the azonal soils comprise alluvial and volcanic soils. There is also intrazonal soil.[53]
Zonal soils are formed under the influence of climate. The two main zonal soils found in Cameroon include ferralitic soil and ferruginous soil, collectively called Latosols.[54]

The ferralitic soil is a reddish or brownish soil found in the Equatorial Rainforest in the southern region of Cameroon between latitude 0° to 5° north of the equator. Its formation is influenced by the climate of the Equatorial Rainforest region characterised by heavy rainfall and high temperatures.[55] There is intense chemical weathering in the region due to heavy rainfall and high temperatures. This results in the formation of deep soil profiles. Owing to heavy rainfall, soluble minerals like calcium and sodium are leached, leaving behind insoluble oxides of iron and aluminium near the surface to form the reddish or brownish soil found in the A-horizon. The B-horizon is made up of silica and base deposited in this layer. This gives the B-horizon a yellowish colour. The C-horizon is made up of small particles of clay regolith as a result of deep chemical weathering.[56]

---

51 Fogwe et al. (2001: 9).
52 Ndzeidze (2008: 6–7, 146).
53 Dobgima (2008: 323); Neba (1987: 74).
54 Dobgima (2008: 120–123, 323).
55 Nchangvi (2010: 46–47, 199).
56 Dobgima (2008: 134–136, 323).

The ferralitic soil is also characterised by low nutrient content due to rapid decomposition. Litter supply is high in the region owing to the presence of a large biomass. The climate of the region, which is warm and humid with heavy rainfall and high temperatures, favours the presence of microorganisms and a high rate of decomposition. As such, the thick litter supply is easily decomposed to form humus, but the humus is quickly washed away by the heavy rainfall in the region through leaching and erosion.[57] The ferralitic soil is not very good for farming, because the moment the land is cleared and exposed to rainfall, the soil minerals are easily washed away. However, the laterite which is a characteristic of this soil makes it good for road construction.

This is a hard and dry soil found mainly in the Adamawa Plateau and the Northern Lowlands where rainfall is low and temperatures are high. With the low rainfall and high temperatures, the movement of soil minerals is more upward. The soil minerals on top are baked by the sun to form a hard layer called hardpan. The ferruginous soil is reddish-brown in colour and has low organic matter and is skeletal in nature. The soil has low nutrients as a result of leaching, which does not support forest vegetation and is used mainly for the cultivation of grain crops such as groundnut, maize and millet.[58]

In Cameroon, azonal soils are young soils without distinct horizons or layers; dark in colour and rich in minerals and are two main types: volcanic soil and alluvial soil.[59] This type of soil is formed as a result of the breakdown of volcanic lava. In Cameroon, volcanic soil can be found around the foot of Mount Cameroon, especially around Buea, Muyuka and Idenau; and in the Western Highlands around Oku, Ijim Mountain region and Foumbot.[60] Volcanic soils are very fertile and are good for farming, which is why there are many large farms and plantations around Mount Cameroon, where both food and cash crops are widely cultivated. The main food crops grown in the area are coco yam, yam, cassava, plantain and maize, while the main cash crops grown in the area are cocoa, oil palm, banana, rubber and tea. In addition, potato and vegetables such as carrot, cabbage and tomato are widely cultivated in the volcanic soils of the Western Highlands.[61]

This type of soil is made up of fine and loose materials broken down and deposited by rivers usually on lowland areas. Alluvial soil is a young soil without distinct horizons. In Cameroon, alluvial soils occur in the Coastal Lowlands and around flood plains. In the Coastal Lowlands, alluvial soil can be found in the Tiko-Douala plain, the Mungo region and the Douala-Kribi plain. Alluvial soils also occur in the flood plains of the Logone valley and Benue plain in the north, the Ndop plain, and Noun valley in the Western Highlands. Alluvial soils are very fertile and good for farming.

57 Neba (1987: 28–30, 71).
58 See generally Nchangvi (2010: 51–62, 199).
59 Ndzeidze (2008: 146).
60 Ibid.: 12–24.
61 See generally Neba (1987: 33–37, 74); Dobgima (2008: 140); and Ndzeidze (2008: 12–24).

There are many large farms and plantations in the Coastal Lowlands. Rice farming is carried out in the Logone valley, Ndop plain and Noun valley because of the fertile alluvial soil.[62]

Intrazonal soils are developed under the influence of local conditions. The main type of intrazonal soil found in some areas in Cameroon is hydromorphic soil which occurs in waterlogged areas of the coastal swamps along the coast of the Atlantic Ocean, the wetlands around the country, and the Mbo plain.[63]

2.3 Main drivers of soil degradation

Cameroon has soil types of varying qualities. While some of these soils are naturally of poor quality, the degradation of some of the soils is attributed to anthropogenic drivers. Contextually, soil degradation is a change in the soil health status resulting in a diminished capacity of the ecosystem to provide goods and services for its beneficiaries. Degraded soils have a health status such that they do not provide the normal goods and services of the particular soil in its ecosystem.[64] Soil degradation in Cameroon is linked to a combination of drivers discussed in the subsections that follow.

2.3.1 Agriculture

The economy of Cameroon is largely agrarian, employing over 80% of the country's population. Agriculture in the country is dominated by subsistence small-scale farming practices, which are unsustainable and are at the forefront of causing massive soil degradation.[65] Some of the common practices include slash-and-burn (also called swidden); bush burning; and the *ankara* system, especially in the Western Highlands of Cameroon. The practice of slash-and-burn, or rotational farming, underpins food production and livelihoods in Cameroon and many other countries. Slash-and-burn farming includes several phases: (i) clearing of a portion of forest; (ii) burning of the plant debris; (iii) cultivation of the land, generally for a brief period; and (iv) leaving the land to fallow, generally for a long period of time. So, it is not a form of permanent farming. When returns from land diminish, farmers shift cultivation to another plot and allow the previous parcel to lie fallow for some years to regain fertility. About 80% of rural populations in Cameroon practice rotation. Slash-and-burn agricultural practice is detrimental for soils. This type of agriculture affects vegetation and soil

62 See generally Nchangvi (2010: 62–66, 199); Neba (1987: 30–38); Dobgima (2008: 145–148); and Ndzeidze (2008: 26-29, 146).
63 See Neba (1987: 28–29); Dobgima (2008: 146–148, 323).
64 FAO (2015: 71).
65 FAO (2009: 192).

carbon stocks. Increasingly, agriculture, especially accompanied by burning, has been contributing to soil degradation and climate change, as clearing – which is being intensified to meet the food demand of the growing population – exerts pressure on vegetation and soil, leading to loss of carbon stored in vegetation and soil in the form of carbon dioxide (CO_2).[66]

On the other hand, *ankara* is a traditional farming method practised by farmers in the Western Highlands of Cameroon with the aim of improving soil fertility and increasing crop production. Here, dry plant waste is put in the middle of beds, then partly covered with soil and then burnt. Then, seeds are planted on the burnt portions. During burning, much smoke is emitted, which indicates emission of carbon into the atmosphere with all that this entails for climate change and also reduction of soil fertility in the long run.[67] In these highlands of Cameroon, agriculture is characterised by extensification and a reduction, and in some cases elimination, of fallow periods, giving rise to continuous use of the soil without significant improvements. The rugged nature of these highlands also exposes the soils to the high-intensity rain drops which easily loosen the particles, giving rise to extensive soil erosion of all types (gully, sheet and rill). Extensive grazing in the region is also a major contributor to soil degradation. Livestock grazing in the region is done using the free-range technique over communally owned lands.[68] This technique of grazing, along with non-respect for carrying capacity, has given rise to overgrazing, soil compaction and soil degradation. This accounts for the persistent reduction in the quality of pastures over the years.

In the South Low Plateau, there is the common occurrence of bush fallowing and shifting of cultivation, especially in the East region of the country, characterised by vast expanses of abundant land and a relatively sparse population density. The northern part of the country, characterised by extensive lowlands, is dominated by mono-cropping such as onion, sorghum, millet and other cereal crops. Most often, owing to the growing demand for land as a result of the continuous growth in the human population, the cultivation does not give adequate time for the soil to reconstitute its natural fertility. Equally, the intense traditional grazing methods, such as transhumance and pastoral nomadism, have led to overgrazing and intense trampling that have exposed the soils to agents of erosion, especially wind erosion. The traditional farming methods and intense cattle-grazing have also exposed the soil to the direct rays of the sun.

The Coastal Lowlands are characterised by large-scale plantations, such as the Cameroon Development Cooperation (CDC), Delmonté, PAMOL, Herakle Farms, and SOCAPALM. They use intense chemical fertilizers and pesticides that are not only harmful to the soil, but equally have detrimental effects on the underground water aquifers and the environment as a whole. The peasant subsistence small-scale farming

66 See Pollini (2015: v); Ministry of the Environment and Nature Protection & FCPF (2008: 4).
67 See Njoh et al. (2018: 24).
68 Fogwe et al. (2001: 10).

practices carried out in this zone suffer considerably as a result of declining soil fertility and a drop in agricultural output. The small-scale farmers in this zone depend largely on the natural resource base for improving livelihood conditions. They have also resorted to extension of farming plots as a means of increasing farm output to meet the food needs of the population. The growing population and demand for food have significantly reduced or completely eradicated fallow periods, giving rise to overuse of soils and resultant degradation.

2.3.2 Mining

Given that Cameroon is richly endowed with mineral deposits, large-scale mining is being carried out in the country. Indeed, huge mining potential exists, as exploration studies have shown that the country is rich in sub-surface precious minerals.[69] The major mining sites in the country include iron ore mining in Mballam and Betare-Oya, which are in the East Region, bauxite at Fongo-Tongo in the West Region around Dschang, and limestone mining around Fugil Hill in the north of Cameroon.[70] Mining has an adverse effect on soil quality in that, during and after mining, toxic chemicals and acidic water are released, contaminating the environment, especially the soil. This changes the chemical composition of the soil and, since the chemicals are poisonous, they make the soil unsuitable for plants to grow. Furthermore, mining disturbance alters the flow of nitrogen through a stable soil-plant-microbial ecosystem. Furthermore, mining activities can result in erosion, sinkholes and the contamination of soils by the chemicals emitted from mining processes. The exploitation of these mineral deposits has generated much solid and liquid waste which has polluted vast expanses of the land. The mining companies in Cameroon exploit the mineral resources with impunity and do not take the protection of the environment into consideration. The environmental feedback in these areas has been reported to be negative with serious implications for soil degradation since the wastes generated are not treated before disposal. The current railway under construction, from Betare-Oya in the East region of Cameroon to the Kribi deep seaport, to ease the evacuation of mining products, has led to large expanses of forestland being cut down and has exposed the soils to agents of degradation in this part of the country.

69 Lambi (2009: 28).

70 Cameroon Tribune No. 8036/4325 of 18 January 2004.

2.3.3 Wildfires, farming, hunting, and cattle rearing

Human-induced wildfires are another significant driver of soil degradation in Cameroon. Uncontrolled wildfires cause massive forest destruction, destroy topsoils and expose land to all forms of erosion, such as wind and rain erosion. Communities use fire for clearing for subsistence farming and hunting. Pastoral lands cover a considerable part of the national territory, but reliable figures on pasture expansion into forested areas are not available. Climate modelling predicts that the extent and severity of wildfires will increase under most climate change scenarios.[71] Cameroon is a leading livestock-farming country with 6 million cattle and 7 million small ruminants on pastoral land covering more than 30% of the national territory and constituting more than 14 million hectares.[72] Livestock farmers keep large livestock, triggering further burning to open up more land, especially in the mountainous forest regions, in order to allow regeneration of vegetation for their livestock, with direct implications for soil degradation.

2.3.4 Industrial sites

Generally, Cameroon is characterised by a very low level of industrialisation. As such, most of the raw materials extracted from the country undergo very little processing within the country. The main industrial sites in Cameroon are the coastal industrial region, with the Douala zone being the largest industrial concentration. There is also the central industrial region that cuts from Yaoundé to Mbandjock and the Belabo-Mbalmayo zone. There is also the Western Highlands industrial zone, such as the Bamenda industrial zone that is yet to be developed; and the northern industrial region, where SODECOTON, a cotton-processing factory, and the cement factory that uses limestone at Fugil Hill are situated. Environmental management by a significant proportion of these manufacturing industries in Cameroon remains an issue that has been shrouded in politics with much lip service while actual implementation has remained a fallacy. Equally, the Chad–Cameroon multi-billion oil pipeline project has had some oil spillage. All these instances contribute significantly to degrading the soils and reducing their quality.

It is important to bring to the fore that a significant proportion of industries in Cameroon are not certified with international environmental management organisations, such as the International Standardized Organization (ISO 14001) series, which requires industries to internalise their externalities on the environment. ISO 14001 is a series of environmental management standards developed and published by the

71 CPF (2008: 13).

72 Forest Carbon Partnership Facility Cameroon (2013: 39).

International Organization for Standardization (ISO) for organisations. The ISO 14001 standards provide a guideline or framework for organisations that need to systematise and improve their environmental management efforts. Simply put, ISO 14001 is an environmental management system (EMS) which ensures "a transparent, systematic process known corporate-wide, with the purpose of prescribing and implementing environmental goals, policies, and responsibilities, as well as regular auditing of its elements".

At present, there seems to be no evidence to show that companies in Cameroon are ISO 14001 certified. However, by 2015, the Cameroon sugar manufacturing company, SOSUCAM, was supposed to have been certified to ISO 14000. Most of these industries therefore generate a lot of air pollutants that cause acid rains that degrade the soils. Similarly, some of the solid and liquid wastes (chemical effluents) are not treated because of lack of certification to ISO 14000 and therefore no management policies to treat wastes or recycle. This greatly degrades the soils, water and the environment where these industries are concentrated.[73] Another soil degradation problem associated with industrialisation in Cameroon relates to oil and gas exploitation, especially refinery activities in the national refining company, SONARA, in Limbe, where the by-product of refined oil, namely sludge, is dumped directly onto the land and into the ocean which contributes to marine and land pollution.[74]

2.3.5 Urban sprawls

Cameroon is a developing country that is experiencing a rapid increase in the population, bringing about urbanisation in the rural areas. The rural areas in Cameroon are rapidly urbanising with significant effects on vegetation cover. This has led to significant transformation of forestland into habitable spaces, as well as space for agriculture to meet the demand food production for urban and rural populations. The expansion of settlements and rapid deforestation are exposing the soil to various forms of erosion. This is visible from the large-scale extensification of subsistence farmlands around the peri-urban areas and the simultaneous use of poor farming methods and chemical fertilizers to grow crops rapidly. These practices have been noted for contaminating soils and reducing its productivity.

Furthermore, urban sprawl, due to the human population explosion and unsustainable socioeconomic development, has led to the degradation of wetlands. This has triggered a decline in the goods and services provided by these ecosystems. In fact, most wetland ecosystems are experiencing accelerated degradation in Cameroon. Reclamation and conversion of wetlands for agriculture, human settlement and industrial

73 Ekane & Oben (2001: 120); and Fogwe et al. (2001: 8).

74 Fogwe et al. (2001: 14).

development constitute a considerable threat to the conservation of wetlands.[75] Large areas of wetlands in Cameroon are being converted to agriculture, grazing, land reclamation or encroachment for development activities and housing, firewood and other construction materials. In recent times in most local communities, the majority of wetlands are being carved out and appropriated by community members because of the increasing value attached to land, generally, and to wetlands, in particular. In fact, pressure on wetlands continues to mount both in rural and urban areas, leading to large-scale drainage and conversion for alternative uses without regard to their ecological and environmental values. As a result, a great number of wetlands in Cameroon are continually being degraded. They face severe and diverse threats with implications for soil degradation.

All these developments have taken place in the absence of an appropriate and comprehensive national legal framework that regulates the management, conservation and wise use[76] of wetlands. This is compounded by the limited understanding of the population of their values and what the impacts of their modification and degradation may be. In fact, most wetlands are under threat owing to unsustainable use – which will continue in the absence of a suitable legal framework. Based on current trends, Cameroon is not doing well in responding to degradation of wetlands. Their management, conservation and wise use therefore deserve proper policy and legal attention. With regard to soil protection, wetlands provide supporting services such as nutrient cycling and soil formation, drought and flood control, soil erosion prevention, nutrient and toxic retention, prevention of saline water intrusion, etc. However, urban and rural encroachment on wetlands is affecting the role these ecosystems play in term of soil protection. Protecting wetlands from degradation can therefore enhance the protection of soils.

2.3.6 Demographic growth rate

Population growth and demographic explosion are a reality in Cameroon with the rural areas experiencing faster growth rates than urban areas. It should be recalled that the impact of the population policies that were initiated in the 1960–1980 period in order to expand the population have continued to date. In the aftermath of independence, Cameroon in its desire to consolidate its newly acquired sovereignty, took pride in having a large population, not only for reasons of national grandeur, but also and above all for the needs of economic development. Population growth was therefore

75 Kang (2013: 3); see also Kwame (2006: 10).

76 In Ramsar terms, wise use means the sustainable utilisation of wetlands for the benefit of mankind in a way compatible with the maintenance of the natural properties of the ecosystem. Thus, wise use of wetlands is the maintenance of the ecological character, achieved through the implementation of ecosystem approaches, within the context of sustainable development.

encouraged, as there was insufficient market for products. Indeed, the general policy report of the Head of State on 25 September 1960 says: “Among the limitations to the incentive to invest, we must mention economic factors such as the low density of the local market, below the break-even point ...”.[77] The alarming growth in the size of the population today was long desired. Indeed, before 1980, the population as a factor of development and as a political asset was highly valued in terms of its contribution to socioeconomic development of the country and to slowing down the aging of the population.[78] It would seem, therefore, that, according to the governmental authorities, the limited population size did not allow two objectives to be adequately met: firstly, to have an economic market sufficient to carry out profitable investments, and secondly, to take the country out of underdevelopment. The moderate figure of the population also did not allow the leaders of Cameroon to satisfy their desire for national greatness, as testified by President Ahmadou Ahidjo in his speech of 21 December 1964:[79]

> Me too, I can dream that my country is as big as the United States of America and as big as Russia, but when I wake up, I see that my country is Cameroon with its four million inhabitants.

This explains why births and population expansion were encouraged. The increasing demographic growth experience, especially in the rural areas where agriculture is the main source of rural livelihood, has led to extensification as well as unsustainable grazing practices to satisfy the food needs of the growing population. The effects have been that vast expanses of forests and wetlands have been cut down for the growth of crops and for housing construction. The exposed environment, void of trees especially on hilly terrain, is thus characterised by intense mass movement processes such as landslides and soil erosion. Population growth is therefore associated with increased environmental degradation and declining productivity of soils. The Cameroonian Government’s new position on demographic issues was made official at the World Population Conference in Mexico in August 1984, in the following words:[80]

> Aware of the impact of the increase in population …, we do not encourage the proliferation of large and needy families. We think of directing our population policy towards the improvement of the quality of the population (…).

2.3.7 Weather and climate factors: The symbiotic relationship between soil and climate change

Weather and climate are related. and they differ in some respects. The distinction between weather and climate lies in the fact that weather is the climatic conditions or patterns seen over a short period of time in a given location, while climate is the

77 Bella (1993: 22).
78 Ibid.: 20.
79 Ibid.
80 Ibid.: 24.

average weather patterns seen over decades. Climate change is caused by the emissions and concentration of greenhouse gases (GHGs), mainly carbon dioxide (CO_2) and methane (CH_4), in the atmosphere. There is a symbiotic relationship between climate change and soil. To better understand the symbiosis, it is appropriate to ask the following questions: What is the impact of climate change on soil? Can soil help combat climate change?

Climate change can affect soil functions directly and indirectly. The direct effects include soil process changes in organic carbon transformations and nutrient cycling through altered moisture in the soil or increased soil erosion rates due to an increased frequency of high-intensity rainfall events.[81] Varying climatic conditions in Cameroon have influenced soil degradation in various ways. In the northern Sudano-Sahelian zone where average temperatures are above 28°C and there is a longer drier season, the common occurrence of droughts has caused soil moisture deficit and a high rate of evapotranspiration, affecting the quality of the soils in this zone. The active hamattan winds in this zone contribute equally significantly to the rapid removal of the topsoil. The equatorial climatic zone of the south, where rainfall is high throughout the year, has increased constant leaching of silica, allowing ions and aluminium compounds to accumulate on the topsoil. This increases the acidic contents of the soils and reduces its productive value. In the Western Highlands, the high rainfall intensities where soils are exposed loosen the soil particles, giving rise to erosion and river siltation (as a result of huge quantities of topsoil being washed into rivers every year). The indirect effects of climate change on soil functions include those that are induced by climate change adaptation options.[82] Since soils are intricately linked to the atmospheric–climate system through the carbon, nitrogen and hydrological cycles, altered climate will have an effect on soil processes and properties and, at the same time, the soils themselves will have an effect on climate.[83] Global climate change is projected to have various important effects on soil processes and properties related to restoring soil fertility and productivity.[84]

On the other hand, soil is one of the carbon sinks and reservoirs whose protection and conservation is critical for climate change mitigation. Substantially more carbon is stored in the world's soils. It is estimated that the global soil carbon pool of one-metre deep, estimated at 2,500 PgC, of which about 1,500 PgC is soil organic carbon, is about 3.2 times the size of the atmospheric pool and 4 times that of the biotic pool.[85] The role of soil organic carbon in global carbon cycles is receiving increasing attention both as a potentially large source of carbon dioxide emissions and as a natural carbon

81 Hamidov et al. (2018).
82 Ibid.
83 Brevik (2012: 1).
84 Pareek (2017: 136).
85 Zomer et al. (2017: 1).

sink capable of reducing the concentration of atmospheric GHGs.[86] It is possible to influence atmospheric levels of carbon- and nitrogen-based gases through soil management.[87] Thus, one of the means to limit temperature increase and fight climate change is avoiding soil degradation. Maintaining soil carbon is a natural and cost-effective way of mitigating climate change.

Where we have the ability to sequester and conserve carbon in the soil, management decisions can lead to the release of carbon from the soil, making it a net source of GHGs.[88] Ploughing native soils for agricultural production, introducing more aggressive forms of tillage, and draining wetlands are examples of management practices that increase GHG emissions from soils.[89] The danger of intensively cultivated areas in Africa has been emphasised.[90]

2.3.8 Topographic constraints

The topography of Cameroon is highly diverse. Topographically, the country is made up of the Coastal Lowlands, the South Cameroon Low Plateau, the Western Highlands, the Adamawa Plateau and the Northern Lowlands. This diverse topographical configuration has given rise to changes in the quality and quantity of soils. In most of the highland areas, the soils are generally eroded. The physiographic configuration of the Western Highlands, characterised by volcanic mountain ranges with very steep slopes, has exposed the soils to natural hazards such as landslides, soil creep and rockfalls, which all reduce soil quality and quantity.[91] Geomorphic agents such as water and wind are also very active in these areas which carry away the topsoils. On the contrary, the low-lying areas of Cameroon such as the Northern Lowlands and the Coastal Plains, as well as broad topographic depressions such as the Ndop, Mbaw and Santchou Plains, are endowed with fertile alluvial soils which are consistently washed away from the adjacent highlands into these plains by streams and rivers.

2.3.9 Land-grabbing

Land-grabbing is arguably defined as the large-scale land acquisitions or the buying or leasing of large expanses of land mostly in developing countries by domestic and

86 Ibid.
87 Brevik (2012: 2).
88 Ibid.: 4.
89 Ibid.
90 Zomer et al. (2017: 1).
91 Lambi (2000: 139).

transnational companies, organisations, and individuals.[92] Land-grabbing is also associated with soil degradation. Soil degradation can be incentivised by the grabbing, appropriation and use of lands by large agro-investors in collusion with the government. Although in most rural areas, most lands are still held under customary tenure systems and administered by traditional rulers, customary tenure no longer provides people with security over their land as vast lands are forcefully acquired by the government and its allies – powerful agro-industrial corporations, influential elites, and some traditional leaders. The large influx of investors in Cameroon and the acquisition of thousands of hectares of land for the establishment of plantations will put more pressure on soils through clearing, the use of toxic and hazardous chemicals and poor waste management. The increased value that these large expanses of land used mainly for agriculture and other economic activities have placed on land constitutes a potential driver of soil degradation.

2.3.10 Other causes or drivers of soil degradation

Soil degradation in Cameroon is also driven by a series of underlying drivers including deforestation, pollution, compaction, salinisation, soil erosion, the loss of soil organic matter and migration.

Deforestation is a threat to soils and exposes these to high temperatures which break down the organic matter, increase evaporation, and make soils vulnerable to erosion. Furthermore, soils around the coastal industrial zones have been contaminated by industrial pollutants involving effluents from industries. In the agro-industrial complexes, the use of chemicals and pesticides has equally given rise to soil degradation and environmental traumatisation in general. This is especially in the agro-industrial establishments in the Coastal Lowlands of the country, where fertilizers and agro-chemicals are used in high-input agriculture, in mining, and for oil spills. The high rate of chemical and pesticide use in agro-industrial establishments has resulted in an increase in the acidic content of soils with enormous impact on the health of the soils. In their study on the biochemical indicators of marine pollution in the Douala Lagoon and Limbe Estuary in Cameroon, Etame and Oben[93] posited that there is a great variety of pollutants produced by human activity, many of which reach the aquatic environment. These pollutants emanate from industrial, agro-industrial, to municipal sources, and others come from mining, silt, oil spillages and leakages, and oil from garages.

Soil compaction in Cameroon is common in the northern Sahel region where the activities of the Fulani cattle herders have caused large sections of the soils to become barren landscape through trampling. This is coupled with the prolonged drought

92 See Fru (undated: 3).

93 Ekane & Oben (2001: 130).

conditions that are common characteristics in this zone. The higher temperatures of this zone have caused the soils to become scorched, so that they can hardly support the growth of some crops.

The low-lying nature of the Cameroon Coastal Lowlands between Douala and Tiko estuaries ensures that inundation remains a constant threat and is expected to get worse with accelerated rise of sea levels. A direct consequence is the continued loss of wetlands dominated in the Cameroon Coastal Lowlands by the mangrove forest vegetation. Salinisation of soils and groundwater is already a huge problem in the Douala–Edea–Kribi area to the east and the Douala–Tiko area to the west of the depositional sedimentary basin of the Cameroon Coastal Lowlands. The Cameroon Coastal Lowlands are floodtide dominated by mangroves that proliferate in the shoaling lagoons, creeks and tidal inlets. There is increasing intrusion of salt water into the shallow aquifers of this coastal area. The visible consequences include hazards such as saline soils and flooding. This is thus a fragile and unstable zone.

Soil erosion is the rapid loss of soil as a result of both natural causes and unprecedented human activities that exceed the rate of soil formation. Soil erosion caused by wind or water leads to the loss of surface soil layers which are rich in organic and mineral nutrient pools, resulting in complete or partial loss of soil horizons and possible exposure of growth-limiting subsoil.[94] The process of soil erosion is accelerated by human activities, resulting in reduced soil stability and leading to soil creep and landslides.[95] Erosion remains one of the principal threats to the soils in Cameroon. The hilly physiographic landscape of Cameroon, especially in the Western Highlands of the country dominated by savannah vegetation, has over the years been exposed to frequent soil erosion during the rainy season where fluvial activities are at their peak. These fluvial processes on the hilly landscapes have accelerated the rate of soil loss through erosion. Apart from the natural processes, anthropogenic activities have equally accelerated the process of soil erosion. The high population density in this part of the country, coupled with the fact that the population relies on natural resources for a livelihood, has led to vast expanses of the vegetation being cleared for agriculture and settlement. Similarly, the various land tenure practices and the decrease in the fallow periods have resulted in a situation where the land is exploited continuously without adequate time for soil restoration. This has accelerated the rate of soil loss through erosion and landslides.[96]

The loss of soil organic matter is common in Cameroon and has for a long time lowered the ability of the soil to maintain its production potential. There has been a loss of soil organic matter in some of the soils in Cameroon, especially in the Coastal Lowlands of the country that play host to large agro-industrial estates characterised by

94 Sanz et al. (2017: 49).
95 Ibid.
96 Tassah (2019).

the high use of chemical fertilizers and pesticides that most often kill the soil microbes. This has also been occurring in the Western Highlands of the country where land-use changes are common. Historically, land-use changes in the Western Highlands, where the highlands were reserved as ancestral sites for the gods during the 1960s, have been characterised by agriculture, grazing and settlement land uses.[97] There has been a reduction in the use of manures and an increase in cultivation depth. These practices have resulted in the reduction of organic inputs and increased decomposition of existing soil organic matter. The topsoils are those most affected, as the topsoil is the main zone affected by land use.

Whether international or national, migration and land/soil degradation are closely interconnected processes, which are triggered by intervening social, economic, political, demographic, and environmental processes, occurring at scales from the local to the international.[98] In developing regions, soil degradation is partly driven by those that are heavily dependent on basic ecosystem goods and services who often resort to migration to diversify their livelihood strategies and sources of income, or do so in response to the exigencies of socioeconomic and political unrest, and environmental conditions.[99] With regard to fertility, migration mostly flows from areas of high degradation to those of less, with low yields often escalating migration flows. Tropical regions covered with forests and wetlands often attract migrants from other areas who seek to establish farmlands – this can further drive deforestation and land/soil degradation. Environmental changes, conditions and processes are negative precursors for migration,[100] which is responsible for soil degradation.

In recent times, mass internal migration caused by social, economic and political factors in Cameroon is a threat to the soils. The case of internally displaced persons (IDPs) in Cameroon as a consequence of a sociopolitical crisis in the Northwest and Southwest, two English-speaking regions of the country, is escalating, with potential significant soil degradation impacts. There is a steady increase in the influx of IDPs from the two regions to other regions of the country, especially to the West, Littoral and Central Regions for resettlement purposes to satisfy their food and socioeconomic needs. The effect is the exposure of soils to serious degradation threats owing to increased encroachment and pressure on land (forests and wetlands), which are being cut down for housing construction and settlement and for agriculture involving the use of unsustainable practices. Migration is therefore associated with increased environmental and soil degradation.

97 Ibid.: 211.
98 McLeman (2017: 3); see also IOM & UNCCD (2019: 1 and 6).
99 McLeman (2017).
100 Olimova & Olimov (2012: 8).

2.4 Key actors in soil degradation

Soil degradation in Cameroon has been facilitated by several actors and therefore it becomes difficult to selectively hold a particular actor to be the main agent accountable for soil degradation. These actors range from foreign investors, to farmers and industrial operators.

The role of foreign investors as actors of soil degradation in Cameroon is deeply felt in the agricultural and mining sectors. The mining of huge mineral deposits in Cameroon have seen large quantities of earth materials excavated, leaving the mining sites bare of fertile land and rendering the landscape desolate. Therefore, foreign investors constitute some of the actors to be considered in the process of developing a model for land management in Cameroon.

Large- and small-scale farmers constitute the principal actors in soil degradation in Cameroon. The large-scale agro-industrial establishment in the Coastal Lowlands of Cameroon and the use of industrial chemicals and pesticides have had serious implications for the soil quality, while small-scale farmers who depend on the soil for basic livelihoods have been noted for degrading the soil as they employ unsustainable practices in the process of crop cultivation. This does not augur well for the health of the soil. The small-scale farmers remain the most implicated actors in soil degradation in Cameroon.

The activities of most of the industries in Cameroon have a deleterious effect on environmental protection and soil restoration. With the discharge of effluents and other waste, the health of the soils is not considered. This is basically due to weak enforcement of environmental laws, institutional lapses and corruption. The growing contamination of the soil and water in Cameroon is attributed to the poor urbanisation and industrialisation processes.[101] Generally, these processes have preceded planning. In the case of Douala, which is the main industrial hub of the country, industries are located on an elevated terrain, while human populations are concentrated in lower-lying areas. As a result of poor planning, it has therefore been difficult to properly address the problems of liquid and solid waste pollution.[102] Industries in Cameroon thus remain some of the actors of soil degradation.

2.5 Conclusion

It should be noted that not all drivers of soil degradation command equal importance, as the impacts of some drivers are greater than others. It would seem that the main drivers and causes are mining and industrial operations which lead to soil

101 Fogwe et al. (2001: 8).
102 Ibid.

contamination; unsustainable agricultural practices by small-scale farmers; pesticide use by both small- and large-scale farmers; demographic growth rate or urbanisation, particularly on wetlands; weather and climate change; wildfires in the course of farming, hunting, and cattle rearing; topographic constraints; and land-grabbing. Apart from the main drivers, other causes or threats to soil degradation include deforestation; contamination by industrial chemicals and pesticides; soil compaction or soil sealing; salinisation; erosion; and loss of organic carbon and soil biodiversity. It should also be noted that foreign investors; small- and large-scale farmers; and industrial operators constitute the key actors in soil degradation in Cameroon.

3 General information on public soil legislation

As the basis of virtually all terrestrial life, without which human and many other forms of life on earth cannot exist, soil is both an inherent part of biodiversity and the major part of its foundation.[103] The crucial ecological and socioeconomic functions of soil and the soil degradation challenges justify or warrant the need for the legal protection of soil. A sound legal and institutional framework for managing soils is critical. The legal framework relating to the protection and sustainable management of soils in Cameroon is not contained in a single legal instrument but is diverse and dispersed in numerous instruments having implications for soil protection. In this regard, the protection and sustainable management of soils in Cameroon is provided for in fundamental legislation as well as in different sectoral laws. At the national level, the legal architecture is organised in a hierarchical manner as follows: The Constitution; duly ratified treaties and international agreements; legislation or laws enacted by Parliament; ordinances of the President; Presidential Decrees; Prime Ministerial Decrees, Orders and Circulars; Ministerial Orders, Decisions and Circulars; Gubernatorial Orders and Circulars; Prefectorial Orders; and Municipal Orders.

Each category of such legal norms has addressed in its own way questions relating to the protection and management of soils. The same is true concerning the institutional framework for the protection and management of soils. In fact, a good number of public administrations have, within the framework of their missions, the protection and sustainable management of soils. However, the Ministry of Environment, Protection of Nature and Sustainable Development (MINEPDED) is the main public administration in charge of questions relating to the protection and sustainable management of soils.

103 Hannam & Boer (2004: 1).

3.1 Policy frameworks, government strategies, action plans, etc.

Soil protection policy was elaborated upon by the Government of Cameroon within the perspective of protecting living beings and the environment in general and particularly zones with high potential for soil degradation. National policy frameworks, government strategies, action plans, etc., relevant to soil protection in Cameroon build on international policy instruments relevant to sustainable soil management. Thus, this section will consider both international and national policies relevant to soil protection in Cameroon.

3.1.1 International policies relevant to soil protection

3.1.1.1 The land degradation neutrality initiative

During its 12th Conference of the Parties (COP), the United Nations Convention to Combat Desertification (UNCCD) defined land degradation neutrality (LDN) as:[104]

> a state whereby the amount and quality of land resources necessary to support ecosystem functions and services and enhance food security remain stable or increase within specified temporal and spatial scales and ecosystems.

The objective of LDN is to maintain and enhance the natural land and its associated ecosystem services. The UNCCD provides the international framework for the ongoing development and implementation of the LDN concept that partly seeks to protect the soil.[105] In this regard, the Science–Policy Interface of the UNCCD led to the development of the so-called 'Scientific Conceptual Framework for Land Degradation Neutrality', which should provide a conceptualised scientific model approach for planning, implementing and monitoring the LDN initiative at national or regional level.[106] Actions to achieve LDN include sustainable land management practices that prevent or mitigate degradation, and all efforts to reverse degradation through rehabilitation or restoration of degraded lands. According to Cowie et al., the response hierarchy of reverse land degradation articulates the priorities in planning LDN interventions.[107] The implementation of LDN is done at the landscape level through integrated land-use planning. The pursuit of LDN requires effort to avoid further net loss of the land-based natural capital.[108]

104 Decision 3/COP.12, UNCCD, 2015.
105 See Cowie et al. (2017: 25).
106 Ibid.
107 Ibid.: 25.
108 See Orr et al. (2017: 3).

3.1.1.2 The 2030 Agenda for Sustainable Development instituting the Sustainable Development Goals

Adopted by the United Nations General Assembly, the global 2030 Agenda for Sustainable Development contains 17 Sustainable Development Goals (SDGs) with 169 associated targets which are integrated and indivisible as commitments for both developing and developed countries. Among the 17 goals, the most relevant for soil protection is Goal 15. It sets out to protect, restore and promote sustainable use of terrestrial ecosystems, sustainably manage forests, combat desertification, and halt and reverse land degradation and halt biodiversity loss. More specifically, Target 15.3 urges states to strive to achieve a land degradation neutral world by 2030, thereby constituting the most critical target for soil protection. Other related goals relevant for soil protection include Goal 12 which sets out to ensure sustainable consumption and production patterns; Goal 13 which encourages everyone to take urgent action to combat climate change and its impacts; and Goal 17 which sets out to strengthen the means of implementation and revitalise the Global Partnership for Sustainable Development. In line with Goal 13, soil is one of the carbon sinks and reservoirs whose protection and conservation is critical for climate change mitigation. Maintaining soil carbon is a natural and cost-effective way of limiting climate change. Thus, one of the means to limit temperature increase and fight climate change is avoiding soil degradation. The SDGs referred to above are therefore a panacea for achieving sustainable soil management.

3.1.1.3 The African Union Vision 2063: The Africa We Want

The African Union (AU) Vision 2063, commonly known as Agenda 2063: 'The Africa We Want', adopted in September 2015, is Africa's blueprint and master plan for transforming Africa into a global powerhouse of the future.[109] It is the continent's strategic framework that aims to deliver on its goal for inclusive and sustainable development. It is a concrete manifestation of the pan-African drive for unity, self-determination, freedom, progress and collective prosperity pursued under Pan-Africanism and the African Renaissance.[110] In fact, Agenda 2063 is the concrete manifestation of how the continent intends to achieve this vision within a 50-year period from 2013 to 2063.[111] Among the seven Aspirations for 'The Africa We Want', the most relevant for soil protection is Aspiration 1 which sets out to achieve 'A prosperous Africa based on inclusive growth and sustainable development'. It however does not specifically mention soil. Paragraph 10 details that Africa will have the means and resources to drive

109 See African Union website, at https://au.int/en/agenda2063/overview, accessed 5 June 2019.
110 Ibid.
111 Ibid.

its own development, with sustainable and long-term stewardship of its resources. Africa's unique natural endowments, its environment and ecosystems, including its wildlife and wild lands, will be healthy, valued and protected, with climate resilient economies and communities. According to Paragraph 72(b), the aspiration is to speed-up actions to ensure effective and territorial planning and land tenure, use and management systems. These are all relevant to soil protection.

3.1.1.4 The Regional Implementation Plan for the African Soil Partnership

Cameroon is a member of the Regional Implementation Plan for the African Soil Partnership (AfSP) adopted in 2016 that recognises the importance of land or soil as the main resource base for many people in sub-Saharan Africa. AfSP calls for the strong support of national governments, as well as national and regional entities involved in natural resource management to contribute to achieving the common goal of improved and sustainable soil management. The implementation of the AfSP in sub-Saharan Africa is structured on five main pillars which are all relevant to sustainable soil management.

Pillar 1 promotes sustainable management of soil resources for soil protection, conservation and sustainable production. Pillar 2 encourages investment, technical cooperation, policy, education, awareness and extension in soil. Pillar 3 promotes targeted soil research and development focusing on identified gaps, priorities, and synergies with related productive, environmental, and social development actions. Pillar 4 enhances the quantity and quality of soil data and information: data collection (generation), analysis, validation, reporting, monitoring and integration with other disciplines. Pillar 5 anchors on the harmonisation of methods, measurements and indicators for the sustainable management and protection of soil resources.

The implementation plan of AfSP also recognises several main areas of action as a priority in sub-Saharan Africa: Addressing soil degradation as a major factor in food insecurity and making country- and region-wide efforts to rehabilitate degraded lands and change them into productive assets through community participation (relates to Pillar 1); guiding and enabling the implementation of sound and sustainable soil management practices and the restoration of soil health at all levels to achieve food security (relates to Pillar 1); developing, updating and disseminating updated and harmonised national and regional soil resource information, addressing all user needs including soil fertility information and making the best use of available science to increase soil productivity (relates to Pillars 4 and 5); addressing climate change and developing resilience to climate change adaptation (relates to Pillars 1 and 3); developing and implementing training and capacity-building programmes in all soil applications for existing and new generations of experts in soil science and land management, taking into account the gender balance (relates to Pillar 2); and establishing linkages and networks with other national, regional and global initiatives that affect soil health (relates to Pillars 1 and 2).

3.1.1.5 The Green Wall for the Sahara Initiative

Furthermore, the Green Wall for the Sahara Initiative, a programme initiated by the African Union and developed by the African Union Commission in collaboration with the Food and Agricultural Organization (FAO), United Nations Environment Programme (UNEP), UNCCD, among others, was launched in December 2006. African heads of state and government in their summit in January 2007 adopted the Decision on the implementation of the initiative. The programme covers a wide group of countries, including Algeria, Tunisia, Libya, Egypt, Mauritania, Mali, Niger, Chad, Sudan, Eritrea, Ethiopia, Djibouti, Cameroon, Nigeria, Benin, Burkina Faso, Senegal, Gambia, and Western Sahara, and Cape Verde. The goals of the programme are to slow the advance of the Sahara Desert, enhance environmental sustainability, control land degradation, promote integrated natural resources management, conserve biological diversity, contribute to poverty reduction, and create jobs.[112] The objectives of this initiative are relevant also to sustainable soil management.

3.1.1.6 Other regional and sub-regional commitments of Cameroon relevant to sustainable soil management

Cameroon subscribes to some sub-regional initiatives which are relevant to sustainable soil management notably within the Economic Community of Central African States (ECCAS), Central African Economic and Monetary Community (CEMAC) and the Congo Basin, all under the framework of the Central African Forests Commission (COMIFAC).[113] In terms of sustainable management of soils, COMIFAC and the treaty[114] establishing it commits state parties to undertake – within the scope of the conservation and sustainable management of forest ecosystems of Central Africa, among others – to include the conservation and sustainable management of forests and the management of the environment in national priorities; and to adopt measures aimed at putting forest conservation and sustainable management actions in line with

112 For information on the Green Wall for the Sahara Initiative Commission of the African Union, see https://www.unccd.int/actions/great-green-wall-initiative, accessed 31 January 2021.

113 COMIFAC is the Central African regional body in charge of forests and environmental policy, coordination and harmonisation, with the objective to promote the conservation and sustainable management of the Congo Basin's forest ecosystems.

114 Treaty on the Conservation and Sustainable Management of Forest Ecosystems in Central Africa, 2005.

development programmes of other sectors, notably, agriculture.[115] These have implications for soil protection.

Furthermore, in the framework of reforestation and management of ecosystems, COMIFAC adopted the Sub-regional Action Plan for Combating Land Degradation and Desertification, known by its French acronym PASR-LCD with implications for soil protection. In this respect, COMIFAC has a thematic working group on land degradation and desertification. Also, Cameroon like all other COMIFAC member states adheres to the Convergence Plan[116] whose objectives are relevant for soil protection. In fact, the 2015 revised COMIFAC Convergence Plan contains relevant indicators for sustainable soil management. One of the six priority axes around which the 2015 revised Convergence Plan is structured is the conservation of biological diversity, which is relevant for soil.[117] Another priority axis is combating the effect of climate change and desertification, which is equally relevant for soil protection. The Operation Plan of the Convergence Plan identifies its priorities for sustainable management of the Central African forests and is organised around the vision that COMIFAC members manage their forest resources in a sustainable and concerted manner for the welfare of their populations, and the conservation of biodiversity and the global environment. As part of the implementation of the COMIFAC Convergence Plan, Cameroon is involved in defining and implementing effective long-term strategies to combat land degradation in the sub-region.[118]

Through its subregional programme, the global mechanism established under the UNCCD is working with subregional institutions such as COMIFAC within the framework of ECCAS, to integrate the UNCCD into existing and emerging subregional development frameworks such as the COMIFAC Convergence Plan and to map the efforts to combat desertification, focusing on success stories in agriculture and natural resources management.[119]

Although some of these instruments do not specifically address soil, soil constitutes the most important element of land and natural resources, and reference to land, natural resources and ecosystems by these instruments provides an indirect means to protect soil. Furthermore, although these policies are not legally binding instruments, they can bring political pressure to bear on states to take appropriate domestic legal measures to achieve their objectives especially the reduction of soil degradation and ensuring its protection.

---

115 See generally Article 1 of the COMIFAC Treaty.

116 The Convergence Plan for the Conservation and Sustainable Management of Forest Ecosystems in Central Africa, February 2005, revised and adopted in July 2015.

117 Hannam & Boer (2004: 1).

118 GEF (2007: 34).

119 UN Economic Commission for Africa (2007: 39).

3.1.2 National policies relevant to soil protection

Policies, government strategies, action plans, etc., relevant to soil protection in Cameroon include:

3.1.2.1 The National Environmental Management Plan

The National Environmental Management Plan (NEMP) established in March 1996, forms part of the policy framework for environmental protection and its overall objective is to guide the development of strategies and actions for environmental protection and the rational management of resources to contribute to sustainable development.[120] It is a general framework of reference for the various sectoral environmental management actions in Cameroon. Its five priority areas include participatory land-use management; sustainable management of natural resources; restoration of degraded land and improvement of soil fertility; capacity-building; and concerted management of shared resources at the subregional level.[121] The NEMP has important implications for sustainable soil management and protection as it provides for the restoration of degraded land and improvement of soil fertility. The NEMP is only a policy instrument with no legal value because its implementation is not binding. Restoration is envisaged in response to natural or voluntary soil degradation. The restoration is done according to the type of degradation in question. If it is an excavation, for example, the degraded site can be transformed into a body of water. If it is deforestation, it can be restored through reforestation. When degradation results from natural causes, it is the responsibility of the state to ensure restoration, but if the degradation occurs after the completion of a project, it is the responsibility of the project promoter to ensure the restoration. It is necessary to distinguish whether it is an improvement of soils based on biological or organic elements (compost, for example) or chemical. Organic matter used to improve soil fertility does not greatly increase production, but it allows soil to retain its fertility. Improving the fertility of chemical-based soils increases soil yield, but these chemicals ultimately degrade the soils. The essence of restoration of degraded land and improvement of soil fertility is to reverse and reduce the environmental impacts caused by a project.

The NEMP has no standards to be achieved for restoration of degraded sites and this is probably a huge weakness because one can never ascertain if restoration has been effectively done in order to reduce soil degradation. It is perhaps important to

120 See the REDD Desk website at http://theredddesk.org/countries/plans/national-plan-environmental-management-cameroon, accessed 3 June 2018.

121 Ibid.

mention that there is an urgent need to update the NEMP and one of the salient issues to rethink in that exercise will be setting standards for restoration of degraded lands.

3.1.2.2 Intended nationally determined contributions of Cameroon

In the lead up to the 2015 United Nations Framework Convention on Climate Change (UNFCCC)[122] COP held in Paris in December 2015 during which the Paris Climate Change Agreement (PCCA)[123] was adopted, parties were urged to submit their intended nationally determined contributions (INDCs)[124] spelling out the actions they intended taking to address climate change – both in terms of adaptation and mitigation. Originally submitted as INDCs, these became binding nationally determined contributions (NDCs) when countries ratified the PCCA, unless they decided to submit new NDCs at the same time. The NDC became the first GHG targets under the UNFCCC for countries upon ratification of the PCCA. On 28 September 2015, Cameroon submitted its INDCs to the secretariat of the UNFCCC, in which it pledged a 32% reduction in carbon emissions by 2035 compared to its business-as-usual levels, taking 2010 as the reference year and conditional upon international support in the form of financing, capacity-building and transfer of technology. As a natural solution in fighting climate change, soils as natural carbon sinks enjoy a degree of protection in the NDC of Cameroon. Through its NDC, Cameroon intends to reduce the carbon footprint of its development without slowing its growth, identifying the soil as a critical component in meeting its carbon emission reduction pledge. Thus, the NDC provides for the promotion and adoption of better soil management practices in order to enhance soil productivity through, for instance, restoration.[125]

3.1.2.3 The National Action Plan for the Fight Against Desertification

The protection of living beings and the environment is partly done within the framework of the fight against desertification. In line with this, the National Action Plan for the Fight Against Desertification (NAP-FAD) was elaborated upon in 2007 by the government under the leadership of MINEPDED in collaboration with sister ministries, civil society, the private sector, and development partners. The action plan is

---

122 United Nations Framework Convention on Climate Change 11771 UNTS 107 (1992).

123 Adopted on 15 December 2015, signed in New York on 22 April 2016, entered into force on 4 November 2016.

124 INDCs is an expression used under the UNFCCC for reductions in greenhouse gas emissions that all countries that signed the UNFCCC were asked to publish in the lead up to the 2015 UN Climate Change Conference held in Paris, France in December 2015.

125 See Republic of Cameroon (2015: 4, 5).

considered as a government policy document within the framework of the fight against desertification, in general, and the protection of soils, in particular. In fact, upon ratifying the UNCCD in 1994, the government committed itself to working out a NAP-FAD – a coherent framework for the control of desertification.[126] The overall goal of the NAP-FAD is to reverse the desertification or degradation trends in order to fight against poverty and encourage sustainable development.[127] The NAP-FAD identifies the Sudano-Sahelian zone of the country as the most affected zone in the desertification process. It is for this reason that the North and the Extreme North regions have been designated as zones for priority intervention. One of the major axes of the action plan is the restoration of degraded lands and the improvement of soil fertility. The objective of this axis is supposed to be achieved through the following results: the fertility of marginal soils is improved; degraded soils are restored; and techniques of soil restoration are mastered and used by the population.

In the present state of affairs, it is difficult to affirm that the foregoing results have been achieved. It is quite a vast project and the process is ongoing. The expected results are likely to be achieved over time. Furthermore, NAP-FAD identifies the level of degradation and the zones that are particularly sensitive to the phenomenon of desertification. This strategy provides a precise inventory of the causes and effects of the degradation of forestry landscapes, according to agro-ecological zones and some action corridors. NAP-FAD is aligned to the Decade Strategy (2008–2018) of the UNCCD and was elaborated upon to update the NAP-FAD of 2007.

Regarding efforts to implement the NAP-FAD in the two regions named above, the Ministry of Environment has, since 2008, executed the Operation Green-Sahel Project in the Extreme North region and the Project for the Development of Waterfalls in the Benoue in the North region of the country. There are a number of stakes to the degradation of soils. In the context of NAP-FAD, the process of desertification and degradation of soils appears complex and diversified. The problems and stakes associated with the phenomenon relate to reduction in the production of foodstuffs and livestock with the risk of famine, the scarcity phenomenon: exacerbated social cost. The manifestations of the phenomenon are more observable through degradation of soils; reduction in the surface area and productivity of useful agricultural soils; wood scarcity owing to reduction of forestry and natural resources training; sandy water plans and reduction in fisheries resources; disappearance of some animal and plant species and loss of biodiversity; and deterioration of living conditions and increasing precarious conditions of the poor rural populations. Considering demographic pressure and the resultant reduction in cultivable surface area, loss of soils in arid and semi-arid zones of Cameroon is estimated at about CFA F100 million, representing about one-third of the annual budget of the country. This must be taken seriously.

---

126 GEF (2007).
127 See Republic of Cameroon (2012: 43).

3.1.2.4 The National Biodiversity Strategy and Action Plan II

As a policy tool, the National Biodiversity Strategy and Action Plan II (NBSAP II) provides an improved vision and a new orientation for interventions to reverse the trend of biodiversity loss.[128] Given that soil is both an inherent part of biodiversity and the major part of its foundation,[129] it can be concluded that the NBSAP II is relevant to soil protection.

3.1.2.5 The Readiness Plan Idea Note and REDD+ Readiness Preparation Proposal of Cameroon

The Readiness Plan Idea Note (R-PIN), 2008, and REDD+ Readiness Preparation Proposal (R-PP), 2013, of Cameroon were prepared in view of the national implementation of the REDD+ initiative. The REDD+ (reducing emissions from deforestation and forest degradation and the role of conservation, sustainable management of forests and enhancement of forest carbon stocks in developing countries) initiative has been conceptualised and operationalised as a scheme that results in the North–South flow of funds to incentivise the requisite sustainable forest management strategies in developing countries. It is a scheme through which developing countries are rewarded financially for any emissions reductions achieved associated with a decrease in the conversion of forests to alternative land uses.[130] It was first negotiated under the UNFCCC in 2005, with the objective of mitigating climate change through reducing net emissions of GHGs through enhanced forest management in developing countries. REDD+ negotiations during the various COPs of the UNFCCC have resulted in a plethora of Decisions that embody a comprehensive approach to mitigating climate change. In effect, REDD+ has the potential to contribute simultaneously to climate change mitigation and poverty alleviation, while also conserving biodiversity and sustaining vital ecosystem services. During the last two decades, various studies estimate that land-use change, including deforestation and forest degradation, accounts for about 12–29% of global GHG emissions. For this reason, reducing emissions from land-use change through the REDD+ mechanism is considered essential to achieve the objectives of the UNFCCC.

Although there is no direct reference to soil in the R-PIN, the document clearly identifies slash-and-burn agriculture in the context of fighting climate change as one of the main sources of deforestation and GHG emissions in Cameroon. The practice

128 See Republic of Cameroon (2012: 43).

129 Hannam & Boer (2004: 1).

130 See the REDD Desk website at https://theredddesk.org/what-redd.

of slash-and-burn is also one of the main drivers of soil degradation.[131] In the same vein, Cameroon's REDD+ R-PP identifies slash-and-burn farming and extensive livestock breeding in the context of fighting climate change as one of the main sources of deforestation and GHG emissions in Cameroon. Slash-and-burn farming and extensive livestock breeding are also some of the drivers of soil degradation – they have as corollary the decrease in soil fertility and desertification.[132] The R-PP further identifies bushfire as a source of soil degradation. The R-PIN and R-PP are therefore relevant for soil protection in Cameroon.

3.1.2.6 Cameroon's National REDD+ Strategy

Regarding soil protection, the National REDD+ Strategy clearly identifies the implementation of a programme on landscape restoration and management for climate change resilience in the Northern regions through the restoration of degraded soils by setting up private plantations for the production of wood energy; regaining soil fertility; and water catchment protection through agroforestry techniques.[133] Within the framework of promoting sustainable agricultural systems, the National REDD+ Strategy makes recommendations for regaining soil fertility and water catchment protection through agroforestry techniques; promotion of food crops with low deforestation and forest degradation effects; promotion of agricultural systems that allow carbon conservation and sequestration (such as cocoa growing and coffee growing); promotion and propagation of improved seeds; promotion of certification of agricultural products; promotion of biofertilization through the recovery of agricultural residues; restoration and enhancement of village hedges around agricultural land; recovery of fallow land; and – for agro-sylvo-pastoral landscapes – support for pastoral landscape management (such as securing and improving pastures to reduce the incidence of bushfires).

3.1.2.7 The 1995 Indicative Land Use Framework or Zoning Plan

Soil constitutes a multiple-use resource requiring the harmonisation or coordination of users' interests, which are sometimes environmentally unsustainable and detrimental to soil quality. The indicative land-use framework or zoning plan – developed and adopted in 1995, aimed at the distribution of land use – makes provisions for

131 See Ministry of the Environment and Nature Protection & FCPF (2008).

132 Forest Carbon Partnership Facility Cameroon (2013).

133 Cameroon's National Strategy for reducing emissions from deforestation and forest degradation, sustainable management of forests, conservation of forest and enhancement of carbon stocks, (national REDD+ Strategy), 2018.

permanent forest estates.[134] This is relevant for the protection of the soil covered by such areas. Permanent forest estates, as protected areas, are meant to remain forested.[135] The zoning plan is believed to be inaccurate because of out-dated information and poor consultation with local communities.[136] Although there have been attempts by government to institute a land-use policy, the efforts are not adequate, especially with regard to soil protection. A robust land-use plan needs to be put in place as a policy measure to respond to soil protection.

3.1.2.8 Other relevant national policy instruments for soil protection in Cameroon

Other important policy documents relevant for soil protection in Cameroon are the 1995 National Forest Action Programme, the 2035 Vision, the Poverty Reduction Strategy Papers (PRSPs) 2003–2010, and the GESP 2010–2020.[137] As Cameroon presses towards becoming an emerging country by 2035, the PRSPs and the GESP, both with a strong focus on ensuring that the rural sector becomes a key driver of the 2035 Vision, and the Rural Sector Development Strategy reinforce this ambition. To realise this, Cameroon intends to modernise its agricultural sector and focus on those value chains with huge potential to contribute to poverty alleviation and reduce rural–urban migration and unemployment in the rural areas. The realisation of these ambitions and objectives will put pressure on soil and are therefore potential soil degradation policy documents. In addition, there is the Cameroon's position paper for international discussions on climate change drawn up by the Ministry of Environment and Nature Protection in 2009, as it then was.

National policy frameworks, government strategies, action plans, etc., relevant to soil protection in Cameroon are anchored in the international policy instruments identified above, which all address the need for sustainable soil management. Regarding the LDN initiative, which is critical for soil protection, one notices that no legislation in Cameroon specifically captures it. Although Cameroon has no specific policy, plan of action or strategy on the implementation of the LDN concept, it is one of the

134 See Articles 1(2) and 6(2) of Decree No. 95/678/PM of 18 December 1995 to institute an indicative land use framework. In addition to Decree No 95/678, there are additional texts addressing zoning and land tenure, including: Decision No. 135/D/MINEF/CAB of 26 November 1999 establishing the procedures for the classification of the forests in the permanent forest areas of the Republic of Cameroon; Ordinances No. 74/2 and No. 74/1.

135 See the REDD desk Website, at http://theredddesk.org/countries/policies/indicative-land-use-framework-cameroon, accessed 17 October 2017.

136 See Forest Legality Initiative website, at http://www.forestlegality.org/risk-tool/country/cameroon-0, accessed 31 January 2021.

137 GESP's first phase in the implementation of the long-term development 2030 vision, is a comprehensive and integrated strategic document, a springboard for all actions to be undertaken over the next ten years. It was prepared in a context marked by the increase in the cost of living at the national level, the financial crisis and the global food and energy crisis.

countries that have been earmarked for the implementation of the LDN project. However, the NAP-FAD is comprehensive enough to address the objectives of the LDN. Thus, to an extent, Cameroon has explicitly and implicitly taken steps to establish policies, strategies, plans and programmes that accommodate the international policies.

3.2 Relevant international law for the protection of soils

National legislation and policies are in respect of international (global, regional and subregional) commitments subscribed to by Cameroon. At present, there is no specific international soil instrument despite an early proposal for a 'convention on sustainable use of soil' made in Tutzing, Germany, in 1998.[138] However, existing international instruments contain provisions relevant to soil protection. Thus, international soil regulation is fragmented and dispersed, with no coherent and comprehensive approach to soil protection.

Regarding the transposition of international law into Cameroon's legal order, Article 45 of the Cameroonian Constitution as discussed in Chapter one above, is instructive. It stipulates that "duly approved or ratified treaties and international agreements shall, following their publication override national laws, provided the other party implements the said treaty or agreement". This constitutional provision seems to imply a direct reception and application of international law into the Cameroon's national legal system. Thus, as per Article 45 of the Cameroonian Constitution, the principle of 'direct applicability' otherwise known as 'direct effect', holds that international law is directly applicable as it is mainstreamed into the national legal order without the need of any national measures of transposition or reception. A corollary of the principle of direct applicability is the principle of 'primacy', according to which in case of any conflicting or contradictory provisions or incompatibility between international law and national law, the former prevails. This principle is well captured within the spirit of Article 45 of the Cameroonian Constitution.

Whether multilateral global or regional and subregional agreements, there is usually a distinction between international 'hard law'[139] and 'soft law'[140] instruments. Relevant international instruments for the protection of soil to which Cameroon is a signatory are presented under the following subsections.

---

138 See Boer et al. (2016: 56).

139 Hard law instruments consist of conventions, protocols, covenants, charters, pacts, constitutive instruments, final acts, etc. See Tamasang (2014: 29).

140 Numerous international initiatives have been taken in the area of environmental law and governance, leading to a body of soft law instruments consisting of declarations, resolutions, recommendations, Directives, statements, guidelines, stipulations, targets, decisions, plans, etc. See Tamasang (2014: 29). International environmental soft law or 'voluntary' standards have persuasive authority and may encourage States to act accordingly or may provide good legal basis for hard law instruments.

3.2.1 Relevant international soft law commitments

Although not binding on state parties, soft law instruments have for the most part inspired most hard law instruments. Relevant international soft law instruments for the protection of soil to which Cameroon is a signatory are the following: The Stockholm Declaration, 16 June 1972; the Rio Declaration on Environment and Development and Agenda 21, 14 June 1992; The Future We Want – Outcome document of the United Nations Conference on Sustainable Development (Rio+20 Conference), 20–22 June 2012; the 2030 Agenda for Sustainable Development, instituting the Sustainable Development Goals (SDGs), 2015; and the Johannesburg Declaration on Sustainable Development, 2002.

3.2.2 Relevant international hard law instruments

Relevant international hard law instruments for the protection of soil to which Cameroon is a signatory are the following:

- The United Nations Convention to Combat Desertification, 1994;
- the Convention on Biological Diversity, 1992;
- the United Nations Framework Convention on Climate Change, 1992;
- the Kyoto Protocol to the United Nations Framework Convention on Climate Change, 1997;
- the Paris Climate Change Agreement, 2015;
- the Rotterdam Convention on Prior Informed Consent Procedure for Certain Hazardous Chemicals and Pesticides in International Trade, 1998 (as amended in 2004, 2008, 2011, 2013 and 2015);
- the Basel Convention on the Control of Transboundary Movement of Hazardous Wastes and Their Disposal, 1989;
- the Stockholm Convention on Persistent Organic Pollutants, 2001;
- the African Convention on the Conservation of Nature and Natural Resources, 1968 (revised by the Maputo Convention in 2003);
- the Bamako Convention on the Ban on the Import into Africa and the Control of Transboundary Movement and Management of Hazardous Wastes within Africa, 1991;
- the Convention for the Establishment of the African Centre for Fertilizer Development, 1985;
- the Phyto-Sanitary Convention for Africa, 1967;
- the Convention on the Prohibition of the Development, Production and Stockpiling of Bacteriological (Biological) and Toxin Weapons and on their Destruction. Opened for Signature at London, Moscow and Washington, 1972;

- the Convention on the Prohibition of the Development, Production, Stockpiling and Use of Chemical Weapons and on their Destruction, Geneva, 1992;
- the Convention on the Prohibition of Military or Any Other Hostile Use of Environmental Modification Techniques, New York, 1976;
- the Convention on the Conservation of Migratory Species of Wild Animals, 1979;
- the Ramsar Convention on Wetlands of International Importance, especially as Waterfowl Habitat, 1971;
- the Cartagena Protocol on Biosafety to the Convention on Biological Diversity, Montreal, 2000;
- the Convention for Co-operation in the Protection and Development of the Marine and Coastal Environment of the West and Central African Region, 1981;
- the Protocol Concerning Co-operation in Combating Pollution in Cases of Emergency, 1981;
- the International Plant Protection Convention, 1951; and
- the African Charter on Human and Peoples' Rights, Banjul, 1981.

3.3 Relevant national legal provisions for the protection of soil

There is an absence of a comprehensive and coherent policy or legislation dealing with soil protection in Cameroon. In the absence of such comprehensive and coherent soil legislation, relevant legal provisions for the protection of soil are embedded within legal and policy instruments such as the Constitution; land tenure regulations; agriculture, environmental and natural resources policies; and laws, urban and spatial planning laws, laws relating to cross-cutting issues such as environmental and social impact assessment (ESIA), public participation, access to environmental information, rights to appeal administrative decisions and access to courts, etc. Thus, the Cameroonian legislative framework has a multitude of texts relating to soils. Although dispersed, such legislation prescribes mode of access to soils, manner of dispossession of land, and also use of land. These legislations contain relevant provisions for soil protection, but also incentivise soil degradation, demonstrating the strengths and weaknesses of such legislations in terms of sustainable soil management.

3.3.1 The Constitution

As the *Grundnorm*, the Constitution addresses important issues relating to national life in a concise manner and other laws then cover them in detail. But in the domain of soils, the drafters of the 1996 Constitution did not specifically envisage any provisions relating to soil protection. Thus, there is no direct or specific constitutional provision that deals with soil in Cameroon. However, when mentioning natural resources,[141] we consider that this relates equally to soils. Such a conclusion is indeed plausible as all-natural resources have their springboard from the land or soils and so the exploitation of these resources has a bearing on soil protection. Incidentally, as indicated above, the Constitution does not address everything in detail, otherwise the legislative power would be rendered redundant or would have very little to do. Notwithstanding this observation, we should argue that soil, being a critically important cross-cutting subject, may require express articulation in the Constitution. In its Preamble, the Constitution provides that:

> Every person shall have a right to a healthy environment. The protection of the environment shall be the duty of every citizen. The State shall ensure the protection and improvement of the environment.

These preambular provisions are a pointer to the fact that the Constitution expressly addresses environmental protection issues, particularly from a human rights perspective, and goes as far as to impose obligations on citizens and the state in connection with the enjoyment of such a so-called third-generational human right. Since the Preamble is now part and parcel of the Constitution,[142] any violation of such a right is tantamount to a violation of the Constitution. An important question that begs for an answer at this juncture is whether the Preamble of the Cameroon's Constitution is binding or is merely aspirational. This question is answered by Article 65 of the Constitution which provides that the Preamble is part and parcel of the Constitution and thus is binding.

The legislative power does not have any specific express powers relating to the issue of environmental protection. However, the Constitution provides, among others, that legislation on natural resources is under the legislative power.[143] Since natural resources form the basis of environmental resources, we can come to a safe conclusion that the Constitution envisages the legislative power's role with regard to environmental protection and by extension soil protection.

3.3.2 Legislation on land tenure (landownership, access and users' rights) an anchor point for soil protection

The right of ownership guaranteed by law enables the holder of the right to use and enjoy the proceeds or dispose of his property. No one is supposed to be deprived of

141 Paragraph 3 of the Preamble and Article 26(2)(d)(5) of Law No 96/06 of 20 January 1996 as amended.

142 Article 65 of Law No 96/06 of 20 January 1996 as amended.

143 Ibid.: Article 26(2)(d).

this right unless on the grounds of public utility and on the basis that the owner is duly compensated in accordance with the modalities spelled out by law.

3.3.2.1 Historical overview of landownership

Landownership directly affects livelihoods and human development, both in urban and rural areas, making landownership a high-stake issue. Discussions here focus on landownership during pre-colonial, colonial and post-colonial periods in Cameroon.

Perhaps because of its low economic investment and commercial value, Belaunde et al. note that land in pre-colonial Cameroon was seldom the object of a scramble, and degradation – indeed, land during this period was owned communally by families or whole villages with traditional leaders acting as custodians for the benefit of all members of the village.[144] These authors also emphasise that, under these conditions, land held significant religious value. As the burial place of generations of ancestors, land was a vital link to, and the primary means of communication with, the dead or ancestors. Within this context, land was handed down from generation to generation within the family and beneficial use rights were only granted to strangers temporarily if the family had no use for the land.[145] The communal system of landownership was largely absorbed into a formalised landownership system with the coming of the colonial system.

Since 1884, following the German annexation of Cameroon until its Independence, Cameroon, like the rest of Africa, was under colonial rule, during which time the colonial masters' laws replaced many traditional or customary land tenure practices that were observed across the different fondoms and chiefdoms.

Under German rule for instance, the Crown Lands Act of 1896 granted state ownership over all lands, giving Germany the power to effectively occupy land and made native farmers wage labourers on German plantations.[146] Thus, under German administration, only Germans could acquire land while the natives were deprived of such rights.[147] The colonists confiscated most of the South West Region of Cameroon to establish industrial plantations. Traditional rulers resisted but the penalties for protesting were execution and deportation.[148] However, the Crown Lands Act recognised customary ownership by excluding from the category of 'vacant land without owners',[149]

144 Belaunde et al. (2010: 18).
145 Ibid.
146 Ibid.
147 See Lemmens (2010).
148 Ibid.
149 Commonly referred to in Cameroon as *terres vacantes et sans maître*.

land which 'private individuals or corporate bodies, chiefs or indigenous communities could show proof of ownership rights or other real rights over.'[150]

France, in contrast, used a system of land registration to formally establish the land rights of French citizens, while the natives retained the right only to occupy and exploit land in their native localities. Belaunde et al. state that, beginning with the French Decree of 1932, a process was established in which individuals could assert their claim over land usage.[151] The land law of 17 June 1959 protected customary landownership stating –[152]

> the customary rights exercised collectively or individually on all land are confirmed, apart from land which forms part of the public and private domains (…) and land which has been appropriated according to the regulation of the civil code or the registration system (…). No collective group or individual can be forced to cede their rights unless for a state-approved purpose and for which they receive fair compensation."

In urban areas natives were not allowed to live in the same areas as whites and were coerced to live in slums.[153]

During the British rule, British Cameroon was subdivided into two regions: British Northern Cameroon that applied regulations of Northern Nigeria, and British Southern Cameroon that applied regulations in use in Eastern Nigeria. Native Rights Decrees were enacted in 1927, enabling the Governor-General of Nigeria to confer statutory rights on non-natives and foreigners, and customary rights of occupancy to natives. In 1956, all lands became the property of customary authorities, except private land called 'freehold' and 'leasehold' lands. The rights of natives were protected by traditional rulers. The representative of the Crown, the 'Commissioner', was charged with ensuring the application of the law and protecting all native rights. The 'Public Land Acquisition Decree' enabled government to acquire land for public purposes.[154]

Thus, given its unique colonial history in Africa, Cameroon inherited a plethora of colonial land laws that have contributed to shaping the current legal regime governing landownership.

Soon after French Cameroon achieved independence in 1960 and the reunification of the French-speaking and English-speaking parts in 1961, two land tenure systems inherited from the colonial masters were established. The first attempt to harmonise the two inherited land tenure systems was on 9 January 1963, by decree, with the aim of laying down rules governing land tenure in Cameroon. The intention of the government was to replace the colonial concept of vacant land without owners with a national land law consisting of classical public and private land. Thus, the post-colonial era witnessed the establishment of modern statutory regulations in 1974 by the

150 Article 1.
151 Belaunde et al. (2010: 18).
152 Land Law of 1959, Article 3.
153 See Lemmens (2010).
154 Ibid.

government of the newly formed state in an attempt to boost economic growth, enabling investors to buy and develop land. For this purpose, land was classified into three categories: private property, national land, and public land, guaranteeing free ownership and issuing of land to all naturalised persons and corporate bodies. Procedures and conditions for obtaining land certificates were put in place. The regulations also empowered the government to act as guardian of all land, thus allowing intervention to ensure the use of land. Regulations confiscated land under the control of native authorities. However, the 1974 land reform regulations appeared ineffective and inefficient, leading to a litany of subsequent legislation to facilitate the acquisition and development of land.[155] While customary ownership rights were severely reduced under the 1974 land tenure ordinances, some use rights remained for the native populations. Specifically –[156]

> use rights are, in accordance with the relevant law, those which are recognised for resident populations to exploit all fauna and fish products in the forest, apart from protected species for their own personal use.

Thus, regarding struggles over land, key actors including 'traditional' authorities and natives (or their civil society representatives) continue to assert their claims based on customary law, which are, of course, recognised within the Cameroonian legal context.[157] The multiplicity of legal instruments on land has implications regarding which forums are available to settle land disputes and also for the relative strength of claims over land. This current practice finds its roots in the pre-colonial and colonial eras. Pre-colonial rights over land were enforced by the traditional authorities that had decision-making authority over village affairs. The 1922 French Civil Code extended to Cameroon established a parallel system of adjudication under which 'natives' were governed by customary law and the modern French metropolitan administration applied to the assimilated Africans[158] who had superior claims over natives.[159] A similar practice exists today in Cameroon that tends to disfavour the poor and those without 'connections'. While Decree No. 77/249 of 15 July 1977 recognises the local customs of traditional chiefdoms,[160] written law prevails over customary practice or claims in the event of any conflict.[161] In brief, as noted by Belaunde et al., "legal pluralism in land law is well established in Cameroon, and the colonial legacy of land tenure reinforces power inequalities to the advantage of the State."[162]

155 Ibid.
156 Article 78 of the 1994 forestry law.
157 Belaunde et al. (2010: 19).
158 Commonly referred to in former French colonies in Africa as *assimilés*.
159 Belaunde et al. (2010: 19).
160 Article 6.
161 Supreme Court Decree 1962.
162 Belaunde et al. (2010: 20).

The Government of Cameroon continues to maintain supremacy in landownership and uses, and defining, complex and expensive processes for private ownership.[163] These costly and cumbersome procedures favour wealthy and well-connected individuals over marginalised people or those with little means.[164] In effect, only those with enough resources or influence have been able to acquire land and enforce their land rights as competition for land increases.[165] In Cameroon, statutory land tenure is thus considered superior to customary land tenure, although the latter was in existence long before the modern state. The conflict between customary and statutory land rights often culminates in the loss of land rights for the poorest and marginalised, with implications for land and soil degradation as they may use unsustainable methods to establish rights and claims to land.

3.3.2.2 Modern landownership

The Constitution of Cameroon guarantees in a general manner the right to ownership. This is affirmed in the declaration of general principles in the Constitution, through which ownership is defined as:

> the right guaranteed every person by law, to use, enjoy and dispose of property. No person shall be deprived thereof, save for public purposes and subject to the payment of compensation under conditions determined by law.

Compensation is not, however, a pre-condition for imposition of environmental obligations, as the same Preamble imposes the responsibility on everyone to protect the environment without any condition. The enjoyment of this constitutional right to ownership in the domain of land is mitigated by the various legal texts relating to access to and use of lands or soils. Ownership of land is recognised for every physical or moral person through a certificate of ownership which in land matters is the land certificate. The conditions for obtaining such a document are not within the reach of the average citizen. The land certificate which is true evidence of landownership under Cameroonian land law is obtainable in three types of procedures depending on the origin of the land. This is well articulated below and is entitled "acquiring land under statutory law in Cameroon".

When it comes to landownership, access to and the use of land in Cameroon, public law on the subject is governed by the following ordinances: Ordinance No 74/2 of 6 July 1974 to establish the rules governing state lands; and Ordinance No 74/1 of 6 July 1974 to establish the rules governing land tenure. These are the texts governing land issues in Cameroon and they are complemented by several other enabling instruments

163 Ibid.: 18.
164 Ibid.
165 Ibid.

such as Decree No. 76/166 of 27April 1976 to establish the terms and conditions for the management of national lands, and Circular No. 001/CAB/PM of 1 April 2014 relating to the provisions applicable to investors on access to land in Cameroon. These legal instruments may be read in conjunction *mutatis mutandis* with the following:

- Decree No. 2003/418/PM of 25 February 2003 to establish the rates for indemnities to landowners whose lands have farmlands and planted trees that have been destroyed on the grounds of public utility;
- Decree No. 87/1872 of 16 December 1987 to enable the application of law No. 85/009 of July 4, 1985 on expropriation on the grounds of public utility;
- Decree No. 214/32111 of 29 September 2014 to establish the minimum prices applicable to transactions on land that falls under the private property of the state;
- Decree No. 2014/3210/PM of 29 September 2014 to establish the conditions for the acquisition of BAUX and the modalities for payment of land taxes in economic areas;
- Decree No. 2014/3209/PM of 29 September 2014 to establish the minimum amounts for annual dues for the occupation of attachments to state lands;
- Decree No. 2015/3580/PM of 11 August 2015 to establish the modalities of registration and the regime of insurance and guarantees applicable to consensus and 'baux domaniaux';
- Decree No. 2016/3058/PM of 28 July 2016 to establish the rules for the use of land and construction;
- Arrête No. 00832/Y.15.1/MINUH/D000 of 20 November 1987 to establish the bases for calculating value of buildings that are expropriated on the grounds of public utility;
- Circular No. 001 of 22 March 1994 to establish the minimum amounts for the sale of national lands; and
- Law No. 85/09 of 4 July 1985 on expropriation for public utility purposes and the compensation regime.

To the above can be added Law No. 96/12 of 5 August 1996, a framework law on environmental management in Cameroon; and Law No. 94/01 of 20 January 1994 on forestry, wildlife, and fisheries regulations. The Cameroonian land-related legislative framework therefore constitutes multiple legal texts relating to soils.

Ordinance No. 74/1 of 6 July 1974, to establish the rules governing land tenure, throws more light on this distinction. After establishing the state as "guardian of all lands", to ensure the "rational use of land in the imperative interest of national defense or the economic policies of the nation" in Section 1(2), the ordinance divides land into three categories: Public lands, which consist of roads, rivers, the seaside and other lands for public use; private lands, which consist of privately held lands under title and private state lands ('domaine privé de l'Etat'). Private state lands include lands acquired by the state (e.g. to support public buildings), degazetted lands and rural lands left "unexploited or abandoned" by the owner or custodian as per Article 10 of Ordinance No. 74/2; and national lands, which is a residual category and consists of land that is neither private nor public, and is considered a land reserve. The law explicitly includes untitled lands occupied or used by rural communities as National Lands. This land is administered by the state "for the public good" and to "guarantee their use and effective exploitation" as per Article 14 of Ordinance No. 74/1. This distinction appears rather confusing to a foreigner who can hardly understand the gist of the distinction between public and private property of the state. One can imagine that this distinction is far from being logical in the sense that the state is a public structure and therefore the notion of private property of the state seems rather contradictory.

3.3.2.3 Acquiring land under statutory law

3.3.2.3.1 Acquiring land from the national domain

The acquisition of land in Cameroon occurs through a concession process, a procedure where the state authorises the acquisition by any person wishing to acquire land and who has a development project to undertake on an unoccupied portion of national domain. There are two phases, namely a provisional phase and a final phase. An application for a provisional concession is deposited at the Department of Lands. The divisional service head in writing informs the administrative authority of that division, the Senior Divisional Officer (SDO), who then convenes a consultative commission. This commission visits the *locus in quo* and subsequently forwards to the Minister of Land Affairs minutes with a reasoned opinion on the legal status of the land in question and feasibility of the project on such a piece of land. The applicant has five years to carry out developments on the land (the so-called *mise en value*) in accordance with a prescription of what is expected of the applicant (the so-called *cahier de charge*). The final concession is obtained only after the competent authorities are satisfied with the *mise en value* (effective use) of the portion of land previously under a provisional concession. In the event of non-respect of the obligations imposed on the concessionaire, he is divested of his rights on the piece of land and the concession comes to an end.

For obtaining a provisional concession, the procedure is as follows: Buying fiscal stamps; obtaining a certified copy of a national identity card; obtaining an Order to pay a fee for the opening of the file; paying the application fee for the file; depositing the application file for the concession; obtaining the Prefectoral Order for the visit to the locus; obtaining the Ministerial Arrête (Order) for the attribution of the provisional concession; and paying the land fee.

For obtaining the final concession, the procedure is as follows: Depositing the application of proof of mise en value; obtaining the convocation of the SDO for the establishment of proof of mise en value (effective use) of the piece of land; obtaining the Ministerial Arrête (Order) of the attribution of the final concession; obtaining an Order for the payment of the land fee; paying the land fee; depositing the application file for a land title/certificate; and collecting thereof.

3.3.2.3.2 Acquiring private land of the state

A private estate of the state can be attributed for use or for ownership to physical or moral persons. Sales documents for the private property of the state are valid only after the authorisation and visa of the minister in charge of state property and land affairs is obtained. Complete payments of the price after authorisation of the Minister gives the right to parcelling out or carving out or to transfering of the land title.

For obtaining ownership by way of sale by negotiation, the procedure is as follows: Buying fiscal stamps; obtaining a certified copy of a national identity card; obtaining an Order to pay a fee for the opening of the file; paying the application fee for the file; depositing the application file mutual consent; obtaining the Prefectoral Order for the visit to the locus; obtaining the Ministerial Authorisation for the sale of state land; obtaining an Order to pay the land fee; paying the land fee; depositing documents for the land title; and collecting thereof.

3.3.2.3.3 Acquiring private land of an individual

'Land title' is the official certification of landownership. Land transactions between private individuals can be done by way of transfer or by parcelling out. The transfer of land title is done after a complete cession, gratuitously or with obligations regarding the land. Still, the separation of the land following successive sales or division leads to parcelling out of the original title to the benefit of the acquirers.

Cameroonian land law prescribes that all land transactions be done through a notary officer. The notary officer is in charge of registration of documents of sale at the taxation office and of the transmission of application for land title to the Department of State Property and Land Affairs. In Cameroon a land certificate, which is the only proof of landownership, can be obtained by the signing of a land transfer agreement, a Deed of Conveyance,[166] and eventually the issuance of a land certificate. Generally, an individual or a moral person desirous of owning land in Cameroon has a duty to consult a property attorney to conduct due diligence and investigate the title of the land at the property land registry so as to ensure that the land is free from all encumbrances

166 A deed of conveyance is a legal document prepared by a notary public to convey absolute rights over a piece of land to a purchaser as per Section 8(1) of Ordinance No 74/1 and Section 74 of Law No. 90/059 of 19th December 1990.

like bank mortgages, court cases, double sales, etc. A notary public is statutorily commissioned to draft and sign all deeds of conveyance in Cameroon after conducting a survey site plan of the parcel of land to ascertain the square metre area of the land or documents evidencing initial sale. The Cameroon Penal Code sanctions any vendor who does not make full disclosure at the negotiation stage before selling the piece of land as per Section 318 of the Cameroon Penal Code.

The law regulating the granting of a land certificate in Cameroon is Decree No. 76/165 of 27 April 1976, which has been modified by Decree No. 2005/481 of 16 December 2005. Landowners mistakenly consider their notarised Deed of Conveyance to be a land certificate. The procedure to obtain a land certificate is strict and detailed. A summary of the procedure comprises an application with attached survey plan describing the land, payment of a processing fee, a visit to the locus for boundary demarcation and cadastral mapping, publication and the eventual issuance of a land certificate.

For obtaining a land title following a transfer, a technical file for transfer must be obtained which requires the following procedure: Buying of fiscal stamps; buying a form for the technical file; depositing the application for obtaining of the technical file for transfer; obtaining the state of cession of survey department; paying the survey fee; and collecting the technical file/dossier.

For the Preparation of the technical file of transfer, signature of Sales Act and collection of land title require the following: Applying for urban certificate; collecting of urban certificate; signing of sales acts at the notary office; obtaining a receipt of deposit of the application of land title; and collecting of the main land title clearly marked 'transfer'.

Obtaining a land title after a parcelling out process and /or obtaining the dossier techniques of parcelling out requires: Buying of fiscal stamps; buying of a form for the technical file; depositing of an application for obtaining the technical file for transfer; obtaining the state of cession of the survey department; paying the survey fee; and collecting the technical file/dossier.

Generally, land titling is fraught with stringent bureaucratic procedures and inefficiencies. The acquisition and establishment of a land certificate is a slow process because of stringent legal requirements, and a cumbersome and costly procedure. Cameroon's land tenure law creates a certain degree of uncertainty regarding tenure rights. Modern landownership under state control is unfair, being beneficial to the state, large corporations, the church, national elites and the rich.[167] This can encourage

---

167 See *Divisional Officer of Ndop v Yenkong*, (1994) CAJ-CLC 56; *C. Chekeba v Divisional Officer of Mezam*. (1994) CAJ-CLC 18. (1994) CAJ-CLC 18; also see *Martin Fobuzie v SDO Mezam* BCA/2/78 unreported decision of the Bamenda Court of Appeal. Cited by Munge (2011: 209).

unsustainable practices by occupiers of land who feel unsecured – which is not healthy for soil protection.

3.3.2.4 Traditional law

Traditional/customary law governs land tenure in Cameroon, as in the rest of Africa. The country has more than 250 ethnic groups, each with its own customs,[168] making the country rich in traditional/customary law. In the area of land tenure, customs recognise customary ownership of land. Such customary tenure was recognised by Ordinance No. 74/1 up to 5 August 1974, but the same legislation stated that, after this date, all lands under customary ownership should be registered or cease to exist under customary tenure.[169] Therefore, according to statutory law, there has been no customary ownership of land after 5 August 1974, and this has been one of the major sources of conflict over landownership in the country. In this regard, the majority of lands in Cameroon are classified as national and state-owned despite century-old claims by communities.

3.3.2.5 Conflicts and means of conflict resolution

In Cameroon, there is a variety of land tenure types including state-owned lands (public lands, private state lands and national lands), private lands and lands owned communally by communities, all of which fall under the two broad classifications of statutory and customary land tenure. These different tenure types constitute a source of conflict and unsustainable land and soil management. The majority of civil cases that come before Cameroonian courts today have their root causes in land and land-related conflicts. This means that land has been and continues to be the critical and core resource and deservedly may be referred to as the bedrock resource. In case of conflicting claims over land, ownership is ascribed to the person that can prove better title to the land. If there is no title document, it is sufficient for a claimant to show that they have been in possession of the land. Evidence of possession includes, but is not limited to, cultivation on the piece of land, erection of buildings or fences, and demarcation of the land with pegs or beacons. The purpose of a survey plan in a land case is to identify the land in dispute because a person who cannot identify a piece of land will hardly convince the court of being the rightful owner. Traditional evidence can also be

168 Ngwafor (1996).

169 Article 17(2) of the Land Tenure Ordinance, 1974 read in conjunction with Article 15 classifying land into two categories.

adduced to prove 'ownership' of land, but the court must be convinced as to who founded the land, how the founder founded the land, and the names of intervening owners.

Resolution of disputes over land falls under the jurisdiction of ordinary law courts or courts of ordinary jurisdiction. The judicial organisation for Cameroon according to the 1972 Judicial Organisation Ordinance as amended in 2006 and 2011 is as follows: At the top, there is the Supreme Court, followed by the Court of Appeal in every region, the High Court in every division, the Court of First Instance in every sub-division and, finally, there are the Traditional or Customary Courts, where applicable. Every Cameroonian citizen who feels that his/her rights have been violated in a land transaction can solicit the appropriate court in their place of residence.

3.3.3 Public environmental law

Public environmental law in Cameroon refers to soil-specific legal acts, environmental law, nature conservation legal acts, subsidiary regulations on environmental thresholds, environmental quality standards, etc. and international law (bilateral and multilateral agreements) and their relevant provisions concerning soils.

3.3.3.1 Soil-specific legal acts

Decree No. 2011/2584/PM of 23 August 2011 on the modalities of protection of soils and sub-soils is the one and only Cameroonian text focusing specifically on the protection of soils and sub-soils. This can be verified in Article 3, which stipulates that "any activity relating to the exploitation of the soil must be done in a manner as to avoid or reduce erosion of soils and desertification". In addition, this decree specifically takes into account lands suitable for agricultural activities. Thus, the protection of arable land is envisaged in Article 5 in the following words: "is forbidden any activity which degrades or modifies the quality and/or the structure of arable lands or contributes to the loss of such lands". Decree No. 2011/2584/PM is an enabling instrument to Law No. 96/12 of 5 August 1996 on framework law on environmental management. The administration in charge of environment is tasked with overseeing the implementation of this legal text. It therefore has to ensure the respect of this piece of legislation, as need be, and to impose administrative sanctions in cases of violation of the text. The decree is even more specific regarding the protection of soils and subsoils to the extent that it particularly preserves risk zones. This is the purport of Article 4(1) which prohibits the exploitation of zones with high risk of erosion. Article 4(2) prohibits any activity that degrades or modifies the quality and/or structure of arable lands or which contributes to the loss of these lands. On the issue of environmental impact assessment (EIA), it is important to note that although the realisation of all development projects is conditional upon the carrying out of EIA, this prescription has already been envisaged in the Framework Law on Environmental Management. The decree has retaken the provisions in order to make this prescription emphatic and to ensure further sensitisation to a better protection regime for soils and sub-soils. This is what seems to be the purport of Article 9, which provides that:

> all physical or moral persons, private or public who undertake agricultural exploitation and practice intensive use of fertilizers and/or pesticides or apparatuses that condition the soil, are obliged to carry out in a regular manner an evaluation of their impacts on the environment in accordance with regulations in force

and Article 10 which provides that:

> all physical or moral persons desirous to manufacture or condition fertilizers and/or pesticides on the national territory are obliged to carry out environmental and social impact assessment in conformity with regulations in force.

There is no gainsaying from the foregoing provisions that environmental and social impact assessments (ESIA) are mandatory under Cameroonian law for any project likely to have deleterious effects on the use of soils. The question remains that of effective implementation of the rules on ESIA. Are the rules strictly respected by the stakeholders? To this question, the answer may be in the negative. Again, does the administration in charge of the environment control project implementation in order to ensure compliance with the undertakings by project promoters (commonly referred to in Cameroon as *cahier de charge*)? We will say that the administration does carry out control, but such a control is usually tainted with corrupt practices as the promoter may grease the palms of the environmental inspectors or controllers, thereby making them biased in their report. This, as a matter of fact, does not augur well for sustainable soil management. Furthermore, where a report identifies violators anyway, the question is whether such violators are sanctioned? Sanctions for violations are administrative and judicial. From an administrative point of view, there is ample evidence that, once identified, the administration sanctions the violators of soil and soil-related legislation. Another disturbing issue has turned on whether the sanctions are sufficient to have a deterrent effect on violators. Most of the cases that go to court are protracted and generally the sanction is not in favour of the administration for at least two reasons. The one is that judges are not sufficiently schooled in this relatively grey area of the law and, second, even when they are, some will give in to corrupt practices. Even when the violators are sanctioned, it has been argued that the sanctions are not heavy enough to deter violators. Again, the provisions above aimed at users practising intensive use of fertilizers and pesticides or apparatus that condition the soil seem impractical because, if read as they stand, any user of pesticides would have to conduct an ESIA. This seems unrealistic. However, the decree specifically mentions 'intensive use' of fertilizers and/or pesticides or apparatus that condition the soil. This may be interpreted to mean that users who do not practise intensive use are not required to carry out ESIA. Nevertheless, their activities may still lead to soil degradation if the sum total of their small-scale projects are taken into account. In the absence of a comprehensive and coherent soil law, the relevant provisions of environmental law, as supplemented by other subsidiary regulations on environmental thresholds and environmental quality, govern soils in Cameroon.

3.3.3.2 Environmental law, relevant provisions concerning soils

In Cameroon, protection of the soil and subsoil is envisaged in Law No. 96/12 of 5 August 1996 relating to the framework law on environmental management and its enabling instrument which is Decree No. 2011/2584/PM of 23 August 2011 Establishing the Modalities for the Protection of the Soil and Subsoil as discussed above. The direct provision of the 1996 Framework Law on Environmental Management is Article 36 which provides that:

> (1) the soil and subsoil, as well as the limited renewable or non-renewable resources contained therein, shall be protected against any form of degradation and jointly managed rationally by the competent Administrations; and
>
> (2) an enabling decree of this law, prepared in collaboration with the Administrative units concerned, shall lay down:
>
> - the specific conditions for the protection and fight against desertification, erosion, loss of arable land and pollution of the soil and its resources by chemicals, pesticides and fertilizers;
>
> - the list of fertilizers, pesticides and other chemical substances whose use shall be authorised or encouraged in agriculture;
>
> - the authorised quantities and the terms and conditions for their use so that the substances do not endanger soil quality or other receptor environments.

With respect to this specific provision of the law, we can praise the fact that the enabling instruments are in force and the only regret is that, like many other instruments, its effective implementation is still doubtful as some unauthorised chemicals and pesticides are still used for agricultural activities thereby degrading the soils and subsoils by way of pollution and other means. There is therefore the need to enhance the implementation of legislation in order to ensure that soils are properly protected.

According to Article 37 of the 1996 Framework Law on Environmental Management, holders of mining or quarrying permits are required to rehabilitate the exploited sites. With regard to this provision, there is good reason to commend the intentions of the legislator for the simple reason that, as one of the mineral destinations in Africa, Cameroon hosts many multinational companies carrying out exploration and exploitation in the extractive sector, especially in the domain of hard minerals. Consequently, the soils are exposed after these activities have taken place and therefore there is the need to rehabilitate. Unfortunately, subsidiary/delegated legislators have not moved the legislative crafting agenda forward as the enabling instruments to the application of this provision relating to soils have not yet seen the light of day in spite of the fact that mining activities have taken place and are still taking place and the soils are exposed to erosion to the same extent as they pollute. The regret is even greater because the law is 23 years old, having entered into force in 1996, and some of its enabling instruments have not yet come into force.

It is important at this point to say a few words regarding the critical issue of enabling instruments in the particular context of Cameroon. The legislative crafting process in Cameroon is one that is significantly inspired by the Continental legal system. Such a legal tradition practices a law-making process where parliament, or any other organ of state entrusted with powers to make laws, crafts a piece of legislation by setting out the main issues of the law and allows subsidiary or delegated legislators to lay down details to complete such a legislation. These details have the following ingredients, namely: clarifying/defining of concepts, phrases and words contained in the main legal instrument; creating institutions for the implementation of the law; outlining the procedure that may be necessary for the effective implementation of the law; and taking any other measures that may be necessary for a complete understanding of the law. The obvious merits of such a legislative crafting process is that: the main piece of legislation itself is not overloaded; it eases understanding and avoids ambiguity in the understanding and interpretation of the legislative piece; it makes for sufficient flexibility in the law-making process as delegated legislators are involved especially from a technical perspective; it saves parliamentary time and obviates boredom; and makes allowance for some urgent matters to be addressed without necessarily convening parliament for the purpose. Despite these advantages, the ugly side of such a process is that legislative implementation is unnecessarily delayed because an enabling instrument has not seen the light of day. The executive power which is usually in charge of putting in place an enabling instrument may deliberately delay the implementation of a law requiring the former probably because that law was not the brainchild of the government, for instance, where a funding institution from which funds are sourced, such as the World Bank or the International Monetary Fund, imposes a conditionality for the grant of a loan. In fact, the absence of an enabling instrument makes the implementation of a piece of legislation practically difficult, if not impossible. It is therefore recommended that enabling instruments should be crafted at the same time as the main law.

Relevant provisions of the 1996 Framework Law on Environmental Management for the conservation of nature, which by extension protects the soil, include: Article 38 regarding the allotment and management of land for agricultural, industrial, urban or other uses, as well as prospecting, research or exploitation of subsoil resources likely to endanger the environment; Article 62 regarding the protection of nature, the preservation of animals and plant species and their habitats, the maintenance of biological balances and ecosystems, and the conservation of biodiversity and genetic diversity against all causes of degradation; Article 63 regarding the rational management of natural resources; Article 64 regarding the sustainable use of biodiversity; Article 65 regarding the exploitation of biological and genetic resources; Article 66 on the recognition and protection of historic, archaeological and scientific sites, as well as sites that are of special panoramic beauty; Article 67 regarding the rational and ecological exploitation of mining resources and quarries in line with environmental considerations; Article 68 regarding protection of land against erosion and prevention and fighting against desertification; and Article 69 requiring states to use shared resources in a sustainable manner and in accordance with international conventions signed between the states sharing such resources.

Natural resources, nature and biodiversity conservation are properly addressed in environmental texts relating thereto as seen in the provisions above. This is not surprising given the fact that the legislation in question is a framework law. Soils form the bedrock of natural resources and nature, including biodiversity. A reading of the environmental legislation above relating to these aspects reveals that sufficient measures are in place to protect soils and soil-related elements which are the habitats of nature and biodiversity resources. Furthermore, while there is ample evidence of national policies on the subject of soil protection, the environmental legislation has gone a step further to put an assent on the application of international conventions duly ratified by Cameroon in keeping with Article 45 of the Constitution given earlier. Cameroon has ratified most, if not all, of the relevant international conventions on soil and soil-related issues. What's more, the country is in the implementation phase of national legislation and international conventions, but with obvious challenges which we think could be addressed in model legislation.

MINEPDED, which is the administration that spearheads the application of this law, encounters many difficulties in its mission of ensuring the protection of the soil and subsoil. In effect, in the organisational structures of many other public administrations, we find some internal services that are specifically in charge of environmental concerns. These services carry out their missions without necessarily seeking the opinion of the ministry in charge of the environment. It is this state of affairs that generally leads to soil degradation in our country. For example, in matters of mineral exploitation or any other industrial activity that affects the soil, MINEPDED requires that all such sites should be returned to their initial state or be restored. This requirement is seldom respected by industrial operators and MINEPDED is handicapped in taking any effective measures against the recalcitrant operators because the industrial activities carried out on these sites do not fall within the area of competence of MINEPDED. The attitudes of these ministries do constitute, in most of the cases, the root causes of the conflicts between the local populations and the industrial operators. This justifies the need for collaboration and coordination among centralised and decentralised territorial collectives. In addition to the aforementioned legal texts, one still finds provisions relating to the protection of soil and subsoil in other legal instruments.

3.3.3.3 Nature conservation

In Cameroon, there is not specific legislation with the direct objective of protecting nature apart from the Framework Law on Environmental Management discussed above. However, there are other sectoral legal texts that deal with the conservation of nature and, by extension, soil protection.

3.3.3.3.1 Law No. 98/005 of 14 April 1998 (Water Code)

With regard to the protection of soil, the following provisions are relevant. Article 2(1) requires the state to ensure the protection of water. Article 4(1) prohibits the emptying, shattering, disposal, infiltration, leakage, direct or indirect deposit into waters of any solid material, liquid or gas, and, in particular, industrial, agricultural and atomic wastes if these are susceptible to: altering the quality of the surface or underground water or the high seas within territorial confines; endangering public health or aquatic or submarine flora and fauna; or compromising the economic and tourism developments of the regions. Under Article 4(2), the minister in charge of water may, after inquiry and opinions of other ministries concerned, authorise and regulate the forms of disposal indicated above, with the possibility of modifying or withdrawing such an authorisation. Article 7, in an attempt to protect the quality of water destined for use, sets a perimeter of protection around the capture points, treatment and stocking points of the water and declares lands found within the perimeters of protection to be of public utility.

The Water Code, which is also a sectoral law, does not ignore soil and soil-related concerns which are addressed not directly but by implication. What matters here is that the water legislator has demonstrated the importance of soil in the water management regime given that water has its source from the soils. Therefore, the soils must be protected if the goal is to ensure access by everyone to water resources either for domestic or industrial uses. In relation to effective water management, we submit that, as a matter of principle, the Water Code and its enabling instruments seem to have captured all the stakes that the exploitation of water may have on soil protection. Since water has its source from the soils, the sustainable exploitation of water by implication means the protection of soils.

3.3.3.3.2 Law No. 94/01 of 20 January 1994 on Forests, Fauna and Fisheries Regulation

Law No. 94/01 is the basic law governing forest exploitation in Cameroon. Desertification and deforestation constitute some of the phenomena that contribute to soil degradation. In effect, when trees are cut without being replaced, the space left behind becomes a stretch of desert. The soils become exposed with attendant consequences. It is in this light that this law makes provision for reforestation and reinstatement of the exploited species. Unfortunately, this requirement is hardly respected especially by clandestine forest exploiters. The state, civil society organisations and partners in development have embarked on a mission to combat this ill through the introduction of licensing and certification procedures in forest exploitation.

3.3.3.4 Subsidiary regulations on environmental thresholds, environmental quality standards, and more

A document relating to the norms of environmental protection has been elaborated upon and is in the process of homologation at the Norms and Quality Agency.

Apart from the Framework Law on Environmental Management, there are other subsidiary regulations on environmental thresholds and environmental quality standards that are equally relevant for soil protection in Cameroon. These include: Law No. 89/027 of 29 December 1989 on toxic and hazardous waste that binds local industries, which by their activities generate toxic and/or dangerous waste, to declare the volume and the nature of their production and to ensure their safe disposal for man and his environment; Law No. 98/015 of 14 July 1998 and its implementing regulations notably Order No. 013/MINMEN/DMG/SL of 19 April 1977 on the nomenclature of establishments classified as dangerous, unhealthy or uncomfortable, as modified and completed by Order No. 02/MINMEE/DMG/SDAMIC of 14 January 1999; Decree No. 99/818/PM of 9 November 1999 laying down the procedures for the establishment and operation of establishments classified as dangerous, unhealthy or uncomfortable; Decree No. 2011/2581/PM of 23 August 2011 regulating harmful and/or dangerous chemical substances; and Decree No. 2012/2809/PM of 26 September 2012 laying down provisions for the sorting, collection, storage, transport, recycling, treatment and disposal of waste. The purpose of these texts is to guarantee environmental and public health protection by establishments considered dangerous, unhealthy or uncomfortable; and Decree No. 2000/092/PM of 27 March 2000, amending Decree No. 95/531/PM of 23 August 1995 setting the terms and conditions of application of the forest regime; Decree No. 95/466/PM of 20 July 1995 to set the terms and conditions of applying the wildlife regime; Decree No. 95/531/PM on the role of ministry of forestry staff to determine modalities for safe and controlled fire, and ministry of territorial administration and decentralisation to issue permits to start fires after consultation with local forestry staff; Decree No. 95/678/PM of 18 December 1995 establishing an incentive framework for the use of Southern Forest Areas and Circular Letter No. 92/LC/MINFOF/SG/DF of 23 September 2009 on procedures for the issuance and monitoring of recuperation of timber permits and selected logging.

The aforementioned legal texts all seek to prevent deforestation and wildlife extinction or the destruction of wildlife habitats. The protection of these ecosystems indirectly also protects their soils.

3.3.4 Environmental monitoring

Environmental monitoring is of fundamental importance to effective environmental management,[170] especially soil protection. With regard to soil, environmental monitoring may be referred to as the systematic sampling of soil in order to establish the ecological state of the soil; to assess the effects of dangerous activities on soils; to ensure compliance with environmental regulations; and to inform policy design and decision-making. Environmental monitoring and compliance is carried out through EIA, which is defined as a way of tracking and addressing changes in the biophysical and social environment during project implementation.[171] In its organisational framework, the ministry in charge of the environment has a service dealing with environmental monitoring. In effect, this service in respect of ecological monitoring and follow-up of climate has the mission to conceive and put in place an ecological survey and alert system; elaborate on, establish and follow-up on programmes relating to climate change; develop strategies of environmental surveys; formulate and put in place the policy for information concerning the environment, nature protection and sustainable development; manage the systems of geographic information on the environment, nature protection and sustainable development; serve as liaison between the networks and information systems existing in the environmental sector, nature protection and sustainable development, both at the national and international level; put in place and animate a platform for information-sharing between the focal points of international agreements and conventions in matters of environment, nature protection and sustainable development; centralise data relating to information and documentation in all sectors of the environment; and participate in the prevention and management of natural or anthropic disasters.

See, generally, Article 45 of Decree No. 2012/431 of 1 October 2012 relating to the Organization of the Ministry of Environment, Protection of Nature and Sustainable Development. Environmental monitoring is contained in Law No. 96/12 of 5 August 1996 relating to the Framework Law on Environmental Management, notably through one of its enabling instruments being Decree No. 2013/0171/PM of 14 February 2013 establishing the conditions for environmental and social impact assessment. Under Cameroonian EIA regulations, Environmental Management Plans (EMP) formullated during the impact assessment (IA) process are subject to administrative and technical

170 FAO (2009: v).

171 Taza-Asaba (2013).

surveillance as defined by Article 27 of the 2013 decree on ESIA. This decree not only requires EMP implementation, but demands the production of semester reports by bodies or companies for projects whose implementation has been subjected to IA. These are all relevant for sustainable soil management and protection. This text in Articles 27, 28 and 29 makes provision for environmental monitoring of projects which implicitly protect the soil. Article 29 gives the latitude to the administration in charge of the environment to make use of recourse to any expertise in order to ensure the effectiveness of the environmental assessment. Thus, environmental monitoring can be conducted by stewardship organisations, concerned individuals, non-governmental environmental organisations, private consulting firms, and government agencies.

3.3.4.1 Execution of the law

The executive arm of government executes or implements the law at the various central and decentralised levels of the administration with the help of law enforcement agents. Government departments[172] are in charge of executing the law at the central level, while regional entities,[173] local councils[174] and traditional authorities[175] oversee the executing of the law at the decentralised level. It should be noted that the decentralised entities referred to above operate within institutional arrangements created by the law, and the question is: Do such arrangements ensure effective collaboration and cooperation that can enhance sustainable management of resources, including soils? This does not seem to be the case as the transfer of competence and management of resources is not total. The government departments overseeing territorial administration continue to control the activities of decentralised entities, rendering the implementation or execution of projects a difficult task.

3.3.4.2 Enforcement issues

One of the difficulties in matters of soil protection is the issue of enforcement of existing legislation. In effect, without prejudice to the prerogatives of the public prosecutor and the judicial police vested with general enforcement competence, the officials under oath in every administration, especially those of the cadastral survey, town planning, public works, forests, merchant, mines, industry, labour and tourism services, are responsible for the application of all the regulations in force in every sector of activity

172 Article 57(2).
173 Law No. 2004/019 of 22 July 2004 fixing the rules applicable to regions.
174 Law No. 2004/018 of 22 July 2004 fixing the rules applicable to councils.
175 Decree No. 77/245 of 15 July 1977 to organise Chiefdoms. See articles 19, 20(1) and (2) and 21.

to which they are party or are connected. In this respect, they oversee the research and establishment of infringements in view of implementing the legal framework governing their domain of interest. This is contained in Article 88 of the 1996 Framework Law on Environmental Management. Similar provisions can be found in Article 202(1) of the Mining Code.[176]

3.3.4.3 Competences of enforcement entities

As stated above, each administration controls its domain of competence. Every administration has a control service. In the administration overseeing the environment, there is an environmental inspection brigade. This unit is in charge of identifying acts that violate the environment. The organ is made up of a body of environmental inspectors and controllers. The environmental brigade is not in charge of administrative monitoring but may be solicited after administrative monitoring where public agents discovered serious environmental violations.

3.3.4.4 Available and accessible data

The ministry in charge of the environment in Cameroon possesses in its organigram a Centre for Information and Environmental Documentation (Centre d'Information et Documentation sur l'Environnement). The centre oversees the collection, stocking and dissemination of information relating to the environment. The centre is also equipped with many clearing house mechanisms (CHMs). The number of these CHMs depends on the number of multilateral environmental agreements ratified by the State of Cameroon and whose implementation requires the use of a CHM. The ministry in charge of the environment also has a website which publishes important information relating to its domain of competence. As a matter of principle, information and data relating to the environment in Cameroon is transparently available to everyone. But information on soil is not available on the website.

3.3.4.5 Sufficient expertise and support by research institutions

For a good number of years now, many research institutions have created study centres in various branches of the environment. It is in this light that we see both state universities and private institutions providing training in matters relating to the environment.

176 Law No. 2016/017 of 14 December 2016 repealing Law No. 001 of 16 April 2001 establishing the Mining Code and its modification by Law No. 2010/011 of 29 July 2010.

Despite the availability of persons trained in matters relating to the environment, the administration in charge of the environment is unable to employ all these persons with good skills in the job market. It is true that the private sector increasingly searches for experts in this domain, but unfortunately the number of experts recruited by this sector still remains modest. In research, state universities are leading in matters of environmental research. The administration in charge of the environment sometimes makes use of recourse to the expertise of these institutions or to their research centres.

3.3.4.6 Staff and technical equipment

MINEPDED was created in 2004 and, since 2012, had a new organigram. To date, many of the offices created within that organigram have still not been occupied. This situation is explained by an insufficiency of personnel. This relatively new field or domain thus faces the challenge of limited personnel. Many explanations may be advanced for this state of affairs, such as MINEPDED does not have a legal framework relating to the professional corps on the environment; training institutions in the various branches of the environment were created in the distant past, and the public service at some point temporarily halted recruitments.

As concerns the technical teams, MINEPDED is lagging behind. This administration which was only recently created was primarily preoccupied with the establishment of its institutional framework, the sensitisation of citizens on matters relating to the environment, and the stakes involved. A whole team was constituted for the realisation of environmental inspections and control, but because they were not renewed, these teams are today obsolete. The administration in charge of the environment is in deep need of technical equipment, as well as training of personnel to use the equipment.

3.3.4.7 Science-policy interface of soil data/information

Scientific data and information are the basis for sustainable soil management and are critical in informing policymaking, but such scientific data on sustainable soil management in Cameroon are not known to the general public. In addition, scientific data on soil status and actual soil degradation or potential degradation threats in the country are limited and not publicly available. Regarding agriculture in particular, scientific information on sustainable soil management is not made available to farmers, especially small-scale farmers who continue to indulge in unsustainable agricultural practices which are detrimental to soil health. Improved and sustainable soil management therefore needs data that speaks of soil degradation and the involvement of scientific institutions through the data they generate from research, which could inform options for model legislation. Within the framework of the science–policy interface, quantified and qualitative soil data and information should be scientifically verified, requiring data collection (generation), analysis, validation, reporting, monitoring and integration with other disciplines.

Generally, the legal requirements and institutional structures for environmental monitoring exist in Cameroon, but their implementation is limited because of weak capacities and conflicts with other sectors owing to poor coordination. Other associated reasons are the lack of EMP implementation follow-up on the part of the administration due to constraints in financial resources allocated to monitoring missions and the unavailability of validated environmental monitoring and compliance methodology for the different industry sectors.[177] Limiting soil degradation requires constant monitoring and regular environment audits, but a robust monitoring system to monitor soil degradation is absent and there is little research or information available about soils. Scientific information is the basis of sustainable soil management, but such scientific information on sustainable soil management in Cameroon is not known to the general public, especially not to small-scale farmers. Environmental monitoring is weak and therefore sustainable soil protection is not promoted. Another major weakness is that different ministerial departments are working from different land-use maps with many hectares of land having more than one land-use status, which is an incentive for soil degradation. In a sustainable context, licences for land use should only be allocated within the appropriate land-use category, but at present this is weakly monitored and enforced, partly as a result of the fact that land-use planning and zoning is inadequately designed. There is also no appropriate body with the power to exercise monitoring and enforcement prerogatives. This could put areas of highly vulnerable soil at risk of degradation.

Furthermore, environmental monitoring in Cameroon is weak and therefore does so far not enhance sustainable soil protection. The current land planning regulatory framework makes it challenging to protect soils, and there is therefore a need for regulatory reforms that would make it easier for project implementers to engage in sustainable activities that protect soils. The main requirements for the monitoring arrangements are that they should be independent, accountable, sustainable, and performed to a reasonably high scientific standard. International NGOs and research institutions have an important role to play in setting up such a monitoring system, including building the capacities of the different stakeholders in monitoring. This is critical in putting any sound management in place. A crucial monitoring criterion with respect to soil protection is the establishment of an appropriate body with the power to exercise monitoring and enforcement prerogatives.

177 Taza-Asaba (2013).

3.3.5 Cross-cutting issues

The need for EIAs, provisions of public participation, access to environmental information, and rights to appeal administrative decisions (access to courts) are some of the cross-cutting issues that underpin soil protection in Cameroon. Their poor implementation is also an incentive for unsustainable soil management that can drive soil degradation.

3.3.5.1 Need for environmental impact assessments

Prescribed by many international legal instruments both of soft and hard law characters,[178] Environmental impact assessment is the systematic review of whether or not a project has adverse effects on the environment. The Framework Law on Environmental Management enforces the prescriptions in Article 17(1) – which requires the promoter or owner of any development, labour equipment or project which may endanger the environment owing to its dimensions, nature or the impacts of its activities on the natural environment – to carry out an EIA in order to determine the direct or indirect effects of the project on the ecology of the zone where the plant is located or other region, the physical environment and quality of life of the populations, and the impact on the environment in general. Under Article 18, an EIA that does not comply with the prescriptions of the specifications will be null and void.

To facilitate the understanding and application of the abovementioned provisions of the law, Decree No. 2013/0171/PM of 2013 lays down rules for conducting ESIA. We notice an innovation in this enabling instrument which introduces a social dimension to the impact assessment process. Another development in this regard came in 2016 with two Ministerial Orders: one to elaborate on the categories of operations subject to ESIA and strategic environmental assessment and the other to define the contents for modelled terms of reference. Given that this is a cross-cutting issue, the grant of a Certificate of Environmental Conformity by the minister in charge of the environment is informed and opined by an Inter-ministerial Committee on the study of the application files for ESIA.

We do not hesitate to state that the effective implementation of the abovementioned legal instruments is fraught with challenges ranging from ineffective public participation, to inadequate personnel and over-centralisation, corruption, and inadequate monitoring by the administration in charge of the environment. Of course, this does not augur well for effective soil protection and the environment in general. Some researchers have highlighted that the conduct of most EIAs is usually on demand by

178 Such as the Rio Declaration on Environment and Development, 1992; the Convention on Biological Diversity, 1992; etc.

development assistance agencies on a project-by-project basis, not as a response to a widespread domestic demand for better environmental protection.[179] The law on ESIA in Cameroon falls short of effective implementation as is evidenced through the numerous environmental and social conflicts arising from projects implemented across the country. It is therefore crucial that the implementation of ESIA should be improved in order to enhance soil protection and the environment in general.

Other impediments to an effective ESIA process include inadequate baseline data, procedural flaws in scoping, exorbitant administrative fees, absence of an appeal procedure, incompetent personnel and over-centralisation of EIA powers.[180] Furthermore, one of the inherent weaknesses of the ESIA law in relation to soil protection is that small-scale agriculture is passing through the sieve of the law on ESIA with serious soil impacts. Although this type of agriculture is usually practised on small scales, the total land surface areas of these activities when summed up for all the farmers is enormous and can produce serious ecological or soil degradation. Small-scale farmers have little or no motivation or incentive to adopt sustainable soil management measures or practices as their immediate concern is feeding their families.[181] It has been estimated that the agricultural sector in general employs more than 70% of Cameroonians.[182] This is enough reason for the inclusion of small-scale agriculture among the categories of agricultural projects which are subject to ESIA. For the purpose of soil protection, all agricultural projects, whether practised on a small or large-scale, need or ought to comply with the law on ESIA. Theoretically, this may make sense, but the critical question is: who should pay for the cost of ESIA given that small-scale farmers cannot afford to pay for such assessment? This is probably what can render such a prescription a non-starter. Another salient question is: who should control the ESIA, given that small-scale farms amount to millions of them, scattered all over the country? One way of resolving this is to provide extension services at local levels to sensitise local famers on the importance of practising sustainable farming and to monitor and control their activities.

3.3.5.2 Provisions of public participation and access to environmental information

Public participation is a key principle of international environmental and sustainable development law,[183] which was enshrined in the 1992 Rio Declaration with reference to three interrelated pillars consisting of 1) the right to participate in environmental

179 Dashaco & Tarh (2018: 196).

180 Alemagi et al. (2007).

181 See Ginzky et al. (2019: 4).

182 Tchoffo (2009: 3).

183 It is reflected in the Rio Declaration 1992; the Non-Legally Binding Instrument on All Types of Forests; the Convention on Biological Diversity, among others.

decision-making, 2) the right for citizens affected by environmental decisions to receive pertinent information, and 3) the right to access judicial and administrative proceedings, including redress or remedy, to enforce these rights.[184] These may loosely be referred to as Environmental Democracy (ED) rights.[185] Public participation has become an indispensable approach to creating a sense of ownership among participating stakeholders, and ultimately to facilitate law enforcement.[186] In line with international guidance, access to environmental information and public participation in Cameroon is guaranteed by the 1996 Framework Law on Environmental Management,[187] the 1994 Forestry Law,[188] and the 2013 ESIA Decree, which also makes public consultation and hearings mandatory during ESIA processes. In fact, consultation with the public is a key feature of EISA procedures.[189] Consultation ensures public participation in decision-making and thereby strengthens the quality of decisions.[190] The Preamble of Cameroon's Constitution similarly provides for public participation in environmental matters by mandating that it is the duty of all citizens to work for the protection of the environment. Information, decision-making and participation are supposed to involve all concerned stakeholders, but, sadly, sometimes there are no consultations when granting concessions over lands.[191] Given that freedom of information laws exists in Cameroon, the government should provide the necessary institutional support for implementation.[192]

Access to information is indispensable for effective public participation in decision-making, which is vital for conservation.[193] Access to information is guaranteed under the Convention on Access to Information, Public Participation in Decision-Making and Access to Justice in Environmental Matters (Aarhus Convention)[194] and in the International Convention on Civil and Political Rights.[195] Under Principle 10 of the 1992 Rio Declaration, access to environmental information is seen as vital to environmental and natural resource management. National legislation would therefore do well to ensure that responsibility for providing information to concerned stakeholders is clearly required from public authorities and all actors who are charged with

184 Report of the UN Conference on Environment and Development: Annex 1. Rio Declaration on Environment and Development, UN Doc A/CONF.151/26 (Vol.I), 12 August 1992, Principle 10.
185 See Ngwome (2018: 257).
186 See Costenbader (2009: 36).
187 See generally Articles 6, 7, 9, 72, 73 and 74.
188 See Articles 51(2), 61 and 142(3).
189 See Ngwome (2018: 130).
190 Ibid.: 131.
191 Tamasang & Ngwome (2018: 951).
192 Ibid.
193 See Ngwome (2018: 297).
194 Adopted on 25 June 1998.
195 Adopted on 16 December 1966. See Article 14 on access to justice.

implementing policies, as well as from economic operators (investors).[196] Information needs to be provided in an effective manner, that is it should be given in forms that are accessible to a variety of actors and allow enough time for consultations.[197] Public access to information is also required so that civil society can effectively carry out its watchdog function in all sectors prone to soil degradation. Access to information is linked with the right of access to justice in environmental matters.[198] The government is required to provide the public with information about the rights they possess and the judicial resources available to protect them.

With regard to sustainable soil management, public participation and access to information is not sufficiently implemented in Cameroon. Information on soil is often inadequate, out-dated, not available in digital format, and not referenced geographically. The danger of soil degradation in the country is little known to the general public or it is underestimated by those who are informed and therefore does not constitute an immediate concern. Information on the status of soil and appropriate measures to achieve sustainable soil management are critical. Adequate information on sustainable soil management is crucial and should be integrated into curricula at all levels of education.

The 1996 Framework Law on Environmental Management prescribes public participation and access to environmental information in Articles 9, 73 and 74, which call for the participation of populations in environmental management, especially through consultation mechanisms to take stock of the opinion and contributions of the populations; free access to environmental information; sensitisation, training, research and education on the environment at all levels, using the media and other means of information; representation of the populations within environmental advisory bodies; and production of environmental information.

Although commendable, the 1996 legislative prescriptions are not exhaustive and require further insights into the understanding and then application of the law by way of an enabling instrument. Again, such an instrument has not been crafted and so this renders the application of these provisions difficult.

There is relevant case law of the African Commission on Human and Peoples' Rights (the African Commission) establishing a procedural aspect of Article 24 of the African Charter on Human and Peoples' Rights (ACHPR) dealing with the obligation to consult and obtain free and prior informed consent – the principles of environmental democracy. In fact, the African Commission has dealt with this on many occasions in the context of land-grabbing, recognising indigenous peoples' rights over ancestral or traditionally owned land. In *Centre for Minority Rights Development & Minority Rights Group International (MRG) on behalf of the Endorois Community v The*

---

196 See Costenbader (2009: 49).
197 Nhantumbo & Marisa (2015: 70).
198 Ngwome (2018: 296).

Republic of Kenya,[199] the Endorois indigenous community in Kenya successfully contested, among other rights, the violation of their land and natural resource rights, and, above all, their expulsion from their ancestral land by the Kenyan Government under the ACHPR, the Constitution of Kenya and international law. In a landmark decision approved by the African Union on 2 February 2010, the African Commission found and ruled that the Kenyan Government had violated the Endorois' rights to religious practice, to property, to culture, to the free disposition of natural resources, and to development, under the ACHPR (Articles 8, 14, 17, 21 and 22, respectively). The Commission declared the eviction of Endorois from their ancestral lands illegal. The summary, the enforcement of the decision, and the significance of the case are stated by the Centre for Minority Rights Development Kenya on their website.[200]

In *Social and Economic Rights Action Centre (SERAC) v Nigeria* (Ogoni case) (2001), SERAC's communication contained, among others, the forced mass eviction of residents of the Maroko community of Lagos State and failure to provide alternative housing in violation of their rights to housing and property, alleging violations of Articles 2, 4, 5, 6, 7, 14, 15, 16, 17, 18, 22, and 24 of the ACHPR and Article 16 of the Protocol to the ACHPR on the Rights of Women in Africa in addition to violations of corresponding provisions of the Universal Declaration of Human Rights (UDHR), the International Covenant on Economic, Social and Cultural Rights (ICESCR), the International Convention on the Rights of the Child, and the International Covenant on Civil and Political Rights (ICCPR).[201] The African Commission, in its ruling in 2001, found the Federal Republic of Nigeria in violation of Articles 2, 4, 14, 16, 18(1), 21 and 24 of the ACHPR and appealed to the government to ensure the protection of the environment, health and livelihood of the people of Ogoni land by stopping all attacks on Ongoni communities and leaders and permitting citizens free access to the territory; undertaking a comprehensive clean-up of lands and rivers damaged by oil operations; ensuring that appropriate ESIAs were prepared for any future oil development; and that the safe operation of any further oil development was guaranteed through effective and independent oversight bodies for the petroleum industry; and providing information on health and environmental risks and meaningful access to regulatory and decision-making bodies to communities likely to be affected by oil operations, etc.

---

199 See 276/2003 – *Centre for Minority Rights Development (Kenya) and Minority Rights Group International on behalf of Endorois Welfare Council v Kenya*, at https://www.hrw.org/sites/default/files/related_material/2010_africa_commission_ruling_0.pdf, accessed 17 October 2019.

200 See the website of the Centre for Minority Rights Development (Kenya) at https://www.escr-net.org/caselaw/2010/centre-minority-rights-development-kenya-and-minority-rights-group-international-behalf, accessed on 17 October 2019.

201 See the Secretary African Commission on Human and Peoples' Rights, Banjul, Communication, *Social and Economic Rights Action Center v Nigeria*, at http://www.hlrn.org/img/documents/SERAC%20v%20%20Nigeria%20Communication.pdf, accessed 17 October 2019.

3.3.5.3 Right to appeal administrative decisions – access to courts

The right to appeal administrative decisions or the right of access to justice is crucial for sustainable environmental and natural resource management and, therefore, soil protection. Environmental and natural resource management, including land and soil, usually create conflicts between the various actors involved. Adequate access to justice is a critical component of effective environmental, natural resources and especially land and soil management, without which stakeholders will be unable to enforce and protect their rights, rendering natural resources governance ineffective. In fact, the ability to enforce rights is one of the critical pillars of any governance system. Poor dispute settlement mechanisms can undermine efforts to ensure accountability, which may weaken the chance of effective participation, especially for vulnerable groups. Generally, environmental justice is not well institutionalised in Cameroon and, therefore, less developed. In fact, an environmental law court in Cameroon is absent. Judges and other court officials are not well-informed about the importance of soil protection. There is therefore the need for strong, independent dispute resolution mechanisms with the capacity to identify and deal with grievances.

Access to courts or justice answers the following concerns: Is there a system for identifying, preventing and resolving conflict between stakeholders such as litigation, alternative dispute resolution, or administrative review? Has awareness of the system's existence been raised? Is it cheap and accessible? Does it provide timely results?[202] Access to courts forms an integral part of a country's governance system and can be understood as the availability of recourses that citizens can make use of in the event of violations of their substantive and procedural rights.[203] Avenues, such as administrative procedures, judicial forums, traditional authorities, and arbitration guaranteed under relevant environmental, natural resources and related laws,[204] are all available for settling disputes. These avenues, however, need to be strengthened in order to guarantee sustainable soil protection. There is therefore the need to organise workshops or other platforms to help develop the requisite capacity among court officials and judges. Under international law,[205] governments have a number of duties and obligations to

202 See Costenbader (2009: 112); Chapman et al. (2014: 28).

203 Ngwome (2018: 318).

204 The 1996 Framework Law on Environmental Management; the 1994 Forestry Law; the 1998 Water Law; the 2003 Biosafety Law; and the 1974 Land Tenure law.

205 Reference to the right of access to justice under international law includes: Principle 10 of the Rio Declaration on Environment and Development; Articles 2, 9, 14, 26 and 50 of the International Convention on Civil and Political Rights and its First Protocol; Articles 8, 11, 13, 20, 28, 32 and 40 of the UN Declaration on the Rights of Indigenous Peoples; Article 15 of the Convention for the Elimination of All Forms of Discrimination Against Women; Articles 9,12 and 14 of the ILO Convention No. 169; Articles 7, 8 and 10 of the Universal Declaration of Human Rights; Article XVI of the 2003 African Convention on the Conservation of Nature and Natural Resources.

ensure adequate access to the essential components of justice. These are access to effective judicial proceedings, and freedom from economic obstacles preventing citizens from accessing the courts, which include free legal services and the strengthening of community support programmes to ensure that marginalised groups that would generally be excluded from accessing the courts, owing to lack of technical or financial means, are able to benefit from the protection of judicial bodies.[206]

Access to an appropriate mechanism for settling disputes is crucial for enforcing rights to participate, access to information, etc. Access to justice also increases the accountability of authorities and project implementers and protects the rights of affected stakeholders as it provides an opportunity to challenge acts and omissions by public authorities and project developers.[207] Dispute settlement mechanisms need to be equitable, transparent, accountable and independent. The government is required to provide the public with information about the rights they possess and the judicial resources available to protect them, such as the right to a fair trial, which includes the right to legal assistance; the right of defence; and the right to reasonable time for the preparation and formalisation of arguments; the right to an effective remedy, which should be “simple, urgent and accessible”.[208] Because it can be difficult for vulnerable groups, such as local communities, to enforce their rights, owing to lack of education and capacity, increasing community-level legal awareness is crucial in helping them to demand their rights.[209] Measures that can be taken by government to ensure that the legal frameworks support and enable access to justice regarding soil protection and beyond have been suggested, among others, to include the existence of clear rules to enable citizens as well as communities to initiate litigation or be parties to a dispute (i.e. legal standing); ensuring that the recognition of the right to judicial review of administrative actions is enshrined in the Constitution; developing programmes to raise awareness among the population of their right to access courts and of any initiatives that can facilitate this access; providing legal aid, i.e. legal support and services for vulnerable and marginalised persons, which could include measures to reduce the costs of accessing the judicial system or the provision of judicial proceedings in local languages; and ensuring that tribunals do not have any substantial interest in the outcome of the matter they are presiding over.[210]

Procedural rights such as full and effective public participation, access to information and access to justice are key to ensuring and enhancing sustainable soil management and protection.

206 Denier et al. (2014: 129).
207 Costenbader (2009: 53).
208 Denier et al. (2014: 129).
209 Ngwome (2018: 318).
210 Denier et al. (2014: 130, 131).

3.3.5.4 Specific instruments to control the behaviour of foreign investors

3.3.5.4.1 Compliance with public law

Every administration must make sure that any investor who is interested in its domain of competence should meet the provisions of the regulation in force in that sector. In effect, the institutional dispositions of Cameroon give latitude to every public administration to control and monitor all investments/investors operating within their respective areas of competence. For instance, the administration in charge of hydrocarbons ensures the respect of the regulation in force in that sector such that every investor must conform to the provisions of the petroleum code. This is the same in the case of soil and subsoil wherein the administration in charge of water makes sure that investors in this domain respect the provisions of the water regulation in force. The administration in charge of mines ensures that investors comply with the provisions of the regulation in force in this sector. This is the same principle applicable in the domains of forestry and environmental protection.

Despite the power given to each administration to ensure the respect of the regulations of the different sectors by investors, it is also common to see clandestine operators who do not conform to these texts in the respective sectors. This is why there are mining exploiters who do not carry out their activities in conformity with the regulation in force in that sector. This situation may be explained through the lack of mastery of the mining cartography as well as the deplorable attitudes of some administrative and traditional authorities. These are some of the situations that cause degradation of soils and environment because once these clandestine operators exploit a given site, they simply abandon it without reinstating or rehabilitating the site in question.

Finally, Cameroon has a law that encourages private investment. The law in question is Law No. 2017/015 of 12 July 2017 to modify and complete some of the provisions of Law No. 2013/004 of 18 April 2013 on the encouragement of private investment in the Republic of Cameroon. This law treats all foreign investors equally without considering their respective countries of origin. Within the prism of this law, there is a unique organ[211] put in place to provide information to any investor with respect to his type of activity. The investor may comply with all the necessary formalities for the creation of an enterprise without having to go from one administration to another.

---

211 The Cameroon National Investment Corporation.

3.3.5.4.2 No unfair or illegal land acquisition

Access to land for foreign investors is governed by texts that we have already cited sufficiently above – Ordinance No. 47/01 of 6 July 1974 to establish the land tenure regime. Article 10 provides that:

> (1) natural persons and corporate bodies of foreign nationality or incorporated bodies wishing to invest in Cameroon may conclude lease agreements or purchase landed property except in the border areas.
>
> (2) deeds drawn up for this purpose must bear the prior approval of the minister in charge of lands or bear the penalty of being declared null and void. As concerns diplomatic and consular missions as well as international organisations, the visa of the minister of external relations and the minister in charge of lands is required.
>
> (3) the state, in the event of a resale, has a pre-emptive right of purchase over the property, taking account of the initial price, developments carried out and amortisation.

The Mining Code similarly provides in Article 106 that upon the signing of the mining agreement, the state will, after consultation with the affected populations, grant to the mining operator the lands necessary for the mining of the discovered mineral substances, in accordance with the laws and regulations in force.

3.3.5.4.3 Fair taxation

Looking at Law No. 2018/012 of 11 July 2018 relating to the financial regime of the state and other public entities, the domain of taxation is regulated by a single administration in Cameroon, being the ministry in charge of finance. In effect, even though it is provided in many legal texts, the financial provisions of these texts are formulated by the ministry in charge of finance, otherwise all the other ministries will have to seek the opinion of the said ministry regarding the financial provisions to be inserted in any legal document. However, at the start of every budgetary exercise, the ministry in charge of finances elaborates upon and prepares the adoption of a finance law. This law is applied by means of a circular providing instructions for the execution of the finance law, the follow-up and control of the budget of the state, public administrative establishments, territorially decentralised entities, and the other organs under subvention. It is these two texts that determine the financial gains expected in the public treasury and in all sectors of activity.

3.4 Relevant ministries and state institutions and their responsibilities

The relevance of discussing ministries and state institutions lies in the fact that they are responsible for the implementation of the law and their absence from this report will definitely paint an incomplete picture. The laws have their gaps, so too do the institutions. Even when laws appear to be complete, it has been established in this report that institutions are critically important for the effective implementation of the law.

3.4.1 Ministry of Agriculture and Rural Development

According to Decree No. 2005/118 of 15 April 2005, the Ministry of Agriculture and Rural Development (MINADER) is in charge of elaborating, implementing and evaluating government policies in the domains of agriculture and rural development. The ministry also has the mandate of developing standards and rules applicable to agriculture. It is the responsibility of the ministry to identify and prepare projects and programmes for investments in the agricultural sector. Since agriculture is associated with soil degradation, the role of this ministerial department is critical for soil protection.

3.4.2 Ministry of State Property, Surveys and Land Tenure

According to Article 1 of Decree No. 2012/390 of 18 September 2012, the Ministry of State Property, Surveys and Land Tenure (MINDCAF) is responsible for elaborating and implementing government policy related to land tenure, land registration and land surveying. This includes the elaboration of legislative and regulatory texts in its different areas of competence; management of government's private and public property; making proposals for the attribution of state lands; and elaboration and conservation of cadastral plans. Since soil degradation-related activities such as mining and agricultural projects begin with the acquisition of land, the role of this ministerial department is crucial for soil protection.

3.4.3 Ministry of Environment, Protection of Nature and Sustainable Development

According to Decree No. 2012/431 of 1 October 2012, the Ministry of Environment, Protection of Nature and Sustainable Development (MINEPDED) has as principal missions: the definition of modalities and principles for the sustainable management of natural resources; the definition of environmental management measures in collaboration with other ministries and concerned specialised institutions; the elaboration of sectoral master plans for the protection of the environment in liaison with other interested ministries; coordination and monitoring of all interventions by regional and international organisations in the areas of environmental and natural resources in liaison with the Ministry of External Relations and concerned administrative bodies;

monitoring of environmental compliance in the implementation of large projects; information and sensitisation of the public to encourage their participation in the management, protection and restoration of the environment and nature; negotiation and implementation of international conventions and treaties related to the protection of environment and nature in liaison with the Ministry of External Relations. Since soil degradation is a subset of environmental degradation, MINEPDED ensures that ESIA, strategic environmental evaluation and other actions are properly conducted. MINEPDED is the overseer ministerial department for monitoring the respect of environmental and social commitments and meting out of administrative sanctions to project implementers violating environmental standards.

3.4.4 Ministry of Forests and Wildlife

The Ministry of Forests and Wildlife (MINFOF) is responsible for elaborating and implementing national policies in matters of forestry and wildlife and is thus charged with the management of protected areas and conservation concessions in the national domain.[212] MINFOF also undertakes regeneration, reforestation, forest inventories, monitoring and application of logging standards, which makes this ministry a crucial stakeholders in issues of soil protection, as sustainable and unsustainable forest management has implications for soil protection and soil degradation, respectively.

3.4.5 Ministry of Economy, Planning and Regional Development

According to Article 1(2) of Decree No 2008/220 of 4 July 2008 relating to the organisation and functioning of the Ministry of Economy, Planning and Regional Development (MINEPAT), the ministry is in charge of developing, monitoring and coordinating government's economic policy; elaborating norms and rules of regional planning, and controlling their application. Poor land-use planning is a driver of soil degradation. MINEPAT's role is therefore relevant for general environmental protection and soil protection, in particular, in the context of establishing and running investments and economic activities likely to contribute to soil degradation.

212 See Decree No. 2005/099 of 6 April 2005 to organise the Ministry of Forest and Wildlife. See also Republic of Cameroon (2012: 48).

3.4.6 Ministry of Urban Development and Housing

Created by Presidential Decree No. 2004/320 of 8 December 2004, the Ministry of Urban Development and Housing (MINDUH) works in collaboration with decentralised territorial entities (urban and rural councils) in redressing urban challenges in order to build well-planned and convenient cities. It is the supervisory ministry to its sub-organisation, the Cameroon Real Estate Company (Société Immobilière du Cameroun). MINDUH and its subordinate bodies are the backbone of urban policy in Cameroon. According to Decree No. 2005/190 of 3 June 2005, MINDUH is in charge of, among others, the elaborating, implementation and evaluation of government policy on urban development and housing; planning and control of the development of cities; development and monitoring of the implementation of urban development strategies and restructuring; definition and monitoring compliance of standards for sanitation and drainage; the beautification of urban centres; and the implementation of the social housing policy. The role of MINDUH is therefore crucial in ensuring that urban development projects do not lead to soil degradation.

3.4.7 Ministry of Trade

By Decree No. 2011/408 of 9 December 2011 on the organisation of the government, the Ministry of Trade is responsible for the development and implementation of government policy in the field of trade. With respect to soil degradation or protection, this ministry is responsible for the promotion and defence of a quality label for products for the local market; monitoring the application of import standards, in liaison with the administrations concerned; monitoring the conservation and distribution circuits of consumer products; monitoring the development and application of the standards of measuring and quality control instruments in conjunction with the administrations concerned; monitoring the development or approval of standards for the presentation, storage and distribution of consumer products and compliance with these standards by economic operators in relation with the administrations concerned; application of administrative sanctions in the event of fraud or non-compliance with the standards set; etc. The role of the Ministry of Trade is therefore relevant for preventing the importation and transportation of products likely to affect the quality of the soils.

3.4.8 Ministry of Mines, Industry and Technological Development

The Ministry of Mines, Industry and Technological Development (MINMIDT) is in charge of the elaboration and implementation of mining and industrial policy and the development of strategies for technological development in the different sectors of the national economy. The activities promoted by this ministry are drivers of soil degradation. The role of MINMIDT is therefore crucial in the context of this discussion and should be given due consideration.

3.4.9 Ministry of Scientific Research and Innovation

The Ministry of Scientific Research and Innovation (MINRESI) is responsible for the elaboration and implementation of national policies in matters of scientific research and innovation and is thus charged, among others, with coordination and control of scientific research activities in collaboration with all sectoral ministerial departments and organisations.[213] Since scientific research has implications for soil protection or degradation, MINRESI's role is also crucial in the context of this assessment and should be strengthened.

3.4.10 Ministry of Livestock, Fisheries and Animal Industries

The relevance of the Ministry of Livestock, Fisheries and Animal Industries (MINEPIA) is in implementing policies aimed at reducing soil degradation caused by animal husbandry practices.

3.4.11 Institute of Research for Agricultural Development

The mandate of the Institute of Research for Agricultural Development (IRAD)[214] is to elaborate and implement high-level scientific research based on the country's key priority axes and needs, taking into consideration agricultural development in the country's five agro-ecological zones. IRAD also ensures the sustainable management of natural resources and conservation of the environment. It therefore plays a relevant role in ensuring that agricultural development does not lead to soil degradation in the country.

---

213 Republic of Cameroon (2012: 48).

214 IRAD was created by Presidential Decree No. 96/050 of 12 March 1996 as modified by Decree No. 2002/230 of 6 September 2002.

3.4.12 Inter-Ministerial Committee for the Environment

Hosted by MINEPDED, the Inter-Ministerial Committee for the Environment consists of 14 key ministerial departments and is responsible for assisting the government in its mission of elaborating, coordinating, executing and controlling environmental policies. Since soil is an integral part of the environment, this committee's role is crucial in guarding against negative soil impacts of sectoral policies and projects.

3.4.13 National Consultative Commission for the Environment and Sustainable Development

The National Consultative Commission for the Environment and Sustainable Development was created by the environmental framework law with the mission of ensuring a wide participation of all stakeholders[215] in the development and implementation of environmental management policies and strategies. In line with its mission, this commission's role is also critical for soil protection.

3.4.14 Regional and local authorities

Regarding the implementation of the existing environmental provisions relevant to soil protection, the regional and local authorities in Cameroon – within the framework of the missions devolved upon them by central government – ensure, through monitoring and inspection, that all activities carried out by individuals and enterprises do not cause environmental damage. They exercise this role concurrently with the relevant central administrative departments, under terms and conditions provided for by law.

3.4.15 National Council for Planning and Sustainable Development of the Territory

The National Council for Planning and Sustainable Development of the Territory is one of the institutions provided for by Law No. 2011/008 of 6 May 2011 laying down guidelines for the planning and sustainable development of the territory of Cameroon.[216] When this is set up, it will be responsible for issuing opinions and suggestions on the orientations and the conditions of implementation of the policy on planning and

215 Such stakeholders include NGOs, associations, the private sector, professional associations, common initiatives groups.

216 See Article 27.

sustainable development of the territory by the state and the decentralised territorial authorities. It also issues opinions, at the request of the government, on major draft laws or regulations relating to spatial planning and sustainable development. In line with its functions, this council's role is equally critical for soil protection.

Generally, the institutional framework lends indirect and minimal support to the protection of soils. The relevant ministries also exercise their functions through regional, divisional and subdivisional delegations. In the framework of the implementation of decentralisation, the relevant ministries are by law required to transfers part of their competencies and resources to decentralised entities for proper regional and local-level development.

3.5 Conclusion

The assessment of Cameroon's environmental and related natural resources policy and legal instruments reveals that there is no comprehensive and coherent soil policy or soil legislation which can inform sectoral laws and legislation incentivising soil degradation in Cameroon. However, the existing environmental and related natural resources laws and policy instruments contain provisions which are relevant to soil protection to an extent. Soil protection-relevant provisions are therefore fragmented and scattered across national legislations which are most often poorly implemented. Consequently, soil protection-related provisions are not effectively implemented and enforced in Cameroon. Soil as a natural resource is thus not sufficiently integrated and protected under the Cameroonian law. The analysis also shows that sustainable soil management is not an immediate concern in Cameroon, especially as it has not been directly addressed by a specific legal instrument and also because the majority of sectoral legal and policy instruments driving soil degradation do not directly refer to the need to protect soils. Furthermore, the institutional framework which is responsible for the effective implementation of the scattered legislative provisions on soil protection operates, in most cases, in isolation. Consequently, there is a veritable problem of collaboration, cooperation and coordination of actions that could improve the health of soils.

4 Legislation on main drivers of soil degradation: Strengths and weaknesses

While some soils in Cameroon are naturally of poor quality, with natural factors accounting for their degradation, such as climatic factors, the degradation of some of the soils is attributed to human or anthropogenic drivers, incentivised by sectoral legislation. Thus, soil degradation in Cameroon is linked to a combination of drivers. This chapter considers all drivers of soil degradation in Cameroon, but from a legal perspective. Legislation on the main drivers of soil degradation in Cameroon are those dealing with agriculture; mining; industrial development; demographic growth, urban sprawl and land planning regulatory framework; climate change; land tenure insecurity; wildfires in farming, hunting, and cattle rearing. Legislation and policies governing these sectors drive or incentivise soil degradation, but also contain relevant provisions for soil protection, demonstrating the strengths and weaknesses of such legislation in terms of soil protection.

4.1 Agriculture

Most agricultural projects are associated with soil degradation, caused either by the misuse of chemical products (pesticides and fertilizers) or unsustainable farming methods such as the slash-and-burn method and bushfire practised by most local communities across the country and the *ankara* system practised in the Western Highlands of Cameroon.

4.1.1 Relevant legal provisions

The matter of soil degradation may be scantly referred to in some legal texts, whereas these texts are expected to protect the soil. Problems arise when it comes to the implementation of these texts. The relevant legal texts and provisions include:

4.1.1.1 Law No. 2003/003 of 21 April 2003 on phytosanitary protection

This law which lays down the principles and rules governing phytosanitary protection specifically relates to matters of agriculture. Section 21(1) provides that only phytosanitary products that have been homologated or wholesales which have been temporarily authorised may be imported, distributed, packaged or used in Cameroon. Also of relevance is Section 19(1) which provides that chemical treatments must be performed in compliance with good agricultural practices with a view to preserving the health of humans and animals and protecting the environment from the hazards caused by the presence or the accumulation of residue of phytosanitary products. Section 2 is also relevant in the context of this discussion. It sets out the various measures to be undertaken by the administration in charge of agriculture to achieve phytosanitary protection such as the setting, adoption and adaptation of norms in the domain; the prevention and control of plant and plant product pests; the use of sanitary products which are safe for humans, animals and the environment; the dissemination and publication of appropriate phytosanitary protection techniques; the control of importation and exportation of phytosanitary products, plants and plant products and other regulated items that may lead to the release of plant pests, and the control, throughout the national territory of phytosanitary products, plants and plant products that may serve as vectors of harmful organisms. Under Sections 5 and 6, the administration in charge of agriculture may request support from relevant ministries and other services in the context of the implementation of phytosanitary legislation and, in this respect, may delegate its powers regarding phytosanitary protection to any natural person or corporate body under the conditions fixed by law.

The implementation of the 2003 law on phytosanitary protection is enabled by a series of decrees.[217] One of the enabling texts or complementary decrees to the law is Decree No. 2005/0770/PM of 6 April 2005 establishing the terms and conditions of the fight against phytosanitary products with the following relevant provisions. Article 9 states that the fight against harmful organisms should be done with respect to the principle of integrated protection with the aim of reducing the reliance on and exercising effective control over the use of phytosanitary products, and to minimise the risks involved with the abusive and inappropriate use of phytosanitary products. Article 10 calls for the implementation of an integrated approach to fight against the use of phytosanitary products as a priority involving the participation of farmers through the provision of assistance and resources necessary to promote initiatives that aim at the adoption and implementation of the integrated fight; support of research activities that involve farmers; support of the organisation of training programmes that bring together farmers, researchers and those who spread the information; sensitisation of consumers on the quality of agricultural products; and training of farmers on the techniques of integrated protection.

In effect, the failure to implement, or poor implementation of these texts may contribute to soil degradation. This is the case with the law on phytosanitary protection,[218] and the sectorial law in the domain of agriculture which is aimed at protection of vegetation and its attendant products through the use of phytosanitary products. The stakeholders in the implementation of this law, that is farmers and economic operators (in phytosanitary products), do not always comply with the regulation in force in this domain. The commercialisation and use of phytosanitary products that are not homologated contributes to soil degradation. The control of phytosanitary products used in the national territory appears to be less efficient because the borders are porous. This situation enables the traffic of all sorts of dangerous phytosanitary products.

The law in this domain aims at effectively regulating phytosanitary products, but still falls short of effective implementation and monitoring. Thus, from a phytosanitary

217 See Decree No. 2005/0771/PM of 06 April 2005 on modalities for plant quarantine operations; Decree No. 2005/0772/PM of 06 April 2005 on the control and registration of phytosanitary products; Decree No. 2005/0770/PM of 06 April 2005 on modalities for phytosanitary control operations; Decree No. 2005/0769/PM of 06 April 2005 Creation of a Phytosanitary Council.

218 Law No. 2003/003 of 21 April 2003 on plant protection.

perspective, the law seems to have covered all the activities that use phytosanitary products, which we have reason to commend, but we must also remark that implementation has remained a problem. In the first place, farmers do not respect existing prescriptions on the use of phytosanitary products because of inadequate monitoring. In the second place, inadequate cooperation or communication between sister administrations renders implementation difficult. Thus, there is an absence of a coordinated approach to sustainable land management as many different ministerial departments are involved with the management of environmental pollution such as causes soil degradation, with poor collaboration. There is therefore a need for government to urge users of phytosanitary products to comply with the relevant regulations, and government institutions responsible for law implementation and enforcement to implement and enforce the relevant regulations in close collaboration.

4.1.1.2 Law No. 2003/007 of 10 July 2003 governing the activities of the fertilizer subsector

This law aims to "increase the productivity of farms and increase agricultural production and the sustainable management of natural resources" in Cameroon through the regulation of the following activities: the production, import, export, packaging, distribution and use of fertilizers.[219] Although this law seeks to avoid the harmful effects of fertilizers, it falls short of halting soil degradation in that the production, import, export, packaging, distribution and use of fertilizers do not always conform to its provisions in Cameroon. Unfortunately, the enabling instrument of this law has not been enacted, making its implementation difficult. This also makes the monitoring and control of fertilizers in the country difficult and opened to corrupt practices. One can find fertilizers that are not homologated being used by farmers. This smacks of illegal practices in the sector regarding the use of these fertilizers. There is therefore a need for the government to urge users of fertilizers to comply with the relevant regulations and government institutions responsible for law implementation and enforcement to implement and enforce the relevant regulations.

4.1.1.3 Decree No. 2011/2584/PM of 23 August 2011 laying down soil and subsoil protection modalities

Most agricultural projects are associated with soil degradation caused either by the misuse of chemical products (pesticides and fertilizers) or by unsustainable farming methods such as slash-and-burn, bushfire or *ankara* methods practised by most local

219 See Article 1.

communities across the country. Decree No. 2011/2584/PM of 23 August 2011, which lays down the soil and subsoil protection modalities, regulates activities related to land use, in order to avoid erosion, desertification, and the loss of arable land. It requires any natural or legal person, public or private, who uses fertilizers and/or pesticides to ensure that these products correspond in quality and quantity to the standards set by national and international legislation. On the one hand, the decree prescribes a preliminary evaluation of the physical and chemical state of the soil and, on the other, a regular evaluation of the impact of these products on the environment. The provisions of this decree are not properly respected by most local farmers who by the misuse of chemical products (pesticides and fertilizers) or unsustainable farming methods, cause soil degradation. In fact, slash-and-burn, bushfire and the *ankara* agricultural practices are detrimental for soils. Consequently, there is the need for policy measures to ensure that the provisions of the decree are complied with by small-scale farmers. This can be done by developing policies that are geared toward the sensitisation of farmers on the danger of using non-homologated chemicals and pesticides and other unsustainable farming practices.

4.1.1.4 Common Provisions on the Homologation of Pesticides in the Economic and Monetary Community of Central Africa Zone

The use of pesticides in Cameroon is governed by a community regulation, namely the Common Provisions on the Homologation of Pesticides in the Economic and Monetary Community of Central Africa (CEMAC) Zone. The aim of this text can be found in its Article 1, which is:

> to bring together experiences and expertise of the member States for the evaluation and homologation of pesticides in order to ensure their rational and judicious use, as well as the protection of human health and the environment.

The scope of application of this regulation can be found in Article 3(1) which includes the:

> experimenting, authorization, importation, exportation, transportation, transit, stocking, marketing, use, control and elimination of active materials and formulated products of pesticides within the States of the CEMAC zone, within the directives adopted by the FAO.

Unfortunately, this community regulation is not always complied with owing to many insufficiencies and difficulties encountered on the ground. In effect, the loose nature of the borders of the CEMAC countries facilitates the entry of contraband pesticides into states. Such products do not pass through the Homologation Committee and, as such, neither the quality nor the efficiency of these products can be asserted. These products find their way into the hands of farmers, notably the local farmers who use them either through ignorance or because of their hugely affordable costs. The second difficulty in the application of this community regulation has to do with the importation of unauthorised products by certain delinquent traders. Chemical products that are toxic to the soil also find their way into the hands of citizens who use them in ignorance or because of their affordable prices. There is therefore a need for the secretariat of CEMAC to urge member states, for instance Cameroon, to comply with and enforce the regulation.

Regarding the legal status of CEMAC regulations and their relationship to national law, it should be noted that in the contemporary world, countries with common boundaries are coming together through regional cooperation and integration to respond to the exigencies of globalisation. In this regard, a supranational structure, the Economic and Monetary Community of Central Africa – known by its French acronym as CEMAC – to replace the Economic and Customs Union of Central Africa was established in 1994. CEMAC aims to promote subregional integration within the framework of economic and monetary union through common political, financial, legal and economic structures and policies. Because of these, community laws have been encouraged and, at times, imposed. The gradual application of CEMAC community laws has led to sovereignty decline of member states. Since CEMAC member states apply legal monism, the treaty instituting CEMAC as superior to all national laws. This implies the subordination of the national law-making bodies to the community. Thus, after the Constitution, CEMAC laws are at the apex of the pyramid of laws in Cameroon as per Article 45 of the Cameroonian Constitution. Thus, by opting for the monist approach in meeting its international commitments, which asserts the supremacy of international law over national law, this constitutional provision implies a direct reception of the CEMAC community laws by member states. The CEMAC treaty goes further, stating that the community regulations are directly applicable. They, therefore, have a supra-constitutional value. By implication, the CEMAC treaty and regulations override any national laws. The superiority of CEMAC laws is guaranteed by the possibility of sanctioning their violation as per Articles 14 and 17 of the additives to the CEMAC treaty. Thus, this implies that the member states are bound to observe them.

The principle of 'direct applicability' otherwise known as 'direct effect'[220] holds that CEMAC regulations are directly applicable as they are mainstreamed into the national legal order without the need of any national measures of transposition or reception. Community laws therefore create rights and obligations for individuals, which national authorities must uphold. The basis of direct applicability is the specificity of the community legal order; it is in the objective of integration that this principle is applied. The CEMAC treaty is silent regarding the principle of 'primacy' according to which, in case of any conflicting or contradictory provisions or incompatibility between community law and national law, the former prevails. However, this issue is settled by Article 45 of the Cameroonian Constitution and therefore by the direct

220 Article 21 of the Additive to the CEMAC treaty. This principle has as its basis the integration of the community legal order.

application of the community regulation on the common provisions on the homologation of pesticides with relevance to soil protection.

Now that the Constitution enables the direct application of this piece of legislation and, of course, its supremacy over national laws, this enhances the available legal arsenal for the protection of soils in Cameroon. It is therefore incumbent on the concerned administrations to ensure its effective implementation to achieve best results in terms of soil protection.

4.1.2 Enforcement issues

Apart from the prerogatives of the public prosecutor, and the judicial police vested with general enforcement competence, the officials under oath in every administration in charge of the environment and other administrative units concerned are in charge of the research and establishment of infringements in view of implementing the legal framework governing their domain of interest. They must ensure the implementation, control and sanction of any defaulter of the regulations in force. For instance, the administration in charge of the environment must ensure the implementation of the laws and texts that are destined for environmental protection. In this light, they must be able to identify and prosecute infringers of these legal norms. This same responsibility must be shouldered by the administration in charge of water, energy resources, and mines, for instance, when it comes to the implementation of the laws in those sectors. Nevertheless, every administration is responsible for the application of all the regulations in force in every sector of activity to which it is party or is connected. This is contained in Article 88 of the 1996 Framework Law on Environmental Management which provides that: (1) without prejudice to the prerogatives of the public prosecutor, and the judicial police vested with general competence, the officials under oath in the administration in charge of the environment and other administrative units concerned, especially those of the cadastral survey, town planning, public works, forests, the merchant, mines, industry, labour and tourism services will be in charge of the research and establishment of infringements in keeping with the provisions of this law and its enabling instruments; and (2) the officials mentioned in subparagraph (1) above will take an oath before the competent court, upon the request of the administration concerned. Similar provisions can be found in Article 202(1) of the Mining Code.[221]

One of the difficulties in matters of soil protection is the issue of enforcing the implementation of the texts in force owing to inadequate monitoring and poor communication between concerned ministries. In addition to these implementation challenges, the law enforcement agents are engaged in corrupt practices that make the enforcement

---

221 Law No. 2016/017 of 14 December 2016 repealing Law No. 001 of 16 April 2001 establishing the Mining Code and its modification by Law No. 2010/011 of 29 July 2010.

of the relevant provisions of the agricultural regulations and other legislation difficult, and by extension, onerous to achieve sustainability in the agricultural sector.

4.1.3 Monitoring

In its organisational framework, the ministry in charge of environment carries out services in respect of environmental monitoring. In effect, the services relating to ecological monitoring and follow-up of climate in this ministerial department have the mission to conceive and put in place an ecological survey and alert system; elaborate, establish and follow-up on programmes relating to climate change; elaborate strategies for environmental surveys; elaborate and put in place the policy for information concerning the environment, nature protection and sustainable development; manage the systems of geographic information on the environment, nature protection and sustainable development; serve as liaison between the networks and information systems existing in the environmental sector, nature protection and sustainable development, both at national and international level; put in place and animate a platform for information-sharing between the focal points of international agreements and conventions in matters of environment, nature protection and sustainable development; centralise data relating to information and documentation in all sectors of the environment; and participate in the prevention and management of natural or anthropic disasters.

See generally, Article 45 of Decree No. 2012/431 of 1 October 2012 relating to the organisation of the ministry of environment, nature protection and sustainable development. Again, corruption, lack of information and available data, as well as poor communication between concerned institutions, render monitoring very difficult, with serious implications for soil degradation.

4.1.4 And what's more?

There is also the National Agriculture Investment Plan (PNIA) for the period 2014–2020, which is the agricultural subsector of the National Rural Sector Development Strategy.[222] PNIA targets second-generation agriculture to increase the growth rate by at least 10% by 2020, at an estimated cost of CFA F3,351 billion.[223] Four thematic areas are involved: (1) develop the production sector and improve food safety and nutrition; (2) modernise production infrastructure in rural areas and improve access to

222 See Ministry of Environment, Protection of Nature and Sustainable Development, 2018, The national strategy for reducing emissions from deforestation and forest degradation, sustainable management of forests, conservation of forest and enhancement of carbon stocks, (National REDD+ Strategy), Final Version.

223 Ibid.

finance; (3) manage sustainably and use natural resources; (4) practise good governance and institutional development. A series of incentives, particularly tax exemptions, have also been initiated to improve the agricultural sector.[224] These will have positive impacts on soil protection. The problem here is that second-generation agriculture targeted by PNIA may be carried out on an unsustainable basis by the use of non-homologated fertilizers, chemicals and phytosanitary plant products which are harmful to soils. Corruption, inadequate monitoring and inadequate communication between concerned institutions must therefore be addressed in order to ensure the protection of soils in the implementation of the PNIA.

The strength of these legal and policy instruments lies in the fact they all envisage and seek to protect soils against chemical inputs and also to ensure the sustainable management and use of soil as a natural resource. Notwithstanding their strength regarding soil protection, these instruments also have some weaknesses that lead to soil degradation. For instance, in order to realise the objectives of increasing agricultural productivity, these laws and policy instruments promote actions that put more pressure on soils through forest clearance and encroachment on other natural ecosystems that protect soil, and also by way of more chemical inputs with soil degradation as the direct consequence. Another critical challenge is the problem of implementation and enforcement of the legal texts in the domain of agriculture.

4.2 Mining

Cameroon is one of Africa's most attractive new destinations for mining. In this respect, the government has developed a minerals policy to ensure the continuous development of the mining industry in the quest to diversify the economy and harness the natural resources for the development of the country. Mining operations take place in the natural environment, with serious threats to soil quality. Although legislation[225] governing mining activities in Cameroon addresses environmental problems, such as soil degradation, and provides for soil protection, it also contains some weaknesses that incentivise soil degradation. The Mining Law regulates the search, discovery, exploitation, detention, transportation, transformation and commercialisation of mineral substances.[226]

224 Ibid.

225 Law No. 2016/017 of 14 December 2016 repealing Law No. 001 of 16 April 2001 establishing the Mining Code and its modification by Law No. 2010/011 of 29 July 2010.

226 See Article 1.

4.2.1 Relevant legal provisions

In connection with the protection of soils, the relevant provisions of the Mining Law[227] seem to be the following: Article 69 institutes the requirement for a mining licence or permit to be obtained by any miner or by a landowner mining quarries for purely domestic use. Quarrying for domestic use is obligatorily subject to regulations governing health, safety, labour and the environment. Under Article 123, landowners are entitled to compensation stemming from, among others, damage caused to the natural surface of the land. Article 126 provides for the establishment of protected zones and closed zones aimed to protect buildings, agglomerations, cultural sites, burial grounds, places of endemism, tourist sites, water points, communication routes, civil engineering works, public utility works, archaeological sites, agricultural concerns, and protected areas, by the minister in charge of mines in conjunction with the relevant government services and prohibits mining or quarry activities within such zones. Similarly, Article 127 prohibits prospection, exploration or mining without authorisation from the competent authorities around built property, villages, houses, protected areas, wells, religious buildings, burial grounds and places considered sacred, without the consent of the owner, and also around communication routes, water pipes, energy and sundry substance carrier systems and, generally, around all public utility sites and civil engineering works. Article 135(1) provides that any mining and quarry operation undertaken (1) must comply with the laws and regulations in force relating to sustainable environmental protection and management; and (2) is subject to the granting of all mining and quarry permits and titles apart from the non-industrial mining licence, and to the prior conduct of an ESIA and a hazard and risk assessment, and the provision of an environmental management plan as provided for by the laws and regulations in force in matters relating to the protection and sustainable management of the environment.

Article 136 provides for the restoration, rehabilitation and closure of mining and quarry sites, including removal of any mining or quarry plant found on the land. In order to ensure the rational use of mineral and quarry resources in line with environmental protection, Article 137 requires holders of mining and quarry titles to prevent geo-hazards and geo-disasters; prevent or minimise the discharge of waste in the open; protect fauna and flora; promote or maintain the general health of the population; reduce waste; dispose of non-recycled waste in such a manner as to ensure the safety of the environment, after informing and receiving the approval of the authorities in charge of mining and the environment; and manage waste in accordance with the laws and regulations in force. Article 138 requires mining companies to ensure the rehabilitation and closure of mining and quarry sites and proper management of waste to ensure safety of the environment; reduce waste; prevent geo-hazards and geo-disasters; and

227 Law No. 2016/17 of 14 December 2016 relating to the Mining Code.

also requires holders of mining or quarry permits to dismantle, in accordance with standard rules, any mining plant liable to payment of duties and taxes. Article 140 requires buildings, outbuildings, wells, galleries and all structures, in general, built and used for the mining or quarry activities to be secured, in accordance with conditions set out in the ESMP and the rehabilitation programme of the mining sites at the end of mining or quarry activities.

We have selected these articles to demonstrate how the legislator intends to maintain the environment through the protection of people and the environment itself.

4.2.2 Monitoring

With regard to the supervision, control and inspection of mining activities, Article 196 provides that sworn civil servants, inspectors and assistant inspectors of the ministry in charge of mines and other relevant authorities or any duly authorised body will supervise and control mining activities within the limit of their prerogatives. Be these provisions as they may in relation to soil protection and related issues, the same regret as was expressed earlier also applies here, namely that this piece of legislation is not being applied for want of an enabling instrument. For example, Article 199 provides that the conditions for supervising and controlling mining, quarries, and spring, mineral and thermo-mineral water tapping activities, as well as the mining of geothermal deposits, and appointing inspectors and assistant inspectors of the ministry in charge of mines will be laid down by regulation. The enabling instruments of this law are still to be signed and published. These instruments are aimed at enhancing the effective implementation of this law. This is one of the difficulties in the legislative crafting process in Cameroon.

4.2.3 The role of foreign investors

The role of foreign investors in the mining sector is significant. In effect, Cameroon does not possess the technical equipment and the necessary technology for mineral exploration and exploitation. Consequently, the country always solicits the intervention of foreign investors. These investors have to comply with the regulations in force relating to their line of activity. The government encourages national investors to collaborate with the foreigners in a bid to ensure transfer of technology and know-how. Unfortunately, these foreign investors are not usually very concerned about environmental protection. It has been noticed that these investors are usually in no hurry to obtain environmental authorisation before launching their activities. This is why, once a site has been exploited, the investors care little about reinstating or rehabilitating the exploited site. These dilapidated sites constitute a threat to the host populations and lead to soil degradation. Moreover, foreign investors – as well as national investors – use chemical products that are unhealthy for people and the environment, such as mercury. This substance, used illegally on sites, is dangerous for the host and local populations. It pollutes the water used by people and also destroys the attendant biodiversity in soils.

From the forgoing, we realise that the responsibility for environmental degradation, notably soil degradation, is shared between the state and the other stakeholders, being the explorers and exploiters. Regarding the strength of mining legislation with respect to soil protection, the numerous Mining Code articles, as stated above, require mining and quarry operations to comply with the laws and regulations in force relating to sustainable environmental protection and management. The essence of these environmental and social management practices for mining and quarry activities is to ensure soil safety, fertility and the physical prospects of the mining site. In general, these provisions require holders of mining and quarry permits to ensure that mineral resources are exploited rationally and in harmony with environmental protection. The provisions cited above are therefore relevant for soil protection.

Notwithstanding the strength of the Mining Code regarding soil protections, it also has some weaknesses that act as a potential driver of soil degradation. The weaknesses lie in the fact that the code is not being applied owing to the lack of an enabling instrument. As pointed out, this is one of the shortcomings in the legislative crafting process in Cameroon, at least as it concerns natural resources and environmental management in general and soil protection in particular. The question is: What accounts for this very disturbing situation? One may be tempted to think that the government which is in charge of the subsidiary legislation (regulatory instruments) deliberately delays the process in order to frustrate the implementation of laws passed by Parliament, as some provisions may be seen as working against the government agenda or the usual government inertia may be at play. Again, the question is: Was the making of the law conditionality from international monetary institutions, like the World Bank or the International Monetary Fund, for an application/negotiation of a loan for development plans in this area? We must, however, be quick to appreciate the fact that, unlike the previous legislation on the subject, this one has considered governance benchmarks in terms of disclosure principles and this, of course, could render greater service to soil protection than was previously the case. That notwithstanding, the question raised regarding the non-application of the Mining Code due to the absence of an enabling instrument is: What can be done to make good the situation? This may be remedied by either enacting complete and detailed legislation that does not require an enabling instrument, or the law and its enabling instrument could be crafted at the same time so as to facilitate the understanding and the immediate implementation of the law.

4.3 Industrial development

Generally, Cameroon is characterised by a very low level of industrialisation. However, the government has committed itself to becoming an emerging economy by 2035, and industrial development has a major role to play in achieving this goal, as outlined in Vision 2035 and the GESP that serve as the country's compass for emergence by 2035. The GESP with a strong focus on making Cameroon an industrialised nation thus becomes a key driver of this vision. Cameroon is also endowed with rich natural resources that will provide industries with raw materials. This government ambition may mean increased pressure on the environment, especially the soil. At present, there is no specific legislation governing the industrial sector in Cameroon. The sector today is regulated through a plethora of laws and regulatory instruments governing other sectors. Concerning the treatment of industrial and other wastes that are dangerous to the soil, the following legislative provisions are relevant in the context of this assessment.

Article 47(3) of the 1996 Framework Law on Environmental Management regulates the treatment of special industrial waste which, by reason of its properties, is dangerous, and may not be deposited in storage facilities receiving other categories of waste. Article 54 of the same law provides for the regulation of classified establishments, factories, workshops, depots, building sites and, in a general way, the industrial, craft or commercial installations that may be dangerous to health, safety, public health, agriculture, nature and the environment in general, or disadvantages for the convenience of the neighbourhood. In the same spirit, the 1994 Forestry Law in Article 18 forbids the dumping of any toxic product or industrial waste in national forests, public waterways, lakes or sea without obtaining the prior permit of the government, and without their proper treatment. Article 4(1) of the Water Code prohibits spills, discharges, jets, infiltrations, landfills, spreading, direct or indirect deposits in the waters of any solid, liquid or gaseous material and, in particular, industrial, agricultural and atomic wastes that are liable to alter the quality of surface or groundwater or seawater within territorial boundaries; harm public health and aquatic and submarine fauna and flora; and jeopardise the economic and tourist development of the regions.

Article 2(1) of Order No. 002/MINEPDED[228] calls on every generator and/or operator in the field of industrial waste (toxic and/or dangerous) to provide at the end of the semester to the administrations in charge of the environment a declaration containing a summary of the information of different manifestos. Article 3 requires any operator of an installation that annually generates more than two tons of such waste to provide the administration responsible for the environment with a management plan for the waste. Article 4 obliges every carrier of such waste to use a manifest of

228 Order No. 002/MINEPDED of 15 October 2012 fixing the specific conditions for the management of industrial waste (toxic or hazardous).

traceability of the waste according to the form in force. Article 5 requires sworn agents of the administration in charge of the environment to prescribe samples and analyses to check the conformity of the loading to the manifest. Articles 6 to 9 provide for the requirements to be met by the generator or shipper of such waste before and during transportation and the conditions under which such waste is transported. Under Article 10, any breach of one or more of the obligations incurs the responsibility of the operator involved.

The Prime Ministerial Order fixing the conditions for the sorting, collection, transport, recovery, recycling, treatment and final disposal of waste[229] also applies to industrial waste. The relevant provisions include: Article 9 subjects those involved in the collection, transport and storage of industrial waste (toxic and/or dangerous) to obtaining an environmental permit issued by the administration in charge of the environment. Article 10 requires the transport of such waste to be accompanied by a manifest of traceability of the waste delivered by the administration in charge of the environment. Article 11 requires every generator, collector, transporter or destroyer of industrial waste (toxic and/or dangerous) to keep a register in which it records the type, nature, quantity, characteristics of danger, and origin of the hazardous waste which it has produced, collected, stored, transported, recovered or disposed of. This register is subject to the control of the administration in charge of the environment.

The Prime Ministerial Order specifying the modalities of protection of surface water and underground water against pollution[230] similarly prohibits in Article 3(1) the spills, discharges, seeps, landfills, spreading, direct or indirect deposits in water of any solid, liquid or gaseous material and, in particular, any industrial, agricultural or atomic waste likely to alter the quality of surface or groundwater or seawater within the territorial limits; to harm public health, aquatic, submarine and land fauna and flora; to jeopardise the economic and tourist development of the regions; and to harm the quality of life and the comfort of residents. Subsection 2 of this article prohibits the discharge, dumping or depositing in surface water, in public sewers or in artificial waterways any solid waste, even if previously subjected to mechanical grinding, any water or other fluids containing such materials or substances, any oils, lubricants and other substances resulting from the cleaning and maintenance of motor vehicles, combustion engines and similar machinery, and any slushes and pesticides.

The concerns relating to soil protection and landownership are also taken on board in the new Petroleum Code[231] in Articles 4, 57 to 77, 91 and 92. The most relevant provisions are: Article 4(1) and (2) requiring any physical or corporate persons, including landowners wishing to carry out petroleum operations, to obtain prior

229 Decree No. 2012/2809/PM of 26 September 2012 fixing the conditions for the sorting, collection, transport, recovery, recycling, treatment and final disposal of waste.

230 Order No. 2001/165/PM of 8 May 2001 specifying the modalities for the protection of surface water and underground water against pollution.

231 Law No. 2019/008 of 25 April 2019 establishing the Petroleum Code.

authorisation from the state and to conform to the legislation on land tenure and state lands in force with respect to the attribution of land for exploitation. In view of attributing lands for exploitation, Article 57 requires the holder of a petroleum authorisation to submit a file for land inquiry, the aim being to identify the status of the parcels of land covered by the authorisation; to carry out a census of those who have rights on the parcel of land in question, and to inform them of the modalities for payment of indemnities as a result of loss of their rights; and to sensitise the surrounding population about the petroleum activity. Article 91 requires holders of petroleum permits to carry out petroleum operations in such a manner as to ensure, under all circumstances, the conservation of natural resources, in particular hydrocarbon deposits, and due protection of essential features of the environment. In this respect, holders are required to take all the necessary measures to preserve the safety of persons and property, and to protect the environment, natural surroundings and ecosystems. Article 92(1) requires holders of petroleum contract to carry out ESIAs with respect to the laws and regulations applicable in matters of environmental protection in order to evaluate the direct or indirect impacts of petroleum operations on the ecological balance of the surrounding areas, the people's living environment and quality of life, and the environment in general. Under subsection 2, the ESIA is to be submitted for public inquiry, where such a procedure is required. Subsection 3 provides that the terms and conditions for implementing the provisions of this Section, in particular the list of petroleum operations, the performance of which is subject to an impact assessment, the contents of the assessment, as well as the conditions under which it is made public, is laid down by regulation.

The legislation described above is the most recent piece of legislation touching on soil protection by implication. Compared to the 1999 Petroleum Code,[232] the present code does not contain innovations in terms of the soil protection paradigm as its provisions have no direct reference to soil apart from general environmental protection provisions. The importance of soil is therefore neglected by this code. Another main shortcoming is, as with other legislation, the lack of enabling instruments needed to complete and implement the law, especially the provisions relevant to soil protection. Furthermore, in the context of environmental protection, Article 30 of Law No. 2012/006 of 19 April 2012 to institute the gas code indirectly protects the soil from all related gas activities, which obliges the operator to comply with environmental protection and safety regulations in force, as well as with internationally accepted environmental protection and safety standards. Law No. 2011/25 of 14 December 2011 on the valorisation of associated gases equally provides indirect protection to soil in the context of environmental and ecosystem protection under Article 11.

Despite the existence of these regulatory instruments which indirectly govern the industrial sector, we still find effluent or liquid and gaseous discharge of industrial

232 Law No. 99/013 of 22 December 1999 to institute the Petroleum Code. See Articles 82 and 83.

origin, treated or untreated, discharged directly or indirectly into the environment in some major cities such as Douala, which may be harmful to soil health. In the absence of appropriate policies and regulations that balance industrial development with environmental exigencies, such development may have negative impacts on the ecosystem resulting in increased deforestation, and emission of harmful gases and industrial spillage leading to soil degradation. There is therefore the need to develop a legal instrument that will govern industrial development in Cameroon. The government should mainstream environmental concerns especially the protection of soils in such an instrument. Cameroon has elaborated and validated its National Industrialisation Plan aiming at translating into practical terms Cameroon's ambition of becoming an emerging economy by 2035. The Plan focuses on three key areas referred to as 'industrial sanctuaries' consisting of agro-industry; energy and digital and five industrial pillars consisting of forest and timber; textile/confection/leather; mining/metallurgy/iron and steel industry; hydrocarbons/petrochemicals/refining; and chemical/pharmacy. These targets all have implications for soil degradation. This therefore requires strong regulation with a particular objective to protect the soil.

4.4 Demographic growth, urban sprawl and land-planning regulatory frameworks

Population increase manifested in the form of urban sprawl is one of the major drivers of environmental degradation, including soil degradation. In fact, demographic growth is putting enormous pressure on the environment through different human activities that are causing soil degradation. Rapid increase in the population coupled with rapid urbanisation has led to significant transformation of natural ecosystems such as forests and wetlands into habitable spaces as well as for industrialisation and agricultural purposes to meet up with food production. These are exerting enormous pressure on natural ecosystems, exposing the soil to various forms of degradation. Urban and spatial planning laws and policies in Cameroon, at least in theory, guarantee sustainable management of natural resources, the environment and the soil in particular. Such planning laws and policies ought to help direct certain activities away from ecosystems that need special protection. The development policy of Cameroon establishes a decentralised approach to natural resources and environmental management. The 1996 Constitution introduces decentralised authorities, whose role is to promote the economic, environmental, social and cultural development of their peoples in line with the principle of sustainability. Thus, in the general framework of decentralisation in Cameroon, one may cite Law No. 2011/008 of 6 May 2011 on the orientation of planning and the sustainable development of the territory of Cameroon. Article 1 of this law sets out its objectives in terms of defining the general legal framework for national spatial planning from the perspective of sustainable development and coverage of all operations relating to the occupation of space, the allocation or balanced distribution of activities, infrastructures, equipment and services in the national territory. To achieve these objectives, the law prescribes concerted and participative development and the implementation of strategic planning and sustainable development tools, based on the needs and available resources, strategic choices and options for coherent regional or subregional development across sectors.[233]

The implementation of regional development policy is also guaranteed by specific regulations, including: Decree No. 77/193 of 23 June 1977 establishing the urban and rural land development and equipment administration; Decree No. 79/189 of 17 May 1979 establishing the rules and regulations governing the demarcation of urban boundaries; Decree No. 79/194 of 19 May 1979 establishing the rules governing the creation of schemes; Decree No. 81/185 of 4 May 1931 establishing rules governing the creation of special layouts by the development of urban and rural land; and Decree No. 79/PM of 10 July 1981 allocating parcels of special provisions.

Upon adoption, the National Land Use Planning for Sustainable Development Scheme (*Schéma National d'Aménagement et de Développement durable du Territoire* – SNADDT) will also be instrumental with respect to the protection of soils as it has an impact on soil. The first phase of the SNADDT identified and zoned the entire territory according to resources and development potential. The second phase is in the process of producing a national indicative land-use plan. Currently, regional land-use plans are being prepared. In addition, the current investment plan to enhance municipal council land-use plans promoted by the National Participative Development Programme is an important planning policy with direct implications for soil and therefore, should align with soil protection objectives. Furthermore, Articles 16 and 17 of Law No. 2004/018 of 22 July 2004, fixing the rules applicable to councils, make provision for the protection of the soil by councils. In the same manner, Article 19 of Law No. 2004/019 of 22 July 2004, fixing the rules applicable to regions, makes provision for the protection of the soil by regions in the framework of environmental and natural resources management. Thus, the urban and spatial planning laws and policies influence land use and natural resource management policies with direct implications for soil protection.

Notwithstanding the foregoing, the current land planning regulatory framework is not being felt on the ground and makes it difficult to protect soils, partly owing to lack of direct references to soil and also because of implementation challenges. The implementation challenges stem from poor coordination between the concerned ministerial departments. There is therefore the need for regulatory reforms that would make it easier for project implementers to engage in sustainable activities that protect soils. One way to do this is to develop and implement a strategy, to formulate legal and institutional frameworks for spatial planning in a participatory manner, taking into account sectoral objectives, and to enhance the capacities of stakeholders.

233 See Article 3(1).

4.5 Climate change law and soil degradation

As discussed in Chapter two, climate change is one of the major causes of soil degradation and soil is one of the natural solutions to mitigate climate change through its carbon sequestration and storage functions. Unfortunately, Cameroon presently has no specific climate change legislation that addresses these issues. Thus, despite the symbiotic relationship between soil and climate change, both international and national politics on climate change have paid little attention to the importance of soil as a natural means of combating climate change and the corresponding negative effects of climate change on soil. The lack of a specific reference to soil as both a sink and source of GHGs in the UNFCCC, the Kyoto Protocol,[234] the PCCA and any other related international and national instrument demonstrates the lack of political will to give more attention to the impact of climate change on soil and also the relevance of soils in fighting climate change.

However, in the absence of a specific climate change law, Cameroon has developed a good number of policy documents to prepare for and implement the REDD+ initiative that was developed and implemented since 2005. Relevant national policy documents and progress in this respect are the 2008 R-PIN and the 2013 R-PP, the NDCs submitted in 2015 to the secretariat of the UNFCCC, and the 2018 National REDD+ Strategy that were prepared in view of the national implementation of the REDD+ initiative. Although there is no direct reference to soil in the R-PIN and the R-PP, the documents clearly identify slash-and-burn agriculture in the context of fighting climate change as one of the main sources of deforestation and GHG emissions in Cameroon – which is also a main driver of soil degradation. The R-PP further identifies bushfire as a driver of soil degradation. The two policy documents are therefore relevant for soil protection in Cameroon. Further, the NDCs spell out the actions Cameroon intends taking to address climate change – both in terms of adaptation and mitigation. Originally submitted as INDCs, they became binding NDCs upon the ratification of the PCCA. Via its NDCs, Cameroon has pledged a 32% reduction in its GHG emissions by 2035 compared to business-as-usual levels, taking 2010 as the reference year and conditional upon international support in the form of financing, capacity-building and transfer of technology. Through its NDCs, Cameroon intends to reduce its development carbon footprint without slowing its growth, identifying the soil as a critical component in meeting its 32% carbon emission reduction pledge. The NDCs therefore provide for good soil management practices through, for instance, restoration.[235]

In terms of soil protection, the National REDD+ Strategy clearly identifies the implementation of a programme on landscape restoration and management for climate

---

234 Adopted in Kyoto, 11 December 1997, UN Doc FCCC/CP/1997/L.7/add.1, entered into force in 2005.

235 See Republic of Cameroon (2015: 4, 5).

change resilience in the Northern Regions through the restoration of degraded soils by setting up private plantations for the production of wood energy; and regaining soil fertility and water catchment protection through agroforestry techniques. In the framework of promoting sustainable agricultural systems, the National REDD+ Strategy makes recommendations for regaining soil fertility and water catchment protection through agroforestry techniques; promoting food crops with low deforestation and forest degradation effects; allowing carbon conservation and sequestration (cocoa and coffee growing, etc.); promoting certification of agricultural products; promoting biofertilization through the recovery of agricultural residues; restoring and enhancing village hedges around agricultural land; recovering of fallow land; and, for agro–sylvo–pastoral landscape management, supporting of pastoral landscape management (securing and improving pastures to reduce the incidence of bushfires).[236] As of now, one may say that the only challenge with the implementation of the National REDD+ Strategy is securing international support in the form of adequate financing, capacity-building and transfer of technology.

Cameroon has a national climate change observatory. This structure has the mission to, among others, follow up the evolution of the climate and alert the government of ecological, sanitary and environmental threats that may be caused by climate change. To this effect, the organ collects information relating to climate and then elaborates and publishes a bulletin of alerts on climate. Despite the relevance of these initiatives for the protection of soil, the importance of soil especially as a carbon sink needs special and specific legal protection. A key message is that climate change is a major threat to soil degradation and soil is also critical for climate change mitigation – which requires that the policy on climate change and soils be appropriately designed to address these challenges.

4.6 Land tenure insecurity: Relevant legal provisions and associated problems

Land tenure insecurity is an important underlying factor of land and soil degradation. The following points constitute the relevant legal provisions and associated challenges in terms of soil protection.

236 Cameroon's National Strategy for reducing emissions from deforestation and forest degradation, sustainable management of forests, conservation of forest and enhancement of carbon stocks, 2018.

4.6.1 Ordinance No. 74/2 of 6 July 1974 establishing the rules governing state lands

Ordinance No. 74/2 governs the public and private property of the state as well as those of other public bodies as contained in its Article 1. This ordinance also enables us to make a distinction between the different types of public properties – i.e., natural and artificial public properties. Natural public property comprises coastlands, waterways, subsoil and airspace. Our interest in this exercise is on the maritime property, landed public property and fluvial public property. In effect, the maritime public property comprises, among others, the soil and subsoil of territorial waters. Even though such property is not exploited by the ordinary population, there is some human presence associated with it, which can be seen through offshore petroleum exploitation and through the disposal of different types of waste, notably plastic waste and any other pollutant affecting this type of property. Landed public property comprises the subsoil. This text therefore showcases the principle of devolution of the subsoil for purposes of its exploitation or its valorisation. The expression 'devolution' here is employed to mean the legal transfer of property from one owner to another. Waterways or fluvial property comprises, among others, marshland. Ordinary populations are usually forbidden from putting such property into use. Such land is considered by Cameroonian law as *non aedificandi* zones, which means lands on which activities such as the construction of buildings are forbidden.

4.6.2 Ordinance No. 74/1 of 6 July 1974 establishing the rules governing land tenure

Just like the previous ordinance on state lands, Ordinance No. 74/1 establishing the land tenure regime lays down the basic principles on the basis of which one can acquire ownership of land. In effect, Article 1(1) of this piece of legislation provides that: "the State guarantees to all-natural persons and corporate bodies having landed property the right to freely enjoy and dispose of such lands". Article 1(2) further makes the state the guardian of all lands and may in this capacity intervene to ensure rational use of land or use of land in the imperative interest of defence or in accord with the economic policies of the nation. This text makes it possible for every physical or corporate body whether of Cameroonian or foreign nationality to acquire land in Cameroon. Unfortunately, it is the application of this provision through the procedure for acquisition of land title over pieces of land that causes some trouble to the populations. These troubles, for instance, include the onerous cost of obtaining land title as well as the formalism associated with it.

In addition, such a general provision has eased the path and procedure for what is now a disturbing situation of 'land grab'. Land-grabbing is the controversial issue of large-scale land acquisitions involving the government leasing large parcels of land to big corporations, mostly of foreign origin, or influential national elites buying and registering large expanses of land in local communities.[237] Tafon and Saunders note that:[238]

> the widespread leasing or sale of lands in the developing world to foreign Governments and companies and to locally owned companies, or the appropriation of such lands by national or local Governments commonly known as land grab has intensified in recent years.

It has also been asserted by Amin and Jaha that this mode of land acquisition constitutes a pattern of economic dispossession throughout the global South.[239] There are numerous cases of land grabs, dispossession and evictions of communities across the country with implications for soil degradation.

The Herakles Farms plantation in the South West Region of Cameroon is one of the well-documented examples involving massive land grabs and environmental problems such as soil degradation. In 2009, the Cameroonian subsidiary of Herakles Farms – SITHE Global Sustainable Oil Cameroon (SGSOC) – signed a convention with the Government of Cameroon to develop a large-scale palm consisting of a 99-year lease for 73,086 hectares of land in the Ndian and Kupe-Manenguba Divisions. Local civil society organisations such as the Upper Balung Cultural and Development Association group representing seven villages mobilised to oppose the project, but with stiff resistance from state institutions. It is reported that SGSOC cleared more than 882 hectares of forest, with serious soil degradation and other environmental problems. The company was further accused of manipulating the content of its EIA to hide the plantation's true impacts and that the company's high conservation value assessment was forged by a panel of experts. SGSOC has also been accused of violating communities' rights to free and prior informed consent by engaging in corrupt land negotiation processes and demarcating its plantation boundaries without consent from locals in Nguti and, in the process, clearing farmlands belonging to communities. The actions of a coalition of over 20 Cameroonian and international NGOs opposing SGSOC's unethical and illegal behaviour were abortive. In fact, it is reported by some researchers[240] that two Cameroonian NGOs – the Struggle to Economise Future Environment and Nature Cameroon, based in the plantation area, suffered administrative and judicial harassment by SGSOC and the Cameroonian Government.

Another case is the Bakweri Land Problem and the Privatization of the CDC. As highlighted by Tande, in reaction to the ministerial visit in early 1999 to consider the planned privatisation of the CDC which had not addressed most of the key concerns of the local population, the Bakweri Land Claim Committee addressed a memorandum to the Cameroonian President in March 1999, in which it reiterated the 50-year-old

237 FAO & ITPS (2015: 92).
238 Tafon & Saunders (2019: 42).
239 Amin & Jaha (2016: 19).
240 See Fraser & Mousseau (2016: 3); Tafon & Saunders (2019: 50); Ndi (2017).

Bakweri claims to the lands on which the CDC had established its agro-industrial complex after the Second World War.[241] The committee demanded, among other things, official recognition that the CDC lands historically and legally belonged to the natives of the Fako Division.[242] In the course of the debates a general agreement was arrived at that the CDC should not be privatised without addressing the long-standing grievances of the Bakweri people, and that being an integral part of their lives, the CDC should not be sold to third parties without taking into account their interests for which the corporation had been established by the British Government.[243] In 2007, some indigenes from 19 villages of the Bakweri tribe in the Fako Division attempted to uproot banana plants on 15 hectares of a CDC plantation at Liongo, claiming that the health hazards of CDC's economic activities on their children, together with its expansionist and expropriationist tendency towards their ancestral lands provoked their hostility.[244] This long conflict was over the ownership, control and use of over 250,000 hectares of ancestral lands from which they had been evicted and relocated to a strange land, where they were deprived of their old hunting grounds and fishing rights.[245] While the Bakweri indigenes had been struggling for decades to have their land rights restituted, the government consistently exerted its authority by invoking the land law of 1974 which declares, among others, that "the State shall be the guardian of all lands". Thus, as highlighted by Tande and Ngwoh, while the Bakweri Land Claim Committee members continued to cite this same law as a confirmation of their customary ownership, the state remained adamant.[246]

According to Lang, religious groups in the country are also associated with the phenomenon of land-grabbing, which has been blamed on the generosity of the land tenure legislation.[247] We beg to differ with this researcher and take the view that the acquisition of lands by the church during the colonial era cannot actually be considered as land grab in the contemporary understanding of the concept. Moreover, unlike the so-called land-grabbers and actors in land and soil degradation, churches are not involved in activities that degrade the soil. Therefore, one may convincingly argue that the church is not a land-grabber and certainly not an actor in soil degradation in Cameroon. That said, land acquisition by churches can be blamed on the generosity of early traditional rulers who carved out large portions of their chiefdoms and fondoms and allocated them to the missionaries. An important goal of the church's mission in Africa was the acquisition of land required for the provision of public services, such as schools, health facilities and cemeteries, which made the church owner of relatively

241 See Tande (1999).
242 Ibid.
243 See generally Tande (1999) and Ngwoh (2019).
244 Ibid.
245 Ibid.
246 Ibid.
247 See Lang (2017: 120).

large parcels of land in communities across Africa. The most implicated of these churches is the Roman Catholic Church, which enjoys a nationwide presence and occupies land in most communities for its numerous evangelical, economic and social engagements. The church has acquired large expanses of land across the country for its huge holistic mission, with associated disputes, most of them over boundaries. According to Lang, a contributing factor to land boundary disputes in Weh was the expansion of the Catholic Church in the Weh community, whose theology went beyond worship, manifesting huge interest in land acquisition.[248] Other instances of land conflicts involving the church have been noted in villages such as Esu, Njinikom, Nkwen, Nso and Baseng. Former President of Kenya, Jomo Kenyatta, is well known for his assertion that:

> When the missionaries came to Africa, they had the Bible, and we had the land. They said let us pray. We closed our eyes. When we opened them, we had the Bible, and they had the land.

The interpretation of this quotation is that the missionaries came to Africa under false pretences. Their real purpose was not to teach the Bible but to lull the people into piety while pursuing their real objective of taking and owning their lands.

The high economic value presently placed on land and its appurtenant resources[249] has invariably increased the tendency of the most powerful to engage in land-grabbing in Cameroon and beyond, to the detriment of the vulnerable groups.[250] These vulnerable groups are increasingly being displaced from their lands, stirring disputes and sometimes bloody conflicts, with devastating effect on all parties involved. In fact, it has been observed by Lang that customary land tenure systems offer weak security, and the modern land law provides huge opportunities for land-grabbing.[251] Land-grabbing and dispossession are serious cause of hardship in vulnerable groups. It has been reported that in the North West Region of Cameroon, such as Bui, Wum and Mezam, to name a few, elites, bureaucrats, and cattle graziers use their positions and wealth to amass large tracts of land, on which they establish cattle ranches and plantations.[252] In many cases, such land grabs deprive the vulnerable groups of land on which they depend for their subsistence.

248 Ibid.

249 Minerals, timber and non-forest timber resources and other related activities such as agricultural development.

250 Local communities and the poor.

251 Lang (2017: 116).

252 Sone (2012).

4.6.3 Decree No. 76/166 of 27 April 1976 establishing the terms and conditions for the management of national lands

Decree No. 76/166 is the enabling instrument for the application of Ordinance No. 74/2 of 6 July 1974 to establish the rules governing state lands. The decree determines the modalities for the attribution of parts of state lands. The text in Article 1 enables individuals and physical or corporate persons to obtain parts of unoccupied or unexploited national lands for developmental projects by means of a temporary grant of rights, which may become a lease or an absolute grant depending on the circumstances and subject to the provisions of the present decree. Article 2 provides that: "temporary rights shall be granted for development projects in line with the economic, social or cultural policies of the nation". A reading of the provisions above may lead one to the conclusion that national lands may be subject to a temporary grant of rights, which could be a lease or absolute grant, depending on the provisions of the decree. A condition for this to happen as per the decree is that such lands are either unoccupied or unexploited. Article 2 is even more emphatic that temporary rights accruing from the grant must be for development projects that respond to economic, social or cultural policies of the country.

But what does this mean for soil management? These pieces of legislation do not place any limit to the amount of land that can be acquired under the temporary grant and the fear is that such lands, once acquired, may be over-exploited to maximise returns, to the extent that they degrade, since land is granted for a limited period of time. However, the law has placed this limit on the number of years rights arising from such grants could last. This seems to suggest that any renewal could be conditioned on the manner in which the uses answer to economic, social or cultural policies, including soil management dimensions. This is the spirit, in our view, behind Article 3 of the decree, namely that: "the duration of the temporary grant may not exceed five years. In exceptional cases it may be extended on reasoned application by the grantee". In addition, the exploitation of lands under this heading for development projects must be done in accordance with conditions laid down in the environmental and social impact assessment (ESIA), which checks negative impact on the environment including soil conservation.

4.6.4 Circular No. 001/CAB/PM of 1 April 2014 relating to measures applicable to investors on access to land

In the hierarchy of norms, circulars are generally not taken into consideration because they do not possess an efficient and evident binding force. In Administrative Law, circulars are of two types, namely interpretative and imperative circulars. The former is a non-Administrative Act and consequently does not create rights and obligations, but its legal value lies in the fact that it gives further meaning to the law in terms of a better understanding and therefore eases the implementation of the main Administrative Act. It resembles an enabling instrument to an Administrative Act only from an interpretative perspective. The latter, on the contrary, is imperative/mandatory because it creates rights and obligations for the parties concerned. Such circulars appear to be veritable legal texts based on their contents and the persons to whom they are addressed. This is the situation with the circular in question, which re-establishes the modalities for allocation of lands to investors. The circular is applicable to all the administrations that are involved in the process of allocation of lands for the purpose of a development project. In effect, this 2014 Prime Ministerial Circular comes as a consequence of a number of irregularities and also malfunctioning in the process of allocating lands to investors for the realisation of their projects. The Prime Minister and Head of Government noticed that:

> certain administration took engagements in matters relating to land contrary to the legislation and regulations in force (…) while investors requested for the allocation of lands with immature projects, that is to say without prior assessment of the feasibility of the projects and their financing meanwhile it is clear that the evaluation of the first pieces of land is strictly dependent on the technical parameters of the project. He further noticed that huge stretches of land demanded by certain investors are generally used for the mobilisation of important financing, which seriously truncates the role that lands play in matters of development.

On the basis of the foregoing, this circular has been useful in redefining rights and obligations, roles and procedure for the allocation of land to investors and consequently has reduced the land-grabbing phenomenon and the illegal occupation of land by investors. This has undoubtedly had an effect on access to and exploitation of soils.

4.6.5 Law No. 85/009 of 4 July 1985 relating to expropriation on grounds of public utility and the modalities for the payment of indemnities

Law No. 85/009 is the most important text in Cameroon relating to the loss of ownership of land. The text enables the state to enter into possession of any piece of land regardless of who the owner is, provided it is for the purpose of a development project that will serve general interest. Article 1(1) provides that: "for the realisation of objectives of general interest, the State may make recourse to the procedure of expropriation on grounds of public utility". This expropriation cannot be done without something in exchange. Article 3(1) in this respect provides that: "expropriation entitles the owner to receive indemnity, be it financial or in kind, in accordance with the conditions laid down by the present law". However, this indemnity will not be paid if the owner is occupied in some illegality in the wording of Article 10(3), such the destruction of buildings that are dilapidated or threatened by ruin or constructing buildings in violation of the urbanisation plan or against legislative or regulatory dispositions on the land tenure regime.

This text appears to be a framework document in that every act of expropriation on grounds of public utility must be preceded by a specific decree from the President of the Republic or the Prime Minister, Head of Government. While this piece of legislation has been applauded by many as it envisages compensation in cases of loss of ownership on the ground already expressed above, we must not lose sight of the fact that litigations abound and are usually articulated around the modalities governed by these specific decrees for calculating dues and the length of time it takes to pay the dues to the victims. The implication of this legal position for the soil is that the length of time it takes to pay compensation to victims is a factor that may incentivise activities that degrade the soil by disgruntled victims.

4.6.6 Traditional law

Traditional law here should be understood as customary law relating to land tenure. We need to state immediately that there is a rich but very slippery debate around customary land tenure in Cameroon, as is probably the case elsewhere on the continent.[253] That Cameroon is Africa in miniature is as true in the domain of customary or traditional law as it is in other domains. The country has more than 250 ethnic groups, each with its own customs.[254] The country is therefore very rich in customary or traditional law. In the area of land tenure, customs hold that there is customary ownership of land. It is important to mention that such customary tenure was recognised by law up to 5 August 1974 where the land tenure legislation so provided, but the same legislation stated that, after this date, all lands under customary ownership should be registered or cease to exist under customary tenure.[255] Of course, this provision could be understood as a transitional measure because before the land tenure legislation was enacted which gives exclusive ownership of land to the state, ownership was purely customary. Therefore, since the coming into force of this legislation, customary landownership ceased to exist. The only rights over such lands now are access and use rights in terms of hunting and fruit-picking,[256] which can have very insignificant negative impacts on the soils. In fact, this has not been a healthy situation as local communities have continued to claim ownership of lands situated within their localities – the so-called rural lands. The result is a continuous conflict, especially when such lands have to be exploited for public purposes and no compensation is to be paid out to communities as they have no ownership over such lands or when the land is allocated to foreign investors for investment purposes. In very few cases are the inhabitants of such lands

253 Elias (1971).

254 Ngwafor (1996).

255 Article 17(2) of the Land Tenure Ordinance, 1974 read in conjunction with Article 15 classifying land into two categories.

256 Article 17(3).

resettled. The attempt to ease land registration through the 2005 legislation has provided only meagre satisfactory results.

Completely ignoring traditional undocumented systems, statutory law makes land titles and leases the only legal means of holding property rights to land. In this regard, most lands in Cameroon are classified as national and state-owned, despite century-old claims by communities. Indeed, there is a general conception that local communities' land tenure rights were established even before the state came into existence. Unfortunately, rural land is hijacked from local communities, making them tenants of the state and subject to state regulation. Formally, most land today, including untitled lands occupied by rural communities, is considered National Land, administered by the state for the public interest. The state can evict communities from these lands and relocate them to guarantee the lands' 'effective exploitation'. Rural communities can title their customary land, and titles are the only protection against such evictions. But communities can only title land that was used and occupied prior to 1974. Neither land occupied after 1974 nor unoccupied non-farmland can be titled, even if it is vital to the community. Land reform in 2005 simplified land titling by reducing the number of steps and departments involved, and cut the time needed to obtain a land title from several years to less than one. Yet, it failed to address significant hurdles, including contradictory legal provisions and poor record-keeping. Sometimes, more than one land title is issued over the same parcel of land, creating conflicts. This can be frustrating and is a potential incentive for unsustainable activities which do not favour soil protection. It is critical that customary ownership by local communities be officially recognised, otherwise they will have little incentive to manage lands sustainably and protect soils. There is a need to strengthen customary landownership. Strengthening customary tenure rights here means the process by which the government legally and unequivocally cedes landownership and management rights to local communities that have historically used and occupied such lands. However, the strengthening of land rights, especially for local communities, should go in tandem with the enforcement and monitoring of the legal reforms.

A new and rampant tendency consists of elites moving to village communities to propose financing the registration of their land. In return, the communities or family members compensate the elites with many hectares of their land. This at least provides some tenure security, compared to customary 'ownership'. However, this has not laid to rest disputes over landownership and use. Today, as the government, elites, agro-industrial companies, and powerful traditional leaders acquire more lands, neither legal processes nor customary tenure systems provide people with adequate security over their land. This can incentivise unsustainable land management by occupiers of land who feel unsecured, which is not healthy for soil protection.

4.6.7 Conflicts and means of resolution

As discussed in Chapter three, there is a variety of land tenure types, giving rise to conflict and unsustainable land and soil management. For instance, there is evidence of customary rules prescribing acceptable claims to lands among members of communities, but where such claims are contradicted or nullified by legislation. Communally owned lands are insecure as such lands can easily be converted into national lands for development purposes. This insufficiency of the law leaves communities vulnerable, which, in turn, may incentivise land and soil degradation by communities who do not feel secured. Lang observed that "this situation of dual co-existing rules causes confusion and difficulties of understanding rules regulating people's rights to land".[257] We believe that apart from the customary argument of giving more land rights to groups who depend directly on the lands for their livelihood, it is also likely that if their rights to land are not legally strengthened, they may thwart soil protection and conservation efforts. We also believe that strengthening customary land tenure rights can guarantee legitimacy and local support for soil protection with positive economic, social and environmental derivatives.

In the land dispute involving *Nkamgang Mingeu Joseph v The State of Cameroon (MINDCAF)*,[258] the petitioner applied and obtained from the Minister of Lands a parcel of 40 hectares of national land for agricultural purposes. The petitioner claimed that having received a land certificate for the parcel of land, the same Provincial Service of Lands at Buea issued a second land certificate for the same piece of land to another party. The petitioner requested the Administrative Court of the South West Region, among other things, to cancel the latter land certificate, which was fraudulently issued, citing case law[259] to show that the only remedy for the fraudulent act was to withdraw the second land certificate. The court in its judgment declared the petition unfounded on its merits. This was because the Tiko Court of First Instance had visited the area in dispute in an earlier action for trespass on land by the petitioner against the defendant and in its reasoned judgment found that "the tort of trespass has not been proven against the defendant and third parties on the balance of probabilities". The Tiko court referred the plaintiff and the third parties to the competent Ministry which issued the land certificates for regularisation and dismissed the claim. The petitioner then applied to the Minister of Town Planning and Housing to apply Section 2(3) and (4) of Decree No. 76/165 of 27 April 1976 and withdraw the second land certificate issued on the land, but the Minister did not respond to the pre-litigation complaint. The fact that the Administrative Court of the South West Region did not find either at the site of the

257 See Lang (2017: 118–119).

258 Suit No. SWAC/LPM/006/2014.

259 See CS/CA Judgment No. 10/91-92 of 26/12/1999 *Aff. BOLLO ETOGO v Etat du Cameroun (MINUH)*; -cs/ca Judgment No. 01/87-88 of 29/10/1988 *Aff. BASSO Theodore et MAKON Daniel v Etat du Cameroun (MINUH).*

encroachment or in both land certificates any point where both pieces of land overlap, and the petitioner's absence during its visit to the scene of the alleged encroachment were proofs of irregularities that caused the court to declare the petition unfounded on its merits.

In *Noumsi Jean Bosco v The State of Cameroon (MINDCAF)*,[260] the plaintiff asked the Supreme Court to withdraw and cancel a land certificate obtained eight years after his on the same piece of property. The plaintiff in this case blamed the administration for having mapped out and issued two land certificates on the same property in violation of the principle of "*bornage sur bornage revant*" (which is the operation by which contiguous landowners agree to recognise the common boundary of their respective landed properties). In its reasoned judgment, the Supreme Court after declaring the petition acceptable in due and proper form ordered the immediate cancellation of the land certificate of the respondent which was obtained eight years after the plaintiff's certificate without the plaintiff's knowledge and under dubious and opaque circumstances.

In *Yongo Marc v The State of Cameroon (MINUH) and Delangue Koloko Michel*,[261] the plaintiff asked the Supreme Court to cancel and nullify the land title obtained by the respondent under conditions that were illegal and attributable to the state's error or fault. The Supreme Court, in granting the plaintiff's request, noted the overlapping registration procedures undertaken on the same land as constituting a fault of the administration and the clandestine contract of fictitious demarcation constituting fraud by the beneficiary Delangue Koloko Michel and that the beneficiary's land title had to be withdrawn pursuant to Article 2, paragraphs 3 and 6 of Decree No. 76/165, fixing the conditions for obtaining the land title.

In another land dispute between *Watson Mbua Maliva and Jakai Joan Limunga v The State of Cameroon (MINDCAF), Tsamo Souna Christian Josue and Souna Edward*,[262] the petitioner requested the court to nullify and cancel an irregular land certificate issued on 13 December 2016 to the respondents on a land surface area of 1,206 m^2 covering portions of land allocated to the petitioners by Chief Kaka Daniel, the head of the Bokwai village land management committee, dated 6 August 2012, following the procedure of land surrendered by the CDC. It was also attested that the land certificate was issued amid a serious dispute over the land and contrary to the law in force. The court declared the claim inadmissible because the petitioners failed to mention in their pre-litigation complaint for the withdrawal of the land certificate to the MINDCAF the fact that the portions of land were allocated to the petitioners by Chief Kaka Daniel, following the procedure of land surrendered by the CDC.

260 CS/CA Judgment No. 34/04-05 of 29 December 2004.
261 CS/CA Judgment No. 76/04-05 of 27 April 2005.
262 Suit No. SWAC/LSP/007/2017, Judgment No. 014/2018.

Other relevant decided cases involving land disputes in Cameroon include:

- Suit No. 01/RG/F/016 of 2 February 2016 *Ousmanou Dairou v The State of Cameroon (MINDCAF)*, Judgment No. 08/AFD/ 2017, delivered by the Maroua Administrative Court;
- Suit No. SWAC/LSP/003/2017 *The University of Buea (Repr. by the Vice Chancellor) v Bulu Village Traditional Council (Repr. by the Chairman Muambo Etonge Paul), Molinge Etonge Ruben, Ngowona Mba She Marie Benoite, Njume George Ndumbe, Fouejeu Tiogo Gabin, Nanfack Tsiguia Frank and Edembat Claude*, Judgment No. 015/2018;
- Suit No. SWAC/PND/001/2016 *Barrister Ebai Helen v The State of Cameroon (Repr. by the Ministry of State Property, Surveys and Land Tenure), The State of Cameroon (Repr. by the Ministry of Territorial Administration and Decentralization), the Governor of the south west region and Chief Kombe Simon*, Judgment No. 006/2018;
- Suit No. SWAC/LPM/006/2014 *Nkamgang Mingeu Joseph v The State of Cameroon (MINDCAF), Sone Ngenye Stephen, Robinson Ebeke Mondo, Ngenye Esoh, and Deutia Noumageu M. (Intervener)*, Judgment No. 018/2018;
- Suit No. 08/RG/F/016 of 15 November 2016 *Ali Née Nkeck Géneviève v The State of Cameroon (MINDCAF) and Hamadou Bako*, Judgment No. 03/AN of 6 February 2018;
- Suit No. 1780/03-04 of 8 October 2003 *Douala Mouteng née Mbara Angandji Germaine v The State of Cameroon (MINDCAF)*, Judgment No. 124/2016/TA-YDE of 19 April 2016;
- Suit No. 377/2013 of 11 October 2013 *Efila Nnah Jean Gabriel v The State of Cameroon (MINDCAF), Judgment No. 133/2016/TA-YDE of 3 May 2016*;
- Suit No. 352/2013 of 19 September 2013 *Eya Ateba Sidoine v Etat du Cameroun (MINDCAF)*, Judgment No. 96/2016/TA-YDE of 5 April 2016;
- Suit No. 259/2013 of 6 June 2013 *Mengue Barbare v The State of Cameroon (MINDCAF)*, Judgment No. 125/2016/TA-YDE of 19 April 2016;
- Suit No. 89/2013 of 5 March 2013 *Syndic de la liquidation des Ets Paul Khoury (Ngoua Elembe) v The State of Cameroon (MINDCAF)*, Judgment No. 131/2016/TA-YDE of 3 May 2016;
- Suit No. 05/2013 of 3 January 2013 *Succession Eyenga Marie Gisèle Béatrice (NKIE Laurent Cyrille Martin) v The State of Cameroon (MINDCAF)*, Judgment No. 130/2016/TA-YDE of 3 May 2016;
- Suit No. 373/06-07 of 16 November 2007 *Noah Soter Isidore and others v The State of Cameroon (MINDCAF)*, Judgment No. 121/2016/TA-YDE/ADD of 19 April 2016;

- Suit No. 41/2010 of 27 January 2010 *Nyemb Jean Baptiste v The State of Cameroon (MINFOPRA)*, Judgment No. 128/2016/TA-YDE of 3 May 2016;
- Suit No. 32/2013 of 25 January 2013 *Onana Onana Roger v The State of Cameroon (MINDCAF)*, Judgment No. 122/2016/TA-YDE of 19 April 2016;
- Suit No. 1569/02-03 of 26 December 2002 *Succession feu Amougou Ambroise v The State of Cameroon (MINDCAF)*, Judgment No. 129/2016/TA-YDE of 3 May 2016;
- Suit No. HCN/03/0S/2011 *Struggle to Economise Future Environment (SEFE) v S.G. Sustainable Oils Cameroon LTD and Dr. Timti Isidore*, Ruling CRNo. 90200251 of 19 March 2012;
- Suit No. 1346/00/01 of 7 August 2001 *Dame Nga Etende Atangana Marie Dame Banga Blandine v The State of Cameroon (MINUH) and Société Industrielle de Mbang S.A*, Judgment No. 111/2016/TA-YDE of 12 April 2016; and
- Suit No. SWAC/PSE/001/2018 *Livanda Village Community v The Minister of State Property, Surveys and Land Tenure*, Ruling No. 005/RPSE/PC/2018 on an application for stay of execution.

The importance of resolving land tenure conflicts and ensuring fair ownership, access and use rights for all is critical for soil protection. Land tenure security guaranteed by land titling is crucial for soil protection, especially as the economic interest in land is constantly on the increase due to much pressure from large-scale investors in agro-industries and related activities. Without secure land tenure, users have no incentive to protect lands and soils. Land tenure security will provide a safeguard against risks of unsustainable land practices by unsecured users and will support more effective land and soil management. Land tenure security for communities, in particular, will support the exercise of traditional knowledge and practices that are good for soil protection.

There seems to be no case law regarding appeals on administrative decisions concerning the use or protection of soil other than land disputes. This is probably because the protection of soil is not a major concern in Cameroon, at least for now.

4.6.8 Land tenure legislation and associated land-grabbing

Land-grabbing is identified as a main driver of soil degradation. The general provision of the land law states that:[263]

> the state shall be the guardian of all lands. It may in this capacity intervene to ensure rational use of land or in the imperative interest of defense or the economic policies of the nation

263 Section 1(2).

has eased the path and procedure for what is now a disturbing situation of 'land-grabbing'. This provision is an enabler of land-grabbing in that it has eased the way for the most powerful (the state, large corporations, the church, influential national elites and the rich) to engage in acquisition of large expanses of land to the detriment of the vulnerable groups (local communities and their poor members). Thus, the generosity of the land tenure legislation may lead to more soil degradation in the country.

4.6.9 Relationship of landownership and environmental responsibility

All the regulatory texts on land tenure in Cameroon guarantee ownership, which gives landowners of the three land categories the right to exclusive possession and use of their land, the right to mortgage the land, and the right to transfer the land, but these texts are silent on the question of owners' responsibility to manage the lands they own sustainably. This is an inherent flaw of the Cameroonian land tenure system. Environmental concerns and, by extension, soil protection is thus not addressed by the Cameroonian legal framework on land tenure. One should expect to see clear and unambiguous provisions apportioning environmental responsibility to owners and users of the three land categories in Cameroon. However, the Preamble of Cameroon's Constitution indirectly imposes such environmental responsibility regarding land by providing that:

> Every person shall have a right to a healthy environment. The protection of the environment shall be the duty of every citizen. The State shall ensure the protection and improvement of the environment.

Although these Constitutional pronouncements are relevant, their impact is less if compared to the direct provisions of specific legal texts on land. Given that land law contains no provision on the environmental responsibility of landowners, the land tenure law of Cameroon must be revised in order to impose such responsibility on landowners and users or to factor in or mainstream environmental protection concerns. This will go a long way to protect the soil.

In the absence of specific provisions establishing the environmental responsibility of landowners and users in the various regulatory and legislative texts governing land in Cameroon, Decree No. 2013/0171/PM of 14 February 2013 fixing modalities for carrying out ESIA seems to assign such environmental responsibility in connection with the use of land. This regulatory prescription ensures environmental responsibility of use of land by requiring the promoter of a project or an establishment to carry out an ESIA, under penalty of the laws and regulations in force.[264]

With respect to environmental protection, important elements of the assessment include the following: The presentation of the establishment, including the promoter,

264 Article 3(1).

location, objectives, justification, facilities, operating processes, processing of raw materials, products, waste and effluents; the description and analysis of the environment of the establishment, including all the natural, human and sociocultural elements affected by the activities of the establishment; identification and analysis of environmental impacts; the field of intervention, including accounting with laws, regulations and policies, management, hygiene, health, safety and environment; the environmental and social management plan; and an information awareness programme, as well as the reports and minutes of public consultations held with the population, unions, opinion leaders and other organised groups concerned with the activities of the business.[265]

In fact, Article 5(1) provides that every promoter of a project subject to an ESIA must submit to the Minister of the Environment, in addition to the general file of the project a request for an ESIA including the sector of activity, and the terms of reference of the impact study accompanied by a project description and justification, with a focus on the preservation of the environment. Upon receipt of the request, the administration in charge of the environment will then give an opinion on the terms of reference of the impact assessment which include among others, the responsibilities and obligations of the promoter.[266]

Articles 5(6) and 15 further oblige every promoter of a project requiring ESIA to obtain a certificate of environmental compliance issued by the minister in charge of the environment to continue to operate, under penalty of the penalties prescribed by the legislation in force. Article 6 complements the provisions above by stipulating that no ESIA can be carried out without the approval of the terms of reference by the minister in charge of the environment. By the provisions of Article 13(1), the inter-ministerial committee of the environment must give its opinion on the ESIA files[267] transmitted to it by the administration in charge of the environment. To ensure that the project promoter respects his environmental responsibility, the decree makes provision for monitoring and follow-up of the effective implementation of the environmental management by an administrative and technical supervision service of the competent administrations as per Article 16(1) and (2). The same Article in its (3) also requires the project promoter to produce a semi-annual report on the implementation of the environmental management plan at the Ministry of the Environment. Under Article 9, (1) the realisation of an ESIA must be done with the participation of the populations concerned through consultations and public hearings, in order to gather the opinions of the populations on the activity; (2) such public consultation consists of meetings during the impact assessment, in the localities affected by the activity; and (3) the

265 Article 4.

266 Article 5(3).

267 Containing the report of the environmental and social audit declared admissible; the assessment report of the environmental and social audit; and the evaluation report and the records of consultations and public hearings.

public hearing is intended to publicise the impact assessment, record any opposition and allow the public to comment on the conclusions of the impact assessment. However, Article 12 excludes public consultation or hearings regarding the conduct of ESIA for activities of security or national defence. This exclusion constitutes a danger to both environment and people.

All the provisions above seek to establish and impute environmental responsibility on those carrying out projects which are likely to cause land degradation and, by extension, soil degradation. But we must be quick to add that such responsibility is for the promoters of large projects. What about those who carry out small projects or who acquire land to use for subsistence agriculture? Those who acquire land for human habitation whose projects have extremely negative impacts on the environment are not within the strict scrutiny of law in the same way as those carrying out subsistence agriculture such as the slash-and-burn and *ankara* systems that have been described above and which are proscribed by the 1994 Forestry Law.

In any event, the Arrête of 2016[268] identifies and categorises those activities on land that require ESIA. The promoters of the activities mentioned above have the responsibility to ensure that such activities do not cause any environmental harm. An inherent weakness of this regulation concerns subsistence farming, such as slash-and-burn and *ankara* agricultural practices, which are mostly practised on small-scales. They are not taken into consideration by this regulation, which may be dangerous for soil health. Although these types of subsistence agriculture are usually practised on small scales, their total land surface area, when summed for all the farmers, is enormous and can lead to soil degradation. This is worsened by the fact that small-scale farmers have little or no incentive or motivation to practise sustainable soil management measures as their immediate concern is feeding their families.[269] The livelihoods of almost all communities – if not all – depend on subsistence agriculture. This is enormous in terms of pressure on the soil and is enough reason for the inclusion of small-scale agriculture among the categories of agricultural projects which are subject to environmental impact assessment. For the purpose of soil protection, all agricultural projects whether practised on a small or large scale ought to comply with the law on environmental impact assessment. This may make sense from a theoretical angle but the critical question that must be answered is: Who should pay for the cost of the impact assessments given that small-scale farmers cannot afford to pay? Another important question is: Who should control the impact assessment process, given that small-scale farms add up to millions, dispersed all over the country? One way of resolving this is to make available extension administrative services at local levels to sensitise and educate local

---

268 See Arrêté No. 00001/MINEPDED of 8 February 2016 establishing the different categories of operations whose realisation is subject to a strategic environmental assessment or an environmental and social impact study.

269 See Ginzky et al. (2019: 4).

famers on the importance of practising sustainable farming and to monitor and control their activities.

Moreover, it is not enough to establish the responsibility of landowners to manage their lands sustainably; incentives are critical tools that can encourage landowners to practise sustainable production methods on their lands. Furthermore, landowners can be educated on the linkages of their activities on land to soil degradation through sensitisation and capacity-building programmes, etc.

Legislation makes the state the primary landowner in Cameroon.[270] While many of the communities occupying national lands claim customary rights or have some access rights to land and resources, these rights are poorly recognised in laws. Tenure insecurity encourages activities that offer more immediate returns from land rather than long-term returns from sustainable land management. The failure of public policies and land law to take into account traditional land rights constitutes a further source of land degradation. Deforestation sometimes is a means to secure land rights as clearance itself can establish proof of occupation and increase tenure security. The land tenure regime has not properly addressed tenure insecurity, especially on communities' lands that host much of the cultivable lands. Furthermore, most of the disjointed, segregated and scattered pieces of legislation were crafted without any consideration for environmental protection and, by extension, no soil protection provisions. The institutional framework for managing land and land-based resources such as minerals and forests is also weak. These challenges are worsened by improper land-use policy, which should instead guide the realisation of a balance between the many competing land uses. Poor land-use policies have led to continued degradation of land and soils.

Land tenure clarification, spatial planning, and mainstreaming of soil protection provisions are important elements of sustainable land use. If communities have undisturbed ownership rights to land, they will consider such rights not only as an economic commodity, but as a social and cultural resource that requires protection. In so doing, they will reduce unsustainable land practices, which are a great driver of soil degradation.

4.7 Wildfires, hunting and cattle rearing

As pointed out in Chapter two of this assessment, human-induced wildfires are another significant driver of soil degradation in Cameroon. Although there are fire management policies in Cameroon, strengthening capacities to prevent wildfires can help to protect soil. The 1994 Forestry Law proscribes fire. Article 14(1) forbids anyone from starting fire that is likely to cause damage to the vegetation of the national forest estate without prior authorisation. Article 80 prohibits hunting with the aid of fire. Article

270 See Section 1(2) of the Land Ordinance No. 74/1.

154 punishes anyone who ignites a fire in a forest of the national domain, as provided for in Article 14 with a fine of CFA F5,000 to CFA F50,000 or imprisonment of 10 days, or both. Article 156 punishes with a fine of CFA F200,000 to CFA F1,000,000 or imprisonment of one month to six months, or both, anyone who makes a fire in a state forest, a protected or ecologically fragile area, in violation of Articles 14, 16(1) and (3), and 17(2) of the same law.

Furthermore, Decree No. 95/531/PM of 23 August 1995 to set the terms and conditions of applying the forest regime in Sections 6–8 recognises the role of the ministry of forestry staff to determine modalities for the safe control of fire, and the ministry of territorial administration and decentralisation to issue permits to start fires after consultation with local forestry staff. Joint MINFOF–community fire prevention and monitoring committees are supposed to be set up at local level, but they have hardly been effective owing to a lack of environmental concerns.

In the case of cattle rearing where the herders burn down both grassland and forests for fresh vegetation, there is a need for policies and strategies to address wildfires. Systems of intensive cattle rearing on ranches that have been successfully used in Indonesia are feasible options.[271] Although such systems will need more financial inputs to enable adaptation with intensive livestock farming, they can greatly reduce pressure on soil.

4.8 Conclusion

An assessment of the sectoral legislations above reveals their strengths and weaknesses in terms of soil protection. Regarding their strengths, the sectoral legislations at least have some minimal soil protection relevance due to the fact that they make references to soil protection incidentally although, in most cases, indirectly. Notwithstanding the strengths of these legislations in terms of soil protection, this assessment also notes their weaknesses. For instance, sustainable land management in Cameroon seems challenging given that majority of the legal instruments for environmental and natural resources lack enabling instruments to complete and transpose the objective of the framework laws. Almost all legislation in Cameroon is incomplete regarding particular subject matter and this often provides that such issues are to be dealt with by decrees. These are the enabling instruments that further detail and complete the legislation. It usually takes months or years for such decrees to be established by the executive power. Such delays, which may be for political reasons, render the implementation of legislation difficult in practical terms. This is the case, for instance, with the current mining law. For the purpose of the effective implementation of a piece of legislation, parliament should always enact detailed and complete legislation like in common law

271 Epule et al. (2014: 412).

countries where the enabling instruments do not exist. This way, the requirement of an enabling instrument can be bypassed. Better still, the text of law and its enabling instrument should be crafted at the same time, so as to facilitate the understanding and the immediate implementation of the law.

Our assessment of Cameroon's land tenure reveals that land access and land rights are a major determinant with regard to sustainable soil management. However, the plurality of land tenure – statutory and customary – is a major challenge that does not enhance soil protection. These drawbacks in the land law are a legacy of colonial history, which has been reinforced by modern post-colonial administration with the objective of exerting supremacy over vulnerable communities. After independence, the Government of Cameroon, like the colonial powers, continues to own most of the lands in Cameroon under the rubric of state lands and national lands. Colonisation has influenced and encouraged the following drawbacks: the non-legalisation of customary land titling; the fact that the state owns most of the land and the practice of land-grabbing and disposition of local communities' land by the state and its powerful allies (natural resource and agricultural investors, and the rich and influential elites); the challenges of land access and rights; and the high costs and cumbersome procedures involved with obtaining land titles. All these factors have serious implications for soil degradation. Furthermore, the various pieces of land legislation in Cameroon are completely devoid of soil protection provisions. On reading through the segregated and disjointed pieces of land legislation, one does not find any express references to the need to protect soil. Thus, land law in Cameroon is not only incoherent in terms of two systems co-existing and governed by segregated and ambiguous pieces of legislation; it is equally incomplete as it fails to address the need to protect soils.

Based on these revelations, our conclusion is that these legislations are devoid of any effective provisions for the protection of soils, especially as most of the legislations promote and encourage activities that drive soil degradation. There is therefore a need for legal reform to properly address soil protection. One way is the formulation of a comprehensive and authoritative framework legislation for land management as well as the establishment of a national environmental protection agency that will supervise all land-use related activities in the country. Furthermore, secured landownership rights can favour the adoption of sustainable soil management practices. In fact, security of tenure is important for the adoption of land conservation practices. A combination of short-term and long-term policy measures that offer incentives for sustainable soil management practices or land conservation, including enhanced security of tenure, government targeting programmes and other policies that reduce household poverty and improve access to education, both formal and informal, is critical.

5 Lessons learnt and recommendations

5.1 Positive lessons learnt and opportunities for soil protection

Regarding the existing enabling legal environment scattered provisions (express and implied) in various pieces of legislation such as the Constitution, Framework Law on Environmental Management, and sectoral laws in agriculture, mining, forestry, water, land tenure. Specific legislation on the protection of soils and subsoils (Decree No. 2011/2584/PM of 23 August 2011 on the modalities for the protection of soils and subsoils which requires any activity relating to the exploitation of the soil to be carried out in a manner that avoids or reduces erosion of soils and desertification), but with the limitation that it is not comprehensive enough. Information, public participation, education, policy advocacy and planning, as well as monitoring of trends and impact of interventions in sustainable soil management, are central to the success of efforts to foster protection of soils. Information and communication technologies, the media, networks and extension services are vital components of improved information systems to enhance sustainable soil management. There are scant policy and legal provisions on these interventions in the 1996 Framework Law on Environmental Management, the ESIA decree and other sectoral legislation and their implementation is weak.

Soil degradation interventions should be designed to ensure their sustainability. The effective involvement of small-scale famers and local communities should be required in land and soil degradation control activities. Their knowledge, skills and adaptive capacities are invaluable in ensuring sustainable land and soil management practices. This is well recognised in the 1996 Framework Law on Environmental Management, but the harnessing of local knowledge and skills and the empowerment of local communities through increased capacity-building that is linked to achieving tangible results is not a reality in Cameroon. Community regulation on pesticides and fertilizers – the Common Provisions on the Homologation of Pesticides in the CEMAC Zone – aims to bring together experiences and expertise of the member states for the evaluation and homologation of pesticides. The objective is to ensure their rational and judicious use, as well as the protection of human health and the environment; and to oversee experimentation, authorisation, importation, exportation, transportation, transit, stocking, marketing, use, control and elimination of active materials and formulated products of pesticides within the states of the CEMAC zone. Regarding industrial development, in the absence of specific legislation governing the industrial sector in Cameroon, the sector today is regulated through a plethora of disjointed and dispersed pieces of regulatory instruments.

Given the cross-cutting nature of soils and the ever-present threat of degradation, it is pertinent that strong and well-functioning institutional frameworks are put in place to coordinate the formulation and implementation of related policies and programmes and to ensure that they are adequately mainstreamed into relevant national sectoral development plans, policies, strategies and legislation. A good number of government ministerial departments (MINADER, MINDCAF, MINEPDED, MINEPAT, MINDUH, Ministry of Trade, MINMIDT, MINRESI, MINEPIA, etc.), whose functions or roles are relevant to soil protection and which are supported by decentralised entities, are in place, albeit with weak powers. Government ministerial departments are supported by public and para-public institutions working in the area of soil protection, such as IRAD, ANAFOR (National Forestry Development Agency)[272], MIDENO (North West Development Authority[273]), the Inter-Ministerial Committee for the Environment, the National Consultative Commission for the Environment and Sustainable Development, and the National Council for Planning and Sustainable Development of the Territory. Examples of further support bodies are development partners via project sponsorship, such as the GIZ (German Agency for International Cooperation) and the AFD (French Development Agency), backed by carefully drafted and signed project agreements.

Sustainable soil management and soil protection are complex issues that need an integrated approach to achieve meaningful and sustainable results. The Inter-Ministerial Committee for the Environment, the National Consultative Commission for the Environment and Sustainable Development, the National Council for Planning and Sustainable Development of the Territory are relevant in this respect, but the functioning of these initiatives are weak.

5.2 Negative lessons learnt

Although access to environmental information, public participation and access to justice in Cameroon is guaranteed by the 1996 Framework Law on Environmental Management and other relevant legislation with regard to sustainable soil management, public participation and access to information is not sufficiently implemented in Cameroon. In fact, information on soil is often inadequate, out-dated, not available in digital format and not referenced geographically. The danger of soil degradation in the country is little known to the general public and is underestimated by those who are

272 ANAFOR was created in 2002 following the restructuring of the former National Forestry Development Agency, ONADEF. It is in charge of supporting stakeholders (collectivities, but also private sectors and communities) in reforestation initiatives. Officially, ANAFOR is in charge of implementing the national programme for the development of private and community forestry plantations. See the REDD desk website, at https://theredddesk.org/countries/actors/national-forestry-development-agency-cameroon, accessed 11 September 2019.

273 MIDENO acts on behalf of the Government of the Republic of Cameroon in the North-West Region as the supervisor of development policy and providing a budgetary, financial and technical mechanism for development projects. See the North-West Region's web portal, at http://www.all-about-cameroon.com/cameroon-north-west-development-authori-tymideno.html, accessed 11 September 2019.

informed, and therefore does not constitute an immediate concern. There is also weak implementation of the scant policy and legislative provisions in the 1996 Framework Law on Environmental Management, the ESIA decree and other sectoral legislation regarding environmental information, public participation and access to justice in Cameroon.

Sectoral activities such as agriculture, mining, demographic growth, industrial development are the main drivers of soil degradation. Sectoral pieces of legislation on these activities are devoid of any specific and effective provision for the protection of soils, especially as most of the legislation promotes and encourages activities that drive soil degradation. Legislation on mining contains provisions relevant to soil protection, but this law, like most pieces of legislation in Cameroon, is paralysed because of the lack of enabling instruments.

Regarding the role of foreign investors in the mining sector in Cameroon, we discovered that they are not usually attentive to the concerns of environmental protection as they care little about reinstating or rehabilitating exploited sites. The degraded sites lead to soil degradation. Such investors use chemical products such as mercury that are unhealthy for the environment in general and soils in particular as it pollutes the water used by the local people and destroys the attendant biodiversity, including soils. Regarding industrial development, Cameroon presently has no specific legislation governing the industrial sector. One finds effluent or liquid and gaseous discharge of industrial origin, treated or untreated, discharged directly or indirectly into the environment in some major cities such as Douala. This is harmful to soil health. This sector constitutes a further danger to the soils given that industrialisation is one of the pillars and the growth engine which the government intends to rely on to achieve its Vision 2035. Despite the symbiotic relationship between soil and climate change, both international and national politics on climate change have paid little attention to the importance of soil as a natural solution when combating climate change. In fact, the symbiotic relationship between soil and climate change has not been captured by legislation. This is not surprising since Cameroon has no climate change legislation that recognises the impacts of climate change on soil and the critical role that soil plays in mitigating climate change. This is clear proof of the inadequate political will to give more attention to the relevance of soils in fighting climate change.

Most agricultural projects are associated with soil degradation caused either by the misuse of chemical products (pesticides and fertilizers) or unsustainable farming methods, such as the slash-and-burn, bushfire and *ankara* methods practised by most local communities across the country. Domestic legislation on water and soil protection and the CEMAC Community Regulation on pesticides and fertilizers are poorly implemented. In addition, legislation on ESIA does not address the slash-and-burn or the *ankara* agricultural methods. Legislation on bushfire also suffers from implementation problems. Agricultural scientific data and information on sustainable soil management are not made available to farmers, and more particularly not to small-scale farmers, who continue to indulge in unsustainable agricultural practices that are detrimental to soil health.

Regarding current land tenure in Cameroon, colonial legislation continues to influence and encourage the following drawbacks: the non-legalisation of customary land tenure; the fact that the state owns all lands and the practice of land grabs and dispossession of local communities' land by the state and its powerful allies (agricultural investors, and the rich and influential elites); the challenges of land access and rights and the high costs and cumbersome procedures involved in obtaining land titles or land registration. All these factors have serious implications for sustainable soil management.

One of the difficulties underpinning soil protection in Cameroon is the absence of a specific law applicable to this critical resource. This is not to say soil is unregulated, but the plethora of laws spread across a wide range of areas and sectors render implementation challenging. This becomes even more intricate because of contradictions in sectoral laws, especially concerning land use and the authority of the state; and duplication of institutional roles, especially for the ministries and community involvement. Such duplication seems to promote conflict between sectoral ministries rather than achieve a coordinated approach to protect the soil. Other core impediments for effective sustainable soil management in Cameroon are institutional and organisational deficiencies. National institutions both at the level of central administration and decentralised entities are charged with the responsibility of law implementation in general and the implementation of laws relating to soil protection in particular. One big challenge, however, is the organisational deficiencies stemming from the challenges of the decentralisation process wherein the central administrative units are reluctant to transfer the necessary resources and competencies to the decentralised entities (regions and councils) to enable them to carry out their functions, including the soil management function, properly. Even where resources and competencies are transferred, the institutional arrangements for such transfers are unclear. Unlike other countries in Africa, for instance, those with decentralised entities having legislative powers, decentralised entities such as regions and councils in Cameroon do not have powers or competence to make laws. Rather, the central administration, which is also slow to act, delegates only law implementation powers to the decentralised entities. Thus, while comprehensive soil legislation is absent, the limited legislation on a matter that is central is only poorly implemented in the country, thus rendering soil protection difficult within the entire administrative set up of the country.

5.3 Recommendations

Given the potential of doubling production in terms of agriculture and natural resources exploitation, there will be increased pressure on soils, necessitating effective soil protection legislation. Throughout this assessment, it has been established that soil is the bedrock of all-natural resources. For this reason, the following recommendations are proffered: Although the Constitution implicitly mentions soil when it speaks of natural resources, a specific constitutional provision addressing soil protection should be enacted. Thereafter, parliament should proceed to craft a comprehensive and coherent piece of legislation that encapsulates all the specific provisions in framework and sectoral laws that relate to or have implications for sustainable soil management.

In order to craft overarching legislation for soils, the following aspects should be considered: Crafting a detailed and comprehensive soil protection law to facilitate understanding and an informed, immediate and effective implementation of such law; including soil management in the academic curricula at the elementary level up to university stage, or at least mainstream soil management issues in teaching at all levels; passing on soil information to small-scale farmers and the part of the population that does not have access to academic education, which should be done through sensitisation and carefully thought-out capacity-building programmes; considering, and mainstreaming soil legislation to all important soil and soil-related governance benchmarks such as contracting processes for soil exploitation activities, corruption, transparency, accountability in soil exploitation arrangements and contracts; involving relevant stakeholders who have fervent concerns about soil protection, such as non-governmental organisations, civil society organisations and environmental protection institutions, in the crafting of soil legislation; improving institutional arrangements through more effective decentralisation consisting of the actual transfer of power and competencies and the necessary resources from the central to decentralised territorial entities, in order to overcome the challenge of 'no one being in charge'. This requires strong political will from the powers-that-be.

Moreover, obtaining clarity from the existing sectoral legal and institutional dispensation is important. A specific soil protection law will provide certainty and clarity on measures of applicability of such provisions. A first step in this direction will be to consolidate all applicable laws to soil. The revision of the different laws on the institutional organisation of the different ministries – mainly the provisions that are at the origin of conflict – is critical. Ensuring legal and institutional certainty and clarity may require the creation at the level of the prime ministry of an inter-ministerial committee in charge of coordinating decision-making related to land-use to ensure effective compliance to the different sectoral laws or simply reinforce the role of coordination of government actions already being ensured by the prime minister, but with particular emphasis on soils as this resource is critical for human survival. Given that Cameroon is characterised by different soil types, it should consider viewing legislation as zonal, addressing specifically the different types of soils, while increasing the sanctions for violators of environmental and soil legislation, which have hitherto been minimal and do not have strong deterrent effects.

Soil protection can be enhanced in the following ways: By adopting a forest strategy including afforestation and reforestation programmes; by formulating an integrated multi-use landscape strategy for restoration of degraded landscapes with a specific focus on soil. This entails taking into consideration all land uses that ensure the participation of all land users; by developing a strategy that engages development partners and funding organisations for projects on sustainable soil protection; by developing a programme of compensation through soil restoration projects; by developing programmes that are geared towards the sensitisation of farmers on the danger of using non-homologated phytosanitary products, chemicals and pesticides and implementing other unsustainable farming practices such as slash-and-burn, bushfires and the *ankara* system; by updating the National Environment Management Plan (NEMP) and rethinking the setting of standards for restoring degraded lands, as a matter of urgency. NEMP has no standards to be achieved for restoration of degraded sites and this is probably a huge weakness because one can never ascertain whether restoration has been effectively achieved to reduce soil degradation.

In terms of improvement of enforcement, monitoring, and access to environmental information it remains key to foster collaboration, cooperation and synergies among centralised and decentralised territorial entities for more effective enforcement of laws and policies through a multi-level committee of representatives of central and decentralised administrative entities. Enhancing access to environmental information and public participation in decision-making are crucial ingredients for environmental and soil enforcement mechanisms. This can be done by elaborating an access to information law that gives everyone the right of access to information held by public bodies and relevant private bodies expeditiously and gratuitously. Public bodies and relevant private bodies must proactively publish information and any refusal to disclose information should be subject to appeal. Of course, disclosure should be subject to security and strategic restrictions. The improvement of government structures charged with monitoring and enforcement of environmental and soil laws and policies is necessary, just as the enhancement of the implementation of existing ESIA measures by engaging independent environmental assessors.

In terms of the improvement of land rights it is important to reduce the multiplicity of legal instruments and requirements on access to land by means of harmonisation and consolidation of the scattered and disjointed pieces of legislation on land tenure in a single land act. Moreover, the recognition of customary laws relating to land tenure must be reflected in modern legislation, or at least modern legislation should ensure that procedures for access to land are comprehensible and accessible to all social groups. Preferably, a land act that harmonises and consolidates the segregated and scattered pieces of legislation on land tenure should be enacted in Cameroon. Such a land act should recognise customary land rights and accord such rights legal protection, and such rights should be considered as a category of private property. This may be accommodated in the ongoing land tenure reform process.

Regarding the control of foreign investors it may be advisable to enact laws imposing an environmental degradation tax, such as a pollution tax; to legalise the certification of commodities whose production or importation are likely to lead to soil degradation; to put in place reforms that limit the amount of land acquired by foreign investors; to commit foreign investors to social responsibility, responsible business or corporate citizenship so as to avoid social conflicts with communities. This is a self-regulating paradigm that helps companies or investors to be socially accountable to the public and commits to corporate environmental responsibility so as to avoid environmental degradation generally and soil degradation specifically.

Incentive mechanisms should be developed that encourage farmers to invest in degraded lands in order to avoid further pressure on such lands by providing them with manure free of charge and granting interest-free loans. Governance and institutional capacity should be enhanced with adequately trained and equipped human resources, especially at decentralised level to ensure effective implementation of monitoring and control activities. Alternative income-generating activities should be provided to small-scale farmers in order to reduce pressure on soil.

The Sub Regional Community Secretariat should urge governments to observe and implement community regulations on soil protection, for instance, the pesticide regulation. Given that climate change is a main driver of soil degradation and that there is a corresponding crucial role of soil in combating climate change through its carbon storage function, both climate change and soil legislation should recognise this symbiosis and mainstream it in climate change and soil legislation.

The detrimental impacts of the misuse of chemical products (pesticides and fertilizers) and unsustainable farming methods (slash-and-burn, bushfire and the *ankara* method) can be averted by developing policies that are geared towards the sensitisation of farmers about the danger of using non- homologated chemicals, phytosanitary products, pesticides and unsustainable farming practices. Thus, it may be advisable to put a moratorium on lands in place, in order to prevent activities that degrade the soil. There is a need for data on soil degradation to be made available to the general public, especially small-scale farmers and for the involvement of science institutions in the model legislation. Information on the status of soil and appropriate measures to achieve sustainable soil management are critical and should be integrated into curricula at all levels of education.

Through a mix of soil conservation techniques such as better tree and pasture management, simple and low-cost farmer-led innovations and technologies can help to achieve sustainable land management and farming systems needed to combat land and soil degradation. Building on and reinforcing these innovations and technologies with expertise and resource support can enhance achievement of better results.

One important challenge to deal with regarding soil protection is obtaining the buy-in of politicians. Soil degradation and its effects need continuous urgent attention, carefully backed up by appropriate, comprehensive and coherent policy, and a legal and institutional framework. A policy and legal framework that defines the activities to be taken and those not to be taken, as well as the institutions and actors and their respective roles, is the foundation of any meaningful step towards sustainable soil management. However, a strong political will is also required to enable the crafting and implementation of such a framework. Any effective measure to manage soils sustainably is contingent on the government's political will to facilitate the measure. It is crucial that politicians buy into and address the political, social and economic importance of soils. The political and socioeconomic exigencies of the population, as highlighted in the country's GESP, National Rural Sector Development Strategy and related documents, are critical factors that can trigger the political will of the government to initiate policy and the legal and institutional changes necessary to enhance sustainable soil management; and to implement good governance for the success of such a policy, as well as legal and institutional changes. There is thus the need for a strong political will to fast track the revision of sectoral legislation, policies and institutional frameworks to include specific soil protection provisions. However, the availability of a comprehensive and coherent policy and a legal and institutional framework does not guarantee successful implementation unless there is also a corresponding political will to ensure the enforcement of the laws and policies. In the absence of political will, the initiative would remain a paper-based idea. The single most important prerequisite for sustainable soil management is thus the political ambition of the state to initiate policies and implement actions on the ground. The political, social and economic relevance of soils are critical levers that can secure the buy-in of politics.

Entrenched vested interests often favour activities that drive soil degradation. To respond effectively to this challenge, a strong political commitment is critical. Buy-in of politics can be ensured by resorting to legislative lobbying and advocacy by identifying politicians, legislators and decision-makers who are sympathetic to soil protection concerns, and who are willing to collaborate, but also by identifying those officials who have opposing views. Sympathetic individuals will then be able to assist advocates in widening the network of policy supporters by recommending others to call, to write to and to lobby. Such contacts can be secured through group or individual meetings or briefings designed to present facts and analysis of proposed legislation. Such facts and proposed legislation should clearly and unambiguously present and demonstrate the political, social and economic importance of soils. Whether advocates meet, call or write to those who support or oppose the advocacy goal, they need to be courteous and respectful towards parliamentarians, government officials and policymakers and consider the importance of long-term relationships.

Public hearings, discussions and forums may also be explored by those leading the advocacy efforts. Since there is strength in numbers, forming alliances with other stakeholders advocating for soil protection can bring more pressure to bear on government officials, legislators and policymakers – which may produce positive outcomes. Network alliances can be formed with the following categories of stakeholders:

legislators, government officials and policymakers who are already in favour of the project; recognised experts in the field; credible celebrities who are sympathetic to the issue; professionals or other organisations concerned with the issue or with the population; supportive community members and investors, as well as others who understand the issue; people who work in organisations offering services aimed at promoting the policy; actual or potential beneficiaries of the policy; and even those who may disagree with the policy. Those advocating and conducting lobbies need to put in place a single coordinating body at the core of the advocacy and lobby effort and be specific and clear about the policy. A well-defined message is easier to pass on to allies, as it is easier for them to understand, and less likely to be misstated. Such a message is easier for government officials, legislators, policymakers and the public to understand, especially if they are unfamiliar with the issue; and it is more likely to be received favourably by government officials, legislators and policymakers, especially if it targets some specific action. The media is also a critical tool in the advocacy campaign to obtain the buy-in of politics.

References

Alemagi, D., V.A. Sondo & J. Ertel, 2007, "Constraints to environmental impact assessment practice: A case study of Cameroon". *Journal of Environmental Assessment Policy and Management* 9 (3), 357, at https://www.worldscientific.com/doi/10.1142/S1464333207002809, accessed 9 May 2019.

Amin, G.F. & I.R. Jaha, 2016, *Land grabs in Africa: Economic imperialism? Critical contributions to a new paradigm*. Saarbrücken: LAP LAMBERT Academic Publishing.

Ayonghe, S.N., 1999, "Statistical analysis of palaeo climatic changes in Cameroon and projections into the 21st Century; causes of observed trends and predictable effects on biodiversity within the Central African Region". In: Nkwi P.N. & D.A. Mbah (eds), *Conserving and managing biodiversity in Central Africa: Global challenges and local solutions*. Yaoundé: Cameroon Academy of Sciences.

Belaunde, S., M. Cortes, J. Hogstad, E. Ku, K. Nascimento & L. Trzcinski, 2010, *Land, legitimacy and governance in Cameroon*. New York: Institute for Research and Debate on Governance & Columbia University School of International and Public Affairs, at http://www.institut-gouvernance.org/docs/sipa_cameroon_land_legitimacy_governance-2010.pdf, accessed 23 January 2021.

Bella, N., 1993, "Cameroun: De L'encouragement des naissances a la maitrise de la fécondité causes et conséquences de l'evolution observée". *African Population Studies*, 20, at http://aps.journals.ac.za/pub/article/download/419/376, accessed 4 August 2019.

Boer, B.W., H. Ginzky & I.L. Heuser, 2016, "International soil protection law: History, concepts and latest developments". In: Ginzky, H., I.L. Heuser, T. Qin, O.C. Ruppel & P. Wegerdt (eds), *International yearbook of soil law and policy*. Cham: Springer, 49.

Brevik, E.C., 2012, "Soils and climate change: Gas fluxes and soil processes". *Soil Horizons* 53 (4), 12.

BUCREP / Bureau Central des Recensements et des Études de Population, 2010, *La population du Cameroun en 2010: Rapport de presentation des resultats definitive*. Yaoundé: République du Cameroon.

Chapman, S., M. Wilder & I. Miller, 2014, "Defining the legal elements of benefit-sharing in the context of REDD+". *Carbon & Climate Law Review* 8 (4), 270.

Costenbader, J. (ed.), 2009, *Legal frameworks for REDD: Design and implementation at the national level*. Gland: IUCN.

Cowie, L.A., B.J. Orr, V.M. Castillo Sanchez, P. Chasek, N.D. Crossman, A. Erlewein, G. Louwagie, M. Maron, G.I. Metternicht, S. Minelli, A.E. Tengberg, S. Walter & S. Welton, 2017, "Land in balance: The scientific conceptual framework for land degradation neutrality". *Environmental Science & Policy* 79, 25.

CPF / Collaborative Partnership on Forests, 2008, *Strategic framework for forests and climate change: A proposal by the Collaborative Partnership on Forests for a coordinated forest-sector response to climate change*, at https://bit.ly/3pzm6db, accessed 4 August 2019.

Dashaco, J.T. & B.G.M. Tarh, 2018, "Understanding the blueprint of environmental impact assessment for developing countries: The headway and impediments in Cameroon". *International Journal of Advanced Research* 6 (5), 194.

Denier, L., S. Korwin, M. Leggett & C. MacFarquhar, 2014, *The little book of legal frameworks for REDD+*. Oxford: Global Canopy Programme.

Dobgima, A., 2008, *Advanced regional geography for Cameroon schools*. Yaoundé: The Leader Print Publishers.

Ekane, D.N. & P.M. Oben, 2001, "Biochemical indicators of marine pollution in the Douala Lagoon and Limbe Estuary". In: Lambi, C.M. (ed.), *Environmental issues: Problems and prospects*. Bamenda: Unique Printers, 119.

Elias, T.O., 1971, *Nigerian land law*. London: Sweet and Maxwell, London.

Epule, T.E., P. Changhui, L. Laurent & C. Zhi, 2014, "Policy options towards deforestation reduction in Cameroon: An analysis based on a systematic approach". *Land Use Policy* 36, 405.

FAO / Food and Agriculture Organization of the United Nations, 2009, *Environmental impact assessment and monitoring in aquaculture: Requirements, practice, effectiveness and improvements*. FAO Fisheries and Aquaculture Technical Paper No. 527, Rome: FAO.

FAO / Food and Agriculture Organization of the United Nations, 2015, *Soil degradation*. Rome: FAO, at http://www.fao.org/soils-portal/soil-degradation-restoration/it/, accessed 21 January 2021.

FAO / Food and Agriculture Organization of the United Nations & ITPS / Intergovernmental Technical Panel on Soils, 2015, *Status of the world's soil resources (SWSR): Main report*. Rome: FAO.

Fogwe, Z.N., F. Ndifor, C.M. Lambi & R.M.E. Etame, 2001, "Industrial water pollution: the case of the Ndogbong Industrial District, Douala (Cameroon)". In: Lambi, C.M. (ed.), *Environmental issues: Problems and prospects*. Bamenda: Unique Printers, 7.

Forest Carbon Partnership Facility Cameroon, 2013, *Readiness Preparation Proposal (R-PP)*. Yaoundé: Forest Carbon Partnership Facility Cameroon.

Fraser, E. & F. Mousseau, 2016, *Background bullying: The role of the US Government in the Herakles Farms' land grab in Cameroon*. Oakland: Oakland Institute, at https://www.oaklandinstitute.org/sites/oaklandinstitute.org/files/backroom-bullying-final.pdf, accessed 13 May 2019.

Fru, V.N., undated, *Land grabbing: The case of Herakles Farms in Cameroon*. Buea: International Centre for Environmental Education and Community Development (ICENECDEV), at https://www.icenecdev.org/Land-Grabbing-in-Cameroon.pdf, accessed 24 January 2021.

GEF / The Global Environment Facility, 2007, *Building Cameroon's capacity to ensure synergy between environmental conventions*. Yaoundé: The National Coordination of the ANCR-NCSA process.

Ginzky, H., O.C. Ruppel, R. Kibugi & W. Engelberg, 2019, *Implementing land degradation neutrality in Africa: Means, legal instruments and institutional challenges*. Outcome summary document of a workshop organised in coorperation between the German Environment Agency (UBA), the Konrad-Adenauer Foundation – Climate Policy and Energy Security Program for Sub-Saharan Africa, the GIZ and University of Nairobi, Nairobi, Kenya, 14 to 15 August 2018, at https://www.umweltbundesamt.de/sites/default/files/medien/2875/dokumente/nairobi_outcome_document.pdf, accessed 31 January 2021.

Hamidov, A., K. Helming, G. Bellocchi, W. Bojar, T. Dalgaard, B.B. Ghaley, C. Hoffmann, I. Holman, A. Holzkämper, D. Krzeminska, S.H. Kværnø, H. Lehtonen, G. Niedrist, L. Øygarden, P. Reidsma, P.P. Roggero, T. Rusu, C. Santos, G. Seddaiu, E. Skarbøvik, D. Ventrella, J. Żarski & M. Schönhart, 2018, "Impact of climate change adaptation options on soil functions: A review of European case-studies". *Land Degradation and Development* 29 (8), 1.

Hannam, I. & B. Boer, 2004, *Drafting legislation for sustainable soils: A guide*. Gland: IUCN.

IOM / International Organization for Migration & UNCCD / United Nations Convention to Combat Desertification, 2019, *Addressing the land degradation – migration nexus: The role of the United Nations Convention to Combat Desertification*. Geneva: IOM.

Kang, A., 2013, *Legal, institutional and technical framework for lake/wetland protection*. Briefing Paper, New Delhi: Centre for Science and Environment.

Kwame, S.A., 2006, "Managing wetlands in Accra, Ghana". African regional workshop: Cities, ecosystems and biodiversity. Nairobi, Side Event at the Africities Summit.

Lambi, C.M. (ed.), *Environmental issues: Problems and prospects*. Bamenda: Unique Printers.

Lang, M.K., 2017, "Land disputes between the catholic church and indigenes of Weh Fondom, 1957–1996". *Ghana Social Science Journal* 14 (1), 109.

Lemmens, M., 2010, "Statutory versus customary land ownership conflicts in Cameroon". *GIM International* 3 December 2010, at https://www.gim-international.com/content/article/land-ownership-conflicts-in-cameroon, accessed 3 June 2019.

Mbu, A.P., 2014, *Regional geography for Cameroon*. Buea: Trinity Ventures Printing and Publishing.

McLeman, R., 2017, *Migration and land degradation: Recent experience and future trends*. Global Land Outlook Working Paper, at https://knowledge.unccd.int/sites/default/files/2018-06/8.%20Migration%2Band%2BLand%2BDegradation__R_McLeman.pdf, accessed on 9 April 2020.

Ministry of the Environment and Nature Protection & FCPF / The Forest Carbon Partnership Facility, 2008, *Readiness Plan Idea Note (R-PIN), Cameroon*. At https://www.forestcarbonpartnership.org/system/files/documents/Cameroon_R-PIN_07-31-08.pdf, accessed 31 January 2021.

Ministry of the Environment, Protection of Nature and Sustainable Development, 2018, *The national strategy for reducing emissions from deforestation and forest degradation, sustainable management of forests, conservation of forest and enhancement of carbon stocks, (National REDD+ Strategy)*. Final Version. Yaoundé: Government of Cameroon.

Munge, S.P., 2011, *The concept of equality and access to land: The case of the anglophone regions of Cameroon*. PhD Thesis, University of Buea.

Nchangvi, S.K., 2010, *Systems analysis in biogeography for advanced learners*. Yaoundé: Grassroot Publishers.

Ndi, F.A., 2017, "Land grabbing, local contestation, and the struggle for economic gain: Insights from Nguti Village, South West Cameroon". *SAGE Open*, 1, at https://journals.sagepub.com/doi/pdf/10.1177/2158244016682997, accessed 13 May 2019.

Ndzeidze, S.K., 2008, *Detecting changes in a wetland: Using multi-spectral and temporal Landsat in the Upper Noun Valley Drainage Basin-Cameroon*. Master of Science, Oregon State University.

Neba, A.S., 1987, *Modern geography of the Republic of Cameroon*. Second edition, Camden: Neba Publishers.

Ngoh, V.J., 1996, *History of Cameroon since 1800*. Limbe: Pressbook.

Ngwafor, E.N., 1996, *Family law in anglophone Cameroon*. Regina: University of Regina Press.

Ngwoh, V.K., 2019, "Cameroon: State policy as grounds for indigenous rebellion. The Bakweri land problem, 1946–2014". *Conflict Studies Quarterly* 27, 39.

Ngwome, G.F., 2018, *The contribution of forest to climate change mitigation under the REDD+ Initiative in Cameroon: The search for an appropriate legal framework*. PhD Thesis, University of Yaoundé.

Nhantumbo, I. & C. Marisa, 2015, *REDD+ for profit or for good? Review of private sector and NGO experience in REDD+ projects*. Natural Resource Issues No. 30, London: IIED.

Njoh, D.B., T. Feldt, C. Seeger, N. Dittrich, H. Karg, E. Gawum, A. Witte & R. van Veenhuizen, 2018, *Urban and peri-urban agriculture in Bamenda: A policy narrative*. For SHUMAS UrbanFoodPlus RUAF Foundation and the Bamenda Multi-Stakeholder Platform, at http://www.urbanfoodplus.org/fileadmin/user_upload/Publications/Policy_Narrative_Bamenda_2018.pdf, accessed 3 July 2019.

Olimova, S. & M. Olimov, 2012, *Environmental degradation, migration, internal displacement, and rural vulnerabilities in Tajikistan*. Grand-Saconnex: International Organization for Migration (IOM), at https://publications.iom.int/system/files/pdf/tajikistan2012envreport_eng.pdf, accessed 9 April 2020.

Orr, B.J., L.A. Cowie, V.M. Castillo Sanchez, P. Chasek, N.D. Crossman, A. Erlewein, G. Louwagie, M. Maron, G.I. Metternicht, S. Minelli, A.E. Tengberg, S. Walter, & S. Welton, 2017, *Scientific conceptual framework for land degradation neutrality*. A report of the science-policy interface, Bonn: United Nations Convention to Combat Desertification (UNCCD).

Pareek, N., 2017, "Climate change impact on soils: adaptation and mitigation". *MOJ Ecology & Environmental Science* 2 (3), 136.

Pollini J., 2015, *Shifting cultivation, gender and REDD+ in Cameroon and the Democratic Republic of Congo*. Washington DC: USAID-supported Forest Carbon Markets and Communities (FCMC) Programme.

Republic of Cameroon, 2012, *National biodiversity strategy and action plan*. Version II. Yaoundé: MINEPDED.

Republic of Cameroon, 2013, *Strategy paper of the education and training sector 2013–2020*. Yaoundé: MINESEC.

Republic of Cammeroon, 2015, *Intended nationally determined contribution (INDC)*. At https://www4.unfccc.int/sites/ndcstaging/PublishedDocuments/Cameroon%20First/CPDN%20CMR%20Final.pdf, accessed 31 January 2021.

Sanz, M.J., J. de Vente, J.-L. Chotte, M. Bernoux, G. Kust, I. Ruiz, M. Almagro, J.-A. Alloza, R. Vallejo, V. Castillo, A. Hebel & M. Akhtar-Schuster, 2017, *Sustainable land management contribution to successful land-based climate change adaptation and mitigation*. A report of the Science-Policy Interface. Bonn: United Nations Convention to Combat Desertification (UNCCD).

Sone, P.M., 2012, "Conflict over landownership: The case of farmers and cattle graziers in the North-West Region of Cameroon". *AJCR* 2012, 1, at https://www.accord.org.za/ajcr-issues/%EF%BF%BCconflict-over-landownership/, accessed 25 July 2019.

Tafon, R. & F. Saunders, 2019, "The politics of land grabbing: State and corporate power and the (trans)nationalization of resistance in Cameroon". *Journal of Agrarian Change* 19, 41.

Tajoche, T., 2008, *Cameroon history in the 19th and 20th centuries*. Buea: Education Book Centre.

Tamasang, C.F., 2014, "Constructing synergies for the conservation and wise use of wetlands in the central African sub-region: Legal and institutional pathways". *Revue Africaine de Droit Public (RADP)* 3 (5), 25.

Tamasang, C.F. & G.F. Ngwome, 2018, "REDD+ implementation in Cameroon's environmental law: The role of indigenous peoples and local communities". In: Ruppel, O.C. & E.D. Kam Yogo (eds), 2018, *Environmental law and policy in Cameroon – Towards making Africa the tree of life*. Baden-Baden: Nomos, 934.

Tande, D. (ed.), 1999, *The Bakweri land problem and the privatization of the Cameroon Development Corporation (CDC): The Internet Debates (August-December 1999)*. At https://bit.ly/2Yu2ZFN, accessed 31 January 2021.

Tassah, I.T., 2019, *Land cover dynamics and agricultural intensification in Momo Division, North-West Region of Cameroon*. Unpublished PhD Thesis, University of Yaoundé I, Cameroon.

Taza-Asaba, J., 2013, *Environmental monitoring and compliance methodology developed through lessons learnt from oil & gas companies in Cameroon*. Calgary: IAIA13 Conference Proceedings 33rd Annual Meeting of the International Association for Impact Assessment, 13–16 May 2013, at https://conferences.iaia.org/2013/pdf/Final%20papers%20review%20process%2013/Environmental%20Monitoring%20and%20Compliance%20Methodology.pdf, accessed 16 May 2019.

Tchoffo, B., 2009, "Shifting cultivation and climate change in Cameroon: What role environmental impact assessment play?". Presentation at the 29th Annual Conference of the International Association for Impact Assessment, Accra International Conference Center, Accra.

UN Economic Commission for Africa, 2007, *African review report on drought and desertification*. Fifth Meeting of the Africa Committee on Sustainable Development (ACSD-5) Regional Implementation Meeting (RIM) for CSD-16 Addis Ababa, 22–25 October 2007.

Yahmed, B.D., N. Houstin & C. Segnobos, 2007, *Atlas of Cameroon*. Yaoundé: Les Editions J.A.

Zomer, R.J., D.A. Bossio, R. Sommer & L.V. Verchot, 2017, *Global sequestration potential of increased organic carbon in cropland soils*. Scientific Report 7, 15554, at www.nature.com/scientificreports/, accessed 4 June 2019.

Country report for Kenya

Patricia Kameri-Mbote (lead author), Irene Kamunge (contributing author) & James Kipkerebulit Yatich (contributing author)

1 Introduction

Soil has ecological, cultural, economic and political dimensions.[1] It provides a wide range of natural habitats for living creatures; it supports diverse ecosystems[2] of interdependent plant and animal life; and it is a source of livelihood for life forms great and small. Despite the recognition and acknowledgement of the critical functions of soil, there is no specific legal regime dealing with it. Owing to the wide range of activities related to environmental systems, soil protection tenets are dispersed across multiple laws and policies. They are found in laws dealing with land rights, land use, environmental and natural resource protection, and health, among others.

The protection of river courses and water bodies from pollution through to soil erosion has, for instance, given rise to different mechanisms, such as bench terraces, to ensure the integrity of the soil. In the public health realm, soil has been secured through protection from vermin harmful to human health. Since soil is not always the primary focus of these mechanisms, sustainable and sound soil management is not canvassed as there are different interests and competing soil uses to be balanced in these complex regimes. This calls for the development of bespoke soil policies, sound governance, and the monitoring of mechanisms to guide the utilisation and sustenance of soil for present and future generations.

This report examines soil protection measures contained in Kenya's laws, policies and programmes with a view to mapping out options for model legislation for sustainable soil management in Africa. It is important to point out at the outset that there is no specific legislation on sustainable management of soil in Kenya. We will discuss explicit or implicit tenets touching on soil protection, drawn from diverse laws addressing other issues. As a prelude to the discussion of legislation, policies and regulations, we describe a variety of relevant aspects of the body of land that makes up Kenya. This discussion covers demography, soil types, climate, rainfall patterns, governance, the economy, and the main drivers of soil degradation. We also look at soil

1 Allan (2008).
2 Howard (2015).

protection in Kenya from a historical perspective, with a view to identifying the different narratives that have shaped soil protection in this country.

The country report for Kenya is structured as follows: Firstly, some background country information will be provided. This is followed by a discussion on the main drivers of soil degradation. Thereafter, we provide background on soil legislation in Kenya from a historical perspective and outline legislation on the main drivers of soil erosion before concluding by making recommendations for future legislation on soil.

2 Country information

Kenya, a former British colony, achieved self-rule in June 1963 and gained independence on 12 December 1963. It lies approximately between Latitudes 4°N and 4°S and Longitudes 33°83' E and 41°75.5' E, straddling the Equator.[3] Kenya shares borders with Uganda to the west, Tanzania to the south, Ethiopia in the north, South Sudan in the northwest, Somalia in the east and the Indian Ocean to the southeast.[4] The country covers a total area of about 582,646 km^2, of which 11,230 km^2 (1.9%) are water bodies, leaving 571,416 km^2 of land. However, some 84% of total land mass (490,000 km^2) comprises arid and semi-arid lands, which are characterised by low, erratic rainfall, high evapotranspiration rates, poor soil fertility and few water resources.[5]

Topographically, the country may be divided into four distinct geographical and ecological regions or zones, with different patterns of land use: the coastal plain, the arid low plateau, the highlands and Lake Victoria basin. The rainfall patterns are extremely varied but generally follow these regions, with Lake Victoria basin receiving the heaviest and most consistent rainfall.[6]

While Kenya retains institutional and economic capacities that make it a pre-eminent country in the region, its historical role as the regional leader is under threat from its neighbours. Kenya needs to address internal challenges, repurpose its infrastructural projects, and focus on wider regional integration to address the rising competition. For a long time, Kenya was the largest and most dominant economy in Eastern Africa in terms of gross domestic product and socioeconomic development in the areas of poverty alleviation, literacy, healthcare, income, civil liberties and freedoms, infrastructure and industry, among others. However, Rwanda and Ethiopia have recently been chipping away at Kenya's dominance. Of particular concern for the country is the need to address corruption and taxation schemes, which have increased the cost of doing business and reduced investment attractiveness.

---

3 Government of Kenya (2016b: 21).
4 Ibid.
5 Ibid.
6 Ibid.: 25, 26.

Kenya is a champion of regional integration, has been host to many refugees from nearby countries, and has played a key role in peace processes of neighbouring Sudan and Somalia. Refugee camps are located on marginal arid and semi-arid lands in the northern part of the country. This has however contributed to further land degradation in these areas.

Like other countries in the region, Kenya faces threats from terror groups. Al-Shabab, a ragtag militia which has set up base in neighbouring Somalia, remains the source of Kenya's greatest threat from terrorism and violent extremism. The majority of al-Shabaab recruits from Kenya come from borderlands or peripheral areas that have suffered generations of marginalisation. While terror attacks have over time spread to various parts of the country, Kenya's coastal counties have taken an interest in dealing specifically with violent counter extremism. This initiative seeks to ensure sustainable development in the region. Kwale County, which is among these counties, has a vibrant agricultural sector that is affected by terrorism through increased insecurity and displacement of people. The county has instituted measures to coordinate multi-stakeholder efforts and approaches to prevent, counter and remove radicalisation and violent extremism.

2.1 Religion

The main religions practised in Kenya include Christianity, Islam, Hinduism and traditional African religions. While Christian churches representing Catholicism and Protestantism have traditionally had wide application since their introduction through colonialism, Pentecostal churches and Islam have attracted more followers in the last couple of decades. This has chipped at the dominance of the traditional churches. Islam has gained ground at the expense of Christianity. Despite efforts of colonial rulers to suppress and eradicate African religions, it remains clear that there are still people who subscribe to traditional religious beliefs, though their number is unclear. These beliefs continue to have an impact on introduced religions and the practice thereof.

2.2 Climatic conditions

Kenya has a moderate tropical climate tempered by topographical relief, especially mountains like Mounts Kenya and Elgon, and the Aberdare and Mau ranges, as well as the movement of the Intertropical Convergence Zone (ITCZ).[7] Large water bodies like Lake Victoria and the Indian Ocean affect the rainfall in Kenya.[8] A relatively wet

7 Ibid.
8 Ibid.

and narrow tropical belt lies along the Indian Ocean coast.[9] Behind the coastline stretch large areas of arid and semi-arid lands.[10] Kenya generally experiences two seasonal rainfall peaks, one of 'long rains' (March–May) and the other of 'short rains' (October–December) in most places.[11] Generally, Kenya is a relatively dry country with mean annual rainfall estimated at 680 mm per year. But this rainfall is unevenly distributed over country on both spatial and temporal scales, varying from about 200 mm in the arid and semi-arid zones to over 2,000 mm in the humid zone.[12] Generally, most of the country suffers from inadequate rainfall and erratic weather, characterised by recurrent droughts and, in some places, floods.[13] These in turn affect the entire economy, which is highly dependent on rain-fed agriculture.[14]

2.3 Population

According to the census carried out in 2009, Kenya's population was 38.6 million.[15] The 2019 census has placed the population at 47.6 million.[16] The total population more than tripled between 1969 and 2009 from 10.9 million in 1969.[17] The country's annual growth rate went down from 2.9% in 2009[18] to 2.2% in 2019.[19] The population of Kenya is concentrated in the central and western parts of the country.[20] The most densely populated counties include Nairobi (4,397,073), Kiambu (2,417,735), Nakuru (2,162,202), Kakamega (1,867,579) and Bungoma (1,670,570), while less populous counties include Lamu (143,920), Isiolo (268,002), Samburu (310,327) and Taita Taveta (340,671).[21] As regards age, those under the age of 15 constitute 40% of the total population.[22] Approximately 75% of the country's population lives within the medium to high potential agricultural areas (consisting of 20% of the land mass), while the rest of the population live in the vast arid and semi-arid lands.[23]

---

9 Ibid.
10 Ibid.
11 Ibid.
12 Ibid.
13 Ibid.
14 Ibid.
15 See https://www.knbs.or.ke/?p=5621, accessed 1 February 2021.
16 Government of Kenya (2019a).
17 Ibid: 5.
18 See https://data.worldbank.org/indicator/SP.POP.GROW?locations=KE, accessed 1 February 2021.
19 Government of Kenya (2019a).
20 Ibid: 11.
21 Ibid.
22 Government of Kenya (2019b:12).
23 Government of Kenya (2019a: 11).

2.4 Literacy levels

The 2015/2016 reveals that in the group of population aged 15 and above the proportion of literate population was 84.5% with a higher proportion of 93.2% in urban areas and a lower proportion in rural areas (78.8%).[24]

2.5 The economy

The economy of Kenya is anchored in agriculture, environment and natural resources, energy and manufacturing, construction, transport and storage, tourism, and information and communication technology. Agriculture, which is climate dependent, directly accounts for 26% of the gross domestic product (GDP) and another 27% indirectly through linkages with other sectors.[25] The sector employs more than 40% of the total population and more than 70% of Kenya's rural people.[26] The sector accounts for 65% of the export earnings, provides a livelihood (employment, income and food security needs) for more than 80% of the Kenyan population, and contributes to nutrition through production of safe, diverse and nutrient-dense foods.[27] The sector is also the main driver of the non-agricultural economy including manufacturing, providing inputs and markets for non-agricultural operations such as building and construction, transportation, tourism, and education and other social services.[28] The reliance of the economy on agriculture has implications for soil management and regulation.

Real GDP is estimated to have expanded by 6.3% in 2018 compared to 4.9% in 2017.[29] The growth was largely attributable to increased agricultural production, accelerated manufacturing activities, sustained growth in transportation, and vibrant service sector activities.[30] Activities in the agriculture, forestry and fishing sectors were vibrant in 2018 mainly on account of favourable weather conditions that characterised the year under review.[31] The sector's growth accelerated from a revised growth of 1.9% in 2017 to 6.4% in 2018.[32] At the end of June 2018, the total stock of public debt stood at KSh4,537.6 billion, of which external debt accounted for 56.6%.[33] The debt from multilateral agencies was KSh829.8 billion, [34] and the stock of external bonds

24 Kenya National Bureau of Statistics (2018: 83).
25 See www.fao.org/kenya/fao-in-kenya/kenya-at-a-glance/en/, accessed 8 May 2019.
26 Ibid.
27 Ibid.
28 Ibid.
29 Kenya National Bureau of Statistics (2019: 1).
30 Ibid: 2.
31 Ibid: 18.
32 Ibid.
33 Ibid: 1.
34 Ibid: 80.

was KSh480.0 billion. In June 2018, the stock of Treasury bonds and Treasury bills accounted for 33.3% and 19.4% of the total debt standing at KSh1,511.9 billion and KSh878.6 billion respectively.[35]

2.6 National debt

Kenya has also borrowed a large sum over the last six years with the overall sovereign stock debt rising from a ratio of nominal debt to GDP of 48.4% in 2013 to a high of around 59.9% of GDP by October 2019.[36] This translates to an amount of debt of KSh1.89 trillion in June 2013, which has since risen to the KSh5.9 trillion mark by October 2019.[37]

2.7 Kenya's political system and governance

Kenya's sovereign power is located in the people of Kenya under the 2010 Constitution.[38] It is exercised either directly or through democratically elected representatives at the national and county levels,[39] following the devolved system of governance. Sovereign power under the Constitution is delegated to Parliament and legislative assemblies in the county governments; the National Executive and the executive structures in the county governments; and the Judiciary and independent tribunals.[40] The governments at the national and county levels are distinct and interdependent and conduct their mutual relationships on the basis of consultation and cooperation.[41]

The National Executive consists of the President, Deputy President and the Cabinet.[42] The President is the head of state and government, and is the Commander-in-Chief of the Kenya Defence Forces.[43] The Cabinet comprises the President, the Deputy President, the Attorney General, and 14 to 22 cabinet secretaries.[44] The President appoints the cabinet secretaries to address diverse sectors, but the National Assembly must approve the appointments.[45] There are, for instance, cabinet secretaries who are responsible for the environment and land. Under the cabinet secretaries are chief

35 Ibid: 80–81.
36 Herbling (2019).
37 Owino & Mutua, (2019: 6).
38 Article 1(1).
39 Article 1(2).
40 Article 1(3).
41 Article 6(2).
42 Article 130(1).
43 Article 131(1).
44 Article 152 (1).
45 Article 152(2).

administrative secretaries and principal secretaries tasked to perform specific functions under designated directorates. Parliament consists of the National Assembly and the Senate with 418 members including the speakers of the two Houses.[46]

The Constitution establishes 47 counties, each with its own government.[47] A county government consists of a county assembly and a county executive.[48] The county assembly is made up of members elected from different wards in the county.[49] The executive authority of the county is vested in, and exercised by, a county executive committee.[50] The county executive committee consists of the county governor, deputy county governor and members appointed by the county governor, with the approval of the county assembly, from among persons who are not members of the assembly.[51] The county governor and the deputy county governor are the chief executive and deputy chief executive of the county, respectively.[52] A county executive committee is responsible for implementing county legislation; implementing national legislation within the county to the extent that this is required; and managing and coordinating the functions of the county administration and its departments, among other functions.[53] A county executive committee may prepare proposed legislation for consideration by the county assembly.[54]

The legislative authority of a county is vested in, and exercised by, its county assembly.[55] A county assembly may make any laws that are necessary for, or incidental to, the effective performance of the functions and exercise of the powers of the county government under the Constitution.[56] Counties have, for instance, legislated on climate change, quarrying, charcoal burning and land use.[57] A county assembly, while respecting the principle of the separation of powers, may exercise oversight over the county executive committee and any other county executive organs.[58] It may receive and approve plans and policies for the management and exploitation of the county's resources and the development and management of its infrastructure and institutions.[59]

46 Articles 93, 97 and 98.
47 Article 6(1).
48 Article 176(1).
49 Article 177.
50 Article 179(1).
51 Article 179(2).
52 Article 179(4).
53 Article 183(1).
54 Article 183(2).
55 Article 185(1).
56 Article 185(2).
57 See the examples of Makueni, Kericho and Kitui. It is worth noting that many of these legislations address collection of fees and not the unsustainability of the practices. Counties like Kitui have however banned charcoal burning.
58 Article 185(3).
59 Article 185(4).

2.8 Legislative authority

Despite the preponderance of different soil types with different management and conservation requirements, Kenya's legal and policy framework on soil governance is largely subsumed in land law. Land law has historically focused on land rights – that is, who holds what interests in what land. Land use was only recently addressed in policy.[60] Accordingly, the law is applied in generic terms, often overlooking the specific requirements of diverse soil types in different parts of the country. As noted above, the Constitution establishes national and county governments as two levels of government with exclusive or concurrent jurisdiction. Until 2010, the National Assembly was the single source of legislation in Kenya. Currently, however, each of the 47 counties has a county assembly. Article 185 of the Constitution mandates the county assembly to make any laws that are necessary for, or incidental to, the effective performance of the functions and exercise of the powers of the county government.

Under the Fourth Schedule, the national government is responsible for development of environmental, land and agricultural policies, while the county governments are tasked with implementation of specific national government policies on natural resources and environmental conservation, including soil and water conservation.

Different parts of the country have different soils types. The protection of these soils therefore requires soil-specific protection measures. Given that the county assemblies can legislate on soil governance, they remain game changers in introducing county soil-specific legislation. In addition, it is expected that with devolved governance will enhance law enforcement and agricultural and soils extension services. As such, the county governments need to monitor soil fertility and the replenishing of nutrients closely. This will assist in reducing soil degradation and will cumulatively increase food production and healthy soils.

2.9 Environmental dispute resolution

The Constitution establishes an independent judiciary[61] consisting of judges of the superior courts, magistrates, and other judicial officers and staff.[62] The superior courts include the Supreme Court, the Court of Appeal, the High Court, the Environment and Land Court[63] and the Employment and Labour Relations Court.[64] The Chief Justice is the head of the Judiciary, and is appointed by the President on the recommendation of the Judicial Service Commission and subject to the approval of the National

60 National Land Policy 2009 and National Land use Policy 2017.
61 Article 160.
62 Article 161(1).
63 Odote (2013).
64 Article 161(1) and (2).

Assembly.[65] The Environment and Land Court is critical in ensuring access to justice in environmental matters.[66] Article 160 of the Constitution of Kenya 2010 provides for the independence of the Judiciary, which means that judicial officers are insulated from interference from various quarters and individuals, including the executive. Some of the mechanisms through which judicial independence is upheld in Kenya include: security of tenure afforded to judicial officers and the restatement that they are not subject to the direction of any person in the conduct of their work; and good remuneration to ensure that judicial officers do not easily fall captive to economic interests.[67] The Kenyan Judiciary has made significant strides in its quest to reform and become independent, a stark contrast to the pre-2010 constitution period when corruption claims were rife, and thus eroding the confidence and the institutional legitimacy of the Judiciary as a whole.[68]

It needs to be mentioned, however, that concerns still remain about the integrity of some judicial officers even at present.[69] On the other hand, the independence of the Judiciary continues to be affected and assailed particularly by the executive arm of government at present, especially in relation to funding. Over the last two years, the Judiciary has only been allocated around half of the budget it requested.[70] For instance, the budget for the Judiciary in the year 2019 was reduced by half, prompting closure of the various tribunals in the country.[71] There have also been some covert and even, on occasion, overt measures to tarnish the names and reputations of particular judges, especially those deemed to have been making decisions that were not in line with the executive's interests. These smear campaigns have largely been conducted on social media by bloggers through various hashtags.[72] This then illustrates the challenges that face the courts in general and this potentially can have an impact on their work.

Notwithstanding this, the Judiciary through the courts has been operating and making decisions in disparate areas of law and has made progressive decisions in the environmental protection sphere. The Environment and Land Court (ELC) has a central role to play in so far as soil governance and conservation is concerned. The court is an important player as it adjudicates disputes over land, issues relating to environmental degradation and environmental protection, and is vested with powers to make various orders including those relating to environmental restoration and rehabilitation. Courts, for instance, have a role to play in giving meaning and effect to environmental rights, which are also human rights, enshrined under Article 42 of the Constitution in the

65 Article 166(1).
66 Odote (2013).
67 Article 160.
68 Shiundu (2018).
69 Uhuru for example refused to gazette judicial officers in 2019.
70 Namusyule & Mueni (2018).
71 Ogemba & Muthoni (2019).
72 See https://bit.ly/3d7B9aQ, accessed 1 November 2019.

chapter on Bill of Rights. The Environment and Land Court has been rather bold in making pronouncements that have had the effect of ensuring environmental protection so as to enable the implementation of the constitutional provisions. To illustrate, in *Patrick Musimba v National Land Commission & 4 Others [2016] eKLR*, which was a case relating to the power of the state to compulsorily acquire land, ELC had this to say on sustainability:

> [T]he State under Article 69 of the Constitution is enjoined to ensure sustainable development. (See also the preamble to the Constitution). The State is also to ensure that every person has a right to a clean and healthy environment. However, physical development must also be allowed to foster to ensure that the other guaranteed rights and freedoms are also achieved. Such physical development must however be undertaken within a Constitutional and Statutory framework to ensure that the environment thrives and survives. It is for such reason that the Constitution provides for public participation in the management, protection and conservation of the environment. It is for the same reason too that the Environmental Management and Co-ordination Act (EMCA has laid out certain statutory safeguards to be observed when a person or the State initiates any physical development. At the core is the Environmental Impact Assessment and Study, which is undertaken under Section 58 of EMCA and the regulations thereunder. Under Regulation 17, the Environmental Impact Assessment Study must involve the public. The inhabitants of any area affected by a physical development must be given an opportunity to air their views on the effects of any such development. After the Environmental Impact Assessment Study report is compiled, the same report must be circulated to the affected persons.

In addition, the National Environment Tribunal, which is a judicial tribunal constituted under EMCA 1999 to adjudicate disputes over the issuance of environmental impact assessment (EIA) licences and other decisions of the National Environmental Management Authority (NEMA), recently stopped the intended construction of a mega-coal project in Lamu in the coastal area of Kenya on the grounds that a proper environmental assessment or audit had not been conducted. In particular, the Tribunal found that the environmental and social impact assessment was inadequate as there were no details on how much pollution from coal, dust and ash the plant would produce. It also stated that the public participation conducted was not sufficient because – though there were meetings held with the local community – appropriate information to enable them to make informed decisions was not made available to the community members. The case, *Save Lamu & 5 Others v National Environmental Management Authority (NEMA) & Another [2019] eKLR*, was a major win in terms of promoting public participation in environmental governance and was a classic case of the powerless citizenry being able to wrestle successfully with the elite in society. What this means is that the courts can be a useful avenue if public-spirited individuals are able to agitate and institute public interest litigation cases grounded in the progressive constitution.

The Environment and Land Court has since restated the minimum basis for adequate public participation in environmental matters in *Mui Coal Basin Local Community & 15 Others v Permanent Secretary Ministry of Energy & 17 Others, Constitutional* Petition No. 305 of 2012 at paragraph 97:

> From our analysis of the case law, international law and comparative law, we find that public participation in the area of environmental governance as implicated in this case, at a minimum, entails the following elements or principles:

> *a.* First, it is incumbent upon the government agency or public official involved to fashion a programme of public participation that accords with the nature of the subject matter. It is the government agency or Public Official who is to craft the modalities of public participation but in so doing the government agency or Public Official must take into account both the quantity and quality of the governed to participate in their own governance. *Yet the government agency enjoys some considerable measure of discretion in fashioning those modalities.*
>
> *b.* Second, public participation calls for innovation and malleability depending on the nature of the subject matter, culture, logistical constraints, and so forth. In other words, no single regime or programme of public participation can be prescribed, and the Courts will not use any litmus test to determine if public participation has been achieved or not. *The only test the Courts use is one of effectiveness. A variety of mechanisms may be used to achieve public participation.*
>
> c. Third, whatever programme of public participation is fashioned, it must include access to and dissemination of relevant information.

It is worth pointing out that the Constitution has made provision for alternative and traditional dispute resolution. In the case of land, the National Land Commission is tasked to promote the resolution of land disputes through traditional dispute resolution. This is especially important because community land comprises over 60% of Kenya's land. Consequently, this mode of dispute resolution has significant potential to have an impact on soil governance.

3 Main drivers and causes of soil degradation

Agriculture – the art and business of soil cultivation, crop production and livestock rearing – is the backbone of the economy of Kenya, a country which was recently ranked as a low middle income economy and the fourth largest economy in sub-Saharan Africa.[73] Its population has nearly doubled since 1989, while arable land – which is 10% of Kenya's land mass – continues to decline as thousands of hectares of highly productive agricultural farmland is converted into satellite cities with massive infrastructure developments in areas like Kiambu and Nakuru counties.[74] Yet these developments, among other natural factors, continue to pile pressure on these finite, yet decreasing agricultural soils to meet food demands of the rising population.

Soil and environmental degeneration in Kenya have been on the rise. Natural factors are partly to blame, while a significant portion of the degradation is attributable to human activities. Climate change, urbanisation, soil erosion, overgrazing, over-cultivation, compaction, industrial activities, illegal land allocations, and encroachment of sensitive environmental areas continue to affect soil fertility negatively and to result in the loss of soil biodiversity.

73 Mohajan (2014).
74 Mwanza (2019).

3.1 Kenya soil profile: Soil types, distribution and degradation vulnerability

Kenya has a wide range of soils owing to the variation in geology (parent material), terrain and climate.[75] Soil resources vary from sandy to clayey, shallow to very deep, and low to high fertility.[76] However, most of these soils have serious problems such as salinity/sodicity, acidity, low fertility and poor drainage. According to the Food and Agriculture Organization (FAO) classification system, the country has 25 major soil types.[77] However, in terms of geographic coverage, about 15 soil types dominate, namely Nitisols, Regosols, Cambisols, Luvisols, Solonetz, Ferralsols, Acrisols, Alisols, Fluvisols, Andosols, Arenosols, Calcisols, Lixisols, Planosols and Vertisols.[78] About 59% of Kenya's soils have moderate to high fertility, meaning that they are theoretically suitable for growing crops.[79] Among these, the major soils used in agriculture in Kenya include:

Nitisols occur in the highlands and on steep volcanic slopes, such as the central highlands of Kenya. For optimal agricultural production, nitisols need the use of manure and inorganic fertilizers.[80] Nitisols often have high clay content of more than 35% and are the most productive agricultural soils found in Kenya.[81] They are used intensely for plantation crops and food production.[82] They have better chemical and physical properties than other tropical soils. These include good moisture-storage capacity and aeration; organic matter content; cation exchange capacity; and percentage base saturation range from low to high.[83] Most Nitisols are acidic (pH < 5.5) owing to the leaching of soluble bases.

As previously observed, the continued optimal productivity of these types of soil requires continuous replenishing of nutrients through manure and inorganic fertilizers. Accordingly, their health depends on the purity of inorganic fertilizers. Counterfeit, substandard chemicals, goods and fertilizers are nothing new in Kenya. In January 2019, top Kenya Bureau of Standards officials, the state corporation mandated to promote standardisation in industry and commerce, were arrested and charged for importation of substandard fertilizer which had a high content of mercury and other metals.[84] Such dubious activities greatly affect the fertility and productivity of these soils. Andosols, young volcanic soils, occur in areas with steep slopes and high rainfall, are

75 Government of Kenya (2016b: 30).
76 Ibid.
77 Ibid.
78 Ibid.: 30-31.
79 Ibid.: 32.
80 Ibid.
81 Ibid.
82 Ibid.
83 Ibid.
84 Karanja (2019).

highly susceptible to erosion.[85] With over 1,000 mm of rainfall per year, Andosols are exposed to excessive leaching.[86] They are porous, have a high water-storage capacity and a low bulk density, and are acidic (low pH) owing to the high leaching tendency of soluble bases and high levels of aluminium (Al).[87] These conditions favour P-fixation, making it no longer available to the plants.[88] Andosols are mainly used for the cultivation of tea, pyrethrum and temperate crops, and for dairy farming. To improve production, liming and the use of fertilizers is necessary.[89] The mapping of soil erosion in Kenya reveals that almost all areas in Kenya are vulnerable to soil erosion, particularly in arid and semi-arid areas. However, erosion is also prevalent in steep, wet soils along Mount Kenya and the Aberdare range, including some parts of Nyeri, Murang'a, Meru, Tharaka Nithi and Nyandarua counties, all of which are in a region predominantly known for high-potential soils.[90]

Acrisols, alisols, lixisols and luvisols occur in the coffee zones in the sub-humid areas, on undulating to hilly topography. They show an increase of clay content in the subsoil (B horizon). The subsoil is often not very porous, impeding root spreading.[91] They have a relatively low water-storage capacity, compared with Nitisols. Acrisols and Alisols in wet areas have a low pH (acid), Al and Mn toxicities, and low levels of nutrients and nutrient reserves.[92] These soils have poor structure and need erosion control measures. Organic and inorganic fertilizers are needed to improve crop production. The soils respond well to fertilizers (especially N, P and K) and to the use of soil organic matter.[93] The use of fertilizers in soils has implications for soil health.[94]

The vulnerability of these soils is increased with the prevalence of the combination of Nitisols and Andosols. This combination tends to be found in areas that are densely populated, a fact that puts pressure on these soils in the course of food production for local communities and the country. As a result, there is a high use of organic fertilizers and chemicals. Coffee and tea cultivation being cash cropping, results in these areas having significant industrial activities, which emit effluents and contribute to air pollution.

Planosols and vertisols occur on very gently undulating to flat topography, mostly in rice-growing areas such as Mwea in Kirinyaga County and Kano plains in Kisumu.[95] They are found in semi-arid and sub-humid environments. Owing to the high clay

85 Government of Kenya (2016b: 32).
86 Ibid.
87 Ibid.
88 Ibid.
89 Ibid.
90 KASLMP & Ministry of Environment and Natural Resources (2016).
91 Government of Kenya (2016b: 32).
92 Ibid.
93 Ibid.
94 David & Edwards (1982).
95 Government of Kenya (2016b: 32).

content in the subsoil (higher than in the topsoil), this layer is impermeable in the B horizon, resulting in very slow and poor vertical and horizontal drainage. Vertisols are dark-coloured, strongly cracking clays, which are best used for irrigated paddy rice and other crops that can withstand temporary waterlogging.[96]

Planosols and Vertisols soils are vulnerable in predominantly two ways. First, their use, through irrigation activities requires a high input of inorganic fertilizers and other chemicals, which, if substandard, end up polluting the soils. Secondly, and more important, a shortage of water in these irrigation areas leads to the use of wastewater/effluent as an alternative to clean and suitable water.[97]

Ferralsols occur on gently undulating to undulating topography.[98] They are very old, highly weathered and leached soils, and therefore have poor fertility, which is restricted to the topsoil, as the subsoil has a low cation exchange capacity.[99] They are deficient in phosphorous (P) and nitrogen (N). Ferralsols are rich in aluminium (Al) and iron (Fe). The nutrient reserves in these soils are easily disturbed by agricultural practices.[100] Important management practices on these soils include the use of fertilizers (such as rock phosphate) and the maintenance of soil organic matter by using green manures, farmyard manures and mulching.[101] Ferralsols have good physical properties including an excellent capacity to hold moisture and are used to grow annual crops.[102]

3.2 The main drivers of soil degradation

3.2.1 Agriculture

Agriculture is the backbone of the Kenyan economy and is practised on large, small and subsistence scales. Arable lands are fast turning into concrete jungles as a result of urbanisation. This has resulted in immense pressure on the remaining agricultural farmlands to produce enough food for the rising population. There is also increased mechanisation and increased use of technology and agricultural chemicals in production in the country. As already observed, there have been several instances of importation of substandard fertilizers and other agrochemicals into Kenya. These substandard agricultural chemicals lead to soil and water pollution. In irrigation schemes for instance, high soil contamination as a result of use of uncertified chemicals has been recorded in paddy rice production in some areas of the Mwea Irrigation Scheme.

96 Government of Kenya (2016b: 32–33).
97 Nyabonyi (2016).
98 Government of Kenya (2016b: 33).
99 Ibid.
100 Ibid.
101 Ibid.
102 Ibid.

Despite agreement and recognition of the fact that extension services, if properly designed and implemented, improve agricultural productivity, the coverage of Kenya's agricultural extension system remains grossly inadequate.[103] This has in turn led to poor and unbalanced soil nutrition. This is exacerbated by mono cropping and the blind use of agrochemicals and fertilizers without knowledge of soil nutrients.

The Third Medium Term Plan (2018–2022) of Kenya's Vision 2030 identifies low and declining soil fertility due to poor farming methods as one of the challenges facing the agricultural sector.[104] Harmful agricultural practices include land clearing, overgrazing caused by large livestock herds, charcoal and wood extraction, cultivation on steep slopes, bush burning and soil nutrient mining.[105] Unsustainable agricultural practices and poor soils necessitate the use of fertilizers to improve productivity, which negatively affect the quality of soils.

Agricultural expansion has escalated over the past 20 years as a consequence of population growth and attendant increased food needs. Limited land resources and over-reliance on land often lead to subdivisions of land into smaller pieces for inheritance purposes.[106] These pressures on land have resulted in high nutrient outflows and the breakdown of former soil fertility maintenance strategies, such as bush fallow cultivation and the opening of new lands.[107]

Most of the agricultural activities in Kenya are subsistence in nature and the farmers are yet to embrace modern methods of food production. As such, practices such as the burning of vegetation cover as a way of cultivating virgin lands is still rampant. Vegetation cover burning leads to huge deposits of carbon on the soil. Most Kenyan farmers are smallholders in rural areas cultivating land parcels measuring two hectares or less.[108] Many of these farmers cultivate on steep slopes and fragile soils, which are highly susceptible to erosion. The farmers depend on already degraded lands to meet their food requirements in a context of increasing demand for food and declining to stagnant agricultural productivity.[109] This has resulted in rapid expansion of agricultural land and reduced rehabilitation of soil fertility through shortening of the uncultivated periods in extensive land use systems.[110] Over-cultivation of the same land for many years leads to a hardpan, which reduces water infiltration, resulting in increased runoff, and hence erosion.[111] The soils are degraded both physically and through nutrient loss, resulting in the decline of land productivity.[112] It has for instance been

103 Muyanga & Thomas (2006).
104 Government of Kenya (2018b: 45).
105 Government of Kenya (2016b: 67).
106 Ibid.: 53.
107 Ibid.
108 Ibid.: 75.
109 Ibid.
110 Ibid.
111 Ibid.
112 Ibid.

estimated that smallholder farming systems in the highlands of Kenya lose an equivalent of 112 kg N, 2.5 kg P and 70 kg K owing to nutrient removals in the form of crop harvesting, leaching and soil erosion.[113] Poor soils result in reduced above-ground productivity with the cascade effects of soil loss, fertility decline, and increased sediment loading in rivers, dams and lakes – further affecting water quality and occasioning loss of revenues.[114]

3.2.2 Mining

Kenya is a mineral-rich country with huge deposits of fluorspar in Kerio Valley, Elgeyo Marakwet County, gold in the western region counties, titanium in coastal areas, coal mining in eastern and coastal areas of the country, and soda ash at the coast and in Kajiado county. Other known minerals include manganese, iron ore, gypsum, diatomite, chromite, limestone, and silica sand.[115] In anticipation of the discovery of new minerals and oil deposits, the country adopted its first ever mining policy in 2016 to enable the country to reap maximum benefits in future.

Heavy mining activities in mineral rich areas and quarrying have led to sizeable losses in biodiversity, increased soil erosion occurrences, contamination of soil due to huge deposits of chemicals used in excavation and mining, and contamination of surface and ground water.[116] Mining and related activities also increase soil erodibility. Although EMCA provides for environmental protection, its enforcement and observance are not as effective as may be expected. For instance, it is a requirement that an EIA be carried out before embarking on any project likely to have a negative impact on the environment. In many cases, no such assessments are carried out in the extractive industry and, if carried out, they do not meet the legal threshold. For instance, in *Cortec Mining Kenya Limited v Cabinet Secretary Ministry of Mining & 9 Others [2017] eKLR*, a titanium extraction licence was cancelled on the grounds that an EIA had not been carried out despite mining having started. The establishment of the Lamu Coal Plant at the Kenyan coast was also halted by the National Environmental Tribunal in *Save Lamu & 5 Others v National Environmental Management Authority (NEMA) & Another [2019] eKLR* for, among other reasons, failure to carry out EIAs to the required legal standards. These cases illustrate how environmental laws that could protect and conserve the environment, including soil, are disregarded.

---

113 Ibid.
114 Ibid.
115 Mining and Minerals Policy 2016, page 4.
116 David et al. (2016); Mutono (2016).

3.2.3 Industrial activities

Kenya is an average industrialised economy serving both local and export markets in sub-Sahara Africa. Although the industries are mainly found in cities and major towns, a sizeable number of industries are found in agriculturally rich areas to cater for the value addition of agricultural produce. The current government has identified industrialisation as one of the major focus areas in the hope that it will create employment opportunities and boost the economy.[117]

Industrial activities produce effluent that is often deposited on soil. A study carried out in 2015 indicates that soils adjacent to industrial areas in Kenya contain persistent organic pollutants. Studies in areas with high industrial activities have also reported reduction in soil fertility and unbalanced soil nutrition. As previously observed, despite the existence of EMCA, which proscribes soil pollution and unlicenced discharge of treated wastes, industries often discharge effluent into rivers and onto soils against set standards and guidelines. For instance, in *Benson Ambuti Adega & 2 Others v Kibos Sugar and Allied Industries Limited & 4 Others; Kenya Union of Sugar Plantation and Allied Workers (Interested Party) [2019] eKLR,* Kibos Sugar Factory was found guilty of polluting the rivers and soils in its areas of operation. This company has on several occasions been closed down for effluent discharge in rivers and soils, with the discharges having had a negative impact on the environment and soil productivity.[118]

Enforcement of law on environmental protection has been somewhat scant, perhaps because of the compartmentalised governance structure. Under EMCA, the National Environment and Coordination Authority is the coordinator of environmental protection. It may lawfully direct lead agencies to take action for the purposes of environmental protection.[119] However, the multiplicity of institutions that deal with environment has resulted in blame games and has not stemmed environmental pollution. *Benson Ambuti Adega & 2 Others v Kibos Sugar and Allied Industries Limited & 4 Others; Kenya Union of Sugar Plantation and Allied Workers (Interested Party) [2019] eKLR* points to the laxity of environmental protection institutions in taking action.

3.2.4 Soil erosion

Soil erosion is both an ecological and socioeconomic problem.[120] The areas with the greatest risk include steep slopes; land usually bare before the onset of rains; soils with surface sealing problems that encourage runoff; bad tillage practices such as

117 Government of Kenya (2017a).

118 Allan (2019).

119 Environmental Management and Coordination Act, 1999, Section 3.

120 Land Use, the Case for National Land Use KLA, page 37.

cultivating up and down slopes; exposure during periods of heavy rain and wind; and inappropriate land use and cultivation of marginal lands.[121] The major erosion types are rill, gully and riverbank.[122] Areas prone to gullies include bare land, animal tracks, faulty road drainage structures, and neglected rills and furrows.[123] Up to 35% of the sediment load from 61 catchments in Kenya originates from roadside gullies. An equal amount is derived from footpaths and cattle tracks.[124]

Two processes cause soil erosion.[125] The first is the loosening or detaching of the topsoil particles when large raindrops fall causing splash erosion, which occurs when vegetation cover has been removed and the soil surface is directly exposed to raindrop impact.[126] If this occurs on sloping ground, the splashed soil particles wash downhill.[127] Secondly, the transportation of such detached particles by flowing water causes rill erosion, which begins when shallow surface flow starts to concentrate in low spots on the soil surface.[128]

Soil erosion occurs when farming practices provide a medium for the two processes to take place.[129] This happens through de-vegetation caused by shifting cultivation, clearance of land, overstocking and overgrazing.[130] Other malpractices that promote soil loss include deep ploughing of land, lack of crop rotation, and ploughing and planting down the contour.[131] In such areas with deep soils and high rainfall, landslide erosion occurs because rainwater infiltrates vertically into the soil up to the bedrock and then moves laterally along the bedrock, causing the soil at the outlet to slide.[132]

Loss of natural habitats has also reduced vegetation cover and exposed soils to extensive wind and soil erosion in many parts of the country.[133] Soil erosion is a major factor in land degradation and has severe effects on soil functions, such as the soil's ability to act as a buffer and filter for pollutants, its role in the hydrological and nitrogen cycle, and its ability to provide habitats and support to diverse forms of life. Soil erosion also causes increased rates of siltation of dams and rivers and increased risk of flooding in rivers and estuaries.[134] It also reduces the productivity of land, requiring farmers to apply more and more fertilizers and other chemicals to improve

121 Ibid.
122 Ibid.
123 Ibid.
124 Ibid.
125 Ibid.: 38.
126 Ibid.
127 Ibid.
128 Ibid.
129 Ibid.
130 Ibid.
131 Ibid.
132 Ibid.
133 Government of Kenya (2016b: 65).
134 Ibid.: 56.

productivity. The resultant excessive use of fertilizers and other chemicals contributes to further soil degradation and water pollution.[135]

On arid and semi-arid land, another cause of soil erosion by water is the opening up of saline and alkaline soils.[136] A study of the erosivity index in Kenya shows that the highest risk of wind erosion is in humid and sub-humid climates on arid and semi-arid land [137] where a high load of sand is suspended in the atmosphere.[138] The highest incidence of wind erosion is most likely to occur in Marsabit, Moyale, Wajir and Garissa,[139] while the lowest risk is around Makindu and Voi.[140]

Soil erosion is exacerbated by unsustainable land use and management practices. Agriculture is a major culprit, as it involves land clearing, overgrazing caused by large livestock herds, charcoal and wood extraction, cultivation on steep slopes, bush burning, and soil nutrient mining.[141] The use of fertilizers to counter land productivity decline, caused by unsustainable agricultural practices and poor soils, negatively affects the quality of soils. Natural disturbances such as drought or flooding exacerbate the unsustainable human activities taking place in already fragile areas. Other human activities contributing to unsustainable land use include cultivation in water catchment areas; deforestation; poorly managed rangelands; encroachment of wetlands; and pollution from agricultural, commercial and industrial activities.[142]

The intersection between physical features and human behaviour produce land cover changes or alterations of the land surface, through conversion or modification, which leads to secondary environmental impacts such as soil erosion.[143]

3.2.5 Unregulated urban and infrastructural development

Over the past 20 years, Kenya's population has doubled.[144] The increase in population has been accompanied by rapid rural to urban migration. The urban population increased from 5.4 million in 1999 to 12.2 million in 2009 and was projected to increase to 17.6 million in 2017. This constitutes an urban population of 39% and an annual urban growth rate of 7.5%.[145] In addition, the creation of counties with autonomous county governments has led to increased urbanisation, at least in the 47-county

135 Ibid.: 58.
136 Land Use, the Case for National Land Use KLA, page 38.
137 Ibid.
138 Ibid.
139 Ibid.
140 Ibid.
141 Government of Kenya (2016b: 67).
142 Ibid.: 71.
143 National Land Use Policy, page 14.
144 Ministry of Land and Urban Planning (2017).
145 Ibid.

headquarters. Unfortunately, planning laws have not kept up with the needed effective planning and management of urbanisation processes through provision of adequate and decent housing, sanitation and infrastructure. As previously observed, Kenya is now losing her rich agricultural lands to concrete jungles to supply housing for the rising urban population. This has led to loss of vegetation and forest cover and has put pressure on the remaining productive soils to cater for this population increase.

The government has continued to support the construction sector by formulating policies and programmes to improve infrastructure to spur economic growth. Programmes include the provision of decent but affordable housing; construction of the single-track standard gauge rail; the expansion and modernisation of the outer ring road; expansion of Ngong road; construction of Kenya's Western bypass, Dongo Kundu bypass and Nuno-Modogashe road; construction of Kisumu oil jetty; and construction of a new 20-inch diameter refined petroleum pipeline (Line 5) from Mombasa to Nairobi, with four new pump stations.[146] These developments have further contributed to increased soil degradation. The laying of an oil pipeline that is not insulated through vast agricultural lands exposes the soil to contamination through leaks. Leaks have already sprung in Makueni in two places, exposing people and livestock to health and fire hazards, while polluting the water and soil.

3.2.6 Climate change

The world over, soil is a larger natural reservoir that stores carbon-containing chemical compounds accumulated over an indefinite period of time than the planet's biomass and atmosphere combined. The organic carbon sources in soil include microbes, fungi and invertebrates, as well as root matter and decomposing vegetation.

Reports indicate that Kenya is extremely vulnerable to climate change, with temperatures expected to rise by about 2.5 °C by the year 2050, while rainfall is expected to become more intense and less predictable.[147] There are reported cases of increasing loss of soil organic carbon in Kenya, which is one of the principal signs of land degradation threatening sustainable development, biodiversity conservation, and mitigation and adaption to climate change.

Furthermore, over 70% of natural disasters in Kenya are related to extreme climate events, which are also key causal factors for some emergencies that lead to disasters.[148] Kenya has, for instance, experienced effects of climate change such as prolonged droughts and floods in recent years. Large areas of Kenya are at risk of flooding, which

146 Kenya National Bureau of Statistics (2018: 174).
147 Ministry of Foreign Affairs of Netherlands (2018).
148 Government of Kenya (2016b: 64).

results in soil erosion and loss of property and even lives.[149] Floods have increasingly become a major threat to life, property and the environment – a factor associated with land degradation and climate change.[150] All the six major drainage basins in Kenya experience different flood magnitudes with statistics indicating that in 1982 and 1985 floods in Nyanza and western Kenya affected about 14,000 people.[151] Generally, the most flood-prone areas are in the counties of Garissa, Tana River, Lamu, Homa Bay, Siaya, Kisumu, Trans Nzoia, Uasin Gishu, Nyandarua and Busia.[152]

The worst floods were however experienced in the 1997/1998 El Niño flood, which covered the entire country and 1.5 million people were affected through displacement, loss of property and livelihoods.[153] Other floods have been experienced in later years, including in 2012 when the long rains came late and caused heavy floods that resulted in displacements, loss of property and lives.[154] Several rivers burst their banks and this can be attributed to reduced vegetation and thus poor rainfall infiltration, resulting in flash floods and soil erosion.

Kenya has suffered periodic droughts throughout its recorded history. The magnitude and severity of these droughts have increased over the years. The areas prone to drought include the arid and semi-arid lands, which are hot and generally receive less rainfall. For instance, serious droughts were recorded in 1972, 1974/75, 1977, 1980, 1982, 1983/84, 1991/92, 1995/96, 1999/2000, 2004, 2006, 2009 and 2010/2011.[155] The average incidence of serious drought has increased from around seven serious droughts during the period 1980–1990 to 10 between 1991 and 2003, with drought occurring every two years in the last decade. Droughts destroy vegetation, making land more vulnerable to erosion by wind and water.[156]

3.2.7 Brownfield sites

Brownfield sites are areas of land that are underutilised or abandoned as a result of actual or perceived contamination associated with previous activities for which they were used but have the potential for redevelopment or reuse. Some brownfield sites – with perceived or real contamination – may have minimal physical constraints, may already have infrastructure, and may be located in desirable areas.[157] In Kenya,

149 Ibid.: 62.
150 Ibid.
151 Ibid.
152 Ibid.
153 Ibid.
154 Ibid.
155 Ibid.: 64.
156 Ibid.
157 Kazungu et al. (2011).

industrial sites, abandoned owing to relocation of industries to other places like Athi River, have land-cover change problems that require concerted redevelopment plans.[158]

3.3 Other threats to soil

3.3.1 Topographic features

Kenya has a varied topography with steeply sloping mountains, hills and highlands that render the country highly susceptible to soil erosion. These steep slopes on mountainous and hilly countryside encourage excessive water runoff, leading to land degradation.[159] For instance, it has been recorded that in the upper Tana River sub-catchments of Thika and Chania, at least 66% of the farmers cultivate very steep slopes, which suffer excessive runoff.[160] Earlier studies reported soil loss amounting to 247 tons per hectare per year on steep slopes of the high-potential areas in the Central Highlands, while on the steep agricultural areas of Taita Taveta up to 50% of agricultural lands suffered interill, rill and gully erosion.[161]

3.3.2 Soil contamination

The use of chemicals, fertilizers and fungicides has poisoned and compacted the soils.[162] Fertilizer is the dominant farm input in Kenya, averaging 275,270 metric tons per year.[163] Chemical discharges from industries and other urban waste contribute to further degradation of the soil. In a study on the concentration distribution and toxicological assessment of eight heavy metals, namely lead (Pb), cadmium (Cd), copper (Cu), chromium (Cr), nickel (Ni), mercury (Hg), arsenic (As), and zinc (Zn), in agricultural soils in Kenya, the results showed mean concentrations of Zn, Pb, Cr, Cu, As, Ni, Hg, and Cd as 247.39, 26.87, 59.69, 88.59, 8.93, 12.56, 8.06, and 0.42mg/kg−1, respectively. These values were close to the toxicity threshold limit of United States Environmental Protection Agency (USEPA) standard values of agricultural soils, indicating potential toxicological risk to the food chain.[164] Intensification of human

158 Ibid.

159 Government of Kenya (2016b: 60).

160 Ibid.

161 Ibid.

162 Land Use, the Case for National Land Use KLA, 43.

163 Ibid.

164 Occurrences and toxicological risk assessment of eight heavy metals in agricultural soils from Kenya, Eastern Africa.

agricultural activities, growing industrialisation, and rapid urbanisation largely influenced the concentration levels of heavy metals in Kenya's soils. Moreover, the lack of agricultural normalisation management and poor enforcement of environmental laws and regulations further intensified the widespread pollution of agricultural soils.

Apart from agriculture, mining is also a driver of soil degradation through contamination. High mercury contents have been found in soil in the Migori–Transmara gold mining areas.[165]

3.3.3 Soil compaction

In Kenya, soil compaction is a major problem in areas with high livestock densities, and especially on denuded dry areas around watering points.[166] Here, excessive trampling by livestock and wildlife compacts the soil, reducing its infiltration capacity and leading to high runoff flows, soil erosion and even gullying.[167]

3.3.4 Salinity and sodicity

Salinity and sodicity problems are common in the arid and semi-arid lands where soils are naturally formed under the prevailing climatic conditions and owing to high rates of evapotranspiration and lack of leaching water.[168] About 40% or 25 million hectares of the land of Kenya is covered with soils that have salinity and/or sodicity problems.[169]

3.3.5 Soil erodibility

Kenya's soils have high erodibility (a natural property of soil), based on soil texture, profile depth, mineralogical composition and structure. Soil erodibility is also influenced by human activities, especially the addition or removal or organic matter.[170] Fragile, easily damaged soils located along steep slopes are often associated with soil erosion, if vegetation cover is poor.[171]

---

165 Impact of gold mining associated with mercury contamination in soil, biota sediments and tailings in Kenya.
166 Government of Kenya (2016b: 66).
167 Ibid.: 67.
168 Ibid.: 68.
169 Ibid.: 66.
170 Ibid.: 65.
171 Ibid.

3.3.6 Poor rangeland management

Rangelands cover about 70% of the total area of Kenya, and are thus of utmost economic importance.[172] Most of the rangelands are in the arid and semi-arid lands where pastoralists and agro-pastoralists face competition from an increasing influx of farmers from the overcrowded higher-potential areas migrating into the dry lands.[173] Rangeland degradation is manifested by the loss of vegetation cover and an increase in the proportion of bare soil surface.[174] Loss of vegetation cover and increased erosion can be attributed to livestock overgrazing.[175] Overgrazing predisposes soil to water and wind erosion.[176] As pointed out above, excessive trampling by livestock and wildlife compacts the soil, reducing its infiltration capacity.

3.3.7 Loss of forest cover

Forest ecosystems are important in conservation of soil, water and biodiversity, as well as in moderating climate.[177] Over the years, forest resources, including wildlife and water, in public and community forests have faced numerous threats arising from human activities, including charcoal burning, illegal logging, overgrazing, and human encroachment of forest areas.[178] Kenya's forest cover has over the years been depleted at a rate of 5,000 hectares per annum.[179] This has led to extensive soil erosion in areas such as Leroghi, Ndoto and Mount Nyiru forest reserves.[180] It is encouraging to note that Kenya's forest cover recorded an estimated increase from 7.2% of the total land area in 2013 to 7.29% in 2017.[181] The government has committed itself to increasing the tree cover to 10% by 2022.[182]

172 Ibid.: 76.
173 Ibid.
174 Ibid.
175 Ibid.
176 Hannam & Boer (2004: 4).
177 National Environment Policy, 11.
178 Government of Kenya (2018c: 28).
179 Ibid: 5.
180 Ibid.: 39–40.
181 Government of Kenya (2018b: 85).
182 See https://bit.ly/3cumZ33, accessed 1 February 2021.

3.3.8 Biodiversity loss

Biodiversity contributes to a wide variety of environmental services including conservation of fertile soils. Kenya has lost considerable biodiversity.[183] The most serious drivers of biodiversity loss are land degradation; climate change; pollution; unsustainable harvesting of natural resources; unsustainable patterns of consumption and production; and introduction of invasive and alien species.[184] The invasive alien species that constitute a major threat to biodiversity in Kenya include *Prosopis juliflora* (Mathenge), *Eichornia crassipes* (water hyacinth), and *Lantana camara*.[185]

3.3.9 Poverty

Poverty is one of the main drivers of soil degradation in Kenya. Poverty has forced the people to encroach on marginal lands and forests, burn charcoal and fetch firewood, which is leading to deforestation and land degradation.

3.3.10 Encroachment of fresh water and wetland ecosystems

Freshwater resources and wetlands form an important part of Kenya's natural resources. The supporting services of these ecosystems are important for soil formation and retention, as well as for nutrient cycling. The ecosystems also provide habitats for plant and animal species. Wetlands act as sponges, absorbing excess stormwater from heavy rainfalls, and thus providing flow regulation, flood control and prevention of soil erosion.[186] Floodwater may be stored in the soils or retained as surface water, thus reducing floodwater volumes downstream.[187] In addition, wetland vegetation slows down the flow of floodwater, resulting in silt and sediment retention and riverbank protection.[188] Besides reduction of flooding events downstream, this also ensures that river flows are maintained for longer periods.[189] Wetland vegetation also protects the soil from damage by strong waves and wind.[190] Wetland ecosystems face numerous threats from human population pressure and land use changes. Some of them have been converted for agricultural use, settlements and commercial developments.[191]

183 National Environment Policy, 19.
184 Government of Kenya (2013a: 14).
185 Ibid: 25.
186 National Wetlands Conservation and Management Policy (2014: 6).
187 Ibid.
188 Ibid.
189 Ibid.
190 Ibid.
191 National Environment Policy, 12.

Other threats include pollution; sedimentation and over-exploitation of wetland resources; introduction of alien species; encroachment on riparian reserves; and adverse effects of climate variability.[192] These have caused extensive degradation, reduction in water quality and quantity, and loss of freshwater and wetland ecosystem goods and services.

A number of illegal allocations of land around riparian sites were recorded in the Report of the Commission of Inquiry into the Illegal/Irregular Allocation of Public Land.[193] The land affected by these allocations is around rivers, lakes and the ocean. Huge commercial, religious and community centres, like Nakumatt Ukay and the Visa Oshwal Centre off Ring Road, Westlands, are constructed on river and wetland systems without any regard for the adverse consequences for the ecosystems.[194] Construction on river and wetland ecosystems has led to clearance of riparian vegetation, which is essential for reducing soil erosion. The Government of Kenya has embarked on reclaiming riparian land with several properties allegedly built on the riparian reserve already brought down.

3.4 Key actors in soil degradation

3.4.1 Investors

Local and international investors engaged in diverse activities, such as agriculture, mining, and infrastructure and housing development, contribute to soil degradation. It is therefore important to include such investors when framing interventions to stem soil degradation. These should include both incentives to elicit sustainable soil management and sanctions to discourage degrading activities.

3.4.2 Government

The national and county governments, as landowners with activities on land and as custodians of land under their jurisdiction, are key actors in soil degradation. Both national and county governments have roles to play in land use planning and allocation. They also have activities on land. Enlisting their leadership in stemming soil degradation is critical if soil degradation is to be addressed holistically.

---

192 National Environment Policy, 12 and 13.
193 Comission of Inquiry (2004).
194 Ibid.: 120.

3.4.3 Farmers

As users of land, farmers on community and private land are actors in soil degradation. Initiatives to stem soil degradation should target farmers through education and extension services that address unsustainable land use practices and soil contamination through the use of chemicals. Enlisting the participation of large- and small-scale farmers is critical to ensuring that soil degradation is stemmed. Any soil law or policy that leaves out farmers excludes a large segment of actors capable of bringing about real change considering their ubiquity in soil-related activities.

3.4.4 Pastoralists

Pastoralists in arid and semi-arid lands contribute to soil degradation through unsustainable rangeland management and overstocking. Many soils in rangelands are degraded and soils in areas around watering points compacted. Education and extension services targeting these practices can greatly enhance soil health and overall ecosystem integrity. This would greatly benefit the users of these lands.

3.5 Conclusion

Soil degradation in a country like Kenya where soil and agriculture accounts for 24% of the country's gross domestic index has drastic consequences. The main drivers of soil degradation are agriculture, mining, unsustainable land use, urban sprawl, climate change, and soil erosion. Soil compaction, sodicity and erodibility, poverty, and loss of biodiversity are also contributors to soil degradation in Kenya. As a developing country, Kenya is witnessing massive development, rapid population increase, and industrialisation. The country must remain cognizant of the biological, natural and physical drivers of soil degradation and must introduce legislation and enforcement measures to address them. The introduction of devolution as a form of governance is a golden opportunity to introduce more specific soil legislation in the 47 counties.

4 Background on soil legislation

4.1 Historical perspective

The reasons for the establishment of Kenya as a British colony have been variously explained to include the strategic significance of the Suez Canal in 1869 and hence the River Nile, and the need for expansion of the British Empire to be able to ward off economic competition from the United States, Canada and the European powers.[195] The legislation passed from the time of the declaration of a protectorate in 1895 to independence in 1963 facilitated the acquisition and consolidation of rights to vast tracts of land by settlers.[196] Africans were moved to native reserves.

The law did not directly address soil conservation. However, the way in which, and the speed at which, colonial policies were implemented destabilised the structures of the local communities and centres of authority, and significantly disrupted the equilibrium between people and their physical environment.[197] The increase in the population of Africans in the reserves without expansion of the land available for their occupation and use resulted in over-use and hence soil deterioration. A number of colonial policies and laws are relevant for soil governance.

Acquisition of land rights for settlers was mainly done through political processes that were followed by legal instruments giving the political acts the requisite binding force. Colonial land policy was thus not systematic. Decisions were made in the face of day-to-day problems whose resolution demanded swift actions.[198] To facilitate the alienation of land, the Indian Lands Acquisition Act of 1894 was extended to the East African Protectorate in 1899. The effect of this was to vest the power of control and disposition over –[199]

> waste and unoccupied land in the protectorates where there was no settled form of government and where land had not been appropriated either to the local sovereign or to individuals. Her Majesty might, if she pleased, declare them to be Crown lands or make grants of them to individuals in fee or for any term.

Pursuant to this, a need arose to define what "Crown lands" meant. The East Africa (Lands) Order-in-Council, 1901 defined Crown lands to mean "all public lands within the East Africa Protectorate, which for the time being are subject to the control of His Majesty by virtue of any Treaty, Convention, or Agreement, or of His Majesty's Protectorate, and all lands which have been or may hereafter be acquired by His Majesty".[200]

While this provision solved the issue of acquisition of land for public purposes, land had to be acquired for private persons and the settlers were dissatisfied with the nature of rights that they had been able to secure thus far.[201] Attempts by the incoming settlers to acquire land through purchase from the native people were frustrated by the lack of

195 Mungeam (1966); Wolff (1974).

196 Ibid.

197 See e.g. Lugard (1929) on the effects of colonialism on the institution of traditional chiefs in Kenya. See also Huxley (1935).

198 Kameri-Mbote (2002).

199 See Palley (1966: 82) quoting the Report of the Foreign Office FOCP 7403 No. 101.

200 See § 1 of the East African Order-in-Council, 1901, passed at the Court of St. James on 8 August 1901.

201 For some time, the colonial officers considered themselves unable to grant anything more than temporary certificates of occupancy which the early settlers found unacceptable.

capacity on the part of the natives to sell land, as the settlers would have wanted. This is a critical aspect of native land tenure that has implications on people's relationship with the land, soil and other resources on the land. To many of the natives, land was inalienable, and the allodium or paramount title vested in the entire community.[202] This mode of holding land led to the general view of the colonial administration that Africans had no rights to land either as individuals or as groups.[203] Their ways of relating with and using land were negated with *terra nullius* as the dominant assumption. This has had implications for Kenyan land law and policy as will become clear from the discussions below.

4.2 Colonial laws, policies and plans

4.2.1 Crown Lands Ordinance, No. 21 of 1902

The Crown Lands Ordinance, No. 21 of 1902 was passed because of increased pressure from the incoming settlers. It vested power in the commissioner to sell freeholds in Crown land to any purchaser in lots not exceeding 1,000 acres.[204] These regulations conferred enormous discretionary power on the colonial authorities that had a virtually free hand to determine what was waste and unoccupied land. The tendency was to treat all native rights to land as temporary and only exercisable if the native was actually occupying the land. Such rights, Lord Haldane contended, could be extinguished by the action of a paramount power taking possession and assuming full control of a country.[205] This view is significant when one considers the plight of nomadic pastoralist communities, such as the Maasai and the agricultural communities where people cultivated different pieces of land and practised shifting cultivation. These practices were coping and adaptation mechanisms for communities using the land and were based on their knowledge of the terrain.

By virtue of the 1902 ordinance, the Crown authorities could grant land, which included native settlements and villages. The ownership of these villages would be vested in the grantee once actual native occupancy ceased. These provisions effectively converted communally managed resources into open access ones, paving the

202 Bentsi-Enchill (1964).

203 See the case of *Mulwa Gwanobi v Alidina Visram* (1913) 5 K.L.R. 141 involving the sale of land by members of the Jibana tribe where the Court held that what the tribe members sold were rights to occupy and reap fruits from the land and not absolute rights as the purchaser would have had the Court believe. In the Judge's view, the members of the tribal community had only a right of occupancy and they could consequently not pass on by sale a right greater than the one of occupancy.

204 See § 4 of the Crown Lands Ordinance 1902.

205 See *Sobhuza II v Miller and others* [1926] A.C. 518 at 525.

way for actual settlement of the protectorate.[206] The price and rent asked for the land was very low so as to attract many settlers since the colonial authorities did not perceive the natives as capable of developing as vibrant an economic state as they envisaged Kenya would become.

4.2.2 Crown Lands Ordinance, 1915

The Crown Lands Ordinance of 1915 declared all land within the protectorate to be Crown land whether or not the natives occupied such land or whether or not it was reserved for native occupation.[207] The ordinance mandated the colonial authorities to grant 999-year leases though the settlers clamoured for perpetual leases.[208] Chief Justice Barth's interpretation of the provisions of this ordinance in the case of *Isaka Wainaina & Another v Murito wa Indagara & Ors* was to the effect that Africans were mere tenants at the will of the Crown, with no more than temporary occupancy rights to land.[209] Section 54 of this ordinance gave powers to the governor to reserve any land for "the use and benefit of native tribes".[210] Exercising this power the governor, in 1926, gazetted 24 African reserves.[211] There was no security of tenure provided in the native reserves.[212] The increase in population in the native reserves led to soil degradation. Dr Leakey's testimony to the Carter Commission of 1933 to the effect that the Kikuyu native reserves were congested bears this out. His opinion was that the Kikuyu would be faced with an identical need for land for subsistence and stock raising[213] and suggested that their reserves be increased by an additional 2,000 square miles of land extracted from the forest reserve located to the north of the Kikuyu native reserves.[214] However, no additional land was granted to the Kikuyu, prompting a protracted war for independence with land as the major point of contention. The undocumented consequence of the forceful taking of natives' land rights was its impact on land, soil and the health and management of land-based resources.

---

206 See, e.g. Bondi & Mugabe (1996) arguing that environmental degradation manifest in regions under customary land tenure is largely due to interference in rural resource management by a "modernising" nation-state rather that the "inherent vices" of customary property relations. See also Gadgil (1989).
207 See § 5 of the Crown Lands Ordinance, 18 May 1915.
208 See § 34 of the Crown Lands Ordinance, 18 May 1915.
209 (1922–23) Kenya Law Reports Vol. IX 102.
210 Kakumu (1996).
211 Ibid: 30.
212 Ibid.
213 Corray (1978).
214 Ibid.

4.2.3 Native Lands Trust Ordinance, 1938

Section 65(1) of the Native Lands Trust Ordinance of 1938[215] bestowed power on the governor to make rules on the following issues that were pertinent to the management of soils when it came to native reserves:

a) Controlling the occupation and use of native reserves for grazing and pasturing stock
b) Compulsorily reducing the number of stocks, flocks and herds in any native land units
c) Regulating the reconditioning of any native land unit and, for such purpose, prohibiting and regulating the occupation of any areas
d) Regulating generally the use and conservation of any area in the native reserves
e) Regulating the issue of licences in the native areas for cattle grazing rights and the removal of timber, forest produce, sand, limestone and other common minerals apart from surface salt
f) Protection of trees and forest produce on land, not within the meaning of the Forest Ordinance and for regulating the felling and removal of such trees or forest produce

4.2.4 Agricultural Policy, 1944

The Agricultural Policy of 1944 came in at the tail end of World War II. Food had become scarce as drought ravaged most African countries.[216] This policy, borrowed from Humphrey Norman's radical proposals, such as that Africans exceeding the carrying capacity of land should be moved to new settlement areas that were not overly populated.[217] The other proposal was that attention be given to new agricultural methods and drought-resistant crops.[218] There was also a proposal for communal cultivation to increase cooperation in soil conservation.[219] In 1945, elders in Nyeri started a six-month trial care for their lands.[220] Labourers, who were mostly women, were required to turn up two mornings a week to dig terraces on family and clan lands.[221] This is said to have produced spectacular results.[222] This move was however stopped in 1948 when Jomo Kenyatta gave a speech at Fort Hall during a Kenya African Union address, stating that women should not be compelled to work on the terraces.[223] It is important to note, first, the communities' eagerness to care for their soils; second, the involvement

215 Native Lands Trust Lands Ordinance 1938, at kenyalaw.org/lex/rest//db/.../Amendment%20Acts/No.%2028%20of%201938.pdf, accessed 17 May 2019.
216 Thurston (1987).
217 Ibid.
218 Ibid.
219 Ibid.
220 Ibid.
221 Ibid.
222 Ibid.
223 Ibid.

of women; and, third, political interference with soil conservation initiatives that did not take into account the value of such initiatives on the ground.

4.2.5 African Courts Ordinance, 1951

The African Courts Ordinance of 1951 stated that the courts should consist of elders appointed by the provincial commissioner, who would have jurisdiction over all Africans.[224] Administrative officers, the district officer and the provincial commissioner supervised these courts.[225] At this time, the Native Authority of the clans was recognised, and they were enabled to make rules and orders on matters vital to the welfare of the people, like soil conservation. The African courts dealt with the breach of these rules and orders.[226]

4.2.6 Swynnerton Plan, 1954

By 1940, there was a severe land shortage within the reserves and the Africans were demanding the restoration of stolen lands. In 1952, these demands culminated in the Mau Mau revolts predominantly led by the Kikuyu. These revolts awakened the colonial administration to the need for tenure reform. Having constructed African tenure systems as 'non-property' or open access, the colonial agronomic experts viewed the solution to the African land problem as one of tenure, namely the structure of access to the use of land in areas occupied by the natives. The existing tenure system was perceived as inimical to proper land use and agricultural development as it encouraged fragmentation of land, which cut down on returns from labour and time expended on the land and led to incessant disputes that were a disincentive to long-term capital investment.[227] The African tenure system of inheritance, characterised by subdivision of land in native reserves, also resulted in reduced productivity due to soil leaching.[228]

The solution to the problem was conceived in terms of individualised title to land and intensified agriculture in African areas through technological improvements. It was hoped that this would increase production and divert the attention of the Africans from the settler occupied areas.[229] A commission was set up to investigate African tenure systems and to make recommendations on ways of improving them and making them contribute to the economic development of the colony.

224 The African Courts Ordinance of 1951, Section 4.
225 Ibid.: Section 1(b).
226 Munro (1959).
227 See Swynnerton (1954).
228 Ibid.
229 Ibid.

The Swynnerton Plan of 1954 recommended the consolidation of land holdings of families into one, followed by the adjudication of property rights to that land and the registration of individuals as absolute owners of land adjudicated as theirs.[230] This was primarily an economic plan whose purpose was to increase productivity in the agricultural sector. Soil conservation was critical if intensified production was to be achieved. Small holdings were consolidated, and a typographical map of the area was drawn, accompanied by a soil conservation plan.[231]

The severity of soil erosion in Kenya was realised as early as the 1920s. In an attempt to arrest the situation, compulsory terracing schemes, such as the Muhiriga system discussed above, were introduced in the 1940s.[232] These were unpopular because their benefits were unclear to the local people. Some techniques developed during this period were effective, but the fact that they were based on enforced communal work meant that soil conservation was bitterly resented by the local people.[233] Many terraces fell into disrepair around the time of independence in the early 1960s.[234] It is instructive to note in this regard that the relative proportions of land that was terraced in Kangundo–Matungulu–Mbiuni agroecological zone 3 (high-potential land) and Masii in zone 4 (semi-arid upland) in 1961 were essentially the same as those of 1948.[235]

4.3 Selected soil conservation initiatives in post-independence Kenya

After independence, terracing was renewed and carried out voluntarily. Farmers began to construct terraces within a few years of opening new land, even in the newly settled areas of Makueni (drier, warmer and lower zone 4 and 5, settled after 1945), where average slopes were less steep.[236] Unterraced arable land had been virtually eliminated in all three areas by 1978, with significant progress made between 1961 and 1978, when arable areas were growing rapidly as a result of the increasing population.[237] Terrace construction continued in the 1980s, and by 1990, erosion on arable land was considered to be under control. The problem was, however, only beginning to be tackled on grazing land.[238]

The soil and water conservation campaign began in the 1970s[239] when people became increasingly concerned about the future of their farmlands and were therefore

230 See Osolo-Nasubo (1977).
231 Ibid.
232 Karuku & International Network for Natural Sciences (2018: 123).
233 Ibid.
234 Ibid.
235 Ibid.
236 Ibid.: 124.
237 Ibid.
238 Ibid.
239 Ibid.

receptive to advice and ready to participate in conservation activities.[240] Erosion was worsening owing to the expanding cropped area, while spells of drought regularly affected yields, especially maize.[241] Enforced conservation did not work in colonial times, but in the 1970s people were ready to respond to the new campaign as they envisaged accrued benefits to their efforts.[242] Awareness and community participation in decision-making, which were previously lacking, bore fruit.[243]

Several projects aimed at improving crop and livestock productivity were initiated. While these were not anchored in any national law or policy, they provided the basis for soil protection and must be canvassed in any discussion on soil protection in Kenya. Indeed, they may provide pointers to what works and what does not, as lessons in framing soil legislation.

4.3.1 National Soil and Water Conservation Project

The Government of Kenya and the Swedish International Development Agency jointly funded the National Soil and Water Conservation Project, which began in 1974 and ended in 1994. Its overall objective was to contribute to food security and to raise the standard of living of the rural population, through suitable conservation practices.[244]

The project was implemented in cropped fields where erosion had the most damaging effect on productivity and farmers' incomes and focused on improving the status of arable land. The main method used was the development of bench terraces using the *fanya juu* (literally do up) terracing technique over a period of time. Soil was thrown up the slope from a ditch to form an earth embankment or bund, with several terrace banks made across a field, on the contour. The land between the bunds levelled off gradually and the field developed the stepped characteristic of bench terraces. Soil and rainwater were conserved between the *fanya juu* bunds.[245]

The technical objective was two-fold: to keep rainfall where it fell, and to keep soil in the field. The end result was better growing conditions for the crop, both immediately, because of an increase in the amount of moisture available, and in the long term, because the soil was conserved.[246] Each farm was surveyed to see whether it required a cut-off drain to protect it from surplus rainfall runoff. The cut-off drain was usually designed to hold all the runoff which flowed into it, and therefore it was sometimes

240 Ibid.
241 Ibid.
242 Ibid.
243 Ibid.
244 Mutisya et al. (2010: 8).
245 Ibid.
246 Ibid.: 9.

known as an 'infiltration ditch'.[247] The alignment of the terraces was surveyed along the contour using a simple line level. The spacing between the terraces depended on the slope of the land. Apart from terracing, other recommended activities, though on a smaller scale, were grass strips along the contour, contour ploughing, simple gully control measures, tree planting, riverbank protection and grazing control.[248]

In 1987, the project changed focus to the catchment approach through farmers' groups, and agroforestry was incorporated as an activity to enhance the soil and water conservation measures. Farmers were organised into groups in each catchment area. A catchment covered an area extending from the hilltop to the riverbank and consisted of either one or two villages sharing common hydrological watersheds and therefore requiring similar soil conservation measures. Each catchment had a committee and a given number of farmers (approximately 200). Individual farmers undertook soil conservation measures on their farms with regular guidance from the extension officers. Communal activities included wetlands management, riverbank protection, communal tree nursery establishment and management, gully erosion control, and the erection of gabions. A shifting catchment approach was adopted through which the project would concentrate activities in one catchment area for one year, then shift to another. Catchment residents were provided with farm tools such as shovels, hoes, pangas (machetes), mattocks, pickaxes, crowbars and wheelbarrows. They were also provided with free agroforestry tree seeds and seedlings, and polythene tubes. The items were given as demonstration materials and the farmers were expected to appreciate the need for these items and then purchase on their own thereafter. After one year, the catchment committee was expected to continue coordinating soil conservation activities.[249]

Regular evaluation of the project was carried out, and the results and recommendations were discussed in workshops where necessary adjustments were made in the project activities. The project was successful in developing simple extension messages, which farmers easily understood. However, the project was rated as poor because most of the community-based activities were not sustainable in the absence of free farm tools and inputs.[250] The groups disintegrated. The soil and water conservation and group agroforestry activities collapsed after the end of donor support and the catchment committees stopped their coordination roles.[251]

---

247 Ibid.
248 Ibid.
249 Ibid.
250 Ibid.
251 Ibid.

4.3.2 Permanent Presidential Commission on Soil Conservation and Afforestation

Pursuant to Section 23 and 24 of the 1969 Constitution, the President had the prerogative to set up and abolish offices in the public interest. Through this power, President Moi set up the Permanent Presidential Commission on Soil Conservation and Afforestation in 1981. This was necessitated because the President felt that the bureaucratic machinery of the Ministry of Agriculture was not adequate to deal specifically with issues of soil conservation.[252] The commission had an open-ended mandate to deal with soil conservation without requiring amendment of objectives.[253] It focused its strategies on afforestation and soil conservation, and formulating appropriate policies.[254] The commission also focused on public education and coordinated government functions dealing with soil conservation.[255] One of the recognisable efforts of this commission was establishing presidential soil conservation sites throughout the country. In Machakos, for instance, there were three sites: Mwanyani site, which started in 1982; Uuni site in 1984; and Masinga site in 1985.[256]

During President Moi's tenure, different authorities were established and tasked with responsibilities, which included conserving and protecting soil. The authorities were established through acts of Parliament as shown below:

Authority	Act of Parliament	Section granting mandate	Areas covered
Ewaso Ng'iro North River Basin Development Authority	Ewaso Ng'iro North River Basin Development Authority Act	Section 8(g)	Isiolo, Laikipia, Samburu, Marsabit, Wajir, Mandera, parts of Nyandarua, Meru and Nyeri.
Tana and Athi Rivers Development Authority	Tana and Athi Rivers Development Authority Act	Section 8(j)	Area bound by and drained by Tana and Athi River together with its tributaries.
Lake Basin Development Authority	Lake Basin Development Authority Act	Section 8(h)	Lake Victoria and Lake Kyoga catchment areas
Ewaso Ng'iro South River Basin Development Authority	Ewaso Ng'iro South River Basin Development Authority Act	Section 8(h)	Ewaso Nyiro South River basin and catchment areas situated within Narok, Kajiado, Nyandarua and Nakuru districts

252 Bragdon (1990).
253 Ibid.
254 Ibid.
255 Ibid.
256 Gichuki (1991).

4.4 Types of conservation measure that have been used in Kenya over the years

4.4.1 Terraces

Levelled bench terraces and earth bunding on existing slopes are common earth structures in Kenya. Sometimes, and especially in the highlands, steps are constructed across hillsides and strips of crop residues are covered with soils dug from above. The resulting incorporation of organic matter increases soil fertility and enhances infiltration through macro porosity as well as increased water retention in soils.[257] The *fanya juu* earth bunding system is now common in Kenya and is designed to trap runoff and suspend sediment.[258] The challenge, however, is the high labour requirement in their construction and maintenance.[259]

A *fanya chini* (do down) is like a *fanya juu*, except that the soil is put on the lower side of the contour trench, not on the upslope side as in a *fanya juu*. *Fanya chini* are used to conserve soil and divert water. The resulting embankment can be used to grow fodder.[260]

4.4.2 Conservation agriculture

There are three major principles of conservation agriculture as practised in Kenya: minimal soil disturbance, permanent soil cover, and crop rotation.[261] Soils under conservation agriculture tend to improve their soil organic matter content considerably after applying the technology for several years.[262] Soil organic matter is the most important soil fertility and quality factor influencing other soil properties such as macro porosity, infiltration, water holding capacity, and soil structure. In conservation agriculture, only minimal or no soil tillage is applied, and it involves crop seeding without mechanical seedbed preparation and with minimal or no soil disturbance since the harvest of the previous crop.[263]

---

257 Karuku & International Network for Natural Sciences (2018: 125).
258 Ibid.
259 Ibid.
260 Ibid.
261 Ibid.
262 Ibid.: 126.
263 Ibid.

4.4.3 Cover crop for soil fertility and erosion control

Cover crops are beneficial in stabilisation of soil moisture and temperature; protection of soil during fallow periods; mobilisation and recycling of nutrients; improvement of soil structure and breaking compacted layers and hard pans; permitting rotation in a monoculture; controlling weeds and pests; and producing additional soil organic matter that improves soil structure.[264] In Kenya smallholders grow velvet bean, hairy vetch (*Vicia villosa*) and sun hemp (*Crotalaria juncea*) as cover crops.[265] Some cover crops have been shown to suppress weeds, reduce nematode loads, improve soil fertility, reduce water leaching, and control erosion. In a study at Matunda farm in Kenya, it was observed that velvet bean produced more biomass than other cover crop species.[266]

4.4.4 Green manure

Green manure consists of plants grown specifically to accumulate nutrients for the main crop. These plants penetrate the soil with their roots, deliver nutrients and support infiltration of water into the soil.[267] The contribution of organic matter to the soil by means of such green manure crops is comparable to the addition of 23 to 33 Mgha-1 of farmyard manure. Leguminous plants, for instance, fix nitrogen (N) from the air into the soil and this N enriches the soil and feeds plants in the area.[268] An alternative to sowing a green manure crop in the field is to collect fresh plant material from elsewhere and to work it into the soil (biomass transfer), as is done in western Kenya. It was observed that trees and shrubs growing alongside crops in agroforestry systems could provide large quantities of green material which could be used as green manure. *Tithonia diversifolia*, for example, accumulates a high concentration of nutrients in its leafy biomass, which then mineralises very rapidly when incorporated in soil. Green leaf biomass of *Tithonia diversifolia* harvested in western Kenya is high in nutrients – in the order of 3.5-4.0%N; 0.35-0.38%P; 3.5-4.1%K; 0.59%Ca and 0.27%Mg on a dry matter basis.[269]

264 Ibid.
265 Ibid.: 127.
266 Ibid.
267 Ibid.: 128.
268 Ibid.
269 Ibid.

4.4.5 Agroforestry

Various agroforestry technologies have been applied in Kenya, such as a) fertilizer trees like *Calliandra* spp., *Leucena leucocephala*, and *Terminalia brownii*, among others, that when combined with inorganic fertilizers double or triple crop yields in degraded lands; b) fodder trees used in smallholder zero-grazing systems in ways that supplement or substitute commercial feeds; c) improved varieties of temperate and tropical fruits used to supplement household incomes and nutrition; d) medicinal trees used on farms and conserved in situ; and e) fast growing timber and fuel trees that can be grown in various niches on the farm and in commercial woodlots and plantations.[270]

4.4.6 Hedges

Hedges are used in Kenya to conserve soils on contours. A contour hedge is a horizontal strip of multipurpose trees or shrubs that are used to control soil erosion on sloping lands.[271] Contour hedges control erosion by providing a physical barrier and also by increasing water infiltration through a leaf litter layer creating good soil structure.[272] Over the long term, these hedges have resulted in the formation of terraces on the upper side of each hedge, which are an added advantage in soil and water conservation.[273]

4.4.7 Improved fallows

Improved fallows have been used in some areas, where land is left to rest (fallow) from cultivation and is enriched with leguminous plants to speed up soil fertility replenishment. In western Kenya, maize yields improved following fallows. Fallows increase the water infiltration capacity of soil and are capable of deep-root development. Fallows also reduce soil erosion, by maintaining a leafy canopy during dry seasons and more vigorous crop growth during rainy seasons.[274] Communities practising shifting cultivation, as noted above, make use of fallow seasons.

270 Ibid.: 129.
271 Ibid.
272 Ibid.: 130.
273 Ibid.
274 Ibid.

4.4.8 Vegetation strips

Vegetation strips are usually narrow grass strips grown across slopes. The grass acts as a barrier to runoff, thus encouraging deposition of sediments and eventually leading to terrace development. The commonly planted grasses in Kenyan degraded lands are *Imperata cylindrica*, *Vetiveria zizanioides* and *Pennisetum purpureum*.[275]

4.4.9 Conservation and regeneration measures

Conservation and regeneration measures such as area closure and rotational grazing management measures are often applied to grazing land in situations where uncontrolled use has led to degradation and where other measures simply do not work without a fundamental change in land management. Enclosures are used to protect land from grazing and thus allow regeneration of vegetation cover. Other measures include intensification of grazing land use where fodder crops are planted and used for cut-and-carry feeding of livestock.[276]

4.4.10 Contour farming

Contour farming involves ploughing, planting and weeding along the contour, across the slope rather than up and down. Contour ridges are commonly used in arid and semi-arid lands to harvest water, and in the humid, higher rainfall areas for growing potatoes.[277] Research has however shown that contour lines can be destroyed by termites eating the trash and thus compromising the conservation agenda envisaged. To overcome this obstacle, grass barrier strips are planted with fodder grass, like Napier, or the contour is left with natural grass.[278] These are effective soil conservation measures on soils that absorb water quickly, and on slopes as steep as 30%.[279]

4.4.11 Trash lines

Trash lines made by laying crop residues, or trash, in lines along the contour have been shown to slow down runoff and trap eroded soil, eventually forming terraces. Apart from impeding runoff and enhancing infiltration, trash lines also increase soil organic

275 Ibid.
276 Ibid.: 131.
277 Ibid.: 132.
278 Ibid.
279 Ibid.

matter content when incorporated into soil during ploughing; enhance soil macro porosity, water holding capacity and soil hydraulic conductivity; and improve soil fertility upon decomposition and mineralisation. Trash lines are extensively used in the Tharaka area of Meru in northern Kenya.[280]

4.4.12 Cut-off drains, retention and infiltration ditches

Cut-off drains are usually dug across a slope to intercept surface runoff and carry it safely to an outlet such as a canal or stream with minimal risk of exacerbating erosion.[281] They are used to protect cultivated land, compounds and roads from uncontrolled runoff, and to divert water from gulley heads.[282]

Retention ditches are dug along a contour to catch and retain incoming runoff and hold it until it seeps into the ground. They are an alternative to cut-off drains when there is no nearby waterway into which to discharge the runoff. They are used to harvest water in semi-arid areas.[283]

4.5 Conclusion

The concerns about soil degradation in Kenya have been recorded since colonial times. Measures to stem soil erosion have been part and parcel of land use for agriculture for a long time. As demonstrated above, a raft of initiatives has been implemented to curb land degradation generally and soil erosion specifically. These initiatives and measures form a good basis for soil legislation. The implementation of legislation is also favoured by the fact that people have experienced the negative effects of land degradation over the years, particularly in agricultural landscapes that have become less productive. Loss of lives due floods and landslides in different parts of the country attributable to land degradation is also a compelling motivation for both the enactment of a soil specific law and its implementation.

5 Legislation on the main drivers of soil degradation

Kenya has a plural legal system whose law comprises the Constitution, which lists the sources of law to include international treaties that Kenya has ratified; religious and

280 Ibid.
281 Ibid.
282 Ibid.
283 Ibid.

customary laws; acts of Parliament (National Assembly and Senate); and county laws. The operationalisation of many laws is usually done through subsidiary legislation in the form of regulations by the line ministries. For soil, these include ministries responsible for environment, mining and agriculture. The inclusion of religious and customary law as sources of law introduces rarely addressed bodies of norms for governing the environment and soil. In dealing with culture,[284] the state is mandated by the Constitution to promote science[285] and recognise the role of science and indigenous technologies in national development. It is also exhorted to protect and enhance intellectual property in, and indigenous knowledge of, biodiversity and the genetic resources of the communities.[286]

Kenya is also party to international treaties addressing soil. These include the United Nations Framework Convention on Climate Change; the United Nations Convention on Biological Diversity, whose Aichi Targets are particularly relevant for sustainable soil management; and the United Nations Convention to Combat Desertification (UNCCD). The Constitution of Kenya provides that "the general rules of international law"[287] and "any treaty or convention ratified by Kenya"[288] is to form part of the law of Kenya. The nature and extent of the application of international law, however, is not as clear-cut as would be expected in the light of these provisions. The ambiguity of the constitutional provisions[289] and the hierarchy of legal norms in municipal legal systems make the application of these constitutional provisions complex.[290] Most legal systems require some act of domestication to bring international law norms into the municipal law, usually through legislation. The implication is that ratification is not enough even where there are provisions for direct application.[291] While Kenyan courts have used international law to come to decisions, the prevalent practice remains that of cascading international law norms into municipal law through national legislation. Kenya's framework environmental law has incorporated many of the international environmental law norms, as we will see below. Kenya is also implementing the United Nations Agenda 2030 and has a robust framework for tracking the achievement of the Sustainable Development Goals (SDGs), which have specific application to soil management.[292]

The Constitution and statutes discussed hereunder impliedly and explicitly regulate the conservation and management of soil in Kenya. This governance regime has to be considered within the context of a long history of the country's engagement and

284 Constitution of Kenya 2010, Article 11.
285 Ibid., Article 11(2)(a).
286 Ibid., Article 69(1)(c).
287 Ibid., Article 2(5).
288 Ibid., Article 2(6).
289 Wabwile (2013); Oduor (2014).
290 Kabau & Njoroge (2011); Kabau & Ambani (2013).
291 Kabau & Ambani (2013); O'Connell (1960: 452).
292 SDG 15 is particularly relevant here.

investment in soil conservation. The measures outlined above, which have been used for protecting the soil, should be integrated into the operative laws as they have been successfully applied over the years. The discussion below highlights laws and policies that can be used for soil protection. It is a matter of grave concern that the detailed measures used for soil conservation are not directly canvassed in these laws. This is a missed opportunity for ingraining soil protection measures in environmental, land and natural resource management laws, policies and guidelines.

5.1 International instruments relevant to soil protection

Kenya has signed and ratified various international treaties, policies and strategies, which have an impact on soil protection and conservation. While some of these international instruments may not have had the protection of soil as their aim, the import of their provisions in the respective territories is to affect the conservation and protection of soil. Below is an overview[293] of the international instruments (laws, policies, strategies, action plans and declarations) that Kenya has ratified or adopted, and which have an impact on soil regulation in Kenya:

The United Nations Sustainable Development Goals, 2030; the Declaration on Environment and Development, Stockholm 1972; The World Heritage Convention, 1972, which Kenya adopted in 1991, which provides for protection of ecosystems and habitats of global scientific value; the Ramsar Convention on Wetlands, 1992; Agenda 21 on Environment and Development, Rio de Janeiro, 1992; the Convention on Biological Diversity, which Kenya ratified in 1994; the United Nations Convention to Combat Desertification, which Kenya ratified in 1997; the United Nations Framework Convention on Climate Change, which Kenya ratified in 1994; the Rotterdam Convention on the Prior Informed Consent Procedure for Certain Hazardous Chemicals and Pesticides in International Trade, 1998; the Millennium Declaration, 2000; the Johannesburg Declaration on Sustainable Development, 2002; the Cartagena Protocol on Biosafety to the Convention on Biological Diversity, 2000; and the Stockholm Convention on Persistent Organic Pollutants, which was ratified by Kenya in 2004. In the following section, the most relevant international law instruments will be highlighted in more detail in terms of national relevance.

293 Adapted and modified from: KASLMP & Ministry of Environment and Natural Resources.

5.1.1 Convention on Biological Diversity

Kenya is a party to the Convention on Biological Diversity (CBD), and is thus bound by the provisions of the treaty.[294] The main objective of the convention is to ensure the conservation of biological diversity in all its various forms, given its importance for sustenance of life on Earth. It reaffirms the responsibility of states to conserve their biological diversity and utilise biological resources in a sustainable manner. Soil forms part of the biological resources whose protection is intended by the convention. Article 3 of the CBD states the guiding principle of the convention, which basically is that states have the sovereign right to exploit their own resources in accordance with their own environmental policies, while bearing the responsibility of ensuring that activities under their jurisdiction do not cause damage to the environment of other states. It follows that while a state may lawfully utilise the soil occurring within its own jurisdiction as a matter of sovereign right, it has a duty to prevent soil degradation.

For purposes of accountability, Article 23 of the convention provides that the Conference of the Parties (COP) has the mandate to review the implementation of the convention in the respective countries. Article 26 of the convention establishes a reporting mechanism and requires all contracting parties to present reports on measures which they have taken for the implementation of the provisions of this convention and their effectiveness in meeting the objectives of the convention to COP. Accordingly, Kenya as a signatory to the convention submits its reports to COP on the extent to which it is implementing the provisions of the convention. To implement the CBD at the national level, Kenya has developed national biodiversity action plans. The first National Biodiversity Action Plan was prepared in 2000. To ensure its effective implementation, various laws, policies and strategies have also been adopted.

5.1.2 Strategic Plan for Biodiversity (2011–2020) and Aichi Biodiversity Targets (2020)

Contracting parties to the CBD adopted a strategic plan for biodiversity in 2010 to run from 2011 to 2020. This plan was to guide the achievement of the objectives of the CBD for the subsequent decade. This was to bring an end to or mitigate the continued biodiversity loss and enhance benefits to the population. The plan included the 2020 Aichi Biodiversity Targets, which would act as an indicator of how much progress was being made towards achievement of the objectives of the CBD. The Aichi Targets comprise five main strategic goals, namely socioeconomic and institutional changes; reducing direct pressures on biodiversity and ecosystems; ensuring the flow of benefits

294 See http://kenyalaw.org/treaties/treaties/87/Convention-on-Biological-Diversity, accessed 10 October 2019.

of biodiversity to people and especially to communities whose subsistence is tied to local ecosystem services; and developing conditions required to implement the strategic plan as well as to develop the knowledge base. When Kenya submitted its Fifth National Report to the CBD it noted that Kenya had not finalised all the measures it had been required to undertake. It had, however, committed to continuing to review and enact various laws and regulations aimed at ensuring the restoration and maintenance of ecosystems.

5.1.3 United Nations Convention to Combat Desertification

The United Nations Convention to Combat Desertification (UNCCD) is another international instrument ratified by Kenya and which is relevant for purposes of soil conservation and protection. The convention defines 'combating desertification' broadly to include activities which are part of the integrated development of land in arid, semi-arid and dry sub-humid areas for sustainable development aimed at: (i) prevention and/or reduction of land degradation; (ii) rehabilitation of partly degraded land; and (iii) reclamation of desert land.[295] The main concern of the convention is the prevention of soil degradation and the restoration of already degraded land. What is more, the convention defines land to include soil as part of the terrestrial bio-productive system.[296] In addition, land degradation that is sought to be curbed by the convention includes soil erosion either by wind or water, deterioration of the chemical, biological and economic properties of soil; and the long-term loss of natural vegetation. Under Article 5 of the convention, some of the obligations of affected parties are to address the underlying causes of desertification and give due priority to actions to combat desertification. Further, Article 10 of the convention requires contracting parties to develop national action programmes whose effect is to identify factors contributing to desertification and practical measures necessary to combat desertification.

Kenya ratified the Convention to Combat Desertification on 24 June 1997. A major commitment on the part of signatories to the convention was to develop national action plans to effectively implement the provisions of the convention. Following the ratification of the convention, Kenya received financial support from the United Nations Development Programme/United Nations Sudano-Sahelian Office (UNDP/UNSO) to facilitate the development of the National Action Programme (NAP).[297] There were various sensitisation efforts and initiatives among stakeholders including government institutions, research institutions, the private sector, non-governmental organisations, community-based organisations and local communities living in the dry lands of the

295 Article 1b.
296 Article 1e.
297 Government of Kenya (2002).

country.[298] Information and data gathered during the sensitisation forums were analysed to help in the development of NAP.[299] There was also support offered to local communities through the various community-based initiatives seeking to combat desertification, on a pilot basis, with a view to teaching the communities how to better manage local natural resources, enhance food security, and form partnerships with local communities.[300] Workshops were then held at both local and national levels for stakeholders to deliberate and make recommendations on NAP.

According to NAP published in 2002,[301] there were various constraints that stood in the way of efforts to combat desertification. These constraints included a sectoral approach that was adopted to programming; low and uncoordinated funding; frequent shifts of the mandate from one institution to another; inadequate legal, policy and regulatory frameworks; inadequate involvement of local communities in programming and decision-making; inadequate capacity for implementation, monitoring and evaluation; and inadequate access to production resources by local communities.[302] Some of the recommendations that came out of NAP include circulation and sensitisation of people on the contents of NAP; development of many viable projects and programmes geared towards implementation of NAP; mobilisation of resources from all possible sources necessary to implement NAP; ensuring that there are mechanisms for integrating NAP into national development processes including budgeting; and integrating NAP into regional and sub-regional programmes.[303]

According to a study conducted by the United Nations Development Programme on efforts to implement the CCD (Convention to Combat Desertification) in Kenya's dry lands[304] and published in 2013,[305] there are a variety of emerging lessons that may be gleaned and which for our purposes can be useful when considering future soil legislation. Some of the lessons drawn from the study are that improvement of livelihood and environmental management reinforce each other and that efforts to improve the former led to the improvement of the latter with the implication that efforts to reduce land degradation can be augmented by improving the economic position of the vulnerable, who then find little reason to further degrade land in search of a livelihood; participatory processes through an integrated approach whereby local communities are engaged by policymakers and development partners leads to better outcomes; local communities through community-based organisations have rich indigenous knowledge that they employed through 'traditional best practices' to avoid land

298 Ibid.
299 Ibid.
300 Ibid.: 4.
301 Ibid.
302 Ibid.
303 Ibid.: 55.
304 The study covered parts of Turkana, Baringo, Narok, Taveta and Malindi.
305 UNDP (2013).

degradation and soil erosion; continuous monitoring of initiatives leads to better outcomes; and practices that took into account the sociocultural perspectives of the local community tended to generate better results.[306]

Kenya as a country has tried to implement the various provisions of the CCD in a bid to prevent land degradation and combat desertification in the process. For instance, Kenya has since partnered with Japan International Cooperation Agency, Senegal and the CCD to launch what is now known as the African Initiative for Combating Desertification and Resilience to Climate Change in Sahel and the Horn of Africa.[307] In addition, Kenya is also undertaking a programme that seeks to promote the growing of drought-resistant trees known as *Melia volkensii,* which is to increase forest cover and therefore reduce soil erosion and land degradation, particularly in the vast dry lands within the country.[308] Furthermore, Kenya hosted the 15th Session of the Committee for the Review of the Implementation of the Convention, which is a subsidiary body of the UNCDD charged with tracking the implementation of the convention by state parties in October 2016.[309] In this session conference, Kenya intimated that it had a month before (in September 2016) launched an ambitious land restoration programme of massive pieces of land by the year 2030.[310]

5.1.4 Land degradation-neutrality

Land degradation neutrality (LDN) was defined in the 12th Session of the Conference of Parties to the UNCCD as "a state whereby the amount and quality of land resources necessary to support ecosystem functions and services and enhance food security remain stable or increase within specified temporal and spatial scales and ecosystems."[311] As a concept, LDN was formulated so as to encourage a good mix of measures that had the effect of reducing, avoiding or even altogether reversing land degradation so as to achieve a state of healthy land or soil.[312] At the core of LDN, then, are sustainable land management practices and better land use planning that takes care of the economic needs of both the present and future generations.[313]

LDN is a scientific conceptual framework within the UNCCD that seeks to ensure that avoidance of land degradation is integrated into planning processes and is supported by an enabling policy environment.[314] Decisions with respect to LDN can be

306 Ibid.: 29–35.
307 See http://www.environment.go.ke/?p=2874, accessed 26 October 2019.
308 Ibid.
309 Ibid.
310 Ibid.
311 UNCCD (2016).
312 Ibid.
313 Ibid.
314 Gichenje et al. (2019).

coordinated through the mechanism of land use planning, which is regulated by a separate and distinct legal regime in Kenya.[315] While there is no piece of legislation that expressly provides for LDN in Kenya, there are a number of laws and policies that either directly or indirectly affect the use of land particularly in the rural context, and which then indirectly may be said to be relevant in the implementation of LDN. It is to these policies and laws that we now devote our attention.

First, the Constitution provides for the right to a clean and healthy environment, including the right to have the environment protected for the benefit of present and future generations; and also has sustainability as one of the key principles of land policy.[316] Chapter five of the Constitution, which is basically devoted to land and environment, provides various principles, including the sustainable use and management of the environment and the sound conservation and protection of ecologically sensitive areas. Land generally, including soil, forms part of the environment and there is thus a constitutional imperative to ensure that the soil is both clean and healthy in a manner that enables it to sustain agricultural productivity. This vision of the environment, articulated in the Constitution, certainly cascades and informs all other policy and legal instruments relating to every sector of the economy and society. On the other hand, the constitutional provision that requires the increase of tree cover to at least 10% of the whole total land mass seeks to reduce or reverse the effects of land degradation that have occurred in the past on account of mass deforestation, and thus fits in well as a measure aimed towards achieving LDN.

The Environment Management and Coordination Act of 1999 (as amended to reflect the Constitution of Kenya 2010), which is the overarching statute with respect to matters relating to environmental management, provides for protection and conservation of the environment, including soil at Part V of the Act. The Act also calls for afforestation and reforestation practices, especially for the maintenance of mountain ecosystems, hilltops and hill slopes.

Other statutes that have provisions relating to soil conservation, and thus form a legal basis for the implementation of LDN, are the Agriculture and Food Authority Act of 2015, which prescribes the preparation of guidelines for purposes of conservation of soil or the prevention of adverse effects of soil erosion on land; and the Community Land Act of 2016, which allows for the making of rules and by-laws to guide the conservation and management of land by registered communities.

In addition, the National Environment Policy calls for the development of the National Soil Conservation Policy, which has yet to be done. The National Land Use Policy of 2017 calls for the strengthening of the regulatory and enforcement agencies to ensure conservation of the environment and proscribes settlement and the undertaking of other activities, such as farming on ecologically sensitive areas. The National

315 Ibid.

316 Constitution of Kenya, Articles 42 and 60.

Spatial Plan[317] contains various policy statements, such as the development of an integrated land-use master plan for arid and semi-arid lands; the need to strictly regulate the subdivision of land in high potential agricultural lands; and the preparation of integrated management plans for environmentally sensitive areas, for example forests, mountains and wetlands. The National Policy for the Sustainable Development of Northern Kenya and other Arid Lands[318] provides for the strengthening of research and extension systems that promote soil and water conservation, agroforestry and organic farming.

There are indeed other legal provisions that seek to offset the effect of land degradation and, as such, form part of the implementation matrix of LDN. For instance, the Environmental Management and Co-ordination Act of 1999 (EMCA) provides for environmental restoration orders, which may be given by NEMA or ELC, requiring a person who has given rise to land degradation or environmental damage to remedy such damage. There are virtually similar provisions in the Forest Management and Conservation Act of 2016 and the Wildlife Management and Conservation Act of 2013, both of which contain restoration orders or clauses with respect to mining and quarrying, which are permitted activities within forests and national parks.

Even at the county level, for instance, some county governments, such as those governing areas which suffer the most significant effects of land degradation, have taken legislative and policy measures. By way of illustration, the Makueni County Assembly passed the Makueni County Sand Conservation and Utilisation Act of 2015, which contains provisions seeking to promote the sustainable use of sand resources through afforestation and building of dams and gabions. These legal measures have the effect of reducing or reversing land degradation in the area and thus fit as LDN implementation measures.

In our view therefore, while there is no particular legislation that specifically speaks to LDN, there are various laws, policies, strategies and action plans, both at the national level and the county level, that contain provisions that advance LDN. This points to the need for policy coherence on issues of land degradation through the development and enactment of a soil conservation policy and law.

5.2 Regional policies and instruments

At the regional level on the African continent, a few treaties or instruments that have a bearing on soil conservation and prevention of land degradation exist. These instruments and initiatives are discussed below.

317 Government of Kenya (2016a).
318 Republic of Kenya, Sessional Paper No. 12 of 2012.

5.2.1 African Convention on the Conservation of Nature and Natural Resources, 1968

The African Convention on the Conservation of Nature and Natural Resources is a regional treaty for the African continent that was signed in Algiers in Algeria in 1968, revised in Maputo in 2003, and again revised and adopted on 7 March 2017. Over 30 countries, including Kenya, have ratified the treaty. The objectives of the convention are to enhance environmental protection; foster the conservation and sustainable use of natural resources; and to harmonise and coordinate policies in those fields – all with a view to achieving ecologically rational, economically sound, and socially acceptable development policies and programmes.[319] Some of the principles to guide state parties to the convention are that it is the right of all people to a satisfactory environment that is favourable to their development, and the individual and collective duty of states to ensure that developmental and environmental needs are met in a sustainable and equitable manner. The convention has defined natural resources that form the subject of protection under the convention as including soil.[320] In our view, it is impossible to achieve the objective and abide by the principle of the convention, namely, to ensure development and environmental needs are met without taking soil conservation into account. This is because soil is an important facet of social and economic development, because it enhances food security. More fundamentally, Article VI contains provisions relating to land and soil, and expressly provides that state parties will take effective measures to prevent land degradation and to that effect will develop long-term strategies for conservation and management of land resources, including soil. The convention further provides that states are to adopt measures for conservation and improvement of soil, including combating its erosion and misuse, and deterioration of its physical, biological, chemical and economic properties.[321] In particular, states are obligated to improve soil conservation, introduce sustainable farming practices, and control erosion caused by land misuse and mismanagement when implementing agricultural practices and undertaking agrarian reforms.[322] To this extent, therefore, it can be argued that this convention both directly and indirectly empowers state parties that have ratified it, including Kenya, to take measures to conserve soil and prevent land degradation.

319 Article II.
320 Article V(1).
321 Article VI(1) and (2).
322 Article VI(3b).

5.2.2 Action Plan of the African Union/New Partnership for Africa's Development Environment Initiative

The Action Plan of the African Union/New Partnership for Africa's Development Environment Initiative was prepared after a consultative and participatory leadership meeting of environment ministers in Africa under the auspices and leadership of the African Ministerial Conference on the Environment (AMCEN) in response to the call of the New Partnership for Africa's Development (NEPAD) for the development and adoption of an environment initiative to deal with Africa's environmental challenges. The action plan was adopted in Maputo on 12 July 2003 by the Summit of the African Heads of State and its implementation began in 2004. AMCEN work programme serves as an integral part of the action plan whose implementation is usually conducted by the United Nations Environment Programme (UNEP) and other collaborative agencies. Programme area 1 under the work programme of AMCEN covers the thematic area of combating desertification, land degradation and drought.

The implementation of the NEPAD initiative in general in Kenya was formalised through an executive order by the President in the year 2002, and a National Steering Committee was put in place to spearhead the participation of Kenya in the process. By the time the Environment Initiative Action Plan was being adopted in the following year, Kenya had already institutionalised the wider NEPAD initiative.

5.2.3 NEPAD's Initiative for the Resilience and Restoration of African Landscapes

The Initiative for the Resilience and Restoration of African Landscapes was launched by NEPAD in Paris on 6 December 2015. It seeks to build the resilience of landscapes on the African continent and particularly those in drylands and other vulnerable areas. The initiative is implemented through restoration efforts and specifically through biodiversity conservation, climate-smart agriculture, rangeland management, and forest and ecosystem conservation. The initiative works closely with the African Forest Landscape Restoration Initiative to bring up to 100 million hectares of degraded and deforested land on the continent under restoration by 2030. It is envisaged that the initiative will lead to improved soil fertility and food security, and combat desertification.

With respect to the level of implementation of the initiative in Kenya, we were unable to ascertain whether any programmes under the initiative have been rolled out. However, it is crucial to note that the Ministry of Environment and Natural Resources is currently spearheading the planting of 10 million trees in the Maasai Mau Forest within the larger Mau Forest Complex that serves as a vital water tower. The programme began with the planting of 3 million trees on 1 November 2019. Apart from ensuring water provision by protecting the water catchment area, the initiative will ensure the conservation of soil through reforestation and restoration programmes.

5.2.4 Protocol Concerning Protected Areas and Wild Fauna and Flora in the Eastern African Region, 1985

The Protocol Concerning Protected Areas and Wild Fauna and Flora in the Eastern African Region was adopted in Nairobi, Kenya, on 21 June 1985 with the objective of protecting threatened and endangered species of flora and fauna and important natural habitats within the East African region. Article 8 of the Protocol provides that parties are to establish protected areas to safeguard important ecosystems, including those that provide habitats for endangered, endemic, migratory and economically important species of flora and fauna. Soil and forests, which ensure soil conservation form important ecosystems or habitats for these species and therefore this Protocol by implication requires the protection of soil, albeit indirectly. The Protocol also prohibits activities that have adverse effects on the habitats of endangered species, including the destruction of critical habitats and, in our view, this subsumes the protection of soil from degradation.

5.3 National policies

5.3.1 National Environment Policy, 2014

The National Environment Policy[323] proposes measures to enhance conservation and management of ecosystems and sustainable use of natural resources. The policy states that urban environmental degradation – through a lack of appropriate waste management and sanitation systems – and industry- and transport-related pollution have an adverse impact on soil quality.[324] The main human activities contributing to environmental degradation in Kenya include unsustainable land use practices, poor soil and water management practices, deforestation, overgrazing and pollution.[325]

The measures proposed in the policy for conservation of soil are: development and implementation of a National Soil Conservation Policy; promotion and support of eco and organic farming so as to maintain soil fertility of wetlands, riverbanks, hilltops and slopes, and to protect them from unsustainable practices and prevent soil erosion and environmental degradation; promotion of good soil management practices to avert

323 Government of Kenya (2013b).
324 Ibid.: vi.
325 Ibid.: 4.

landslides, mudslides, floods and other disasters that are preventable; and involvement and empowerment of communities in soil conservation.[326]

5.3.2 National Land Policy, 2009

The National Land Policy was Kenya's first ever land policy. It provides policy direction for land administration, access to land, land-use planning, restitution of historical injustices, environmental degradation, land-use conflicts, control of unplanned proliferation of informal urban settlements, and a legal and institutional framework for land governance and management and land information management. It also addresses issues of tenure, compulsory acquisition and development control.

The policy states that sustainable land-use practices are key to the provision of food security and attainment of food self-sufficiency. It identifies key problems that need to be resolved at the level of policy and law, which include: land deterioration due to population pressure, massive soil erosion and variability in climatic patterns, among other things; uncontrolled subdivision of land; overstocking in rangelands; and lack of alternative innovative land uses and planning for diversification of the rural economy.[327] The policy also states that the government must ensure that all land is put into productive use on a sustainable basis by facilitating the implementation of key land policy principles on conservation of land quality, environmental audit and assessment, productivity targets and guidelines, land sizes and land-use planning.[328]

The policy stipulates that to restore the environmental integrity of land and facilitate sustainable management of land-based resources, the government will introduce incentives to encourage use of technology and scientific methods for soil conservation; encourage use of traditional land conservation methods; establish measures to control degradation of land through abuse of inputs and inappropriate land-use practices; and establish institutional mechanisms for conservation of the quality of land for environmental conservation purposes.[329]

The policy identifies the environmental problems Kenya faces as including the degradation of natural resources such as forests, wildlife, water, and marine and coastal resources, as well as soil erosion and the pollution of air, water and land. It calls for measures on conservation and sustainable management of the environment, ecosystem protection, urban environment management, and environmental assessment and audits, to address these problems.[330]

326 Ibid.: 18.
327 Government of Kenya (2009: 28).
328 Ibid.: 28.
329 Ibid.: 30.
330 Ibid.

EIAs and audits are also identified as tools for land management that the government should implement for all proposed projects, programmes and activities on land that have a likelihood to degrade the environment. Monitoring of urban and rural environmental degradation is also required to be done regularly: encouraging public participation in the monitoring and protection of the environment; instituting enforcement mechanisms such as the 'polluter pays principle'; and providing incentives to promote cleaner production and prevent pollution of soil, water and air.

5.3.3 National Land Use Policy, 2017

The overall goal of the National Land Use Policy[331] is to provide the legal, administrative, institutional and technological framework for optimal utilisation and productivity of land-related resources in a sustainable and desirable manner at the national, county and community levels.[332] The policy is premised on the philosophy of economic productivity, social responsibility, environmental sustainability and cultural conservation. Key principles informing it include efficiency, access to land-use information, equity, elimination of discrimination, and public benefit-sharing.[333]

The policy notes that the interaction between physical processes and human activities produce land cover changes or alterations of the properties of the land surface. These take different forms, such as conversion or modification, which leads to secondary environmental impacts (such as soil erosion, microclimatic changes and changes in water quality, among others) and reflects human goals mirrored on land use and land-use changes.[334] It points out that in several parts of the country, agricultural potential is limited because of erosion, low fertility, rockiness and acidity of the soils, and the danger of landslides.[335] Land deterioration has also occurred due to population pressure, massive soil erosion arising from poor land-use practices and variability in climatic patterns. This has led to rapid depletion of land cover and creeping desertification in arid and semi-arid lands, which has in turn affected the capacity for regeneration of the country's water catchment areas.[336] It notes that the country's coastal region is affected by soil erosion.[337] Further, cultivation on marginal lands and fragile ecosystems lead to environmental degradation and other challenges such as: loose soils, destruction of ecosystems and microclimatic conditions, soil erosion,

331 Government of Kenya (2017b).
332 Ibid.: v.
333 Ibid.
334 Ibid.: 14.
335 Ibid.: 16.
336 Ibid.: 17.
337 Ibid.

eutrophication and increased rainwater runoff.[338] Unsustainable farming methods in these sensitive areas have resulted in severe soil erosion and degradation, which has reduced the overall capacity for sustainable food production in the country,[339] massive soil erosion arising from bad land-use practices, and variability in climatic patterns.[340]

To promote and ensure productive and sustainable use of land, the policy exhorts the government to develop a framework to facilitate an assessment of land resources, including basic soil surveys, farming systems, soil degradation surveys, and production potentials of the soils in the country.[341] To address the problem of cultivation on marginal lands and fragile ecosystems, the government is required to encourage the use of modern farming practices that sustain crop yields and soil fertility.[342] The policy notes that soil mapping is done by different organisations, which affects coordinated action to sustainably manage soils. There is, therefore, a need for unified mechanisms for collection, storage and dissemination of environmental and natural resources information.[343]

5.3.4 National Climate Change Action Plan, 2013

The National Climate Change Action Plan aims to further develop Kenya's development goals by providing mechanisms and measures to achieve low-carbon climate-resilient development in a manner that prioritises adaptation. Priority adaptation actions identified in the plan which affect soil include increasing forest cover to 10% of total land area and rehabilitation of degraded lands.[344]

5.4 National Laws

5.4.1 The Constitution of Kenya, 2010

Kenya's 2010 Constitution fundamentally changed the legal landscape for environmental conservation, management, and dispute resolution mechanisms and processes in Kenya. In its preamble, the Constitution recognises the need to respect and sustain the environment for the benefit of current and future generations.

338 Ibid.: 23.
339 Ibid.: 24.
340 Ibid.: 37.
341 Ibid.: 38.
342 Ibid.: 44.
343 Ibid.: 53.
344 Government of Kenya (2018b: 37).

At the heart of the national values and principles of governance, which bind all persons and state organs, spelt out in the Constitution, is the principle of sustainable development.[345] Sustainable development is development that meets the needs of the present without compromising the ability of future generations to meet their own needs.[346]

The Constitution enhances access to environmental justice. For the first time in the history of Kenya, environmental rights are classified as fundamental human rights in the Constitution.[347] In this regard, every person in Kenya is entitled to a healthy soil environment and to be informed of the ecological state and condition of the soil. The Constitution also tempers the rigours of the doctrine of *locus standi* that had hitherto hampered access to environmental justice.[348] If a person alleges that a right to a clean and healthy environment has been, is being or is likely to be denied, violated, infringed or threatened, the person may apply to a court for redress in addition to any other legal remedies that are available in respect to these issues.[349]

Every citizen has the right of access to information held by the state and information held by another person and required for the exercise or protection of any right or fundamental freedom.[350] The need for a person to expressly make an application for access to information was affirmed by Mumbi Ngugi J. in *Nairobi Law Monthly Company Limited v Kenya Electricity Generating Company & 2 Others [2013]* eKLR, where she held that:

> what is required is for the person seeking information to make a request for such information. A violation of the right to information cannot be alleged before a request for information has been made.

However, while there is a condition for parties to expressly apply for such information, the High Court in *Nairobi Law Monthly Company Limited v Kenya Electricity Generating Company* held that even though the right to information implies entitlements to the citizen to information, it also imposes a duty on the state with regard to provision of information. Thus, the state has a duty not only to publish information proactively in the public interest, which in the judge's view is the import of Article 35(3) of the Constitution of Kenya. This provision imposes an obligation on the state to "publish and publicize any important information affecting the nation", and also to "provide open access to such specific information as people may require from the State".[351]

The Constitution establishes the Environment and Land Court (ELC),[352] a superior court of record, where all environment and land matters are to be adjudicated. The

345 Article 10(2)(d).
346 World Commission on Environment and Development (1987).
347 Article 42.
348 Article 70.
349 Article 70(1).
350 Article 35(1)(9)(a) and (b).
351 *Nairobi Law Monthly Company Limited v Kenya Electricity Generating Company & 2 Others [2013]* eKLR.
352 Article 162(2)(b).

court has powers to hear and determine disputes relating to soil conservation and management.

According to Article 60 of the Constitution, land in Kenya is held, used and managed in a manner that is equitable, efficient, productive and sustainable, and in accordance with the principles of sustainable and productive management of land resources as well as sound conservation and protection of ecologically sensitive areas. These principles are to be implemented through a national land policy developed and reviewed regularly by the national government and through legislation. Land is defined in the Constitution to include the surface of the earth and the subsurface rock and natural resources completely contained on or under the surface.[353] The state is given powers to regulate use of any land and property.[354]

The National Land Commission is mandated under Article 67 of the Constitution, to conduct research related to land and natural resources and to make recommendations to appropriate authorities. The commission could study specific aspects of soil and carry out ecological surveys to inform decision-making.

To manage and conserve the environment, the state is obliged under Article 69 of the Constitution to: ensure sustainable exploitation, utilisation, management and conservation of the environment and natural resources and ensure the equitable sharing of the accruing benefits; to work to achieve and maintain a tree cover of at least 10% of the land area of Kenya; to protect and enhance intellectual property in, and indigenous knowledge of, biodiversity and genetic resources, and biological diversity; to establish systems of environmental impact assessment, environmental audit and monitoring of the environment; to eliminate processes and activities that are likely to endanger the environment; and to utilise the environment and natural resources for the benefit of the people of Kenya.

These provisions have implications for soil governance. Further, every person has a duty to cooperate with state organs and other persons to protect and conserve the environment and ensure ecologically sustainable development and use of natural resources.[355] Consequently, every person has a duty to protect and conserve soil for the benefit of current and future generations. The state's obligations under Article 69 of the Constitution can be invoked for sustainable management of soil. For instance, given the importance of soil in maintenance of biodiversity, the state should, in particular, protect and manage soil biodiversity.

In regard to the distribution of functions between the national and county governments, the national government is responsible for the protection of the environment and natural resources with a view to establishing a durable and sustainable system of development, including, in particular fishing and hunting; protection of animals and

---

353 Article 260.

354 Article 66.

355 Article 69(2).

wildlife; water protection, securing efficient residual water, hydraulic engineering and the safety of dams; and energy policy.

The county governments are charged with the responsibility of implementing specific national government policies on natural resources and environmental conservation, including soil and water conservation, and forestry.[356] Soil conservation is therefore a shared function of both the national and county governments and they should work cooperatively and collaboratively to ensure sustainability.

The sharing of responsibilities between the two levels of government and the overall transition to the new form of governance have been slow and a source of conflict. County governments have had to force the national government to transfer the functions through courts.[357] The unwillingness of the national government to cede functions to counties and the uncertainty about the scope of the transferred functions have greatly hampered environmental conservation and efficient delivery of services, including disaster management.[358]

Although soil conservation is primarily a county government function, in practice the national government has retained most soil conservation activities. In areas where the function has been devolved to the counties, county governments have inadequate capacity and funds to adequately conserve the soil. It is worth noting that requisite resources to perform functions should accompany devolution. Further, the national government is obligated by the Constitution to build the capacity of counties to perform devolved functions. The retention of funds at the national level and devolution without capacity-building makes devolution ineffective and affects sectors such as land and soil.

Soil conservation, like other concurrent functions of both levels of government, has not been given much attention by either the national or the county government because of lack of clear role mapping.[359] The end result has been blame games, with each side evading their role. It is a matter of grave concern that the national government and county governments each have officers and institutions charged with performing the concurrent functions. For instance, the national government and the county governments have employed agricultural extension officers in respect of the same areas. The setting up of parallel systems has adversely affected service delivery in the agricultural sector where the two systems end up not delivering the much-needed services.

Sustainable soil governance hinges on cooperation between the two governments. The Supreme Court has held that this cooperation is inextricably linked to the proper harmonized formulation of policies, management, development and planning of land.[360]

---

356 Fourth Schedule.

357 *Kenya Ferry Services Limited v Mombasa County Government & 2 others* [2016] eKLR.

358 *Johnson Kamau Njuguna & another v Director of Public Prosecutions* [2018] eKLR.

359 Mulinge et al. (2016).

360 *Council of Governors & 3 others v Senate & 53 others* [2015] eKLR.

5.4.2 Environmental Management and Coordination Act, 1999 (as amended)

The Environmental Management and Co-ordination Act (EMCA) is the framework environmental law for Kenya. It establishes the legal and institutional framework for managing the environment. According to Section 2 of EMCA, 'environment' includes the physical factors of the surroundings of human beings including land, water, atmosphere, climate, sound, odour, taste, the biological factors of animals and plants and the social factor of aesthetics and includes both the natural and the built environment.

Section 5 of EMCA empowers the cabinet secretary in charge of environment and natural resources to formulate policies and set priorities for the protection of the environment. Section 5 also requires the cabinet secretary to promote cooperation among public departments, local authorities, private sector, non-governmental organisations and such other organisations engaged in environmental protection programmes. Implicitly, the cabinet secretary may formulate policies on soil management and protection.

EMCA establishes NEMA,[361] which exercises general supervision and coordination over all matters relating to the environment and is the principal instrument of government in the implementation of all policies relating to the environment.[362] Since soil issues are multidisciplinary in nature, NEMA can therefore coordinate activities being undertaken by public entities on protection and management of soil. Other functions of the authority include coordinating environmental management activities being undertaken by the lead agencies; taking stock of the natural resources; advising on land-use planning; undertaking research, investigating and surveying in the field of environment; and disseminating information on the findings; mobilising and monitoring the use of financial and human resources for environmental management; regulating, monitoring and assessing activities to ensure that the environment is not degraded; enforcing environmental standards; undertaking environmental education, public awareness and public participation programmes; developing, publishing and disseminating manuals, codes and guidelines relating to environmental management; preparing the State of the Environment in Kenya Report; and development and implementation of the national environment action plans.[363]

NEMA's functions under EMCA can be applied to protect and manage soils. NEMA can undertake soil research and prepare information on the ecological condition of the soil environment. Information on the soil environment forms part of the State of the Environment Report, which is prepared by NEMA bi-annually. In addition, NEMA can develop and implement educational and sensitisation programmes on

361 Section 7.
362 Section 9(1).
363 Section 9(2).

sustainable management of soils. NEMA can also prepare and disseminate information to the public on protection of soils.

In the following, some mechanisms and institutions provided for in EMCA that have the potential to protect soil shall be examined in more detail. These are general environmental protection mechanisms not specifically tailored to soil protection.

5.4.2.1 National Environment Trust Fund (NETFUND)

The National Environment Trust Fund is established under Section 24 of EMCA, 1999. A board of trustees administers the fund in accordance with a trust deed, which constitutes the rules and regulations that govern the operations and functions of the fund. The object and purpose of the fund is to facilitate research intended to further the requirements of environmental management, capacity-building, environmental awards, environmental publications, scholarships and grants. [364] Hence, the fund can support research on soil protection.

5.4.2.2 National Environment Restoration Fund

The 1999 EMCA also established the National Environment Restoration Fund.[365] Deposit bonds consist of such proportion of fees as may be determined by NEMA from time to time, as well as such sums as may be donated or levied from industries and other project proponents as a contribution towards the restoration fund. The restoration fund is vested in the authority and is administered by the director-general.[366] The restoration fund acts as supplementary insurance for the mitigation of environmental degradation where the perpetrator is not identifiable or where exceptional circumstances require the authority to intervene towards the control or mitigation of environmental degradation. Consequently, the restoration fund may be used to control to mitigate soil degradation. The cabinet secretary may, by notice in the *Gazette*, issue orders for the levying of funds from project proponents towards the restoration fund. Administrative procedures for undertaking soil rehabilitation and restoration should however be developed.

364 Section 24(4).

365 Section 25(1).

366 Section 25(3).

5.4.2.3 Deposit bonds

Under Section 28 of EMCA, the authority is required to create a register of those activities and industrial plants and undertakings which have or are most likely to have significant adverse effects on the environment when operated in a manner that is not in conformity with good environmental practices. The cabinet secretary responsible for finance may, on the recommendations of the cabinet secretary in charge of environment and natural resources, prescribe that persons engaged in activities or operating industrial plants and other undertakings identified in the register pay such deposit bonds as may constitute appropriate security for good environmental practice. The deposit bond determined should be refunded to the operator of the activity, industrial plant or any other undertaking by the authority after such duration not exceeding six months without interest where the operator has observed good environmental practices to the satisfaction of the authority. The authority may, after giving the operator an opportunity to be heard, confiscate a deposit bond where the operator is responsible for environmental practice that is in breach of the provisions of EMCA. The authority may in addition cancel any licence issued to the operator under this act if the authority is satisfied that the operator has become a habitual offender. Where operators are dissatisfied with the confiscation of their deposit bonds, they may refer the matter to a competent court of law. The proceeds of every refundable deposit bond levied are paid into the restoration fund and are treated as part of the restoration fund until refunded to the depositor. Any interest accruing from monies deposited into the restoration fund are for the benefit of the authority.

5.4.2.4 County environment committees

EMCA establishes the county environment committees (CECs).[367] The committees are constituted by the governor through a *Gazette* notice and are chaired by members of the executive committee in charge of environmental matters. Other members of the committee include one representative for each of the ministries responsible for the matters specified in the First Schedule of EMCA at the county level; two representatives of farmers or pastoralists within the county to be appointed by the governor; two representatives of the business community operating within the concerned county appointed by the governor; two representatives of the public benefits organisations engaged in environmental management programmes within the county. An officer of NEMA whose area of jurisdiction falls wholly or partially within the county is the secretary to the CEC.

367 Section 30.

In making the appointments, the governor should ensure that there are equal opportunities for persons with disabilities and other marginalised groups; and that not more than two-thirds of the members are of the same gender. Members of the CECs, except the chairperson and the secretary, are required to hold office for a period of three years and are eligible for re-appointment for one further term. The provision on the term of office for representatives of the ministries at the county level assumes that the length of posting of the representatives runs concurrently with the appointment as member of the CEC. However, this is not the case and there is a possibility that a ministerial representative continues to perform the functions of the Ministry at county level after their term as a member of the county environment committee has expired.

CECs are responsible for proper management of the environment within the county. They are also responsible for development of county strategic environmental action plans every five years. The committees may also perform such additional functions as are prescribed by EMCA or as may, from time to time, be assigned by the governor by notice in the *Gazette*. Soil protection could be one such additional function.

5.4.2.5 National Environment Complaints Committee (NECC)

The National Environment Complaints Commission is mandated to investigate any allegations or complaints against any person or against the authority in relation to the condition of the environment in Kenya. The NECC was established under Section 31 of the EMCA, 1999. It was formerly known as the Public Complaints Committee (PCC) but its name changed in the EMCA (Amendment) No. 5 of 2015). It is an important institution in the assessment of the condition of the environment in Kenya. It plays an important role in the facilitation of alternative dispute resolution mechanisms relating to environmental matters. The NECC makes recommendations to the Cabinet Secretary and thus contributes significantly to the formulation and development of environmental policy. The commission is also mandated on its own motion, to investigate any suspected case of environmental degradation, and to make a report of its findings together with its recommendations thereon to the council. It can also undertake public interest litigation on behalf of the citizens in environmental matters. Hence the commission can take legal action against any person who causes soil degradation.

5.4.2.6 National Environment Action Plans

The authority is required to formulate the National Environmental Action Plan every six years through a participatory process. The authority is required to submit the plan to the cabinet secretary for approval. Upon approval of the plan, the cabinet secretary has an obligation to submit the plan to the National Land Commission and the Ministry responsible for land. The cabinet secretary is required to publish the plan in the *Gazette*. NEMA should review the National Environment Action Plan every three years. The plan is binding on all persons, government departments, agencies, state corporations and other organs of government upon adoption by the National Assembly.

The purpose of environmental action plans is to coordinate and harmonise environmental policies, plans, programmes and decisions of the national and county governments, as the case may be, in order to minimise the duplication of procedures and functions; promote consistency in the exercise of functions that may affect the environment; secure the protection of the environment across the country; and prevent unreasonable actions by any person, state organ or public entity in respect of the environment that are prejudicial to the economic or health interests of other counties or the country.[368] Soil plans could be integrated in the National Environmental Action Plans.

5.4.2.7 County Environment Action Plans

Every county environment committee is required to develop a county environmental action plan in respect of the county every five years through a participatory process. This action plan is considered and adopted by the County Assembly. In preparing a county environment plan, the County Environment Committee should take into consideration every other county environment action plan already adopted, with a view to achieving consistency among such plans. Upon adoption by the County Assembly, the County Environment Action Plan should be submitted to the cabinet secretary for incorporation into the national environment action plan. Every county environment action plan should contain provisions dealing with matters contained in the National Environment Action Plan in relation to their respective county.[369]

The authority is obligated to consider every county environment action plan and either recommend incorporation of such plan into the National Environment Action Plan or specify changes to be incorporated into a county environmental plan. The cabinet secretary is empowered, on the recommendation of NEMA, to issue guidelines and prescribe measures for the preparation of environmental action plans. The guidelines and measures may include guidelines on soil planning, ecological limits of use of soil, soil zoning and soil classification. The contents of the county environmental plans are similar to those of the National Environment Action Plan.

368 Section 41(A).
369 Section 40.

5.4.2.8 Monitoring compliance with Environmental Plans

The obligation for monitoring compliance with national and county environmental action plans rests with NEMA.[370] NEMA may take any steps or make any inquiries that it may consider necessary in order to determine if the plans are being complied with. If as a result of any action taken or inquiry, NEMA is of the opinion that a plan is not substantially being complied with, NEMA will serve a written notice to the organ concerned, calling on it to take such specified steps NEMA may consider necessary to remedy noncompliance. Within 30 days of the receipt of the notice, the organ will respond to the notice in writing, setting out any objections to the notice; the action that will be taken to ensure compliance with the plan; or other information that the organ considers relevant to the notice.

After considering the representations from the organ and any other relevant information, NEMA will within 30 days of receiving the response issue a final notice to either confirm amend or cancel the notice or to specify any action and a time period within which such action must be taken to remedy non-compliance. The authority should keep a record of all environmental action plans and ensure that such plans are available for inspection by the public.

5.4.2.9 Protection and conservation of the environment

Part V of EMCA deals with the conservation and management of various aspects of the environment. These include the rivers, lakes, wetlands, genetic resources, hill tops, hill sides, mountain areas and forests. Section 44 requires the authority, in consultation with the relevant lead agencies, to develop, issue and implement regulations, procedures, guidelines and measures for the sustainable use of hill sides, hill tops, mountain areas and forests, and such regulations, guidelines, procedures and measures will control the harvesting of forests and any natural resources located in or on a hill side, hill top or mountain area so as to protect water catchment areas, prevent soil erosion and regulate human settlement. Under Section 45(1), every county environment committee is required to identify the hilly and mountainous areas under their jurisdiction which are at risk of environmental degradation. A hilly or mountainous area is at risk of environmental degradation if it is prone to soil erosion; landslides have occurred in such areas; vegetation cover has been removed or is likely to be removed from the area at a rate faster than it is being replaced; or any other land-use activity in such an area is likely to lead to environment degradation.

Every county environment committee must specify which of the areas identified are to be targeted for afforestation or reforestation. Every committee must take measures,

370 Section 41(B).

through encouraging voluntary self-help activities in its local community, to plant trees or other vegetation which are within the limits of its jurisdiction. Where the areas specified are subject to leasehold or any other interest in land, including customary tenure, the holder of that interest must implement measures required to be implemented by the county environment committee, including measures to plant trees and other vegetation in those areas.[371]

Section 47 of EMCA obligates the authority, in consultation with the relevant lead agencies, to issue guidelines and prescribe measures for the sustainable use of hill tops, hill slides and mountainous areas. The guidelines issued and measures prescribed by the authority must be by way of *Gazette* notice and must include those relating to appropriate farming methods; carrying capacity of the hill tops, hill slides and mountainous areas in relation to animal husbandry; measures to curb soil erosion; disaster preparedness in areas prone to landslides; the protection of the hill tops, hill slides and mountainous areas from human settlements; the protection of water catchment areas; and any other measures the authority considers necessary. The county environment committee is responsible for ensuring that the guidelines issued, and measures prescribed in respect of their counties are implemented. Any person who contravenes any measure prescribed by the authority or who fails to comply with a lawful direction issued by a county environment committee is guilty of an offence.

5.4.2.10 Integrated environmental impact assessment

According to Section 57A of EMCA, all policies, plans and programmes for implementation must be subjected to strategic environmental assessment. Strategic environmental assessment is a formal and systematic process to analyse and address the environmental effects of policies, plans, programmes and other strategic initiatives.[372] The plans, programmes and policies that are subject to strategic environmental assessment are those that are prepared or adopted by an authority or parliament at national, county and regional levels. The authority may also determine the policies, plans and programmes which should be subjected to strategic environmental assessment because they are likely to have significant effects on the environment.[373] The costs of undertaking the strategic environmental assessments are to be borne by the entities preparing the plans, programmes and policies.[374] The assessments are submitted to the authority for approval.[375] The authority, in consultation with lead agencies and relevant

371 Section 46.
372 Section 2.
373 Section 57(A)(2).
374 Section 57(A)(3).
375 Section 57(A)(3).

stakeholders, is required to prescribe rules and guidelines in respect of strategic environmental assessments.[376]

Notwithstanding any approval, permit or licence granted under this Act or any other law in force in Kenya, any proponent of a project must, before applying for any financing, commencing, proceeding with, carrying out, executing, conducting or causing to be financed, commenced, proceeded with, carried out, executed or conducted by another person any undertaking specified in the Second Schedule of the Act, submit a project report to the authority, in the prescribed form, giving the prescribed information and accompanied by the prescribed fee.[377] The proponent of any project specified in the Second Schedule[378] must undertake a full environmental impact assessment study and submit an environmental impact assessment study report to the authority prior to being issued with any licence by the authority provided that the authority may direct that the proponent forego the submission of the environmental impact assessment study report in certain cases.[379] In undertaking environmental impact assessments, proponents of projects have been undertaking soil environmental impact assessments.

To regulate the practice of integrated environmental assessments, the cabinet secretary is mandated, in consultation with NEMA, to make regulations and formulate guidelines for the practice of integrated environmental impact assessments and environmental audits.[380] The cabinet secretary is also mandated to make regulations for the accreditation of experts on environmental impact assessments.[381] A person who knowingly submits a report which contains information that is false or misleading commits an offence and is liable, on conviction, to a term of imprisonment of not more than three years, or to a fine of not more than five million shillings, or to both the fine and imprisonment, and in addition his licence will be revoked.[382]

NEMA may cancel or revoke a licence; suspend such licence, for such time, not more than 24 months, where the licensee contravenes the provisions of the licence. Where the authority cancels, revokes or suspends a licence in accordance with this section, the reasons for such action must be given to the licensee in writing.

To enhance public access to information contained in the environmental impact assessment reports, the authority is required to cause to be published a notice of a proposed project not only in the *Gazette* and at least two newspapers circulating in the

376 Section 57(A)(4).
377 Section 58(1).
378 The activities listed in the Second Schedule which impact on soils include changes in land use, urban development, transportation and related infrastructure projects, mining activities and hydrocarbon projects.
379 Section 58(2).
380 Section 58(6)(A).
381 Section 58 (6)(B).
382 Section 58(10).

area or proposed area of the project, but also over the radio.[383] NEMA is furthermore obliged to ensure that its website contains a summary of the environmental impact assessment reports.[384] This presents an opportunity to members of the public to access information on soil and involve themselves in decision-making.

5.4.2.11 Environmental monitoring

The authority, in consultation with the relevant lead agencies, is mandated to monitor all environmental phenomena with a view to making an assessment of any possible changes in the environment and their possible impacts; or the operation of any industry, project or activity with a view of determining its immediate and long-term effects on the environment.[385] An environmental inspector appointed under EMCA may enter any land or premises for the purposes of determining how far the activities carried out on that land or premises conform to the statements made in the Environmental Impact Assessment Study Report issued in respect of that land or those premises.[386] The owner of the premises or the operator of a project for which an environmental impact assessment study report has been made must keep accurate records and make annual reports to the authority describing how far the project conforms in operation with the statements made in the Environmental Impact Assessment Study Report.[387] The owner of a premises or the operator of a project must take all reasonable measures to mitigate any undesirable effects not contemplated in the Environmental Impact Assessment Study Report and must prepare and submit an environmental audit report on those measures to the authority annually or as the authority may, in writing, require.[388]

5.4.2.12 Environmental quality standards

The cabinet secretary in charge of environment and natural resources on recommendation of the authority is empowered to prescribe minimum water quality standards;[389] minimum air quality standards;[390] standards for waste; their classification and analysis;[391] standard criteria for the classification of hazardous wastes;[392] standards for the

383 Section 59(1).
384 Section 59(3).
385 Section 69(1).
386 Section 68(2).
387 Section 68(3).
388 Section 68(4).
389 Section 71.
390 Section 78.
391 Section 85.
392 Section 91.

concentration of pesticide residues in raw agricultural commodities;[393] minimum standards for emissions of noise and vibration pollution;[394] and standards for setting acceptable levels of ionizing and other radiation in the environment.[395] Regarding standards for waste, the cabinet secretary must, on the recommendation of the authority identify materials and processes that are dangerous to human health and the environment; issue guidelines and prescribe measures for the management of the materials and processes identified to be injurious to the environment; prescribe standards for waste, their classification and analysis, and formulate and advise on standards of disposal methods and means for such wastes; or issue regulations for the handling, storage, transportation, segregation and destruction of any waste. It is an offence for any person to discharge or dispose of any wastes, whether generated within or outside Kenya, in such manner as to cause pollution to the environment or ill health to any person.[396] It is an offence for any person to discharge a hazardous substance, chemical, oil or mixture containing oil into any waters or other areas of the environment.[397] A person convicted of the offence will, in addition to any other sentence imposed by the court, pay the cost of the removal of the hazardous substance, chemical, oil or mixture containing oil including any costs which may be incurred by any government agency or organ in the restoration of the environment damaged or destroyed as a result of the discharge; and the costs of third parties in the form of reparation, restoration, restitution or compensation, as may be determined by a competent court on application by such third parties.[398]

With regard to pesticides and toxic substances, the cabinet secretary must, on the recommendation of the authority, establish standards to regulate the importation, exportation, manufacture, storage, distribution, sale, use, packaging, transportation, disposal and advertisement of pesticides and toxic substances in consultation with the relevant organisations, determine measures for monitoring the effects of pesticides and toxic substances on the environment; determine measures for the establishment and maintenance of laboratories to operate as standards laboratories for pesticides and toxic substances; and determine measures for the establishment of enforcement procedures and regulations for the storage, packaging and transportation of pesticides and toxic substances.

393 Section 94.
394 Section 101.
395 Section 104.
396 Section 87(1).
397 Section 93(2).
398 Section 93(3).

5.4.2.13 Environmental restoration orders

The authority may issue and serve on any person an environmental restoration order in respect of any matter relating to the management of the environment.[399] An environmental restoration order requires the person on whom it is served to restore the environment to as near as it may be to the state in which it was before the taking of the action which is the subject of the order; prevents the person on whom it is served from taking any action which would or is reasonably likely to cause harm to the environment; awards compensation to be paid by the person on whom it is served to other persons whose environment or livelihood has been harmed by the action which is the subject of the order; and levies a charge on the person on whom it is served which in the opinion of the authority represents a reasonable estimate of the costs of any action taken by an authorised person or organisation to restore the environment to the state in which it was before the taking of the action which is the subject of the order.

An environmental restoration order may require a person on whom it is served to take such action as will prevent the commencement or continuation or cause of pollution; restore land, including the replacement of soil, the replanting of trees and other flora; and the restoration, as far as may be, of outstanding geological, archaeological or historical features of the land or the area contiguous to the land or sea, as may be specified in the particular order; take such action to prevent the commencement or continuation or cause of environmental hazard; cease to take any action which is causing or may contribute to causing pollution or an environmental hazard; remove or alleviate any injury to land or the environment or to the amenities of the area; prevent damage to the land or the environment, aquifers beneath the land and flora and fauna in, on or under or about the land or sea specified in the order or land or the environment contiguous to the land or sea specified in the order; remove any waste or refuse deposited on the land or sea specified in the order and dispose of the same in accordance with the provisions of the order; pay any compensation specified in the order.

5.4.2.14 Environmental easements and environmental conservation orders

A court may grant an environmental easement or an environmental conservation order.[400] An environmental conservation order may be imposed on burdened land so as to preserve flora and fauna; preserve the quality and flow of water in a dam, lake, river or aquifer; preserve any outstanding geological, physiographical, ecological, archaeological or historical features of the burdened land; preserve scenic view; preserve open space; permit persons to walk in a defined path across the burdened land; preserve the

399 Section 108.
400 Section 112.

natural contours and features of the burdened land; prevent or restrict the scope of any activity on the burdened land which has as its object the mining and working of mineral aggregates; prevent or restrict the scope of an agricultural activity on the burdened land; create and maintain works on the burdened land so as to limit or prevent harm to the environment; or create or maintain migration corridors for wildlife.

5.4.2.15 Integrated National Land Use Guidelines

In the exercise of its powers under Section 9(2) of EMCA, NEMA has developed the Integrated National Land Use Guidelines.[401] The guidelines are for rivers and lakes and propose a buffer zone of 30 m for lakes for purposes of minimising soil erosion.[402] Guidelines for coastal zone areas include protecting near-shore coral reefs from damaging activities such as soil erosion. With regard to agricultural land, the guidelines propose the development and mapping of soil capability profiles for the country in order to carry out different sustainable agricultural activities.[403] In addition, the guidelines provide that crop production should be done depending on adaptation to designated agro-ecological zones, soil characteristics, recommended agricultural practices and appropriate technologies.[404] With cultivation on slopes from 0% – 12%, contour farming and the use of soil conservation measures are recommended; at 12% – 55% soil conservation measures are compulsory; and above 55% perennial/permanent crops (such as Napier grass, tea, bananas and trees) should be planted.[405] To protect soil against erosion, the guidelines recommend ploughing and planting along the contours, practising crop rotation, applying manure to crops, leaving crop residue on the ground and practising terracing.[406]

The guidelines make specific mention of red soil harvesting. The guidelines encourage the rehabilitation of degraded areas as recommended in environmental impact assessments, environmental audits and environmental management or as per restoration provisions of EMCA.[407] The guidelines prohibit loose hanging material near or on the face of excavations and quarries. Red soil harvesting should not be carried out in road reserves, near dwellings, and in other environmentally sensitive areas.[408] The guidelines prohibit vertical faces exceeding 2.5 m when quarrying on red soil.[409]

---

401 National Environment Management Authority (2011).
402 Ibid.: 6.
403 Ibid.: 20.
404 Ibid.
405 Ibid.
406 Ibid.: 21.
407 Ibid.: 28.
408 Ibid.
409 Ibid.

On flood-prone areas, the guidelines recommend afforestation, tree planting, and water and soil conservation in catchment areas and along watercourses.[410] On landside-prone areas, the guidelines recommend intensification of soil and water conservation measures in already settled landslide-prone areas.[411] Siting of infrastructure in landslide-prone areas should be determined by slope, soil characteristics and vegetation cover.[412]

5.4.2.16 Assessment of the effectiveness of the Environmental Manangement and Co-ordination Act

NEMA is tasked to study and examine land-use patterns to determine their impact on the quality and quantity of the natural resources, including soil, and to make recommendations on land planning in Kenya.[413] The proper performance of this function requires coordination with other government land-use players, such as the Ministry of Lands and Physical Planning, the National Land Commission and county governments. According to the National Land Use Policy, lack of institutional coordination and harmony in the various statutes establishing various government institutions poses a challenge to the overall management of land use in the country.[414] Accordingly, the government through the National Land Use Policy passed in 2017 aims at providing institutional coordination in land-use planning across all relevant sectors where lack of coordination has led to infringement of agricultural areas, urban sprawl and environmental degradation.[415]

Another factor that has an impact on the effectiveness of EMCA is inadequate resource mapping in Kenya, which limits the effectiveness of environmental conservation measures. Soil conservation requires physical information of vulnerable land and the identifying of available land, and the protection of watersheds, vegetation, topography and drainage courses. Notably, the focus has been on land (mostly water, forests and land accessibility), but not on soils. [416]

As mentioned, the effectiveness of EIA as a tool for balancing development and environmental conservation to mitigate environmental degradation can be enhanced.[417] EIA can, for instance, be used to address soil pollution from industrial and urban activity. In reality, however, either no EIA is undertaken in many instances where capital

410 Ibid.
411 Ibid.: 29.
412 Ibid.
413 Environment Management and Coordination Act, 1999, Section 9.
414 Government of Kenya, National Land Use Policy, Sessional Paper, No. 1 of 2017, 20.
415 Government of Kenya, National Land Use Policy, Sessional Paper, No. 1 of 2017.
416 Government of Kenya, Royal Netherlands Government & UNEP "National Land Degradation Assessment and Mapping in Kenya" 1997.
417 Environment Management and Coordination Act, 1999, Section 57.

intensive projects are carried out or, if undertaken, EIA does not meet the legal threshold. This was the case in *Cortec Mining Kenya Limited v Cabinet Secretary Ministry of Mining & 9 Others [2015] eKLR* where mining licences were cancelled on account of failure to conduct EIA.[418] In instances where the EIA does not meet the legal threshold or is not undertaken at all, the projects have an unmitigated negative impact on the environment. Soil and water resources have been on the receiving end in this regard.

Cognizant of the fact that poor water quality could be the source of the soil degradation, EMCA requires that the cabinet secretary in charge of the environment, in consultation with NEMA, establishes the water quality for agricultural purposes.[419] Such water quality precludes the use of contaminated water in irrigation. In this regard, the Environmental Management and Coordination Quality Regulations, 2006, were promulgated. Regulation 19 prohibits the use of wastewater for irrigation purposes, unless such water complies with standards set out in the Eighth Schedule of these regulations. A study carried out on the quality of water used in Kenya's largest irrigation scheme, Mwea Irrigation Scheme, revealed that wastewater with high toxic chemicals was widely used in the irrigation scheme, lowering the quality of soils and leading to low productivity.[420]

The law also prohibits disposal of hazardous waste into the environment without a valid permit. The law defines the term hazardous waste as any chemical, waste, gas, medicine, drug, plant, animal or microorganism which is likely to be injurious to human health or the environment.[421] Ideally, the issuance of a licence ensures that the waste is properly disposed of to minimise environmental impact. Despite the heavy penalty imposed for disposing hazardous waste into the environment without a permit, this provision is barely observed.[422] Unfortunately, even government entities do not manage the dumpsites and wastes properly, which leads to further environmental degradation. In many instances, citizens have had to force the government to manage waste properly through court actions.[423]

On regulation of standards of pesticides and toxic substances, the law mandates the cabinet secretary, on the recommendation of NEMA, to determine standards to regulate the importation, exportation, manufacture, storage, distribution, sale, use, packaging, transportation, disposal and advertisement of pesticides and toxic substances.[424] Although Kenya has launched various measures to combat illicit trading of chemicals

---

418 See also *Save Lamu & 5 others v National Environmental Management Authority (NEMA) & another [2019] eKLR*, where National Environment Tribunal nullified an EIA licence on the grounds that due process of undertaking the EIA was not followed.

419 Environment Management and Coordination Act, 1999, Section 71.

420 Nyabonyi (2016).

421 Environment Management and Coordination Act, 1999, Section 91.

422 Wasilwa & Nanjala (2019).

423 *African Centre for Rights and Governance (ACRAG) & 3 others v Municipal Council of Naivasha* [2017] eKLR.

424 Environment Management and Coordination Act, 1999, Section 94.

and fertilizers, it is still widespread and the agricultural sector is negatively affected by substandard products, as will be discussed below.

5.4.3 Forest Conservation and Management Act, 2016

The Forest Conservation and Management Act[425] provides for the development and sustainable management, including conservation and rational utilisation, of all forest resources for the socioeconomic development of the country and related purposes. According to the Act, 'forest produce' includes, among other things, limestone, murram and soil.[426]

Section 7 of the Act establishes the Kenya Forest Service. The functions of the service are to conserve, protect and manage all public forests in accordance with the provisions of the Act; prepare and implement management plans for all public forests; and, where requested, assist in preparation of management plans for community forests or private forests in consultation with the relevant owners; receive and consider applications for licences or permits in relation to forest resources or management of forests or any other relevant matter in accordance with this Act; establish and implement benefit-sharing arrangements in accordance with the provisions of the Act; assist county governments to build capacity in forestry and forest management in the counties; develop, in consultation with relevant stakeholders, programmes for tourism and recreational and ceremonial use of public forests; promote forestry education and training; register and maintain a register of all forest management plans prepared for public forests; collaborate with relevant persons in identifying research needs and applying research findings in relation to forests and forestry; and manage water catchment areas in relation to soil and water conservation, carbon sequestration and other environmental services in collaboration with relevant stakeholders.

All indigenous forests and woodlands will be managed on a sustainable basis for purposes of conservation of water, soil and biodiversity, as well as riparian and shoreline protection.[427]

5.4.3.1.1 Quarrying

The Kenya Forest Service should only grant its consent for quarrying operations in a forest area where an independent environmental impact assessment or audit has been

425 No. 34 of 2016.
426 Section 2.
427 Section 42(1)(a) and (b).

carried out.[428] The cabinet secretary will, on the recommendation of the service, and in consultation with the cabinet secretary responsible for the environment and the relevant government agencies, publish rules to regulate and govern quarrying operations in forest areas. The conditions on which a licence for quarrying any allied activity carried out in the forest, will, where the activity concerned is likely to result in the depletion of forest cover in any forest, include a condition requiring the licensee to undertake compulsory restoration and re-vegetation immediately upon the completion of the activity.[429] Re-vegetation will be undertaken in consultation with the service, which will determine the seeds and seedlings proposed to be used in the re-vegetation.[430]

5.4.3.1.2 Incentives for increasing forest and tree cover

The cabinet secretary for the National Treasury may propose tax and other fiscal incentives to increase investments in forestland use and forest resource utilisation in order to promote forest conservation and management, and to prevent or arrest forest degradation.[431] The tax and fiscal incentives may include the following: a customs and excise waiver in respect of imported capital goods or tax rebates to forest industries and other establishments investing in plants, equipment and machinery for improved resource utilisation and for using other energy resources as substitutes for hydrocarbons; exemption from payment of all or part of the land rates and other such charges as may be levied in respect of the land on which a private forest is established; and income and other tax deductions to landowners in exchange for the establishment of a forest conservation easement.[432] The cabinet secretary will plan and execute programmes necessary for observing the national tree-planting week and the International Day of Forests.[433]

Section 64 of the Act prohibits certain activities in the forest, except under a licence or permit or a management agreement issued or entered into under the Act. No person is permitted, in a public or provisional forest, to fell, cut, take, burn, injure or remove any forest produce; smoke, where smoking is prohibited by notice, or kindle, carry or throw down any fire, match or other lighted material; de-pasture or allow any livestock to run there; clear, cultivate or break up land for cultivation or for any other purpose; construct any road or path; or set fire, or assist any person to set fire, to any grass or undergrowth or any forest produce. Any person who undertakes any of the prohibited

428 Section 46(1)(c).
429 Section 46(4).
430 Section 46(5).
431 Section 54(1).
432 Section 54(2).
433 Section 55.

activities commits an offence and is liable, on conviction, to a fine not exceeding 100,000 shillings or to imprisonment for a term not exceeding six months, or to both the fine and imprisonment.

5.4.4 Water Act, 2016

The Water Act[434] provides for the regulation, management and development of water resources, water and sewerage services, and other related purposes. According to the Act, 'water resource management' means the conservation, including soil and water conservation, protection, development and utilisation of water resources.[435] A person may not provide water services except under a licence issued by the Regulatory Board, upon submission of an application and such supporting documents as the board may require.[436] A licensee may enter into an agreement with any person with respect to the execution and maintenance, by any party to the agreement, of such works as the licensee considers necessary or as the conditions of the licence may require for the purpose of protecting the catchment areas, draining of land, carrying out soil conservation measures, controlling vegetation or effectively collecting, conveying or preserving the purity and quantity of water which the licensee is for the time being authorised to take.[437]

5.4.5 Climate Change Act, 2016

Kenya has a National Climate Change Action Plan,[438] a National Climate Change Framework Policy[439] and a Climate Change Act.[440] These legal instruments seek to reduce causes of climate change, to create climate change resilience, to enable climate financing, to manage knowledge, to develop capacity, and to cater for technology requirements, monitoring and reporting.

The Climate Change Act applies to the development, management, implementation and regulation of mechanisms to enhance climate change resilience and low carbon development for the sustainable development of Kenya. It applies in all sectors of the economy and is implemented by the national and county governments to mainstream climate change responses in development planning, decision-making and

434 No. 43 of 2016.
435 Section 2.
436 Section 85(1).
437 Section 104(1).
438 2013.
439 2016.
440 No. 11 of 2016.

implementation; to build resilience and enhance adaptive capacity to the impacts of climate change; to formulate programmes and plans to enhance the resilience and adaptive capacity of human and ecological systems to the impacts of climate change; to mainstream and reinforce climate change disaster risk reduction into strategies and actions of public and private entities; and to mainstream intergenerational and gender equity in all aspects of climate change responses, among others.[441]

The Act establishes the Climate Change Council, which provides an overarching national climate change coordination mechanism. The council is required to ensure the mainstreaming of the climate change function by the national and county governments and to approve and oversee implementation of the National Climate Change Action Plan.[442] The Act also establishes the Climate Change Directorate, which provides analytical support on climate change to the various sector ministries, agencies and county governments.[443]

Kenya has positioned itself as a global leader in sustainable development of energy production by greening the energy sector. In this regard, Kenya currently hosts the largest wind power plant in Africa.[444] The country's bourse regulator, the Capital Markets Authority, has approved the trading of Kenya's first green bond to build environmentally friendly student accommodation.[445] Lending institutions, cognizant of the threat posed by climate change, have been offering credit guidance to land and soil conservation. For instance, F3 Life, a private lender, offers farmers affordable green loans whose interest rates are determined by the quality of soil conservation practised by the farmer. This is a transformative integrated agenda that combines credit and soil conservation.[446]

5.4.6 Land laws

Land tenure types and policies usually influence land-use practices and hence affect the quality of soils. All land in Kenya belongs to the people of Kenya collectively as a nation, as communities and as individuals.[447] Land is classified as public, community or private.[448]

---

441 Section 2.
442 Section 6.
443 Section 9.
444 Salaudeen (2019).
445 See https://www.cma.or.ke/index.php?option=com_content&view=article&id=591:press-release-cma-approves-kenya-s-first-green-bond&catid=12:press-center&Itemid=207 accessed 6 November 2019.
446 See http://farmbizafrica.com/profit-boosters/1434-farm-loan-pegs-interest-on-soil-conservation, accessed 3 November 2019.
447 Article 61(1) of the Constitution.
448 Article 61(2) of the Constitution.

Public land comprises alienated government land used or occupied by any state organ, except land that is occupied by the state organ as lessee under a private lease; land transferred to the state by way of sale, reversion or surrender; and land in respect of which no individual or community ownership can be established by any legal process; land in respect of which no heir can be identified by any legal process; all minerals and mineral oils; government forests and other community forests; game reserves, water catchment areas, national parks, government animal sanctuaries, and specially protected areas; all roads and thoroughfares; all rivers, lakes and other water bodies; the territorial sea, the exclusive economic zone and the sea bed; the continental shelf; all land between the high and low water marks; any land not classified as private or community land under the Constitution; and any other land declared to be public land by an act of Parliament.[449]

Public land vests in and is held by a county government in trust for the people resident in the county, and is administered on their behalf by the National Land Commission, if it is classified as alienated government land; land transferred to the state by way of sale, reversion or surrender; land in respect of which no individual or community ownership can be established by any legal process; and land in respect of which no heir can be identified by any legal process and land lawfully held, used or occupied by any state organ, except any such land that is occupied by the state organ as lessee under a private lease other than land held, used or occupied by a national state organ.[450] All other public land vests in and is held by the national government in trust for the people of Kenya and is administered on their behalf by the National Land Commission.[451] Public land, especially forestland is often invaded by individuals or groups because of insecurity of tenure. The invaders usually over-exploit the resources, leading to soil degradation.

Community land vests in and is held by communities identified on the basis of ethnicity, culture or similar communities of interest.[452] Community land consists of land lawfully registered in the name of group representatives under the provisions of any law; land lawfully transferred to a specific community by any process of law; any other land declared to be community land by an act of Parliament; land that is lawfully held, managed or used by specific communities as community forests, grazing areas or shrines; ancestral lands and lands traditionally occupied by hunter-gatherer communities; or land lawfully held as trust land by the county governments, but not including any public land held in trust by the county government.[453] Any unregistered community land is held in trust by county governments on behalf of the communities for which

449 Article 62(1) of the Constitution.
450 Article 62(2) of the Constitution.
451 Article 62(3) of the Constitution.
452 Article 63(1) of the Constitution.
453 Article 63(2) of the Constitution.

it is held.[454] Private land consists of registered land held by any person under any freehold tenure; land held by any person under leasehold tenure; and any other land declared private land under an act of Parliament.[455]

5.4.6.1 Land Act, 2012

The Land Act[456] gives effect to Article 68 of the Constitution. It also consolidates and rationalises land laws and provides for the sustainable administration and management of land and land-based resources. Article 68 empowers Parliament to revise, consolidate and rationalise existing land laws; revise sectoral land-use laws in accordance with the principles set out in Article 60(1); enact legislation to, among others, prescribe minimum and maximum land-holding acreages in respect of private land; regulate the manner in which any land may be converted from one category to another; and protect, conserve and provide access to all public land.

With regard to management and administration of land, the cabinet secretary is empowered to develop policies on land, upon the recommendation of the National Land Commission; facilitate the implementation of land policy and reforms; coordinate the management of the National Spatial Data Infrastructure; monitor and evaluate land sector performance; provide policy direction regarding all classes of land in consultation with the commission, where appropriate; and coordinate the development and implementation of a National Land Information System in collaboration with the commission.[457]

In managing public land on behalf of the national and county governments, the commission evaluates all parcels of public land based on land capability classification, land resources mapping considerations, overall potential for use, and resource evaluation data for land-use planning. The commission may require the land to be used for specified purposes subject to such conditions, covenants, encumbrances or reservations specified in the relevant order or other instrument.[458] The commission prescribes guidelines for the management of public land by all public agencies, statutory bodies and state corporations in actual occupation or use of public land. The guidelines must indicate management priorities and operational principles for the management of public land resources for identified uses.[459]

454 Article 63(3) of the Constitution.
455 Article 64 of the Constitution.
456 No. 6 of 2012.
457 Section 6.
458 Section 8.
459 Section 10.

5.4.6.1.1 Development plans

The commission will, upon request by the national or county government, by order in the *Gazette*, reserve public land located in the public interest.[460] A management body will, on its own motion or at the request of the commission, submit to the commission for approval a plan for the development, management and use of the reserved public land vested in the management body.[461] Before submitting a plan to the commission, a management body will consider any conservation, environmental or heritage issues relevant to the development, management or use of the public land in its managed reserve for the purpose of that managed reserve; incorporate in the plan a statement that it has considered those issues in drawing up the plan; submit an environmental impact assessment plan pursuant to existing law on environment; and comply with the values and principles of the constitution.[462] If a management body submits a plan to the commission and the commission approves that plan and notifies the management body of that fact, the management body may develop, manage and use the public land concerned in accordance with the plan as approved or subsequently varied, as the case may be.[463] If a management body does not comply with guidelines or directions issued by the commission in writing, or does not submit a development plan in compliance with a request made, the commission, by order in the *Gazette*, may revoke that management order.[464] If the commission considers that it is in the public interest to revoke a management order, the commission may, by order in the *Gazette*, revoke the management order.[465] The preparation and implementation of development plans will be in accordance with the physical planning regulations and any other relevant law.[466]

5.4.6.1.2 Conservation of land-based natural resources

The commission makes rules and regulations for the sustainable conservation of land-based natural resources. The rules and regulations may contain measures to protect critical ecosystems and habitats; incentives for communities and individuals to invest in income-generating natural resource conservation programmes; measures to facilitate the access, use and co-management of forests, water and other resources by communities who have customary rights to these resources; procedures for the registration of natural resources in an appropriate register; procedures on the involvement of

460 Section 15.
461 Section 17(1).
462 Section 17(2).
463 Section 17(3).
464 Section 18(1).
465 Section 18(2).
466 Section 18(3).

stakeholders in the management and utilisation of land-based natural resources; and measures to ensure benefit-sharing to the affected communities.[467]

Section 135 of the Land Act establishes the Land Settlement Fund administered by the Land Settlement Fund Board of Trustees. The board is responsible for the provision of access to land for, among other things, conservation. Any monies appropriated by Parliament for the purposes of the fund must be paid into the fund, as also funds provided by bilateral or multilateral donors for the purpose of the fund; gifts, grants, donations or endowments as may be given to the board for the purpose of the fund; monies that may be borrowed by the board for the purposes of the fund; the rates, charges, dues or fees levied by the board of the Land Settlement Fund Trustees under this Act; all monies derived from the payment made by beneficiaries of settlement schemes; and such sums as may be payable to the board of the Land Settlement Fund Trustees pursuant to this Act or any other written law.

5.4.6.2 Land Regulations

The Land Regulations, 2017, deal with the management and administration of public, private and community land. An application for subdivision, amalgamation, partition and reparcellation of freehold land is submitted to the county government and is processed and approved in accordance with the laws relating to physical planning.[468] The county government ascertains the viability of the subdivision, amalgamation, partition and reparcellation and, in that regard, seeks representations from the relevant authorities including, but not limited to, an officer representing the national director of Surveys at the county; an officer representing the national director of Physical Planning at the county; the land administration officer of the national government at the county; representative of the Land Control Board, where applicable; and any other relevant authority.[469] An application for subdivision, amalgamation, partition and reparcellation of leasehold land is submitted to the county government.[470] The county government, before granting approval for subdivision, amalgamation, partition and reparcellation, seeks representations from the officer representing the national director of Surveys at the county; the officer representing the national director of Physical Planning at the county; the land administration officer of the commission and of national government at the county; the Land Control Board, where applicable; and any other relevant authority.[471]

467 Section 19.
468 Regulation 16(1).
469 Regulation 16(2).
470 Regulation 17(1).
471 Regulation 17(2).

An application for building plans on leasehold land is submitted to the relevant county government.[472] Where the county government has approved building plans or any other development on leasehold land, it communicates the approval to the cabinet secretary and the commission for purposes of noting that the conditions of the lease have been met.[473]

5.4.6.3 Guidelines for management of public land held by public agencies, statutory bodies and state corporations

Public agencies, statutory bodies and state bodies vested with the control, care and management of reserved land under Section 16 of the Land Act are required to carry out their mandate in accordance with the guidelines set out in the First Schedule of the Land Regulations.[474] The guidelines stipulate that the institutions undertake to prepare long-term land-use and management plans for the land and deposit the plans with the commission.

5.4.6.4 Community Land Act, 2016

The Community Land Act[475] provides for the recognition, protection and registration of community land rights; management and administration of community land; and the role of county governments in relation to unregistered community land. The Act establishes community land management committees, whose functions and powers include responsibility for the running of the day-to-day functions of the community; management and administration of registered community land on behalf of the respective communities; coordination of the development of community land-use plans in collaboration with the relevant authorities; promotion of cooperation and participation among community members in dealing with matters pertaining to registered community land; and prescribing of rules and regulations, to be ratified by the community assembly; and governing of operations of the community.[476] A registered community must have a community assembly, which consists of adult members of the community.[477] The quorum for decision-making by the community must not be less than two-thirds of the community assembly.[478] The community assembly must elect between

472 Regulation 20(1).
473 Regulation 20(2).
474 Regulation 5.
475 No. 27 of 2016.
476 Section 15(4).
477 Section 15(1).
478 Ibid.

seven and 15 members of the community assembly to constitute the community land management committee.[479] Provisions in the Community Land Act outlined below provide an opportunity to embed sustainable soil management.

5.4.6.4.1 Land use and development planning of community land

A registered community may, on its own motion or at the request of the county government, submit to the county government a plan for the development, management and use of the community land administered by the registered community, for approval.[480] Before submitting a plan to the county government, a registered community must consider any conservation, environmental or heritage issues relevant to the development, management or use of the land; incorporate in the plan a statement that it has considered those issues when drawing up the plan; consider any environmental impact plan pursuant to existing laws on environment; comply with the values and principles of the Constitution; seek ratification from the members of the registered community; and be bound by any approved relevant physical development plan.[481] If a registered community submits a plan to the county government and the government approves and notifies the registered community of that fact, the registered community must develop, manage and use the land concerned in accordance with the plan as approved or subsequently amended, as the case may be.[482] The county government must, in considering a plan submitted to it, comply with the relevant law relating to development planning.[483] The county government needs to, on request of the commission, submit records of development plans lodged with the county government in accordance with this section.[484]

5.4.6.4.2 Conservation and management of resources in community land

For purposes of the sustainable conservation of land-based natural resources in community land across counties, every respective registered community must abide by the applicable laws, policies and standards on natural resources.[485] The communities must establish measures to protect critical ecosystems and habitats; incentives for communities and individuals to invest in income-generating natural resource conservation

479 Section 15(3).
480 Section 19(1).
481 Section 19(2).
482 Section 19(3).
483 Section 19(4).
484 Section 19(5).
485 Section 20(1).

programmes; measures to facilitate the access, use and co-management of forests, water and other resources by communities who have customary rights to these resources; procedures for the registration of natural resources in an appropriate register; and procedures for the involvement of communities and other stakeholders in the management and utilisation of land-based natural resources.[486]A registered community must put in place measures necessary to conserve resources on community land.[487]

5.4.6.4.3 Grazing rights

A registered community must take the customs and practices of pastoral communities relating to land into consideration as long as they are consistent with the provisions of this Act or other applicable law.[488] Community land in a pastoral community must be available for use by members of the community for the grazing of their livestock, subject to such conditions as the respective registered community may impose, including conditions relating to the kind and number of livestock that may be grazed; the section or sections of the land where livestock may be grazed and the grazing in rotation on different sections; a grazing plan; and the right of the community to utilise the portion of land in accordance with this Act.[489] This is an important provision, as overgrazing is one of the causes of soil degradation on rangelands. The registered community may, upon application by any person who is not a member of the registered community, grant grazing rights and, upon such grant, that person must exercise the rights subject to the conditions mentioned.[490] The registered community must, subject to the approval of the members of the registered community in a meeting convened for that purpose, withdraw a grazing right if, owing to drought or any other reasonable cause, the registered community considers such cancellation to be in the interest of the residents of the community concerned.[491] In addition, a registered community may withdraw the grazing right of any member who fails to observe in a material respect any condition or contravenes the provision of the Act.[492]

A person may not, except with the written authority of the registered community, erect or occupy any building or other structure on the designated grazing land; plough or cultivate any portion of the land; take up abode on or occupy any portion of the grazing land; or obstruct the access to any watering place on the land, prevent or attempt to prevent any person from drawing water from, or watering stock at a watering

486 Section 20(2).
487 Section 20(3).
488 Section 28(1).
489 Section 28(2).
490 Section 28(3).
491 Section 28(4).
492 Section 28(5)

place, pollute the water at a watering place or interfere with the operation of any windmill, water-pump, water-pipe, dam or storage tank or other appurtenance installed or constructed at such a watering place.[493]

5.4.6.4.4 Land use rights on community land

A registered community may reserve special purpose areas including farming areas; settlement areas; community conservation areas; access and rights of way; cultural and religious sites; urban development; or any other purpose as the community, county government or national government may determine for the promotion of public interest.[494] An area designated for special purposes must be used exclusively for the designated purposes.[495]

5.4.6.4.5 Natural resources on community land

Natural resources found on community land must be used and managed sustainably and productively for the benefit of the whole community, including future generations; with transparency and accountability; and on the basis of equitable sharing of accruing benefits.[496]

5.4.6.4.6 Rules and by-laws

A registered community may make rules or by-laws for regulating the management and administration of its land. Such rules or by-laws may provide for the regulation of investments in the land; the determination of terms of any leases granted for purposes of investment; the conservation and rehabilitation of the land; land use and physical planning; and any other relevant matter.[497]

5.4.6.4.7 Regulation of community land-use planning

The state has the power to regulate the use of any land, or interest in or right over land, in the interest of defence, public safety, public order, public morality, public health or

493 Section 28(6).
494 Section 29(1).
495 Section 29(2).
496 Section 35.
497 Section 37.

land-use planning.[498] The management of community land is subject to national and county government laws and policies relating to fishing, hunting and gathering; protection of animals and wildlife; water protection, securing sufficient residual water, hydraulic engineering and safety of dams; forestry; environmental laws; energy policy; and exploitation of minerals and natural resources.[499]

5.4.6.5 Land Control Act

The Land Control Act, Cap 302, regulates the development, use and subdivision of agricultural land. It establishes the Land Control Board for the land control area or division in which the land is situated, which must grant consent for any of the following transactions:

- The sale, transfer, lease, mortgage, exchange, partition or other disposal of or dealing with any agricultural land which is situated within a land control area.
- The division of any such agricultural land into two or more parcels to be held under separate titles, other than the division of an area of less than 20 acres into plots in an area to which the Development and Use of Land (Planning) Regulations, 1961 (L.N. 516/1961), for the time being, apply.
- The issue, sale, transfer, mortgage or any other disposal of or dealing with any share in a private company or cooperative society which, for the time being, owns agricultural land situated within a land control area.[500]

In deciding whether to grant or refuse consent in respect of a controlled transaction, a land control board must have regard for the effect which the grant or refusal of consent is likely to have on the economic development of the land concerned or on the maintenance or improvement of standards of good husbandry in the land control area. In addition, the land control board must act on the principle that consent ought generally to be refused where the terms and conditions of the transaction (including the price to be paid) are markedly unfair or disadvantageous to one of the parties to the transaction, or, in the case of the division of land into two or more parcels, the division would be likely to reduce the productivity of the land.[501]

Although the required consent is an excellent tool for soil conservation, the land control boards have not been as effective as they could be. Their activities have been marred by corruption with 'consent to the highest bidder' being the operative principle. On several occasions, the government has been forced to disband boards.[502]

498 Section 38(1).
499 Section 38(2).
500 Section 6(1).
501 Section 9(1).
502 Maina (2016).

5.4.6.6 Physical and Land Use Planning Act, 2019

The Physical and Land Use Planning Act repealed the Physical Planning Act of 1996 in a bid to conform to the Constitution of Kenya, 2010. As pointed out above, the Constitution of Kenya, 2010, created two levels of government and distributed specific functions to each of the governments.[503] Section 3 of the Act outlines the objectives of the Act including to provide for principles, procedures and standards for preparation and implementation of physical and land-use development plans at the national, county urban and rural levels; to provide for the administration and management of physical and land-use planning in Kenya; and to provide a framework for equitable and sustainable use, planning and management of land, among others. Under the Act, all state organs, state officers and public officers engaged in regulation of land use or physical planning are bound by the Constitution and, in particular, are required to abide by the national values articulated under Article 10 of the Constitution, which includes sustainable development, as well as Article 60 of the Constitution, which provides sustainable land use as one of the principles of land policy. Some of the principles of physical and land-use planning articulated in Section 5 of the Act are that development activities must be planned in a manner that integrates economic, social and environmental needs of present and future generations.

Under Section 6 of the Act, a National Physical and Land Use Planning Consultative Forum is established, whose functions include: providing a forum for consultations on the national physical and land-use development plan and promoting effective coordination of planning, among other functions. Section 9 of the Act also requires the National Land Commission to monitor and oversee land-use planning throughout the country; prepare reports on the status of land-use planning in the country and present such reports to the President and Parliament; and develop a monitoring framework and oversight parameters for land-use planning. The cabinet secretary of matters relating to land is, on the other hand, vested under Section 10 of the Act with various responsibilities including: formulation of a national policy on physical and land-use planning; approval and oversight over the preparation of national physical and land-use development plans; issuance in the Kenya *Gazette* policy statements, guidelines and circulars on general and specific aspects of physical and land-use planning; and coordination of national and county levels of physical and land-use planning.

Cooperation of both the national and county governments is inextricably linked to the proper harmonised formulation of policies, management, development and planning of land.[504] One pillar of devolution in the Kenyan set up is to ensure increased public participation in the management of county affairs at every stage of decision-making. This mandates the planning authority to develop plans and only invite

503 Article 1.

504 *Council of Governors & 3 others v Senate & 53 others* [2015] eKLR.

objections to an already developed plan.[505] In Article 10 and indeed as an object of devolution, the public must be involved in the formulation of such development plans for effective plans to be achieved. Participation should be in good faith and substantial, as opposed to tokenism. These contributions must be considered.[506] The procedure for application and approval of development does not envisage public participation.[507]

The office of the Director of Physical and Land Use Planning is established under Section 13 of the Act and is given powers to: prepare national physical and land-use plans; prepare development plans for strategic national installations and projects; formulate policies, guidelines and standards relating to physical and land-use planning; coordinate the preparation of inter-county physical and land-use development plans; and advise the government on these matters, among other functions. Section 18 of the Act also establishes a county director of Physical and Land Use Planning for each county, who performs similar roles but at the county level. Furthermore, at the devolved unit level, the counties, a County Physical and Land Use Planning Consultative Forum has been established under Section 14 of the Act. This forum is tasked to operate in each county and has similar functions to the national forum.

There is a requirement in Section 21 of the Act to have national physical and land-use development plans, which cover an implementation period of 20 years and may be reviewed every 10 years. It is precisely this development plan that forms the basis for environmental conservation, protection and improvement, which include soil conservation and protection. Section 24 of the Act further provides that such plans must include a situation analysis of the state of physical and land-use development in the country and the various relevant studies and reports that may have been done. A spatial analysis – accompanied by physical, land use and suitability maps and charts that focus on soil, among other aspects of the environment – is required, as spelt out in the Second Schedule to the Act regarding the outline and format of local physical and land-use development plans.

Sections 57 and 58 of the Act requires a person wishing to make developments on their land to obtain development permission from the respective county executive committee member by applying for development permission, upon payment of the necessary fees. This is a means of development control – it is a right of the state to regulate the use of land as provided for under Article 66 of the Constitution. The purpose of development control is to ensure economic land use by allocating the resources to maximise benefits.[508] Soil protection easily falls within this mandate. Article 60 requires that land be managed in an equitable, efficient, productive and sustainable manner. In addition, the use of land should ensure sustainable, productive, transparent

505 Section 9.
506 *Robert N. Gakuru & Others v Governor Kiambu County & 3 others* [2014] eKLR.
507 Section 33.
508 Mativo (2015).

and cost-effective management of land. Article 10 contains principles such as social justice, equality, inclusiveness, integrity and sustainable development. These are binding principles that should be adhered to in land planning.

Kenya has had physical planning laws that have not been effective in the management of land. The main challenges bedevilling land planning in Kenya have been disregard of planning, and multiple land tenure regimes that create loopholes, conflicts and contradictions.[509] Corruption, political patronage, weak institutions, and ineffective development control institutions have also affected land-use planning. In addition, the repealed Physical Planning Act was not clear on the classification of land use, particularly in mixed developments in residential areas.[510] The Act was inflexible and unresponsive to the dynamics of development. In this regard, the law did not have effective regulatory mechanisms to deal with rapid urbanisation, population pressure and emergent land development dynamics, such as sectional properties.

This has led to indiscriminate extension of urban boundaries in areas of land which are still used predominantly for farming and livestock-keeping. Indeed, the land use in Kenya's urban areas does not conform to existing zoning and building regulations. Agricultural lands have rapidly been converted into concrete jungles and industries have sprung up in areas zoned for agriculture. [511]

The 2019 Physical and Land Use Planning Act has addressed some of these issues. Effective implementation of the Act will contribute to sustainable soil management. Of concern, however, is the failure of the Act to address the duplication and parallel setting up of institutions in the county government and national government. This is likely to continue to affect sustainable soil governance.

5.4.7 Agriculture, Fisheries and Food Authority Act, 2013

The Agricultural, Fisheries and Food Authority Act[512] establishes the agriculture and food authority and makes provision for the respective roles of the national and county governments in agriculture, excluding livestock. The agriculture and food authority is established to promote best practices in, and regulate, the production, processing, marketing, grading, storage, collection, transportation and warehousing of agricultural products as may be provided for under the Crops Act, No. 16 of 2013.[513] It is also mandated to collect and collate data, maintain a database on agricultural products, document and monitor agriculture through registration of players, as provided for in the

509 Ibid.; Institute of Social Accountability (2017).
510 Mativo (2015: 37).
511 Ndegwa (2001).
512 No. 13 of 2013.
513 Section 4(b).

Crops Act.[514] In addition, the authority is responsible for determining the research priorities in agriculture and to advise generally on this research.[515]

5.4.7.1 Development, preservation and utilisation of agricultural land

In regard to policy on development, preservation and utilisation of agricultural land, The cabinet secretary, on the advice of the authority, and in consultation with the National Land Commission, is empowered to provide general guidelines, referred to as land development guidelines, which are applicable to all categories of agricultural land.[516] The land guidelines are to be implemented by the respective county governments, taking into account the circumstances of the respective areas under their jurisdiction.[517] The guidelines may require the adoption of such system of management or farming practice or other system in relation to the land in question, including the execution of such work and the placing of such things in, on or over the land as may be necessary for the proper development of land for agricultural purposes.[518]

5.4.7.2 Rules on preservation, utilisation and development of agricultural land

The cabinet secretary is empowered on the advice of the authority, and in consultation with the National Land Commission, to make general rules for the preservation, utilisation and development of agricultural land.[519] The rules may prescribe the manner in which owners, whether or not they are also occupiers, should manage their land in accordance with rules of good estate management; prescribe the manner in which occupiers should farm their land in accordance with the rules of good husbandry; advise on the control or prohibition of the cultivation of land or the keeping of stock or any particular kind of stock; advise on the kinds of crops which may be grown on land; provide controls on the erection of buildings and other works on agricultural land; and provide for such exemptions or conditional exemptions from the these provisions as may be desirable or necessary for vulnerable groups, including women.[520]

An owner of agricultural land is deemed to fulfil his or her responsibilities to manage the land in accordance with the rules of good estate management if, having regard for the character and situation of the land and other relevant circumstances, it enables

514 Ibid.
515 Section 4(b).
516 Section 21(1).
517 Section 21(2).
518 Section 21(3).
519 Section 22(1).
520 Section 22(2).

an occupier of the land reasonably skilled in husbandry to maintain efficient production of kind, quality and quantity of produce.[521] The occupier of agricultural land is deemed to fulfil his or her responsibilities to farm the land in accordance with the rules of good husbandry if the occupier is maintaining a reasonable standard of production, as regards both the kind of produce and the quality and quantity thereof, while keeping the land in a condition which enables this standard to be maintained in the future.[522]

5.4.7.3 Soil conservation

Section 23(1) of the Agriculture, Fisheries and Food Authority Act provides that the cabinet secretary, on the advice of the authority and in consultation with the National Land Commission, may prescribe national guidelines for the purposes of the conservation of the soil and the prevention of the adverse effects of soil erosion on any land. The guidelines may address any of the following matters:

- Prohibit, regulate or control the undertaking of any agricultural activity, including the firing, clearing or destruction of vegetation when such prohibiting, regulating or controlling is deemed by the cabinet secretary to be necessary for the protection of land against degradation and the protection of water catchment areas or otherwise, for the preservation of the soil and its fertility.
- Require, regulate or control the afforestation or re-afforestation of land in respect of the drainage of land, including the construction, maintenance or repair of drains, gullies, contour banks, terraces and diversion ditches; and salination, acidification and saltification of soil.
- Require the uprooting or destruction, without payment of any compensation therefor, of any vegetation which has been planted in contravention of a land preservation order.
- Require the supervision of unoccupied land.
- Prohibit, restrict or control the use of land for any agricultural purpose excluding livestock.

The guidelines may provide for such exemptions or conditional exemptions from the operation thereof as may be specified. The guidelines may also provide for the granting of permits or conditional permits of exemption from the operation thereof, its application to certain periods or seasons of the year, restricting its application to specified persons or any class or description of person, or to any area or areas, and requiring or prohibiting any act or thing to be done to or in respect of any land, notwithstanding

521 Section 22(3)(a).
522 Section 22(3)(b).

that the purpose of such a rule or order or its carrying into effect is or will be to the benefit of any other land or land in the ownership or occupation of another person.[523]

5.4.8 Crops Act, 2013

The objective of the Crops Act[524] is to accelerate the growth and development of agriculture in general, enhance productivity and incomes of farmers and the rural population, improve the investment climate and efficiency of agribusiness, and develop agricultural crops as export crops that will augment the foreign exchange earnings of the country. Landowners and lessees of agricultural land, being stewards, have the obligation to cultivate the lands they own or lease and make the land economically productive in a sustainable and environmentally friendly manner.[525]

5.4.9 Irrigation Act, 2019

The Irrigation Act[526] is an act of Parliament to provide for the development, control and improvement of irrigation schemes, and for incidental and connected purposes. Section 3 of the Act establishes the National Irrigation Board, which is responsible for the development, control and improvement of national irrigation schemes in Kenya.[527] The cabinet secretary may, after consultation with the board, make regulations generally, which may provide for the standards of good husbandry and the control of pests and diseases in national irrigation schemes.[528] The regulations may also provide for the methods of harvesting, collection, storage, transport, processing, marketing and sale of produce grown on national irrigation schemes.[529]

In this regard, the cabinet secretary promulgated the Irrigation (National Irrigation Schemes) Regulations, 1977. Any person who resides in, carries on business in, or occupies any part of the scheme, or grazes any stock thereon must, unless he is the holder of a valid licence granted to him under the regulations by the manager in charge of an irrigation scheme with the approval of the committee or is the authorised dependent of the licensee, be guilty of an offence.[530] One of the conditions for granting the licence is that a licensee must comply with all instructions given by the manager with

523 Section 23(2).
524 No. 16 of 2013.
525 Section 4(b).
526 No. 14 of 2019.
527 Section 15(1).
528 Section 27(1)(b).
529 Section 27(1)(e).
530 Regulation 4.

regard to good husbandry; the branding, dipping, inoculating, herding, grazing or watering of stock; the production and use of manure and compost; the preservation of the fertility of the soil; the prevention of soil erosion; the planting, felling, stumping and clearing of trees and vegetation; and the production of silage and hay.[531] Any licensee who refuses, or without reasonable excuse fails, to comply with any of the conditions of the regulation must, in addition to any penalty that may be imposed, be liable to have his licence terminated by the cabinet secretary.[532] A licensee may not construct buildings or other works of any kind on his holding or elsewhere in the scheme without the prior consent, in writing, of the manager and, in the event of his having erected a structure or building without such consent, the manager may direct, in writing, that the structure be removed and the land returned to its original state; and, if the licensee fails to comply with this direction within one month, the manager may enter the building or structure for the purpose of demolition and any expenses incurred by the manager for the removal of the building or structure may be recovered from the licensee.[533] The requirement to restore the land to its original state implies that the licensee should undertake remedial action to redress soil degradation.

The Irrigation Act also prohibits the use of any prohibited chemicals or substances in the schemes. As previously observed, substandard fertilizers, chemicals and polluted water are illegally used in some irrigation schemes in Kenya. This points to ineffective implementation of the law.

5.4.10 Plant Protection Act, 2012

The Plant Protection Act[534] provides that the Minister may make rules for preventing and controlling attacks by or the spread of pests or diseases on plants.[535] Consequently, the act indirectly assists in soil protection by protecting crop cover, which is essential for preventing soil erosion.

5.4.11 Mining Act, 2016

The Mining Act[536] applies to minerals specified in the First Schedule of the Act. The Act does not to apply to petroleum and hydrocarbon gases.[537] A mineral right or other

531 Regulation 8(1)(f).
532 Regulation 8(3).
533 Regulation 10(5).
534 Cap. 324 of 2012.
535 Section 3.
536 No. 12 of 2016.
537 Section 3.

licence or permit granted under this Act must not exempt a person from complying with any law concerning the protection of the environment.[538] A mining licence will not be granted to a person under the Act unless the person has obtained an environmental impact assessment licence and social heritage assessment, and the environmental management plan has been approved.[539]

5.4.11.1 Land use

Section 179 of the Mining Act stipulates that the holder of a permit or licence under the Act is required to use the land in accordance with the terms of the permit or licence and should ensure the sustainable use of land through restoration of abandoned mines and quarries; that the seepage of toxic waste into streams, rivers, lakes and wetlands is avoided and that disposal of any toxic waste is done in the approved areas only; that blasting and all works that cause massive vibration is properly carried out and muffled to keep such vibrations and blasts to reasonable and permissible levels in conformity with the Environmental Management and Co-ordination Act; and that upon completion of prospecting or mining, the land in question must be restored to its original status or to an acceptable and reasonable condition as close as possible to its original state.

5.4.11.2 Requirement of site restoration and mine-closure plans

The cabinet secretary will not grant a prospecting licence, a retention licence or a mining licence to an applicant, unless the applicant has submitted site mitigation and rehabilitation, or mine-closure plans for approval.[540] The cabinet secretary may prescribe regulations for site rehabilitation and mine-closure obligations.[541]

5.4.11.3 Environmental protection bonds

An applicant for a prospecting licence, a retention licence or a mining licence must provide a bond or some other form of financial security, called an environmental protection bond, sufficient to cover the costs associated with the implementation of the environmental and rehabilitation obligations of the holder under the Mining Act.[542] The required environmental protection bond must be in a form and for an amount as

538 Section 176(1).
539 Section 176(2).
540 Section 180(1).
541 Section 180(2).
542 Section 181(1).

may be determined by the cabinet secretary, having regard for the particular characteristics of the project.[543] In determining the form and amount of the bond, the cabinet secretary will take into account the amount that the applicant is required to provide by way of a bond or some other form of financial security under the provisions of the Environmental Management and Co-ordination Act.[544] The cabinet secretary may release, in part, an environmental protection bond upon the satisfactory completion of rehabilitation measures undertaken within the duration of a licence and may release the bond in full following the successful completion of all environmental and rehabilitation obligations.[545] In the case of soil pollution, the environmental protection bond may be used to restore and rehabilitate the soil.

As observed above, Kenya has large deposits of minerals. Under the Mining Act, a holder of a mining licence should observe environmental conditions and environmental laws. As highlighted in the *Mui*[546] *case*, mining companies do not always carry out EIAs before mining operations begin. It is important to note that most of the mining operations in Kenya are small scale, artisanal and informal. As such, the majority of the small-scale miners do not obtain mining licences. For instance, the artisanal gold mining areas of western Kenya have reported high soil pollution as miners continue to use metals such as mercury and lead illegally in gold prospecting.[547]

The Petroleum Act[548] provides a framework for the contracting, exploration, development and production of petroleum. It also provides the framework for the cessation of upstream petroleum operations and gives effect to relevant articles of the Constitution in so far as they apply to upstream petroleum operations, and regulation of midstream and downstream petroleum operations.

A person with whom the national government concludes a petroleum agreement is required to carry out upstream petroleum operations in the contract area in accordance with all the applicable environment, health, safety and maritime laws and best petroleum industry practices.[549] The contractor should deploy the best available technology to ensure quality, environment, health and safety requirements are met; control the flow and prevent the waste or escape in the contract area of petroleum, gas (not being petroleum) or water; prevent the escape in the contract area of any mixture of water or drilling fluid and petroleum or any other matter; prevent damage to petroleum-bearing strata in any area in respect of which the petroleum agreement is not in force; prevent the pollution of any soil, air, biodiversity, brine, water well, spring, stream, river, lake, reservoir, sea, forest, wildlife and marine, estuary or harbour by the escape of

543 Section 181(2).
544 Section 181(3).
545 Section 181(4).
546 Constitutional Petition No. 305 of 2012.
547 Odinga (2018).
548 No. 2 of 2019.
549 Section 59(1).

petroleum, salt water, drilling fluid, chemical additive, gas (not being petroleum) or any other waste product or effluent; and, where pollution occurs, treat or disperse it in an environmentally acceptable manner. Finally, a contractor must furnish to the authority, prior to the drilling of any well, a detailed report on the technique to be employed, an estimate of the time to be taken, the material to be used and the safety measures to be employed, in the drilling of the well.[550] A contractor must ensure that the management of production, transportation, storage, treatment and disposal of waste arising out of upstream petroleum operations are carried out in accordance with all the applicable environmental, health, safety and maritime laws and best petroleum industry practices.[551]

A contractor and any other participant in upstream petroleum operations must, at all times maintain efficient measures for emergency preparedness with a view to dealing with incidents which may lead to loss of life or personal injury, pollution or damage to property.[552] The contractor must ensure that the measures taken to prevent or reduce harmful effects include measures to ensure that the environment is restored as far as possible to its original condition prior to commencement of operations.[553]

The cabinet secretary is obligated to establish a disaster preparedness, prevention and management unit within the Ministry to coordinate response to accidents, disasters and other emergencies that may occur in upstream petroleum operations.[554] The disaster preparedness, prevention and management unit should collaborate with the National Disaster Operations Centre, county governments and other relevant institutions to ensure a timely response and emergency preparedness for resource sharing.[555] The cabinet secretary must formulate and periodically update a risk assessment of upstream petroleum operations and implement appropriate risk mitigation programmes.[556] The disaster preparedness, prevention and management unit must in liaison with the contractor carry out public awareness and sensitisation forums for local communities resident in areas surrounding ongoing upstream operations.[557] Where an accident or an emergency occurs, the contractor or other person responsible for the operation and use of the facility must, to the extent necessary, suspend the upstream petroleum operations for as long as the requirement of prudent operations warrants.[558] Where special circumstances exist, the cabinet secretary may order that upstream petroleum operations

---

550 Section 59(2).
551 Section 60(1).
552 Section 67(1).
553 Section 67(2).
554 Section 69(1).
555 Section 69(2).
556 Section 69(3).
557 Section 69(4).
558 Section 71(1).

be suspended to the extent necessary, or may impose particular conditions to allow continuation of the activities.[559]

A person who wishes to undertake refining, importation, export, bulk storage or transportation of petroleum crude or products must have a valid licence issued by the Energy Regulatory Commission.[560] The licencing authority must, in granting or rejecting an application for a licence or permit, take into consideration the need to protect the environment and to conserve the natural resources in accordance with the environmental laws, maritime laws and international maritime treaties ratified by Kenya and other guidelines developed by the commission.[561] A licence or permit issued by the licencing authority needs to set out a requirement that the licensee must comply with all applicable environmental, health and safety laws.[562] An application for a licence must be accompanied by an environmental liability policy as may be prescribed by the authority.[563]

5.4.11.4 Liability for damage

The contractor is liable for damage from pollution, without regard to fault from whichever source, related to the upstream petroleum operations of the contractor when the damage occurs in Kenya or within its territorial waters.[564] A person engaged in the petroleum business must comply with the applicable environmental, health and safety laws.[565] In the event of a fire, explosion, oil spill, injury or fatality occurring in the course of operating a petroleum logistics facility, transportation or sale of petroleum, either by accident or through negligence, the operator or person transporting or selling the petroleum must forthwith clean up the polluted or damaged environment, at the operator's own expense, to the satisfaction of the licencing authority and any other relevant authority. Any person engaged in the storage, transportation or sale of petroleum and petroleum products must have an oil clean-up plan in compliance with the National Oil Spill Policy, relevant environmental health and safety regulations or guidelines.[566] If the operator or person transporting or selling petroleum fails, or unreasonably delays, to carry out the work, the licencing authority may cause any work not carried out to be executed at the expense of the operator or person transporting or selling the petroleum.[567]

559 Section 71(2).
560 Section 74(1).
561 Section 75(1)(b).
562 Section 76(2).
563 Section 79.
564 Section 72.
565 Section 97(1).
566 Section 97(2).
567 Section 97(3).

5.4.12 Environment and Land Court Act, 2011

The 2010 Constitution established a specialised court to deal with the environment and land. The promulgation of the Environment and Land Court Act[568] illustrates the importance of land and natural resources in Kenya. This court has been in existence for close on nine years. Much time was spent defining the jurisdiction of the court and its relationship with the High Court. Cases revolving around jurisdiction bogged down the court for a while, slowing the rate at which it delivered judgements on land, land planning, land use and environmental protection. The court has also been under-staffed considering the preponderance of land and environment matters requiring adjudication.[569] While many applicants for posts in the court are well versed with land matters, as this is a required course in all law schools, the number of lawyers with environment and land competence remains low. This denies the court a much-needed specialisation. These factors have indirectly contributed to environmental degradation because of the slow rate at which environmental and land-use disputes are resolved.

5.4.13 Fertilizers and Animal Foodstuffs Act

The Fertilizers and Animal Foodstuffs Act[570] establishes the Fertilizer and Animal Foodstuffs Board of Kenya, whose functions include ensuring that fertilizers imported, manufactured or distributed in Kenya meet the standards of quality and safety prescribed by law.[571] It also prohibits the importation, manufacture, compounding, mixing, or sale of any fertilizer or animal foodstuff that is not approved.

As was observed in Chapter two, the majority of the soils used for agriculture in Kenya require constant replenishing of nutrients. The application of substandard fertilizers has greatly contributed to soil degradation. Smuggling of substandard fertilizers into Kenya is sometimes carried out in collusion with government institutions.[572]

5.5 Jurisprudence on environmental protection

The courts of law in Kenya have attempted to interpret the various provisions of the law and the Constitution discussed in the foregoing section. The jurisprudence emanating from these decisions indicates that the courts are ready and willing to give effect to environmental principles and sustainable development. In this section, we review

568 No.19 of 2011.
569 See https://bit.ly/3pp4W1f, accessed 6 November 2019.
570 Cap 345.
571 Fertilizers and Animal Foodstuffs Act, Section 2(A) and (B).
572 *Afri Ventures (Kenya) Limited v Turbo Highway Eldoret Limited* [2014] eKLR; Ombati (2018).

select cases so as to illustrate how courts have understood the right to a clean and healthy environment as well as the various statutory and constitutional provisions, and how this has affected or has the potential to affect soil conservation and improvement.

5.5.1 *John Mutungu Waititu v China Wuyi (Kenya) Co. Limited [2018] eKLR*

In this case filed at the ELC in Nyahururu, the appellant (John Mutungu Waititu) brought an action against the respondent claiming, among other things, that the respondent had failed to restore his land after excavating soil, thus leaving his land vulnerable to soil erosion, especially since it was on a hilly slope. The appellant argued that under the one-year lease agreement, both parties had agreed that upon excavation of the murram on the appellant's land, the respondent would push back the topsoil to fill any hole that may have remained so as to leave the land as flat as possible. The respondent did not honour this agreement. The court found that the respondent had contributed to environmental degradation, which it defined at paragraph 79 of the decision as "deterioration of the environment through depletion of natural resources such as air, water and soil; the destruction of ecosystems and the extinction of wildlife". The appellant had contested the award of 200,000 Kenyan shillings by the lower court as damages to the appellant for the environmental damage, arguing that no amount of money could compensate for the environmental damage and asked the court to issue an environmental restoration order. The court agreed with the appellant, set aside the order for compensation and substituted it with an order compelling the respondent to restore the land by topping up the soil as had been agreed under the agreement.

5.5.2 *African Centre for Rights and Governance (ACRAG) & 3 Others v Municipal Council of Naivasha [2017] eKLR*

In this case, the petitioner lodged a constitutional petition at the ELC in Nakuru, arguing that the continued operation of a dumpsite near Naivasha was a constitutional violation of the right of the inhabitants to a clean and healthy environment. The court made its finding at paragraph 43 as follows:

> After considering all issues, I think in my view, this court ought to make some orders, some of which ought to take place immediately and some of which can be graduated over time. The immediate step is of course to order the respondent, now the County Government of Nakuru, to engage personnel and measures to immediately collect all plastic bags littering the area and to ensure that on a daily and continuous basis, plastic bags will continue being put aside for incineration or other forms of destruction so that the area is not prone to these. The County Government of Nakuru, must also forthwith, if it intends to continue using the site as a dump, apply for the requisite licence from NEMA, as required by Sections 87 and 88 of EMCA and such application must be made within 14 days from today. If such application is made, NEMA must proceed to assess this application having in mind all requisite criteria, and either decline or permit it

> with the necessary conditions for operations. In assessing the application, I direct NEMA, to ensure that a thorough Environmental Impact Assessment is done, with a consideration of among other things, alternative sites; all necessary mitigation measures including fencing of the site, and annual auditing. The option of having a landfill other than an open dumpsite should also be considered, for a landfill is a more modern and less environmentally destructive method of waste disposal.

Justice Munyao Sila further ordered for the judgement to be served upon the cabinet secretary responsible for environment matters to consider issues of policy and compliance with proper solid waste management, among other matters.

5.5.3 *Martin Osano Rabera, John Ndungu Kinyanjui v Municipal Council of Nakuru, NEMA & County Government of Nakuru*

In this case[573], the petitioners were residents of Nakuru living near Gioto waste disposal site. They sought a declaration that their right to a clean and healthy environment under Article 42 of the Constitution of Kenya 2010 had been violated. In his judgement, Ohungo J. observed that the obligation to ensure a clean and healthy environment was for everybody – from the state to all persons be they of natural or juridical association or of another group of persons, whether incorporated or not.[574] The court found that while the 2nd respondent had a statutory mandate to offer technical support on environmental matters in Kenya, including waste disposal, the primary obligation in waste disposal and management rested with the county governments.[575] He found for the petitioners. This case lays out the principle under the Fourth Schedule of the Constitution which makes it the responsibility of county governments to deal with all waste management.

5.5.4 *Moffat Kamau & 9 Others v Aeolus Kenya Limited & 9 Others (the Kinangop Wind Park Project case)*

In this case,[576] a company called Ecogen sought to have a wind power park in Kinangop area initially for the production of up to 30 MW of power from turbines to be located in a single parcel of land. The company applied for and was issued with an EIA licence. This licence was later transferred to Aeolus Limited. Aeolus upscaled the project to 61 MW and the project coverage was expanded from 2 sq km to 16 sq km. To continue with this project, Aeolus did not apply for a new EIA licence, nor did it

573 Petition No. 53 of 2012 eKLR.

574 Ibid at para. 49.

575 The Judgement at para. 47

576 Nakuru ELC Petition No. 13 of 2015 (2016) eKLR.

conduct a new EIA. Instead, it applied for, and was granted a variation of the original EIA licence without the necessity of conducting a fresh EIA. The petitioners successfully challenged this. The court held that where there was a substantial change in the character of the project, a variation of the original licence, which without a fresh EIA, was wrongful. The court held that where circumstances exist that would entitle NEMA to cancel the original licence, then NEMA must at least seek a fresh EIA before issuing a variation. In this instance, the court felt that the character of the project had changed so fundamentally that it was wrong for NEMA to only issue a variation of the original EIA licence, without a fresh EIA being conducted. The court also pointed out situations when it would be wrong for NEMA to only vary a licence without requiring a fresh EIA, including a change in the site of the project, a change in law, a change in technology to be used, or a change in the environmental effects.[577]

5.5.5 *John K. Kibicho & Others (suing on behalf of the Milimani Residents Welfare Association) v County Government of Nakuru & Others*

The residents of Milimani in Nakuru, through their association, filed a suit to oppose the construction of a multiple storey residential block of flats in an area that predominantly consisted of bungalows. The evidence showed that the developer had applied for a change of user, which was opposed by the plaintiff but, despite this opposition, the county government of Nakuru (sued as the 1st respondent) gave the go-ahead for the development without giving the petitioners a hearing.

The court held that a change of use of land was applied for because the intended use of the land was not in conformity with the conditions attached to the holding of the title, and thus it was among the applications that needed to be served on owners or occupiers of adjacent land. A further notice also needed to be placed in the Kenya *Gazette*, in two local dailies, and a notice served upon the chief as required by Section 41 of the Physical Planning Act. In the case at hand, there was only one advertisement in one English daily newspaper, and the court was of the view that the provisions of the Physical Planning Act had not been complied with. The court cancelled the change of user licence.[578]

---

577 Ibid.: para. 85.

578 See also *Koome Mwambia & Others suing on behalf of Kunde Road Residents Association v Deshun Properties Company Limited & 4 Others,* Nairobi ELC Petition No. 1433 of 2013 (2014) eKLR.

5.5.6 *Justus Irungu Githae & 12 Others v Attorney General & 4 Others*[579]

In this case, an injunction was issued against the county government of Kirinyaga, stopping it from dumping waste on land that was neighbouring that of the petitioners who argued that the county government's action of dumping waste in their neighbourhood threatened their right to a clean and healthy environment. The county government conceded in their reply that they had not conducted any EIA before starting to dump waste and the court was of the view that any further dumping should be stopped pending the hearing of the petition.

5.5.7 *Joseph Leboo & 2 Others v Director Kenya Forest Service & Another*

The plaintiffs in this case complained about the issuance of licences for the felling of trees in Lembus Forest by the Kenya Forest Service (KFS). They complained that KFS had illegally allocated pre-qualified and unqualified saw millers to harvest timber and fuel materials from the Lembus Forest, without involving the community, in accordance with the law governing the harvesting of timber and firewood from forests. They also complained that the saw millers were harvesting trees that had not been allocated to them and were also harvesting unspecified trees. The court found that indeed there was no management plan for the forest despite this being an explicit requirement in the Forest Act, 2005.[580] The rules required a five-year management plan for every forest[581] and also barred KFS from issuing any authorisation without a site-specific plan in place.[582] These were found to be lacking and the court issued an injunction stopping any further harvesting of trees.

5.5.8 *Raycon Limited v Superply Limited & 2 Others*[583]

The plaintiff claimed to have been granted harvesting rights over exotic timber in the Mau Forest by KFS. The plaintiff claimed that the 1st and 2nd defendants had encroached on its allocated portion and were harvesting trees illegally and thus sought an injunction against the first and second defendants to stop them from any further harvesting of trees pending the hearing of the suit. It emerged in the course of the hearing that the plaintiff did not in fact have any licence to harvest trees, and yet had been allowed to harvest trees by KFS. The court also wondered how the 1st and 2nd

579 ELC at Kerugoya, Case No. 804 of 2013 (2016) eKLR.
580 The Forest Protection and Sustainable Management Rules in the Forest Act, 2005.
581 Ibid.: Rule 5(1).
582 Ibid.: Rule 5(6).
583 ELC at Nakuru, Case No. 39 of 2017 (2017) eKLR (ruling of Sila J).

defendants were allowed to harvest timber despite clear provisions in the Forest Act of 2016 barring the harvesting of trees in a forest without a licence.[584] The court was not persuaded that either the plaintiff or the 1st and 2nd defendants had any licence to harvest trees and issued summons to the director of KFS to explain why these companies were being allowed to harvest trees in the Mau forest.

5.6 Conclusion

Soil conservation in Kenya is incidental to land and environmental protection in general. An appraisal of the legal framework reveals that although Kenya has many laws that have an impact on soil conservation, the institutional weakness, poor state of implementation and corruption contribute to the laws' inefficiency. In addition, soil conservation has not been a key consideration in the development landscape.

The recent ranking of Kenya as a lower middle-income country, its rapid massive infrastructural development and population growth, as well as its strategic location as the East African region's business and transport hub, have placed increased pressure on the country's finite natural resources, including land.[585] Population increase, uncontrolled urban sprawl and industrialisation continue to mount pressure on land and soil, contributing its degradation.[586] Unfortunately, the law has not evolved fast enough to protect the natural resources, particularly the soil and its components, as more attention is diverted to production, thus relegating sustainability and conservation of soil to the back burner. Considering the analysis above, we recommend the tightening of loose ends in the implementation of laws and enhanced capacity-building and institutional coordination.

A review of the legal, policy and regulatory environment relating to soil protection and conservation reveals that there is indeed a legal basis for ensuring soil protection in Kenya. While there is no single legal framework that expressly provides for protection of soil, there are various policies, strategies, national statutes, national constitution, regional and international instruments that Kenya has ratified which all speak to the protection of soil and improvement of its fertility. Put differently, the law on soil protection and improvement in Kenya may be found in ad hoc and fragmented pieces of legislation and policy documents.

While this fragmented nature of the legal framework does not in and of itself rob the legal framework on soil protection of its potency and utility, it certainly takes away the much-needed focus, creates overlaps among various institutions, and does not

584 The Forest Conservation and Management Act, 2016, Section 64(1)(a), which makes it mandatory for one to have a licence before harvesting any trees in a forest and Section 64(2) which provides that it is an offence for any one to undertake those activities without a licence.

585 Mwanza (2019).

586 Mundia & Murayama. (2010).

establish clear responsibilities for particular institutions and individuals. There is potential for conflict among institutions or even dereliction of duty, as each institution expects the other to act. A single legal framework that speaks specifically and solely about the protection and improvement of soil as a component of the environment will signal more urgency, and the various players involved will tend to give such laws much more attention and resources to drive their implementation.

ELC has taken on the mandate of protecting the environment and has made bold decisions. ELC is evolving into a critical player in the sustainable management of Kenya's land and environment, as was envisaged under the Constitution. The court would definitely make decisions for sustainable soil management if such issues were brought before it. A specific soil law would elicit such causes from the citizenry and lead to a robust soil jurisprudence as is emerging in the case of the environment.

6 Lessons learnt and recommendations for future legislation

Soil protection has featured in Kenya's policy and law terrain from colonial times. Soil has indeed been addressed historically at the highest political levels. As pointed out at the outset, however, there is currently no specific law on soil protection in Kenya. There are many provisions dispersed in different laws that can be used to protect soil. But, with no specific law on soil protection and with the various existing laws focusing principally on other issues, soil may be neglected. This gives rise to the need to consolidate soil protection measures in a dedicated law incorporating the measures that have been used for soil protection over the years.

6.1 Lessons learnt

The Constitution of Kenya, 2010, recognises the right to a clean and healthy environment, which includes the right to have the environment protected for the benefit of present and future generations through legislative and other measures. Okpara is of the opinion that the right to a clean and healthy environment includes a habitable human environment with, among other things, clean water, and soil and air free from toxins or other hazardous matter that threaten human health.[587] As such, the recognition of the right to a clean environment is of fundamental importance to soil conservation and protection, as is the realisation of other constitutionally recognised human rights, including the right to be free from hunger, to have adequate food of acceptable quality, and to have the highest attainable standard of health. This constitutional provision

587 Okpara (2012).

provides an excellent platform and tools to demand the protection and conservation of soil as part of the environment.

A related matter is that the Kenyan Judiciary in the post-2010 period has been progressive and has shown remarkable dedication to a holistic, purposeful constitutional interpretation and the willingness to enforce the right to a clean and healthy environment. First, the courts are increasingly recognising the interconnection between the right to a clean environment and other social economic rights. In *Friends of Lake Turkana Trust v Attorney General & 2 Others,*[588] the court held that the right to life, dignity and economic and social rights are all connected and indivisible, and it cannot be said that one set of rights is more important than another. All these rights of necessity need to be observed for persons to attain a reasonable livelihood. Such a broad approach allows a multidisciplinary application of laws, creating a wider protection of human rights. Second, the courts have in their holistic interpretation of the right to a clean environment held that this right inherently proscribes pollution of the environment.[589] Third, despite the uncertainty about which court between the High Court and the Environment and Land Court has the jurisdiction to rule on disputes on environmental law protection, there is a general consensus that either of the courts should interpret the right to environment as protecting all components of the environment to the fullest extent permissible in law.[590] Fourth, the courts and tribunals have boldly ruled on controversial government-sponsored projects that have negative impacts on the environment. In *Save Lamu & 5 Others v National Environmental Management Authority (NEMA) & Another,*[591] the National Environment Tribunal nullified an environment impact assessment licence because of inadequate public participation by the residents of Lamu on the environmental impact of the project. Evidently, the Judiciary has been in the forefront in the protection of the environment. Accordingly, the courts present a strategic opportunity to enforce the right to a clean environment in soil governance and protection.

Manifestly, Kenya *contains a comprehensive and robust environmental protection and conservation legal framework,* particularly the Environment Management and Coordination Act, 1999. Although, soil conservation has not attained the level and robustness of protection that other components of the environment have, such as water, air, forests and wildlife, there is room, in the little avenue provided, to advocate proper soil management and protection within the broader ambit of the environment.

As previously noted, Kenya's soil profile and types require constant replenishing with nutrients. Accordingly, ideal soil legislation in Kenya should provide for standard fertilizers and chemicals of high quality that do not contribute to soil degradation. In

588 *Friends of Lake Turkana Trust v Attorney General & 2 others* [2014] eKLR.

589 *Pastor James Jessie Gitahi & 202 Others v Attorney General* [2013] eKLR.

590 *Said Tahir & 2 others v County Government of Mombasa & 5 others* [2015] eKLR.

591 *Save Lamu & 5 others v National Environmental Management Authority (NEMA) & another* [2019] eKLR.

this regard, Kenya has in place the Fertilizers and Animal Foodstuffs Act that establishes the Fertilizer and Animal Foodstuffs Board of Kenya, whose functions include ensuring that fertilizers imported, manufactured or distributed in Kenya meet the standards of quality and safety standards prescribed by law.592 It also prohibits the importation, manufacture, compounding, mixing, and selling of any fertilizer or animal foodstuff that is not approved. Similarly, there is the Irrigation Act, 2019, which prohibits the use of any chemicals or substances unapproved for use in the schemes. As previously observed, wastewater and substandard chemicals are often used illegally in Kenya.

The Kenyan land tenure system recognises the private, public and community land systems. It behoves the government as the custodian of public land and in the interest of the public to conserve and protect the soils of public land. Specifically, Article 69 obligates the state to ensure that there is sustainable exploitation, utilisation, management and conservation of the environment and natural resources, and equitable sharing of the accruing benefits. On private land, Article 66 gives the state and the police powers to control use of the land for public benefit. Notably, Kenya, an inherently communal society, now has the opportunity to collectively and collaboratively conserve the environment and soils within community lands as part of Kenyan African heritage.

Access to information on environment and soil, in particular, is of utmost importance in soil conservation and protection. First, given that Articles 22 and 70 of the Constitution give every person the right to approach the court to enforce human rights, access to information remains a vital component of this right. Second, courts have been consistent that adequate, timely and accessible information and awareness are critical elements of participatory governance. Article 35 of the Constitution provides the right of access to information held by the state, as well as information held by another person and required for the exercise or protection of any right or fundamental freedom. In *Friends of Lake Turkana Trust v Attorney General & 2 Others [2014] eKLR*, the court held that "it is also now an accepted principle in international law that such access to environmental information is necessary to meet the goals of sustainable development". Kenya has the Access to Information Act, 2016, whose legislation provides for mechanisms for access of information. Evidently, the right to access to information as a component of soil conservation and protection is well protected in Kenyan laws. Unfortunately, there is still inadequate and out-dated information that lacks geographical contextual analysis.

Sustainable soil management requires an integrated approach that builds on both local and natural resources with appropriate use of targeted inputs and management practices. There is a need to quantify the costs of land degradation so that it becomes feasible to assign a value to land degradation. Attributing a value to land degradation

592 Fertilizers and Animal Foodstuffs Act, Section 2(A) and (B).

will also help policymakers to understand the benefits that would accrue from improvement of soil fertility and soil conservation in terms of improved food security. Doing this economic calculation would help to focus and reinforce attention on land degradation as a pressing policy challenge that requires urgent remedial action.

Environmental protection, including protecting the soils of Kenya, is compartmentalised and governed by sectoral laws. The sectoral pieces of legislation range from laws on land, air, water, environment, agriculture, forests and wildlife. Unfortunately, these laws do not adequately and effectively provide for soil-specific provisions. Instead, soil governance, protection and conservation have become secondary or an incidental aspect of environmental protection. This has led to relegation of soil conservation and little attention has been paid to its conservation.

Despite the inadequate soil-specific provisions in the sectoral laws highlighted above, each of the pieces of legislation creates an institutional framework to implement and enforce the specific legislation. For instance, the National Environment Management Authority established under the Environment Management and Coordination Act, 1999, is the lead agency in environmental protection; the Agriculture and Food Authority Act establishes the Agriculture and Food Authority to implement the Crops Act, 2013; the Irrigation Act, 2019, establishes the National Irrigation Authority to implement the Irrigation Act; and the Fertilizers and Animal Foodstuffs Act establishes the Fertilizer and Animal Foodstuffs Board of Kenya to oversee the standards of fertilizers imported or manufactured in Kenya, among other institutions. However, as was noted in Chapter four of this report, the National Land Use Policy recognises that there has been inadequate institutional coordination, and this impedes soil conservation and protection.

Related to inadequate institutional coordination is the uncertainty surrounding the scope of county and national government roles, as contained in the Fourth Schedule of the Constitution. As was highlighted in Chapter two and three of this report, there have been conflicts between the national government and county government on the scope of each level of government's responsibility in agriculture. While the Constitution devolves actual implementation of agricultural activities to county governments, the national government has been reluctant to fund and devolve agricultural activities. In addition, both levels of government have established parallel institutions in the agricultural sector, which creates conflicts and duplication of roles leading to blame games and inefficiency in soil protection and agriculture in general.[593]

Despite the various environmental laws in Kenya that would protect the soil, these laws are poorly implemented. In the earlier sections of this report, we gave instances where illicit trading has led to smuggling of substandard fertilizers in huge volumes, despite the existence of the Fertilizer and Animal Foodstuffs Board of Kenya, Kenya

593 *County Government of Migori & 4 others v Privatization Commission of Kenya & another* [2017] eKLR.

Bureau of Standards, an overzealous Kenya Revenue Authority Custom Department, the National Cereals Board, and the Directorate of Criminal Investigations, among other notable institutions. Similarly, environmental impact assessment licences are rarely obtained before the commencement of mega projects that have negative impacts on soil and, if obtained, they are irregularly issued.

Regarding the National Environment and Management Authority, there have been challenges in this institution's enforcement mechanism as other lead agencies do not cooperate or enforce environmental laws in their respective divisions. In respect of irrigation, we highlighted instances of use of wastewater in irrigation schemes, which then pollute the soil despite clear legal provisions. On land planning and urban sprawl, corruption has invaded the developmental control departments in the country and the planning laws are rarely followed. Cumulatively, the omissions, inactions and actions by various stakeholders have led to soil degradation.

On access to information as a powerful tool to soil conservation, we have observed elsewhere that soil information in Kenya is generally outdated and inaccessible. The inadequate information, particularly to farmers, sees the continued practice of unsustainable agricultural activities that pollute the soil.

Processes such as urbanisation have contributed to degradation of agricultural soils, in particular; thus, threatening food security. The nature, extent, severity and degree of soil degradation varies and changes, based on location, community, and use to which the particular land is put. This therefore requires specific measures based on the vulnerability of each soil. For instance, counties such as Kitui, Machakos and Makueni, which receive little to no rainfall and which have sandy soil, among other types of soil, are more susceptible to erosion and therefore require more stringent measures to avert continued degradation.

There are also linkages between soil degradation and poverty, particularly among the rural poor who depend mainly on the productivity of soil for their livelihood. As such, any efforts to improve the economic lot of the people and eradicate poverty must encompass reforms geared towards improving soil fertility and ensuring soil protection.

On climate, Kenya is quickly positioning itself as a world leader in green economy and clean energy. However, and as observed earlier in this report, there have not been efforts to conserve the soils, given that loss of soil carbon contributes to climate change.

A significant level of consideration of the political context of any particular society is critical if there are to be any successful legal and policy reforms. This is largely because much of policy and legislative reforms turns on the political goodwill that may be afforded to any such legislative initiatives by the executive and parliamentary arms of government, which almost invariably comprise politicians. In particular, all policy documents originate from the Cabinet, which is part of the Executive, and are then taken to Parliament for adoption. Equally, only the legislative assemblies (Parliament and County Assemblies) are vested with the exclusive legislative authority. The Executive represented by the President has the power to assent to all bills passed by Parliament, essentially giving the bills the force of law. Similarly, various delegated pieces of legislation are usually the product of the executive branch of government, mainly the cabinet secretaries, who draft the regulations. Realisation of this fact then means that it is of significant moment to ensure the buy-in of politics as this is necessary to ensure that various proposals relating to soil conservation are transmuted into legislative proposals. It is not all legislative and policy proposals that are put forward or even desired in particular quarters that find expression in law. A lot depends on whether proposals secure the goodwill and support of politicians in Parliament and the Executive.

The upshot of the foregoing is that a political economy analysis in any particular society is necessary if there are to be successful legislative and policy reforms. Attempts to construe legislative reforms to ensure soil conservation and prevention of soil degradation as merely technical rather than a political process is bound to fail. It is essential that these changes be viewed within their wider political context and that an assessment of the various incentives that face all the various stakeholders be done. Some of these stakeholders, including Parliament, Executive, Ministry of Agriculture, county governments, farmers, agricultural officers, and agrochemical industries, have various and sometimes conflicting interests that must be considered if reforms are to be successful. Where particular stakeholders' interests are not considered or views of particular stakeholders are ignored, there is usually a tendency for such groups of stakeholders to create hindrances to successful reforms. A large part of the success that may be experienced in reforms geared towards enhancing soil conservation depends on engagement with counterparts in government.

In addition, a lack of appreciation of the political context or the lack of buy-in by politicians is likely to lead to challenges in implementation of laws and policies geared towards ensuring soil protection. This is partly because politicians head the Executive, which will be responsible for implementing laws that call for soil conservation. Deployment of the financial and technical resources necessary for ensuring the implementation of laws that promote soil conservation is similarly largely dependent on the goodwill of politicians in charge of the relevant department within the Executive and Parliament.

In our view, a detailed analysis of the underlying motivations of the key actors and institutions within the soil sector is an imperative for successful legislative reforms. A proper understanding of these motivations and incentives of the various stakeholders and institutions will help those in charge of pushing for a soil law to manage their interests and expectations and lobby them so as to garner their much-needed political support. For instance, given the strong linkage between soil fertility and agricultural output and the need for food security among the electorate, this may be framed in such a manner that the politicians become aware that soil conservation is a politically live issue that can form a campaign issue – so much so that issues of soil conservation and improving soil fertility form part of the agenda of politicians even as they go and seek out the support of the electorate. Moreover, in Kenya the President has set out an ambitious target of meeting four main agendas, one of which is food security. Yet, food security is impossible in the absence of improved soil fertility and the control of soil degradation. Massive resources are being allocated and considerable attention is being paid to measures that can ensure the achievement of food security. In these circumstances, there is hardly a better opportunity for lobbying for a soil-specific soil law in Kenya than during this period.

6.2 Recommendations

In view of the foregoing and the contents of this report, the following recommendations are made with respect to enhancing soil conservation and protection in Kenya: There is a need for the country to develop a comprehensive soil policy which brings together all stakeholders to develop the principles and policies to govern soil management in Kenya. At the national level, the country should in a participatory manner enact comprehensive soil legislation that implements the principles of soil conservation and management in Kenya. With the devolution of agriculture as a function of county governments under the Fourth Schedule of the Constitution, county assemblies should also development county-specific legislation on soil management and governance. This will assist in the development soil legislations that are specific to soils in various regions.

In developing soil conservation measures, given the cross-cutting role of soil, there is a need to develop an integrated approach and to legislate having regard to other important components of the environment. Moreover, there is a need to set out clearly the roles of the national and county governments and create institutions. To avoid an uncoordinated institutional framework, there is a need to have harmonised institutional coordination.

In terms of enhanced enforcement of environmental laws and environmental rights it has also been noted that there is laxity in enforcement of laws by mandated institutions. It is therefore recommended that the National Environment and Management Authority and other institutions should coordinate and collaboratively implement environmental laws on protection and conservation of the soil. Soil being a cross-cutting natural resource, there is a need to create an integrated approach of enforcement to abolish the sectoral implementation of environmental laws. There is a need to enhance the penalties set out in law for breaches and introduce restoration taxes that should be paid by those guilty of degrading soils, over and above the restoration orders that may be ordered by courts or tribunals against such persons. In addition, there is a need to ensure that issues of sustainable soil management are inculcated into school-going learners by integrating this matter into the school or educational curriculum. Such a move would ensure that children and young learners become champions of soil management, similar to the efforts to integrate climate change awareness into school learning. The net effect of this is to cause young learners to be agents of soil protection, which would ensure that soil is protected for the forthcoming generations.

It is critical that updated information on the quality of soil is easily accessible to the general public, many of whom are small-scale farmers who depend daily on soil for their economic livelihood and sustenance. There is need to adopt various techniques such as afforestation and reforestation, and the use of low-cost technologies as these methods and techniques have the potential to improve soil protection. Some incentive schemes should be developed such as fertilizer and manure subsidies for local small-scale farmers who would otherwise ill-afford these nutrients as this would help improve soil fertility. There is a need to take a holistic approach to soil conservation in law by taking note of the fact that soil is degraded through a variety of ways and means, including through erosion, acidification, salinisation, compaction, contamination, and loss of nutrients and organic matter. Any attempt to prevent soil degradation and improve the status of soil through legislation must therefore encompass measures geared towards arresting the factors that result in soil degradation.

Policymakers ought to realise, while drafting soil legislation, that a number of activities including land-use changes, urban expansion, intensification of agriculture, particular farming methods, and deforestation result in biodiversity loss and soil degradation and thus need to be taken care of in law. There should be a recognition that issues relating to soil protection are transboundary in nature and that they should be independent of any political boundaries if they are to be handled successfully and effectively.

The enumerated recommendations could inform the legislation enacted to regulate soil. Below, we set out some of the key features or elements that should be contained in soil-specific legislation in Kenya.

6.3 Elements of a soil-specific legislation

There are various essential features or elements that a soil-specific law in Kenya should contain including the following: The purpose of the law be clearly stated and which should ideally be on the sustainable management of soils. The statement of purpose may speak about the need for a competent organisation charged with managing soils, setting of priorities, the geographical area of interest of the law, and areas of application of the law. A definitional section should provide definitions of various concepts to provide clarity as to the meaning of the words used and the context in which such words and phrases are employed. The objective of the law should be devoted to the conservation of soil, the prevention of soil degradation, and the improvement of soil fertility in order to ensure food security. The law should also contain principles that undergird its application on soil and which can serve as an interpretive guide to the courts in the event of conflicts over interpretation. Another section shall set out rights and responsibilities accruing to various parties and actors. This delineation of rights and responsibilities is important in ensuring accountability of functions. In terms of the protection of marginalised persons and communities it is essential that the law encompasses special provisions on the rights of marginalised groups, especially bearing in mind the critical role of soil for livelihood sustenance. It often happens that marginalised groups, which include the poor, women, and persons living in arid and semi-arid areas that rarely experience adequate rainfall, suffer long periods of droughts and occasional flash floods, which result in soil erosion and degradation. The law should, therefore, make special provision to enhance soil conservation and soil fertility in these areas to ensure food security. In the section on national authorities and focal points the law should outline the institutional framework responsible for soil conservation and protection and necessarily comprising various ministries and state agencies charged with agriculture, land, water and irrigation, among others.

Regarding public and community participation the law should have provisions requiring involvement of the people (as the public or the community), given that it is the people who are most affected by the state of the soil. This is especially critical in constitutional democracies such as Kenya and would also be in conformity with the constitutional provision which lists public participation as a national value. The utility of this provision is that the views and insights of the public are captured and implemented for the better management of soils.

In the developmental interest of national soil strategies, the law ought to provide for the development of soil strategies at the national level, preferably by the ministry. These soil strategies should then act as a reference point for all the various actions that would be done. The law should provide for periodic reviews of the soil strategies to help the law align with changes that occur in the soil sector.

In determination of national soil authority, the law should preferably establish a national soil authority, which should be a state agency resourced by the national government. The soil authority should be the overarching body mandated with various functions including soil information, soil planning, executive and financial administration, and conducting of soil evaluation and assessment, among a variety of other functions. The authority should have a head, who will be the titular head and executive officer of the authority to ensure the achievement of its functions. The law should also establish a national soil advisory body which should also be devolved to the various counties. Principally, the advisory body should be made up of a group of high-level experts well-versed in soil science, agriculture, herbicides, crop science, land, physical planning and other related disciplines. The mandate of the advisory body should be to advise on legal, strategic, administrative, political and financial issues relating to the sustainable management of soils. The body would serve as the intellectual nerve centre and would be concerned with preparing, implementing and reviewing soil strategies and other policies relating to sustainable management of soils.

Linked to the national soil strategy is the need to develop a national soil policy, which may be reviewed every 10 years. The soil policy would encapsulate the main principles that should guide the management of soils and would precede any subsequent ruling on the subject of soil that may be enacted. The law should proscribe a list of activities. The prohibited or outlawed activities should be those that have a deleterious effect on soil. The power to punish for violation of this provision should be vested in the national soil authority.

Given the importance of conducting soil research and investigating developments to improve soil status, and the need to build the technical capacity of persons involved in the management of soil, there ought to be a provision in the law for these express mandates. For the effective and sustainable management of soils, the law ought to devise and provide for a monitoring framework that regularly assesses the state of soil, particularly in erosion prone areas. This kind of monitoring would then help the soil authority, and the government in general, to take corrective measures that are geared to restoring the health and fertility of the soil.

Soil protection, conservation, prevention of soil degradation, and improvement of soil fertility entail resource-intensive exercises that require a huge mobilisation of resources. This is especially so given the level and extent of land degradation in particular areas of the country. It is therefore critical that there be a guaranteed financing scheme from government. The law should make provision to deal with the right of citizens and other concerned persons to soil information. This would in essence be a restatement of the constitutional right to information. This right would ensure that the government is held accountable for all actions relating to soil and would ensure that it would seek to comply with the law. As soil degradation is transboundary in nature in that effects of soil erosion occurring in one country or county can spill over into the territory of another country or county, proper soil conservation will necessarily entail a coordinated approach that is cross-border in nature, and which seeks the support of other neighbouring countries and counties.

Women tend to be the managers within the household responsible for providing food to the family. Evidence shows that in most of sub-Saharan Africa it is the women who manage land and farms for subsistence, even in cases where they do not hold titles to the land. It therefore means that when soil is degraded, women are disproportionately harmed compared to men, as it is women who are charged with the duty of ensuring that there is food security in the household.

The legal framework on soil should have both a liability and redress mechanism. Such a framework would ensure that for each liability, there is a legal remedy that can be afforded to the injured party. The law should explicitly vest the National Environment Tribunal with the original jurisdiction to adjudicate disputes relating to soil, being an environmental matter, and decisions should be appealed before the Environment and Land Court to enable expeditious resolution of disputes.

References

Allan, C., 2008, "Can adaptive management help us embrace the Murray-darling basin's wicked problems?". In: Pahl-Wostl, C., P. Kabat & J. Möltgen (eds), *Adaptive and integrated water management*, Berlin: Springer, 61.

Allan, O., 2019, "High Court orders closure of Kibos sugar factory over pollution". *Citizen Digital* 31 July 2019, at https://citizentv.co.ke/news/high-court-orders-closure-of-kibos-sugar-factory-over-pollution-266894/ accessed 10 October 2019.

Bailey, T.A., 2018, "The curious case of substandard fertilizers in Kenya". *International Policy Digest* 30 June 2018.

Bentsi-Enchill, K., 1964, *An exposition, analysis and critique*. London: Sweet & Maxwell.

Bondi, D.O. & J. Mugabe, 1996, "Land tenure systems and natural resource management". In: Calestous, J. & J.B. Ojwang (eds), *In land we trust: Environment, private property and constitutional change*. Nairobi: Initiatives, 85.

Bragdon, S.H., 1990, *Kenya's legal and institutional structure for environmental protection and natural resource management*. Washington: Economic Development Institute of the World Bank, at http://documents.worldbank.org/curated/en/278671468774886535/pdf/multi-page.pdf, accessed 18 May 2019.

Commission of Inquiry, 2004, *Report of the Commission of Inquiry into the illegal/irregular allocation of public land*. Nairobi: Commission of Inquiry, at https://bit.ly/3prdvIB, accessed 15 February 2021.

Corray, M.S., 1978, "The Kenya Land Commission and the Kikuyu of Kiambu". *Agricultural History* 52, 179.

David, P. & C.A. Edwards, 1982, "Pesticides and Ecosystems". *Issues in Biology Education Oxford University Press on behalf of the American Institute of Biological Sciences* (32) 7, 595.

David, M., D. Ndirangu, M. Mangala, J. Boman, K. Shepherd & M. Gichuru, 2016, "Environmental implications of high metal content in soils of a titanium mining zone in Kenya". *Environmental Science and Pollution Research* 23, 21431.

Gadgil, M., 1989, "On the diversification of common property". In: Berkes, F. (ed.), *Common property resources: Ecology and community-based sustainable development*, 240.

Gichenje, H., J. Muñoz-Rojas & T. Pinto-Correia, 2019, "Opportunities and limitations for achieving land". *Land* 8 (8), 115.

Gichuki, F.N., 1991, *Environmental change and dryland management in Machakos district, Kenya 1930–1990 conservation profile*. Working Paper 56, University of Nairobi, at https://www.odi.org/sites/odi.org.uk/files/odi-assets/publications-opinion-files/6951.pdf, accessed 18 May 2019.

Government of Kenya, 2002, *National action programme: A framework for combating desertification in Kenya in the context of the United Nations Convention to Combat Desertification*. Nairobi: Ministry of Environment and Natural Resources & National Environment Secretariat.

Government of Kenya, 2009, *National land policy*. Nairobi: Ministry of Lands, at https://www.refworld.org/docid/5b3e29474.html, accessed 2 February 2021.

Government of Kenya, 2013a, The state of the world's biodiversity for food and agriculture – Kenya report. Nairobi: Government of Kenya, at http://www.fao.org/3/CA3473EN/ca3473en.pdf, accessed 2 February 2021.

Government of Kenya, 2013b, *National environment policy*. Nairobi: Ministry of Environment, Water and Natural Resources, at https://bit.ly/37gN3LI, accessed 15 February 2021.

Government of Kenya, 2014, *Kenya demographic and health survey*. Nairobi: Government of Kenya.

Government of Kenya, 2016a, *National spatial plan 2015-2045*. Nairobi: Government of Kenya.

Government of Kenya, 2016b, *Report of the land degradation assessment (LADA) in Kenya based on a study of land degradation assessment (LADA) with remote sensing and GIS, for sustainable land management (SLM) in Kenya*. Nairobi: Ministry of Environment and Natural Resources.

Government of Kenya, 2017a, *The Big Four Agenda*, at https://www.president.go.ke, accessed 18 January 2021.

Government of Kenya, 2017b, *National land use policy*. Nairobi: Ministry of Lands and Physical Planning, at https://lands.go.ke/wp-content/uploads/2018/06/SESSIONAL-PAPER-NO.-1-OF-2017-ON-NATIONAL-LAND-USE-POLICY.pdf, accessed 2 February 2021.

Government of Kenya, 2018a, *Kenya integrated household and expenditure survey 2015/2016 basic report*. Nairobi: National Bureau of Statistics.

Government of Kenya, 2018b, *Kenya Vision 2030: Third medium term plan 2018–2022*. Nairobi: Government of the Republic of Kenya, at http://vision2030.go.ke/wp-content/uploads/2019/01/THIRD-MEDIUM-TERM-PLAN-2018-2022.pdf, accessed 1 February 2021.

Government of Kenya, 2018c, *Taskforce report on forest resources management and logging activities in Kenya*. Nairobi: Government of Kenya.

Government of Kenya, 2019a, *Kenya population and housing census. Volume I: Population by county and sub county* Nairobi: National Bureau of Statistics.

Government of Kenya, 2019b, *Kenya population and housing census. Volume III: Distribution of population by age and sex*. Nairobi: National Bureau of Statistics.

Government of Kenya, Royal Netherlands Government & UNEP, 1997, *National land degradation assessment and mapping in Kenya*. Nairobi: Government of Kenya.

Hannam, I. & B. Boer, 2004, *Drafting legislation for sustainable soils: A guide*. Gland: IUCN.

Herbling, D., 2019, "Kenya to double debt ceiling to almost match economy's size". *Bloomberg News* 16 October 2019, at https://www.bloomberg.com/news/articles/2019-10-16/kenya-to-double-debt-ceiling-to-almost-match-economy-s-size, accessed 1 February 2021.

Howard, T.M. & A. Lawson, 2015, "Soil governance: Accessing cross-disciplinary perspectives". *International Journal of Rural Law and Policy* 1, 3776.

Huxley, E., 1935, *White man's country: Lord Delamere and the making of Kenya*. London: Macmillan and Co., Limited.

Institute of Social Accountability, 2017, *Memorandum on Physical Planning Bill 2017*, at https://www.tisa.or.ke/images/uploads/Memorandum_on_the_Physical_Planning_Bill_2017.pdf accessed November 2019.

Kabau, T. & C. Njoroge, 2011, "Application of international law in Kenya under the 2010 Constitution: Critical issues in the harmonisation of the legal system". *Comparative and International Law Journal of Southern Africa* 44 (3), 293.

Kabau, T.J.O. & Ambani, 2013, "The 2010 Constitution and the application of international law in Kenya: A Case of migration to monism or regression to dualism?". *Africa Nazarene University Law Journal* 1(1), 36.

Kakumu, O.A., 1996, *The impact of land acquisition problems on plan project implementation.* Thesis submitted in partial requirement of Master of Arts in Planning, University of Nairobi.

Kameri- Mbote, P., 2002, *Property rights and biodiversity management in Kenya.* Nairobi: ACTS Press.

Karanja, F., 2019, "Top KEBs officials in court seeking re-test of alleged substandard fertilizer". *Standard Digital* 9 January 2019, at https://www.standardmedia.co.ke/article/2001308784/top-kebs-officials-seek-fresh-test-on-fertiliser, accessed 20 October 2019.

Karuku, G.N. & INNSPUB / International Network for Natural Sciences, 2018, "Soil and water conservation measures and challenges in Kenya". *Current Investigations in Agriculture and Current Research* 2 (5), 259.

Kazungu, R., J. Gitau & P. Gichuru, 2011, "Application of GIS in identification, documentation and monitoring Brownfield land". Paper presented at the 47th ISOCARP Congress 2011.

KASLMP / Kenya Agricultural Productivity and Sustainable Land Management Project & Ministry of Environment and Natural Resources, 2016, *Land degradation assessment in Kenya report.* Nairobi: KASLMP, at http://www.environment.go.ke/wp-content/uploads/2018/08/LADA-Land-Degradation-Assessment-in-Kenya-March-2016.pdf, accessed 1 February 2021.

Kenya National Bureau of Statistics, 2018, *Economic Survey 2018.* Nairobi: Kenya National Bureau of Statistics.

Kenya National Bureau of Statistics, 2019, *Economic Survey 2019.* Nairobi: Kenya National Bureau of Statistics.

Lugard, F.D., 1929, *The dual mandate in British tropical Africa.* London: W. Blackwood.

Maina, W., 2016, "Why dissolution of land control boards will not cure corruption, disbanding land boards won't end corruption". *Daily Nation* 24 June 2016, at https://mobile.nation.co.ke/blogs/dissolution-of-land-control-boards-will-not-cure-corruption/1949942-3266160-mklifp/index.html accessed 6th November 2019.

Mativo, J.M., 2015, *The role of law in urban planning in Kenya: Towards norms of good urban governance.* LLM Thesis, University of Nairobi.

Ministry of Foreign Affairs of Netherlands, 2018, *Climate change profile: Kenya.* The Hague: Ministry of Foreign Affairs, at https://www.government.nl/documents/publications/2019/02/05/climate-change-profiles, accessed 18 January 2021.

Ministry of Land and Urban Planning, 2017, *Sector Plan for Population, Urbanization and Housing 2013-2017.* Nairobi: Ministry of Land and Urban Planning.

Mohajan, H., 2014, "Food and nutrition scenario of Kenya". *American Journal of Food and Nutrition* 2 (2), 28.

Mulinge, W., P. Gicheru, F. Murithi, P. Maingi, E. Kihiu, O.K. Kirui & A. Mirzabaev, 2016, "Economics of land degradation and improvement in Kenya". In: Nkonya, E., A. Mirzabaev & J. von Braun, 2016, *Economics of land degradation and improvement–A global assessment for sustainable development.* Cham: Springer, 471.

Mundia, C.N. & Y. Murayama, 2010, "Modelling spatial processes of urban growth in African cities: A case study of Nairobi city". *Urban Geography* 31 (2), 259.

Mungeam, G.H., 1966, *British rule in Kenya, 1895-1912: The establishment of administration in the East Africa Protectorate.* Oxford: Clarendon Press.

Munro, A.P., 1959, *The land tenure revolution in Kenya 1954–1959: Legal and political implications.* Master Thesis, Columbia University, at http://erepository.uonbi.ac.ke/bitstream/handle/11295/96147/A.P.%20MUNRO%20M.A%201960.pdf?sequence=4&isAllowed=y, accessed 18 May 2019.

Mutisya, T., K. Juma & L. Zejiao, 2010, "Soil and water conservation in Kenya-operations, achievements and challenges of the National Agriculture and Livestock Extension Programme (NALEP)". *Journal of American Science* 6 (3), 7.

Mutono, N.R., 2016, *Environmental and health problems associated with artisanal mining in Kenya: A case study of Macalder mines in Migori*. Master Thesis Environmental Governance, University of Nairobi.

Muyanga, M. & J. Thomas, 2006, *Agricultural extension in Kenya: Practice and policy lessons*. Working Paper 26, Tegemeo Institute of Agricultural Policy and Development, Egerton University.

Mwanza, K., 2019, "Thousands of acres of farmland are being turned into satellite cities". *How we made it in Africa* 31 March 2019, at https://www.howwemadeitinafrica.com/thousands-of-acres-of-kenyan-farmland-are-being-turned-into-satellite-cities/63097/, accessed 20 October 2019.

Namusyule, S. & L. Mueni, 2018, "Impact of Judiciary budget cut". *Judiciary* 21 August 2018, at https://www.judiciary.go.ke/impact-of-judiciary-budget-cut/, accessed 1 November 2019.

National Environment Management Authority, 2011, *Integrated national landuse guidelines*. Nairobi: NEMA.

Ndegwa, E.N., 2001, "Making Kenya a planning society: Challenges and opportunities". Paper presented during the Launch Workshop of the Kenya Institute of Planners held at Nairobi Safari Club on 8 March 2001, unpublished.

Nyabonyi, J., 2016, *Suitability assessment of effluents from Mwea irrigation scheme for reuse in irrigation for rice production, Kirinyaga County, Kenya*. Master Thesis Master of Sciene, Kenyatta University.

O'Connell, D.P., 1960, "The relationship between international law and municipal law". *Georgetown Law Journal* 48 (3), 431.

Odinga, T., 2018, "Focus on miners, farmers as soil pollution rises". *Business Daily* 4 December 2018, at https://www.businessdailyafrica.com/datahub/3815418-4881226-11dxf1kz/index.html, accessed 3 November 2018.

Odote, C., 2013, "Kenya: The new Environment and Land Court". *IUCN Academy of Environmental Law E-Journal* 1.

Oduor, M., 2014, "The status of international law in Kenya". *Africa Nazarene University Law Journal* 2 (2), 97.

Ogemba, P. & K. Muthoni, 2019, "Budget cuts: Treasury slashed Judiciary's budget by Sh3 billion". *Standard Digital* 29 October 2019, at https://www.standardmedia.co.ke/article/2001347258/judiciary-on-trial-as-cash-crisis-hits-hard, accessed 1 November 2019.

Okpara, C.I., 2012, "Right to a clean and healthy environment: The Panacea to the Niger Delta struggle". *Journal of Politics and Law* 5 (1), 3.

Ombati, C., 2018, "Firm denies claims into fertilizer accusations amid KEBS arrests". *Standard Digital* 24 June 2018, at https://www.standardmedia.co.ke/article/2001285333/firm-denies-claims-into-fertilizer-accusations-amid-kebs-arrests, accessed 6 November 2019.2

Osolo-Nasubo, N.A., 1977, *Socio-economic study of the Kenya highlands from 1900-1970: A case-study of the Uhuru government*. Washington: University Press of America.

Owino, K. & J. Mutua, 2019, "Analysis of trends in Kenya's public debt". Presentation, Institute of Economic Affairs-Kenya 24 April 2019.

Palley, C., 1966, *The constitutional history and law of Southern Rhodesia 1880–1965*. Oxford: Oxford University Press.

Salaudeen, A., 2019, "Kenya launches largest wind power plant in Africa". *CNN Marketplace Africa* 20 July 2019, at https://edition.cnn.com/2019/07/20/africa/africas-largest-wind-farm-intl/index.html, accessed 2 February 2021.

Shiundu, A., 2018, "Long road to Independence". *Development and Cooperation* 12 December 2018.

Swynnerton, R.J.M., 1954, *A plan to intensify the development of African agriculture in Kenya*. Nairobi: Government Printer.

Thurston, A., 1987, *Smallholder agriculture in colonial Kenya: The official mind and the Swynnerton Plan*. Cambridge: African Studies Center, at https://www.african.cam.ac.uk/images/files/titles/smallholder, accessed 17 May 2019.

UNCCD / United Nations Convention to Combat Desertification, 2016, *Achieving land degradation neutrality at the country level: Building blocks for LDN target setting*. Bonn: Global Mechanism of the UNCCD, at https://bit.ly/2M2Ks0C, accessed 26 October 2019.

UNDP / United Nations Development Programme, 2013, *Combating desertification in Kenya: emerging lessons from empowering local communities*. Nairobi: UNDP, at https://bit.ly/2N5u00b accessed 26 October 2019.

Wabwile, M., 2013, "The emerging juridical status of international law in Kenya". *Oxford University Commonwealth Law Journal* 13 (1), 167.

Wasilwa, C. & S. Nanjala, 2019, "Stop pollution or face legal action, MP tells firm – toxic waste disposal war nets 9, factories shut". *Daily Nation* 28 August 2019, at https://bit.ly/3bihHW8, accessed 6 November 2019.

Wolff, R.D., 1974, *The economics of colonialism: Britain and Kenya 1870–1930*. Yale: Yale University Press.

World Commission on Environment and Development, 1987, *Our common future*. Oxford: Oxford University Press.

Country report for Zambia

Pamela Towela Sambo (lead author), Andrew Nkunika (contributing author) & Nelly Zulu (contributing author)

1 Introduction

The purpose of this report is to evaluate the provisions of relevant laws and policies in Zambia in order to ascertain whether sustainable soil management is being implemented in the country. This is against the background that the Intergovernmental Panel on Climate Change (IPCC), has recently published a report which re-affirms that effective land management, among other measures, can contribute to tackling climate change.[1] The IPCC is the world's leading body in assessing the state of scientific knowledge related to climate change, its impacts, potential future risks, and possible response options.

Sustainable soil management is important for Zambia and other countries because it is one definite pathway to achieving some of the Sustainable Development Goals (SDGs).[2] The relevant SDGs include: ending all forms of poverty and hunger; achieving food security through improved nutrition; promoting sustainable agriculture; and taking urgent action to combat climate change and its impacts.[3]

This report is divided into main sections which provide insight into government structure which deal with the way Zambia is set up for governance through three organs, the Executive, Legislature and Judicature; as well as the main drivers of soil degradation and the applicable laws and policies to safeguard the soil.

1.1 Geographic and climatic information

The Republic of Zambia is a landlocked country in Southern Africa covering a surface area of 752,972 km^2 located roughly between latitudes 8° and 18° south of the equator.[4] The country is surrounded by the Democratic Republic of Congo, Tanzania, Malawi, Mozambique, Zimbabwe, Botswana, Namibia and Angola.

1 IPCC (2019: 2).
2 The sustainable development goals (SDGs) are discussed more substantively below.
3 See https://bit.ly/3cRsOYw, accessed 3 February 2021.
4 Japan Association for International Collaboration of Agriculture and Forestry (2008).

Generally, there are three seasons in Zambia, a summer rainy season (November to April); a cool, dry winter season (May to August); and a hot dry season (September and October).

Zambia is located in the tropical climatic zone, approximately 900–1,500 metres above sea level, excluding the basins of the Zambezi, Luangwa and Kafue rivers, and the areas around Lakes Tanganyika, Mweru and Bangweulu, which are relatively cool.[5] The country's geographical position and high altitude provides it with sub-tropical vegetation and climatic conditions.

The season with the highest temperature is the month of October. The rainy season extends from November/December to around April, and the dry season from around May to around November. The average annual rainfall amounts to around 1,000 mm but varies by region. The rainfall in the south and south-west regions is around 900 mm, but in the north and north-west regions it exceeds 1,400 mm. After the cool season from May to mid-August, the temperatures start rising. In the capital, Lusaka, the minimum and maximum average temperatures in July are 9 degrees Celsius and 23 degrees Celsius respectively; and in January 17 degrees Celsius and 26 degrees Celsius respectively. Normally, the annual average rainfall per annum is about 810 mm.[6]

As with the rest of Africa, and particularly the sub-Saharan region, Zambia has been experiencing the effects of climate change resulting in extreme weather conditions, such as droughts, rising temperatures and unpredictable rainfall patterns.[7] The frequency and intensity of climate events is expected to rise in future, with negative impacts on the economy and consequently people's livelihoods.[8]

1.2 Historical background, demographic information and level of education

Zambia attained its political independence from Britain in 1964. The country's political history spans the era of multiparty democracy from 1964 to 1972; one-party rule thereafter until 1990; and a multiparty democracy system of governance from 1991 to date.[9] Administratively, the country is divided into 10 provinces, namely Central, Copperbelt, Eastern, Luapula, Lusaka, Muchinga, Northern, North-Western, Southern and Western. These provinces are further subdivided into districts, constituencies and wards.[10]

---

5 Plisnier et al. (2018).
6 Resilience and Economic Inclusion Team (2016).
7 Ministry of National Development Planning (2016: 2–3).
8 Plisnier et al. (2018); Sintayehu (2018: 225–227); Ministry of National Development Planning (2016: 4).
9 Phiri (2006: 1–5).
10 Central Statistical Office (2015: 1).

It has been noted that after political independence in the 1960s, Zambia enjoyed a strategic role as supporter of the liberation movements in Southern Africa. Zambia gradually lost its strategic importance over the years following the deterioration of African economies, the demise of the Soviet Union and the fragmentation of the 'Third World' as countries in South-East Asia grew rapidly and drew away. Zambia has also had enduring relationships with China and India since its independence.[11] These relationships resulted in a number of projects to support the Zambian economy. The Tanzania–Zambia (TAZARA) railway, for example, was the first and probably best-known example of China's engagement in Africa.[12] In trade terms, Zambia's loss of strategic importance has resulted in negative consequences for the country's negotiating power in both traditional and non-traditional development assistance.

According to the Population and Demographic Projections for 2011–2035 Report (Projections Report), Zambia's population was estimated to stand at 15.9 million in 2016, out of which 7.9 million would be males and 8.0 million females.[13] Also, 9.2 million would reside in rural areas and 6.7 million in urban areas. The population is expected to continue growing at an average annual rate of around 2.8% during the projection period 2011–2035.[14] The population in rural areas is expected to grow at a relatively stable average rate of 2.4% per annum, while the urban population is expected to grow at 3.5% per annum during the same period.

At provincial level, Lusaka has the largest population with 2,888,575 persons, while the North-Western Province has the smallest population with 856,286 persons. The population was expected to grow to 17.9 million by 2020 of which 10.1 million would reside in rural areas, while 7.8 million would reside in urban areas.[15] During the projection years, the age structure was expected to remain relatively unchanged although the proportion of children in the population would fall. The young population was expected to result in growth in the reproductive age group (15–49) and the economically active age group (15–64).[16]

The Projections Report further stated that in 2016 the estimated or average life expectancy at birth would be 53.7 years. Females had a higher life expectancy at birth of 56.1 years compared to 51.5 years for males. The projected decline in fertility and mortality was expected to lead to an increase in life expectancy at birth and at different ages, as well as an increase in the proportion of the elderly of 65 years and older, in the long run.[17]

11 Prizzon (2013: iv).
12 Monson (2013: 52).
13 See https://bit.ly/3tsja4H, accessed 3 February 2021.
14 Ibid.
15 See https://bit.ly/2YHQ1En, accessed 3 February 2021.
16 Ministry of Finance (2017: 31).
17 Ibid.: 33.

The country's average population density is 20.6 persons per km², while Lusaka Province has the highest density of 126.8 persons per km². There are 73 ethnic groups in Zambia with seven major languages used besides English, which is the official language. The seven major languages are Bemba, Kaonde, Lozi, Lunda, Luvale, Nyanja and Tonga.[18]

Zambia's Vision 2030, the long-term national development plan, provides a strategic focus for the country to become "a prosperous middle-income nation."[19] In order to attain this vision, the role of quality education is critical. In 2015, the Ministry of Education, Science, Vocational Training and Early Education was split into two distinct parts – the Ministry of Higher Education and the Ministry of General Education. The Education System consists of early childhood education (ECE), primary, and secondary under the Ministry of General Education. ECE (pre-school) provides education for children aged 3–6 years, while primary level runs from grades 1 to 7 (7–13 years old) and the secondary level runs from grades 8 to 12 (14–18 years old). The professional or tertiary levels include universities and colleges and fall under the jurisdiction of the Ministry of Higher Education.[20]

The adult literacy in Zambia currently stands at 68%[21] and can be related to the generally low awareness levels about the environment, let alone its constituent elements like soil. The priority areas for the general education subsector have been access and participation, quality and relevance of education and equity. The targets by the end of the Revised Sixth National Development Plan period were to attain net enrolment ratio (NER) of 100%. With regard to the transition rate, the targets for 2016 were 68% at Grade 7 and 50% at Grade 9.[22] These targets were to be achieved through the construction of new schools and additional classrooms in existing schools in order to enhance access. Significant investment was made in strategies to promote equity in access to education during the period of the Fifth and Sixth National Development Plans.

According to the Ministry of General Education, the Early Childhood Education (ECE) level made notable achievements with the shifting of the mandate of providing ECE from the Ministry of Local Government and Housing to the Ministry of Education. The proportion of learners with ECE experience rose from 20.3% in 2005 to 24.4% in 2015.[23]

There is, however, much more that needs to be done to enhance access to ECE, in order to meet the target of 30% of new Grade 1 entrants with ECE experience. Overall, the education sector benefits an average of about 15–17% of the national budget or

18 Central Statistical Office, (2013: 1).
19 Ministry of National Development Planning (2006: 1–2).
20 Ministry of General Education (2017).
21 Ibid.; Fadjukoff (2015: 127).
22 Ministry of Finance (2011: 41).
23 Ministry of General Education (2017).

about 2–4% of the GDP – lower than the SADC recommended minimum threshold of 20% of national budget or 6% of GDP.[24]

1.3 Main economic activities

This section discusses the main economic activities in Zambia, and their impact on the general environmental well-being and, more specifically, sustainable soil management. The highest environmental impact stems from mining, while the tourism sector complements environmental sustainability because it is premised on preserving biological diversity, such as wildlife and the floral kingdom, among others.

1.3.1 Mining

Zambia is the seventh largest copper producer globally,[25] and mining contributes over 75% of the country's total export value. It has been observed that the total contribution of mining to gross domestic product (GDP) averaged at 12.9% for the period 2006–2015 and that the sector created 56,227 jobs in 2005, which increased to 82,725 in 2014.[26] In recognition of the important national economic role that mining continues to play, such as employment creation, revenue generation and rural-urban development, Zambia continues to make efforts to reduce copper dependence and support the diversification to other minerals, such as gemstones and other industrial minerals. Although minerals such as cobalt, coal, emeralds and gold are mined in Zambia, their contribution to the country's total export value is not clear. Generally, the mineral output in the sector has been lower than it was historically. For example, the 2015 copper output of 710,560 metric tonnes was below government's projection of 800,000 metric tonnes.[27]

1.3.2 Agriculture

Owing to the falling prices of copper on the global market, Zambia has embarked on a programme to diversify its economy in order to reduce overdependence on copper. Copper- price fluctuations have presented a risk and have led to a sharp decline in

24 OSISA (2015: 10–18).

25 Major countries in copper mine production worldwide from 2010 to 2018, see https://www.statista.com/statistics/264626/copper-production-by-country/, accessed 12 April 2019.

26 Mining Partnerships for Development (2014: 11).

27 Ministry of National Development Planning (2017: 26).

revenue from export over the years. This economic meltdown also happened in Zambia during the Fifth National Development Plan (FNDP) period between 2007 and 2009, when copper prices fell by 28%. This in turn led to a corresponding foreign direct investment (FDI) fall of 47%. The FDI flows into Zambia remained highly concentrated in the copper mining sector. The agriculture, manufacturing and tourism sectors, which create and sustain productive employment, received only negligible investments.[28]

About 58% of Zambia's total land area of 75 million hectares is potentially good for agricultural production, although most of this arable land is yet to be fully utilised for the purpose of increasing the contribution of the agricultural sector to the national economy. Zambia's agricultural activities are mainly rain-fed despite having large water bodies that can easily be tapped for irrigation purposes.[29] Against this, it has widely been observed that Zambia has the potential to increase its agricultural output.[30] While arable land is plentiful in the country, only about 15% of it is under cultivation. In recent years, the promotion of the agricultural sector has been one of government's top priorities in a bid to diversify the economy and reduce overreliance on its traditional products and exports, such as copper and cobalt. The total contribution of agriculture to GDP averaged at 9.8% in the period 2006 to 2015.[31] With a combination of arable land and an annual rainfall ranging from 800 to 1,400 mm[32], the country has medium-to high-potential for agriculture; yet maintains a high underutilised acreage. In the unused arable land area, however, a reduction of forest area could lead to destruction of the natural environment, thus the extent of this transformation to farmland should be carefully examined.[33]

The Zambian agricultural sector comprises crops, livestock, and fisheries.[34] There are three broad categories of farmers: small-scale, medium, and large-scale. Small-scale farmers are generally subsistence producers of staple foods such as maize, sorghum, millet, and cassava, with occasional marketable surplus. Most Zambians are subsistence farmers. Medium-scale farmers produce maize and a few other cash crops such as cotton, groundnuts, sorghum, rice, sunflower seeds, coffee, sugar and fruits. Large-scale farmers produce various crops such as sugar, soybeans, coffee, groundnuts, rice, tobacco, paprika, wheat and cotton, as well as horticultural produce. A small percentage of produce from large-scale farmers is sold on the local markets while the bulk of the high-grade produce is reserved for export.[35] While the country enjoys 40%

---

28 ZDA (2017: 3)
29 Central Statistical Office (2015: 1).
30 ZEMA (2017: 46); Chapoto & Chisanga (2016: 7–10).
31 Ministry of Agriculture (2016: 1–3).
32 ZEMA (2017: 33).
33 Japan Association for International Collaboration of Agriculture and Forestry (2008: 36).
34 See http://www.zda.org.zm/index.php/agriculture/, accessed 2 February 2021.
35 Chapoto & Chisanga (2016: 30–42).

of sub-Saharan water resources, there is very little mechanical irrigation and most farms are dependent on rain-fed growing cycles.[36] This presents insurmountable challenges when the rain patterns fluctuate, as has been seen in recent times owing to the effects of climate change.

For instance, during the period 2006–2015, output for 13 of the 18 major crops declined largely as a result of erratic rainfall, which in recent times has negatively affected the yield rates. For example, in the 2015–2016 farming season, maize production decreased by 21.9% from 3,350,671 to 2,618,221 metric tonnes (MT). Such a drastic decline has the potential to affect the rural economy in the country, because most of the agricultural activities are undertaken in these areas. Further, with the high employment opportunities offered by the agricultural sector, it is likely that such dramatic declines in production could further spur the rural–urban drift in Zambia. At the heart of addressing these challenges, there are multi-pronged efforts at mitigating the effects of climate change across all sectors.[37]

1.3.3 Manufacturing

The manufacturing sector accounted for about 7.8% of the country's GDP and an average annual growth rate of 3% from 2006 to 2015. The 2005 and 2014 Labour Force Surveys showed that there were 166,143 persons employed in the manufacturing sector in 2005, which increased to 223, 681in 2014. The manufacturing sector was pivotal in economic development as it played a key role in the backward and forward linkages to economic growth. It has been further noted that in the latter years of the Sixth National Development Plan (SNDP) 2011–2015, there was slow growth in the manufacturing sector owing to some of the constraints to growth such as the energy deficit and high production costs which contributed to a drop of output of between 60% and 70%.[38]

The sector is largely driven by the agro-processing (food and beverages), textile, and leather subsectors. There is also secondary processing of metals, smelting and refining of copper, which have led to the manufacturing of metal products. The sector also benefits from the emerald mining industry and manufactures a number of ornaments for export purposes. Fertilizers, chemicals, explosives and construction materials such as cement are also produced. Other activities include producing wood and paper products, vehicle parts and assembly, refining petroleum and light engineering.[39]

36 See http://www.fao.org/3/t0800e/t0800e0a.htm, accessed 2 February 2021.
37 Ministry of Finance (2017: 25).
38 Energy Regulation Board (2017: 1).
39 BoZ (2017a: 5).

1.3.4 Energy

The country's demand for electricity stood at 1,949 megawatts (MW) in 2015, while the sector was only able to produce 1,281 MW, thus giving a deficit of 668 MW.[40] This situation resulted from limited investment over the years, which was also compounded by non-cost-reflective tariffs. Further, the deficit was worsened by the effects of climate change on the availability of water, since Zambia's electricity generation is predominantly through hydropower.[41] The current projections indicate that growth in demand will increase by 150 MW to 200 MW per annum. The peak demand for electricity in the country was projected at 3,000 MW by 2020.[42] The increase in energy demand in Zambia is the result of the improved economic outlook.

The leading sectors in relation to electricity consumption were mining, construction, agriculture and services. Side by side with the expansion of the domestic economy, the national electricity consumption increased from 10,857.54 GWh in 2016 to 12,191.86 GWh in 2017, thus reflecting 12.3% growth.[43] Of this 2017 consumption, the mining sector accounted for 6,202.0 GWh of total consumption representing 50.9% of the total electricity output.[44] The demand for energy has steadily been rising with the increase in population and urbanisation, and the growth of industry and resultant energy needs.

In 2016, the country had installed energy capacity of 2,493 MW with hydro generation accounting for 97%, while other sources were at 3%. It was envisaged that other sources of energy, which include geothermal, wind, solar and coal, would grow to about 15% by 2030.[45] To increase supply, there was a need for additional investment in hydro, geothermal, wind and solar energy generation.[46] This would have a further bearing on the fuel used for domestic purposes, especially in rural areas where the absence of electricity forces people to use charcoal as a source of fuel. The increased generational capacity of electricity, coupled with the increase in rural electrification, means that there will be a decreased use of fossil fuels, resulting in reduction in deforestation and emission of greenhouse gases, as well as the reduction of soil erosion. It has been noted for example that in 2017, the Rural Electrification Authority (REA) continued to implement rural electrification projects nationally and had successfully completed 14 rural electrification projects, 11 being grid extensions and three solar projects.[47] Energy generation in Zambia is not without impact on soil sustainability and the environment generally. For example, persistent organic pollutants (POPs),

40 Ministry of Finance (2017: 27).
41 Ministry of National Development Planning (2016: 7).
42 Ministry of Energy (2008: 3).
43 Energy Regulation Board (2017: 1–3).
44 ZDA (2017: 1).
45 Ministry of Energy (2008: 3–8).
46 Ministry of Finance (2017: 26).
47 Ibid.

which are chemicals that have toxic properties and do not easily decompose in the environment are used as coolants and lubricants in electricity generation equipment such as transformers, capacitors and switches. They may include polychlorinated biphenyls (PCBs). These materials accumulate in the soil and organisms by ingestion through the food chain, thereby posing a hazard for human beings and animals.[48]

Further, according to ZEMA, as of 2016, Zambia had 16,000 transformers owned by electrical and mining companies of which 326 were identified as potentially containing PCBs. Some capacitors and oil circuit breakers were believed to contain PCBs. Furthermore, about 196 tonnes of PCB-contaminated soil was stored at the Kariba North Bank PCB storage facility, while some other PCB-contaminated oil, polythene sheets and personal protective equipment (PPE), and transformer shells were found. Of greatest concern to this discussion is that, at present, Zambia has no capacity for disposal of PCB materials.[49] This is an immensely worrisome situation for soil sustainability and general environmental well-being.

In addition, the fall in the country's hydropower generation in recent years by about 600 MW, mainly attributed to poor rainfall patterns, has hampered the country's economic growth prospects in agriculture, manufacturing, mining and other services. Other adverse effects have led to increased costs of treating climate-related diseases such as malaria, the loss of natural environments, damage to infrastructure and disruption of biodiversity.[50] Climate change adaptation and mitigation will, therefore, promote social well-being, including better health, growth of the economy and at the same time reduce environmental risks, such as shortage of water, air pollution and other effects.[51]

1.3.5 Construction

The construction industry continues to play an integral part in the development of the economy and is one of the important catalysts for growth. Activities in the subsector are driven by public and private projects, such as roads, stadiums, hospitals, schools, and residential and commercial property. As noted in the section on mining, the construction industry has fuelled illegal quarrying, which in turn has severe impacts on soil sustainability. The construction industry continued to grow over the past 12 years at a steady annual average rate of 17.5%. This growth can be directly attributed to increased public and private sector investment on infrastructure development.[52] With

48 ZEMA (2017: 113).

49 Ibid.

50 Sintayehu (2018: 225–227).

51 Ministry of National Development Planning (2016: 7).

52 ZDA (2017).

inadequate safeguards, the growth of the construction sector is projected to cause further strain on soil sustainability.

1.3.6 Tourism

Government has identified tourism as an area of priority.[53] Zambia's total annual international tourist arrivals increased from 668,862 in 2005 to 931,782 in 2015, representing a 39% increment. Tourism's average GDP contribution over the 5-year period from 2010 to 2014 was around 1.76% per annum. With regard to accommodation establishments, the sector recorded an increase of 25.6% from 933 in 2012 to 1,172 in 2015, with a corresponding 45.6% increase in bed spaces from 51,662 in 2012 to 75,253 in 2015.[54] The increase was attributed to high demand for tourism enterprise businesses, mostly by local citizens. The room occupancy rate improved from 54.9% in 2012 to 68.9% in 2015 owing to increased tourist arrivals.[55]

Despite these positive strides in the tourism sector, Zambia has continued to face stiff competition from other African countries in attracting tourists. For instance, in 2013, a total of 55.8 million arrivals were recorded in Africa, out of which Zambia only recorded 914,576, representing 1.63%. The number of foreign visitors to the country rose from 814,140 in 2010 to 914,576 in 2013. From these arrivals, the country recorded annual direct earnings of US$441,062,536 (K2,271,472,063) in 2012, which rose to US$540,209,718 (K2,971,153,451) in 2013. The number of jobs in the sector rose from 44,292 in 2012 to 57,337 in 2013. The top holiday markers for tourism to Zambia were Africans, accounting for 79% of the 914,576 visitors in 2013.[56]

During the Sixth National Development Plan period (2011–2015), a marginal increase in the average length of stay for tourists was recorded – from 5 days in 2012 to 6 days in 2013. This was attributed to inadequate diversification of tourism products, underdeveloped tourism circuits and tour packages, among others.[57]

1.4 Gross national product

It has been noted that Zambia's economy during the period 2000–2005 grew at an annual average of about 5.8%, while the 2006–2015 period saw an upward and sustained growth averaging 6.9%.

---

53 Ministry of Finance (2017: 27–28).
54 Ibid.
55 Ministry of Tourism (2016: 12–17).
56 Ministry of Finance (2017: 28).
57 Ibid.: 35.

Zambia's gross domestic product in December 2017 was US$25.81 billion. The economy is predominantly driven by the agricultural and mining industries. The largest proportion of Zambia's exports go to Non-European Union Organisation for Economic Co-operation and Development (Non-EU OECD) countries, like Switzerland, followed by Asia (China), Southern African Development Community (SADC) and Common Market for Eastern and Southern Africa (COMESA) countries, while Switzerland and China are the main consumers of copper.[58]

The forestry industry contributes at least 3.7% to the GDP. Within this industry, the largest part is wood fuel, including commercial charcoal production of 2.2% and subsistence wood collection of 0.8%, with about 90% of the people using the fuelwood thus produced. The productivity of the forestry industry, however, is low throughout all stages from production to processing and distribution. This is because of the underdevelopment of infrastructure such as roads and communications, which leads to transaction costs becoming high. For this reason, the improvement of efficiency in the forestry industry, including small-scale enterprises, would bring great benefits to the economy and environment.[59]

1.5 National debt

Zambia's stock of external debt has been rising since 2012. At the end of 2014, external debt stock was at US$4.81 billion, representing 24.0% of GDP, compared to US$3.18 billion which was 17.2% of GDP in 2012. In 2015, external debt was US$6.41 billion, and in September 2016 the external debt had reached US$6.7 billion, representing 35% of GDP. By 2018, the debt had increased to 72% of GDP.[60] The International Monetary Fund (IMF) predicts that if the country maintains its current path without fiscal policy adjustments, debt will increase to a high of 84% of GDP by 2021, well above the threshold of so-called debt sustainability (very roughly the threshold is around 60%).[61]

The historical perspective to the foregoing is that, in 1991, Zambia moved from a single-party state dominated by the United National Independence Party (UNIP), to a multiparty state led by the Movement for Multiparty Democracy (MMD). The MMD inherited a huge public (or government) debt from the former ruling party, UNIP. At that time, the size of the debt was not known (mainly owing to impasses between the UNIP government and multilateral institutions like the IMF). After 1991, the MMD government's willingness to address the debt situation, coupled with their more

58 BoZ (2017b: 3).
59 Japan Association for International Collaboration of Agriculture and Forestry (2008: 39).
60 Ministry of Finance (2017: 19).
61 Personal communication with Ministry of Finance Economists (June, 2019).

favourable stance on the IMF and World Bank, led to the establishment of the exact debt size by 2000.[62] Around the same time, the MMD government and civil society, both in Zambia and internationally, mounted a vigorous debt forgiveness campaign called Jubilee 2000. At that point, the debt was estimated at K29.2 billion, which accounted for 261% of GDP (or more than two and a half times the size of the economy).[63]

Zambia reached the Highly Indebted Poor Country (HIPC) completion point in 2004 and a big chunk of its debt was written off. The debt burden fell from K38.6 billion (or 130% of GDP) in 2004 to K28.2 billion (76% of GDP) by 2005.[64] The country had at that time attracted further debt relief under the Multilateral Debt Reduction Initiative (MDRI) and its debt dropped further to a moderate 25% of GDP. During the remainder of the MMD government era, there were sustained prudent fiscal and monetary policies, including tight debt management, thus reducing the debt to 19% of GDP by 2010.[65] Zambia was assigned lower middle-income country status in 2011, along with Ghana, which facilitated extensive borrowing on the private markets (Eurobonds) and numerous non-concessional loans from China.[66]

The year 2011 saw a regime shift to the Patriotic Front (PF) government. The then new government inherited a healthy economy with a good fiscal position. The national debt increased sharply from 21% of GDP in 2011 to a remarkable 62% in 2015. In the interim, the government had, among other things, borrowed three Eurobonds, one in 2012 worth US$750 million, another in 2013 worth US$1 billion and the third in 2015 worth US$1.25 billion (making the total Eurobond issuance to US$3 billion).[67] Despite an economic downturn and GDP growth slowdown in 2015, the government kept borrowing, treating the downturn as a temporary thing, which it was not, as has been seen in the current debt burden and gloomy predictions. According to the IMF, this debt scenario is being fueled by the country's development strategy which has seen rapid scaling-up in infrastructure spending and consequent large fiscal deficits, financed by non-concessional debt.[68]

---

62 See https://www.oecd.org/countries/zambia/2497663.pdf; https://www.afdb.org/fileadmin/uploads/afdb/Documents/Generic-Documents/Zambia_Country_Profile.pdf, both accessed 2 February 2021.

63 See https://jubileedebt.org.uk/countries/zambia, accessed 2 February 2021.

64 IMF (2005).

65 AFRODAD (2003: 11–15).

66 Hinfelaar & Sichone (2019: 6).

67 Nalishebo (2015).

68 Hinfelaar & Sichone (2019: 5–6).

1.6 Foreign investments

Foreign investments in developing economies such as Zambia mostly hinge on natural resources exploitation, which in turn may have adverse environmental effects. Some of these adverse environmental effects affect soil quality, for instance in mining. Foreign direct investment (FDI) is an important source of development in most countries as it facilitates access to international markets, the creation of more skilled jobs, and technological and innovative advancements.[69]

Research conducted by the central bank on foreign assets and liabilities during the period 2016–2017 provided highlights on the magnitude, types and direction of foreign private capital assets and liabilities, Foreign Affiliates Trade in Services (FATS) and investor perceptions in Zambia.[70] It was found that Zambia's net foreign direct investment inflows declined by 58.7% to US$486.1 million from US$1,177.4 million in 2015, mainly explained by a reduction in FDI liabilities by 49.2% to US$662.8 million from US$1,304.9 million.[71] Net acquisition of FDI assets, however, rose by 38.6% to US$176.7 million. The fall in FDI liabilities was largely driven by reduced growth in foreign borrowing from related parties and retained earnings in various industries.[72]

Value addition in the mining and manufacturing industries improved. Borrowing from affiliates continued to be the major form of FDI liabilities, with British Virgin Islands as the major source country, accounting for 37.0% of the total inflows, while the manufacturing industry was the major recipient of the inflows. In 2016, Zambia's private sector foreign assets transactions increased by 94.9% to US$407.5 million explained by an increased accumulation of assets in other investments and direct investments. Switzerland was the major destination, accounting for 87.7% of the flows, largely for the mining and quarrying industry. As noted throughout this report, mining is the mainstay of the Zambian economy,[73] despite intense efforts at diversification.

In a report examining how Zambia can leverage the benefits and mitigate the risks of Chinese foreign direct investment to support its long-standing objective of diversified growth, it was found that:[74]

> Zambia needs foreign capital to catalyze diversification, while China is seeking destinations and projects that will generate profits; the intersection of which may constitute a viable Zambian growth strategy, provided the country can both attract Chinese FDI and ensure that the domestic economy benefits from the investments.

For the purposes of this research, diversification was taken as "an effort to target investment in and modernization of priority non-mining sectors that have hitherto been

69 UNCTAD (2017: 3); Mabey & McNally (1999: 3–8).
70 BoZ (2015: 3–6); BoZ (2017a: 9).
71 BoZ (2017a: 1–3).
72 Ibid.
73 Ndaba (2015: 7).
74 Abdelghaffar et al. (2016: 10).

underdeveloped – in particular agriculture, manufacturing, energy, transport and infrastructure."[75]

In line with Zambia's development agenda after 2017, a successful implementation of the diversification strategy stimulated growth and created jobs in these sectors of the economy. Investment opportunities included potential for manufacturing based on agricultural produce as inputs for crop-processing plants, such as canning factories and oil-processing plants. Further, large tracts of land have been reserved as farming blocks earmarked for large-scale farming and, in such areas, government is providing basic infrastructure such as feeder roads, communication and power.[76] In the mining sector, exploitation of gold, zinc, coal, nickel and gemstones (emeralds, aquamarine, topaz, opal, amethyst) offers great opportunities for potential investors.

2 Information on government organisational structure

The organisational structure discussed in this section is important for understanding the enforcement of soil-relevant laws and policies in Zambia.

The Constitution establishes Zambia as a "sovereign Republic under a constitutional form of governance."[77] In line with legal expectation, the Constitution "sets forth the basic postulates of a free society", meaning that it establishes "the basic structure of government ..."[78] The present Patriotic Front government has been in office since September 2011, with changes in leadership owing to death in 2008 and 2014. The next general elections are scheduled for 2021.[79]

The Republic of Zambia is a unitary, multiparty democracy with a distinct separation of powers between the executive, legislative and judicial arms of government and an executive president.[80] The President and members of parliament are elected by the people through direct elections;[81] and the President in turn appoints cabinet ministers from the elected and nominated members of parliament. Zambia has a unicameral parliament, which is presided over by the Speaker of the National Assembly, while the Judicature of Zambia is headed by the Chief Justice.[82]

75 Ibid.: 4.
76 ZDA (2017).
77 Article 4(1) and (2).
78 Ndulo & Kent (1996: 256).
79 Prizzon (2013: 4).
80 Article 4(3) of the Constitution (2016).
81 Article 47(1).
82 The Commonwealth: (2019).

2.1 Legal system / tradition

Zambia has a dual legal system in which written law operates side by side with customary law.[83] Other authors have also described the country's legal system as "deeply plural" in its nature owing to its colonial past.[84] The Constitution of Zambia (Amendment) Act, No. 2 of 2016 provides that the laws of Zambia consist of the Constitution, laws enacted by Parliament, statutory instruments, Zambian customary law that is consistent with the Constitution and the laws and statutes, which apply or extend to Zambia, as prescribed.[85]

Customary law is generally administered by lower courts in the judicial hierarchy and it consists of matters of a personal nature, such as marriage, inheritance and land.[86] In the context of land, it must be emphasised that this law only applies with respect to customary tenure. It is interesting to note that matters of soil sustainability would most likely be addressed under written environmental law, regardless of the fact that the land in question is subject to customary tenure. Customary laws are not codified and as such the phrase 'customary law' does not refer to a single system but instead a set of rights, liabilities and duties across diverse ethnic groups.[87]

According to Munalula, the case of English law in Zambia, like other former British colonies, is different from the legacy inherited by former French colonies: English law was "never imposed … in such a way as to oust the indigenous customary law."[88] Common law utilises a system of judicial precedent which binds judges to prior decisions and doctrines developed over time by judges in earlier and more superior courts, rather than being derived exclusively from statutes or legislation. As such, judges determine the answers to legal questions through the review of previous judicial decisions and accordingly build analogies to the facts of the case before them.[89] In Zambia, common law is generally administered in the hierarchically higher courts, known as superior courts and in which both civil and criminal cases are heard, as well as appeals from the first instance courts.

Most Zambians resort to applicable customary law in case of disputes. This is attributable to the fact that almost 60% of the Zambian population resides in rural and peri-urban areas, where the majority of traditional and local courts are situated.[90] Against this background, some authors conclude that statutory courts are therefore "irrelevant" for a sizeable part of the population.[91]

83 Munalula (2004: 54).
84 Gloppen (2003: 11); Ige (2015: 59).
85 Article 7.
86 Gloppen (2003: 113).
87 See https://issafrica.org/chapter-6-customary-justice, accessed 5 February 2021.
88 Munalula (2004: 53).
89 Church (1974: 2).
90 AFRONET (1998).
91 Gloppen (2003: 131).

As a core feature of the country's legal system, the Judiciary is created under the Constitution as a neutral and independent arbiter, thus: "in the exercise of the judicial authority, the Judiciary shall be subject only to this Constitution and the law and not be subject to the control or direction of a person or an authority."[92] According to Article 120(1), the Judiciary consists of the superior courts and subordinate courts, small claims courts, local courts, and courts as prescribed. The superior courts are the Supreme Court, Constitutional Court, Court of Appeal, and High Court. Article 121 provides that the Supreme Court and Constitutional Court rank as equivalents.

2.2 Competence of legislation and enforcement

Zambia has a unicameral parliament that consists of the President and members of Parliament. According to Article 61 of the Constitution, the legislative authority of the Republic derives from the people of Zambia and is exercised in a manner that protects the Constitution and promotes democratic governance. Parliament consists of the President and the National Assembly. The Constitution provides that the legislative authority of the Republic is vested in and exercised by Parliament,[93] and further that no person or body, other than Parliament, has the power to enact legislation, except as conferred by the Constitution.[94] Article 63(1) provides that in exercise of its legislative function, Parliament enacts legislation through bills passed by the National Assembly and assented to by the President. Article 64(1) empowers a member of Parliament or Minister to introduce a bill in the National Assembly.

The legislative-making powers of Parliament have been subject to judicial interpretation in the past giving the Supreme Court an opportunity to assert the legislative power of Parliament in the *Zambia Democratic Congress v Attorney-General.*[95] This was an appeal case against the judgement of the High Court dismissing the appellant's application for judicial review. The original application for judicial review challenged the decision by the President and the Cabinet to amend the Constitution in the manner suggested in Constitution of Zambia (Amendment) Act, No. 17 of 1996, which was published in the *Government Gazette* as required by Article 79 of the Constitution. The applicants averred that the change sought to alter or destroy the basic structure or framework of the Constitution. The Supreme Court held that the Constitution of Zambia itself gives Parliament powers to make laws and that Parliament could not be equated to an inferior tribunal or body when exercising its legislative powers. In

92 Article 122(1).
93 Article 62(2).
94 Article 62(3).
95 SCZ Judgment No. 37 of 1999.

appropriate cases, however, actions, but not by judicial review, could be commenced against it.

The enforcement of the legislative framework in Zambia is performed by various law enforcement agencies and any other authorised persons under the various applicable laws. Most of the soil-relevant legislative provisions analysed in this report are subject to enforcement by the Zambia Environmental Management Authority (ZEMA) established under the Environmental Management Act (EMA), 2011.

2.3 Role of traditional entities

Traditional leaders in Zambia play a vital role in the administration of customary law generally and, more specifically, land rights, which are critical to the soil sustainability discussion in this report.

Historically, all the constitutional regimes in Zambia since 1965 have recognised the role of traditional authorities in national affairs. The current Constitution recognises the role of traditional entities in Zambia. Article 165(1) provides that the "chieftaincy and other traditional institutions are guaranteed and shall exist in accordance with the culture, customs and traditions of the people to whom they apply." Further, in support of the existence of these traditional institutions, Parliament will not enact legislation which "confers on a person or authority the right to recognize or withdraw the recognition of a chief or derogates from the honour and dignity of the institution of chieftaincy."[96]

The institution of chieftaincy is recognised in Article 166 as a "corporation sole with perpetual succession and capacity to sue and be sued and has capacity to hold property in trust for its subjects." The administration of traditional land has been highlighted as one of the major challenges that the traditional leadership in Zambia faces. Most of the contention surrounding this provision relates to land and resources that are land-based. In this context, soil sustainability interests are also affected. It is arguable that the chiefs must exercise leadership and decision-making powers related to ensuring the well-being of the natural resources they hold in trust for their subjects.

Further, a chief may own property in a personal capacity and is constitutionally empowered to enjoy privileges and benefits either bestowed on the office of chief by or under culture, custom and tradition and/or attached to the office of chief, as may be prescribed.[97] Furthermore, the Constitution allows chiefs to participate in the running of public affairs by seeking and holding public office, provided they abdicate the chief's throne, in all cases, except in the case of appointment as councillor.

---

96 Article 165(2).
97 Article 167.

Of further relevance to this discussion, the Constitution provides that the role of a chief in the management, control and sharing of natural and other resources in the chiefdom will be prescribed.[98] There is no further information of this detail in the Constitution, except in the provisions of The Chiefs Act, which is discussed below.

Article 169 establishes a House of Chiefs to consist of five chiefs from each province, elected by the chiefs in that Province. The functions of the House of Chiefs are to:

> (a) consider and discuss Bills relating to custom or tradition referred to it by the President, before the Bill is introduced into the National Assembly; (b) initiate, discuss and make recommendations to the National Assembly regarding socio-economic development in the Province; (c) initiate, discuss and decide on matters relating to customary law and practice; (d) initiate, discuss and make recommendations to a local authority regarding the welfare of communities in a local authority; (e) make proposals on areas in customary law that require codification; (f) advise the Government on traditional and customary matters; and (g) perform other functions as prescribed.[99]

The preamble to the Chiefs Act, Chapter 287 provides that it is purposed to make provision for the recognition, appointment and functions of chiefs and their deputies, and other incidental matters. Historically, chiefs and traditional authorities have been active participants in natural resources management in Zambia.[100]

Section 3 outlines the chiefs who are recognised in Zambia, while Section 10 outlines the chiefs' functions:

> The traditional functions under African Customary Law in so far as the discharge of such functions is not contrary to the Constitution or any written law and is not repugnant to natural justice or morality and such functions as may be conferred or imposed by this Act or any other written law.

In practice, this provision applies by operation of unwritten customary law, and provisions of written law such as the Local Government Act[101] and the Registration and Development of Villages Act, both of which ensure that chiefs and other traditional leaders are involved in the management of natural resources generally in the rural areas where most of their jurisdiction applies.

The general view of traditional leaders over time has been that their traditional authority is at best ignored in land transactions involving large-scale investment. For instance, it has been observed that potential investors usually acquire land only to resell it at exorbitant prices, sometimes without ever developing it. The House of Chiefs, in line with its constitutional mandate, has in the past proposed that the Ministry of Lands needed to be strengthened at provincial level by increasing personnel so that it could undertake periodic land development inspections in all districts.[102] This would

98 Article 68(3).
99 Article 169(5).
100 Munyinda & Habasonda (2013: 24–27).
101 Sections 36 and 37.
102 Zambia Environmental Management Agency (2017: 41–57); Ministry of Lands and Natural Resources (2017).

hopefully compel investors to develop the land within a specified period. It has further been proposed that standard guidelines be developed on acquiring land from traditional leaders across the country, to improve land administration.[103]

Another area of concern for traditional leaders is the high poverty levels in rural districts and it has accordingly been proposed that government should put in place policies to ensure that rural areas are opened up for development by ensuring that essential services such as electricity, transport network, schools and hospitals are available.[104]

2.4 Religious considerations

Article 4(3) of the Constitution provides that "the Republic is a unitary, indivisible, multi- ethnic, multi-racial, *multi-religious*, multi-cultural and multi-party democratic State." The multi-religious nature of the Zambian population is confirmed by statistics, which indicate that Protestants comprise 75.3% of the total population, Roman Catholics 20.2%, others 2.7% (which includes Muslims, Buddhists, Hindus and Baha'i), while 1% covers the non-religious.[105]

Each of the country's religions have an approach towards soil and environmental protection. In a 2016 newspaper article, it was reported that government had declared that there was need for more organisations to promote organic farming among farmers in order to protect the environment from chemical fertilizers and improve yields.[106] Organic farming promotes the natural regeneration of humus in the soil thereby helping the earth to support growth that feeds living organisms on the land.

Speaking at a conference under the theme: "Care of our common home in the context of large- scale investments: mining and agriculture," the Deputy Minister of the then Ministry of Lands, Natural Resources and Environmental Protection had said that government recognised and appreciated the work that the Catholic Church had continued doing in Zambia, in terms of promoting organic farming among small-scale farmers. Government went on recommend the Catholic Church for running the Kasisi Agricultural Research Institute, which was spearheading the promotion of organic farming among small-scale farmers by teaching them how to improve their yields without doing harm to the soil through the use of chemical fertilizers.

In the previous year, 2015, Pope Francis had called on all people to "enter into dialogue about the common home planet [E]arth to [promote] environmental management."[107]

---

103 World Bank (2016: 7–10).

104 See generally Ministry of Chiefs and Traditional Affairs (2016).

105 See https://www.indexmundi.com/zambia/religions.html, accessed 5 February 2021.

106 Tembo (2016).

107 Pope Francis (2015); van Tine (2017: 141–178).

Further, the government shared the concerns expressed by Pope Francis on the plight of the earth and the need to take action and was committed to protecting the environment. The government effected several policies, strategies and programmes to help manage the environment and natural resources prudently.

Some of the policies and legislation were to ensure that development actions, including mining and other extractive industries, did not result in environmental liabilities. This newspaper article shows that from the Christian Catholic perspective, soil conservation and environmental protection are important considerations.

Furthermore, in 2018, the Catholic Church augmented practical measures towards soil conservation by coining the "Prayer for the year of the environment, 2018," which was recited on every day of prayer throughout that year. The acts of praying faithfully and actually taking practical steps towards environmental protection from the religious perspective is one way of ensuring that more community members are aware of the urgent need to preserve the environment for future generations.

The perspective of the Catholic Church is reinforced by the argument of Hansjürgens that soil is of central importance to the global provision of food and in the fight against hunger, climate change, loss of biodiversity and deterioration of water bodies. The author traverses the other legal and ethical considerations and concludes that:[108]

> More than ever, sustainable soil conservation requires (improved) social integration. Soil is not only part of God's creation, but also constitutes valuable "natural capital" from an economic perspective, that is worthy of protection.

This conclusion can be taken as a summation of the position of all other Christian denominations in relation to soil preservation. In relation to other religions, the belief that a higher being or force created the universe and all things contained therein would be taken as the basis for ensuring that the environment and its constituent components such as soil are well maintained. The responsibility for caring for the environment would naturally rest on human beings as custodians.

3 Main drivers of soil degradation

This section analyses the main drivers of soil degradation in Zambia. The main constraints to sustainable soil management in the country have generally been identified as soil erosion and degradation and are also closely linked to deforestation. In addition, the huge energy deficit in the country has brought renewed pressure on wood fuel and consequently on sustainable soil management.

Soil erosion refers to the wearing away of a field's topsoil by the natural and physical forces of water and wind, or through farming activities such as tillage.[109] Soil

108 Hansjürgens et al. (2018: 1–9).
109 Ul Zaman et al. (2018: 1114).

erosion is a natural, essential process for the formation of soil.[110] As a naturally occurring phenomenon, soil erosion affects all landforms. It occurs when soil is removed through the action of wind and water at a greater rate than it is formed. Erosion involves the three distinct actions of soil detachment, movement and deposition, whether it is caused by water wind or tillage.[111] Soil erosion has occurred throughout the history of agriculture; however, in recent years the rate at which soil is eroding has intensified and, as such, it is one of the major causes of land degradation.[112]

The concerns related to erosion as a factor contributing to the degradation of soil are due to the accelerated rate at which it is taking place, where the natural rate at which it ordinarily occurs has been significantly increased mostly by human activity.[113] In relation to the agricultural use of land, land degradation involves deterioration in soil properties related to crop production.[114]

In addition to the foregoing, other industrial sectors such as manufacturing also have significant impact of soil health. For instance, some manufacturing processes involve the use of various chemical processes which may contribute to soil contamination, especially where there are ineffective waste management mechanisms. On another limb, the increased role of foreign investors across many economic activities may possibly lead to spiral effects of land and soil degradation.

Other sectors such as tourism may also put pressure on soil. Tourism is dependent on natural and man-made environmental quality. This means that tourism and the environment sustain a delicate relationship. On one hand, tourism puts significant stress on land-use practices, soil erosion, pollution, natural habitat loss and, on the other, potentially contributes to environmental protection and conservation, and raises environmental awareness and economic importance of natural areas.[115]

3.1 Mining and soil sustainability

Despite the economic benefits associated with mining activities, there are a number of negative impacts. The mining industry exerts enormous pressure on land and soil resources in the country. It has been noted that the mining sector has contributed to the contamination of soils and vegetation through dust fall-out from smelters, crushers and dry beaches of tailing impoundments.[116] Additionally, quarrying activities in Zambia

110 Stanchi et al. (2015: 403–408).
111 Ul Zaman et al. (2018: 1116).
112 Pimentel & Kounang (1995) 1117.
113 Stanchi et al. (2015: 403).
114 Alori & Nwapi (2014: 98–114).
115 Sunlu (2003: 263–270).
116 Kříbek et al. (2008: 24–26).

have been acknowledged to be increasing as a result of heightened demand for aggregate materials for use in construction.

Although quarrying has brought socioeconomic benefits especially for the informal sector, uncontrolled and illegal quarrying, particularly in urban areas, has resulted in negative environmental impacts including land degradation and groundwater quality deterioration.[117] The resultant effects include soil contamination; air, ground- and surface-water pollution; formation of sinkholes; erosion; and loss of biodiversity. Other notable environmental impacts include deforestation and the formation of acid rain, which results from sulphur dioxide emissions reacting with rain in the atmosphere to form weak acid. This correspondingly reduces soil fertility and compromises crop production.[118]

3.2 Unsustainable agricultural practices

Other causes of soil degradation are non-sustainable cultivation practices such as cultivation rows which run parallel to a slope resulting in automatically concentrating water flow in a manner that produces soil erosion. Traditional cultivation systems like shifting cultivation or 'slash and burn' also have a negative impact on the environment and result in soil degradation. When the yield declines, a new area is cleared for shifting cultivation, and the initial site is left to lie fallow.

Soil acidity is also a serious problem, particularly in the heavily leached soils of the higher rainfall zones of northern Zambia. Phosphates become insoluble and unavailable to the plants even when present in the soil under conditions of high acidity.[119]According to the Ministry of Water Development, Sanitation and Environmental Protection, it is estimated that acidification due to fertilizer accounted for the loss of up to 15% of arable land in 20 years in the Northern Province.[120] Although the use of nitrogen fertilizer increases soil organic matter, there are cases where continuous use of nitrogen fertilizer destabilises the clay soils and enhances pan formation, which impairs plant root growth while up to 80% losses in organic matter may occur.[121]

3.2.1 Overstocking and overgrazing of animals

Other causes of soil degradation and soil erosion are bush fires and overstocking of and overgrazing by livestock. Bush fires are not necessarily linked to overgrazing and

117 ZEMA (2017: 84); Dymond, et al. (2007: 19–22).
118 ZEMA (2017: 84).
119 Chidumayo (1987: 15–18).
120 Blackwell et al. (1991).
121 Ibid.; ZEMA (2017: 47).

overstocking of animals. According to research, bush fires are deliberately started in certain regions of central to northern Zambia as a traditional practice over many years.[122] Eriksen argues that bush fires are:[123]

> a major feature in the seasonal land management calendar … the local communities use fire to obtain desired natural resources and to shape the natural environment and further their agricultural and other objectives, such as bush clearance, fire break creation, charcoal production, hunting, weed and disease control, caterpillar breeding, honey collection and pasture regeneration.

From the foregoing, it is clear that local communities appreciate the direct benefits of bush fires to their immediate needs but are oblivious to the long-term adverse effects of bush fires on soil sustainability.

In Zambia, both wild and domestic animals, which are carnivorous, herbivorous and omnivorous abound. The keeping of domestic animals and the presence and keeping of significant numbers of herbivorous and omnivorous wildlife in the country means that there is pressure on grazing lands. The use of land for human activities such as crop farming in most rural areas and mining have also placed added pressure on grazing land and in some cases has resulted in overstocking and overgrazing of land, with adverse effects on ecosystems, notably, wildlife depletion and loss of biodiversity.[124]

Overall, livestock accounts for about 35% of the national agricultural output and is mainly concentrated in the Western and Southern Provinces of the country. The animal population comprises largely of goats and cattle, whose numbers have been rising steadily over the years.[125] With increased animal populations, the carrying capacity of most rural communal land has become inadequate, and thus susceptible to overuse, leading to land and soil degradation.

In addition to the natural factors, such as water and wind, that cause soil erosion, several human activities have contributed to soil erosion, and are the major cause of the accelerated rate at which soil is eroding.[126] Erosion caused by human activities occurs with farming practices that are not compatible with the fact that soil can be washed away or blown away. In Zambia, one of the major causes of soil erosion and degradation is deforestation caused by the practice of clearing new land for agriculture when old fields lose their fertility. This is practised under the traditional 'slash and burn' *Chitemene* system of shifting cultivation.[127]

Chitemene is the main traditional agricultural system that has adversely affected soil health in Zambia. *Chitemene* is a Zambian Bemba word which refers to the system of slashing and burning agricultural vegetation. The system is widely practised throughout northern Zambia and is known to have contributed to the loss of half the Miombo

122 Eriksen (2007: 242–247).
123 Ibid.: 249.
124 ZEMA (2017: 84).
125 Ibid.: 48.
126 Ul, Zaman (2018: 1114).
127 Eriksen (2007: 243–248).

woodlands, closely followed by charcoal burning.[128] While governments, donors and other stakeholders have expended huge sums of money in order to reduce climate change, land degradation and deforestation, old farming methods are still being practised by most small scale farmers.[129] Further, about 90% of deforestation in Zambia is attributable to clearing of land for agricultural purposes, especially through the *Chitemene* system of farming.[130]

Arguably, the continued practice of the *Chitemene* system is, in the long term, unsustainable. As the rural population continues to grow, complete deforestation may occur in the coming decades. It is also estimated that northern Zambia has lost more than 35% of its biomass as a result of the *Chitemene* farming system, representing a total of about 43,000 square kilometres of forest land over the past 40 years.[131] It has further been observed that with the number of small-scale farmers engaged in this practice, there is no doubt that the impact that is left on the environment is vast and devastating.[132]

The additional adverse effects of the *Chitemene* system include loss of biological diversity within the forests, increased water runoff and soil erosion, and soil fertility depletion due to the leaching of nutrition. Apart from wildlife depletion, soil erosion and a settlement problem, deforestation is one of the major environmental problems arising from *Chitemene*.[133]

Although the slash and burn system may lead to a more fertile soil in the form of ashes in the short term and therefore compare favourably to inorganic fertilizers purchased at high cost, those temporary benefits cannot outweigh its devastating long-term effects.[134] Slash and burn, shifting cultivation has been the dominant traditional land use in the Miombo woodlands of northern Zambia. This type of cultivation is characterised by short cropping periods of two to six years which are followed by long fallow periods of ten to twenty years.[135] These periods are too short for the indigenous species of trees to grow and mature to replace the trees originally felled.

3.2.2 Wrong use of fertilizers and pesticides

In Zambia, agriculture is largely classified into: (a) traditional agriculture mainly for producing subsistence food; and (b) commercial agriculture basically for commercial

---

128 ZEMA (2017: 51).

129 See http://www.bailiffafrica.org/the-extent-of-slash-and-burn-agriculture-in-zambia-by-clifford-malambo/, accessed 15 April 2019.

130 Ibid.

131 Engel et al. (2017: 13).

132 Ministry of Lands and Natural Resources (2017: i—iii; 1–5); Young (1989: 11–17).

133 Ministry of Lands and Natural Resources (2017).

134 Chidumayo (1987: 15–18).

135 Neubert et al. (2011: 91–100); Gumbo et al. (2018: 12–21).

production. This dual structure of agriculture can be traced back to the economic structure formulated during the colonial era. Against this background, the general system of agriculture that has developed places heavy reliance on the use of non-organic fertilizers which ultimately cause environmental damage and soil degradation in themselves and when coupled with wrong usage.[136] The use of pesticides which leech into the soil is also a hazard in relation to soil sustainability:[137]

> Usage of pesticides, insecticides and other various chemicals in agriculture is very easy, quick and inexpensive solution for controlling weeds and insect pests. However, use of chemicals comes with a significant cost. They have contaminated almost every part of our environment and their residues are found in soil, water, land and air.

In order to boost agricultural output, a shift of cultivation methods from indiscriminate chemical fertilizer usage to conservation farming is currently being advocated in Zambia. Among the manifold efforts to facilitate a change towards more sustainable and climate-smart farming practices, conservation farming is the most prominent.

Conservation farming aims at improved soil and water conservation combined with reduced dependence on chemical fertilizers resulting in increased and more stable yields.[138] Further, conservation farming restores soil fertility damaged by years of continuous ploughing, and the application of destructive inorganic fertilizers. These soil conservation techniques are however not being undertaken on the basis of legislative coercion. It is worth restating here that the agricultural legislation has been earmarked for review to bring it in line with the projected 2030 developmental agenda for the country. It is expected that once this is achieved, the relevant legislation will incorporate international best practices in the use of inorganic fertilizers.

3.3 Deforestation

Zambia is one of the Southern African countries that has a large area of forests totalling an area of 45,610 hectares, which accounts for about 60% of the total land area (752,600 km²) of Zambia. It is acknowledged that within the forest area, the government, on a priority basis, carries out forest conservation in the forest reserves and national parks.[139]

The forest vegetation in Zambia is largely classified into two groups, the first consists of closed forests, mainly comprising evergreen trees of the cryptosepalum and deciduous trees of the baikiaea, while the second group is the open forests sometimes called the Savanna woodlands.[140] This accounts for 87.5% of the total Zambian forests,

136 Shitumbanuma et al. (undated).
137 Sharma & Singhvi (2017: 677).
138 Engel et al. (2017: 13) ; Neubert et al. (2011: 87); Ayub (2020: 31–33).
139 Ministry of National Development Planning (2016: 5–6); Gumbo et al. (2018: 10–11).
140 Gumbo et al. (2018: 1–3).

including the Miombo woodlands, the Kalahari woodlands, the Mopane woodlands and the Munga woodlands.[141] One of the main causes of forest reduction and degradation is charcoal production, which is widely used by poor households in urban areas.[142]

Among these woodlands, the Miombo woodlands account for about 60% of the total forest area, constituting the main part of Zambian forests. This type of woodland is subject to the practice of the *Chitemene* system explained in the previous section. The Miombo woodlands are not limited to Zambia but cover the vast area of Southern Africa including Angola, Zimbabwe, Malawi, Mozambique, Tanzania, and the Democratic Republic of the Congo, thus the typical woodlands of the region.[143]

The government started reforestation in the 1960s. Although it was conducted on a pilot basis at the beginning, the area has over time, under industrial reforestation, covered over 55,000 hectares. Reforestation has been done through the planting of Pine (79%) and Eucalyptus (20%).[144] However, new reforestation and its expansion are not enough to meet demand; consequently, the commercial reforested acreage is currently decreasing. It has been postulated that reforestation has substantially reduced the pressure on the native forests in Copperbelt Province, the main copper-producing area.[145]

Deforestation is presently exacerbated by the consumption of charcoal which is a major source of energy. This report has identified increased energy demand as a driver of soil degradation. As an ecological issue, the reduction in forests has become an increasingly serious problem owing to various causes including charcoal production, inadequate farming techniques, uncontrolled bush fires, uncontrolled forest cutting for construction uses, and overgrazing of animals as explained earlier in the previous sections. Moreover, the illegal cutting and unlawful trading of timber has further added to the problem of deforestation. It is estimated that about 250,000 hectares of forests are lost annually as a result of uncontrolled development of forestry products, illegal settlements and transfers from forests to farmlands.[146] It has further been observed that Zambia's forests are under tremendous pressure, because the deforestation rate is well above the global and regional average.[147] Additionally, deforestation threatens biodiversity and undermines key ecosystem services such as climate and water regulation. Shortened flow of seasonal streams and the drying up of formerly permanent rivers have also been observed.[148]

Throughout Zambia, degrading land resources and poor water management are serious impediments to the development of agriculture. This has a further impact on the

141 Japan Association for International Collaboration of Agriculture and Forestry (2008: 21).
142 Chidumayo & Gumbo (2013: 86–89).
143 Ministry of Agriculture (2017: 1); Gumbo et. al. (2018: 1–3).
144 Chileshe (2001: 20).
145 Japan Association for International Collaboration of Agriculture and Forestry (2008: 25); Chileshe (2001: 20–23).
146 UNEP (2015: 12–25).
147 Mudenda (2010: 6); Ministry of National Development Planning (2016: 6); UNEP (2015: 12).
148 Gumbo et al. (2018: 2, 35, 44–48).

quality of soil. Inappropriate farming practices have numerous negative impacts on soil, such as soil erosion, loss of soil organic matter, declining fertility, and capacity to retain water. Once fertile soils become compacted and crusted, they cause valuable rainwater to run off rather than seep into the ground, carrying with it precious topsoil and nutrients. The results are unhealthy crops due to water and nutrient deficits and the build-up of weeds and diseases, poor and unreliable yields, and chronic water shortages resulting from lack of recharge of groundwater.[149]

3.4 Climate change effects

Climate change is presenting significant challenges the world over, although, in the case of Zambia, these have not been directly related to soil sustainability. It is recognised in the country's National Policy on Climate Change that:

> evidence shows that Zambia has, over the past years experienced a number of climate related hazards, including droughts and dry spells, seasonal and flash floods, and extreme temperatures (…) and have adversely impacted on food and water security, energy and livelihoods of communities, land degradation and desertification.[150]

The meaning of this realisation from the scientific perspective is that natural resources, more specifically soil and ecosystems, are under serious threat. By way of recapitulation, soil is the basis of entire ecosystems and services, and having climate-related hazards such as droughts and dry spells, among others, creates an unfavourable environment for sustainable soil management.

From the global perspective, the Intergovernmental Panel on Climate Change (IPCC) defines climate change as "a change in the state of climate that can be identified (statistics test by the mean/and or variability of its properties that persists for an extended period, typically or longer."[151] It refers to any change in climate over time, whether due to natural variability or human activity. Article 2 of the United Nations Framework Convention on Climate Change, to which Zambia is a party, refers to "a change of climate indirectly or directly as a result of human activity that alters the composition of the global atmosphere and that in addition to natural climate variability observed over comparable time periods."[152]

From the local perspective, addressing the effects of climate change is one of the core features that has direct relevance to soil sustainability in Zambia. Adaptation is also key in the country context, being defined as "adjustment to natural or human

149 Mudenda (2010: 7).

150 Ministry of National Development Planning (2016: 2).

151 See https://unfccc.int/files/press/backgrounders/application/pdf/press_factsh_science.pdf, accessed 3 February 2021.

152 See https://unfccc.int/resource/ccsites/zimbab/conven/text/art01.htm, accessed 3 February 2021.

system in response to experience or future variability and extreme events which may be beneficial or adverse."[153]

Previously, Zambian institutions considered climate change using different lenses. For instance, the Ministry of Finance focused mainly on disaster risk management and economic growth, framing the environment as a "reservoir of natural resources which could provide an impetus to economic development"[154] By contrast, the Ministry responsible for the environment proposed a more holistic perspective of "equal and sustainable management of resources and on climate change, maintained the mission is to ensure that the most vulnerable sectors of the economy are climate proofed."[155]

3.5 Poverty and demographic growth

Since attaining political independence, Zambia has had mixed economic fortunes as a result of the policies that the country has pursued. More recently, it has been observed that although the country recorded steady economic growth during the period 1990–2015, poverty remained the greatest challenge to national development.[156] It has further been observed that poverty trends suggest that, overall, income poverty prevalence was reduced between 1991 and 2015 by 24.6%, although an increase was observed in the late 1990s. The reduction in poverty was more significant in urban areas, where it declined by 25.6%, from 49% in 1991 to 23.4% in 2015. Income poverty in rural areas decreased from 88% to 76.6%.[157]

The impact of population growth on soil sustainability is intertwined with the agricultural and industrial practices relating to land use in Zambia. It must be noted that since only 10% of land in Zambia is under statutory tenure and about 90% is customary law, the increasing urbanisation means that there is more pressure being placed on the land. If the practices that have a negative impact on soils are not changed or resolved, then the impact on soils and the environment generally will be extremely grave.

Furthermore, the increasing population has placed pressure for settlement on ecologically sensitive areas such as wetlands and game management areas, affecting both customary and statutory land. These settlements have also had an impact on the generation and disposal of waste. According to ZEMA,[158] improper waste disposal has contributed to pollution through soil, water and air contamination. The concomitant

153 Ministry of National Development Planning (2016: v, 12–13).

154 Ministry of Finance and National Planning (2011), this Ministry has now been split into two, namely the Ministry of Finance and the Ministry of National Development Planning.

155 Ministry of Tourism Environment and Natural Resources (2010: ii), which was also split into Ministry of Tourism and Arts, Ministry of Water Development, Sanitation and Environmental Protection and Ministry of Lands and Natural Resources.

156 Ministry of National Development Planning (2017: 13).

157 Central Statistical Office (2016: 9).

158 ZEMA (2017).

effects of this have included public health challenges such as the outbreak of diseases like dysentery and cholera; expenditure and infrastructure challenges resulting from the need for water treatment and addressing blockages in drainage systems, which also accelerates infrastructural damage to roads. Overall, this has contributed to the proliferation of pests and vermin, and the loss of aesthetic beauty.

According to official statistics, the percentage distribution of the population by level of poverty in 2015 showed that 40.8% of the population was extremely poor, while 13.6% was moderately poor.[159] The proportion of the non-poor was 45.6%. With the 2015 projected national population at 15.9 million, this meant that 8.5 million people lived in poverty, with 3.5 million of those living in extreme poverty.[160] It is clear that economic growth did not translate into significant poverty reduction, especially in rural areas.[161]

It has been observed that the pattern of economic growth in Zambia is highly unequal and has not increased the incomes of the poor rapidly enough to lift them out of poverty, mainly for three reasons. First, economic growth has historically been concentrated in capital-intensive industries such as construction, mining and transport. Secondly, and in relation to the geographical component of growth, urban areas have gained more than rural areas. Thirdly, and in relation to the structure of the economy, economic growth in the country has not been associated with labour-intensive sectors in which the poor tend to work, such as agriculture.[162]

3.6 Urbanisation

Zambia is one of the most urbanised sub-Saharan African countries, with 42.1% of the population living in urban areas.[163] Urbanisation in Zambia is characterised by linear growth along the line of rail, where most urban centres are located – the largest being Lusaka, Ndola and Kitwe. Urban residents generally have relatively better access to public services and infrastructure compared to their rural counterparts and experience greater development, resulting in clear distinctions in human settlements between urban and rural areas and between different regions of the country.[164] The high levels of urbanisation place immense pressure on the government to find land for new settlements, and at times at the expense of land designated for ecological preservation such as forests and protected areas.

---

159 See www.stats.gov.zm for this and further information.
160 Central Statistical Office (2016: 23).
161 Ministry of National Development Planning (2017: 11).
162 Ministry of Finance (2017: 5).
163 Mususa (2012: 571–573); Osei-Hwedi (1996); Huth (1984: 1–16).
164 Ministry of Finance (2017: 35).

Water scarcity is already a major problem for the world's poor. The number of people affected by water scarcity is projected to increase from about 1.7 billion people at the present time to around 5 billion people by 2025. This is independent of climate change, which is projected to further reduce water availability in many water scarce regions, particularly in the subtropics, owing to increased evaporation and changes in rainfall patterns. Close to two million more Africans are expected to find themselves without adequate clean water as early as 2021. This will most likely lead to an increase in poverty and pandemics such as malaria and cholera.[165] These public health concerns will further put pressure on natural resources such as water and soil.[166]

3.7 Weak governance systems

Weak governance systems across all the sectors has been noted as a key challenge affecting environmental well-being in Zambia.[167] Some of the main deficiencies in the general environmental law framework and soil-relevant governance systems include gaps in policy frameworks and institutions, and poor linkages between those at the grassroots who are in direct contact with natural resources and state institutions that ultimately enact laws.[168]

In the forestry sector, weak levels of policy implementation have been identified as a challenge in the prevention of deforestation and forest degeneration, which in turn are a driver for soil degradation. In addition, in forestry, like other sectors, factors such as inadequate institutional capacity and legal framework and a lack of intersectoral coordination among stakeholders are responsible for hampering policy implementation generally.[169] Other weaknesses in the environmental and soil governance systems include corruption and political influences, insecure land tenure and poor funding.[170]

In terms of the climate change debate, research in the context of Nepal, Uganda, Vietnam and Zambia has shown that:[171]

> While there is little ambiguity within the science community regarding whether climate change is real, uncertainty concerning the implications of climate change in the policy arena is widespread among politicians and bureaucrats at all levels of governance. In our district-level cases we found widespread indecision over the implications of climate change for institutional roles and responsibilities. Most local government staff were introduced to the idea of climate change relatively recently. The international narrative of climate change that has filtered down to local

165 Mudenda (2010: 5–7).
166 Addaney et al. (2018: 182–184).
167 Reublic of Zambia (2009: 7).
168 Madzudzo et al. (2013: 10–11).
169 Kalaba (2016: 42–43).
170 Ibid.
171 Christoplos et al. (2016: 55–56).

> government staff is dominated by technical and infrastructural investment packages in which their own roles are ignored or undefined.

These research findings in the context of the named developing countries, which include Zambia, indicate that there are challenges in implementing climate change laws and policies. It has been shown in this report that the effects of climate change will lead to soil and land degradation. Accordingly, the challenges of implementing climate change laws and policies have a bearing on the argument for sustainable soil management in Zambia. Given the many sector-specific strides currently being undertaken, it is possible that enhanced and coordinated systems of monitoring and enforcement of environment-specific measures would also ultimately enhance sustainable soil management in Zambia. It is however hoped that, with the more coordinated approach towards climate change introduced by the National Climate Change Policy, these challenges and shortcomings will be resolved.

4 Relevant legislative framework on the main drivers of soil degradation

This section analyses the legislative framework relating to the main drivers of soil degradation in Zambia. This section starts by recapping that there are no legislative provisions dedicated to sustainable soil management in Zambia. However, there are many legislative provisions that relate to the conservation of biological diversity and environmental well-being and that are therefore relevant, by implication. The section specifically analyses relevant constitutional provisions and legislation related to mining, agriculture, land tenure and the environment, and natural resources.

4.1 Constitutional provisions on soil sustainability

To start with, the current Constitution is relatively new, having been enacted only in 2016. Therefore, most of the environmental provisions that can enhance soil sustainability in Zambia have not as yet generated any jurisprudence.

Article 147 of the Constitution makes provision for a devolved governance system. To this end, the concurrent and exclusive functions of the national, provincial and local government levels are outlined. Article 147(2) prescribes the annex of these functions, and the prevention of soil erosion is listed as a concurrent national and provincial function.

Further, Part XIX of the Constitution contains provisions relating to land, environment and natural resources.[172] The salient provisions of the Constitution relating to land are contained in Article 253, which provides that "land shall be held, used and managed" in accordance with the following principles: Equitable access to land and associated resources; security of tenure for lawful land holders; recognition of indigenous cultural rites; sustainable use of land; transparent, effective and efficient administration of land; effective and efficient settlement of land disputes; river frontages, islands, lakeshores and ecologically and culturally sensitive areas to be accessible to the public; not to be leased, fenced or sold; and to be maintained and used for conservation and preservation activities; investments in land to also benefit local communities and their economy; and plans for land use to be done in a consultative and participatory manner.

The entirety of Article 253 is critical in the promotion of the sustainable use of soil as it provides for the general principle for the sustainable use of land. This means that the use of land should be intergenerational in nature and should be predicated on the balancing of the various competing interests of society and the need to preserve the diversity and integrity of the country's flora and fauna. As was earlier alluded, it remains unclear how far this provision empowers state agencies in enforcing sustainable soil usage.

Article 255 of the Constitution is also instructive and relates to the management and development of the environment and natural resources, which will be governed by the following principles: Natural resources have an environmental, economic, social and cultural value and this must be reflected in their use. The person responsible for polluting or degrading the environment is responsible for paying for the damage done to the environment. Where there are threats of serious or irreversible damage to the environment, lack of full scientific certainty cannot be used as a reason for postponing cost-effective measures to prevent environmental degradation. The conservation and protection of ecologically sensitive areas, habitats, species and other environmental resources must be done in a sustainable manner. The integrity of natural processes and ecological communities must be respected. Benefits accruing from the exploitation and utilisation of the environment and natural resources must be shared equitably among the people of Zambia. Saving of energy and the sustainable use of renewable energy sources must be promoted. Reclaiming and rehabilitation of degraded areas and those prone to disasters must be promoted. Unfair trade practices in the production, processing, distribution and marketing of natural resources must be eliminated; and origin, quality, methods of production, harvesting and processing of natural resources must be regulated.

---

172 This covers Articles 253 to 257 of the Constitution; See also to Sambo (2019: 655–656) analysing these constitutional provisions in the light of their relevance in creating an 'environmental ethos' in Zambia.

In relation to environmental sustainability, the Constitution also contains principles that are designed to prevent irreversible damage to the environment, such as Article 256, which provides that a person has a duty to cooperate with state organs, state institutions and other persons to maintain a clean, safe and healthy environment; to ensure ecologically sustainable development and use of natural resources; to respect, protect and safeguard the environment; and to prevent or discontinue an act which is harmful to the environment.

The obligations placed on citizens under Article 256 are meant to ensure greater citizen social responsibility. These provisions are progressively being integrated into subordinate legislation such as the Solid Waste Management Act. The requirement to ensure ecologically sustainable development is especially important in order to ensure that the environment generally and soil and land generally are also sustainably utilised.

Article 257 makes provision for the state, in the utilisation of natural resources and management of the environment, as to protect genetic resources and biological diversity; to implement mechanisms that minimise waste; to promote appropriate environment management systems and tools; to encourage public participation; to protect and enhance the intellectual property in, and indigenous knowledge of, biodiversity and genetic resources of local communities; to ensure that the environmental standards enforced in Zambia are of essential benefit to citizens; and to establish and implement mechanisms that address climate change.

4.2 Mining legislation

The mining industry is governed by a number of pieces of legislation. This section focuses on the Acts of Parliament and subsidiary legislation that have relevance to sustainable soil management. The Mines and Minerals Development Act, No. 11 of 2015 (MMDA) is the main legislation governing mining in Zambia, read together with the Mines and Minerals Development (Amendment) Act, No. 14 of 2016, which reduced the percentage of royalties' payable on production of minerals. The MMDA applies to the exploration for, and mining and processing of, minerals and makes provision for safety, health and environmental protection in mining operations. In addition, the mining legal framework incorporates some statutory instruments.[173] Of direct

173 Some of the subsidiary legislation include, but are not limited to (i) Mines and Minerals Development (Application for Mining Rights) Regulations SI No.123 of 1996 (ii) Mines and Minerals (Application for Mining Rights) (Amendment) Regulations SI No. 29 of 1997 (iii) Mines and Minerals Development (Environment Protection Fund) Regulations SI No. 102 of 1998 (iv) Mines and Mineral (Environment) (Exemption) (Amendment) Order, SI No. 31 of 2000 (v) Mines and Minerals Development (General) Regulations SI No. 84 of 2008 (vi) Mines and Minerals Development (Prospecting, Mining and Milling of Uranium ores and other Radioactive

relevance to the soil sustainability discourse are the safety, health and environmental protection provisions under Sections 80 to 87 contained in Part VI of the MMDA. To start with, Section 4 provides for general principles applicable to the mining and development of minerals, among others:

> Mineral resources are a non-renewable resource and shall be conserved, developed and used prudently, taking into account the needs of the present and future generations; mineral resources shall be explored and developed in a manner that promotes and contributes to socio-economic development and in accordance with international conventions to which Zambia is a party; the exploitation of minerals shall ensure safety, health and environmental protection; wasteful mining practices shall be avoided so as to promote sustainable development and prevent adverse environmental effects; citizens shall have equitable access to mineral resources and benefit from mineral resources development; and development of local communities in areas surrounding the mining area based on prioritization of community needs, health and safety.

These principles borrow heavily from international best practices on mining and the environment and are almost a replica of the provisions of the EMA. Overall, these principles are relevant for the protection of soil in mining areas and generally in Zambia. Section 6 establishes the Mining Licensing Committee which is tasked with considering applications for mining rights and non-mining rights and the grant, renewal or refusal of mining rights and non-mining rights in Zambia. The Committee is also responsible for terminating, suspending or cancelling mining rights and non-mining rights, amending terms and conditions of mining rights and non-mining rights; and advising the Minister on matters relating to its functions under MMDA. These outlined functions do not specifically point out that soil sustainability matters are at the fore of the conditions to consider before granting or varying a mining right. Given the nature of mining activities, however, it is argued that failure to implement measures aimed at securing soil sustainability must be explicitly stated as a condition for denying mining rights.

Section 12 prohibits exploration, mining and mineral processing without a licence or environmental impact assessment (EIA) granted by the Zambia Environmental Management Agency (ZEMA). Any person who contravenes this requirement commits an offence and is liable, upon conviction, to payment of a fine or imprisonment for a term not exceeding seven years, or to both.[174] This provision is important for averting future environmental damage but cannot forestall historical contraventions that have yet to be remediated. Further sanction is provided for in Section 36.

Production of mining may be suspended, or a mine closed where a mining rights holder fails to comply with the conditions of the mining right or mineral processing licence. Some of the omissions for which mining rights can be suspended or withdrawn include the creation of an unsafe environment or causing uncontrollable pollution from

---

Mineral Ores) Regulations, SI No. 85 of 2000 (vii) Mines and Minerals Development (Mining Rights and Non- Mining Rights) Order, SI No. 27 of 2009 (viii) Mines and Minerals Development (General) Regulations SI No. 7 of 2016.

174 Section 29(3) EMA, 2011.

mining operations, among other reasons. It is clear that if such a provision is to be enforced, soil sustainability can be enhanced in mining and surrounding areas. Since the enactment of the MMDA, a number of mining companies have been held accountable for ongoing pollution, through court prosecutions.[175]

The provisions of Section 80 are also relevant in respect of soil sustainability as the Committee is mandated to take the following into account when granting mining rights:

> The need to conserve and protect the air, water, soil, flora, fauna, fish, fisheries and scenic attractions; and the features of cultural, architectural, archaeological, historical or geological interests; and the need to ensure that any mining or mineral processing activity prevents any adverse socio-economic impact or harm to human health, in or on the land over which the right or licence is sought.

This provision is purposed to ensure that there is wholesome environmental well-being irrespective of the mining activities that are undertaken in area. This provision makes specific reference to soil conservation and protection as a consideration. Furthermore, this provision means that a mining licence will not be granted where the applicant is unable to show evidence of measures that will be taken to guarantee soil conservation and environmental protection.

Section 80 also makes provision that the Director of Mines Safety and the Zambia Environmental Management Agency ensure that applicants undertake all such environmental impact studies and other studies to be carried out as are considered necessary for ensuring that negative environmental impacts are mitigated in the interest of environmental protection.[176]

The MMDA empowers the Minister of Mines to propose additional conditions subject to which a mining right can be granted or renewed.[177] The Minister is obliged to ensure that such conditions are prescribed in a statutory instrument and include:

> the conservation and protection of (i) the air, water, soil, flora, fauna, fish, fisheries and scenic attractions; (ii) the features of cultural, architectural, archaeological, historical or geological interest; and (iii) in or on the land subject to the right or licence; *(b)* the protection of human health, in consultation with the Minister responsible for health; *(c)* the rehabilitation, levelling, regrassing, reforesting or contouring of such part of the land over which the right or licence has effect as may have been damaged or adversely affected by exploration operations, mining operations or mineral processing operations; and *(d)* the filling in, sealing or fencing of excavations, shafts and tunnels.

A close examination of these conditions shows that these conditions are the same ones that the Committee is obliged to enforce under Section 80. The importance of enforcing these environmental conditions necessitates that the Minister is also given an opportunity to ensure that they have been adhered to at the time of granting the mining right.

---

175 Mulenga (2019: 3, 12–15).

176 Section 80(2).

177 Section 81(1).

Section 81(2)(b) requires an applicant for a mining right to pay deposits of cash as may be prescribed, for the purpose of "securing the performance by that applicant or holder of a licence of all or any such conditions" as have been set. Some of the conditions may relate to soil conservation. In the event that the applicant does not fulfil those conditions, then the moneys paid are forfeited to the Environment Fund established under Section 86(1) discussed below.

Under Section 84, if a mining licence holder appears to be using wasteful mining practices, the Director of Mines or Director of Mines Safety is empowered to:

> Give notice to the holder specifying the particulars of the wasteful mining practices; (b) request the holder to cease the wasteful mining practices and remedy any damage caused by the practices; (c) require the holder to reply, in writing, showing cause, within a time specified by the notice, why the holder's licence should not be revoked; and (d) suspend the mining operations until the holder takes remedial measures.

The MMDA does not define "wasteful mining practices" and there is no jurisprudence on this yet. It is, however, open to argument that such mining practices are obviously harmful to the environment. Given the proximity of mining activities to land and soil, it can be concluded that these are mining practices that are likely to contaminate soil and the environment in general. This legal provision is therefore progressive in sustaining soil health. In the event that the mining rights holder fails to remediate the environment, the Committee will cancel the licence.[178] In addition, a mining holder is under legal duty to inform the Director of Mines Safety of any accident that occurs at a mining site,[179] presumably to facilitate urgent remedial measures on the soil and immediate surroundings.

An Environmental Protection Fund is established in Section 86(1) administered and managed by the Environmental Protection Fund Committee appointed by the Minister. The funds in this Fund may be refunded to the holder in the event that there are no breaches of the conditions imposed in the mining right.

A holder of a mining right is "strictly liable" for any harm or damage caused by mining operations or mineral processing operations and must compensate any person to whom the harm or damage is caused.[180] Further, Article 87(4) provides that where any harm or damage is caused to the environment or biological diversity, compensation must include the cost of reinstatement, rehabilitation or clean-up measures which are incurred and, where applicable, the costs of preventive measures. Liability extends to "any air, water or soil contamination or damage to biological diversity; or any other consequential disorder", among many others.[181]

178 Section 84(2).
179 Section 85.
180 Section 87(1).
181 Section 87(5)(e) and (g).

The provisions of Section 87(1) introduce the notion of strict liability under the law of tort based on the rule in *Rylands v Fletcher.*[182] Strict liability ensures that the polluter, in this case, is liable independent of any wrongful intent or negligence. This is a progressive provision because mining is known to be a source of wide-ranging pollution, which ought to put holders of mining rights under a higher general duty of care to persons and the environment. Further, the monetary benefits that accrue from marketing minerals at international markets should be re-invested to mitigate negative environmental impacts.

Section 87(6) provides that, notwithstanding any other law to the contrary, the right to bring any action in respect of harm caused by mining or mineral processing operations should lapse after a *reasonable period* from the date on which the affected person or the community could reasonably be expected to have learned of the harm or damage. This provision is a marked departure from the position in Zambia where any personal injury cases must be litigated within three years.[183] The section instead provides for a *reasonable period* within which to initiate litigation. The reasonableness of the period can be interpreted with reference to what environmental damage consists of. More specifically, if issues of soil contamination are at issue, scientific evidence would be required, and this would require long periods of time and processes to conclude. Section 87(6)(a) and (b) provide a guide on determining the reasonableness of the delay, namely consideration should be given to "the time the harm or damage may take to manifest itself and the time that it may take to correlate the harm with the mining or mineral processing operations, having regard to the situation or circumstance of the person or community affected."

Section 87(7) allows a "person, group of persons or a private or state organization" to bring a claim and seek redress in respect of the breach or threatened breach of any provision relating to damage to the environment, biological diversity, human and animal health or to socioeconomic conditions. According to this section, the cause of action may be brought in the interest of a person or group of persons; in the interest of or on behalf of, a person who is, for practical reasons, unable to institute such proceedings; in the interest of, or on behalf of, a group or class of persons whose interests are affected; in the public interest; and in the interest of protecting the environment or biological diversity.

Looking at these instances, the argument in favour of soil sustainability and the environment can be made by any interested party.

Further, legal costs must not be awarded against any of the persons specified under Section 87(7) who fail in any action if the action were instituted reasonably out of concern for the public interest or the interest of protecting human health, biological diversity and, in general, the environment. It is worth noting here that the provisions

182 *Rylands v Fletcher* (1868) LR 3HC 330.

183 Section 3(a) Law Reform (Limitation of Actions) Act, chapter 72 of the laws of Zambia.

of Section 87(7) and 87(8), in particular, remove some legal barriers that hinder justice for the environment.

First, Section 87(7) addresses *locus standi* or 'the right to bring an action or to be heard' in a given forum. This provision has broadened the rule on *locus standi* by allowing any other party other than the affected person(s) to bring an action. In this regard, any interested person including environmental non-governmental organisations can bring an action in respect of breach or threatened breach of any provision relating to damage to environmental and biological diversity, human and animal health, and socioeconomic conditions. In light of this, this provision is a potent mechanism for advocating soil sustainability in mining areas in Zambia.

Secondly, Section 87(8) is also progressive because it provides that costs will not be awarded against any of the persons specified under Section 87(7) who do not succeed in an action instituted reasonably out of concern for the public interest or the interest of protecting human health, biological diversity and, in general, the environment.

While some of the provisions are quite unspecific, leaving room for interpretation, which could stand in the way of an effective implementation, the provisions of the MMDA, are – overall – progressive. In this vein, the provisions of the MMDA are likely to be effective in sustainable soil management and environmental protection, especially when read together with the provisions of the equally progressive, overarching Environmental Management Act. The enforcement provisions of both pieces of legislation are equally forward-looking. This said, it will be important to see how these laws will be utilised in the interests of the soil sustainability agenda and environmental protection, in the wake of the country's projected development trajectory.

4.3 Agricultural legislation

The projected development trajectory of the country rests on agriculture. It is expected that there will be further strain on agriculture in order to achieve the country's SDG targets. Despite this expectation, most of the sector legislation does not specifically address soil-related issues that have been pointed out as driving soil degradation.[184] One reason for this is that the sector is still addressing one of its policy targets of reviewing its legislative and policy framework. Further, it is important to point out that the provisions of the Environmental Management Act (EMA), 2011 take precedence over other laws with regard to environmental matters. To this end, the shortcomings

184 These are the other pieces of sector legislation without clear relevance to sustainable soil management- The Cotton Act, chapter 227; Tobacco Act, chapter 237; Coffee Act, chapter 228; Plant Variety and Seeds Act; chapter 236; Plant Pests and Diseases Act, chapter 233; Food Reserve Act, chapter 225; Animal Health Act, 2010; Agricultural Institute of Zambia No. 2 of 2017; Agricultural Lands Act, chapter 187; Agricultural Credits Act No. 35 of 2010.

of legislation in agriculture can be remedied by the EMA, 2011, where necessary. From the current legal framework, it is only possible to discuss two pieces of legislation.

4.3.1 Fencing Act, Chapter 190

The erection and maintenance of dividing fences is regulated by this piece of legislation. By implication, the Fencing Act may be relevant to soil sustainability in so far as environmental assessments may be necessary to undertake such developments.

4.3.2 Agriculture (Fertilizers and Feed) Act, Chapter 226

The preamble to the Agriculture Act provides that it is purposed to regulate and control the manufacture, processing, importation and sale of agricultural fertilizers and farm feed as well as provide for minimum standards of effectiveness and purity of such fertilizers and feed and other connected matters. The Act does not provide for standards relevant to soil quality or impact of fertilizers on the soil.

Public environmental legislation and soil sustainability

Public environmental law in the context of Zambia refers to the framework and sectoral natural resources legislation. These pieces of legislation are relevant in the quest for sustainable soil management. First and foremost, it is important to understand the Zambian land tenure system before focusing on the environmental and natural resources legislation. The discussion in the next section will be progress under the ambit of the relevant overarching constitutional provisions.

4.3.3 Land tenure system

The legal framework on land is governed by the Constitution and Acts of Parliament which are analysed in this section. From the constitutional perspective, Article 254 provides for classification and alienation of land and land tenure, which "land shall be delimited and classified as state land, customary land and such other classifications as provided."[185] The President, through the Lands Commission, is empowered to "alienate land to citizens and non- citizens for a prescribed tenure."[186]

Further, the Constitution makes provision for the protection from deprivation of property, which includes land. The relevant Article provides that:

185 Article 254(1).

186 Article 254(2) and (3).

> no property of any description shall be compulsorily taken possession of, and no interest in or right over property of any description shall be compulsorily acquired, unless by or under the authority of an Act of Parliament which provides for payment of adequate compensation for the property or interest or right to be taken possession of or acquired.[187]

The key point to note from this is that the land rights that are conferred on the strength of the constitutional right to property safeguard security of tenure, irrespective of whether the land is held under customary or state land tenure. By implication, soil sustainability is protected as an incidental benefit to land ownership.

The land tenure system in Zambia is generally acknowledged to be dualist in character and as a result, many issues arise with regard to land use and sustainability. The pre-colonial history of modernday Zambia was characterised by land being held on a usufructuary basis. This meant that individuals and families were connected to particular tracts of land for usage through their membership of communities.[188] The right to claim land came with citizenship in a village, through registration in the village register. In essence, membership of the village could be given, or denied, by a headperson. This registration was carried out pursuant to the provisions of the Registration and Development of Villages Act, which is still in force and whose relevance to the soil sustainability discourse in Zambia has been discussed in relation to traditional authorities.

Customary tenure was largely influenced by social status and, as a result, security of tenure was a secondary consideration to social relationships rather than property rights.[189] It has been argued that links to persons through whom land was acquired and by whom it could be used were crucial, and not the rights to land as such. The ability to control significant portions of land is closely associated with, and identified as an important source of, wealth, which becomes the subject of specific rights.[190]

Following the arrival of the British colonists, the Western concept of freehold land tenure and registration of individual property rights to Zambia was introduced. In 1911 the British South African Company (BSA Co.) was given royal authority to explore for minerals.[191] The company thought that the declaration of a protectorate and a granting of land concessions were sufficient sources of title.[192] The BSA Co. was authorised to apportion land to the indigenous people for their occupation. The indigenous people were not allowed to obtain title whereas the British settlers obtained land on either freehold or leasehold tenure. This has been attributed to the strong belief that, under African traditions, individuals did not own land.[193]

---

187 Article 16 of the Constitution of Zambia (as amended by Act No. 18 of 1996).
188 Loenen (1999: 5).
189 Mvunga (1980: 17).
190 Loenen (1999: 3–4).
191 Mvunga (1978: 54).
192 Loenen (1999: 9).
193 Mvunga (1980: 12).

In 1924 the British Crown took over the administration of the Protectorate of Northern Rhodesia, now Zambia. The introduction of Crown land and Native Reserves by Council-in-Order in 1928 arguably clarified the uncertainty about which land was vested in the Crown, and that the occupation of Crown land was for the white settlers only.[194] These lands were governed by statute, with tenure running for 999 years, while it was 99 years for agricultural land.[195]

Native Reserves were designated for the exclusive use of Africans and customary law applied to those areas. Further, non-natives were allowed to hold land in reserves for not more than five years.[196] In 1947, the administration introduced Trust land in the law, out of Crown land and intended for the occupation of indigenous people.[197] The difference between Trust Land and Native Reserves was the duration of a non-native interest of 99 years in Trust Land. In Trust Land non-natives could be granted land if it was determined to be in the interest of both races. Alienation of land in Reserves and Trust Land required the consent of the native authority.

It has further been observed that the colonial government ensured that the most valuable land used primarily for farming and minerals was made available to settler farmers, and although a large proportion of those settlers left when Zambia gained its independence in 1964, most of the best farmland remained in the hands of the absentee landlord settlers. It should be noted that until 1970, the Western Province, formerly Barotseland, had a special status: it was the exclusive domain of the Lozi Litunga and his subjects.[198] In 1970, an amendment to the Constitution of Zambia allowed uniformity in the land tenure system. Parts of the Western Province or Lozi area were formally ranked on a par with Reserves and Trust land elsewhere in the country.[199]

The country witnessed land reforms in 1975 through a new land policy which radically reviewed land tenure through the Land (Conversion of Titles) Act. Under these reforms, all land in Zambia became vested in the President, and freehold tenure was converted to statutory leasehold for a term of years not exceeding 100 years. Further, all vacant land was nationalised together with undeveloped plots, and the subdivision and sublease of land without the President's consent was prohibited. Furthermore, private ownership of land ceased to exist, and all land was declared to have no value. Since land had no more value, it ceased to be a saleable and mortgageable commodity.[200]

In 1991 Zambia returned to multiparty politics and established a market-oriented government with corresponding economic policies which saw the need for a land

194 Mvunga (1978: 39).
195 Loenen (1999: 2).
196 Chinene et al. (1998: 9).
197 Mudenda (2007: 351–358).
198 Ibid.: 353.
199 Bull (2014: 27).
200 Mudenda (2007: 377).

tenure reform to increase private sector development, and generate private and foreign investment.[201] This led to the passage of the Lands Act 1995, which repealed the Land (Conversion of Titles) Act of 1975, the Zambia (State lands and Reserves) Orders, 1928 to 1964, the Zambia (Trust Land) Orders, 1947 to 1964 and other previous land laws. The Lands Act 1995 is the basis of the current land tenure system, although it is also fraught with numerous challenges.[202]

Leasehold tenure applies to state land and whatever pieces of customary land are on registered lease. There were about 200,000 leaseholds on 7 million hectares, about 9% of the country in 2016.[203] There are four different types of state registered leases: first, a 10-year renewable Land Record Card issued on municipal land; secondly, a 14-year interim lease based on a sketch pending a registered boundary survey; thirdly, a 30-year Land Occupancy License in municipal areas and settlement schemes; and fourthly, 10- and 30-year leases which the local authorities give without requirement for legally approved boundaries. A 99-year leasehold period is typical for all surveyed land.[204]

Approximately 40% of the country's population is on state land and it has been noted that this is a considerable proportion of the population to be on less than 10% of the country's available land.[205] Customary land occupation accounts for a little less than 60% of the population, covering 90% of the country's area. Customary tenure is also home to the country's protected areas, wildlife estates, national parks, game management areas, and about 74% of protected forest areas.[206]

Public land in Zambia refers to those areas that are owned and taken care of by the government; it is simply all land that is neither private nor community land and is any other land declared to be public by an Act of Parliament.[207] Common lands refer to grazing lands, grave sites, village woodlands, river frontages or any other classification reserved for community use by a group of people in a particular settlement area. The main Acts of Parliament relevant to land tenure in Zambia include those listed below.

4.3.3.1 Lands Act, Chapter 184

The Lands Act provides for the continuation of leaseholds and leasehold tenure and the continued vesting of land in the President and alienation of land by the President. The Act further provides for the statutory recognition and continuation of customary

201 Mudenda (2007: 405–407).
202 Loenen (1999: 7).
203 Ministry of Lands and Natural Resources (2017: 1).
204 Chinene et al. (1998: 4).
205 Ministry of National Development Planning (2006: 7).
206 Chinene et al. (1998: 7).
207 Sections 4(1) of the Lands Act.

tenure, and conversion of customary tenure into leasehold tenure. The Lands Act, like the other pieces of legislation on land matters does not expressly make any reference to soil sustainability matters. As noted earlier, the legal and policy framework relating to land is earmarked for revision. It is hoped that the soil sustainability discourse can be incorporated into the ongoing consultations.

4.3.3.2 Lands and Deeds Registry Act, Chapter 185

The Lands and Deeds Registry Act provides for the registration of documents and the issuance of Provisional Certificates of Title and Certificates of Title, as well as the transfer and transmission of registered land.

4.3.3.3 Land (Perpetual Succession) Act, Chapter 186

The Land (Perpetual Succession) Act provides for perpetual succession to land and allows for the holding of land in trust as a body corporate.

4.3.3.4 Land Survey Act, Chapter 188

The Land Survey Act makes comprehensive provision for the registration and licensing of land surveyors, the manner in which land surveys should be carried out and diagrams and plans connected with land surveys should be prepared. The Act does not have any direct soil-relevant provisions.

4.3.3.5 Lands Acquisition Act, Chapter 189

The Lands Acquisition Act provides for the compulsory acquisition of land and other property. The Act ensures that adequate and prompt compensation is paid where it is liable to be paid or alternative land is provided as a replacement for the land compulsorily acquired. By implication, this piece of legislation might be relevant if the purpose for compulsory acquisition is about or related to soil conservation.

4.3.4 Environmental Management Act, 2011

The Environmental Management Act (EMA), 2011, is the framework environmental legislation in Zambia and makes innovative and progressive provisions in relation to the environment.[208] This section analyses the provisions of the EMA through the sustainable soil management lens.

According to the preamble, the purpose of the EMA is to provide for "integrated environmental management" and the "protection and conservation of the environment and the sustainable management and use of natural resources". The EMA also provides for the preparation of the *State of the Environment Report*, environmental management strategies and other plans for environmental management and sustainable development. Further, the EMA is relevant for sustainable soil management in light of its provisions on the conduct of strategic environmental assessments of proposed policies, plans and programmes likely to have an impact on environmental management, prevention and control of pollution and environmental degradation. In an attempt to enhance environmental democracy in Zambia, the EMA also provides for public participation in environmental decision-making and access to environmental information.

The enforcement provisions of the EMA range from the establishment of the Environment Fund, which is yet to be operationalised, and environmental audit and monitoring, among others. One of the strongest features of the EMA is that it places national environmental protection in the context of international environmental agreements and conventions to which Zambia is a party, and which are critical in addressing land and soil degradation in particular.

In respect of all environmental matters, the provisions of the EMA, 2011, are only secondary to the Constitution.[209] The EMA, 2011, has robust provisions for the protection of all aspects of the environment, including soil.[210]

Section 2 of the EMA, 2011, defines a number of terms that are used in legislation, two of which have direct relevance to soils. First, the term "element" in relation to the environment means "any of the principal constituent parts of the environment including water, atmosphere, soil, vegetation, climate, sound, odour, aesthetics, fish and wildlife". Secondly, "sustainable management" means the protection and management of the use of the environment, in a manner that, while enabling human beings to provide for their health, safety, social, cultural and economic well-being, (a) safeguards the life-supporting capacity of air, water, soil and ecosystems; and (b) maintains the life-supporting capacity and quality of air, water, soil and ecosystems, including living organisms, to enable future generations to meet their reasonably foreseeable needs. This explanation of terminologies underscores the importance of soil and ecosystems to the sustenance of all forms of life for the present and future generations.

The other references to soil in the EMA, 2011, are in Sections 75 and 76 of the EMA. Section 75 provides that the Zambia Environmental Management Agency

208 Sambo (2019: 651–654) offers an extensive review and analysis of the provisions of the EMA and whether or not it is succeeding in creating an 'environmental ethos' in Zambia.

209 Section 5.

210 Sambo (2019: 647–664).

(ZEMA) should work in consultation with local authorities and other appropriate authorities, within five years of the commencement of the Act, which lapsed in 2016, to identify hilly areas at risk from environmental degradation. The EMA, 2011, further identifies hilly areas as at risk from environmental degradation by being prone to soil erosion, landslides occurring or being likely to occur, vegetation cover being removed or being likely to be removed from the area at a rate faster than it is being replaced; or any other land-use activity in that area being likely to lead to environmental degradation. The Minister of Environment is accordingly empowered to issue a list of landscapes and hilly areas that are regarded as being at risk from environmental degradation, and ZEMA must maintain a record of all these matters and devise strategies to ameliorate these soil-related problems.

The totality of the provisions under Section 75 of the EMA are very progressive and proactive. A search in the ZEMA registry, however, revealed that there is no record of such hilly areas that are at risk of environmental degradation, nor are there strategies devised to address the causes of such degradation. Further, ZEMA working in collaboration with the local authorities and the Minister responsible for the environment are supposed to facilitate public awareness of how to address the problem of environmental degradation. The EMA, 2011, creates a sound basis upon which the main drivers of land degradation in Zambia can be addressed, in the quest for general environmental well-being. It is, however, yet to be seen how these provisions will be implemented, especially in relation to soil governance.[211]

Section 76(1) of EMA, 2011, relates to the management of fisheries, water, forestry and wildlife resources, and provides that they will be managed in accordance with the provisions of the respective pieces of sectoral legislation. It can therefore be inferred that in relation to the protection of natural resources such as water, fish and other aquatic life, forests, and wildlife, due regard must be given to soil sustainability. Such provisions need to be clearly made in the legislation so that there is coordination in all policies and regulations that can foster soil sustainability in Zambia.

Section 105 is also relevant to sustainable soil management in Zambia in as far as it makes provision for the enforcement of environmental restoration orders. Here, if there is a discharge of a contaminant or pollutant into the environment in an amount, concentration or manner that constitutes a risk to human health or property, or that causes or has the potential to cause adverse effects, an environmental restoration order will be served to take any measures that will assist in reducing or eliminating the risk or harm and to take any measures to (a) take such action as will prevent the continuation or cause of pollution; and (b) restore land, including the replacement of soil, the replanting of trees and other flora and the restoration as far as may be, of outstanding geological, archaeological or historical features of the land or the area contiguous to the land.

211 Sambo (2019: 662–663).

4.3.5 Forests Act, No. 4 of 2015

The Forests Act No. 4 of 2015 provides for the establishment and declaration of national forests, local forests, joint forest management areas, botanical reserves, private forests and community forests. It also provides for the participation of local communities, local authorities, traditional institutions, non-governmental organisations and other stakeholders in sustainable forest management. The Act also focuses on the implementation of the United Nations Framework Convention on Climate Change, the Convention on International Trade in Endangered Species of Wild Flora and Fauna, the Convention on Wetlands of International Importance, especially as Water Fowl Habitat, the Convention on Biological Diversity, the Convention to Combat Desertification in those Countries experiencing Serious Drought and/or Desertification, particularly in Africa, and any other relevant international agreements to which Zambia is a party.

The Forest Act is also a relatively new piece of legislation that has not yet aided the evolution of jurisprudence. It must however be noted that at the beginning of 2019, one important forest reserve in the regeneration of water resources in Lusaka district has been degazetted to pave the way for infrastructural developments.[212] Given the importance of forest reserves in the sustenance of soil, ecosystems and the services they support, it is reasonable to conclude that the scientific perspectives that cause phenomena such as climate change are not well understood and assimilated into policy action. This is also evidence that there is no political buy-in in respect of natural resources management in Zambia.

Section 2 of the Act defines "forest produce" to include soil, among many other things, and also defines "forest resources" to include soil, in addition to vegetation, wood and non-wood products, and forest ecological services, including the maintenance of soil quality, control of erosion, provision of organic materials and modulating climate.

Section 45(1) empowers the Minister to issue, by statutory instrument, orders to the occupier of any land to undertake or adopt such measures necessary for the conservation of natural resources on land in an open area and the prevention of injury to natural resources by the acts or omissions of the occupier. An order issued pursuant to this section is known as a conservation order and may relate to:

> (a) the allocation of the uses of land for arable, pasture, woodland or forest purposes or for water catchment; (b) the construction and maintenance of works for conserving water or soil and other works to preserve or improve natural resources; (c) the prohibition or restriction of cultivation of any part of the land; (d) the method of cultivation of land and the system of farming to be used on the land; (e) the manner of watering, managing, pasturing and moving livestock; (f) the preservation and protection of the source, course and banks of any stream; (g) the control of water,

212 See https://tizambia.org.zm/transparency-international-zambias-statement-on-leaders-acquisition-of-land-on-forest-27/, accessed 2 February 2021.

including storm water, drainage water and floods; (h) the prevention of pollution or fouling of public water as defined in the Water Resources Management Act, 2011; (i) the preservation of trees and other vegetation and the method and systems by which forest produce may be taken and used; (j) measures to prevent, control or combat fires, including the making of firebreaks and carrying out controlled burning.

The Act also provides for the implementation of several MEAs, which are specified in the preamble. This piece of legislation is relevant to soil sustainability, as shown in Section 45 where a conservation order may be enforced.

4.3.6 Urban and Regional Planning Act, No. 3 of 2015

The Urban and Regional Planning Act No. 3 of 2015 provides for development, planning and administration principles, standards and requirements for urban and regional planning processes and systems. It operates as a framework for administering and managing urban and regional planning in Zambia and establishes a democratic, accountable, transparent, participatory and inclusive regime for urban and regional planning. One important principle that is embedded in this legislation is broad-based participation of communities, private sector, interest groups and other stakeholders in the planning, implementation and operation of human settlement development. By implication, this should cover a multisectoral interest group which should also have a focus on soil sustainability because the geographical sensitivity of all areas is taken into consideration. This is not mentioned in the Urban and Regional Planning Act, which however, recognises the interconnected nature of issues that arise out of human settlements by making cross reference to other regulatory instruments such as the Environmental Management Act, the National Council for Construction Act, the Public Health Act, the Water Resources Management Act, and many others.

Not only does the Act establish procedures for integrated urban and regional planning in a devolved system of governance, but it also guarantees sustainable urban and rural development by promoting environmental, social and economic sustainability in development initiatives and controls at all levels of urban and regional planning.[213] The Act further makes allowance for locational prerequisites for development, and the characteristics and diversity of particular areas are enhanced and protected. Ideally, the ability of particular soil types to withstand certain developmental processes should be taken into consideration as part of the environmental impact assessment (EIA) process. The question on whether soil sustainability is currently taken into consideration in the EIA process in Zambia is more specifically addressed in a later section of this chapter.

213 See http://www.daily-mail.co.zm/a-look-at-regional-and-urban-planning-act/, accessed 3 February 2021.

4.3.7 Local Government Act, No. 2 of 2019

Section 16(2) of the Local Government Act outlines the functions of local authorities thus:[214]

> With respect to agriculture, a local authority shall (a) establish and maintain farms and allotment gardens; (b) take and cause the taking of measures for the – (i) storage, market and preservation of agricultural produce; (ii) *conservation of natural resources; and* (iii) *prevention of soil erosion, including the prohibition and control of cultivation;* (c) take and cause the taking of measures for the control of grass weeds and wild vegetation and for the suppression and control of plant and insect pests and diseases … (Emphasis supplied).

This provision shows that local authorities, first and foremost, have responsibilities in environmental management as also outlined in the Constitution. Further, these responsibilities extend to conservation of natural resources and particularly to prevention of soil erosion. It however remains unclear whether the local authorities actually carry out these functions.

4.3.8 Solid Waste Regulation and Management Act, No. 20 of 2018

The Solid Waste Regulation and Management Act No. 20 of 2018 makes provision for the sustainable regulation and management of solid waste, general and self-service solid waste services, the regulation, operation, maintenance and construction of landfills and other disposal facilities and other related aspects. The Act does not apply to hazardous waste, e-waste, healthcare waste or waste regulated under the EMA, 2011. Section 5 outlines key concepts and principles in the management and regulation of solid waste, which are recognised as a resource. Some of the concepts and principles relevant to soil sustainability include the restriction of landfills and other disposal facilities near airdromes, wetlands, flood plains and ecologically sensitive areas. In addition, the Act prioritises the protection of the interests of consumers through effective participation of consumers in the management and decision-making processes for solid waste management.

Section 6(5) of the Act empowers local authorities to provide solid waste services in accordance with the Constitution. The functions of a local authority, with respect to solid waste, are described as "facilitating and managing activities that promote the key concepts and principles of solid waste management" as specified in Section 5 of the Act and "determining the location of landfills and other disposal facilities in accordance with international best practice, in consultation with the Zambia Environmental Management Agency". In carrying out the impact assessments that are mandatory in

214 First Schedule to the Local Government Act.

the planning stages of the projects, soil management mechanisms need to be spelt out in order to ensure that there is no disturbance or pollution to the natural environment.

Sections 33 and 34 respectively prohibit the burning of solid waste other than in a prescribed manner and the burying of non-organic waste. The Act does not provide any explanation for this prohibition. However, in a similar vein to the unsustainable agricultural practice of 'slash and burn', unabated burning and burying of non-organic substances would inevitably lead to soil contamination, the environmental effects of which are far-reaching.

Section 78(2) on enforcement of the provisions of the Act provides that:

> For the purposes of implementing and enforcing this Act, monitoring and containing the effects of solid waste on human health and the environment, an authorized person may enter on any land, with a warrant or with the consent of the owner or occupier, enter a private property or premise, after notifying the owner or occupier of the intention to do so; take samples of solid waste, soil and water for testing and analysis ...

This provision shows that soil evaluation is one of the main mechanisms for achieving the objectives of the Act, such as monitoring the effects of solid waste on human health and the environment. Given that the Solid Waste Regulation and Management Act is a relatively new enactment, it was not possible to ascertain whether the soil evaluations have actually been carried out pursuant to the provisions of Section 78(2).

5 Relevant policy framework on the main drivers of soil degradation

The legal and policy framework in Zambia does not directly address soil sustainability issues per se, but rather focuses on land tenure and usage systems, agriculture, forests, water and environmental protection generally. In examining the relevant legislation, particular focus is directed at the soil-relevant provisions, their enforceability and any applicable subsidiary legislation. This section starts by examining the policy framework in relation to the overall developmental agenda of the country. This is followed by a consideration of policies as they relate to the main drivers of soil degradation, namely land, environment, climate change, agriculture and mining, before examining the applicable legislative framework.

5.1 Vision 2030

Zambia's Vision 2030 (2006–2030) aims to transform Zambia into a prosperous middle-income nation by 2030 and to create a new Zambia which is a "strong and dynamic middle-income industrial nation that provides opportunities for improving the well-being of all, embodying values of socio-economic justice."[215] It comprises three priority sectors, namely economic growth and wealth creation; social investment and human development; and the creation of an enabling environment for sustainable social economic development.

Vision 2030 articulates long-term plans for development to achieve desirable socioeconomic outcomes by 2030. The Vision is operationalised through five-year national development plans, the current being the Seventh National Development Plan (SNDP) for the period 2017 to 2021. Implementation of Vision 2030 mandates the involvement of a variety of stakeholders including government, the private sector, cooperating partners, civil society, communities and individuals. Three-year medium-term expenditure frameworks and annual budgets are also developed as part of the process.

Vision 2030 promotes a decentralised governance system and sets out specific goals and targets for different sectors, e.g., for the Energy sector, the target is to reduce the share of wood fuel to 40% by 2030. This is one of the specific goals that is relevant for sustainable natural resources management, specifically for forests and soils.

Further, Vision 2030 recognises the abundance of land in Zambia, which is a necessary economic resource with potential to spur the country's growth. On one hand the abundance of the land resource is advantageous for enhancing a variety of developmental plans and, on the other, spells potential risk for soil protection. In achieving the development targets set in Vision 2030, it is important to ensure that environmental assessments are carried out and enforced in relation to protection of all-natural resources and soil in particular. It is envisioned that, by 2030, there will be access for all to good quality basic human necessities such as shelter and titled land. In the land sector, the Vision is to "secure fair and equitable access and control of land for sustainable socio-economic development by 2030".[216]

Zambia is currently implementing the Seventh National Development Plan (SNDP) which incorporates and localises the United Nations Sustainable Development Goals (SDGs) and Agenda 2063, which is the current model for –[217]

> transforming Africa into the global powerhouse of the future; the continent's strategic framework that aims to deliver on its goal for inclusive and sustainable development and is a concrete manifestation of the pan-African drive for unity, self-determination, freedom, progress and collective prosperity pursued under Pan-Africanism and African Renaissance.

Taken together, the SNDP and Agenda 2063 create and provide an entry point for further mainstreaming and road-mapping for the implementation of the United Nations SDGs in Zambia.

---

215 Ministry of National Development Planning (2006).

216 Ibid.: 33.

217 See https://au.int/en/agenda2063/overview, accessed 3 February 2021; Stevens (2019: 470–472).

5.2 Sustainable Development Goals

The background to the 17 Sustainable Development Goals (SDGs) can be traced to the process leading to the 2012 United Nations Conference on Sustainable Development (UNCSD), whose outcome document *The Future We Want*, was used to negotiate and develop consensus on them.[218] The set of 17 SDGs has 169 targets, many of which look quite similar to their predecessor, the Millennium Development Goals (MDGs), 2000–2015.[219]

The content of the SDGs spans environmental considerations such as land degradation, climate change and challenges such as the interrelated aspects of poverty and gender and other forms of marginalisation. It is this array of themes that links SDGs to sustainable soil management. Despite not being legally binding, the SDGs have since 2015 met global acceptance, and mechanisms of implementing them through national plans and strategies have been underway in Africa and the rest of the world.

Healthy soils and land resources are crucial to the achievement of the objectives and targets of many of the SDGs set out in Agenda 2030. More specifically, the SDGs relating to food security, water security/resources, climate change, biodiversity, and land management are directly related to securing global soil sustainability.[220] Even though each of the SDGs can be summarised in terms of food, health, water, climate and ecosystems, the descriptions cover a wide variety of subtopics that require input by many different disciplines. For the purposes of this analysis, SDG 15 and its objective, Target 15.3 on land degradation neutrality (LDN)[221] are the most relevant to sustainable soil management.

SDG 15 is targeted at protecting, restoring and promoting sustainable use of terrestrial ecosystems, sustainably managing forests, combatting desertification, halting and reversing land degradation and halting loss of biological diversity. Target 15.3 envisages that by 2030 desertification will have been combatted, and degraded land and soil restored, including land affected by desertification, drought and floods, and that the global community would strive to achieve a land degradation-neutral world.[222]

With these globally agreed targets, each country has devised plans and strategies on achieving land degradation neutrality, which is "a state whereby the amount and quality of land resources necessary to support ecosystem functions and services and enhance food security remain stable or increase within specified temporal and spatial

---

218 See https://bit.ly/2YWbJVj, accessed 3 February 2021.

219 Stevens & Kanie (2016: 393–396).

220 Orr et al. (2017: 72–73).

221 For further reading on land degradation neutrality see: Metternicht et al. (2019: 189–191); Gilbey et al. (2019: 230–237); Von Malitz et al. (2019: 54–62).

222 See https://knowledge.unccd.int/knowledge-products-and-pillars/ldn-target-setting-building-blocks/land-degradation-neutrality-ldn, accessed 3 February 2021.

scales and ecosystems."[223] This is against the background that the health and productivity of land globally is declining and, at the same time, demand for land resources is increasing. [224]

The problem of land degradation is particularly pronounced in Africa, and, for this reason, Zambia and other African countries need to utilise the opportunity given by SDGs and the concept of land degradation neutrality (LDN) to evaluate indigenous interventions.[225] In terms of setting LDN targets, Zambia together with UNCCD and the International Union for Conservation of Nature (IUCN) has devised programmes engaging women farmers, project implementers, policymakers and NGOs with a view to mainstreaming gender in projects that support land degradation neutrality (LDN).[226] There are presently no dedicated legal provisions that directly address the challenge of LDN except in so far as environmental well-being is concerned. It will therefore be important to ensure that the country targets for meeting LDN are given effect through specific and deliberate provision in relevant law and policy.

5.3 Seventh National Development Plan

The Seventh National Development Plan (SNDP) emphasises that Zambia's comparative advantage lies in its endowment of renewable and natural resources which can be productively harnessed. There is no concerted focus on the importance of soil sustainability, however. Further, the plan indicates that Zambia is competitive on tourism, greenhousing, and forestry and fishery sectors. The natural beauty makes tourism unique. The fact that Zambia is one of the most water-rich countries in Africa with a high intensity of sunshine opens new avenues for renewable energy generation. Low-cost greenhousing and construction have competitive edges because of the perfect soils for stabilised earth blocks. Forestry and fisheries, if sustainably managed, also have high potential. In addition to integrating development across key sectors for pro-poor economic growth, tackling vulnerabilities is poised to reduce social exclusion.

The plan further reveals that Zambia has to make fundamental policy shifts, particularly to food security and developmental projects, if the country is to achieve the objectives of Vision 2030. Actualising these shifts requires placing enormous pressure on the soil resource and there are no mitigatory factors alluded to in the plan.

According to the plan, accelerating economic diversification for shielding the economy from the effects of adverse commodity price fluctuations is cardinal. Progress

223 Orr et al. (2017: 15)

224 Smith (2018: 285–287).

225 Kibugi (2018: 387–390).

226 See https://www.unccd.int/news-events/ldn-projects-zambia-amplifying-gender-dimension, accessed 3 February 2021.

towards diversification should show a much bigger reduction in the contribution of mining to the gross domestic product and increases in other sectors.

Lastly, the plan proposes building a strong manufacturing and industrial base, which is key to maintaining a strong export-oriented economy that can create resilience in the economy to both external and domestic shocks. This is crucial to ensuring a stable foreign exchange, enhanced foreign currency reserves, stable inflation, more decent jobs and an expanded capital base for the economy, among other things. A strong manufacturing and industrial base also help in forging backward and forward linkages between primary, secondary and tertiary industries and ensures sustained circular flow of resources within the economy, while bolstering job creation. The positive aspects of the national manufacturing and industrial base notwithstanding, it must be acknowledged that these sectors would pose contamination threats to the soil resources.

5.4 Draft National Land Policy, 2017

Primarily, land is the most important aspect that needs evaluation in order to understand its soil component. Regrettably, the National Land Policy (2017) is still in draft form. It has been subject of protracted discussions between stakeholders.[227] The draft National Land Policy recognises that soil quality and fertility is declining, and measures need to be put in place to prohibit practices that contribute to this trend.

One of the major challenges in reaching consensus on the Draft National Land Policy is that the traditional leadership was of the general view that the proposals therein have the effect of usurping their authority over land administration in the country.[228] For instance, one long-held observation is that the rights of landowners under customary law are undefined and sometimes contradictory. Further, there are no clear guidelines on the role and functions of traditional authorities and local authorities in the administration of customary land. Any attempts to resolve these matters which hinge on controlling the authority of traditional entities need to adopt a consultative and consensual approach; and the resultant decision would work in the interests of environmental sustainability.

5.5 National Policy on Environment, 2009

The National Policy on Environment identifies two main soil-relevant environmental challenges in Zambia, namely natural disaster risk and climate change effects. First,

227 The draft document is clearly marked as a working document and not a final policy, it should not be quoted and interpreted as government policy until finally agreed to and adopted.

228 Ministry of Lands and Natural Resources (2018: 1–3).

Zambia is prone to extreme meteorological events such as droughts and floods, with major impacts on food security and public health. Climate change adds to existing environmental stress and is likely to affect Zambia's natural resource base negatively and exacerbate existing problems of land degradation, flood regulation, water purification, and droughts. Secondly, Zambia has been experiencing the effects of climate change resulting in extreme weather conditions, such as droughts, rising temperatures and unpredictable rainfall patterns. The frequency and intensity of climate events is expected to rise in future, with negative impacts on the economy and consequently people's livelihoods.[229]

It is estimated that the impact of climate change will cost Zambia approximately 0.4% of annual economic growth. It is further estimated that without action, rainfall variability alone could lead to losses of 0.9% of GDP growth over the next decade, thereby keeping a significant section of Zambia's population below the poverty line.[230]

In addition, the fall in the country's hydropower generation in recent times by about 600 MW is mainly attributed to poor rainfall patterns. The lower supply of electricity has hampered growth prospects of Zambia's productive sectors of the economy, including agriculture, manufacturing, mining and services. Other adverse effects have led to increased costs of treating climate-related diseases such as malaria and the loss of natural environments, damage to infrastructure and disruption of biodiversity. Climate change adaptation and mitigation will, therefore, promote social well-being, including better health, growth of the economy and at the same time reduce environmental risks, such as shortage of water, air pollution and other effects.[231]

5.6 National Climate Change Policy, 2016

The long-awaited National Climate Change Policy (NCCP) for Zambia was finally launched in March 2017. It is aimed at addressing the impact of climate change and imminent reduction of the country's annual economic growth due to crop failure and the impact of climate change on energy production. The NCCP is long-awaited owing to the global urgency placed on individual countries to start initiatives aimed at fulfilling the objectives of the UNFCCC. The NCCP acknowledges that climate change has been widely recognised as one of the major challenges facing mankind at present, and Zambia is not exempt.[232]

229 Ministry of National Development Planning (2016: 2–8 and 34–36).
230 Zambia Country Climate Risk Assessment Report (2018) at https://www.climatelearningplatform.org/sites/default/files/resources/zambia_climate_risk_screening_report_-_final.pdf, accessed 3 February 2021.
231 Ministry of National Development Planning (2017: 54).
232 Ministry of National Development Planning (2016: 3).

The NCCP is an important policy development that introduces a well-structured and coordinated national strategy to effectively tackle the adverse effects of climate change. Driven by the Ministry of National Development and Planning, it represents the much-needed broad-based consultative process involving all key stakeholders in Zambia. The NCCP recognises the need to ensure stronger collaboration among all ministries that have a role to play in climate change mitigation and adaptation, and special consideration of vulnerable groups such as poor rural women, children and the youth in Zambia.

One key feature of the NCCP is that it facilitates coherence between successive National Development Plans and all climate change programmes in the country.[233] The multisectoral approach is an important ingredient for success in implementing projects and programmes because it is hinged on coordination through an established institutional framework. This is critical to achieving developmental goals through adaptation and mitigation interventions. The entire climate policy for Zambia is relevant to the soil sustainability discourse because the overall objective of the policy is to:

> [p]rovide a framework for coordinating climate change programmes in order to ensure climate resilient and low carbon development pathways for sustainable development towards the attainment of Zambia's Vision 2030.[234]

Some of the specific objectives of the NCCP that are relevant to soil conservation include the promotion of implementation of sustainable land-use management practices in order to contribute toward reducing GHG emissions from land use and land-use change and forestry; and mainstreaming climate change into policies, plans and strategies at all levels in order to account for climate change risks and opportunities in decision-making and implementation.[235]

The NCCP lists the pieces of legislation that complement its implementation, notably, the EMA, 2011, and sectoral legislation such as the Forest, Wildlife, Lands, Agriculture, Energy, Mines and Minerals, Urban and Regional Planning, Water Resources and Fisheries Acts, which have been enacted and are currently in force. In addition, government is in the process of enacting new legislation, such as, more specifically, on climate change, in order to ensure effective implementation of the objectives and measures proposed in the NCCP.[236]

Some of the measures that have already been implemented, and are on course, include the provision of a framework for coordination of climate change programmes,[237] enactment of climate change-specific legislation, promotion and strengthening implementation of adaptation and disaster risk-reduction measures to reduce vulnerability,

233 Ministry of National Development Planning (2016: 18–25).

234 Ibid.: 11.

235 Ibid.

236 Ibid.: 11–26.

237 Dupuy et al. (2019: 1).

promotion of investments in climate resilient and low-carbon development pathways, and promotion and implementation of sustainable land-use management.[238]

Lastly, there are practical challenges in implementing the NCCP, which hinge on climate finance coordination. There is "no publicly accessible database containing a geo-located master list of all current and previously funded projects at either the national or sub-national level." There is also an absence of vulnerability assessment data, with international donors in some cases not utilising the coordinating centre in the Ministry of National Development Planning in the process of establishing and implementing climate-related projects and activities.

5.7 National Agricultural Policy, 2016

The First National Agricultural Policy 2004–2015 was established, based on the principles of liberalisation, commercialisation, linking the public and private sectors, and provision of effective services. The policy envisaged securing food supplies and developing an efficient, competitive and sustainable agricultural sector, able to contribute meaningfully to GDP, on the basis of five priority objectives, namely ensuring national and household food security; contributing to industrial development; increasing agricultural exports; generating income and employment opportunities; and maintaining and improving the agricultural resource base.[239]

In order to achieve these objectives, 19 strategies were devised. Some of the soil-relevant strategies included securing the quality, and sanitary and phytosanitary requirements of agricultural products for exports; strengthening agricultural services for small-scale farmers; arrangement of the institutional and legal framework; access to land, and pursuit of sustainable and environmentally sound agriculture.

The Second National Agricultural Policy (SNAP, 2016–2020) is being implemented at present. One of the priorities of SNAP is to ensure that the agricultural legislative framework is urgently overhauled. At the time of writing, none of the relevant pieces of legislation have been overhauled in line with this priority. As a result of failure to implement the important measure of legislative overhaul, SNAP seems not to have met most of its aspirations. It must however be noted that a number of positive initiatives have been undertaken in the agricultural sector, even in the absence of supporting legislation, such as conservation farming, which is relevant to sustainable soil management.

SNAP has 10 objectives and the formulation of four of these is directly relevant to soil sustainability, namely increasing agricultural production and productivity by promoting improved seed, efficient use of fertilizers and agrochemicals, efficient water

238 Personal communication with officers at the Disaster Management and Mitigation Unit.
239 Ministry of Agriculture and Cooperatives (2004: 1–4).

resources usage and promotion of mechanisation in farming areas; ensuring the sustainable use and management of natural resources across the agricultural sector; improving food and nutrition security through the promotion and diversification of agricultural production and utilisation; and increasing private sector participation in agricultural development by strengthening the legal and regulatory framework which includes the formulation of new legislation.

The Second National Agricultural Policy, 2016–2020, is operationalised through the Ministry of Agriculture and local authorities. Among other objectives, SNAP promotes the sustainable management and use of natural resources through sustainable land management technologies such as conservation agriculture and appropriate stock densities. These measures are important for facilitating sustainable soil management. Some of the advantages of conservation farming that enhance sustainable soil management are that water infiltration and root development of plants are improved.[240]

Conservation farming also ensures the precise application of fertilizer and other inputs next to the plants where it is most likely to be beneficial to the plant and surrounding soils. Further, conservation farming is recommended by agricultural experts since it has the potential to restore soil fertility to land damaged by years of excessive ploughing and heavy applications of chemical fertilizer. Furthermore, conservation farming improves farm yields and incomes with moderate input, whereas conventional hand-hoe technologies that are steadily being replaced, are responsible for unnecessary soil removal.[241]

6 Relevant international soil commitments

Zambia is involved in diverse initiatives and commitments at both regional and global levels. These initiatives and commitments operate in the realm of international law. State parties to international treaties must enter into the obligations created with a view to maintaining them.

With the exception of customary international law, Zambia follows the doctrine of dualism where international instruments are not self-executing.[242] Accordingly, the Executive wing of government does not have law-making powers in this context. The law-making function is vested in the Legislature.[243] Further, an examination of Article 7 of the Constitution, which outlines the sources of law in Zambia, shows that international law is not included. This is because international agreements and treaties, as

240 Shitumbanuma et al. (undated).
241 See http://www.fao.org/conservation-agriculture/en/, accessed 3 February 2021.
242 Munalula (2004: 89–90).
243 Article 62(2) and (3).

sources of international law, are subject to National Assembly approval and domestication into national statutes.

The constitutional process for negotiating and signing international commitments is an Executive function of the President, subject to National Assembly oversight, as outlined in Article 92(2)(c) of the Constitution. Further, in accordance with Articles 63 and 114(1)(d), Cabinet may recommend the accession and ratification of international agreements to the National Assembly.

In order to streamline implementation of these constitutional provisions and facilitate the domestication of international commitments, the Ratification of International Agreements Act, No. 34 of 2016, was enacted. Section 3(1) of this Act provides that whenever the question of ratification of an international agreement arises, the Minister responsible for the subject matter of the international agreement must undertake a due diligence exercise and consider whether it would be in the "best interests of the State to ratify the international agreement". The due diligence exercise essentially requires of the proposing Ministry to make a case for the subject matter of the international agreement. Thereafter, such a report is presented to Cabinet and subsequently to the National Assembly.

Article 12(1) provides that where the National Assembly approves the ratification of an international agreement, the responsible Ministry must, where necessary, initiate the domestication process. The domestication process may involve a number of processes which may include the enactment of local legislation that sets out the international agreement in a schedule; setting out salient provisions of the international agreement, in the substantive part of an Act, that will require specific interventions or measures to be undertaken, and annexing the international agreement to the Act; rephrasing the terms of the international agreement in an Act and annexing the agreement to the Act; adopting, in an Act, the terms of the international agreement in its entirety; or the use of any other enforceable means, where applicable.

In relation to international environmental agreements that undoubtedly also incorporate soil sustainability mechanisms, the provisions of the EMA, 2011, are more apt. Section 84 of the EMA provides that the government will exercise and give effect to Zambia's sovereignty over its environment and natural resources, including its genetic resources, and its powers and rights to manage the living and non-living natural resources within its territories and in areas over which it exercises rights of sovereignty, to the fullest extent permitted under international law.

Further, the EMA provides that government will cooperate with other governments, and with local and international organisations in order to protect the regional and global environment. The Minister will, after signing an international agreement designed to protect the environment, as soon as is practicable: *(a)* cause the agreement to be ratified; and *(b)* take appropriate measures to give effect to the agreement. The Minister may delegate to ZEMA, an appropriate authority, a conservancy authority or other relevant institution, the implementation of any international agreement relating to the environment to which Zambia is a party.

Against this legal background, any international obligations that are relevant to sustainable soil management in Zambia may be considered for implementation as national legislation, subject to completion of the processes outlined in the Constitution, the EMA and the Ratification of International Agreements Act. The following section analyses some of the international obligations which are applicable in Zambia, subject to domestication.

6.1 Regional commitments

At subregional level (i.e., SADC), Zambia is signatory to agreements and protocols on forests, wildlife, water, energy, agriculture, and others that fall under trade through COMESA. Some of these are relevant to soil sustainability and are analysed below.

6.1.1 Common Market for Eastern and Southern Africa

The Common Market for Eastern and Southern Africa (COMESA) is an organisation of free independent sovereign states, including Zambia which have agreed to cooperate in developing their natural and human resources for the good of all their people.[244] The primary objective of the COMESA Treaty is to enhance trade and economic cooperation amongst the state parties. The COMESA state parties have, however, committed themselves to specific undertakings in order to achieve their organisational objectives. Of relevance to the soil sustainability discourse are undertakings in respect of the fields of agriculture and economic and social development.

In relation to agriculture, each state party undertakes to cooperate in agricultural development, adoption of a common agricultural policy, regional food sufficiency, enhancement of rural development, and cooperation in agricultural research and extension.[245] All of these undertakings primarily depend on soil sustainability because soil is the basis of agricultural production and food security. The economic and social development undertaking mainly envisages cooperation in the development and management of natural resources, energy and environment.[246] This undertaking is the umbrella commitment to ensure natural resource conservation and sustainability, and ultimately environmental well-being. It must be re-emphasised at this juncture that soil is the nexus of all life-giving necessities such as water, food and opportunities.

---

244 See https://www.comesa.int/comesa-treaty/, accessed 3 February 2021.
245 Article 4(1)(5)(a) to (g) of the COMESA Treaty.
246 Article 4(1)(6)(h) of the COMESA Treaty.

One observation to make about the cooperation and integration in COMESA with regard to soil sustainability is that there is no deliberate focus and attention drawn to soil health. There are however many opportunities that can be exploited to realise soil sustainability within and beyond the geographical parameters of the member states of COMESA. The framework for regional cooperation and integration has already been established and the COMESA Treaty has provisions that can be interpreted to mean that the windows of cooperation are not closed in respect of other relevant aspects that are likely to enhance the economic and social development of the member states. Further, in the event that these windows of opportunity are open for advancement of the soil sustainability discourse, the question of effective enforcement of the ensuing commitments would arise. Implementation and enforcement issues would range from economic, political and institutional constraints, as are common in most economic integration treaties.[247] In this context, one problem would be that soil sustainability may not be viewed as a very direct priority towards enhancing trade.

6.1.2 Southern African Development Community

The Southern African Development Community (SADC) is a regional economic community of which the Republic of Zambia is a member. The objectives of SADC include the promotion of sustainable and equitable economic growth and socioeconomic development as a way of alleviating poverty through regional integration.[248] Additionally, the sustainable utilisation of natural resources and *effective* protection of the environment are among the other main objectives of SADC.[249] At this point, it is noteworthy that there is no dedicated focus on soil sustainability in the SADC objectives. It must however be mentioned that "effective protection of the environment" can be interpreted to mean that. In achieving its objectives, SADC gives priority to improved utilisation and stewardship of natural resources, by focusing on key areas, namely forests, wildlife, fisheries, trans-frontier conservation areas, and water.[250]

6.1.3 African Union

The African Union (AU) launched in 2002 as a successor to the Organisation of African Unity (OAU, 1963–1999), is a 55-member state continental body.[251] Zambia is among the 55- member states of the AU, which was established with a view to

247 Geda & Kebret (2008: 357–360).
248 Zongwe (2011: 12).
249 Article 5(1)(a) and (g) of the SADC Treaty.
250 Zongwe (2011: 17).
251 See https://au.int/en/overview, accessed 3 February 2021.

accelerating the process of integration on the continent to enable Africa to play its rightful role in the global economy, while addressing multifaceted social, economic and political problems compounded by certain negative aspects of globalisation. This was a build-up on the OAU Pan-Africanism which centred around African socialism and promoted African unity, the communal characteristic and practices of African communities, and a drive to embrace Africa's culture and common heritage.

Some of the objectives of the AU that are directly relevant to sustainable soil management in Zambia and Africa generally include promoting sustainable development at the economic, social and cultural levels, as well as the integration of African economies; promoting cooperation in all fields of human activity to raise the living standards of African peoples; advancing the development of the continent by promoting research in all fields, in particular in science and technology; and promoting and defending Africa's common positions on issues of interest to the continent and its peoples.[252]

Given this basis for cooperation in respect of these objectives, notably promotion of sustainable development, it is clear that African states are of one mind regarding advancing the needs of the continent such as natural resources conservation and environmental sustainability.

In order to achieve its aspirations, the AU has a continental strategic framework, Agenda 2063 that aims to deliver the goal for inclusive and sustainable development in Africa.[253] It is interesting to note that at this juncture, African states are required to implement both Agenda 2063 as part of AU commitment and Vision 2030 in response to global international law. Agenda 2063 and the 2030 Agenda have a broad nexus on social development (people), on inclusive economic development (prosperity), on peaceful and inclusive societies and responsive institutions (peace), and on a number of environmental sustainability issues (planet).[254] This creates a foundation for implementing both initiatives in African countries without compromising the achievement of sustainable development. Against this background, there is an opportunity for African countries to cooperate towards introducing and sustaining the soil conservation agenda.

6.2 Multilateral environmental treaties

Zambia has either ratified or signed the conventions listed in this section which are generally and specifically relevant to enhancing soil sustainability both in Zambia and

252 See https://au.int/en/overview, accessed 3 February 2021.
253 See https://www.un.org/en/africa/osaa/pdf/au/agenda2063-presentation.pdf, accessed 3 February 2021.
254 See https://bit.ly/3txZPip, accessed 3 February 2021.

internationally. Some pieces of legislation in Zambia, like the environmental framework legislation EMA, 2011, and others such as those relating to water, fisheries, forests and wildlife, to name but a few, have provisions for implementing some of these multilateral environmental agreements (MEAs). This section specifies the provisions of the various pieces of legislation that implement the MEAs under discussion.

The Convention on Biological Diversity (CBD) came into force in 1993. Its objective is to conserve biological diversity as a way of achieving sustainable development. Some of the strategies in place to achieve this are to decrease the rate of loss of natural habitats, to establish conservation areas, to restore degraded areas and to protect environments susceptible to human impacts.

The United Nations Convention to Combat Desertification (UNCCD) was established in 1994 with the objective of improving the living conditions of vulnerable populations living in arid, semi-arid and dry subhumid areas.

The Convention on International Trade in Endangered Species of Wild Fauna and Flora (CITES) entered into force in 1975 and is aimed at ensuring that the international trade of specimens (fauna and flora) does not threaten their survival.

The Ramsar Convention on Wetlands of National Importance especially as Waterfowl Habitat, adopted in 1971, was established for international cooperation and national action to protect wetlands and their resources.

The United Nations Framework Convention on Climate Change (UNFCCC) was negotiated under the auspices of the United Nations in 1992, upon global recognition of the need to limit human activities which contribute to climate change and to negotiate immediate measures for addressing climate change together with its negative effects. The overall objective of the UNFCCC is "stabilization of greenhouse gas concentrations in the atmosphere at a level that would prevent dangerous anthropogenic interference with the climate system".[255]

Others include the Montreal Protocol on Substances that Deplete the Ozone Layer; the Vienna Convention on the Protection of the Ozone Layer; the Basel Convention; the Bamako Convention; the Rotterdam Convention; and the Stockholm Convention. From the international legal framework, it must be noted that there is no single convention that is dedicated to soil sustainability matters, although most of them have provisions that can be adapted to do so.

7 Cross-cutting issues

This section analyses cross-cutting issues that have an impact on the achievement of soil sustainability in Zambia.

255 Article 2 of the UNFCCC.

7.1 Environmental impact assessments

The EMA, 2011, makes provision for environmental impact assessments (EIAs) as systematic examinations which must be conducted to determine whether or not an activity or a project has or will have any adverse effects on the environment. Section 117 of the EMA provides that a person who:

> wilfully fails to undertake an environmental impact assessment contrary to the provisions of this Act; fails to prepare and submit a project brief or an environmental impact assessment report as required under this Act; or recklessly or fraudulently makes a false statement on an environmental impact assessment report submitted under this Act; commits an offence and is liable, upon conviction, to a fine not exceeding seven hundred thousand penalty units or to imprisonment for a period not exceeding seven years, or to both.

In a nutshell, the provisions of Section 117 mean that the conduct of EIAs before undertaking any activity as prescribed under the EMA, 2011, is mandatory, the breach of which renders one to be criminally liable, as prescribed. EIA regulations exist under the EMA, 2011, in order to support the enforcement of the provisions of the principal legislation.[256] The applicable 1997 EIA regulations were issued pursuant to the repealed Environmental Protection and Pollution Control Act (EPPCA), 1999.

From a strictly environmental rationale, these regulations should not be in force, having been technically repealed together with the outdated parent legislation in 2011. This is because the EPPCA, 1990, was repealed on account of the fact that it no longer represented the aspirations of present-day environmental discourse. On technical legalities, the regulations have force of law on the basis that where any Act of Parliament is repealed, any statutory instrument issued thereunder remains in force as long as it is not inconsistent with the repealing written law.[257] As the current regulations have not yet been challenged for being inconsistent with the aspirations of the EMA, 2001, they remain in force for the time being.

The Environmental Protection and Pollution Control (EIA) Regulations, 1997, are relevant to sustainable soil management in Zambia because they make provision to consider soil fertility as a possible adverse environmental effect. Regulation 8(3) refers to ecological considerations which must be taken into consideration when effecting development activities as follows:

> (a) Biological diversity such as effect on number, diversity, breeding sites, etc. of flora and fauna, breeding populations of fish and game; and effects on the gene pools of domesticated and wild sustainable yield.
>
> (b) Sustainable use including the effects on soil fertility, nutrient cycles, aquifer recharge, water run-off rates, aerial extent of habitats; and bio-geographical processes.

256 Statutory Instrument No. 28 of 1997, the Environmental Protection and Pollution Control (Environmental Impact Assessment) Regulations, 1997.

257 Section 15, Interpretation and General Provisions Act, chapter 2 of the Laws of Zambia.

This provision shows that EIAs are purposed to protect the totality of biological diversity and ensure sustainability. It has been noted in the earlier discussions that soil is important to the ecosystem–balance equation. The provisions of regulation 8(3) outline the components of ecosystems that need to be protected. The regulations, however, underestimate the value of soils by only considering their fertility, and not necessarily their sustainability. As pointed out, these regulations were made pursuant to a repealed piece of legislation, which was repealed to pave the way for the enactment of a more forward-looking framework legislation. Indeed, there is evidence that the EMA, 2011, is forward-looking and encompasses current global trends in environmental well-being.

Against this background, the 1997 regulations must be immediately replaced by more robust and modern provisions, which can be used to anchor the sustainable soil management campaign in Zambia.

7.2 Public participation

Public participation in environmental decision-making in Zambia is provided for under the constitutional provisions, read together with those in the EMA, the Water Resources Act and almost all the natural resource legislation enacted after 2011.[258] This section analyses the public participation provisions of the Constitution and the EMA.

Article 255(l) of the Constitution makes provision for principles of environmental and natural resources management and development while Article 257(d) refers to modalities for utilisation of natural resources and management of environment. Both Article 255(l) and 257(d) refer to public participation as an important consideration in the management and utilisation of natural resources and can both be interpreted with soil sustainability in mind. The Constitution, however, does not define what amounts to 'public participation' in the management of the environment. This constitutional provision is amplified by the provisions of the environmental framework legislation, EMA, which is discussed below.

Sections 91–94 of the EMA make provision for public participation in all environmental matters. This includes the use and management of soil as a natural resource. To start with, Section 91 provides that the public has the right to be informed of the intention of public authorities to make decisions affecting the environment and of available opportunities to participate in such decisions. The public has the right to participate in decisions concerning the formulation of environmental policies, strategies, plans and programmes and to participate in the preparation of laws and regulations relating to the environment.[259]

258 Munyinda & Habasonda (2013: 10–28).
259 Section 91(2).

Section 91(3) mandates ZEMA and any other appropriate authorities to establish mechanisms for collecting and responding to public comments, concerns and questions relating to the environment, including public debates and hearings. This provision is relevant in understanding the measures that are in place for soil sustainability in Zambia. Further, the general public is entitled to review documents relating to environmental well-being and conduct public hearings on any document under public review.[260] This innovation has been implemented but it is not accessible to members of the general public as there is no publicity about it. Further, the use of such an innovation must be understood against the backdrop of low awareness levels about environmental matters in Zambia.[261]

7.3 Access to information

The EMA has innovative provisions on access to environmental information, which is relevant for sustainable soil management in Zambia, although no specific reference is made to the concept. Sections 86–90 of the EMA are the relevant provisions in relation to environmental information. Section 86 of the EMA is worth reproducing in full; it provides that ZEMA will gather information on the environment and natural resources; subject to any other written law, have access to any data collected on the environment and natural resources; analyse information relating to the environment and natural resources; disseminate information to public and private users; commission studies in demography and trends impacting on environmental and development issues; carry out public information and education campaigns in the field of environment; exchange information relating to the environment with non-governmental organisations and any other regional and international organisations; co-ordinate the management of environmental information with sector ministries; advise the Minister on existing information gaps and needs; and establish, in consultation with sector ministries, guidelines and principles for the gathering, processing and dissemination of environmental information.

The duty placed on ZEMA in this provision means that environmental information of a wide- ranging ambit must be made accessible to the public. For instance, if members of the public wish to access and review any information or data on soil and related matters, ZEMA should oblige. Further, Section 86(2) mandates the Director-General of ZEMA to publish "any information on the protection, conservation, management and utilization of the environment and natural resources as the Director-General considers necessary for public education and awareness". This is an especially important provision, which if well utilised could be the entry point, in addition to many other

260 Munyinda & Habasonde (2013: 20–28); Sambo (2019: 653).
261 Sambo (2019: 658).

provisions, for a dedicated focus on soil sustainability as it promotes general environmental well-being.

Section 87 provides that ZEMA "shall establish and operate a Central Environmental Information System in which shall be stored any findings, data and statistics generated by both public and private bodies in the course of environmental observation and management." This is another progressive provision that can be relied on in making an argument for information on soil protection to be centrally managed and utilised in conjunction with other agencies.

Section 88 empowers the Director-General of ZEMA, in consultation with the relevant appropriate authorities, to take measures for the integration of environment matters in schools, colleges and institutions of higher learning. Further, the EMA places a duty on the Director- General of ZEMA to "plan and conduct programmes aimed at raising awareness of the public on sustainable development and environmental management". This section can also be used to ensure that there is wide publicity and awareness on soil matters as they relate to environmental protection and sustainable development.

Under Section 89, ZEMA is mandated to conduct surveys on the state of the environment, to conduct research, to forecast environmental changes, and to undertake other studies that may contribute to the formulation of policies and preparation of action plans and strategies with regard to environmental protection, conservation and management. This is important for soil management because it is a multi-sectoral subject that requires concerted efforts and coordination of many players. Notwithstanding the provisions of section 89, the Minister responsible for the environment may designate any institution as an advisory body charged with the responsibility of enhancing of targeted scientific research, and information generation in the field of environment and the monitoring and assessment of effectiveness of actions taken.

Section 90 mandates ZEMA to create and maintain an environmental information registry which contains information relating to the environment, including a list of the Acts of Parliament, statutory instruments, international environmental agreements to which Zambia is a party, and any policies, plans, guidelines, studies, reports, decisions, recommendations and other publications relating to the environment published by ZEMA, the Minister or the government; a list of every environmental management strategy and environmental management strategy review report issued by any Ministry; every State of the Environment Report and every National Environmental Action Plan; every National Waste Management Strategy; a list of each application for a licence or approval under the EMA; a list of each licence, order and approval issued under the EMA; and details of all charges laid and convictions entered for contravention of the EMA.

Further, ZEMA is expected to keep all these documents in the form of paper documents, in one location, copies and information documents of the matters listed in the registry which must be accessible for public viewing during ordinary business hours.

The mandatory wording of the relevant sections on environmental information in the EMA show that this is an important matter that the general public must utilise in the quest for sustainable environmental management. There is no jurisprudence at the moment to show how this provision has been implemented, save that records at the ZEMA offices show that there is minimal use of the environmental information registry by local communities.

8 Law concerning foreign investors

The current legal and institutional framework concerning foreign investors in Zambia comprises the Constitution, applicable sectoral and tax legislation, the Zambia Development Agency Act, Companies and Business Regulatory Acts, and all other allied policies and institutions created thereunder.[262] Research was conducted between 2013 and 2015 to understand how strengthening law and policy frameworks and the regulatory and governance capacity of officials and civil society could enable Zambia to manage investments, so that they contribute to sustainable development outcomes. It was found that such investments were on the increase in Zambia. There were both foreign and domestic private investors contributing to the Zambian economy, which is heavily reliant on land use and natural resource capital.[263] Most of the targeted investment opportunities in Zambia are in key economic sectors, namely energy, forestry, mining and agriculture. As these sectors are land- and soil-related, it is critical to enhance the sustainability measures that are in place.

It is acknowledged that "land-use investments can activate development and boost the economy by creating direct benefits such as local employment and infrastructure",[264] however, economic, social and environmental inequities can arise from investments, including breach of property rights, unsustainable land use and environmental degradation and labour rights abuses, among others.

There are inadequate regulatory frameworks and weaknesses in the rule of law which have allowed investors and the Zambian 'elite' to circumvent legal requirements.[265] Four major challenges can be mentioned, which are common to all four key sectors, which limit the capacity of the country to attract and regulate sustainable investments: There are very few incentives that support sustainable land-use investments; customary land tenure remains insecure, with limited processes enshrined in the legal framework to uphold social safeguards, such as consultation with land users; there is low institutional capacity to enforce the social and environmental

262 Sambo et al. (2015: 7–9).
263 Ibid.: 1, 10.
264 Ibid.: 2–3.
265 Ibid.: 10–54.

safeguards that are established in the law; and access to information on investments is limited in Zambia, which reduces the potential for public scrutiny and participation.[266] The research concluded that the legal and institutional framework on Zambia, particularly its implementation and enforcement, should be strengthened. This will lead to more effective regulation of sustainable investments that adhere to social and environmental safeguards. The ultimate success of adopting these recommendations would be seen in the strides that would be made towards achieving the SDGs.

9 Competence of environmental enforcement

The enforcement of laws generally in Zambia has not been without administrative and other challenges. In many country reports on access to justice, it has been noted generally that inadequacy of expertise in specialised legal areas and inadequate staffing levels have continued to hamper competence of enforcement. With specific reference to enforcement of environmental matters, and soil sustainability in particular, the EMA makes provision for the establishment of the Environmental Fund as well as several other enforcement mechanisms, discussed below.

9.1 The Environment Fund

According to Section 95, the Environment Fund consists of such moneys as Parliament may appropriate for its purpose; voluntary contributions to the Fund from any person or organisation; such sums as may be levied from, or donated by, a person, industry or developer conducting an activity which has, or is likely to have, an adverse effect on the environment; any grants mobilised from any source, within or outside Zambia, for the purpose of environmental management and protection; and other sources. It is noted here that a provision exists for accumulating levies collected from any developer conducting activities that have, or are likely to have, an adverse environmental impact. Of relevance to this report, are activities that have a negative impact on soil sustainability. Section 95(3) provides that the Environment Fund established pursuant to the EMA does not apply to industries, facilities and activities covered by the Environmental Protection Fund established under the Mines and Minerals Development Act, 2015, and the Petroleum (Exploration and Production) Act, 2008, which have other guidelines, as discussed under the respective sectoral sections in this report.

The Environment Fund, as part of the enforcement mechanisms of the frame environmental law, the EMA, is purposed for:

266 Ibid.

> [m]itigating or restoring environmental degradation and adverse effects on the environment; facilitating research to further the requirements of environmental management and sustainable natural resource management; and such other purpose as may be prescribed.[267]

The management and administration of the Environment Fund is vested in ZEMA. Under Section 98, ZEMA is mandated to create a register of the activities, industrial facilities and plants, undertakings and businesses which have, or are likely to have, adverse effects on the environment when operated in a manner that is not in conformity with good environmental practices.

The other environmental enforcement provisions in the EMA relate to audits, monitoring, prevention orders, protection orders, restoration orders, compliance orders, cost orders and prosecution, which can be either civil or criminal. These enforcement mechanisms are now analysed in the context of soil sustainability.

9.2 Environmental audits

Section 101(1) provides that "an owner of premises or a person undertaking a project shall take all reasonable measures to mitigate any adverse effects not contemplated in the environmental impact assessment" in respect of their premises or the project, and "shall prepare and submit an environmental audit report on the measures to ZEMA annually or as ZEMA may, in writing, require." The section also mandates ZEMA to carry out an environmental audit of all the activities that are likely to have an adverse effect on the environment. This provision of the EMA can be used to enhance soil protection. It is arguable that, in a number of instances, soil conservation may be overlooked as an important consideration in EIAs for development projects. This provision therefore allows for soil sustainability issues to be incorporated for consideration after the inception of the project.

In order to enhance enforcement, ZEMA inspectors may enter any land or premises for the purpose of determining the extent to which the activities carried out on the land or premises conform with the environmental impact assessment made in respect of the land or premises. This enforcement mechanism can be applied to all development projects that have since commenced but did not initially take negative impacts on soil sustainability into account. Any owner of premises or person undertaking a project for which an environmental impact assessment is conducted must keep accurate records and make annual reports to ZEMA, describing the extent to which the project conforms, in operation, to the environmental impact assessment. Suffice it to mention that this is yet another opportunity that can be used to report adverse impacts on soil sustainability and remediation effected.

267 Section 97.

9.3 Environmental monitoring

Section 102(1) empowers ZEMA, in consultation with other relevant agencies or bodies, to monitor:

> [a]ll environmental phenomena with a view to making assessments of any possible changes in the environment and their possible impacts; or the operation of any industry, project or activity with a view of determining its immediate and long-term effects on the environment.

This provision means that environmental monitoring can be extended to "any possible changes in the environment" which include changes in soil composition, fertility and sustainability. This enforcement mechanism can be used to ensure that soil matters are also given priority as they contribute towards sustaining a clean and healthy environment. Further, ZEMA inspectors may enter any land or premises for the purposes of monitoring the effects upon the environment of any activities carried out on that land or premises.

9.4 Prevention orders

Section 103(1) provides that where the Director-General has "reasonable grounds to believe that a person is, or will be, conducting an activity, or is or will be in possession or control of a substance or thing that may result in an adverse effect", the Director-General may serve a prevention order on that person. Section 103(2) further provides that a prevention order served on a person under subsection (1) may require that person to:

> [p]repare a written emergency response plan to reduce or eliminate the risk and provide a copy of the plan to the Director-General; have any necessary equipment, facilities and trained personnel available to deal with the risk; upon an identified event or set of circumstances occurring, implement the plan; and take measures that are necessary to ensure that any emergency can be effectively dealt with.

Any person served with a prevention order must comply with its requirements by the date or dates specified in the order and, if no date is specified, the person must comply with the order immediately.[268] Failure to comply with this provision renders one liable, upon conviction, to a fine and/or imprisonment, or both.[269] There is currently no available jurisprudence on this legal provision. In severe breaches of soil management, it is arguable that these legal sanctions can be imposed to serve as deterrents to the general public.

268 Section 103(3).
269 Section 103(4).

9.5 Protection orders

Protection orders are another enforcement mechanism that is available and currently being issued under the EMA, 2011. There is no jurisprudence specific to sustainable soil management yet. Under Section 104 of the EMA, 2011, the Director-General of ZEMA may, where considered necessary to conserve, protect and enhance the environment and natural resources in an area, serve a protection order on the owner, manager or person in control of the premises, vehicle, vessel, aircraft or equipment where the activity is occurring or will occur, or on any person who caused or permitted the activity. According to Section 104(2), a protection order may require the person on whom it is served to:

> [t]ake any measures to avoid, remedy or mitigate any adverse effects and to (i) stop the activity that is resulting or is likely to result in, an adverse effect; (ii) control the activity; (iii) assess the actual or anticipated extent of the adverse effect; (iv) remedy any adverse effects caused by the activity; or (v) prevent a recurrence of the activity or the adverse effect.

Further, Section 104(3) requires that a person on whom a protection order is served complies with the requirements of the order by the date or dates specified in the order and if no date is specified, the person must comply with the order immediately. Contravention of this subsection is an offence, and the offender is liable, upon conviction, to a fine and imprisonment for a period not exceeding one year, or to both.

9.6 Restoration orders

Environmental restoration orders may be served on the owner, manager or person in control of the premises, vehicle, vessel, aircraft or equipment from which the discharge was or is being made; on any person who, at the time the discharge occurred, was the owner, manager or person in control of the premises, vehicle, vessel, aircraft or equipment from which the discharge was made; or on any person who caused or permitted the discharge.[270] An environmental restoration order may require the person on whom it is served to take any measures that will assist in reducing or eliminating the risk or harm and to take any measures to:

> (a) take such action as will prevent the continuation or cause of pollution; (b) restore land, including the replacement of soil, the replanting of trees and other flora and the restoration as far as may be, of outstanding geological, archaeological or historical features of the land or the area contiguous to the land or area as may be specified in the particular order; (c) take such action to prevent the commencement or continuation or cause of environmental hazard; (d) cease to take any action which is causing or may contribute to causing pollution or an environmental hazard; (e) remove or alleviate any injury to land or the environment or to the amenities of the area; (f) prevent damage to the land or the environment, aquifers beneath the land and flora and fauna in, on or under or about the land specified in the order or land or the environment contiguous to the

270 Section 105(1).

land specified in the order; (g) remove any waste or refuse deposited on the land or sea specified in the order and dispose of the same in accordance with the provisions of the order

From the foregoing, environmental restoration orders may be instrumental in sustainable soil management, as seen in this provision which specifically identifies land restoration and soil replacement. However, it would be a challenge to enforce this provision owing to the requirement for scientific proof of degradation requiring restoration. In addition, the enforcement of this provision across the country would need skilled manpower, which the relevant institutions are lacking. At present, there is no jurisprudence on how this provision has been enforced. In like manner with other environmental orders, any person who contravenes these provisions commits an offence and is liable, upon conviction, to a fine or to imprisonment or to both.

9.7 Compliance orders

Section 106 empowers the ZEMA Director-General who may, when reasonable grounds exist that any condition of a licence issued under the EMA has been breached, to serve a compliance order on the licensee requiring the licensee to remedy the breach within the period stipulated in the order. A compliance order may require the suspension of the licence with immediate effect if necessary, to prevent or mitigate an imminent risk of significant adverse effects to the environment or to human health occurring; or may require the licensee to take specified measures to prevent or abate any adverse effect. These adverse effects may relate to soil as this provision is not specific to any aspect of the environment. Where a licensee fails to comply with a compliance order, ZEMA is empowered to take the necessary steps to remedy the breach and recover the cost from the licensee or vary the conditions of the licence; or revoke the whole licence.[271] Failure to comply with a compliance order is an offence for which the offender may be fined or imprisoned, or both.

9.8 Cost orders

Where a person fails to comply with a requirement in an order, licence or approval issued under the EMA, 2011, ZEMA may issue a cost order requiring that person to reimburse ZEMA for the cost of taking the measures, as provided for under Section 107(1). A cost order is enforced as if it were an order of court if no application for the review of the cost order is made.[272]

271 Section 106(3).
272 Section 107(2).

9.9 Civil and criminal prosecution

Section 109 mandates any person to write to and request ZEMA to investigate an alleged contravention of the EMA. This requirement may not be possible for the illiterate and semi-literate, thus reducing accessibility. Such a written request must set out the reasons therefor, including the detailed factual grounds for believing that a contravention has occurred. Although the nature of the contravention in this section is not specific, it is arguable that it may relate to soil contamination or any other adverse occurrence that may be likely to compromise soil quality. The Director-General of ZEMA is mandated to consider the written request and, within 30 days, to decide whether or not to commence an investigation, and then accordingly notify the requesting person, in writing, of that decision, stating the reasons therefor, and, if applicable, the date upon which the Director-General intends to commence the investigation.[273]

In the event that the Director-General decides not to commence an investigation, the requesting person may lay a charge and initiate and conduct the prosecution on their own and may obtain the assistance of any other person in doing so.[274] This is a very important provision as it gives leeway to private citizens to participate in ensuring that they have an environment that is clean and healthy. This provision can also be used to enhance soil protection. Where the charge is followed through in the courts of law:

> The court shall not award any costs or damages against a person who initiates a prosecution after informing the Director-General in accordance with this section, unless the court finds that the primary motivation for the prosecution was not a concern for the public interest or for the enhancement, protection and conservation of the environment.[275]

While this section empowers private citizens to take part in environmental protection without fear of legal consequences such as costs, it also aims at ensuring that the progressive legal provisions are not abused by persons with frivolous, vexatious or malicious allegations. This provision is also important in advocating a culture of wholesome environmental well-being as it can readily accommodate causes of action in the interest of soil sustainability.

Section 110 empowers any person to sue for damages in respect of an act or omission that constitutes a contravention of the EMA or that is likely to have an adverse effect, whether or not that person or any other person has suffered, or is likely to suffer, any loss or harm from the act or omission. This right of action is in addition to any other legal rights or remedies available to a plaintiff or applicant.[276] Further, Section 111 provides that a court that convicts a person of an offence under the EMA may, in addition to any other penalty imposed, order the person to take and pay for measures

273 Section 109(3).
274 Section 109(4).
275 Section 109(5).
276 Section 110(2).

to avoid, remedy or mitigate any adverse effects arising from, or likely to arise from, the offence. These measures are also likely to be applicable in the preservation of soil quality.

The EMA makes provision for environmental crimes in Sections 117 and 119. The provisions of Section 117 relate to failure to undertake an EIA and these have been discussed in the section on EIAs. Section 119 provides that a person who:

> (a) contravenes any environmental standards or guidelines established or prescribed under the EMA; (b) contravenes a measure prescribed or ordered under this Act; or (c) uses the environmental or natural resources in a wasteful or destructive manner contrary to the prescribed standards, measures or guidelines; commits an offence and is liable, upon conviction, to a fine not exceeding seven hundred thousand penalty units or to imprisonment for a period not exceeding seven years, or to both.

Although this provision does not specifically refer to any adverse effects on soil quality and quantity, it remains a possible solution in efforts to ameliorate the worsening challenge of soil degradation in Zambia. For example, in the agricultural sector, numerous non-legal interventions have been introduced to curb the widespread practice of 'slash and burn' or *chitemene* owing to its long-term negative impacts on the environment generally and soil sustainability specifically. In the event that some farmers remain averse to embracing the more sustainable farming practices being introduced, the provisions of Section 119 can be applicable for deterrence.

10 Lessons learnt and recommendations

This section outlines some possible recommendations on addressing the challenges of soil sustainability legislation in Zambia. It has been noted that apart from some of the provisions of the EMA, there is presently no other legislation that can be used effectively to advance the soil cause in Zambia. Although the EMA contains progressive provisions that are relevant in the context of sustainable soil management, it has been observed that there are no provisions dedicated to soil as a natural resource. Most of the provisions of the EMA can be adapted to apply directly to soil with positive results. This analysis of soil-related legislation in Zambia has encountered some important lessons which need to be followed up.

There are positive and progressive provisions in the Constitution, EMA, 2011, mining legislation and other post-2010 sectoral legislation that need to be harnessed and coordinated into the country's soil legislation. It is remarkable that the National Climate Change Policy has been adopted and promises the enactment of climate-specific legislation in Zambia. This, together with prospects of new legislation in the agricultural and land sectors are opportunities to legislate in the interest of sustainable soil management in Zambia.

Control of foreign investors is required in order to ensure that land-use investments are sustainable and that the laws of the country are being observed. International cooperation and regional integration must be enhanced. For instance, the findings of international research entities must be implemented through regional cooperation. To illustrate, this report has shown that the recent IPCC Report findings (2019) connect climate change and land degradation, and ultimately soil health. It is important that such findings be tabled before regional meetings so that countries that are similarly affected are able to devise common and specific ways of implementation.

Political buy-in must be sought in all the different sectors, capitalising on the initiatives being spearheaded under the National Climate Change Policy (2016). There is a need to ensure political buy-in in environmental sustainability and natural resources issues, more particularly in soil sustainability as the 'cradle of ecosystem services'. This can be achieved through mechanisms of reducing institutional and system bureaucracy between local communities and the ultimate decisionmakers. Without effective community representation, citizen-power, and strong environmental NGOs to assist in ensuring checks and balances, effective environmental stewardship cannot be achieved. Ultimately, environmental and natural resources issues must be introduced on the agenda of political demands that political players in Zambia need to meet. Outdated legislation in the agricultural and land sectors, which are more directly aligned to soil conservation, is a major drawback, while the absence of a constitutional environmental right is a challenge that detracts from the positive provisions in the EMA, 2011.

The constitutional framework, sectoral and subsidiary legislation in Zambia have all been analysed with a view to pointing out how and whether soil sustainability matters are taken into consideration. It has been shown with absolute certainty that, while the Constitution and framework environmental legislation make provision for wholesome environmental well- being and define soil as an important constituent element of the environment, there are no clear and definite provisions on soil sustainability.

It is therefore recommended that, given the importance of soil to environmental well-being, there must be dedicated legislation cutting across all sectors. In the specific case of Zambia, it has been shown that the EMA has remarkable provisions in relation to other elements of the environment, such as water. In the same vein, there could either be a separate Act of Parliament outlining the importance of soil sustainability to all sectors of the economy or subsidiary legislation similar to the EIA and other regulations promulgated under the EMA. The content of the envisaged legislation could then be subjected to multiple stakeholders' input and approval. This could follow the usual process for the enactment of legislation.

The policy framework in the relevant sectors and cross-cutting issues have been evaluated. It has been noted that the policy framework refers to the main drivers of land/soil degradation but does not go further to prescribe mechanisms for addressing them in a more concerted manner. In the agricultural sector, for instance, there are ongoing initiatives to overhaul the entire legislative framework. This is an opportune time to ensure that interventions, such as conservation farming, are incentivised and that other unsustainable practices, such as the *chitemene,* are outlawed or discouraged with legal sanctions. In the Draft National Land Policy, it has also been noted that there are subtle provisions on how to encourage sustainable land use. This can be extended to soil conservation. In relation to land, and quite apart from tenure issues, it is possible to identify soil as an integral part that needs to be protected. This is another window of opportunity as the Lands Act (1995) has for some time been earmarked for overhaul.

Other more specific recommendations can be summarised as follows: There is no soil-specific legislation in Zambia. However, there are several provisions in many sectoral laws that can be used to ensure a sustainable soil regime. The Constitution, with its framework environmental legislation, has robust provisions for agriculture, mining, forestry and water resources. It is 'merely' the political will for enforcement that is still lacking.

Conservation farming could be a way of enhancing soil health. There is a need to identify and consolidate the numerous soil protection initiatives currently running in the agricultural sector into soil-specific legislation that will cut across all sectors. It is also important to enhance the establishment and coordination of a national soil information system covering various environmental issues pursuant to the EMA, 2011, while the Ministries of Agriculture and Lands and Natural Resources also operate others. Arising from this is the need for a centralised national institutional framework for sustainable soil management in Zambia.

Moreover, there is a need to infuse soil impact assessments in the various environmental assessments currently being implemented in the country. In relation to this, soil standards will need to be prescribed in relation to any developmental or other activities. Most farmers have already adopted sustainable farming practices that can be used to promote soil health. However, these initiatives are not coordinated.

In order to incentivise sustainable agricultural practices, sustainable soil mechanisms must be incorporated as a prerequisite for access to the Environment Fund established under the EMA, 2011, which makes provision for several innovative enforcement mechanisms, such as environmental audits and monitoring, restoration, protection, prevention, compliance and other orders, which are relevant for sustainable soil management. This prompts the need to survey ways of 'breathing life' into these provisions. Zambia still has very low awareness levels in relation to environmental issues in general which necessitates raising community awareness and educational activities on sustainable soil use to be introduced.

The agricultural, environment, land and mining sectors have research or monitoring units that generate a lot of data relevant to sustainable soil management. Furthermore, access to environmental information related to sustainable soil management is facilitated both by the Constitution and the EMA. There must be enhanced collaboration and cooperation as envisaged by the EMA in relation to all aspects of the environment. The creation and enforcement of a constitutional human rights paradigm for the environment is essential. The right to a clean, safe and healthy environment, the duty to conserve and protect the environment for the current and future generations, environmental procedural rights, climate justice and property rights would also assist with the inculcation of responsibility towards the environment and natural resources. In this light it is important to mention the threats to soil, which are both global and locally significant.

It is acknowledged that the law is but one of the myriad measures that can be employed to safeguard soil sustainability. Research has shown that approximately 20% of the world's land is degraded.[277] It is imperative to recognise that land degradation is affecting almost all the world regions and could result in many human rights issues, specifically in sub-Saharan Africa, which has been identified as one of the hotspots of soil and land degradation.[278] The negative effects which have a bearing on human rights compromise will affect a large portion of the world's poor population, resulting in a human rights crisis. On this score, it is essential to look at soil sustainability more holistically from different sectoral, disciplinary and geaographical perspectives.

References

Abdelghaffar, N., K. Bryant, C. Siang Bu, M. Campbell, B. Lewis, R. Low, K. Namit, D. Paredes, A. Silva & C. Yu, 2016, *Leveraging Chinese FDI for diversified growth in Zambia*. Princeton University, Graduate School Policy Workshop, at https://wws.princeton.edu/sites/default/files/content/Zambia%20Final%20Final%20Report_27Apr2016.pdf, accessed 29 July 2019.

Addaney, M, E. Boshoff & M. Gyan Nyarko, 2018, "Protection of environmental assets in urban Africa: Regional and sub-regional human rights and practical environmental protection mechanisms". *Australian Journal of Human Rights* 24 (2), 182, at https://doi.org/10.1080/1323238X.2018.1480235, accessed 28 July 2019.

AFRODAD / African Forum and Network on Dept and Development, 2003, *A critical analysis of the poverty reduction strategy papers: Processes and outcomes. The Case of Zambia*, at https://bit.ly/3oX6gbs, accessed 16 January 2021.

AFRONET / Inter-African Network for Human Rights and Development, 1998, *The dilemma of local courts in Zambia. A question of colonial legal continuity or deliberate customary law marginalisation?* Lusaka: AFRONET.

Alori, E.T. & C. Nwapi, 2014, "The international legal regime for sustainable soil". In: Huks, R., T. Ako & D. Olawuyi (eds), *Food and agricultural law: Readings on sustainable agriculture and the law in Nigeria*. Afebabalola University: Ado Ekiti, 98.

Ayub M.A., M. Usman, T. Faiz, M. Umair, M. Anwar ul Haq, M. Rizwan, S. Ali & M. Zia ur Rehman, 2020, "Restoration of degraded soil for sustainable agriculture". In: Meena R.S. (ed.), *Soil health restoration and management*. Singapore: Springer, at https://doi.org/10.1007/978-981-13-8570-4_2, accessed 16 November 2019.

Blackwell, J.M., R.N. Goodwillie & R. Webb, 1998, *Environment and development in Africa*. New York: World Bank, at https://doi.org/10.1596/0-8213-1608-7, accessed 5 February 2021.

277 Addaney et al. (2018: 186).

278 See https://bit.ly/3pXI7CX; and https://bit.ly/3rutI1d, both accessed 3 February 2021.

BoZ / Bank of Zambia, 2015, *Foreign private investment and investor perceptions in Zambia: Re-thinking, refocusing and implementing investment and export diversification strategies*, at https://www.boz.zm/ForeignPrivateInvestmentReport2015.pdf, accessed 16 January 2021.

BoZ / Bank of Zambia, 2017a, *Foreign private investment and investor perceptions in Zambia: Enhancing invest for export promotion and industrialisation towards inclusive growth*, at https://www.boz.zm/report.pdf, accessed 30 June 2019.

BoZ / Bank of Zambia, 2017b, *Bank of Zambia annual report*. Lusaka: BOZ, at https://www.boz.zm/annual-reports.htm, accessed 30 June 2019.

Bull, M.M., 2014, "Reserved area: Barotseland of the 1964 agreement". *Zambia Social Science Journal* 5 (1), at http://scholarship.law.cornell.edu/zssj/vol5/iss1/4, accessed 15 January 2021.

Central Statistical Office, 2013, *Population and demographic projections 2011–2035*. Lusaka: Central Statistical Office.

Central Statistical Office, 2016, *2015 Living Conditions Monitoring Survey*. Lusaka: Central Statistical Office.

Central Statistical Office, 2018, "Zambia in figures", at www.zamstats.gov.zm, accessed 20 August 2019.

Chapoto, A. & B. Chisanga, 2016, *Zambia agriculture status report 2016*. Lusaka: Indaba Agricultural Policy Research Institute (IAPRI).

Chidumayo, E.N., 1987, "A shifting cultivation land use system under population pressure in Zambia". *Agroforest Systems* 5, 15, at https://doi.org/10.1007/BF00046411, accessed 17 July 2019.

Chidumayo, E.N. & D. Gumbo, 2013, "The environmental impacts of charcoal production in tropical ecosystems of the world: A synthesis". *Energy for Sustainable Development* 17 (2), 86, at https://doi.org/10.1016/j.esd.2012.07.004, accessed 15 January 2021.

Chileshe, A., 2001, *Forestry outlook studies in Africa (FOSA) – Zambia*. Rome: FAO.

Chinene, V.R.N., F. Maimbo, D.J. Banda, S.C. Msune, 1998, "A comparison of customary and leasehold tenure: Agriculture and development in Zambia". In: Groppo, P., *Land reform, land settlement and cooperatives*, 88, at http://www.fao.org/3/x1372t/x1372t07.htm, accessed 15 January 2021.

Christopolos, I., C. Aben, B. Bashaasha, H. Dhungana, E. Friis-Hansen, M. Funder, N. Thi Thanh Huong, D. Bahadur Khatri, L. Salloum Lindegaard, C. Mweemba, L. Duc Ngoan, I. Nyambe, H. Ojha, J. Okiror, A. Pain, L. Thi Hoa Sen, 2016, *Understanding sub-national climate governance – Findings from Nepal, Uganda, Vietnam and Zambia*. Copenhagen: DIIS, at https://pure.diis.dk/ws/files/614369/DIIS_RP_2016_5_WEB.pdf, accessed 5 February 2021.

Church, W.L., 1974, "The common law and Zambia". *Zambia Law Journal* 6, 1.

Dupuy, K., P.T. Sambo, M. Funder & E. Chama, 2019, *Coordinating climate finance: Lessons from Zambia*. PRIO Paper. Oslo: PRIO, at https://www.prio.org/utility/DownloadFile.ashx?id=1895&type=publicationfile, accessed 5 November 2019.

Dymond, A., 2007, *Undermining development? Copper mining in Zambia*, at https://www.banktrack.org/download/undermining_development_copper_mining_in_zambia/underminingdevelopment.pdf, accessed 21 August 2019.

Engel, E., S. Rettberg, T. Rauch, S. Neubert, D. Richter, M. Minah & C. Berg, 2017, *Towards inclusive and sustainable rural transformation in Sub-sahara Africa*. Berlin: Centre for Rural Development, at https://bit.ly/3txUGa1, accessed 9 May 2019.

Eriksen, C., 2007, "Why do they burn the 'bush'? Fire, rural livelihoods, and conservation in Zambia". *The Geographical Journal* 173 (3), 242.

Fadjukoff, P., 2015, "Promoting 21st Century literacy education in Zambia". In: Hölttä, S., A. Moore & E. Pekkola (eds), *Higher education institutions – partnering for development and change:*

Reflections of the first round of the Finnish HEI ICI Programme, 124, at https://bit.ly/3joVSIl, accessed 15 January 2021.

Geda, A. & H. Kebret, 2008, "Regional economic integration in Africa: A review of problems and prospects with a case study of COMESA". *Journal of African Economies* 17 (3), 357, at https://doi.org/10.1093/jae/ejm021, accessed 15 January 2021.

Gilbey, B., J. Davies, G. Metternicht & C. Magero, 2019, "Taking land degradation neutrality from concept to practice: Early Reflections on LDN target setting and planning". *Environmental Science and Policy* 100, 230.

Gloppen, S., 2003, "The accountability function of the courts in Tanzania and Zambia". *Democratization* 10 (4), 112.

Gumbo, D.J., M. Dumas-Johansen, G. Muir, F. Boerstler & Z. Xia, 2018, *Sustainable management of Miombo woodlands – Food security, nutrition and wood energy*. Rome: Food and Agriculture Organization of the United Nations, at http://www.fao.org/3/i8852en/I8852EN.pdf, accessed 28 October 2019.

Hansjürgens, B., A. Lienkamp & S. Möckel, 2018, "Justifying soil protection and sustainable soil management: Creation-ethical, legal and economic considerations". *Sustainability* 10 (10) 3807, at https://doi.org/10.3390/su10103807, accessed 20 August 2019.

Hinfelaar, M. & J. Sichone, 2019, *The challenge of sustaining a professional civil service amidst shifting political coalitions: The case of the Ministry of Finance in Zambia, 1991-2018*. ESID Working Paper No. 122. Manchester: The University of Manchester, at www.effective-states.org, accessed 31 July 2019.

Huth, M.J., 1984, "The impact of rapid population growth, expanding urbanisation, and other factors on development in sub-saharan Africa: The contrasting responses of Tanzania and Kenya". *International Journal of Sociology and Social Policy* 4 (2), 1, at https://doi.org/10.1108/eb012963, accessed 1 May 2019.

Ige, R.A., 2015, "Legal pluralism in Africa: Challenges, conflicts and adaption in a global village". *Journal of Law, Policy and Globalization* 34, 59.

IMF / International Monetary Fund, 2005, *Zambia: Enhanced initiative for heavily indebted poor countries*. Country Report No. 05/137, Completion Point Document, at https://www.imf.org/external/pubs/ft/scr/2005/cr05137.pdf, accessed 15 January 2021.

IPCC / International Panel on Climate Change, 2019, *Climate change and land*. An IPCC special report on climate change, desertification, land degradation, sustainable land management, food security and greenhouse gas fluxes in terrestrial ecosystems, at https://www.ipcc.ch/srccl-report-download-page/, accessed 16 August 2019.

Japan Association for International Collaboration of Agriculture and Forestry, 2008, *Agriculture and forestry in Zambia: Present situation and issues for development*, at http://www.jaicaf.or.jp/publications/zanbia_agri.pdf, accessed 1 May 2019.

Kalaba, K.F., 2016, "Barriers to policy implementation and implications for Zambia's forest ecosystems". *Forest Policy and Economics* 69, 40.

Kibugi R., 2018, "Soil health, sustainable land management and land degradation in Africa: Legal options on the need for a specific African soil convention or protocol". In: Ginzky H., E. Dooley, I. Heuser, E. Kasimbazi, T. Markus & T. Qin (eds), *International yearbook of soil law and policy 2017*. Cham: Springer, 387.

Křībek B., V. Majer, P. Bezuško, J. Pašava, J. Adamovič, I. Nyambe, K. Liyungu & F. Chibesakunda, 2006, "Impact assessment of mining and processing of copper and cobalt ores on the environment in the Copperbelt, Zambia". *Geoscience Research Reports* 40, 160, at http://www.geology.cz/zpravy/en/detail/2006-str-160-162, accessed 16 January 2021.

Loenen, B., 1999, *Land tenure in Zambia,* at https://www.researchgate.net/publication/242672704_Land_tenure_in_Zambia, accessed 20 July 2019.

Mabey, N. & R. McNally, 1999, *Foreign investment and the environment: From pollution havens to sustainable development.* London: WWF.

Madzudzo, E., A. Mulanda, J. Nagoli, J. Lunda, & B.D. Ratner, 2013, *A governance analysis of the Barotse floodplain system, Zambia: Identifying obstacles and opportunities.* Penang: CGIAR Research Program on Aquatic Agricultural Systems.

Metternicht, G., M. Akhtar-Schuster & V. Castillo, 2019, "Implementing land degradation neutrality: From policy challenges to policy opportunities for national sustainable development". *Environmental Science and Policy* 100, 189.

Mining Partnerships for Development, 2014, *Enhancing mining's contribution to the Zambian economy and society,* at https://miningforzambia.com/wp-content/uploads/2016/11/ICMM-Report-on-Mining-in-Zambia.pdf, accessed 10 May 2019.

Ministry of Agriculture and Cooperatives, 2004, *First national agricultural policy 2004–2015.* Lusaka: Ministry of Agriculture and Cooperatives.

Ministry of Agriculture, 2016, *Second national agriculture policy 2016- 2020.* Lusaka: Ministry of Agriculture.

Ministry of Chiefs and Traditional Affairs, 2016, *Ministerial statement on increased membership of the House of Chiefs,* at https://bit.ly/2Lu4fFP, accessed 15 January 2021.

Ministry of Energy, 2008, *National energy policy.* Lusaka: Ministry of Energy.

Ministry of Finance, 2011, *Sixth national development plan.* Lusaka: Ministry of Finance.

Ministry of Finance, 2017, *Seventh national development plan.* Lusaka: Ministry of Finance.

Ministry of General Education, 2017, *Educational statistical bulletin,* at https://bit.ly/3rt5gxl, accessed 15 January 2021.

Ministry of Lands and Natural Resources, 2017, *National investment plan to reduce deforestation and forest degradation (2018–2022).* Lusaka: Ministry of Lands and Natural Resources.

Ministry of Lands and Natural Resources, 2018, *Ministerial statement on the outcome of the national validation meeting for the draft national land policy.* Lusaka: Ministry of Lands and Natural Resources.

Ministry of National Development Planning, 2006, *Vision 2030.* Lusaka: Ministry of National Development Planning, at https://www.mndp.gov.zm/wp-content/uploads/2018/05/Vision-2030.pdf, accessed 15 January 2021.

Ministry of National Development Planning, 2016, *National policy on climate change.* Lusaka: Ministry of National Development Planning.

Ministry of National Development Planning, 2017, *Seventh national development plan (2017–2021).* Lusaka: Ministry of National Development Planning, at https://www.mndp.gov.zm/wp-content/uploads/2018/05/7NDP.pdf, accessed 3 February 2021.

Ministry of Tourism, Environment and Natural Resources, 2010, *National climate change response strategy (NCCRS).* Lusaka: Government of the Republic of Zambia, at https://www.adaptation-undp.org/sites/default/files/downloads/zambia-climate_change_response_strategy.pdf, accessed 5 February 2021.

Ministry of Tourism and Arts, 2016, *Tourism statistical digest 2015.* Lusaka: Ministry of Tourism and Arts, at https://www.mota.gov.zm/?wpfb_dl=65, accessed 15 January 2021.

Monson, J., 2013, "Remembering work on the Tazara railway in Africa and China, 1965–2011: When "new men" grow old". *African Studies Review* 56 (1), 45, at https://doi:10.1017/asr.2013.5, accessed 15 January 2021.

Mudenda, F.S., 2007, *Land law in Zambia – cases and materials*. Lusaka: University of Zambia Press.

Mudenda, M., 2010, *Climate change and environmental threats, (Zambia): Climate change and urban slums in Lusaka, Zambia: Ignore, mitigate or adapt*. FIG Congress, Facing the Challenges – Building the Capacity Sydney, Australia, 11–16 April 2010, at https://bit.ly/3cRDuX2, accessed 15 January 2021.

Mulenga, C., 2019, "Judicial mandate in safeguarding environmental rights from the adverse effects of mining activities in Zambia". *Potchefstroom Electronic Law Journal* 22, at https://ssrn.com/abstract=3377116, accessed 10 July 2019.

Munalula, M.M., 2004, *Legal process-cases, statutes and materials*. Lusaka: University of Zambia Press.

Munyinda, N. & L. Habasonda, 2013, *Public participation in Zambia – The case of natural resources management*. Copenhagen: Danish Institute for Human Rights, at https://menneskeret.dk/files/media/dokumenter/udgivelser/public_participation_study_final-nov2013.pdf, accessed 15 January 2021.

Mususa, P., 2012, "Mining, welfare and urbanisation: the wavering urban character of Zambia's Copperbelt". *Journal of Contemporary African Studies* 30 (4), 571.

Mvunga, M.P., 1978, *Land law and policy in Zambia*. Ph.D. thesis, London: University of London.

Mvunga, M.P., 1980, *The colonial foundations of Zambia's land tenure system*. Lusaka: National Educational Company of Zambia Limited (NECZAM).

Nalishebo, S., 2015, *Lowering the repayment risk of Zambia's Eurobonds*. Lusaka: ZIPAR, at http://www.zipar.org.zm/17-lowering-the-repay.ment-risk-of-zambia-s-eurobonds, accessed 15 January 2021.

Ndaba, S., 2015, *The impact of foreign direct investment on economic growth in Zambia – A study in the context of a natural resource dependent economy*. Research Paper presented in partial fulfilment of the requirements for obtaining the degree of Master of Arts in Development Studies, The Hague: Institute of Social Studies, at https://bit.ly/3s55co1, accessed 15 January 2021.

Ndulo, M. & R.B. Kent, 1996, "Constitutionalism in Zambia: Past, present and future". *Journal of African Law* 40 (2), 256.

Neubert, S., M. Kömm, A. Krumsiek, A. Schulte, N. & L. Zeppenfeld Tatge, 2011, *Agricultural development in a changing climate – Increasing resilience to climate change and economic shocks in crop production*. Bonn: DIE, at https://www.files.ethz.ch/isn/128010/Studies%2057.pdf, accessed 17 January 2021.

Orr, B.J., A.L. Cowie, V.M. Castillo Sanchez, P. Chasek, N.D. Crossman, A. Erlewein, G. Louwagie, M. Maron, G.I. Metternicht, S. Minelli, A.E. Tengberg, S. Walter & S. Welton, 2017, *Scientific conceptual framework for land degradation neutrality*. A Report of the Science-Policy Interface, Bonn: United Nations Convention to Combat Desertification, at http://catalogue.unccd.int/814_LDN_CF_report_web-english.pdf, accessed 17 January 2021.

Osei-Hwedie B.Z., 1996, "Environmental protection and economic development in Zambia". *Journal of Social Development in Africa* 11 (2), 57, at https://bit.ly/3cO3R08, accessed 18 January 2021.

OSISA / Open Society Initiative for Southern Africa, 2015, *Effective delivery of public education services in Zambia*. Lusaka: OSISA.

Phiri, B.J., 2006, *A political history of Zambia*. Trenton: Africa World Press, Inc.

Pimentel, D. & N. Kounang, 1998, "Ecology of soil erosion in ecosystems". *Ecosystems* 1 (5), 416.

Plisnier, D.P., M. Nshombo, H. Mgana & G. Ntakimazi, 2018, "Monitoring climate change and anthropogenic pressure at Lake Tanganyika". *Journal of Great Lakes Research* 44 (6), 1194, at https://doi.org/10.1016/j.jglr.2018.05.019, accessed 17 January 2021.

Pope Francis, 2015, *Laudato Si*. San Francisco: Ignatius Press.

Prizzon, A., 2013, *The age of choice: Zambia in the new aid landscape*. London: Overseas Development Institute, at https://www.odi.org/sites/odi.org.uk/files/odi-assets/publications-opinion-files/9107.pdf, accessed 18 January 2021.

Republic of Zambia, 2009, *The national policy on environment*. Lusaka: Government of the Republic of Zambia, at https://www.oneplanetnetwork.org/sites/default/files/national_policy_on_environment_2009.pdf, accessed 2 February 2021.

Resilience and Economic Inclusion Team, 2016, *Zambia climate action report*. Dublin: Irish Aid, at https://www.irishaid.ie/media/irishaid/allwebsitemedia/30whatwedo/climatechange/Zambia-Country-Climate-Action-Report-2016.pdf, accessed 18 January 2021.

Sambo, P.T., 2019, "The Environmental Management Act (2011): A basis for the growth of an environmental ethos and good environmental governance in Zambia?". In: Kameri-Mbote, P., A. Paterson, O.C. Ruppel & B.B. Orubebe (eds), *Law | Environment | Africa*. Baden-Baden: Nomos Publishers, 647.

Sambo, P.T., C. Haywood, D.A. Wardell, R. Kibugi & M.-C. Cordonier Segger, 2015, *Enabling legal frameworks for sustainable land-use investments in Zambia – Legal assessment report*, at https://bit.ly/3rwFtV4, accessed 17 January 2021.

Sharma, N. & R. Singhvi, 2017, "Effects of chemical fertilizers and pesticides on human health and environment: A review". *International Journal of Agriculture, Environment and Biotechnology* 10 (6), 675, at https://ndpublisher.in/admin/issues/IJAEBv10n6f.pdf, accessed 16 October 2019.

Shitumbanuma, V., P. Simfukwe, D. Kalala, B. Kaninga, B. Gondwe, M. Nambala, S. Kabwe, G. Siulemba, N. Kapulu, O. Lungu & J. Mutegi, undated, *Integrated soil fertility management in Zambia*. Lusaka: The Soil Health Consortium, at https://bit.ly/3q46aQw, accessed 20 October 2019.

Sintayehu, D.W., 2018, "Impact of climate change on biodiversity and associated key ecosystem services in Africa: a systematic review". *Ecosystem Health and Sustainability* 4 (9), 225, at https://www.tandfonline.com/doi/full/10.1080/20964129.2018.1530054, accessed 15 January 2021.

Smith, P., 2018, "Managing the global land resource". *Biological Sciences* 285 (1874), at http://doi.org/10.1098/rspb.2017.2798, accessed 20 October 2019.

Stanchi, S., G. Falsone & E. Bonifacio, 2015, "Soil aggregation, erodibility, and erosion rates in mountain soils (NW Alps, Italy)". *Solid Earth* 6, 403, at https://doi.org/10.5194/se-6-403, accessed 20 August 2019.

Stevens, C., 2019, "Reviving the right to development within the multilateral trade framework affecting (African) countries to actualize Agenda 2063". *African Human Rights Law Journal* 19 (1), 470, at https://dx.doi.org/10.17159/1996-2096/2019/v19n1a22, accessed 20 October 2019.

Stevens, C. & N. Kanie, 2016, "The transformative potential of the Sustainable Development Goals (SDGs)". *International Environmental Agreements: Politics, Law and Economics* 16, 393, at https://doi.org/10.1007/s10784-016-9324-y, accessed 21 October 2019.

Sunlu U., 2003, "Environmental impacts of tourism". In: Camarda D. & L. Grassini (eds), *Local resources and global trades: Environments and agriculture in the Mediterranean region*. Bari: CIHEAM, 263, at http://om.ciheam.org/om/pdf/a57/04001977.pdf, accessed 31 October 2019.

Tembo, T., 2016, "Protect environment from chemical fertilizers". *Zambia Daily Mail*, 2 May 2016.

The Commonwealth, 2019, "Zambia – Constitution and politics", at http://thecommonwealth.org/our-member-countries/zambia/constitution-politics, accessed 15 April 2019.

Ul Zaman, M., S. Bhat, S. Sharma & O. Bhat, 2018, "Methods to control soil erosion – A review". *International Journal of Pure and Applied Bioscience* 6 (2), 1114, at http://dx.doi.org/10.18782/2320-7051.6462, accessed 18 January 2021.

UNCTAD / United Nations Conference on Trade and Development, 2017, *Promoting foreign investment in the Sustainable Development Goals (SDGs)*. Geneva: UNCTAD, at https://unctad.org/system/files/official-document/diaepcb2018d4_en.pdf, accessed 18 January 2021.

UNEP / United Nations Environment Programme, 2015, *Benefits of forests ecosystems in Zambia and the role of REDD+ in a green economy transformation*. Nairobi: UNEP, at https://bit.ly/3quTbaR, accessed 18 January 2021.

United States Agency for International Development, 2010, *Zambia: Land tenure and property rights profile*, at http://www.usaidlandtenure.net/sites/default/files/country-profiles/full-reports/USAID_Land_Tenure_Zambia_Profile.pdf, accessed 3 February 2021.

United States Department of State, 2015, *Zambia investment climate statement*, at http://www.state.gov/documents/organization/242010.pdf

van Tine, R., 2017, "Reflections, analysis, and significance for human ecology of Pope Francis's encyclical letter 'Laudato Si': On care for our common home". *Human Ecology Review* 23 (1), 141.

Von Malitz, G., J. Gambiza, K. Kellner, T. Rambau, L. Lindeque & B. Kgope. 2019, "Experiences from South African land degradation neutrality target setting process". *Environmental Science and Policy* 101, 54.

World Bank, 2015, "Doing business 2016: Economy profile 2016 – Zambia", at https://bit.ly/37oj5Fz, accessed 15 February 2021.

World Bank, 2016, *Land governance assessment – Zambia*. Country Report, Lusaka: World Bank.

Young, A., 1989, *Agroforestry for soil conservation*. Wallingford: International Council for Research in Agroforestry, at http://old.worldagroforestry.org/downloads/Publications/PDFS/03_Agroforestry_for_soil_conservation.pdf, accessed 11 October 2019.

ZDA / Zambia Development Agency, 2017, *Zambia's investor guide handbook*, at http://impactcapafrica.com/resources/pdf/Investor%20Guide%20Handbook%20-%20April2017.pdf.

ZEMA / Zambia Environmental Management Agency, 2017, *Zambia environment outlook report*, at http://www.zema.org.zm/index.php/download/zambia-environment-outlook-report-3/, accessed 11 October 2019.

Zongwe, D.P., 2011, *An introduction to the law of the Southern African Development Community*. New York: Hauser Global Law School Programme, at https://www.nyulawglobal.org/globalex/Southern_African_Development_Community.html, accessed 18 January 2021.

Mapping out options for model legislation for sustainable soil management in Africa

Harald Ginzky, Patricia Kameri-Mbote, Oliver C. Ruppel, Pamela Towela Sambo & Christopher F. Tamasang[1]

1 Introduction

Africa is the continent with the least soil degradation, while at the same time the pressure on soils is extremely high. Factors such as poverty, hunger, overuse, overpopulation and climate change are exacerbating this pressure. Hunger and poverty in Africa can only be overcome with fertile soil.

The protection of soil and the sustainable management of soils are preconditions for sustainable development and ultimately for the survival of humankind. Without sufficient areas of fertile soils, there is no food security and no chance to mitigate climate change. Degraded soils result in hunger, famine, migration and, under certain circumstances, even wars. Africa has experienced such deprivations in the past and, with increasing climate change, these hardships can even be exacerbated. Land preservation – and thus the sustainable management of soils – is required in order to achieve most of the Sustainable Development Goals of the United Nations 2030 Sustainable Development Agenda, and in particular the land degradation neutrality objective.

Although the effects of soil degradation are global, the appropriate management of soils must be implemented locally. The challenges are multifactorial, including ecological, social, cultural, economic, political and legal. Africa is the continent with the least land degradation, yet the pressure on soils is already enormous and continually increasing owing to a range of factors, including poverty, over-exploitation, population growth and climate change. Drivers of unsustainable soil management include overstocking, overgrazing, water erosion, landslides, and over-application of agrochemicals. Moreover, poor populations lacking the means to conserve often depend directly on land and other natural resources for immediate needs, which is an additional driver for land and soil degradation.

Sustainable soil management is an essential factor in overcoming the major challenges that confront African countries in the face of climate change, limited food supplies and declining biodiversity. Soil degradation causes hunger, poverty, migration and sometimes even conflict.

1 The authors wish to thank Mr Georg Junger for his support with this chapter.

Soil is a matter that is affected by a multitude of interests. In addition to the ecological and developmental dimensions, numerous economic, cultural and social interests are relevant to soil. Despite the overwhelming importance of soil, there is no uniform soil protection law in any African country. Rather, the protection of soil is often found in a variety of sectoral laws that are not primarily concerned with soil protection.

Based on a selection of three African countries (Cameroon, Zambia and Kenya), soil protection in Africa was analysed comparatively and by mapping out options for model legislation for sustainable soil management in Africa. This chapter reflects the underlying findings comparatively in view of the possible preparation of an African soil protection law.[2] The distinct country studies from Kenya, Cameroon and Zambia serve to com6paratively expose the serious vulnerabilities of soil in Africa.

Relevant aspects covered are the lack of soil data and soil research, and its frequent unavailability or inadequacy. Existing laws are not sufficiently implemented in agricultural practices, while coherent soil policy is often still lacking in the legislation of many African countries. Finally, insecure land tenure rights pose numerous uncertainties in the presence of African legal pluralism. A common perception in African societies is linked to the presumption that landowners are entitled to use their land as they wish. And although governments have attempted to put legally binding standards for soil management in place, governmental entities often tend to lack the competence and financial means to enforce such standards. Finally, legal pluralism in many African societies between traditional and modern law leads to considerable legal uncertainties, especially regarding – but in no way limited to – land-use rights.

While mapping out options for model legislation for improved sustainable soil management in Africa, the chapter addresses intertwined, interdisciplinary and complex questions pertaining to soils, which may also be of comparative interest to the jurisdictions of other continents. The chapter provides special insights and recommendations that may be useful for African countries, Regional Economic Communities and African Union institutions in the consideration of establishing a framework protection basis for the benefit of generations to come.

2 Setting the scene

This section provides some background information which is relevant to understanding the various dimensions of the challenge to establish good governance to achieve

2 Regarding the footnoting of sources in this chapter, only those sources which have not already been referenced in the country studies will be explicitly acknowledged in this chapter. Where sections of the chapter draw on information from the country studies, the relevant and underlying sources will not be repeated in this chapter and the reader is referred to the respective country study for further reference.

sustainable soil management in Africa. In the following sections, options to improve current overarching and sectoral legislation are presented.
First, some information is given about Africa's natural, economic and historical conditions. Secondly, the importance of soils for sustainable development in Africa is explained. Thirdly, the main drivers of soil degradation are outlined. Fourthly, the structure of continental and regional cooperation in Africa and the international governance of soil management is briefly described.

2.1 Africa in natural, historical, economic and political terms

The size of Africa is 30 million square kilometres, which makes it the world's second largest continent. The continent's population was estimated to be 1.2 billion in 2016. The major economic activity in Africa is agriculture and that is why soil protection is a pertinent issue on this continent. Other economic activities include mining, energy and investments. Africa also has a range of climatic conditions such as an equatorial climate, tropical climate, arid and semi-arid conditions, and subtropical conditions in the highlands. The vegetation in Africa reflects the climate but, generally, the continent is vegetative.[3]

With regard to the establishment of good governance to achieve sustainable soil management, it is important to mention that Africa has been colonised for centuries and that independence in most African states was achieved relatively recently at the beginning of the 1960s.

The very long period marked by the lack of freedom and sovereignty has left traces in various aspects of the African societal fabric, e.g., random state borders, pluralism of tenure rights, strong role of tribes, illegal and/or illegitimate foreign investment in land and soil, unfair trade practices, unfinished unification of African states, people's inferiority complex, and many more. This statement does not mean to convey that the colonial period is the only cause of the current challenges in Africa, particularly those just mentioned. But it would certainly not be appropriate to ignore the 'colonial hangover effect'.

The economies of the more than 50 African states have developed differently. In some countries, industrialisation is already well-established. But several conditions prevail in most, if not all, African states: Large portions of the population make their living from agriculture, and the gross domestic product (GDP) is largely based on agricultural activities. Often, the majority of farmers are small-scale and thus vulnerable to external shocks due to climate or economic changes. National income often depends on the export of natural resources. The level of domestic processing is usually low. Foreign investment in land, agriculture and extraction of natural resources is an

3 Detailed information can be found in the three country studies.

important economic factor. African states often face a high or very high level of debt, which strongly hampers the ability to vitalise economic development by stimulus programmes.

Most African states have developed a democratic and modern system separating legislative, executive and juridical powers. Some have approved very modern constitutions, in particular with regard to environmental protection and management of natural resources. Core challenges are the lack of sufficient resources and little clarity regarding the roles and responsibilities of ministries and other governmental and administrative entities. Thus, law implementation and enforcement often remain weak and ineffective. In addition, sustainable development efforts often lack attention to societal (justice) issues, e.g. inequality, discrimination, stigmatisation, tribalism and marginalisation.

2.2 Importance of soil

Soil is one of the most crucial natural resources. Despite its importance, the preservation of soil in Africa is precarious and this, in turn, places the future of all ecological functions in the very bedrock, as reported in the Cameroonian report. Soil is used in agriculture in the production of crops and other agricultural products; thus, it provides a solution to food insecurity. In this context, sustainable soil management is certainly required to end hunger in Africa – and is therefore the baseline challenge for all humans. Soil is the basis of all terrestrial life. In the Kenyan report, soil was described as the source of livelihood for organisms and humans. Soil also provides a habitat for innumerable living things that form part of the ecosystem. Soil is used in building infrastructure such as buildings, roads and other economic structures. In Kenya, soil has been recognised as having ecological, cultural and political dimensions.[4] The ecological usefulness of soil includes water and moisture retention, habitats for living organisms, and the decomposition of waste materials.[5]

The cultural usefulness of soil varies from one culture to another. Soil has a religious significance in some communities and is used for cultural decorations in other communities. Soil also has economic value. It stores numerous minerals and other natural resources that are useful to the economies of countries. Soil is also sold in the form of land as property. Indeed, as stated in the Cameroonian report, soil has crucial ecological and socioeconomic functions.

---

4 Allan (2008: 61).
5 Howard & Lawson (2015).

2.3 Main soil threats, degradation drivers and challenges

In the following paragraphs, the threats, degradation drivers and challenges of soil degradation relevant to Africa are summarised. Soil degradation is a change in soil health status resulting in a diminished capacity of the ecosystem to provide goods and services for its beneficiaries. From the three reports provided by Kenya, Cameroon and Zambia, there are numerous factors that affect the nature, quality and structure of soil.

2.3.1 Agriculture

In Kenya and Cameroon, agriculture is a major economic activity. Poor agricultural practices are one of the threats to soil structure and its functions, in particular the application of agrochemicals and fertilizer without knowledge of existing soil nutrients and farming with no rotational practices or seasonal breaks. Poor methods of bush and forest clearing, such as burning, leads to the death of soil organisms that contribute to its nutrients. Overgrazing by running excessive livestock numbers per unit area not only destroys protective vegetative cover, but also leads to soil compaction – thus negatively affecting soil profile and aeration. In contrast, Zambia maintains a high acreage of underutilised land, and has a medium to high potential for agriculture. Within the unused arable land area, however, a reduction of forest area may lead to the destruction of the natural environment.[6]

2.3.2 Mining

Mining is the excavation of mineral resources from their natural setting, which is usually soil. The economic activity of mining is useful but its effect on soil is alarming. Mining leads to soil degradation through the excavation process. Cameroon, Kenya and Zambia are richly endowed with mineral deposits and the mining of those ores leads to destruction of soil profile and productivity.

2.3.3 Industrialisation

The growth of industries is another threat to soil. Industrial processes and products affect the quality of soil in several ways. Industries deposit their waste and effluents on soil according to set standards and guidelines. The waste contains dangerous

6 Japan Association for International Collaboration of Agriculture and Forestry (2008: 36).

chemicals and non-biodegradable substances, which negatively affect soil decomposition. Greenhouse gases cause acidic rain that affects soil pH. In addition, industrial activities require a large operation area, which necessitates the clearing of land, and this may require deforestation. It is important to bring to the fore that a significant proportion of industries in Cameroon are not certified by international environmental management organisations which require industries to internalise their external effects on the environment.

2.3.4 Urbanisation

Urbanisation refers to increasing population growth in urban areas. Most cities in Africa are highly populated and have extreme population densities. This is because most people migrate from rural to urban areas in search of employment. The high population density in urban areas, as well as the increase in development in these areas, has led to deforestation and also soil compaction. Urban sprawl leads to the conversion of agricultural land and wetlands into settlement areas, thus affecting soil use.

2.3.5 Weather and climate change

Climate change, meaning changed temperatures and weather events (timing, duration and strengths), directly and indirectly affects soil functions. Flooding which erodes soil, as well as water scarcity and droughts, may affect the availability of fertile soils and the structure and quality of soils. Floods may also have the effect of increasing contamination by spreading contaminants. Even the timing of rainfall may have detrimental effects on soil quality. Non-resilient small-scale farmers, particularly, may be unable to cope with these changes. By contrast, sustainable soil management may cause an increased uptake of carbon and could thus be regarded as a mitigation or adaptation measure to fight climate change.

2.3.6 Topographical constraints

Topography may exacerbate soil erosion and floods. Uneven topography, as found in Kenya, Cameroon and Zambia, causes rainwater to flow down steep gradients, thus washing soil from the highland areas and later depositing it on the lowland areas. This erosion therefore affects the soil structure of the highland areas.

2.3.7 Poverty

Poverty is a social factor that affects the quality of soil. Poverty has forced humans to encroach on marginal lands and forests, where they burn charcoal and gather firewood, which leads to deforestation and land degradation. Furthermore, poverty is often associated with poor agricultural practices and overuse of natural resources. Finally, poverty increases the proclivity of local communities to engage in illegal and illegitimate land acquisition.

2.3.8 Poor law implementation and enforcement

Weak law implementation and enforcement is an additional social driver of soil degradation.

2.3.9 Illegal or illegitimate foreign investment in land

Finally, foreign investment in land that is illegal or illegitimate often widely ignores existing legal requirements to protect soil quality. Thus, these forms of investment constitute an additional driver of soil degradation.

3 Framework for soil legislation

3.1 International framework

There are various international instruments and so-called soft laws that create the obligation of soil protection. The first important obligation relating to soil protection is the 2030 Agenda for Sustainable Development which institutes the Sustainable Development Goals (SDGs). It sets out obligations that help with soil conservation and management. These include Goal 12, which aims to ensure sustainable consumption and production patterns, and Goal 13, which encourages urgent action to combat climate change and its impacts. Furthermore, and most relevant, Target 15.3, which requests states "to strive to achieve a land degradation neutral world by 2030" needs to be highlighted. The United Nations Convention to Combat Desertification (UNCCD) has declared itself as lead organisation to implement the land degradation neutrality (LDN) objective. Certain overlaps with the Convention on Biological Diversity (CBD) in terms of legal scope and mandate regarding soil biodiversity may occur, while the United Nations Framework Convention on Climate Change (UNFCCC) also creates obligations that reduce climate change thus reducing the threat of soil degradation. The

Ramsar Convention on Wetlands requires contracting parties to formulate and implement plans that ensure conservation and wise use of wetlands within their boundaries.

3.2 National framework

The following section addresses whether and what overarching provisions are required in order to have a solid baseline for sectoral provisions dealing with specific soil threats such as urbanisation, industrial facilities, use of fertilizers, pesticides and more. These overarching provisions might form a kind of framework soil legislation. To this end, first a short summary of the three country studies will document the current legal situation in the three countries, identifying substantial shortcomings concerning both a coherent soil policy and legislation. Before the specific options are presented, the objective and value of overarching provisions and the political buy-in are explained. Overarching provisions may be in the form of constitutional provisions or as a legislative act which is regarded as a leading framework for sectoral provisions.

3.3 The country studies' findings

None of the national constitutions of the three countries entails explicit or substantial provisions on sustainable soil management. This is actually not surprising since – as far as is known – no constitution worldwide provides such norms. Moreover, the relationship of sustainable soil management to poverty and hunger prevention and to climate change is not mentioned in the constitutions of the three countries. To a certain extent, it appears that the importance of soils as a natural resource was not fully understood when the constitutions were drafted and adopted. However, all three constitutions set out ambitious provisions on natural resources, on environmental protection and, partly, even on benefit-sharing. The term 'resource' needs to be understood widely to encompass also soils. The constitutions also do not cover specific provisions on the responsibilities of foreign investors. Furthermore, the three country studies conclude that there is no overarching policy on sustainable soil management and thus no overarching and coherent soil legislation. The criticism finds a sectoralisation and compartmentalisation regarding air, water and other natural resources have been put in place, which leads to a kind of fragmentation of sectoral provisions regarding the various soil threats.

Furthermore, it seems that none of the analysed legislation entails provisions on the implementation of the objective "land degradation neutrality". This objective is one of the 169 targets of the 2030 Agenda for Sustainable Development which has been adopted by the United Nations General Assembly adopted on 25 September 2015.[7] The Agenda includes 17 SDGs and 169 accompanying targets. Importantly, the Agenda stipulates commitments for both developing and developed countries. SDG 15 and Target 15.3 are the most pertinent ones as SDG 15 requests states "to halt and reverse land degradation" and Target 15.3 demands that states "by 2030, combat desertification, and restore degraded land and soil, including land affected by desertification, drought and floods, and strive to achieve a land-degradation neutral world".

The UNCCD, which has established itself as the international lead organisation for the land degradation neutrality (LDN) objective,[8] has interpreted the term as follows:[9]

> Land degradation neutrality is a state whereby the amount and quality of land resources necessary to support ecosystem functions and services and enhance food security remain stable or increase within specified temporal and spatial scales and ecosystems.

As soil is an essential element of land, the LDN objective is directly applicable to soils. In addition, the definition underlines that the "amount and quality" has to "remain stable or increase." That means essentially that the amount and quality of soil must not diminish. As land/soil degradation cannot be avoided completely, restoration or rehabilitation interventions must be in place in order to achieve neutrality.[10] Thus, the investigated legislation entails neither an obligation to achieve LDN within a specific timeframe, nor a requirement to set specific targets based on agreed indicators, and there are no specific LDN-related planning instruments.

3.4 Recommendations

The following sub-section first addresses the objective and value of overarching provisions on sustainable soil management (framework legislation) and discusses the advantages from the perspective of policymakers (political buy-in). Secondly, specific options with regard to constitutional provisions, soil policies and legislation are put forward. Finally, some thoughts are provided on the use of sanctions and penalties.

3.4.1 Objective and value of framework legislation and political buy-in

A framework legislation on sustainable soil management could and should stress the ecological functions of soils and the dimensions affecting society. The ecological function could be summarised as follows: Soils are the basis for food production and the

---

7 See https://bit.ly/3p24MMY, accessed 10 February 2021.
8 Boer et al. (2016: 63).
9 See https://www.unccd.int/actions/achieving-land-degradation-neutrality, accessed 10 February 2021.
10 Ehlers (2016: 75).

production of plants for renewable energy. Soils sequester carbon and are therefore crucial in the fight against climate change. Soils host biodiversity and thus play a vital role in the world's biological cycle by, among other things, storing nutrients or filtering hazardous substances from groundwater. They also have cultural and biological significance.

Thus, the dimension of soils relating to society is in safeguarding human welfare in general, and more particularly in preventing hunger and eradicating poverty. Furthermore, soils play a role in the mitigation and adaptation to climate change, as well as the maintenance and fostering of biodiversity. Finally, healthy soils play a part in the prevention of forced displacements, societal tensions, and political or even military conflicts. In order to fulfil these ecological functions and the dimension relating to society, soil needs to be legally regarded as a natural resource whose ecological services have to be maintained and fostered.

Moreover, the objective of LDN could be established as a binding obligation. In addition, the overarching planning instruments to achieve LDN could be clarified and established by a framework legislation. A framework legislation could also clarify the general institutional roles, competencies and responsibilities, including the establishment of a permission regime (prior written authorisation) for activities with severe risks for soils.

With respect to the advantage of such overarching provisions, three primary aspects should be mentioned in legally declaring soil as a natural resource and stressing its ecological functions: First, the costs of rehabilitation or restoration by far exceed the costs of sustainable management – which has been evidenced by the results of the Deutsche Gesellschaft für Internationale Zusammenarbeit (GIZ) initiative, *Economics of Land Degradation.*[11] In that regard, it is simply good sense to impose a general obligation to manage soil sustainably and to achieve land degradation neutrality.

Second, owing to the interconnectedness of combating the climate crisis and poverty, and safe-guarding natural resources and development options with soils, sustainable soil management is one more required ingredient – along with, among others, avoidance of societal tensions and political and military conflicts, birth control, and fair-trade patterns – to achieve an improvement in the economic conditions in African countries and to realise sustainable development.

Thirdly, as climate change is very high on the international political agenda, a number of international funds have been established and made accessible for climate mitigation and adaptation projects. As projects to improve soil quality mostly, if not always, have a positive effect on the carbon sequestration function of soils, international funds supporting climate mitigation and adaptation could also be used for soil-related projects.

---

11 Initiative "Economics of Land degradation", further information to be found at https://www.eld-initiative.org/, accessed 10 February 2021.

3.4.2 Constitutional provisions

Sustainable soil management and LDN implementation could be addressed by constitutional provisions. The constitutions of the three countries analysed already entail strong provisions on natural resources. It is clear that the term 'natural resources' encompasses soil.

First of all, it needs to be stated that an analysis of the valid national provisions is necessary before deciding on amending the existing rules. Two options to strengthen sustainable soil management should be recommended here. In any case, it seems to be reasonable to emphasise legally that soil is a natural resource which carries out essential ecological functions which are linked to most relevant social and societal implications, as outlined above. In particular, the interface of sustainable soil management to climate change should be explicitly mentioned by constitutional provisions. A second option which has to be seen as an additional bid would be to integrate the LDN objective as a constitutional obligation for all governmental entities. This obligation could also be extended to all relevant actors in society.

Finally, the imposition of a particular responsibility towards the sustainable development of the national economy could be considered for foreign investors. The supporting argument would be that foreign investors are usually in a very strong position. Thus, binding them by constitutional obligation would be appropriate. A negative consequence of such a provision could be that a country would need to document its dependence on foreign investment. On the whole, such a provision could be beneficial, but would need to be carefully drafted.

3.4.3 Soil-related policies

Comprehensive and coherent soil policies are a further option to promote sustainable soil management in African countries. Such policies must clearly be based on constitutional provisions. The advantage of soil policies is that they fill the gap between legal norm and subsidiary standards and indicators. They could address how to get the 'soil engine' established and continuously running. Obviously, in order to be comprehensive and coherent, the policies need to address all soil health drivers and all threats. In addition, they need to provide an approach to LDN implementation – including measurement of the status quo, indicators, targets, measures and institutions. The same goes for sustainable soil management in general. The necessary scientific bodies must be established, personnel recruited, information gathered, and compilation and synthetisation need to be organised. In addition, soil policy could also address the involvement of private actors and civil society.

3.4.4 Overarching soil provisions

It has been argued that overarching provisions on sustainable soil management would be beneficial. Overarching provisions could be included in the constitutions. The provisions should be accompanied by coherent soil policies. In addition, or even instead of the constitutional provisions, overarching provisions could be imposed via legal instruments, such as acts, depending on the constitutional requirements. Basically, there are two options for overarching provisions via a framework legislation.

Option 1 is a framework legislation that entails the crucial framing requirements, which would then coordinate sectoral provisions with respect to all soil drivers. Such a framing legislation would have to clarify that soils are a natural resource which provides ecological services. Furthermore, the services for the environment also need to be addressed if this has not already been implemented by the constitution. Finally, the obligation to achieve LDN could also be mentioned in the framing legislation.

With regard to the control mechanism, the framing act should establish a permission regime for activities with severe risks for soils. The activities for which an *ex-ante* permission is required need to be undoubtably determined in order to avoid any misunderstanding. In order to achieve LDN and to implement this objective, planning instruments to calculate the ongoing degradation and the envisaged restoration need to be established as well. It would also be beneficial if the framing legislation determines – at least roughly – the roles, competencies and responsibilities of the various governmental entities with regard to LDN management; the environmental quality standards, emission limit values and technical standards; the regional standards which fit the regional specificities; and the permission regime.

Particular regulatory provisions concerning the various drivers of soil degradation should not be part of the framework legislation. However, it should be ensured that soil management-related environmental and technical requirements are implemented through the other sectoral provisions. This approach has been successfully applied by Germany's soil protection governance – at least with regard to soil contamination.[12] The German federal Soil Protection Ordinance entails specified and legally binding environmental quality standards and emission limit values. These standards have to be complied with through the implementation of other sectoral provisions, for example the mining act. It is important to note that this regulatory approach will only work if specified standards are adopted by the framework legislation for both contamination and all other forms of soil degradation and if these standards are legally binding – so that these standards have to be enforced via the sectoral provisions.[13]

Option 2 would be a kind of holistic soil legislation for all drivers and sectors which regulate all aspects mentioned for option 1. In addition, all regulatory instruments for

12 Ginzky et al. (forthcoming 2021).
13 Ibid.

all soil drivers and all soil threats could be integrated in this framework legislation. It seems that this would perhaps be an opportunity if in an African country no regulation on sustainable soil management exists, which is highly unlikely. Thus, this option would lead to much duplication of existing regulations, which has occurred, for example, with regard to the regulation of pesticides. Furthermore, a purely soil-oriented regulation of activities which actually affect several environmental aspects would simply be inappropriate. Thus, in the case of advanced legislation on the protection of the environment, option 1 clearly seems to be more reasonable.

3.4.5 Penalties and sanctions

Next to all these planning and prior control instruments it is also reasonable to consider incentives for compliance. From a legal perspective, incentives could primarily be sanctions in all legal forms: fines, civil rights obligation to restore land/soil degradation and even criminal sanctions such as penalties. All these sanctions must be both proportionate and severe enough in order to set an incentive to avoid these sanctions. A fine for a foreign investor which is related to the average income of the national population would probably not severe enough, for example. Next to the sanctions mentioned above the threat to blame the reputation of an enterprise and/or a politician could also be a quite effective instrument to foster the motivation for compliance.

4 Climate change, land and soil

4.1 Intergovernmental Panel on Climate Change findings

Soil protection is imperative in light of the far-reaching and heavily adverse social and economic effects that result from its neglect. This seems particularly important in the light of Africa's extreme vulnerability to the impacts of climate change.[14] This can also be said with reference to the Intergovernmental Panel on Climate Change (IPCC). Because of its scientific and intergovernmental nature, the IPCC provides rigorous and balanced scientific information. In the UNFCCC, explicit reference is made to the IPCC under Article 21 in "that the Panel can respond to the need for objective scientific and technical advice."

With its *5th Assessment Report (AR5) on Climate Change,*[15] the IPCC has most rigorously reviewed and assessed scientific, technical and socioeconomic information produced worldwide relevant to the understanding of climate change. The

14 Ruppel & von Finckenstein (2017: 343).

15 Report available from http://www.ipcc.ch/report/ar5/, accessed 28 May 2020.

aforementioned report is of great relevance with regard to all aspects of climate change and contains a solid base for further debate on this important topic. Robust scientific knowledge about climate change plays an overarching role. By means of effectively and objectively assessing such scientific knowledge and the prevailing uncertainty, the IPCC can provide the world with the best possible and much-needed evidence of climate change-related impacts.

The IPCC's analysis of observed climate trends and future projections reveals that it is very likely that mean annual temperature has increased over the past century over most of the African continent,[16] and that temperatures on the continent will rise faster than the global average increase during the 21st century.

Selected executive summary statements of the IPCC AR5 Africa chapter[17]

Evidence of warming over land regions across Africa, consistent with anthropogenic climate change, has increased (high confidence).

Mean annual temperature rise over Africa, relative to the late 20th century mean annual temperature, is likely to exceed 2°C in the Special Report on Emissions Scenarios (SRES) A1B and A2 scenarios by the end of this century (medium confidence).

A reduction in precipitation is likely over Northern Africa and the southwestern parts of South Africa by the end of the 21st century under the SRES A1B and A2 scenarios (medium to high confidence).

African ecosystems are already being affected by climate change, and future impacts are expected to be substantial (high confidence).

Climate change will amplify existing stress on water availability in Africa (high confidence).

Climate change will interact with non-climate drivers and stressors to exacerbate vulnerability of agricultural systems, particularly in semi-arid areas (high confidence).

Climate change may increase the burden of a range of climate-relevant health outcomes (medium confidence). Climate change is a multiplier of existing health vulnerabilities (high confidence), including insufficient access to safe water and improved sanitation, food insecurity, and limited access to health care and education.

Growing understanding of the multiple interlinked constraints on increasing adaptive capacity is beginning to indicate potential limits to adaptation in Africa (medium confidence).

There is increased evidence of the significant financial resources, technological support, and investment in institutional and capacity development needed to address

16 With the exception of areas of the interior of the continent, where the data coverage has been determined to be insufficient. See Niang et al. (2014: 1206).

17 Extract from Niang et al. (2014: 1202–1204).

climate risk, build adaptive capacity, and implement robust adaptation strategies (high confidence).

Climate change and climate variability have the potential to exacerbate or multiply existing threats to human security including food, health, and economic insecurity, all being of particular concern for Africa (medium confidence).

AR5 presents strong evidence that the impacts[18] of climate change in Africa are already being felt across various sectors. Climate change poses challenges to economic growth and sustainable development and to the various facets of human security. Although detection of and attribution to climate change are often difficult given the role of drivers other than climate change, there are substantially more impacts in recent decades now attributed to climate change.[19] Various examples, however, show that climate change exerts extensive pressure on different ecosystems such as terrestrial, freshwater, and coastal/ocean ecosystems.[20] The health, livelihoods and food security of people in Africa are all affected by climate change. And as "Africa as a whole is one of the most vulnerable continents due to its high exposure and low adaptive capacity",[21] innovation and technology, smart policymaking, high levels of government attention, effective diplomacy, and international cooperation are required in order to effectively address the current and future challenges related to climate change.

> Climate change will amplify existing risks and create new risks for natural and human systems. Risks are unevenly distributed and are generally greater for disadvantaged people and communities in countries at all levels of development.[22]

Africa is most vulnerable to climate change owing to the existence and interaction of multiple stresses – endemic poverty; complex governance and institutional dimensions; limited access to capital, markets, infrastructure and technology; ecosystem degradation; complex disasters and conflicts; and low adaptive capacity. Yet, as a global problem, climate change calls for multilateral solutions as opposed to unilateral approaches, in particular if these are confrontational. It is clear that required global emissions reductions cannot be achieved in developed countries alone. As a consequence, both developed and developing countries will have to transform themselves into low-carbon economies. This will require efforts at various levels, including substantial

18 Impacts of climate change are the "effects on natural and human systems of extreme weather and climate events and of climate change. Impacts generally refer to effects on lives, livelihoods, health, ecosystems, economies, societies, cultures, services, and infrastructure due to the interaction of climate changes or hazardous climate events occurring within a specific time period and the vulnerability of an exposed society or system. Impacts are also referred to as consequences and outcomes. The impacts of climate change on geophysical systems, including floods, droughts, and sea level rise, are a subset of impacts called physical impacts." IPCC (2014b: 5).

19 IPCC (2014a: 7).

20 See Niang et al. (2014: 1214).

21 Ibid.: 1205.

22 IPCC (2014b: 13).

changes in lifestyle, in particular in industrialised countries. Equally important is major investment in low-carbon technology and modern technology transfer to, and capacity-building in, Africa.

The IPCC, in its findings on global warming of 1.5°C (2018 Report),[23] and climate change and land (2019 Report),[24] looked closely at the relationship between soil and the impact of climate change. It acknowledges that human changes in land use result in atmospheric carbon being stored in plants and soil and this is differentiated from natural CO_2 stored in the land.[25] Drought and dryness due to global warming – an increase in global temperatures of 1.5°C to 2°C – is said to have an impact on soil moisture, particularly in areas of the southern African region.[26]

Soil degradation is a way in which terrestrial carbon can be returned to the atmosphere.[27] The ocean provides important services, including the regulation of atmospheric composition via gas exchange across the boundary between ocean and atmosphere, and the storage of carbon in vegetation and soils associated with ecosystems such as mangroves, salt marshes and coastal peatlands.[28] As such, soil degradation upsets the balance of terrestrial carbon and causes this carbon, once previously stored, to return to the atmosphere.[29]

Soil degradation in the form of soil erosion can be expected to occur in areas where there is higher rainfall than is usually expected, thus wearing away the soil deposits present.[30] Soil degradation refers to a subset of land degradation processes that directly affect soil.[31]

Soil desertification is discussed in detail in Chapter 3 of the 2019 Report.[32] The first mention of soil carbon sequestration can be found in the 2018 Report where the IPCC makes mention of soil carbon sequestration as a method of accumulating negative carbon emissions through the Carbon Dioxide Removal Project.[33] In an attempt to keep global temperatures below 2°C, the use of soil carbon sequestration is the process of "enhanced weathering of minerals where natural weathering to remove CO_2 from the

---

23 The full title of the report being: An IPCC Special Report on the impacts of global warming of 1.5°C above pre-industrial levels and related global greenhouse gas emission pathways, in the context of strengthening the global response to the threat of climate change, sustainable development, and efforts to eradicate poverty. See IPCC (2018).

24 The full title of the report being: An IPCC Special Report on climate change, desertification, land degradation, sustainable land management, food security, and greenhouse gas fluxes in terrestrial ecosystems. See IPCC (2019).

25 IPCC (2018: 114).

26 Ibid.: 196.

27 Ibid.: 125 and 219.

28 Ibid.: 227.

29 Govind & Kumari (2014: 2).

30 IPCC (2018: 216).

31 IPCC (2019: 350).

32 Ibid.: 251–306.

33 IPCC (2018: 17).

atmosphere is accelerated, and the products stored in soils, or buried in land/deep ocean".[34] Soil carbon sequestration, although a rather scientific methodology, has proved to be an example of a negative emission technology (NET) that would be beneficial in mitigating CO_2 emissions and decreasing climate change impacts.[35] The IPCC also acknowledges the benefits of soil carbon sequestration provided that it can result in "improved biodiversity, soil quality, and local food security".[36] Soil carbon sequestration and biochar were discussed under Section 4.3.7.3. of the 2018 Report.[37] According to the IPCC, "[t]he potential for soil carbon sequestration and storage varies considerably depending on prior and current land management approaches, soil type, resource availability, environmental conditions, microbial composition and nutrient availability among other factors".[38]

Sustainable land management describes "the stewardship and use of land resources, including soils, water, animals and plants, to meet changing human needs while simultaneously assuring the long-term productive potential of these resources and the maintenance of their environmental functions".[39] By introducing soil management practices on an extensive scale, soils can be used as a global carbon sink to help achieve a net removal, depletion or mitigation of overall CO_2 levels within the atmosphere.[40] Exercising sustainable soil management practices can help to tackle food security and climate change challenges faced by agricultural systems.[41]

> Agricultural land use contributes significantly towards the emission of greenhouse gases; at the same time, agriculture has enormous mitigation potential. Agriculture is susceptible to impacts of climate change such as water shortages, extreme weather and other factors that affect productivity. Smallholder agricultural systems can adapt to climate change by adopting climate-smart practices, increasing the resilience of agricultural systems by protecting natural resources and related livelihoods, particularly of the most vulnerable, through adaptation measures. Addressing global poverty requires addressing the resilience of smallholder agriculture to climate change impacts. While these are often rather technical to include in primary legislation, laws can identify these matters as a priority for the competent authority or provide indication that subsidiary legislation will provide further details. While improvements in carbon and nitrogen management will contribute to the reduction of emissions, climate adaptation and food security objectives should also be policy imperatives.[42]

All three country reports reflect the interrelatedness of soil and climate change. And while the climatic conditions differ across the African continent, it becomes most apparent that – from a policy perspective – both sustainable soil management and the protection against the impacts of climate change reflect two sides of the same coin.

---

34 Smith (2016: 1315).
35 Ibid.: 1316–1319.
36 IPCC (2018: 17).
37 Ibid.: 345.
38 IPCC (2019: 192).
39 Ibid.: 100.
40 Paustian et al. (2019: 568).
41 IPCC (2019: 500).
42 FAO & UNEP (2020: 630–632).

4.2 Recommendations

More research is required to understand the complex interconnections of land, soil, climate, water, society, sustainability and food, especially in Africa. In terms of technical and legal principles on adapting to climate change from the point of view of soil protection, further action on how to implement climate protection in soil protection law becomes apparent. The aims of climate-related soil protection should be introduced in accordance with other protected natural resources and political objectives, while the measures should be introduced into an assessment framework.

The measures should provide a basis for the legal analysis and evaluation of the feasibility of soil protection related to climate functions. In this light and also in support of the Nationally Determined Contributions (NDCs), a legal framework should be established to offer effective instruments in order to implement climate ambitions in Africa. Significant gaps in the NDCs and contained commitments need to be bridged and national governments might consider (re-)evaluating national, regional and transformative response options and policy instruments. More inclusive forms of socially just and more equitable governance processes and institutions should also be considered.

5 Agriculture

Agriculture in this section is split in two – crop growing and livestock. The first part of this section addresses crop growing while the second focuses on livestock.

5.1 Agriculture – crop growing

This section starts with a summary of the agriculture sector in Cameroon, Kenya and Zambia, with specific focus on crop growing.

5.1.1 Cameroon

The economy of Cameroon is largely agrarian, employing over 80% of the country's population. It is dominated by subsistence small-scale farming practices which are unsustainable and are at the forefront of massive soil degradation such as 'slash-and-burn' – which underpins food production and livelihoods in Cameroon and many other countries. The slash and burn farming practice includes several phases: (i) clearing of a portion of forest; (ii) burning of the plant debris; (iii) cultivation of the land, generally for a brief period; (iv) leaving the land fallow, generally for a long period of time.

In the coastal lowlands, intense chemical fertilizers and pesticides are used on large-scale plantations. These fertilizers and pesticides are not only harmful to the soil but also have detrimental effects on the underground water aquifers and the environment as a whole. The peasant subsistence small-scale farming practices carried out in this zone suffer a lot owing to declining soil fertility and a drop in agricultural output.

5.1.2 Kenya

Kenya has recently been ranked as a low middle-income economy and the fourth largest economy in sub-Saharan Africa. Inevitably, thousands of hectares of highly productive agricultural farmland have been converted into satellite cities with massive infrastructural developments which continue to pile pressure on decreasing agricultural soils to meet food demands of the growing population, with the consequence that soil and environmental degradation in Kenya have been on the rise in recent years.

Agriculture is the backbone of the Kenyan economy and is practised on large, small and subsistence scales. In order to boost production, there has been an increase in mechanisation, use of technology, and agricultural chemicals in the country, as well as importation of sub-standard fertilizers and other agrochemicals, leading to soil and water pollution. In irrigation schemes, for instance, high soil contamination as a result of using uncertified chemicals has been recorded in paddy rice production in some areas of the Mwea Irrigation Scheme.

Most of the soils used for agriculture in Kenya require constant nutrient replenishing, whereas the application of sub-standard fertilizers greatly contributes to soil degradation. One point to note in terms of understanding the political will to regulate the effect of fertilizers on soils in Kenya is that smuggling of sub-standard fertilizers in Kenya is sometimes done in collusion with government institutions. The Third Medium Term Plan (2018–2022) of Kenya's Vision 2030 identifies low and declining soil fertility due to poor farming methods as one of the main challenges facing the agricultural sector. Extension services, if properly designed and implemented, can improve agricultural productivity; however, the coverage of Kenya's agricultural extension system remains grossly inadequate.

Agriculture in itself may be counter-productive to soil health, as it involves land clearing, overgrazing caused by large livestock herds, charcoal and wood extraction, cultivation on steep slopes, bush burning and soil nutrient mining, among many other uses. Unsustainable agricultural practices and poor soils necessitate the use of fertilizers to improve productivity, but these fertilizers, as pointed out above, negatively affect the quality of soils. Most of the agricultural activities in Kenya are subsistence in nature and the farmers have yet to embrace modern methods of food production. As such, practices such as vegetation cover burning, as a way of cultivating virgin lands, is still rampant.

5.1.3 Zambia

Zambia is the seventh largest copper producer globally, and mining contributes over 75% to the country's total export value. Owing to the falling prices of copper on the global market, the country has over the years embarked on programmes to diversify its economy in order to reduce overdependence on copper. Agriculture has been tipped to supplement the copper contribution to the national economy. The quantity and nutritional quality of agricultural products for supporting human health largely depend on soils. Only healthy soils can provide the needed ecosystem services and secure increased supplies of agricultural produce to support a country's economy. Despite this expectation from agriculture, most of the sector legislation does not specifically address soil-related issues that have been pointed out as driving soil degradation. One reason for this is that the sector is still addressing one of its policy targets of reviewing its legislative and policy framework. It is hoped that this process can be completed speedily in order to ameliorate major challenges in the sector.

While about 58% of Zambia's total land area is potentially suitable for agricultural production, only about 15% of this area is under cultivation. This means that the country has a medium to high potential for agriculture; yet a high underutilised acreage continues to exist and, in turn, creates undue soil pressure for the limited land parcels that are used. The Zambian agricultural sector comprises crops, livestock and fisheries, with three broad categories of farmers: small-, medium-, and large-scale. Most Zambians are subsistence farmers, generally producing staple foods such as maize, sorghum, millet and cassava, with occasional marketable surplus. Medium-scale farmers produce maize and a few other cash crops such as cotton, groundnuts, sorghum, rice, sunflower seed, coffee, as well as sugar and fruits, while large-scale farmers produce various crops such as sugar, soybeans, coffee, groundnuts, rice, tobacco, paprika, wheat and cotton as well as horticultural produce. Owing to low crop yields, there is heightened use of chemical fertilizers, which in the long run compromise soil fertility.

Similar to the cases of both Cameroon and Kenya, traditional cultivation systems like shifting cultivation and slash and burn, also known locally as *chitemene,* have resulted in soil degradation and other negative impacts on the general environment. Further, unsustainable practices in crop cultivation, involving tillage rows which run against, rather than along, the natural contours of slopes, end up concentrating waterflow in such a manner as to cause soil erosion. Soil acidity, also a documented problem in Zambia, is caused by the injudicious sustained use of inorganic fertilizers in order to improve crop yields.

The current Second National Agricultural Policy (SNAP 2016–2020) has not achieved the much-needed sector legislative reform that was set as a target, although a number of positive initiatives such as conservation farming have been implemented. Conservation farming is relevant to sustainable soil management and consists of a farming system suited to the needs of crops and the prevailing conditions of a locality, thus enhancing resource-saving agricultural crop production, while concurrently protecting the environment from soil erosion and land degradation. The principles of conservation agriculture mainly consist of three linked components: reduced soil disturbance, maintenance of permanent soil covers, and species diversification which is favourable for sustainable soil management.

5.1.4 Public law

In the case of Kenya and Zambia, devolution as a form of governance is a golden opportunity to introduce more specific soil legislation.

In all the three countries, slash and burn practices have been identified as detrimental to soil health. In Zambia these practices are prohibited by the Environmental Management Act, while in Kenya the prohibition is pursuant to the Forest Conservation and Management Act.

In the case of Cameroon, the 1994 Forest Act proscribes slash and burn practices, although the legislation on environmental and social impact assessment does not address slash and burn practices or the related Ankara agricultural methods, a traditional farming method practised by farmers in the Western Highlands of Cameroon. Ankara involves dry plant waste being placed in the middle of beds, then partly covered with soil and burnt.

The impact of misusing chemical products (pesticides and fertilizers) on soil health is well noted and articulated in all three country reports and is rightly identified under "low hanging fruits". All three country reports explain the deliberate country initiatives instituted to address this soil- specific challenge. The monitoring and control of fertilizers in Cameroon is reportedly difficult and open to corrupt practices, as is also pointed out in the case of Kenya, where some level of illegal practices in the sector renders law implementation and enforcement extremely difficult.

In Kenya, as in the other two countries, the use of sub-standard fertilizers has negatively affected soil sustainability, especially since smuggling of sub-standard fertilizers and other illegal practices are prevalent in the government procurement processes.

In Zambia, in order to boost agricultural output, a shift in cultivation methods from indiscriminate chemical fertilizer usage to conservation farming is currently being advocated. Among the manifold efforts to facilitate a change towards more sustainable and climate-smart farming practices, conservation farming is the most prominent. Conservation farming aims at improved soil and water conservation combined with reduced dependence on chemical fertilizers, resulting in increased and more stable yields.

5.1.5 Findings

Extension services focusing on raising awareness of the importance of soil in the agricultural sector and beyond is necessary. These extension services must be multidisciplinary and touch on all the following aspects and more: Findings of soil science research need to be incorporated into day-to-day understanding based on the following questioning: What are the physical and chemical components of soil that are relevant to enhancing sustainable soil management?

Farmers' awareness of the exact importance of physical soil health beyond favourable crop yields should be heightened, in particular with regard to hunger alleviation, sustainability for future use, and achievement of a number of SDGs.

In all three countries, the discussion on the importance of soil reveals that there is a disconnect between (environmental) science and (environmental) law which needs to be addressed if soil sustainability is to be realised. This will involve using the opportunities and overcoming the numerous challenges pointed out in relation to science, on one hand, and policy and law, on the other. Assessing soil-related risks means that, based on scientific evidence, the likelihood of a certain outcome and its gravity can be estimated, and the resultant knowledge used to formulate policy and decision-making for soil sustainability.

There are opportunities and challenges associated with addressing the science–law interface which offer helpful insights to those involved in this endeavour, especially external scientists not directly involved in government.[43] For instance, there is a need to consider the real-world application of scientific research into soil and how best to transfer this knowledge to decision makers.

In the case of Kenya, the state is mandated by its constitution to promote science and recognise the role of science and indigenous technologies in national development. The state is also exhorted to protect and enhance intellectual property in, and indigenous knowledge of, biodiversity and the genetic resources of the communities. This is an important premise upon which to build the law and science interface with respect to the importance of soil. There is a need for data that speak of soil degradation to edify the general public, especially small-scale farmers, and for the involvement of science institutions in model legislation.

In relation to Zambia, the country's constitution makes reference to scientific research within the context of environment and natural resources generally, while the Environmental Management Act has several provisions that encourage the use of scientific research in sustainable environmental management. These provisions, however, do not make specific reference to soil sustainability, while in Cameroon it is noted that there is a need for data that speak of soil degradation to edify the general public,

43 Moore et al. (2018).

especially small-scale farmers, and for the involvement of science institutions in model legislation.

The fundamental importance of soils in supporting agriculture and forestry is widely recognised, with many examples of the drastic consequences of soil loss. However, in addition to the basic functions of supplying essential nutrients, water, oxygen and support for plants, we now better understand the many other essential services provided by soils in terrestrial ecosystems. Soils are a critical part of the hydrological cycle and can moderate flood risk and contribute to water purification. Moreover, soils contain massive quantities of carbon which, if released into the atmosphere, substantially accelerate the pace of global warming and associated climate change. Fully functional soils support a biodiverse ecosystem, which is essential for the stability of ecosystem functions and to suppress soil-borne diseases, while also providing a potential source of genetic resources. Moreover, although soils are the result of natural processes, these processes are exceedingly slow and – from the perspective of human lifetimes – soils need to be regarded as a non-renewable resource. Some of the scientific processes that affect soil health negatively include erosion, compaction, decline in organic matter content, loss of soil biota, and diffuse contamination. Soils play an important role in achieving half of the United Nations Sustainable Development Goals (SDGs), specifically SDGs 2, 3, 6, 7 and 12–15, which relate to food security, human health, land management including land restoration, water security, climate change and biodiversity preservation.

Intensive farming often leads to the depletion of soil nutrients. Conventional wisdom holds that farmers have a direct interest in maintaining the productivity of their soils (an argument often used politically as to why there is no need for governments to intervene), but the scale of erosion suggests that soil conservation measures are not being properly adopted or implemented.

All the different kinds of practices in crop growing that result in soil degradation need to be monitored. Information and communication technologies should be used in communications and data collection relating to different soil-related agricultural practices across the different ethnic and cultural set ups in the countries and regions of Africa.

5.1.6 Recommendations

Generally, it is to be recommended that national governments implement regulations on soil pollution and limit the accumulation of contaminants beyond established levels in order to guarantee human health and well-being, a healthy environment and safe food. The lack of awareness about the significance of soil is an obstacle against achieving sustainable soil management. There is a need to increase awareness and understanding of the profound importance of soil for human life, and to educate the public about the crucial role soil plays in food security, climate change adaptation and mitigation, essential ecosystem services, poverty alleviation and sustainable development. This can be effected through agricultural legislation which takes into account or addresses the fact, that practices that may compromise or restore soil health and sustainability are well known; standards on good practices are needed to establish clear requirements regarding impacts, monitoring, effectiveness and implementation; while some unsustainable practices such as the use of chemical fertilizers and pesticides and the slash and burn technique are *stricto sensu* illegal in terms of already existing legislation in the three countries. It is recommended that such unsustainable practices should be prohibited first. Secondly, there is a need to establish adequate mechanisms to ensure enforcement of such prohibitions.

The Stockholm and Rotterdam Conventions on the control of pesticides and chemical fertilizers should be implemented in national provisions. Thereby, adequate standards for fertilizers and pesticides could be set. The inclusion of adequate sanctions in legal regulations such as fines or imprisonment is recommended. There is a need for qualitative and quantitative communication on what soil is, and how soil relates to sustainability, crop production and economic development. Lack of communication limits the consideration of the role of soil as an answer to sustainable economic development.

Extension services are an appropriate means of overcoming these kinds of communications challenges. Besides information dissemination, extension services can provide guidance and support in respect of actual physical soil health and agricultural practices.

Information derived from soil research must be made available to the scientific community, soil users (e.g., farmers, agronomists, foresters, civil engineers) and society as a whole. This would ensure that knowledge is transferred and shared with stakeholders, decision makers, land-use planners, politicians and others.

Traditional knowledge could be an important source for setting adequate standards and to ensure respect for cultural perceptions of land. Thus, there is a need to systematically collect and synthetise traditional knowledge in order to preserve cultural heritage and to balance modern and traditional attitudes and approaches.

The soil–science discourse must continue to expand beyond its traditional identification with agriculture as it becomes a partner in the earth, ecological and environmental sciences.[44] Adequate institutional settings are required for law implementation and enforcement. Here the recommendations in the respective country reports should be considered. Continuous monitoring is needed. Soil testing on a regular basis would be one option. As unsustainable practices are often caused by poverty and insecure living conditions, a system of soil stewardship payment or other economic incentives should be considered.

44 Usman & Kundiri (2016: 66–70).

5.2 Agriculture – livestock

5.2.1 Summary of three country reports

Livestock keeping is practised in many countries because of the suitability of the climate and the availability of vast grazing lands in Africa. Livestock farming has been a main driver of soil degradation because of the large numbers of cattle that most farmers keep. Overstocking has led to erosion and lack of soil protection, leading to the destruction of important ecosystems.

In Kenya, the Third Millennium Term Plan (2018–2022) notes that low soil fertility is one of the main challenges that agriculture faces. Kenya is the fourth largest livestock farming country in Africa. The rangelands in most pastoral farming regions tend to be stocked with large herds of cattle. The high livestock densities cause soil compaction which renders the environment conducive to soil erosion. In order to avert this mismanagement by pastoral communities, a number of projects have been adopted to improve soil fertility and ensure sustainable livestock farming in the region, such as the National Soil and Water Conservation Project (NSCWP) and a clear definition of grazing rights on community land.

In Cameroon, livestock farming is conducted mainly by using free-range techniques on communally owned lands. This leads to a reduction of quality pastures available for these animals. Cameroon is a leading livestock farming country, according to its report. Livestock farmers keep large numbers of cattle and other ruminants, which trigger burning of more natural vegetation, especially forests, in order to allow for the expansion of grazing areas. Livestock keeping, being a main driver of soil degeneration, leads to a reduction in food production and stocking capacity. In order to curb these problems, the country has established the Ministry of Livestock, Fisheries and Animal Industries to ensure mass tracts of land are established for effective cattle farming.

In Zambia, livestock accounts for about 35% of the national agricultural output. The main concentration areas are the western and southern provinces of the country. The animals kept are mainly goats and cattle, which are run in increasing numbers every year. Owing to this increase, the rural communal lands have become inadequate for animal rearing, thereby increasing their susceptibility to overuse – which results in unsustainable land use. A number of laws have therefore been put in place to ensure that livestock agriculture is regulated, and this ensures the curbing of soil degradation.

5.2.2 Public law

There are a number of laws that have been enacted in each country to ensure that livestock farming is regulated. In Kenya, certain activities that degrade the soil have been prohibited. Section 64 of the Forest Act prohibits practices such as de-pasturing or allowing livestock in any forest areas in order, with the aim of keeping the tree cover at an acceptable percentage. Any person who cuts down trees for livestock purposes will be liable, on conviction, to imprisonment and/or a fine. The Community Land Act provides that grazing rights be consistent with the community grazing routine. Grazing rights may be granted to a non-member subject to the conditions set out by the members. The Physical and Land Use Planning Act does not extensively cover land-use practices nor, owing to population pressure, land predominantly for livestock keeping and farming affected by urbanisation. Large numbers of livestock are seen in urban areas due to inefficient zoning regulations. Deforestation is a serious issue in Kenya and reforestation initiatives are a major focus of the government's forestry policy. This is a vital intervention in the quest for soil health.

In Cameroon, there are a number of policies in respect of livestock keeping regulations. The National Action Plan for the Fight against Desertification (NAP-FAD) identifies a couple of activities that may cause desertification. The objective of the policy is to reduce the effects of the problems associated with livestock farming.

In Zambia, the following practices have been adopted. Section 45 of the Forest Act of 2015 provides that the minister may issue a conservatory order for natural resources on land in open areas to ensure that they are conserved. This includes the manner in which livestock are watered, managed, pastured and moved. This ensures that soil is conserved. Animal health is equally important in ensuring sustainable land practices as provided for in the Animal Health Act. In ensuring soil protection, any other practice on land should be considerate of animal health to prevent the reduction of livestock.

5.2.3 Findings

Extension services are crucial in providing important information to farmers and livestock keepers, and especially in encouraging successful adoption of new research findings to ensure effective land use practices in order to conserve the soil.

Kenya generally has a weak extension service system. However, efforts have been made to ensure the protection of the soil. Extension officers offer guidance to livestock farmers on the sustainable use and conservation of soil. The National Policy for the Sustainable Development of Northern Kenya and Other Arid Lands also provides a platform for strengthened research and extension systems for soil conservation. The government has ensured that funds are provided for effective soil protection through the National Environmental Trust Fund. Cameroon, being a member of the African Soil Partnership, has reached a great milestone. One pillar of soil conservation is that it encourages investment, technical cooperation, policy, education, awareness and extension in respect of soil. This ensures that any livestock practices carried out consider the need for physical soil protection.

In Zambia, extension services are important in ensuring that farmers are sensitised to the right way to use land for grazing purposes while protecting soil. Any farmers found in contravention may be liable for criminal and civil prosecution.

In the three countries, farmers can adopt certain appropriate agricultural practices to prevent soil degradation. These may include extensive livestock farming, rotational grazing, agroforestry (which may promote the use of livestock manure as fertilizer), strategic placement of livestock watering points and adherence to judicious stocking rates and carrying capacity. An agricultural area plan may be adopted setting out the areas where grazing may be carried out. With this, soil will be well conserved.

In the three countries, extension officers have been employed to ensure that information is effectively conveyed to the farmers. This information concerns appropriate agricultural practices, soil protection and the different causes of soil degradation. The information also covers the available laws and policies that govern livestock farming. A thorough training may be offered to the farmers in their different regions. The main problem with this is an overlap of roles between the national and county extension officers (in Kenya), which may lead to some not performing their duties or an exchange of roles.

The involvement of researchers is to identify the possible causes of soil degeneration through livestock keeping and to come up with possible solutions, which policy makers then extract and look into as they formulate different policies. This approach ensures that a scientific model is adopted for the planning, implementation and monitoring of land-use practices. A mix of agriculture and pastoralism may be adopted as per the sustainable land management report. This will ensure that greater productivity of the land, reduced soil erosion, improved soil nutrient status and efficient water use are achieved. Grazing pressure management may also be employed. It ensures that the number of livestock that can be accommodated in a given area is assessed in order to protect the vegetation cover, soil and water in a given area. It may also be useful to improve the soil–carbon dynamics protecting the soil structure. The science–policy interface also arises in considering the impacts of the use of chemicals for animal health on soil health.

Kenya has a number of institutions and administrative bodies, from governmental bodies, research organisations, the private sector, non-governmental organisations and local community structures. Communities have the advantage of ensuring administration over grazing lands by determining the activities that are carried out and who is to carry out the activities. This is as per the Community Land Act. This ensures that any livestock activities degrading land are evaded. The involvement of different extension officers also ensures that the livestock practices carried out on land are in accordance with the set-out standards. Involvement of all the institutions ensure that soil is protected, and that livestock increase is regulated. The Agriculture, Fisheries and Food Authorities Act should ensure that it includes the subject of livestock in order to ensure a synchronised soil protection system.

Cameroon has different systems to ensure a smooth system of soil administration in livestock governance. The Ministry of Agriculture and Rural Development oversees the implementation and evaluation of different government policies. This ensures that soil protection is observed in all agricultural spheres, which includes livestock keeping. The Ministry of Livestock, Fisheries and Animal Industries is largely involved in the implementation of policies that look into reducing soil degradation caused by animal husbandry practices. This ensures that soil is conserved. The different extension services also offer a smooth administration of livestock practices which are friendly to the land.

Zambia has different local authorities, local communities, non-governmental organisations and traditional institutions that oversee the need for administration of land-use practices in respect of livestock use. The Minister for Forestry is instrumental in drawing conservatory orders with regard to watering, moving and pasturing livestock. There are a number of skilled personnel with the task of ensuring that the policies are implemented. This ensures that soil is conserved.

5.2.4 Recommendations

Taking the analysis of the three country studies into account, the following recommendations were drawn up: First, environmentally unsound practices should at best be prohibited. In this context, negative effects on forests and effects which may risk increased desertification should be scrutinised. As far as possible, environmentally sound practices with regard to the protection of soils should be determined and approved as legally binding standards. Extension services need to be strengthened in order to better inform and consult to farmers concerning legal standards and acceptable practices. To establish clear incentives, sanctions such as fines and imprisonment should be part of the whole regulatory concept. As provisions are senseless without implementation, an appropriate institutional setting is required. The science–policy interface is important in this context as well. Finally, as settlements such as villages and cities will be subject to sprawl over the next years, a zoning concept needs to be established and enforced in the context of spatial planning on a regional level and for town planning.

6 Industry, mining, infrastructure and urbanisation

6.1 Industrial facilities

Industry is a potential further driver of soil degradation. The magnitude and the degree of the potentially negative effects depend on the level of industrialisation in a particular country and on the regulatory approach to deal with the effects. Generally speaking, the level of industrialisation in African countries is low although it needs to be recognised that there are quite big differences. Nevertheless, most African countries strive to accelerate the establishment of additional industrial plants first in order to allow for processing of raw material to increase income by experts, and second and more generally to increase national wealth. Thus, the industrialisation, the potential effects on soils and the appropriate regulatory approaches are important topics with regard to achieving sustainable soil management.

The following sections will provide for the three countries, Cameroon, Kenya and Zambia, a summary of their levels of industrialisation and their current legislation with regard to industrial facilities. Thereafter, options on how to establish an appropriate regulatory regime to ensure sustainable management of soils relating to industrial facilities will be presented. To this end, concepts established in other national legislation will be consulted.

6.1.1 The country studies' findings

6.1.1.1 Cameroon

Generally, Cameroon is characterised by a very low level of industrialisation. As such, most of the raw materials extracted from the country undergo very little transformation within the country. The main industrial sites in Cameroon are the coastal industrial region with the Douala zone being the largest industrial concentration. It is important to bring to the fore that as a significant proportion of the industries in Cameroon are not certified with an international environmental management organisation such as the International Organization for Standardization (ISO 140001) series, which states that industries have to internalise their externalities on the environment. Thus, some of the solid and liquid wastes (chemical effluents) are not treated appropriately.[45]

Another soil degradation problem relates to oil and gas exploitation refinery activities by the National Refining Company (SONARA) in Limbe. The government has committed to becoming an emerging economy by 2035, and industrial development has a major role to play in achieving this goal, as outlined in the Vision 2035 and the Growth and Employment Strategy Paper (GESP) that serves as the country's compass for emergence by 2035. Cameroon is also endowed with rich natural resources that will provide industries with raw materials.

At present, there is no specific legislation governing the industrial sector in Cameroon. The sector today is regulated through an array of laws and regulatory instruments governing other sectors such as forests, water and waste management provisions. For a specific industrial activity, such as a petroleum operation, a prior authorisation is

45 Ekane & Oben (2001); Fogwe et al. (2001).

required under the new Petroleum Code.[46] The operator is obliged "to carry out, at his own expense, an environmental and social impact assessment" pursuant to Article 92 of the Petroleum Code. There is therefore the need to develop a legal instrument that will govern industrial development in Cameroon.

6.1.1.2 Kenya

Kenya is an average industrialised economy serving both local and export markets in sub-Saharan Africa. Although the industries are mainly found in cities and major towns, a sizeable number of industries are found in agriculture-rich areas to cater for the value addition of agricultural produce.[47] Industrial activities produce effluent that is often deposited on soil. Persistent organic pollutants are often found adjacent to industrial facilities. As a consequence, reduction in soil fertility and unbalanced soil nutrition has also been reported frequently.

The current government has identified industrialisation as one of the major focus areas with the hope that industry will create employment opportunities and boost the economy. It thus sees industrialisation as a key development option. The proponent of any project specified in the Second Schedule will undertake a full environmental impact assessment study and submit an environmental impact assessment study report to the authority prior to being issued with any licence by the authority, provided that the authority may direct that the proponent forego the submission of the environmental impact assessment study report in certain cases. In undertaking environmental impact assessments, proponents of projects have automatically been undertaking soil environmental impact assessments.

The public needs to be involved during the assessment of the environmental impacts. For establishment and operation of industrial facilities, a prior authorisation taking into account the results of the environment impact assessment is required. Suitable standards could be determined by the competent authority. The competent authority could impose "environment restoration orders".

6.1.1.3 Zambia

The manufacturing sector accounted for about 7.8% of the country's GDP and an average annual growth rate of 3% from 2006 to 2015. The 2005 and 2014 Labour Force Surveys showed that there were 166,143 persons employed in the manufacturing sector in 2005, which increased to 223, 681in 2014. The manufacturing sector was pivotal in

46 Article 4 of the Law No. 2019/008 of 25 April 2019: Establishing the Petroleum Code.
47 Government of Kenya, The Presidency (2017).

economic development as it played a key role in the backward and forward linkages to economic growth. Zambia has a National Industrial Policy which took effect in March 2018 and recognises the vast natural resources wealth of the country. The vision of the country is to be an industrialised and competitive nation with a diversified, innovative and globally competitive industrial base which contributes to sustainable growth and employment creation by 2027.[48]

The National Industrial Policy is motivated by the aspirations of the Country's Vision 2030 which aims at transforming Zambia into a prosperous middle-income economy. The policy identifies nine specific objectives, one of which is central to sustainable soil management: to promote environmentally sustainable industrial production through the adoption of cleaner technologies; promotion of environmental certification; streamlining environmental impact assessment procedures; promoting compliance to environment management regulations by enterprises; and promoting capacity-building and awareness in industries to enhance environmental protection.

Pursuant to Article 29 and 26 of the Zambian Environmental Management Act, projects that may have an effect on the environment require a written approval by the competent agency. For all industrial facilities which potentially discharge contaminants, an environmental impact assessment is required. The law furthermore requires the establishment of a strong inspectorate system.

6.1.2 Recommendations

In order to determine the potential options for good soil governance with regard to industrial facilities, it is necessary to elucidate the major soil threats involved with industrial activities. Industrial facilities may primarily cause contamination via the emission of hazardous substances via air, water or other means. In addition, physical soil threats like compaction may be caused by the establishment and operation of industrial facilities. The establishment of industrial facilities may also give rise to detrimental effects on particularly valuable compartments of soil – taking into account the particular fertility of soils, a high level of soil carbon or of biodiversity – e.g. swamps or other compartments. The three country studies have documented that, first, there are already many industrial facilities and that, second, all three countries intend to promote industrialisation of their economies.

It could be recommended that a regulatory regime should first address soil degradation, in particular by contaminants, which has already been caused by existing facilities, and, second, should avoid future negative effects by both existing and new facilities. In order to set clear requirements with regard to contamination, soil quality standards for the most crucial parameters such as lead, cadmium, mercury, benzopyrene and

48 Mulimbika & Mahbub Karim (2018).

others should be adopted. The soil quality standards should be conceptualised as maximum tolerable concentrations in the soils in order to ensure that the ecological functions of soils are maintained. The standards could be adopted by subordinated legal instruments such as ordinances. Experience clearly documents that standards are much more effective if they are legally binding.

In case of already existing contamination, the regulatory regime should require the restoration of the contaminated area. Usually, the operator should be held responsible and should bear the costs of the rehabilitation measures according to the 'polluter pays' principle. The above-mentioned standards are of eminent importance as they determine generally the required level of restoration. Furthermore, the future use of a specific spot should be taken into account owing to the potential negative effects on human health. A site which is to be used for food production or for the establishment of a kindergarten requires a higher soil quality than a future industrial installation.

In addition, a soil restoration fund to which all operators of industrial installations should contribute financially seems to be a reasonable proposition. In cases where the operator responsible for the restoration is insolvent or cannot be identified or has left the country, the restoration measures can be financed by the resources available in the soil restoration fund. Alternatively, or even additionally, the obligation of operators to submit securities may be advisable.

In order to avoid or at least reduce future soil contamination by industrial facilities, it is essential to establish a regulatory regime that such a facility must not be established or operated without prior written authorisation – which is the case in Cameroon (only for petroleum activities), Kenya and Zambia. Such a regime should be clear, ambitious and participatory. For the sake of clarity, it is recommended that the categories of industrial installations for which an authorisation is required should be listed in a subordinated legal instrument such as an ordinance. Such a list which could determine the relevant industrial activities which may cause negative effects for the environment, and thus, for soils too, would be extremely helpful for the competent authorities and would help to improve law implementation and enforcement. From the perspective of operators, it would be very instructive and would ensure clarity.

An environmental impact assessment, including an environmental impact study, should be used as baseline to decide whether an industrial activity can be permitted or not. In this context again, the above-mentioned standards for soil quality are of eminent importance. Taking these standards into account, the competent authority is in a position to decide whether the emissions to be expected from an industrial facility are acceptable or not.

The environmental impact assessment (EIA) should be conducted by the operator and at his or her expense, as in most African states governmental institutions lack financial resources. It could be assumed that foreign investors, in particular, are usually able to bear these costs.

General public and civil society organisations should be involved in the permission procedure. They need to be invited to comment on the plans of the operator and, in particular, on the environmental impact study. Their comments should be taken into account by the competent authority. A new industrial facility is an important issue in most African countries; thus, society needs to be involved in the decision-making.

Furthermore, the operator should be committed to monitoring continually whether the requirements which have been included in the authorisation are complied with. The monitoring should be at the expense of the operators. The competent authorities should be empowered to control the industrial activities in order to check whether they are in line with the legal requirements and, if necessary, to enforce measures in case of non-compliance.

In addition, a regulatory instrument could be established which clearly sets an economic incentive for the operators of new industrial installations to avoid negative effects on soils. In order to maintain soil functions, the operator could be required – before production starts – to examine and document the status of soils beneath the industrial site in a so-called 'baseline report'. The baseline report should be part of the documents required for the application for a prior written authorisation. Furthermore, it should be regulated that after the closure of the site, the operator has to rehabilitate the site to the original status of the soil and groundwater, if significant negative effects have been caused.

This regulatory concept was first adopted by the Industrial Emissions Directive of the European Union in 2010. The combination of the baseline report and the obligation to rehabilitate the site to its original status, create an incentive to avoid negative effects on soils. It seems to be important that the public is involved in the decision-making process after the closure of the site in order to ensure a regular pattern of behaviour of the authorities in charge.

This conceptual approach is probably only applicable in cases where the soil threat is relatively limited in terms of spatial extension. It cannot be applied in cases of diffuse sources or very large areas, e.g., agriculturally used plots, as the assessment and documentation of the status of larger parts of soil compartments would simply be too time-, resource- and cost-consuming. With regard to the protection of particularly valuable soil compartments, planning instruments seem to be necessary. Competent administrative bodies should be empowered to determine areas which should be excluded from industrial uses and potentially also to determine go-areas for industrial facilities. Thereby, it could be ensured that particularly valuable soil compartments could be protected.

6.2 Mining

Mining has had a major impact on soil, water and biota since ancient times,[49] and documented examples from around the world abound of heavily contaminated soils associated with mining activities.[50] The mining process includes metal smelting to separate minerals – which introduces many pollutants into the soil through the release of huge quantities of heavy metals and other toxic elements into the environment which persist for long periods, and can be dispersed by wind and water erosion over long distances to eventually reach agricultural soils. For example, high levels of lead and copper have been found in agricultural fields located near a tailings dam in Namibia[51] and toxic concentrations occurred in agricultural soils and crops in India, resulting in a high risk to human and livestock health.[52] This situation is similar to the general outlook in Cameroon, Kenya and Zambia. Moreover, mining leads to the removal of topsoil and to the use of wide plots on the surface which could be used for other purposes. From a practical point of view, after closure, mining areas should be rehabilitated to a good environmental status.

6.2.1 The country studies' findings

6.2.1.1 Cameroon

Cameroon is richly endowed with vast mineral deposits which facilitate the ongoing large-scale mining in the country. The country has huge mining potential, as exploration studies have shown a wide range of sub-surface precious minerals. As noted in the opening remarks to this section, mining presents numerous adverse effects on soil quality, owing to toxic chemicals and acidic water which are released into the environment during and long after mining processes. These changes affect the chemical composition of the soil and the high toxicity of chemicals makes the soils unsuitable for plants to thrive. Furthermore, mining alters the flow of nitrogen through a stable soil-plant-microbial ecosystem. Most of the mining companies in Cameroon exploit the mineral resources with impunity and do not take into consideration the protection of the environment. The environmental status in these areas have been reported to be negative with serious implications for soil degradation since the wastes generated are not treated before disposal.

49 FAO & ITPS (2015).
50 Alloway (2013).
51 Mileusnić et al. (2014).
52 Kumar & Maiti (2015).

Cameroon is one of Africa's most attractive new mining destinations for international investors. In this respect, the government has developed a Minerals Policy to ensure the continual development of the mining industry in the quest to diversify the economy and harness the natural resources for the development of the country. Mining operations take place in the natural environment with serious threats to soil quality. Although legislation governing mining activities in Cameroon addresses environmental problems such as soil degradation and provides for soil protection, it also contains some weaknesses that incentivise soil degradation.

Mining law regulates the search for, discovery, exploitation, detention, transportation, transformation and commercialisation of mineral substances. The role of foreign investors in mining in Cameroon is significant; local Cameroonians do not possess the technical equipment and the necessary technology for mineral exploration and exploitation. Consequently, the country always solicits the intervention of foreign investors. These investors have to comply with the regulations in force relating to their line of activity. Unfortunately, these foreign investors are not usually preoccupied with the responsibilities of environmental protection. It has been noticed that investors are usually in no hurry to obtain environmental authorisations before launching their activities. This is why, once a site has been exploited, the investors care little about reinstating or rehabilitating the exploited site. These dilapidated sites constitute a threat to the host populations and lead to soil degradation. In addition, both foreign and local investors use chemical products that are unhealthy for humans and the environment, such as mercury which is used illegally on sites. Therefore, the responsibility for environmental degradation, notably soil degradation, is shared between the state and the other stakeholders, who are both explorers and exploiters.

6.2.1.2 Kenya

Kenya is a mineral rich country with huge deposits of fluorspar, gold, soda ash, coal and titanium in coastal areas. Other known minerals include manganese, iron ore, gypsum, diatomite, chromite, limestone, and silica sand. In anticipation of the discovery of new minerals and oil deposits, the country adopted its first-ever Mining Policy in 2016 to enable the country to reap maximum benefits in future. As already noted, mining and related activities are responsible for loss of biological diversity, increased soil erosion, contamination of soil due to huge deposits of chemicals used in excavation and mining, and contamination of surface and groundwater.

Although the EMCA provides for environmental protection, its enforcement and observance are not as effective as would be expected. For instance, it is a requirement that an environmental impact assessment (EIA) should be carried out before embarking on any project likely to have a negative impact on the environment. In many cases, no such assessments are carried out in the extractive industry and, if carried out, they do not meet the legal threshold. For instance, in *Cortec Mining Kenya Limited v Cabinet Secretary Ministry of Mining & 9 Others,* a titanium extraction licence was cancelled on the grounds that an EIA had not been carried out despite mining having started. The establishment of the Lamu Coal Plant at the Kenyan coast was also halted by the National Environmental Tribunal in *Save Lamu & 5 Others v National Environmental Management Authority (NEMA) & Another* for, among other reasons, failure to carry out an EIA to the required legal standards. These cases illustrate how environmental laws that could protect and conserve the environment, including soil, are disregarded.

The law lays down requirements for site restoration and mine-closure plans. The Cabinet Secretary will not grant a prospecting licence, a retention licence or a mining licence to an applicant, unless the applicant has submitted site mitigation and rehabilitation, or mine-closure plans for approval. The Cabinet Secretary may prescribe regulations for site rehabilitation and mine-closure obligations, which are relevant to soil sustainability. The law also provides for Environmental Protection Bonds.

It is important to note that most of the mining operations in Kenya are small-scale, artisanal and informal, and, as such, the majority do not obtain mining licences. For instance, the artisanal gold mining areas of western Kenya have reported high soil pollution as miners continue to use metals illegally, such as mercury and lead in gold prospecting. Therefore, the environmental impacts arising from this can be unmitigated and, in mining, soil is the most compromised natural resource.

6.2.1.3 Zambia

Mining plays an important economic role in Zambia through employment creation, revenue generation and rural urban development, among others. With little success, the country has continued to make efforts to reduce copper dependence and support the diversification of the economy to other minerals, such as gemstones and other minerals outside of mining. Despite the enormous economic benefits associated with mining activities, there are a number of negative impacts. Additionally, quarrying is increasing as a result of heightened demand for aggregate materials for use in the booming construction industry. Although quarrying has brought socioeconomic benefits, especially for the informal sector, it is usually uncontrolled and illegal, particularly in urban areas. Rising negative environmental impacts include land degradation, groundwater quality deterioration, soil contamination, air and surface and groundwater pollution, formation of sinkholes and erosion. Other notable environmental impacts include deforestation, loss of biodiversity and formation of acid rain.

The Mines and Minerals Development Act, No. 11 of 2015 (MMDA) is the main legislation governing mining in Zambia, read together with the Mines and Minerals Development (Amendment) Act, No. 14 of 2016. The MMDA establishes the Mining

Licensing Committee which considers applications for mining rights and non-mining rights, and the grant, renewal and refusal of mining rights and non-mining rights in Zambia. The committee is also responsible for terminating, suspending and cancelling mining rights and non-mining rights, amending terms and conditions of mining rights and non-mining rights, and advising the Minister on matters relating to its functions under the MMDA. These outlined functions do not specifically point out that soil sustainability matters are at the forefront of the conditions to consider before granting or varying a mining right. Given the nature of mining activities, however, it is argued that failure to implement measures aimed at securing soil sustainability must be explicitly stated as a condition for denying mining rights.

Further, the MMDA prohibits exploration, mining or mineral processing without a licence or environmental impact assessment granted by the Zambia Environmental Management Agency (ZEMA). Furthermore, the MMDA mandates the committee to take the following into consideration: the need to conserve and protect the air, water, soil, flora, fauna, fish, fisheries and scenic attractions; the features of cultural, architectural, archaeological, historical and geological interests; and the need to ensure that any mining or mineral processing activity prevents any adverse socioeconomic impact or harm to human health, in or on the land over which the right or licence is sought. While some of the provisions are quite unspecific and leave room for interpretation which could stand in the way of an effective implementation, the provisions of the MMDA are, overall, progressive and would be effective in sustainable soil management and environmental protection.

6.2.2 Recommendations

The challenges with regard to the implementation of environmentally sound mining are diverse. First of all, mining activities by foreign investors need to be treated differently from national enterprises and small-scale mining. With regard to mining operations by foreign investors, the recommendations about tenure rights and control of foreign investors have to be considered and applied. More generally, further recommendations could be made. All recommendations which have been submitted with regard to industrial installations are equally valid for mining operations, such as the restoration obligation for already occurred soil contamination; the requirement of a written prior authorisation based on an environmental impact assessment and involving the public; and the establishment of effective monitoring.

It is important that the maintenance of soil quality is established as one assessment criterion for granting permission, either via an environmental impact assessment or as a single legal requirement. Law enforcement seems to be a specific challenge. A specific challenge is the regulation and control of small-scale mining. It is hardly possible to allocate sufficient resources so that the effective enforcement of 'good provisions' is doable and small-scale mining becomes well controlled. Three measures seem to be more promising: First, security of land tenure could avoid wild and uncontrolled mining as people would be certain about their possession and this would hinder negative effects on their property. Secondly, awareness-raising might offer a chance that people would look for other opportunities to make their living. Thirdly, if the carrot does not provide sufficient incentive, the stick might work. In other words, severe penalties in case of law infringements around mining operations may create a public perception that illegal small-scale mining is risky and thus less attractive owing to probable penalties.

Functioning land administration systems play a vital role in providing land tenure security. Outdated, non-transparent and overlapping land tenure laws can weaken community property rights and foster corruption. Understanding the complexity of African land tenure systems can also harness the increase in large-scale land acquisitions, often also referred to as land-grabbing in various African countries.

6.3 Infrastructure

6.3.1 The country studies' findings

In Zambia the infrastructure such as roads and communication facilities are underdeveloped. This is mostly in the rural areas. Lusaka plays a significant role in regional air transportation. There are poor network facilities in most of the rural areas. The main mode of transport is via road, and most of the roads are not well developed. The use of roads seems to affect soil structure and quality owing to compaction. The railways built in Zambia mainly serve the needs of the mining sector. The Ministry of Housing and Infrastructure Development manages Zambian infrastructure. Some of the challenges facing the infrastructure system in Zambia are the over-investment in road networks, which then affect soil use, and the subsequent neglect of these rural networks. The railways attract low traffic volumes, and the Lusaka airline connectivity is declining owing to competition from other counties such as Kenya and Tanzania. In addition, access to electricity is only at 20% in Zambia. This therefore lags behind the utilisation of soil and also development in the rural areas.[53]

In Kenya, as in Zambia, the main form of infrastructure is roads. The rate of infrastructural development in Kenya is a bit more moderate than in other countries such as Zambia and Cameroon. The state of roads is not too bad, and the road transport network covers a larger area in the country. Energy production is also good in Kenya, and power is supplemented by neighbouring countries. Railway transport is being improved and Kenya now has a standard gage railway. Air transport is well-developed,

53 Foster & Dominguez (2011).

and Kenya Airways is one of the most developed airline companies in the region. Internet connectivity is faster in the urban areas and internet accessibility is fair across the country.

Some of the challenges that affect the Kenyan infrastructure are the poor drainage system, adverse weather conditions, and poor management. Roads management also faces challenges of governance between the county government and the national government. The managing body that regulates infrastructure in Kenya is the Ministry of Transport, Infrastructure, Housing, Urban Development and Public Works.

In Cameroon roads are the main form of transport infrastructure. Cameroon also makes use of a relatively high performance CAMRAIL. CAMRAIL is one of the most intensely used transport networks in sub-Saharan Africa. Cameroon further has port services similar to those of Kenya, and the country is a natural air-traffic hub for central Africa, as demonstrated by relatively high traffic levels.

The summary outcome of the three countries concludes that their main transport network is road. Other forms of infrastructure such as buildings and internet accessibility experience various challenges, which are relatively similar. Negative effects on soils are mainly caused by degradation of valuable soil compartments through sealing, compaction and contamination. The challenges are comparable to those of mining and industrial installation, both from the perspective of environmental protection and from the fact that foreign investors are often involved in constructing infrastructure such as roads.

6.3.2 Recommendations

First of all, it is recommended that the measures suggested to control foreign investors need to be implemented. Furthermore, the recommendations with respect to industrial installations should also apply for better protection of soils threatened by the construction of infrastructure. The effective protection of soil quality needs to be a crucial criterion, either through an environmental impact assessment or as one of the legal requirements of a permission procedure. Along with these governance-related recommendations, it seems to be advisable that African governments consider investing in other forms of transport, such as railways to reduce CO_2 emissions and potentially negative effects on soils. Finally, increased internet connectivity is important to develop a basis for gathering, and to synthesise and publish data on soil quality and status. Through internet, awareness can also be increased.

6.4 Urbanisation

Africa is an exceptionally biodiversity-rich continent which is urbanising rapidly, to the detriment of its natural resources. Currently, the continent has "seven megacities, that is cities with populations over 10 million: Cairo, Kinshasa, Lagos, Accra, Johannesburg–Pretoria, Khartoum, and Nairobi. In 15 years, Luanda and Dar es Salaam will be added to this list."[54] Although urbanisation is a necessary condition for modernisation, there is an increasing need to account for its direct and indirect impacts on the continent. With soil being the lifeline of biological diversity and ecosystem services, it is clear that there is an urgent need for sustainable urbanisation in Africa.

The high levels of urbanisation in Africa have led to the development of slums, in which high poverty levels; poor air, soil and water quality; insufficient water availability; waste-disposal problems; and diseases manifest themselves.[55] This generally contributes to greater demand for land for commercial use, social and economic support institutions, transportation, and residential developments – with the consequence of rapid environmental degradation. Eventually, these activities put pressure on sustainable soil management. Urban expansion that takes place in forests, wetlands and agricultural systems leads to habitat clearing, degradation and fragmentation of landscapes. Urban lifestyles are largely consumptive, requiring vast quantities of natural resources and generating increasing amounts of waste, and also lead to increased levels of air, water, and soil pollution. As the global urban population increases, so does the generation of waste. In both developing and least developed countries, high rates of population growth and increasing waste and sludge production, combined with lack of municipal services to deal with waste management, create a dangerous situation in many ways, and particularly as a breeding ground for diseases that are also likely to contaminate soils.

6.4.1 The country studies' findings

Poor urbanisation and industrialisation processes are singled out as not auguring well for environmental protection and soil restoration in Cameroon. The consequential pressure to discharge significant volumes of effluent and other wastes leaves soil health out of the equation, owing to weak enforcement of environmental laws, institutional lapses, and corruption. In addition, poor planning is one of the major reasons for soil contamination. For instance, in Douala, industries are located on a more elevated terrain while the human population is concentrated downstream. The ensuing challenge of managing liquid waste becomes difficult and culminates in a negative impact

54 Güneralp et al. (2017).
55 Koop & van Leeuwen (2017: 387).

on public health and sustainable soil management. In theory, urban and spatial planning laws and policies in Cameroon guarantee sustainable management of natural resources – the environment and soil resources in particular. Such planning laws and policies ought to help direct certain activities away from ecosystems that need special protection.

Rapid urbanisation is among several drivers of soil degradation in Kenya, just like in the other two African countries. Urbanisation contributes to degradation of agricultural soils – which in turn threatens food security. In summary, the ensuing pressure on natural resources and the wider environment weakens soil sustainability. In addition, Kenyan planning laws have historically not kept up with the needed effective planning and management of urbanisation processes through provision of adequate and decent housing, sanitation and infrastructure. In this regard, the law did not have effective regulatory mechanisms to deal with rapid urbanisation, population pressure and emergent land.

Zambia is one of the most urbanised sub-Saharan African countries, with 42.1% of its population living in urban areas. The country has a characteristic linear population growth along railway lines, where most urban centres are located. Urban residents generally have relatively better access to public services and infrastructure compared to their rural counterparts and experience greater development, resulting in clear distinctions in human settlements between urban and rural areas and between different regions of the country. The ensuing high levels of urbanisation place immense pressure on the government to find land for new settlements, and at times at the expense of land designated for ecological preservation, such as forests, protected areas and other ecologically sensitive hotspots. Further, high levels of urbanisation influence a number of other activities which have a negative impact on the physical properties and pollution levels in soil. For instance, water scarcity is already a major problem for the world's poor, independent of the effects of climate change – which is projected to further reduce water availability in many water-scarce regions, particularly the subtropics. Meanwhile, water availability is a significant factor in maintaining soil sustainability, and close to two million more Africans are expected to find themselves without adequate clean water in the near future, as a result of unsustainable urbanisation. This will most likely lead to an increase in poverty and pandemics, such as malaria and cholera. These public health concerns will put further pressure on natural resources such as water and soil.

6.4.2 Recommendations

In order to manage the effects of urbanisation processes in African states, routine, well-coordinated town mapping needs to be put in place. To come up with effective town planning, the required information on natural resources (soil) and human population needs to be available and to be taken into account.

Legal instruments such as mandatory town planning can only be effective if they are applied reasonably with a long-term development perspective, if sufficient information is available in order to justify decisions, and if the town planning is accepted as stirring for the subsequent authorisation of buildings and infrastructure. In addition, it should be obligatory to base town planning decisions on environmental impact assessments which necessarily include soil quality.

To achieve sustainable soil management, enhanced digital soil mapping tools could provide a cost-effective means of determining soil geographical distributions.

7 Clarity of land tenure

7.1 The country studies findings

Land tenure types and policies strongly influence land-use practices and hence affect the quality of soils in Africa. Land tenure in Africa – both statutory and customary – is characterised by insecurity, constituting a potential underlying driver of soil degradation in general and specifically in Cameroon, Kenya and Zambia. There are different kinds of land tenure types giving rise to conflict and unsustainable land and soil management in these countries, which may arguably be a reflection of what obtains on the entire continent. For instance, there is ample evidence where customary rules prescribe acceptable claims to land among members of communities, but such claims are contradicted or nullified by national legislation. Communally 'owned' lands, in particular in Cameroon and Zambia, are insecure. Consequently, such lands are easily converted into national lands for development purposes. This conflict between the land tenure systems, both statutory and customary, leads to rising land tenure conflicts.

One reason for the insecurity of owned land is the high economic value presently placed on land and its appurtenant resources. This has invariably increased the tendency of the most powerful to engage in land grabbing and dispossession in Africa. This is to the detriment of the vulnerable groups that are increasingly being displaced from their lands, which triggers disputes and conflicts. In fact, customary land tenure systems offer weak security, and the modern land law provides huge opportunities for land grabbing. For instance, there is a law in Cameroon which enables the state to obtain possession of any piece of land regardless of who the owner is. This law thus not only completely ignores traditional undocumented systems of land ownership, but it is also questionable in terms of the rules of legitimate expropriation. Land titles and leases are the only legal means of claiming property rights to land. Even though it is generally known that the tenure rights of the land of local communities were established long before the state came into existence, most lands are classified as national and state-owned despite century-old claims by communities.

In addition, all three countries have weak governments and a problem with corruption. All three countries' soil management systems are linked to corruption, which contributes to the inefficiency of the law. Especially in Cameroon, land register registration processes are therefore often incorrect. Sometimes, for instance, more than one land title is given for the same property, which leads to conflict. The generosity of land tenure legislation in Africa to the most powerful leads to the insecurity of owned land.

The various pieces of land legislation in Cameroon and Zambia are completely devoid of soil protection provisions. This means, in particular, that the land tenure systems of Cameroon and Zambia are silent regarding the question of the environmental landowners' and users' responsibilities. Reading through the segregated and dispersed pieces of national legislation on land, one does not find much expressed or implied that refers to the need to protect soil. Thus, land law in some countries is not only incoherent in terms of two systems co-existing and governed by segregated and ambiguous pieces of legislation, but it is also equally incomplete as it fails to address the need to protect soils.

These drawbacks in the land laws are not infrequently a legacy of colonial history, which has been reinforced by the modern post-colonial administration with the objective of exerting supremacy over vulnerable communities and for economic interests without due consideration of the need to protect the environment. Colonisation has influenced and encouraged the following drawbacks: the non-legalisation of customary land holding; the fact that the state owns most of the land; and the practice of land grabbing and dispossession of local communities' land by the state and its powerful allies; the challenges of land access and rights; and the high costs and cumbersome procedures involved with obtaining land titles. All of these factors have serious implications for soil degradation.

In contrast to Cameroon and Zambia, Kenya to a large extent has a rich land law with socioeconomic and ecological aspects that decisively support sustainable soil management and protection. In terms of ownership and rights over land, in particular, Kenya's land law seems exemplary. Land law takes into account aspects of conservation, environment and cultural heritage that are relevant to soil protection when developing, cultivating or using public land. This includes, for example, the conservation and management of land-based natural resources and makes provisions for grazing rights (overgrazing is one of the causes of soil degradation on rangelands on the continent). Environmental impacts have to be taken into account in the development, management and use of the land, according to the applicable environmental laws. Furthermore, the Community Land Act empowers registered communities to make rules or by-laws for regulating the management and administration of their land. These rules may provide for the regulation of investments into the land; the determination of terms for any leases granted for purposes of investment; the conservation and rehabilitation of the land; land use and physical planning; and any other relevant matter.

Despite the environmental considerations of land use guaranteed by the Kenyan land tenure system, the various pieces of statute have not yet been effective in the management of land and, by extension, have not enhanced the protection of soil in Kenya.

Corruption, political patronage, weak institutions, and ineffective development control institutions have also affected land-use planning and therefore poor soil management. In addition, the legislature's planning laws were too slow to respond to dynamic development to cope with rapid urbanisation, population pressures, and emerging rural development. This has led to indiscriminate extension of urban boundaries in areas of land, which are still used predominantly for farming and livestock keeping. Land use in Kenya's urban areas does not conform to existing zoning and building regulations. Agricultural lands have rapidly been converted into concrete jungles and industries have sprung up in areas zoned for agriculture.

The 2019 Physical and Land Use Planning Act has addressed some of these issues. Effective implementation of the Act will contribute to sustainable soil management. Of concern, however, is the failure of the Act to address the duplication and parallel setting up of institutions in the county government and national government. This is likely to continue to affect sustainable soil governance, because there is no guaranteed vertical and horizontal institutional coordination. Such coordination would bring the administration closer to the population and lead to effective public participation in decision-making.

7.2 Recommendations

With the exception of Kenya, one does not find a strong anchor point for soil protection when perusing the countries' legislation on land tenure. None of the scattered pieces of related legislation in Cameroon and Zambia make any direct or implicit reference to the need to protect soils. Also, despite Kenya's rich land law that lends support to sustainable soil management and protection, the various statutes have not been effective in the management of land and, by extension, have not enhanced the protection of soil in Kenya.

The main challenges of poor planning, corruption, political patronage, weak institutions and institutional conflicts have been largely disregarded. It is these shortcomings that prompted the following recommendations: It is recommended to reduce the multiplicity of legal instruments and requirements on access to land by means of harmonisation and consolidation of the fragmented and dispersed pieces of legislation on land tenure in a single and comprehensive overarching land act. Moreover it may be advisable to formulate new legislation in such a way that it recognises customary laws relating to land tenure or, at least, so that it ensures that procedures for access to land are comprehensible and accessible to all social groups. Preferably, land acts that harmonise and consolidate the fragmented and scattered pieces of legislation on land tenure should be enacted in these countries and customary and statutory land tenure should be given equal status. Alternatively, such land acts should recognise and accord legal protection to customary land rights and consider such rights as a category of private property existing alongside national lands and state-owned lands. This may be accommodated within ongoing land tenure reform processes.

It is important to mainstream the responsibility to protect the environment, especially soils, in the harmonised and consolidated legislation on land tenure. Therefore appropriate and clear vertical and horizontal institutional arrangements need to be crafted that make for a win-win situation in order to curb or completely put an end to institutional conflicts, as these are negative precursors to sustainable soil management initiatives. This needs to be complemented by means of enhanced measures to fight corruption and to build institutional capacity in land administration matters.

8 Control of foreign investors

Foreign investors constitute one of the main groups of actors responsible for soil degradation in many African countries such as Cameroon, Kenya and Zambia, necessitating their effective control. The increased role of foreign investors across many economic activities in these countries can possibly lead to downward spiralling effects in land and soil degradation. Their role as main actors of soil degradation in these countries is much felt in the mining and agricultural sectors. Therefore, foreign investors constitute some of the actors to be considered in the process of developing model legislation for soil protection in these countries and the whole of Africa. The role of foreign investors in the mining sector is significant.

Cameroon, in particular, is endowed with huge deposits of liquid, solid and gaseous minerals that have attracted a handful of foreign investors. In the same vein, Kenya and Zambia are endowed with hard minerals that have in equal measure attracted foreign investors to the mining sector. All three countries have extensive fertile lands that favour large-scale agriculture.

In fact, Africa is considered today as the new preferred destination for agricultural investments, but this brings serious environmental impacts such as deforestation and soil destruction. It is quite unfortunate that foreign investors are often not preoccupied with the concerns of environmental protection. Not only that they are usually in a mad rush to launch their activities before obtaining environmental authorisations, and once they have exploited mining sites, the investors care little about reinstating or rehabilitating the exploited sites. These neglected sites lead to soil degradation. Foreign investors are also involved in the illegal use of chemical products such as mercury in the mining sector and fertilizers and pesticides in the agricultural sector, which are unhealthy for the environment, polluting water bodies used by communities and destroying soils and attendant biodiversity.

8.1 The country studies' findings

8.1.1 Cameroon

Regarding the control of foreign investors, especially as far as compliance with public law is concerned, the institutional dispositions of Cameroon give every public administration operating within their respective areas of competence the power to control and monitor all investments and investors, including foreign investors. For instance, the administration in charge of hydrocarbons ensures the respect of the regulation in force in that sector such that every investor must conform to the provisions of the petroleum code. This equally applies to soil and subsoil wherein the administration in charge of water makes sure that investors in this domain respect the provisions of the water regulation in force. The administration in charge of mines ensures that investors comply with the provisions of the regulation in force in this sector. This same principle applies in the domains of agriculture, forestry and environmental protection. Despite the power given to each administration to ensure the respect of the regulations of the different sectors by investors, it is common to see clandestine operators who do not carry out their activities in conformity with the regulation in force or who do not comply with legal texts in the respective sectors. This situation may be due to the deplorable and corrupt attitudes of some administrative authorities charged with the responsibility to oversee these situations. These are some of the situations that cause environment degradation in general and the degradation of soils in particular. For instance, once these clandestine operators exploit a given site, they usually abandon it without reinstating or rehabilitating it.

The Law on private investment[56] in Cameroon treats all foreign investors equally irrespective of their countries of origin. This law makes reference to an organ[57] that provides information to any foreign investor with respect to his or her type of activity.

Regarding the acquisition of land for investment, the land tenure laws of the three countries give equal access to both nationals and foreigners. All applicants are required

56 Law No. 2017 / 015 of July 12, 2017 to modify and complete some of the provisions of Law No. 2013 / 004 of April 18, 2013 on the encouragement of private investment in the Republic of Cameroon.

57 The Cameroon National Investment Corporation.

to consult with communities occupying or harbouring a parcel of land which is an object of acquisition.

In Cameroon, for instance, Ordinance No. 47/01 of 6 July 1974 to establish the land tenure regime in Article 10 provides the following: Natural persons and corporate bodies of foreign nationality or incorporations wishing to invest in Cameroon may conclude lease agreements or purchase landed property except in the border areas. Deeds drawn up for this purpose will bear the prior approval of the minister in charge of lands, under penalty of being declared null and void. The visa of the minister of external relations and the minister in charge of lands is required when diplomatic and consular missions as well as international organisations seek to acquire land in Cameroon. In the event of resale, the state always has a pre-emptive right of purchase over the property, taking account of the initial price, developments carried out and amortisation.

The Cameroon Mining Code[58] equally provides in Article 106 that upon the signing of the mining agreement, the state, after consultation with the affected populations, can grant to the mining operator the lands necessary for the mining of the discovered mineral substances, in accordance with the laws and regulations in force. However, practices do not always match legal prescriptions as there are usually some unfair or illegal land dealings in which, in collusion with the government, foreign investors enter into possession of lands and mining concessions without complying with legislation requiring "free prior and informed consent" (FPIC) from affected or concerned communities. Such practices have been known to degrade the environment in general and soils in particular.

The taxation system in Cameroon is fair towards foreign investors who are subjected to the general tax regime in the same way as national investors. There is a sole tax code that applies to all investors – both national and foreign – in a uniform manner. For each budgetary year, the draft finance bill, which contains the tax provisions/column to be levied on all investments, is prepared by a single authority – the Ministry of Finance and voted into law as the Finance Law by Parliament. According to Law No. 2018/012 of 11 July 2018 relating to the financial regime of the state and other public entities, the domain of taxation is regulated by a single administration in Cameroon which is the Ministry of Finance. In effect, even though it is provided in many legal texts, the tax provisions of these texts are elaborated upon by the ministry in charge of finance, otherwise all the other ministries will have to seek the opinion of the said ministry regarding the financial provisions to be inserted in any legal document. It is these two texts that determine the financial gains expected to be paid into the public treasury and in all sectors of activity. It should however not be that some legal instruments grant tax exemption for a certain period and tax reduction to

58 Law No. 2016/017 of 14 December 2016 repealing Law No. 001 of 16 April 2001 establishing the Mining Code and its modification by Law No. 2010/011 of 29 July 2010.

both national and foreign investors exercising in specific domains or exporting their products, etc.

8.1.2 Kenya

Kenya has enjoyed a steadily improving environment for foreign direct investment (FDI). Yet, corporate social responsibility (CSR) efforts in applying international standards relating to human rights, business ethics, environmental policies, community development, and corporate governance can still be improved.[59] Moreover, Kenya needs to address internal challenges, repurpose its infrastructural projects, and focus on wider regional integration to address the rising competition. For a long time, Kenya was the largest and most dominant economy in eastern Africa in terms of gross domestic product and socioeconomic development in the areas of poverty alleviation, literacy, healthcare, income, civil liberties and freedoms, infrastructure, and industry, among others. However, Rwanda and Ethiopia have recently been chipping away at Kenya's dominance. Of particular concern for the country is the need to address corruption and taxation schemes, which have increased the cost of doing business and reduced foreign investment attractiveness.

8.1.3 Zambia

The current legal and institutional framework concerning foreign investors in Zambia comprises the Constitution, applicable sectoral and tax legislation, the Zambia Development Agency Act, Companies and Business Regulatory Acts, and all other allied policies and institutions created thereunder. Foreign investment in Zambia is heavily reliant on land use and natural resource capital. Most of the targeted investment opportunities in Zambia are in key economic sectors, namely energy, forestry, mining and agriculture. As these sectors are land–soil related, it makes it critical to enhance the sustainability measures that are in place. There are inadequate regulatory frameworks and weaknesses in the rule of law which have allowed investors and the Zambian elite to circumvent legal requirements. Four major challenges which are common to all four key sectors (energy, forestry, mining and agriculture) in Zambia limit the capacity of the country to regulate sustainable investment, including limited incentives that support sustainable land-use investments; insecure customary land tenure with limited processes enshrined in the legal framework to uphold social safeguards, such as consultation with land users; low institutional capacity to enforce the social and

59 See https://www.state.gov/reports/2019-investment-climate-statements/kenya/, accessed 5 September 2020.

environmental safeguards that are established in the law; and limited access to information on investments in Zambia, which reduces the potential for public scrutiny and participation. Thus, the legal and institutional framework in Zambia, particularly its implementation and enforcement should be strengthened. This will lead to more effective regulation of sustainable investments that adhere to social and environmental safeguards.

8.2 Recommendations

Improving the legal control of foreign investors is critical to guarantee the effective protection of soils. Such control is crucial in order to ensure that land-use investments are sustainable and that the laws of the countries are being observed. This can be done through the enactment of laws imposing environmental degradation taxation, such as for pollution or soil contamination, to be paid by all (foreign and domestic) investors. Legalisation of certification schemes of commodities production susceptible to causing soil degradation is need as is the promotion of land reforms that limit the amount of land that can be acquired by foreign investors or specifying area of land depending on the activity to be carried out. Fostering commitment of foreign investors to corporate social and environmental responsibility or business/corporate citizenship needs to be achieved so as to avoid social conflicts with communities. This is a self-regulating paradigm, which can help foreign corporate investors to be socially accountable to the public, thereby avoiding activities that are likely to degrade the soils on which the public depends. Therefore, corporate social responsibility (CSR) should result in foreign investors increasingly respecting the environment and promoting sustainable development practices. In the era of globalisation, different approaches to such practices will also allow a more effective protection of soils. In this light, CSR must go beyond legal obligations, but cannot be reduced to an expression of charitable compassion. It must penetrate all foreign investment practices in Africa, placing the peculiarities of the continent in relation to the benefit of any undertaking.[60]

Lastly, mobilising investment for sustainable development in Africa requires political commitment to overcome substantial barriers at various levels. To enable new markets for sustainable development requires adequate regulatory frameworks (international, regional and national) in order to give investors, the necessary confidence. The national state has to balance the interest of attracting (and securing) international investment while promoting peace and security for its population. The most appropriate approach for achieving both of the aforementioned is adherence to and promotion of the rule of law, while creating incentive structures for investors to act sustainably

60 Ruppel & Tchuente (2018).

and to respect national social development goals, empowerment policies, labour standards and human rights.[61]

9 Institutional and procedural aspects

9.1 Institutional arrangements

The focus of the following section is on the implementation, control, monitoring and enforcement of the substantial provisions. This is a trivial statement which is at the same time both factually correct and important. Good governance depends on both good regulations and effective implementation. In other words, without effective implementation, the law itself is useless. Insufficient or ineffectual law enforcement is often a core issue in developing countries, in particular in counties of sub-Saharan Africa.[62] The following section is thus of great importance. The section is spilt into two subsections. In the first, options for more effectively arranging and coordinating the competencies and roles of the authorities are discussed. In the second, the procedural rights of citizens and civil society organisations, such as access to information, public participation and access to justice, are analysed and recommendations are presented.

9.1.1 Competent authorities: Responsibilities, coordination and internal procedures

The following subsection discusses how effective implementation and enforcement of the substantial provisions of governmental institutions, meaning competent authorities, can be achieved. Thus, the subsection deals with the internal arrangements of the governmental institutions and provides recommendations on how these arrangements can be structured in order to heighten efficiency. Each country study reflects its own internal organisation of governmental entities (ministries, agencies and authorities) and the respective competencies and rights of these entities. Moreover, the organisational structure is undergoing constant change for pure political reasons, but also for reasons of efficiency and more. It would therefore not be particularly instructive to inform about the specific current situation in the three countries. It is of more informative value to inform about the most important, most pertinent challenges in the three countries. Overall, although to a different extent, implementation and enforcement of

61 Ruppel & Shifotoka (2017).

62 Cf. for example: Kameri-Mbote et al. (2019); Ruppel & Kam Yogo (2018); Ruppel et al. (2017); Ruppel & Ruppel-Schlichting (2016).

existing provisions are weak. Essentially, several reasons are mentioned: lack of personal and financial resources, lack of expertise, and insufficient equipment. However, these aspects belong more to the endowment of the governmental entities and will not be discussed further in this subsection.

As one internal constraint to an effective and efficient management (i.e., the precondition of law implementation and enforcement) overlapping competencies have been reported. Often, several ministries are responsible for the same issues and they work in parallel. Simultaneously, non-existent and insufficient coordination between entities on the same level (ministries and federation) is a further reason for inappropriate law enforcement. Having ministries working on the same issue is, per se, not a big issue. It only becomes an issue if these actions remain uncoordinated. Furthermore, the competencies of different levels (federation, regions and municipalities) are often not clearly defined, which weakens effective law enforcement. To sum up, going by the three country studies, it appears that insufficient decentralisation of competencies is – generally speaking – an issue that needs to be addressed.

9.1.2 Recommendations

As already stated, the efficiency on the ground depends on both appropriate provisions and effective law enforcement. In order to be effective, several management tasks have to be implemented by governmental bodies (or private institutions have to be managed by the governmental bodies in order to fulfil the specific tasks). The most relevant tasks should be elucidated. An appropriate arrangement of institutional roles and competencies requires that these tasks are clearly and undisputedly attributed to specific entities. First of all, information on soil conditions and soil quality associated with ongoing activities which might affect soils and technological options needs to be gathered and disseminated among at least the competent authorities. In particular, the information gathering on soil conditions and soil quality is demanding in terms of time and human and financial resources. It requires a lot of measurements, in a high spatial solution. Without this information effective soil management could hardly be established.

Secondly, the management task requires standard setting. This, again, is a complex, demanding and time- and resource-intensive task. Standards are important as they enable competent authorities to implement the quite vague legal provisions (e.g., protection of soils). Furthermore, standards inform potential operators what they have to comply with. Standards should, in particular, be established for soil quality with regard to soil health and physical parameters (e.g., for soil carbon, biodiversity and organic matter). These quality standards are particularly important as they define what level of interference is tolerable. In addition, emission limit values for contamination and technical standards for used equipment can also be helpful and instructive for the competent authority.

Thirdly, soil authorities need to be involved in prior permission regimes for activities which might have negative effects on soils, such as industrial installations, the use of pesticides, and the construction of roads, highways and railways. Soil authorities should be able to identify soil concerns based on their particular soil protection expertise. Monitoring of soils is a further important task. This means that a competent authority should observe how specific soil compartments develop over time. This task is interlinked with the task of information gathering.

Finally, competent authorities need to control compliance and have substantial provisions to do so, and, where necessary, to enforce compliance by operators, in particular, and citizens, in general. Chiefs of local communities usually have quite a strong position in African countries. It would be beneficial if their roles, responsibilities and oversight are clearly regulated and would dovetail with the existing arrangements of other governmental powers.

Sustainable soil management must be achieved taking into account the local specificities. From this perspective, it seems to be reasonable to strengthen the decentralised entities, at least at the level of regions and to a certain extent at the level of municipalities or local communities. It nevertheless needs to be ensured that the legal provisions have to be considered and to be abided by. To re-arrange the institutional settings and to clearly define the competencies and roles of the various entities and, further, to decide which entity is superior and has a control function over another is, all in all, a process that courts dispute, as clarity also may mean not being responsible for specific aspects and to lose (or have no) power over certain aspects. Thus, in order to provide incentives for such a decision-making process, clear advantages and benefits need to be shown for society and, at best, for all actors concerned. These advantages and benefits will gain the political buy-in which is needed to be successful.
In the following list the potential advantages and benefits are highlighted: Clarity concerning the procedures should inspire trust in the process. People tend to regard a decision as legitimate if it is taken because of already established procedure. Clarity concerning the procedures also enables good governance. If the procedure is clearly and appropriately defined, it seems likely that decisions are taken on the basis of reason as the required information and expertise have been considered. Clarity concerning the procedures allows for accountability, reliability and transparency – all of which are ingredients of a modern and well-established civil society.

While the reputation of states could be enhanced – even at international level, more clarity would also establish a level playing field for all – including foreign investors.

A positive regulatory environment for fair and responsible investors should be formed, in order to expel detrimental foreign investments. Workable arrangements for institutions and procedures would ensure that respective states would probably be in a better position to deal with future challenges – such as the effects of climate crisis, poverty and hunger and more.

9.2 Institutional setting and more effective procedures

In the following sections, various options are recommended. All these recommendations should be considered in order to achieve effective law implementation and law enforcement.

9.2.1 Drafting legislation in institutional settings is important and demanding

As mentioned above, the detailed determination of the specific roles, competencies and responsibilities of the various governmental entities is extremely important, in order to be able to implement the substantial provisions effectively. The determination has, at best, been made by legal provisions in order to have a clear system in place which cannot be questioned, and entities can rely on. It is important to stress that the determination of the specific roles, competencies and responsibilities is a demanding issue. This determination on its own is a political and substantive matter. It makes a real difference whether experts with pure agricultural expertise implement soil protection provisions or whether experts with specific environmental knowledge are in charge. It is also crucial which level (federal, regional or local) is considered responsible. It is clear that the procedure determines the outcomes. Thus, although this decision-making process could be time- consuming and pretty conflicting, experience clearly shows that it is worth the effort invested.

9.2.2 Coordination and clear distinction of competencies are essential

It needs to be underlined that a precise determination of roles, competencies and responsibilities is of enormous importance. It has to be legally stipulated which ministry is responsible for which driver and for which task. Only via such a clear and legal determination of roles, competencies and responsibilities can conflicts and overlaps in competencies be avoided. Conflicts could cause major disputes, which require effort and energy to resolve – energy which could be better invested in supporting, fostering and finally achieving sustainable soil management. Overlaps in competencies can immediately lead to conflicts, but they can also give rise to a situation where none of the competent bodies actually deal with an issue, as they await a move from another entity.

Moreover, it needs to be clarified how governmental bodies should and could cooperate. It needs to be determined whether another body has to be involved and consulted, and what rights this other body has in legal terms. One option is that another body should be consulted, meaning it should be heard. There would then be no obligation to follow the statements of the other body. A second option is that the other body should have a veto right. That would mean that the authority in charge has to follow the advice of another body. Both aspects – which body should be involved, and what rights this body has – should be legally fixed.

9.2.3 Decentralisation of responsibilities is key

A further point to be considered is whether and to what extent competencies and responsibilities should be attributed to decentralised governmental entities. In general, decentralised competencies seem to be more effective mainly for two reasons. First, the regional specificities can be better assessed and taken into account by a competent authority which is familiar with the regional conditions. The alternative is a central body. It seems quite unlikely that a central body could be structurally in a position to be knowledgeable on the local and regional specificities throughout the country. The same is true for the involvement of local and regional stakeholders. Secondly, trust in decentralised administrative expertise and responsible behaviour is likely to be stronger. A precondition however is that the decentralised governmental entities responsible for sustainable soil management are sufficiently equipped with respect to competent staff and hardware.

9.2.4 Determination of appropriate level that is necessary depending on the management tasks

As pointed out above, there are several management tasks which governmental entities should be responsible for. The following tasks have been identified: Information gathering; standard setting; involvement of soil authorities in prior written authorisation procedures; monitoring; and control and enforcement.

It needs to be decided which would be the appropriate level to take on the various tasks. The final decision certainly depends on the specific conditions in the various countries. Nevertheless, in the following paragraphs an option is presented to underline the importance of considering the right level of competence and responsibility. Information gathering is both a management and a scientific task. As stated above, information is essential for good governance. As information on the status of soils can only be gathered at local level, local or regional entities need to be in charge of collecting this information. The compilation and synthesis should be done at national level. In this way it can be ensured that the information is made available and accessible for all local and regional entities. Concerning information gathering, cooperation between the national, regional and local level has to be established.

Standard setting must primarily be allotted to the national level. Standards should be applicable throughout the country. Concerning the involvement of soil authorities in prior written authorisation procedures, it seems to be reasonable to relegate this task to the regional or local level. In the decision-making procedure for an industrial installation, for example, the local conditions and specificities need to be taken into account. A competent authority on regional or local level should usually be better equipped to deal with local challenges and to involve local stakeholders.

The same goes for environmental monitoring, as well as for control and enforcement. Also, in the context of these tasks, the allocation to local or regional level seems to be more efficient as the knowledge on local specificities should usually be with the respective competent local or regional bodies.

9.2.5 Further mechanisms to avoid poor law enforcement

Further mechanisms to avoid poor law enforcement – which seems to be a challenge throughout Africa – comprise two aspects. First, bodies need to be equipped with sufficient resources with regard to both staff and hardware like furniture, IT equipment and computers. Secondly, the mechanisms required all seem to be instruments of public control, such as access information, public participation and access to justice. These aspects are considered in the following subsection.

9.2.6 Specific control mechanisms of communities' chiefs

Local chiefs play an important role in most African countries with regard to the living conditions in the local communities. Their roles, competencies and responsibilities vary considerably, also the mechanisms to keep them accountable via instruments like documentation of their decisions, reporting to governmental entities, and random control. Cases have been reported where local chiefs have misused their powers either to neglect the requirements of environmental protection or to make short-term and unjustified earnings – sometimes to the disadvantage of the local communities which they represent.

Sustainable soil management on the local level (in the local communities or the villages) needs full awareness, support and fostering by local chiefs. Soils provide ecological functions for all, but sustainable soil management must be implemented locally. Thus, there is room for improvement. First, it seems to be reasonable that local chiefs receive more support and advice from soil scientists. Second, local chiefs must be seen as part of the whole soil-related administrative structure. Third, decisions by local chiefs must be taken via a transparent and inclusive procedure. Fourth, similar procedural rights of citizens and the general public should apply to decisions by local chiefs about, among others, access to justice. The general aspiration should not be to more severely control local chiefs, but to enable them to do more for sustainable soil management.

9.2.7 Optional: extension of water authorities to water and soil authorities

Water is an issue in most African countries, thus in most, if not all, African countries there are water ministries and a complex administrative setting of competent authorities. A simple and perhaps promising approach would be to add the responsibility for sustainable soil management to the water-related entities. From a scientific point of view, this seems to be well-founded, as soil and the aquatic compartments like surface and groundwater bodies are very much interlinked and interdependent. If there is water scarcity, for example, soils are immediately affected. Thus, to manage soil and water compartments in an integrated manner is at least possible, if not reasonable. Therefore, the awareness of soil issues can be strengthened and there would be no need to establish a new administrative structure. The existing structure would just be extended with the topic of sustainable soil management. It would certainly to be discussed whether such an extension is politically acceptable. However, such an extension would also underline that soils are as important to the welfare of an African society as water, owing to the ecological services which are provided by soils.

9.2.8 National circumstances need to be considered and accordingly adapted

The recommendations presented before must be adapted on a case-by-case basis, because of differing national preconditions. There is no single blueprint which fits all systems. However, the options should be considered seriously.

9.3 Procedures and procedural rights

Effective procedures which allow for a thorough assessment of all relevant aspects before taking decisions and procedural rights of potentially concerned citizens are generally regarded as essential in order to achieve good protection. Procedural requirements and procedural rights can only be effective if implemented in practice, a challenge which has been addressed in the following subsection. In the following subsection four aspects are discussed: environmental impact assessment, access to information, public participation and access to justice. At the end, a recommendation is provided.

9.3.1 Environmental impact assessment

Environmental impact assessments (EIAs) in Zambia are under the responsibility of the Zambia Environmental Management Agency (ZEMA). An EIA is a requirement before any investment in land can be made. There needs to be an assessment of the effect of that investment or project on land and its components. An investment that has an adverse impact on the environment is not permitted. In Zambia, failure to undertake an environmental impact assessment contrary to law is a criminal offence. The importance of environmental impact assessments is that they enable the conservation of soil and the environment at large.

In Cameroon, it is a requirement for any developer or owner of a project to carry out an environmental impact assessment that evaluates the negative effect of the project on the environment. Both soft laws (policies) and hard laws (statutes) regulate EIA in Zambia. The procedures are clear and are well laid down, as are rules of conducting environmental and social impact assessment.

In Kenya, environmental impact assessments are an important issue cross-cutting all sectors. It is a requirement that any project must be subjected to an environmental impact assessment in order to evaluate its impact on the ecological system. This procedural right is managed by NEMA, which is an institution created under the EMCA statute. Soft law and hard law regulate EIAs in Cameroon, Zambia and Kenya.

In summary, all three countries have comprehensive legislation on environmental impact assessment. Failure to conduct an environmental impact assessment leads to a criminal offence. The regulatory bodies that manage environmental impact assessments are all created under a statute. The rationale of EIA in all three countries is to protect environment and to enhance sustainable development. However, there are some common challenges faced by the environmental impact assessment obligation in the three countries. The challenges include ineffective public participation in carrying out EIAs; inadequate personnel and over-centralisation; corruption; inadequate monitoring by the administration in charge of the environment; and procedural flaws in scoping, exorbitant administrative fees, and absence of an effective appeal procedure.

9.3.2 Access to information

The right of access to information is both an international right and a domestic right. It is an inherent right that is necessary in public participation and also in furthering other rights. In Cameroon, several international laws relating to access to information are recognised. The right is guaranteed under the Convention on Access to Information, Public Participation and Access to Justice in Environmental Matters (Aarhus Convention). The right is also guaranteed under the International Covenant on Civil and Political Rights (ICCPR). Principle 10 of the Rio Declaration also calls for access to environmental information.

In Kenya, access to information is a constitutional right provided in Article 35 of the Constitution of Kenya. The procedural right is also provided for in the Access to Information Act. Access to information is limited because of some reasons such as privacy and security threats. The problem with the access to information right in Kenya is that it is only guaranteed to citizens as per the dictates of the Constitution.

In Zambia, environmental information and other rights are analogous to access to information. These rights are not stipulated outright in any legal document, but they can be inferred from the mandate of ZEMA, which is required to disseminate environmental information. In the three countries, access to information seems to be an essential right in protecting other rights. Information is power and one cannot act without information.

Some of the common problems experienced in the procedural right of access to information among the three countries include limitations by law on the right to access information; inadequate legislation as seen in Cameroon and Zambia on access to information; secrecy and the unwilling nature of the government to provide information; and restriction of the right to specific cadres of people such as citizens in the Kenyan context.

9.3.3 Public participation

Public participation is one of the essential elements of good and democratic governance. It is the involvement of stakeholders in decision-making. In Zambia, public participation is a constitutional requirement and is also embedded in statutory law. The requirement is that, before any law or decision affecting the environment is made, public consultation must be done. In Zambia, public participation can be done directly or through elected representatives. In Kenya, public participation is also a requirement that has been mainstreamed in almost all forms and activities of governance. It is also provided both in the Constitution of Kenya and in numerous other relevant statutes.

In Cameroon, the requirement of public participation is provided in the preamble of its Constitution and also in statutes. It is a requirement that any decision that concerns environment needs to take into consideration the views and concerns of the public. In summary, the three countries recognise the duty of public participation in making decisions.

This procedural right is embedded in both the constitution and statutory laws of the respective countries. Public participation seems to be mainstreamed in various sectors in the three countries. It is also a tenet of good governance embraced by the three countries. It has also been used as a tool to protect the environment (including soil) from several threats such as overexploitation and abuse.

However, there are some common challenges experienced around the concept of public participation in the three countries. These include – among others - amorphous structures constituting public participation. In Kenya, there has been inconsistency in respect of the judicial decision on what constitutes public participation. This in turn requires legislation for clarity purposes in terms of implementation and enforcement issues; to address inadequate information affecting the quality of public participation, which undermine rights of minorities and marginalised, hinder governance issues and the rule of law.

9.3.4 Access to justice

Access to justice is one of the elements of natural justice. Justice needs to be served to all regardless of societal status. Access to justice in this sense is the access to courts of law or alternative dispute resolution mechanisms that are fair and impartial. Access to courts or justice must answers the following questions: Is there a system for identifying, preventing and resolving conflict between stakeholders such as litigation, alternative dispute resolution and administrative review? Has awareness of the system's existence been raised? Is it affordable and accessible? Does it provide timely results?

In Zambia, anyone who infringes laws that protect the environment (including soil) can be prosecuted in a court of law. Anyone whose bundle of rights has been infringed can also obtain justice from the ZEMA tribunal or courts. In Kenya, one has to exhaust other non-judicial means before approaching the court. This means that the tribunal and other administrative organs have to be contacted before heading to court.

The right to appeal decisions made by tribunals is guaranteed in Kenya, Zambia and Cameroon. Some of the challenges that affect the right of access to justice in the three countries include corruption; lagging of cases in courts; inadequate judicial officers; inadequate infrastructure and funds to support the justice system; and political influence in the administration of justice.

9.3.5 Recommendations

First of all, it needs to be stated that the four instruments, namely environmental impact assessment, access to justice, access to information and public participation should be part of the legal system to ensure that environmental effects are assessed systematically and comprehensively, and that citizens have the opportunity to obtain information, to participate in permission procedure on activities which are of concern to them, and to have access to justice. Moreover, it must be ensured that these instruments are effectively implemented. These are some of the proposals that may help to reduce the challenges that affect procedural rights: EIAs, access to information, public participation and access to justice.

The recommendations that pertain to the strengthening of these rights and, in particular, to ensure an effective soil protection environmental impact assessment should be mandatory by law for all activities which might have significant effects on soils; access to information on soil quality needs to be guaranteed; legislation should be enacted that defines the scope and structure of public participation in soil protection decision-making; resources should be invested in infrastructure that supports access to justice and other procedural rights in matters pertaining to soil protection; specialised courts on environment and land seem to be one option to strengthen the expertise of judges on soil and land topics both from a scientific and a legal point of view; programmes should be developed to raise awareness among the population of their right to access courts, to engage in public participation, and to access information and any initiatives that can facilitate the protection of soil.

Moreover, marginalised people, indigenous groups, minorities, women, youth and people with disabilities should be particularly educated and encouraged in the attainment of procedural rights such as EIAs, access to information, public participation and access to justice. The ministries of justice could be obliged to monitor the implementation of the procedural rights and to provide reports with regard to this implementation on a regular basis. Ultimately, legislation that consolidates and harmonises soil rights in African legal systems is an option that could create uniformity and cooperation in the advancement of soil protection. The African Union could play a specific role in this regard.

10 The role of science

10.1 The science and society interface

Soil science can raise awareness on soil organic matter as a key attribute of soils to illustrate its importance for soil functions and ecosystem services. Soil science can, among others, improve the transfer of knowledge about soils; contribute to educational programmes; facilitate communication with policymakers by framing research in terms that resonate with politicians in respect of the policy cycle or by considering drivers, pressures and responses affecting impacts of land use change; and help to realise the United Nations Sustainable Development Goals (SDGs) in the most effective manner.[63]

In his encyclical letter *Laudato Si*, Pope Francis in 2015 made a pronouncement on the care of our common home, stating "that human beings, endowed with intelligence, must respect the laws of nature and the delicate equilibria existing between the creatures of this world". He went on to say that "one authoritative source of oversight and coordination is the law, which lays down rules for admissible conduct in the light of the common good."[64] He further stated that "science and technology are wonderful products of a God-given human creativity" and "science which would offer solutions to the great issues would necessarily have to take into account the data generated by other fields of knowledge, including philosophy and social ethics".[65] Therefore, continued the Pope, "dialogue among the various sciences is likewise needed, since each can tend to become enclosed in its own language, while specialization leads to a certain isolation and the absolutization of its own field of knowledge."[66]

Increasing climate change has an impact on soils, slows economic growth, threatens food security, exacerbates social inequalities, harbours the risk of violent conflicts, and increases migration movements. Many countries have implemented national climate policies to accomplish pledged Nationally Determined Contributions and to contribute to the temperature objectives of the Paris Agreement on Climate Change. And while, in 2023, the global stocktaking will assess the combined effort of countries, it is already apparent that the implementation of those policies will leave a significant emissions gap towards the well below 2 °C and 1.5 °C Paris goals.

The question arises as to how legal systems can contribute to framework conditions, for example to better protect particularly vulnerable ecosystems and groups from the consequences of climate change. Legal systems are based on certainties and not uncertainties, while science can afford certain levels of uncertainty. In order to avert the climate crisis effectively and protect soils, the right degree of legal regulations and shifted incentives seem to be crucial in motivating individual and national action for more collective success. After all, the law depends on the statements and warnings of science. If the law reaches the limits of knowledge and thus certainty, it depends on references generated in other knowledge systems (science, economy, technology, ecology, etc.).

Given the complexity of soils and the degree of uncertainty around climate change, expert systems must serve the law to provide possible reliable references. Such high complexity levels are, of course, non-linear in nature and the types of prognosis possibilistic, probabilistic or conditional. And as such science must contribute to

63 Keesstra et al. (2016).

64 Cf. https://bit.ly/3tN9r9i, accessed 11 February 2021.

65 Ibid.

66 Ibid.

strengthen the resilience of individuals, societies and economies to systemic climate crisis phenomena. Science needs to inform the law and society of what cause is expected to have which effect and which concerted effects can either be prevented or constructed, and perhaps, above all, who determines what can be disregarded in the process.[67]

Crossing the divide between law and science raises the inevitable question of whether the legal profession is skilled enough to address the scientific needs of the legal system. After all, science and law have always existed together, and it is science which can enlighten the legal profession in revealing the truth to legislators and the courts in complex matters and by means of scientific advancement having an impact on the administration of justice.

10.2 Recommendations

The science and society interface is key in shaping effective laws and policies. Science must also inform the discourse on soil protection in Africa, which in turn must inspire new laws, policies and procedures that can deal with the state of crisis and enlighten a system that ensures that we 'leave no one behind' in the transformation towards more soil sustainability, resilience, equity, and justice.

In this light, science can help to develop indicators and standards that can guide the process towards more sustainable practices. Land degradation neutrality (LDN) interventions must be informed by science–policy interaction as a basis of responsible land governance and soil management. Effective cooperation between scientific institutions can contribute to an advancement of understanding and commitment through greater scientific engagement with stakeholders.

While universities are actors and institutions for academic and scientific diplomacy, the African Academy of Sciences and its various country chapters, the Council for Scientific and Industrial Research in South Africa, the Ghana Soil Information Service, the Cameroonian National Observatory for Climate Change and the Global Alliance of Universities on Climate are but a few examples of such emerging cooperation networks which can inform and promote research, policy development and implementation, technological innovation and entrepreneurship, and creation of jobs and relevant knowledge and skills, and also develop education and exchange programmes.

Ultimately, the independence of scientists from governmental influence and political agendas must be preserved, so as to avoid the perception that they are working towards preconceived political goals or agendas. Responsible decision-making processes also need to integrate traditional knowledge systems and citizen science.

67 Renn (2019: 26).

11 Global, continental and regional cooperation

Knowledge systems and infrastructure, citizen engagement, and international cooperation gain increasing importance in the protection of ecosystems, the mitigation of natural disasters, and the halting of biodiversity loss caused by changes in land use, direct exploitation of natural resources, and climate change. In this light, a green transition and energy access can foster partnerships with and within Africa and contribute to building a low-carbon, climate resilient future and fostering sustainable development.

11.1 The African Union

The African Union is the core mode of continental cooperation with its several organs – among them the Pan-African Parliament, and its various programmes. The Regional Economic Communities (RECS) allow for economic cooperation on a regional level. In particular, the recently approved Agreement Establishing the African Continental Free Trade Area may pave the way for intensified regional and continental cooperation, especially in economic terms.

There are 55 sovereign states which have committed themselves to be part of the African Union – with the African Union placing these states into five regional groups: Central, Eastern, Northern, Southern and Western Africa.[68] In order to be admitted as member state of the African Union, three requirements must be satisfied.[69] The first requirement is that the state wishing to join the African Union must be African; the second requires a majority vote of approval taken by the current member states for the inclusion of the would-be member; and finally the prospective member needs to sign and ratify the Constitutive Act[70] of the African Union of 2001.

Articles 3 and 4 of the Constitutive Act enumerate the objectives and principles of the regional organisation, namely: regional integration; peace and security; protection of human rights; non-intervention or promotion of state sovereignty; intervention in grave circumstances within member states; and respect for democracy and rule of law.

The Constitutive Act provides in Article 13 that the Executive Council coordinates and takes decisions on policies in areas of common interest to the member states. This includes foreign trade; energy, industry and mineral resources; food and agricultural and animal resources; livestock production and forestry; water resources and irrigation; and the environment and its protection.

68 African Union Commission and New Zealand Crown (2020).
69 Lamikanra (2018: 2).
70 Ibid.

Article 5 of the African Union Constitutive Act provides for the establishment of the following institutions: The Assembly; the Executive Council; the specialised technical committees; the Pan-African Parliament;[71] the African Court of Justice (and Human Rights); the financial institutions; the Commission; the Permanent Representatives Committee; the Economic, Social and Cultural Council; and other organs that the Assembly may decide to establish. Each of these has its own mandate and focus areas within the African Union.

African unity and solidarity outlined by the African Union's framework provides the continent with mutually beneficial scientific and technological advancements; a synergetic international cooperation policy; and significant economic development.[72] The African Union looks to intrinsically bind natural rights of the people and any right a member state may have when dealing with its sovereign development.

The African Charter for Human and Peoples' Rights has progressively taken up the issue of environmental protection by explicitly incorporating a human right to environment, a third-generation human right.[73] Article 24 of the African Charter for Human and Peoples' Rights reads, "All peoples shall have the right to a general satisfactory environment favourable to their development".

11.1.1 Vision 2063

The African Union Vision 2063: The Africa We Want. It obligates its signatories to speed up actions to ensure effective and territorial planning, land tenure use and management systems. The Regional Implementation Plan for African Soil Partnership provides several pillars and guidelines that help in the preservation and management of soil in Africa. For example, Pillar one promotes sustainable management of soil resources for soil protection, conservation and sustainable production.

Agenda 2063 has been lauded as the common continental framework for socioeconomic development. This framework strives to realise the African Union's fundamental goals of creating a union that has inclusive policies which are sustainable in their development and maintenance and implement policies to entrench pan-Africanism and ensure continent-wide prosperity. In this light, the African continent and its regions are also called upon to cooperate in ensuring that, among others, soil is conserved. This is done through legislation and numerous policies that ensure that all African countries are united in the struggle to preserve and manage soil use.

71 Also see chapter on the Pan-African Parliament of the African Union: Composition, mandate, partnerships and its quest for sustainable development in this volume.

72 Lamikanra (2018: 3).

73 See Ruppel (2008).

Agenda 2063 is rooted in the principles of the Constitutive Act, among other instruments, and it is said to be the 'blueprint for progress'. The First Ten-Year Implementation Plan of Agenda 2063, spanning 2014 to 2023, outlines a set of goals, priority areas and targets that the continent aims to achieve at regional, national and continental levels. Some of the past and current initiatives it builds on include the Lagos Plan of Action; the Abuja Treaty; the Minimum Integration Programme; the Programme for Infrastructural Development in Africa (PIDA); the Comprehensive Africa Agricultural Development Programme (CAADP); and the New Partnership for Africa's Development (NEPAD).[74]

11.1.2 African Convention on the Conservation of Nature and Natural Resources

The 1968 African Convention on the Conservation of Nature and Natural Resources (also referred to as the African Nature Convention or the Algiers Convention), and the forerunner to the 2003 Revised Algiers Convention, which is outlined in the next paragraph, is arguably one of the centrepieces of the African Union's environmental texts. This regional African Convention was originally adopted in Algiers in 1968 under the auspices of the Organisation of African Unity (OAU) and came into force in 1969. As such, it was the successor of the 1900 Convention for the Preservation of Wild Animals, Birds and Fish in Africa, which was later superseded by the 1933 Convention Relative to the Preservation of Fauna and Flora in their Natural State (also known as the London Convention). The need for a treaty to address nature conservation had already been expressed in the Arusha Manifesto of 1961. Hence, in 1963, the African Charter for the Protection and the Conservation of Nature was adopted, followed soon after by the Algiers Convention.[75]

The objectives of the 1968 Convention encouraged individual and joint action for the conservation, utilisation and development of soil for the present and future welfare of humankind, from an economic, nutritional, scientific, educational, cultural and aesthetic point of view. To this end, states undertake to adopt the measures necessary to ensure conservation, utilisation and development of soil in accordance with scientific principles and with due regard to the best interests of the people (Article II); to take effective measures to conserve and improve the soil and to control erosion and land use (Article IV); and to establish policies to conserve, utilise and develop water resources, prevent pollution and control water use (Article V). Furthermore, the Convention imposes on states the obligation to, among other things, protect flora and ensure their best utilisation, the management of forests and control of burning, land

74 See https://www.nepad.org/agenda-2063/about, accessed 12 July 2020.

75 Ruppel (2018: 124).

clearance and overgrazing (Article VI); and to conserve faunal resources and use them wisely (Article VII).[76]

The African Convention on the Conservation of Nature and Natural Resources of 1968 is one of the legislations that shows the cooperation in soil management in Africa. The legislation provides that state parties will take effective measures to prevent land degradation and to that effect will develop long-term strategies for conservation and management of land resources, including soil.

11.1.3 The African Ministerial Conference on the Environment

The African Ministerial Conference on the Environment (AMCEN) has a strong regional and sub-regional focus.[77] AMCEN thus builds on the potential that the RECs have to integrate adaptation measures into regional policies and socioeconomic development.[78] AMCEN is a permanent forum where African ministers of the environment discuss matters of relevance to the environment of the continent. It was established in 1985 when African ministers met in Egypt and adopted the Cairo Programme for African cooperation. The Conference is convened every second year. In the 2010 Bamako Declaration on the Environment for Sustainable Development, at the thirteenth session of the African Ministerial Conference on the Environment, the Conference's contribution in providing political guidance and leadership on environmental management to Africa since its creation in 1985 in Cairo was appreciated. AMCEN was established to provide advocacy for environmental protection in Africa to ensure that basic human needs are met adequately and in a sustainable manner; to ensure that social and economic development is realised at all levels; and to ensure that agricultural activities and practices meet the food security needs of the region. AMCEN's mandate includes guidance in respect of key issues related to multilateral environmental agreements, towards translating available climate science and current international climate policies in their effort to move towards practical implementation in the context of sustainable development.[79]

11.1.4 The African Continental Free Trade Area

On 21 March 2018, the Agreement Establishing the African Continental Free Trade Area (AfCFTA) was adopted by 44 African countries at a summit of the African Union

---

76 Ibid.
77 Ruppel (2018: 133).
78 Scholtz (2010).
79 Cf. AMCEN (2011).

in Kigali, Rwanda. This marked another significant milestone in the history of the African Union and an important step in achieving an African Economic Community (AEC) as envisaged by the Lagos Plan of Action and Abuja Treaty. The AfCFTA was created to bolster regional and continental economic integration. It is the largest free trade area outside the World Trade Organization (WTO) and a milestone set by Agenda 2063.[80]

As the focal point of African trade,[81] the AfCFTA is a framework agreement consisting of the Agreement Establishing the Continental Free Trade Area, Protocol on Trade in Goods, Protocol on Trade in Services, and Protocol on Rules and Procedures on the Settlement of Disputes.[82] It also envisages protocols on investment, intellectual property rights, and competition policy.[83] As an 'umbrella', the AfCFTA's goal is to harmonise trade by placing certain obligations on all signatory members with regards to a larger continental FTA.[84] It is expected that, under the AfCFTA, restrictions on direct foreign investment will be lifted, which will add capital to expand local industries and boost domestic businesses. Not only will the economy be stimulated by the upward productivity cycle caused by new capital, also banking systems could be stimulated, leading to more investment and consumer lending.[85] African companies will be able to enter new markets, which will expand their customer base and result in new products and services.[86] Importing raw materials from other African countries will become less cumbersome.[87]

Implementing the AfCFTA will also allow Africa to keep its global commitments under the Sustainable Development Goals (SDGs). In agriculture – still the largest employer on the continent – small-scale farms form about 80% of the production.[88] Many emerging African markets are traditional economies that rely on farming for employment. Small family farms cannot compete with large agribusinesses in high-income African countries such as South Africa, Kenya, Egypt and Nigeria.[89]

80 Magwape (2018: 355–357).
81 Ibid.
82 Tralac (2019: 1–4).
83 Ibid.
84 Magwape (2018).
85 Akeyewale (2018: 14).
86 Ibid.
87 Akeyewale (2018: 15).
88 Songwe (2018).
89 Akeyewale (2018: 14).

11.1.5 New Partnership for Africa's Development[90]

Another indication of cooperation is the Action Plan of the African Union New Partnership for Africa's Development (NEPAD) Environment Initiative. The plan seeks to build the resilience of landscapes within the African continent and particularly drylands and other vulnerable areas. NEPAD was initially adopted in 2001 in Lusaka, Zambia, by African Heads of State and the government of the OAU in 2001 and was ratified by the African Union in 2002. Its overall aim is to promote partnership and cooperation between Africa and the developed world, and it envisages the economic and social revival of Africa. Its founding document states:[91]

> This New Partnership for Africa's Development is a pledge by African leaders, based on a common vision and a firm and shared conviction, that they have a pressing duty to eradicate poverty and to place their countries, both individually and collectively, on a path of sustainable growth and development, and at the same time to participate actively in the world economy and body politic. The Programme is anchored on the determination of Africans to extricate themselves and the continent from the malaise of underdevelopment and exclusion in a globalising world.

A healthy and productive environment is a prerequisite for NEPAD.[92] Relevant to soil protection, NEPAD recognises that the region's environmental base must be nurtured, while promoting the sustainable use of its natural resources. To this end, the initiative targets eight subthemes for priority intervention: combating desertification; wetland conservation; invasive alien species control; coastal management; global warming; cross-border conservation areas; environmental governance; and financing. NEPAD is underpinned by the notion of sustainable development in that it takes account of sustainable economic growth, income distribution, poverty eradication, social equity and better governance. NEPAD is primarily implemented at the Regional Economic Community (REC) level. It is widely used by international financial institutions, United Nations agencies and Africa's development cooperation partners as a mechanism to support African developmental efforts.[93]

11.2 Regional Economic Communities

The Regional Economic Communities (RECs) also constitute pillars of African Union cooperation. The Abuja Treaty, which was adopted in June 1991, came into force in 1994. Since then, most African Union member states have signed the Treaty and several RECs have been established on the continent. At the seventh ordinary session of

90 Ruppel (2018: 135).
91 NEPAD founding document available at http://www.nepad.org/resource/new-partnership-africas-development, accessed 25 June 2020.
92 Preamble to Chapter 8 of the NEPAD documentation, titled The Environmental Initiative.
93 Cf. https://au.int/en/organs/nepad, accessed 12 July 2020.

the African Union's Assembly of Heads of State and Government in Banjul, The Gambia, in July 2006, the African Union officially recognised eight such communities, namely, the Arab Maghreb Union (AMU); the Community of Sahel-Saharan States (CEN-SAD); the Common Market for Eastern and Southern Africa (COMESA); the East African Community (EAC); the Economic Community of Central African States (ECCAS); the Economic Community of West African States (ECOWAS); the Intergovernmental Authority on Development (IGAD); and the Southern African Development Community (SADC),[94]

Originally established for mutual economic gain within the geographic communities, these RECs now aim to promote wider economic growth through the auspices of the African Economic Community (AEC) and are instrumental in the cultivation of norms and institutions centred on security.[95] Environmental concerns have, at least to some extent, found their way into the legal framework of many RECs.[96]

In SADC for example, with the 2003 Declaration on Agriculture and Food Security, Heads of State and government gave substantial means to some specific objectives laid down in Article 5 of the SADC Treaty, namely the promotion of sustainable and equitable economic growth and socioeconomic development to ensure poverty alleviation, with the ultimate objective of its eradication and the achievement of sustainable utilisation of natural resources and effective protection of the environment. With this Declaration, SADC member states committed themselves to promoting agriculture as a pillar of strength in national and regional development strategies and programmes, in order to attain their short-, medium-, and long-term objectives relating to agriculture and food security. Moreover, the SADC Protocol on Environmental Management for Sustainable Development, which was adopted in 2014, provides a basis for future avenues of tackling matters related to environmental impact assessment with a transboundary approach. The overall objective of the Protocol is to promote sustainable utilisation and transboundary management of the environment, in the interests of SADC member states. The Protocol covers a wide range of environmental issues, including climate change, waste and pollution, chemicals management, biodiversity and natural heritage, sustainable land management, and marine and inland water resources, as well as cross-cutting issues such as gender, science and technology, and trade and investment. The Protocol, which has yet to come into force, may become relevant for soils protection as it provides that state parties cooperate, among others, by facilitating the development, implementation and coordination of environmental assessment procedures, environmental management instruments and standards with the aim of enhancing the protection of the environment, to promote equitable and sustainable use of natural resources, to promote the shared management of transboundary environment

94 Ruppel (2009: 276).
95 Lamikanra (2018: 6).
96 Ruppel (2016: 100).

and natural resources, and to promote effective management and responses to the impacts of climate change.

11.3 Recommendations

While improving soil law and governance under the structures of the African Union and Regional Economic Communities (RECs), new legislative frameworks need to be developed to strengthen national strategies and policies and fill existing gaps in terms of implementation, among other things. For this matter, channels for finance and other support are needed also to enhance the capacity on the ground. Improving African soil governance must further address options for enhancing coordination and coherence between the national policymakers, RECs parliamentary forums and the African Union structures at large.

The African Continental Free Trade Area (AfCFTA) agreement will create the largest free trade area in the world, measured by the number of countries participating. The pact will connect 1.3 billion people across 55 countries with a combined GDP valued at US$3.4 trillion. It has the potential to lift 30 million people out of extreme poverty but achieving its full potential will depend on putting in place significant policy reforms and trade facilitation measures.[97]

Enabling free trade needs hand-in-hand action at both the supranational and national levels. Potential negative externalities of trade on soils should not be neglected. Moreover, regional communities can provide framework potential for reform, for example, by bringing together regulators to define harmonised standards or to agree on mutual protection interests. In this light, the African Union and particularly its Pan-African Parliament and its members can play a role to ensure harmonisation with Agenda 2063 thorough integration of the SDG indicators.[98]

In the UNFCCC process, feed in through the African Group of Negotiators should strengthen the views on soil protection, also using the findings of this project. With a view to fulfilling obligations related to the Paris Agreement, Nationally Determined Contributions (NDC) cooperation opportunities may contribute to fostering long-term climate action and mobilising means of implementation – finance, capacity-building, technology development, and transfer – on the continent. While all 54 countries have signed the Paris Agreement and submitted NDCs, many have also ratified them. However, in numerous instances, NDCs were drafted hastily, not fully taking all related interests into consideration.

97 World Bank (2020).

98 Also see chapter on the Pan-African Parliament of the African Union: Composition, mandate, partnerships and its quest for sustainable development in this volume.

Lastly, for African and existing REC courts to contribute successfully to dispute settlement (which could also become relevant in the context of soil protection and management) there is great opportunity and potential for the future. Until now, however, frequent failures often prevented the attainment thereof.[99]

12 Outlook

This chapter contains a collection of options through which legislation on soil protection in African states could be enhanced and improved. This collection is based on a summary of recommendations set out in the three country studies and on a synthetisation of consultative suggestions – for the various sectoral regulations relevant for sustainable soil management. The chapter is encouraging, as has been the entire project "Mapping out options for model legislation for sustainable soil management in Africa". The recommendations form an excellent starting point for future improvements of national legislation in the various African states and for the development of a specific model law, which could be elaborated upon, as well as adopted and promoted by the Pan-African Parliament.

It needs to be mentioned, at this juncture, that the – intentionally chosen – consultative bottom-up approach has been a major success factor in the development of such a convincing set of recommendations. It is certainly recommended that this approach – with the involvement of African experts and local stakeholders – should also be applied when working on national level legislation or while drafting a model law for the African continent. In addition, such a consultative approach should not be limited to African states only. The issue of establishing sustainable soil management addresses transnational and international interests, such as foreign investments in land, intracontinental and international trade or financial aspects. Thus, our African project has the quality to serve as an incentive and model for other countries in the world, promoting a vivid exchange of views and experiences while comparatively analysing the various facets of sustainable soil management in their full complexity.

In conclusion it can be stated without prejudice, that both this chapter and the project in its entirety distilled valuable information and workable recommendations. However, a long journey begins with but a single step and much more needs to be done to bring justice to Africa, and in particular to its women, children and the youth. The pristine nature and magnitude of the wonder of this continent oblige all of us to protect Africa as the cradle of humankind, and its soil, of which we are but custodians.

99 Cf. Ruppel (2012).

References

African Union Commission and New Zealand Crown, 2020, *African Union Handbook 2020*. Addis Ababa: African Union Commission and Wellington: New Zealand Ministry of Foreign Affairs and Trade/Manatū Aorere.

Akeyewale, R., 2018, "Winners and losers in Africa's Continental Free Trade Area". *International Trade Forum* 4, 14.

Allan, C., 2008, "Can adaptive management help us embrace the Murray-darling basin's wicked problems?". In: Pahl-Wostl, C., P. Kabat & J. Möltgen (eds), *Adaptive and integrated water management*. Berlin: Springer, 61.

Alloway, B.J., 2013, "Sources of heavy metals and metalloids in soils". In: Alloway, B. (ed.), *Heavy metals in soils. Environmental pollution*. Dordrecht: Springer, 11.

AMCEN / African Ministerial Conference on the Environment, 2011, *Addressing climate change challenges in Africa, a practical guide towards sustainable development*, at http://www.africa-adapt.net/media/resources/778/guidebook_CLimateChange.pdf, accessed 24 June 2020.

Boer, B.W., H. Ginzky & I.L. Heuser, 2016, "International soil protection law: History, concepts and latest developments". In: Ginzky, H., I.L. Heuser, T. Qin, O.C. Ruppel & P. Wegerdt (eds), *International yearbook of soil law and policy*. Cham: Springer, 49.

Ekane, D.N. & P.M. Oben, 2001, "Biochemical indicators of marine pollution in the Douala Lagoon and Limbe Estuary". In: Lambi, C.M. (ed.), *Environmental issues: Problems and prospects*. Bamenda: Unique Printers, 119.

FAO / Food and Agriculture Organization & ITPS / Intergovernmental Technical Panel on Soils, 2015, *Main report: Food and Agriculture Organization of the United Nations and Intergovernmental Technical Panel on Soils, Status of the World's Soil Resources (SWSR)*, at http://www.fao.org/3/a-bc590e.pdf, accessed 14 September 2020.

FAO / Food and Agriculture Organization & UNEP / United Nations Environment Programme, 2020, *Legislative approaches to sustainable agriculture and natural resources governance*. FAO Legislative Study No. 114, at http://www.fao.org/3/ca8728en/CA8728EN.pdf, accessed 14 September 2020.

Fogwe, Z.N., F. Ndifor, C.M. Lambi & R.M.E. Etame, 2001, Industrial water pollution: the case of the Ndogbong Industrial District, Douala (Cameroon). In: Lambi, C.M. (ed.), *Environmental issues: Problems and prospects*. Bamenda: Unique Printers, 7.

Foster, V. & C. Dominguez, 2011, *Zambia's infrastructure: A continental perspective*. World Bank Policy Research Working Paper No. 5599, at https://papers.ssrn.com/sol3/papers.cfm?abstract_id=1792257, accessed 14 September 2020.

Ginzky, H., E. Dooley, I.L. Heuser, E. Kasimbazi, R. Kibugi, T. Markus, T. Qin & O.C. Ruppel, forthcoming 2021, *International yearbook of soil law and policy 2019*. Cham: Springer.

Government of Kenya, The Presidency, 2017, *The Big Four Agenda*. Government of Kenya, at https://www.president.go.ke/, accessed 14 September 2020.

Govind, A. & J. Kumari, 2014, "Understanding the terrestrial carbon cycle: An ecohydrological perspective". *International Journal of Ecology*, 1.

Güneralp, B., S. Lwasa, H. Masundire, S. Parnell & K.C. Seto, 2017, "Urbanisation in Africa: Challenges and opportunities for conservation". *Environmental Research Letters* 13 (1), 1.

Howard, T.M. & A. Lawson, 2015, "Soil governance: Accessing cross-disciplinary perspectives". Special edition 1 *International Journal of Rural and Policy Soil Governance*, 1.

IPCC / Intergovernmental Panel on Climate Change, 2014a. *Climate Change 2014: Synthesis Report*. Contribution of working groups I, II and III to the fifth assessment report of the Intergovernmental

Panel on Climate Change, at http://www.ipcc.ch/pdf/assessment-report/ar5/syr/SYR_AR5_FINAL_full.pdf, accessed 15 June 2020.

IPCC / Intergovernmental Panel on Climate Change, 2014b, "Summary for policy makers". In: Field, C.B., V.R. Barros, D.J. Dokken, K.J. Mach, M.D. Mastrandrea, T.E. Bilir, M. Chatterjee, K.L. Ebi, Y.O. Estrada, R.C. Genova, B. Girma, E.S. Kissel, A.N. Levy, S. MacCracken, P.R. Mastrandrea & L.L. White (eds), *Climate change: Impacts, adaptation, and vulnerability*. Contribution of working group II to the fifth assessment report of the Intergovernmental Panel on Climate Change. Cambridge: Cambridge University Press.

IPCC / Intergovernmental Panel on Climate Change, 2018, *Special report on global warming of 1.5°C*. IPCC special report on the impacts of global warming of 1.5°C above pre-industrial levels and related global greenhouse gas emission pathways, in the context of strengthening the global response to the threat of climate change, sustainable development, and efforts to eradicate poverty, at https://www.ipcc.ch/sr15/, accessed 14 September 2020.

IPCC / Intergovernmental Panel on Climate Change, 2019, *Special report on climate change and land*. IPCC special report on climate change, desertification, land degradation, sustainable land management, food security, and greenhouse gas fluxes in terrestrial ecosystems, at https://www.ipcc.ch/srccl/, accessed 14 September 2020.

Japan Association for International Collaboration of Agriculture and Forestry, 2008, *Agriculture and forestry in Zambia: Present situation and issues for development*, at http://www.jaicaf.or.jp/publications/zanbia_agri.pdf, accessed 1 May 2019.

Kameri-Mbote, P., A. Paterson, O.C. Ruppel & B.B. Orubebe (eds), 2019, *Law | Environment | Africa*. Baden-Baden: Nomos Publishers.

Keesstra, S.D., J. Bouma, J. Wallinga, P. Tittonell, P. Smith, A. Cerdà, L. Montanarella, J.N. Quinton, Y. Pachepsky, W.H. van der Putten, R.D. Bardgett, S. Moolenaar, G. Mol, B. Jansen & L.O. Fresco, 2016, "The significance of soils and soil science towards realization of the United Nations sustainable development goals". *Soil Journal*, 2 (2), 111.

Koop, S.H.A. & C.J. van Leeuwen, 2017, "The challenges of water, waste and climate change in cities". *Environment, Development and Sustainability* 19, 385.

Kumar, A. & S.K. Maiti, 2015, "Assessment of potentially toxic heavy metal contamination in agricultural fields, sediment, and water from an abandoned chromite-asbestos mine waste of Roro hill, Chaibasa, India". *Environmental Earth Science* 74, 2617.

Lamikanra, U., 2018, "Update: Introduction to the norms and institutions in the African Union by Girmachew Alemu Aneme". *NYU Law Global*, 30 June 2018, at https://www.nyulawglobal.org/globalex/African_Union1.html, accessed 14 September 2020.

Mileusnić, M., B.S. Mapani, A.F. Kamona, S. Ružičić, I. Mapaure & P.M. Chimwamurombe, 2014, "Assessment of agricultural soil contamination by potentially toxic metals dispersed from improperly disposed tailings, Kombat mine, Namibia". *Journal of Geochemical Exploration* 144 (C), 409.

Moore, J.W., L. Nowlan, M. Olszynski, A.L. Jacob, B. Favaro, L. Collins, G.L.T. Williams-Davidson & J. Weitz, 2018, "Towards linking environmental law and science". *Facets* 3, 630.

Mulimbika, F. & A. Mahbub Karim, 2018, "Zambia's industrialization agenda: A case for local content in the mining industry". *International Journal of Academic Research and Development* 3 (2), 416.

Niang, I., O.C. Ruppel, M.A. Abdrabo, A. Essel, C. Lennard, J. Padgham & P. Urquhart, 2014, "Africa". In: Field, C.B., V.R. Barros, D.J. Dokken, K.J. Mach, M.D. Mastrandrea, T.E. Bilir, M. Chatterjee, K.L. Ebi, Y.O. Estrada, R.C. Genova, B. Girma, E.S. Kissel, A.N. Levy, S. MacCracken, P.R. Mastrandrea & L.L. White (eds), *Climate change 2014: Impacts, adaptation, and vulnerability*. Contribution of working group II to the fifth assessment report of the Intergovernmental Panel on Climate Change, Cambridge: Cambridge University Press, 1199.

Paustian, K., S. Collier, J. Baldock, R. Burgess, J. Creque, M. DeLonge, J. Dungait, B. Ellert, S. Frank, T. Goddard, B. Govaerts, M. Grundy, M. Henning, R.C. Izaurralde, M. Madaras, B. McConkey, E. Porzig, C. Rice, R. Searle, N. Seavy, R. Skalsky, W. Mulhern & M. Jahn, 2019. "Quantifying carbon for agricultural soil management: From the current status toward a global soil information system". *Carbon Management* 10 (6), 567.

Renn, O., 2019, *Gefühlte Wahrheiten: Orientierung in Zeiten postfaktischer Verunsicherung*. 2. Ausgabe, Opladen: Verlag Barbara Budrich.

Ruppel, O.C., 2008, "Third-generation human rights and the protection of the environment in Namibia". In: Horn, N. & A. Bösl (eds), *Human rights and the rule of law in Namibia*. Windhoek: Macmillan Education, 101.

Ruppel, O.C., 2009, "Regional economic communities and human rights in east and southern Africa". In: Bösl A. & J. Diescho (eds), *Human rights in Africa*. Windhoek: Macmillan Education Namibia, 275.

Ruppel, O.C., 2012, "SADC land issues before the SADC Tribunal – A case for human rights?". In: Chigara, B. (ed.), 2012, *Southern Africa Development Community land issues. A new, sustainable land relations policy*. London: Routledge, 89.

Ruppel, O.C. & E.D. Kam Yogo (eds), 2018, *Environmental law and policy in Cameroon – Towards making Africa the tree of life*. Recht und Verfassung in Afrika – Law and Constitution in Africa, Vol. 37. Baden-Baden: Nomos.

Ruppel, O.C. & K. Ruppel-Schlichting (eds), 2016, *Environmental law and policy in Namibia – Towards making Africa the tree of life*. 3rd edition. Windhoek: Hanns Seidel Foundation.

Ruppel, O.C., K.M. Scherr & A.D. Berndt (eds), 2017, *Assessing progress in the implementation of Zimbabwe's new Constitution. National, regional and global perspectives*. Law and Constitution in Africa, No. 32, Baden-Baden: Nomos.

Ruppel, O.C. & F. Shifotoka, 2017, "Foreign direct investment protection in Africa – Contemporary legal aspects between BITS and BRICS". *African Yearbook of International Law* 21 (1), 5.

Ruppel, O.C. & M.S. Tchuente, 2018, "Responsabilité sociétale et environnementale des entreprises: Normes et Régulations – perspective Africaine, cas du Cameroun". In: Kinhoun, E. & O.C. Ruppel (eds), *La question de la responsabilité sociale et environnementale de l'entreprise - perspective Africaine, cas du Cameroun*. Yaoundé: UCAC Presses, 13.

Ruppel, O.C. & A. von Finckenstein, 2017, "The protection of soil under Namibian law". In: Ginzky, H., I. Heuser, T. Qin, O.C. Ruppel & P. Wegerdt (eds), *International yearbook of soil law and policy*. Cham: Springer, 309.

Scholtz, W., 2010, "The promotion of regional environmental security and Africa's common position on climate change". *African Human Rights Law Journal* 10, 1.

Smith, P., 2016, "Soil carbon sequestration and biochar as negative emission technologies". *Global Change Biology* 22, 1315.

Songwe, V., 2019, "Trade value for prosperity: The value of open markets". In: Gonzalez, A. & M. Jansen (eds), 2019, *Women shaping economic governance*. London: CEPR Press, 61.

Tralac, 2019, *The African Continental Free Trade Area*. A Tralac guide. 5th edition, at https://www.tralac.org/documents/resources/booklets/2878-afcfta-a-tralac-guide-5th-edition-june-2019/file.html, accessed 14 September 2020.

Usman, S. & A.M. Kundiri, 2016, "Role of soil science: An answer to sustainable crop production for economic development in Sub-saharan Africa". *International Journal of Soil Science* 11, 61.

World Bank, 2020, *The African Continental Free Trade Area: Economic and distributional effects*. Washington, DC: World Bank.

Soil protection across Africa: Taking a glimpse at Namibia, Uganda, Mozambique, Nigeria, Ghana and South Africa

Oliver C. Ruppel, Katharina Ruppel-Schlichting, Larissa-Jane Houston & Yvonne Nana Afua

1 Introduction

This chapter addresses soil protection across Africa. In this regard it is important to note that 'soil' is not synonymous with 'land'. Of course, soil is a constituent of land but, while soil is movable, land is not. Moreover, soil protection is closely related to and even overlaps with land use and land management. The chapter provides an overview of national soil protection across Africa, while taking a glimpse at Namibia, Uganda, Mozambique, Nigeria, Ghana, and South Africa. It will also briefly cover the most soil-relevant international law instruments. The chapter is, however, neither meant to be comprehensive nor comparative in nature. In order to deliver a thorough legislative soil review, a more holistic approach would be necessary as has been conducted in the chapters on Cameroon, Kenya and Zambia in this volume.

Such comprehensive legislative soil reviews require an analysis of the Constitution (in respect of social, economic and environmental rights, and responsible branches of government for legislating and enforcing those rights); the examination of the country's international (monist or dualist), regional and bilateral agreements, and legally binding obligations reflected or not reflected in national legislation (including conflicting and ambiguous legislation); an analysis of existing regulatory (sectoral and cross-sectoral) policy, legal and institutional frameworks; the identification of existing regulatory gaps, bad practices and responsibility overlaps; the identification of institutional and governance frameworks; the scrutiny of implementation, monitoring, standardisation and enforcement challenges and pinpointing of the reasons (cost, lack of capacity, political will, human resources, etc.) thereof.[1]

Moreover, such legal reviews should take into consideration aspects related to dispute resolution (courts and tribunals, administrative environmental tribunals, alternative dispute resolution, customary courts); and access to justice (standing, costs, geographic accessibility, timeliness, availability of counsel, and non-governmental advocacy organisations).[2]

1 FAO & UNEP (2020: 63).
2 UNEP (2019: 235).

Apart from the legislative review, contextual factors also play a role in the assessment of optimal soil protection. These include demography (distribution of wealth, population density, age structure, urban/rural split, education and literacy, gender equity); economy (contribution of natural resource/extractive sector to the state economy, per capita income, evenness of development); politics (fragility, corruption perception, rule of law generally); corruption (in the control of natural resources/concessions, in management of natural resource revenues, in the enforcement process); and civic engagement.[3]

2 Namibia[4]

Namibia is one of the driest countries in the world with two of the largest deserts, namely the Kalahari Desert and the Namib Coastal Desert. Namibia has a generally low vegetation cover, thus making soil degradation one of the major environmental challenges facing the country. A sound legal and policy framework is essential to preserve and stabilise fragile soils, to protect biological diversity, and to ensure that the socioeconomic value of the soil is maintained for the benefit of the people living in Namibia, especially those in rural areas of whom most are directly dependent on the soil. This section seeks to provide an overview of Namibia's varied legal and policy frameworks pertaining to soil protection, which span various sectors and institutions.

The inhospitable desert constituted a barrier to European colonisation of south-western Africa until the late 18th century when traders and missionaries first explored the area. Soon the territory fell under German administration and became known as German South West Africa. German domination ended during World War I in the wake of South Africa's military occupation of the German colony. On 17 December 1920, South Africa took over South West Africa in terms of Article 22 of the 1919 Peace Treaty of Versailles. From this point South Africa was mandated with the power of administration and legislation over the territory.[5]

In 1946, the League of Nations was superseded by the newly formed United Nations (UN). When the UN requested South Africa to place the territory under a trusteeship agreement, South Africa refused. After more than a century of foreign domination and a long struggle on both diplomatic and military levels, Namibian independence was achieved and officially declared on 21 March 1990.[6]

Namibian law reflects the country's history and is the product of different sources: Roman law; the fusion of Roman law and Roman Dutch customary law – hence the

3 Ibid.: 235.
4 Ruppel & von Finckenstein (2016).
5 Ruppel & Ruppel-Schlichting (2016: 1).
6 Ibid.

term Roman Dutch law – which came in the wake of the Dutch colonisation of the Cape of Good Hope; English law asserted itself from the early 19th century onwards, leaving deep traces in Roman Dutch law after British hegemony in southern Africa had been established; and indigenous customary law from time immemorial.[7]

With the effect of Proclamation 21 of 1919, the Roman Dutch law developed by South African courts became the common law of the territory, binding on the Namibian courts until Independence. This position was affirmed by Article 66(1) of the Namibian Constitution of 1990, which provides that:

> both the customary law and the common law of Namibia in force on the date of Independence shall remain valid to the extent to which such customary or common law does not conflict with this Constitution or any other statutory law.

With a few exceptions, German legal influence has disappeared completely. Today, the Namibian legal system is an object of fascination for comparative lawyers, legal ethnologists and sociologists. The concept of legal pluralism – a situation in which more than one type of law or legal tradition operates simultaneously – is commonplace in Namibia.[8] The sources of law are statute law or legislation; judgements of the courts; international law (Article 144 of the Constitution); common and customary law (Article 66 of the Constitution), and to some extent legal writing.[9]

The major driving forces of land degradation in Namibia include poverty in rural areas; population pressure; land management policies; unsustainable use of water; limited capacity and cross-sectoral collaborations to effectively prevent land degradation; limited financial and technical resources; and climate change.[10]

Some of the main causes of soil degradation recognised by policymakers and affected persons are overstocking and overgrazing. The most vulnerable and poor groups in Namibia are disproportionately affected by the adverse effects of land degradation. In Namibia, the agricultural use of land, commercially and communally, is widespread. Even though many commercial farmers are able to mitigate negative impacts by means of rotational grazing and continuous monitoring, these opportunities do not generally exist for communal farmers.[11]

The era of colonial reign over Namibia has skewed landownership in the country in favour of the white minority. After Namibia acquired independence, the government promulgated several laws aimed to implement a comprehensive plan of land reform. The National Land Policy of 1998 intended to address the social injustices of the past and encapsulates constitutional principles. The policy goes so far as to state that the failure to practise sustainable environmental practices may be a ground to deny or

---

7 With further references: Ruppel & Ruppel-Schlichting (2016: 4).

8 Ruppel & Ruppel-Schlichting (2012: 33–64).

9 With further references: Ruppel (2016a: 49).

10 Government of the Republic of Namibia (2014).

11 Ibid.: 28. Communal farmers are generally restricted by the size of the land allocated to them, as well as with regard to technical knowledge and fiscal means.

terminate a title. This approach is in line with Article 95(1) of the Constitution, which promotes environmental sustainability.

The name of the Ministry of Agriculture, Water and Forestry changed to the Ministry of Agriculture, Water and Land Reform in 2020. It is responsible for soil management and the promotion and development of sustainable soil management practices in the agriculture, water and forestry sectors through appropriate policy and legal instruments. The directorate for Agriculture Research and Development aims to facilitate the development and management of human resources at all levels and in all disciplines, and to undertake well-balanced crop, livestock and natural resource research within the communal and commercial sectors, with the goal of contributing to increased productivity and sustainable utilisation of natural resources under arid, semi-arid and sub-humid conditions, and thereby improving the living standards of the Namibian population.[12]

According to Article 1(6) of the Namibian Constitution of 1990, the Constitution is the law above all laws. Therefore, all legislation ought to be consistent with the provisions of the Constitution. The Constitution lays the foundation for all policies and legislation in Namibia and contains three key environmental clauses relevant to sustainable use of natural resources.[13]

Article 100 of the Constitution vests all-natural resources in the state, unless otherwise legally owned. Thus, unless legal ownership in a specific locality is proved, such natural resources are owned by the state. The provision thus implies that natural resources can be legally owned as private property. The land (and the soil on the land) belongs to the state in terms of Article 100 of the Constitution, if not otherwise lawfully owned. By means of Article 95(l), Namibia is obliged to protect its environment and to promote a sustainable use of its natural resources.[14] It compels state organs to be directed by the environmental principle of state policy.

The Third National Action Programme for Namibia is the framework intended to aid in the implementation of the United Nations Convention to Combat Desertification (UNCCD) between 2014 and 2024. Here the focus is placed on illustrating the present obstacles which Namibia faces with regard to the environment, desertification, land degradation and drought processes, and how these pose an immediate danger to Namibia's land-based agricultural sector.[15] While the Namibian Programme to Combat Desertification has subsequently been established, various other national policies, strategies and action plans complement the most relevant pieces of legislation for the

12 See http://www.mawf.gov.na/directorate-research-and-development, accessed 12 July 2020.
13 Ruppel (2016b: 30).
14 Ibid.
15 Government of the Republic of Namibia (2014: 3).

protection of soil in Namibia.[16] The environmental framework legislation of cross-sectoral nature such as the Environmental Management Act, No. 7 of 2007 is rather broad in scope, while sectoral legislation such as the Soil Conservation Act, No. 76 of 1969 and the Agricultural (Commercial) Land Reform Act, No. 6 of 1995 is more specific in nature. Apart from the aforementioned pieces of legislation, the Communal Land Reform Act, No. 5 of 2002, the Minerals (Prospecting and Mining) Act, No. 33 of 1992, the Forest Act, No. 12 of 2001, the Agricultural Pests Act, No. 3 of 1973, and the Plant Quarantine Act, No. 7 of 2008 will also be relevant to soil protection.

The Soil Conservation Act of 1969 remains applicable in Namibia and is specifically referred to in the Communal Land Reform Act, No. 5 of 2002. The Soil Conservation Act gives wide ranging powers to the Minister, which includes powers to issue directives relating to the cultivation of land,[17] the management of water and drainage,[18] and the protection and stabilisation of soil surfaces.[19] One of the biggest obstacles which hinders effective soil conservation in Namibia is the fragmentation of responsibilities relating to soil. As yet, there is no cohesive policy to coordinate the effectiveness of existing laws and regulations with regard to soil protection in Namibia.

Article 144 of the Namibian Constitution incorporates international law explicitly as the law of the land. International law is thus integrated into domestic law.[20] Where possible national authorities and the judiciary, in particular, can therefore apply international law directly on the national level, before cases are taken to regional or international judicial or quasi-judicial bodies. International agreements become Namibian law when they come into force for Namibia. The conclusion of or accession to an international agreement is governed by Articles 32(3)(e), 40(i) and 63(2)(e) of the Namibian Constitution. It is important to mention that the Constitution does not require the promulgation of an international agreement for it to become part of the law of the land.[21]

16 These include inter alia the Third National Action Programme for Namibia to Implement the United Nations Convention to Combat Desertification 2014-2024 (NAP3); the National Biodiversity Strategy and Action Plan (NBSAP) 2013-2022; the National Climate Change Strategy and Action Plan (2013-2020); the Forestry Strategic Plan 1996; the National Drought Policy and Strategy 1997; and the Strategic Action Plan for the Implementation of Renewable Energy Policy 2006.

17 Section 3(1)(a).

18 Section 3(1)(c), (d), (f).

19 Section 3(1)(e), (g) and (h).

20 Article 144 reads as follows: "Unless otherwise provided by this Constitution or Act of Parliament, the general rules of public international law and international agreements binding upon Namibia under this Constitution shall form part of the law of Namibia."

21 Ruppel (2016b: 55ff).

3 Uganda[22]

Most of Uganda's land is a plateau, consisting of low savanna with a tall reed-like grass known as elephant grass, and is surrounded by mountains. There are some small areas of equatorial forest.[23] Large deposits of copper and cobalt are Uganda's most important natural resources, along with arable land and regular rainfall. Other minerals mined in Uganda include gold, limestone, and salt. Just over 34% of the land is arable, and about 13% of the land is composed of wetlands.[24] Uganda faces a number of environmental concerns, including deforestation and the draining of the wetlands.

Soil is a fundamental resource for development in Uganda and supports grazing, cultivation, energy provision and settlement, however, communities and households take land-use decisions without due consideration to the delicate balance between productivity, ecosystem health, changing land uses and human welfare.[25] Soil degradation stemming from –[26]

> deforestation, burning of grasslands and organic residues, and continuous cultivation with minimum soil fertility enhancement leads to soil erosion and organic matter and nutrient depletion in these areas. Other unsustainable land-use practices, such as overgrazing, have produced compacted soil layers and often bare grounds in extreme cases in the country.

Uganda was a British colony, which has influenced its legal system that is based on British common law and African customary law. The latter is brought into effect only when it does not conflict with statutory law. In this regard, Uganda today applies statutory law, common law, doctrines of equity, and customary law. The Constitution of Uganda[27] and the Land Act[28] provide that land in Uganda may be owned in accordance with the following four systems: freehold, leasehold, *mailo* and customary. The breakdown in land tenure and management systems is causing land degradation, which is evidenced by loss of vegetation, soil erosion and soil fertility loss in most of the districts in Uganda.[29] Having ownership or tenure of land means that persons can adopt sustainable soil practices and are responsible for maintaining effective soil management over their own land, which ensures accountability for unsustainable land-use and soil practices.

Uganda has ratified several international and regional conventions that recognise the importance of soil conservation, such as the Convention on Biological Diversity (CBD) (1992);[30] the United Nations Framework Convention on Climate Change

22 Cf. Kasimbazi (2019: 315).
23 Tumuhairwe et al. (2003: 35).
24 Ibid.
25 Kasimbazi (2019: 315).
26 Ibid: 316.
27 Constitution of 1995.
28 No. 16 of 1998 Chapter 227, Section 2.
29 Kasimbazi (2019: 316).
30 The Convention on Biological Diversity, 5 June 1992, 31 I.L.M. 818, ratified 8 September 1993.

(UNFCCC);[31] the UNCCD (1994);[32] the Revised African Convention on Nature and Natural Resources (2003);[33] the Treaty for the Establishment of the East African Community (1999);[34] and the Protocol on Environment and Natural Resources Management (2006).[35]

Soil protection in Uganda is traceable in the various environmental and natural resource legal instruments, namely the Constitution; the National Environment Act;[36] the Land Act; the National Forestry and Tree Planting Act;[37] the Prohibition of the Burning of Grass Act;[38] and the Cattle Grazing Act.[39] Uganda has various soil-relevant policies in place, such as the Ugandan Vision 2040;[40] the National Land Policy;[41] the National Agriculture Policy;[42] the Forestry Policy;[43] and the National Environment Management Policy.[44]

Land tenure in Uganda can be a tool for soil conservation since it involves sets of rules and regulations used to control and manage natural resources, biodiversity and the general environment.[45] Although elements relating to soil protection are evident in many pieces of environmental legislation, the consequential and effective implementation and enforcement is yet to be achieved.[46] There is no unified policy that coordinates effectiveness among existing laws, regulations and government initiatives with regard to soil protection in Uganda. Therefore, security of land tenure remains a prerequisite for long-term soil protection, regardless of whether ownership is in individual or collective hands.[47]

---

31 The United Nations Framework Convention on Climate Change I.L.M. 31 (1992), ratified 8 September 1993.
32 The United Nations Convention to Combat Desertification 33 ILM 1328 (1994), ratified 25 June 1997.
33 The Revised African Convention on Nature and Natural Resources (2003), signed 18 December 2003, yet to be ratified.
34 The Treaty for the Establishment of the East African Community (1999), ratified 7 July 2000.
35 The Protocol has since been ratified by the Republic of Uganda and the Republic of Kenya in 2010 and 2011 respectively.
36 The National Environment Act 1995 Chapter 153.
37 The National Forestry and Tree Planting Act No. 8 of 2003.
38 The Prohibition of the Burning of Grass Act 1974 Chapter 33.
39 The Cattle Grazing Act 1945 Chapter 42.
40 Uganda Vision 2040.
41 National Land Policy, 2013.
42 The National Agriculture Policy, 2013.
43 Uganda Forestry Policy, 2001.
44 The National Environment Management Policy for Uganda, 1994.
45 Kasimbazi (2019: 316).
46 Ibid: 330.
47 Ibid.

4 Mozambique[48]

Mozambique enjoys extraordinary natural conditions owing to a diverse natural resource base and geographical position, affording access to regional and international markets by both sea and land.[49] Mozambique's ecological make-up and natural potential is determined by specific features of the agroecological zones into which the country is divided.[50] Each region contains different and specific climate, geomorphology, soils and agricultural production systems, and as such each region must be viewed and considered with its own merits, and soil conservation and protection must also be viewed with this consideration in mind.[51] Mozambique has a relative abundance of resources, including soil, water, fauna and flora. Its major weaknesses, however, are an ineffective system of land-use planning and severe environmental degradation.[52]

With regard to soil, there are 10 zones in the country, from zone R1 to R10.[53] These agroecological zones of Mozambique have been identified, based on climate, soil type, elevation, and farming system.[54] Soil texture analysis indicates that most of the soils fall in the loamy sand, sandy loam, and sandy clay loam classes.[55] Several previous field surveys have indicated that soil fertility is a fundamental problem to food production in Mozambique.[56] Mozambique's soils are diverse in quality and type, but the northern and central provinces generally have more fertile, water-retentive soils than does the south, where sandy, infertile soils prevail.[57] The northern soils, whose qualities allow agricultural potential to extend beyond the river valleys, have a higher content of red clay, with a varying range of fertility. In contrast, the central region has a broad expanse of rich alluvial soils along the Zambezi Delta.[58]

Until independence, Mozambique was predominantly governed by Portuguese law. Thereafter it first repealed the colonial system while the Portuguese legal tradition was revived after the end to the 16-year-long civil war, when the 1990 Constitution and the Rome Peace Accords paved the way to the first democratic elections in 1994. Today, Mozambique's formal legal system can be considered as civil law with statutory

---

48 Cf. Chiziane (2019: 331).

49 According to Mozambique's Agrarian Policy of 1995: "the natural basis of Mozambique roughly consists of: (i) 36 million hectares of arable land, of which about 5 million are currently cultivated, (ii) 3.3 million hectares, of which only about 50,000 are Plains, are currently irrigated"; Chiziane (2019: 331).

50 República de Moçambique (2007: 12).

51 Chiziane (2019: 333).

52 The Resolution (Council of Ministers) No. 10/95, of 17 October approved the National Land Policy and its implementation strategies.

53 Ibid.

54 Maria & Yost (2006: 903).

55 Ibid: 905.

56 Ibid: 913.

57 See https://www.britannica.com/place/Mozambique, accessed 4 June 2020.

58 Ibid.

legislation as its primary source of law. There is no binding precedent (*stare decisis*) as understood in most common law systems. The 2004 Constitution recognises the existence of legal pluralism with African customary law.

There are several provisions within the 2004 Constitution which refer directly or indirectly to soil conservation and addressing issues pertaining to soil conservation in the country, in particular Articles 11(d); 90(1)–(2); 98; 102; 103(1)–(2); 109(1)–(3); 110(1)–(2); 111; and 117(1)–(2). Mozambique has also put together a statutory draft on agriculture to provide a legal framework for the sustainable development of the agricultural sector and the rural environment, which needs to be established and aimed at the promotion and progressive improvement of food and nutritional security of Mozambicans pursuant to paragraph 1 of Article 179 of the Constitution.

Several governmental and non-governmental bodies dealing with soil conservation issues exist in the country.[59] Mozambique's Agrarian Policy,[60] among others, outlines fundamental principles of sustainable use of natural resources, which include land, soil, water, forests, wildlife and genetic resources. Moreover, Mozambique, implemented the principles provided for under the United Nations Conference on Environment and Development (also known as, Rio+20),[61] dealing specifically with desertification, soil degradation and drought, emphasising that these are global challenges presenting serious obstacles for sustainable development.[62]

Mozambique has demonstrated commitment towards soil conservation. However, the work remains unfinished. Full soil conservation, for instance, implies:[63] defining a road map for the introduction of legislation on the conservation of soils and biodiversity; realising agroecological zoning; establishing criteria for the harmonisation and regulation of spatial occupation by various productive activities; and installing hydroelectric infrastructures, while taking into account the agroecological fitness criteria and sociocultural habits of local populations; improving institutional coordination in the sector of land management; and increasing research on soils by the Agricultural Research Institute of Mozambique.

5 Nigeria[64]

The Federal Republic of Nigeria is located in western Africa. Nigeria's climate and ecology is diverse, with the Sahel Desert to the north, tropical forest in the south,

---

59 Rees (2018: 24).

60 Point 13 of the Agrarian Policy of 1995.

61 Resolução (Assembleia da Republica) No. 2/94, de 24 de Agosto, ratifica a Convenção das Nações Unidas sobre a diversidade biológica, de 5 de Junho de 1992.

62 Chiziane (2019: 340).

63 Ibid.: 343.

64 Cf. Orubebe (2020: 157).

mountains in the east and mangrove swamps in the core Niger Delta where the River Niger meets the Atlantic Ocean.[65] A shift in laws has created a conflict of interest among states, ethnic nationalities, communities, families, and individuals, which has been aggravated by the negative impact of climate change and global warming, a fact that has necessitated an unprecedented migration of people and livestock to other parts of the country.[66] Land in Nigeria is predominantly used for activities such as farming and cattle rearing, which both require cultivation of the land and rely on richness of the soil.[67]

Nigeria enjoys a diversity of climates and marked environmental features, including oil- and gas-rich and sensitive wetlands.[68] The country consists of several extensive physiographical plateau surfaces including the Jos Plateau, the Udi Plateau, the Manbila Plateau and the North-Central High Plains.[69] Nigeria, like most African countries, is facing the problem of food insecurity, degradation of land, desertification, pollution, and creation of wasteland. Nigeria is a member of the Global Soil Partnership (GSP) by virtue of its membership of the Food and Agriculture Organization (FAO).[70] GSP was initiated to improve the governance of the limited soil resources of the planet, in order to guarantee healthy and productive soils for a food-secured world, as well as supporting other essential ecosystem services.[71]

After British colonisation, Nigeria became independent on 1 October 1960. The Nigerian legal system is still based on British common law legal tradition. Contemporary sources of Nigerian law include the Constitution, statutory legislation, British common law, African customary law, Islamic law, and judicial precedents. The current constitution is the 1999 Constitution. The Nigerian Land Use Act of 1978, which is regarded as the central statute laying out the legal and governance structure of land, does not define what constitutes land or soil. Notwithstanding, Nigeria federal law that governs soil and land tenure is the Land Use Act. It has been stated that this piece of legislation does not do enough to address the issues associated with sustainable soil and land development.[72] In order to develop sustainable use of soil conditions, "governance programs must be integrated from the local to global level, across a range of sectors, and over a substantial time frame to enable effective soil policy making."[73] Further, "soil

65 Ibid.
66 Ibid.: 158.
67 Ibid.: 159.
68 Ibid.: 157.
69 Ibid.
70 See http://www.fao.org/global-soil-partnership/partners/country-focal-points/en/, accessed 4 June 2020.
71 Orubebe (2020: 170).
72 Ibid.: 174.
73 Boer & Hannam (2015: 5).

protection and rehabilitation policies need to be based on a human rights framework, principally emphasising land rights for marginal and vulnerable groups in society".[74]

In the light of the situation described above, the following recommendations are necessary and ought to be taken seriously:[75] review of current soil or land governance structures and ownership principles; an enabling framework for holistic soil governance legislation; a mutually beneficial land tenure system; an authority avoiding sectionalism; a new legal framework on soil or land governance; impartial enforcement or implementation of detailed soil governance standards; a sustainable and responsible land and soil agenda; more sustainable use of natural resources; and respect by the Federal Government ensuring neutrality of all its law enforcement agencies.

Nigeria is a party to international conventions such as the UNCCD, the CBD and the UNFCCC, and the Paris Agreement on Climate Change.[76]

6 Ghana

The Republic of Ghana has often been branded as an anchor ensuring stability in West Africa, where democracy is well-established. Ghana's economy is heavily dependent on export earnings from just a few commodities, such as gold, crude oil and cocoa. In terms of development cooperation, agriculture and sustainable economic development are focus areas.[77]

On 6 March 1957, the former Gold Coast was led to independence from Britain by Kwame Nkrumah, who transformed the country into a Republic. Ghana's legal system was built on a foundation of received common law, statutory law, and other documents, such as those heralding the legal existence of various military regimes. In addition to this received and imposed law, there is an enduring body of largely unwritten customary usages and practices that still are a contextual feature of today's legal system of Ghana. Legal pluralism is evidenced by a coexistence of indigenous customary laws and practice, which shaped Ghana's legal system, including the impact of British colonialism and, more recently, its constitutional evolution, following independence.[78]

Ghana's Constitution of 1992[79] was adopted just before Ghana's 1995 Environmental Policy was formulated.[80] The new Constitution has made government accountable to the people of Ghana. It identifies the Legislature, the Executive and the Judiciary as

74 Ibid.
75 Orubebe (2020: 176).
76 Ibid.: 174.
77 See https://www.bmz.de/en/countries_regions/subsahara/ghana/index.html, accessed 11 August 2020.
78 See http://judicial.gov.gh/index.php/summary, accessed 11 August 2020.
79 The Constitution of the Republic of Ghana 1992.
80 Ayee (1998: 113).

the different arms of government within the framework of cooperative governance. The starting point for developing a new environmental policy for Ghana, therefore, is the Constitution from which the powers of government and the Ghanaian population at large derives.[81]

Article 11 of the 1992 Constitution provides that the laws of Ghana comprise the Constitution, statutes, orders, rules, regulations, and common law, which includes customary law.

> It thereby establishes a pluralist legal system without establishing a hierarchy among the various, potentially conflicting, sources of law. As an outsider, one might expect that land is governed either by customary law or by a combination of common law and statutes. The reality is more complex, with overlapping claims, multiple systems of customary laws, boundary disputes, lack of written records, an inefficient registration system, no clear choice of law rules, and overlapping jurisdictions for dispute resolution ... Approximately 80% of the land in Ghana is held under customary land tenure systems.[82]

Article 41(k) of the 1992 Constitution regulates soil pollution through environmental protection:

> The exercise and enjoyment of rights and freedoms is inseparable from the performance of duties and obligations, and accordingly, it shall be the duty of every citizen to protect and safeguard the environment.

Article 269 of Ghana's 1992 Constitution provides for the establishment, composition and functions of this country's Forestry Commission. It also gives the Ghanaian President control over all mineral resources, to be managed on behalf of the people, thereby, promoting environmental law principles of the public trust doctrine as far as the exploitation of mineral resources is concerned.

The Forestry Commission of Ghana (re-established under the Forestry Commission Act[83]) is the subdivision under the respective Ministry and is responsible for the sustainable development and management of Ghana's forests and wildlife.

Core objectives of Ghana's revised 2011 policy include managing and enhancing the ecological integrity of forest, savannah, wetlands and other ecosystems; promoting the rehabilitation and restoration of degraded landscapes through plantation development and community forestry; promoting the development of viable forest and wildlife-based industries and livelihoods, particularly in the value-added processing of forest and wildlife resources; promoting and developing mechanisms for transparent governance, equity sharing and peoples' participation in forest and wildlife resource management; and promoting training, research and technology development that supports sustainable forest management.

The Legislative Instrument 1721 Timber Resources Management (Amendment of 2003) plans and manages the use of soil in a comprehensive manner. More specifically,

81 Ibid.: 100.

82 Higgins & Fenrich (2012: 8).

83 Act 571 of 1999.

Sections 3(3)(b) of the Timber Resources Management Act make reference to environmental assessments which can be useful in measuring soil impacts and determining whether practices meet soil protection standards. When it comes to spatial planning instruments or urban planning, the Land Use and Spatial Planning Act,[84] also has relevant legal provisions, namely:

> to prevent soil degradation by inter-alia promoting permission regimes including environmental impact assessment for potentially detrimental environmental uses.

Article 73 of Ghana's 1992 Constitution stipulates that the government must conduct its international affairs in consonance with the accepted principles of public international law and diplomacy in a manner consistent with the national interest of Ghana. Ghana has, of course, acceded to major international agreements and United Nations conventions, of which some have been translated into national action, as reflected in certain legislation.[85] These international conventions deal with the responsibilities which Ghana and other states need to carry out in preventing trends such as waste burning, and the release of excessive concentrations of poisonous gases and heavy metals in the soil, atmosphere, sea and ecosystems in a generic sense. Furthermore, relevant African Union and regional Economic Community of West African States (ECOWAS) treaties also serve to ensure harmonisation at the respective national, subregional and regional levels, as far as soil pollution is concerned.

The National Environmental Policy and National Environment Action Plan[86] seek to improve living conditions and the quality of life of the entire citizenry and to harmonise economic development with natural resource conservation. The following specific purposes are exhibited in the policy: maintaining ecosystems and ecological processes essential for the functioning of the biosphere; ensuring sound management of natural resources and the environment; protecting humans, animals and plants with respect to biodiversity conservation; and minimising pollution and public nuisance stemming from development activity.

The Action Plan is the first comprehensive plan for environmental protection for Ghana, in which the following activities are proposed: Investment related to environmental protection; institutional building; and commitment of the government to policy-making, legislation and management in respect of land resources, forests and wildlife, water, marine and coastal ecosystems, human settlements, and pollution control.

Ghana's Environmental Resource Management Programme,[87] under the Ministry of Environment, Science and Technology, was formulated as an actual programme along

84 Act 925 of 2016.
85 Government of the Republic of Ghana (2009).
86 Government of the Republic of Ghana (1990).
87 Government of the Republic of Ghana (1992).

the lines of the National Environment Action Plan. The Environment Protection Agency was established according to this programme.

The Forest and Wildlife Policy[88] comprehensively covers all aspects of forestry and wildlife conservation. It seeks compatibility between forest conservation and the increasing industrial demand for forest resources in order to ensure rural livelihoods on a limited resource base, exhibiting activities including conservation and good management of forest and wildlife resources in Ghana; promotion of viable and efficient forest-based industries, particularly in secondary and tertiary processing; raising people's awareness to involve rural people in forest conservation and wildlife protection; facilitation of research-based and technology-oriented management of forest and wildlife for their utilisation and development; and enhancement of capability of national, regional and district agencies for sustainable forest and wildlife management.

The Environmental Sanitation Policy[89] aimed at developing and maintaining a clean, safe and pleasant physical environment in all human settlements, as well as promoting the social, economic and physical well-being of all the people. The policy includes the following principal components: Collection and sanitary disposal of wastes including solid waste, liquid waste, excreta, industrial waste, hospital waste and other hazardous waste; drainage of stormwater; street sweeping and cleansing of public spaces including markets; pest control and vector control; education on environmental sanitation; inspection and enforcement of sanitary regulations; burial of the dead; domestic animal control; and monitoring environmental quality with respect to environmental standards.

The Mineral and Mining Act[90] and the Pesticide Control and Management Act[91] are also relevant when it comes to soils. The Minerals and Mining Act makes no explicit mention of soil, however environmental considerations are mentioned in a number of sections throughout the Act. Section 18 pertains to forestry and environmental protection and provides for approvals and permits required from the Forestry Commission and the Environmental Protection Agency prior to activity and action on a mineral right. Section 46 goes further to provide for rights conferred by a mining lease. Section 49 provides that any development agreements may contain provisions pertaining to environmental regulations. Sections 92 and 93 deal rather specifically with small-scale mining committees and the operations of small-scale miners. Section 110 allows the Minister to make additional regulations pertaining to environmental considerations. Unlike the Mining and Minerals Act, the Pesticides Control and Management Act explicitly mentions soil in Section 7(d):

---

88 Government of the Republic of Ghana (2012).
89 Government of the Republic of Ghana (1999a).
90 Act 703 of 2006.
91 Act 528 of 1996.

> In determining whether or not to approve the registration of a pesticide and what classification to give a registered pesticide, the Agency shall consider relevant matters including – the relative hazards of its patterns of use, such as granular soil applications, ultra low volume or dust aerial applications or air blast sprayer applications ...

Ghana's Environmental Protection Agency monitors air quality in industrial and mining areas. Industries and mining operators are required to submit Environmental Management Plans to the EPA to control pollution, while emission standards are under preparation.[92]

Looking more specifically at legislative mandates for soil and environmental protection, the Environmental Protection Agency Act,[93] under Section 2(h), provides the Environmental Protection Agency with the mandate to "provide standards and guidelines relating to the pollution of air, water, land and other forms of environmental pollution including the discharge of wastes and the control of toxic substances". Reference to what land entails is not provided for in the legislation; however, the broad nature of Section 2(h) can be read to include soil preservation.

More recently, the Petroleum (Exploration and Production) Act,[94] Section 95, has provided for the interpretation of land to include subsoil, thus ensuring that subsoil is protected and considered in environmental efforts regarding petroleum exploration and production in Ghana. Numerous environmental considerations are identified equally in specific sections, such as Section 7. Each of the following sections, although mentioned briefly, provide a consideration for environmental protection and ensure environmental assessments that prevent further environmental harm as a result of petroleum exploration and production: Opening of an area; 9. Reconnaissance licence; 24. Exploration drilling; 27. Plan of development and operation; 33. Restrictions on flaring; 39. Application to install and operate facilities; 43. Decommissioning plan; 44. Decision on the decommissioning plan; 47. Restoration of affected areas; 50. Petroleum operating standards; 75. Emergency preparedness; 81. Environmental principles and protection; 82. Impact assessment; 94. Authority to issue regulations and guidelines and stipulate conditions; 95. Interpretation. There are a multitude of NGOs including international NGOs, registered with the Environmental Protection Agency, working on soil pollution and related issues such as the use of pesticides and other chemicals. Owing to the low levels of public illumination on the hazards associated with the use of certain chemical and farming practices on the soil, the implementation of sound pollution laws becomes difficult. The solution to this would be to have more training programmes for farmers and other users of land and soil.

Owing to the lack of adequate penalties, laws are not abided by. One good way to rectify this could be to use the 'carrots and sticks' approach by granting incentives and

92 See http://www.epa.gov.gh/epa/, accessed 11 August 2020.
93 Act 490 of 1994.
94 Act 919 of 2016.

awards to users of best practices. This method could even encourage otherwise illegal offenders to conform to the stipulations of soil pollution laws, as Ghana

> perceives an increasing resource scarcity, competition and use of the available resource are likely to intensify. In this sense, the need for soil security can be conceived of as akin to the turning of a screw. The perception of scarcity (availability) reinforces intense competition use (accessibility and utilization), which in turn speeds up or intensifies degradation, scarcity, inequity, injustice, and ultimately conflicts (stability). Economic development imperatives and urbanization, for example, put manifold pressure on soils available for agriculture and forest. In jurisdictions where land administration and general governance systems are weak, arable lands are being lost rapidly to uses that can potentially make the soils permanently unavailable.[95]

Lastly, there has been no comprehensive legislation on various aspects of environmental problems in Ghana so far. However, while a number of laws touch on the exploitation of natural resources and specific aspects of the environment such as soil pollution, some of the existing laws overlap in their implementation. Consequently, more comprehensive environmental laws, which are under preparation, may be necessary to complement the Environmental Assessment Regulations,[96] as promulgated in 1999 and the Environmental Quality Standard Regulation (water, air and noise) as drafted in the same year. Ultimately, more light should be shed on soil pollution through the provision of relevant sector-specific regulations. In such processes the Soils Science Society of Ghana (SSSG) seems well-equipped to advise on pertinent issues relating to soil health and management; soil degradation and reclamation; agricultural intensification and the environment; and climate smart agriculture.

7 South Africa[97]

Traditionally, South Africa's economy has been rooted in the primary sectors as a result of a wealth of mineral resources and favourable agricultural conditions.[98] Agriculture is one of the main sectors of the economy in South Africa – it is at the same time diverse, and ranges from the intensive, large-scale, commercial agricultural sector to the low-intensity, small-scale, and subsistence farming sector. Moreover, South Africa is facing a mushrooming of new mining ventures, particularly in coal, platinum group metals and other precious metals that are placing a heavy burden on land and which have a significant impact on soil. Mining activities have significant impacts on air and water quality, biodiversity and productivity of soil, by causing erosion, sedimentation, subsidence and landslides.

Pre-1994 land policies led to the crowding of people into 'homelands'. These rural areas constitute shared access to land resources, commonly referred to as communal

---

95 Ywason et al. (2016: 15).
96 Government of the Republic of Ghana (1999b).
97 Cf. Ruppel et al. (2021 forthcoming).
98 See https://bit.ly/3cObmmk, accessed 10 March 2020.

use. These communal areas are used for producing crops and livestock, mainly for subsistence and livelihood security. Communal areas have long been neglected, which has resulted in overgrazing, overharvesting and soil erosion.[99]

The progress towards South Africa's current constitutional dispensation was a journey that was filled with challenges based on a mixture of legal regimes. Colonisation, settlement and Apartheid are major influences on the current multifaceted nature of South Africa's legal system. However, the introduction of the 1996 Constitution has meant extensive change to South Africa's previous legal and political system. Today, South African law consists of the Constitution, legislation, judicial precedent, common law (rules developed from Roman-Dutch and British authorities), (African) customary law, and international law. The "common and customary law embodies official legal pluralism, whilst those two 'official' legal systems, together with all other 'unofficial' legal systems (e.g. Hindu law, Jewish law and Muslim law) embody 'deep' legal pluralism."[100] The diverse nature of the system is mirrored by the inclusion of African customary law, Roman-Dutch law and British common law in pluralistic practice.[101] Traditional leaders are recognised by the Constitution, with Chapter 12 providing for recognition and the role of traditional leaders.[102] South African courts follow the rule of precedent, whereby courts are bound by their own decisions unless and until they are overruled by a superior court. It is, however, conceivable that circumstances arise that would render it possible for a court to override its own legal opinion.[103]

Since the end of Apartheid, South Africa has often been at the forefront of international law efforts. As such, South Africa signed the UNFCCC in 1993 and ratified it in 1997. South Africa acceded to the Kyoto Protocol in 2002 and ratified the Paris Agreement in 2016.[104] South Africa also ratified the UNCCD in 1997. South Africa further recognises the role of SDG 15 (Life on Land), as well as target 15.3 of the same goal, which envisages

> [b]y 2030 [to] combat desertification, restore degraded land and soil, including land affected by desertification, drought and floods, and [to] strive to achieve a land degradation-neutral world. South Africa is committed to setting its voluntary targets for achieving land degradation neutrality (LDN) by 2030.[105]

The Constitution distinguishes between the obligations of the Republic of South Africa on an international level that derive from international agreements to which South

99 Department of Environmental Affairs (2012).

100 Rautenbach (2010: 145).

101 Du Plessis (2019: 15).

102 Constitution of the Republic of South Africa of 1996.

103 Havenga et al. (2002: 8).

104 See https://www.sanbi.org/wp-content/uploads/2018/09/Strategic-Framework-and-Overarching-Implementation-Plan-for-EbA-in-SA.pdf, accessed 20 May 2020.

105 See https://sustainabledevelopment.un.org/content/documents/26158Final_SG_SDG_Progress_Report_14052020.pdf, accessed 20 May 2020.

Africa is a party and their applicability in the domestic legal system.[106] Section 231(2) of the Constitution requires the ratification of an international treaty by both the National Assembly and the National Council of Provinces except in the case of those agreements that can be classified as technical, administrative or executive.[107] The Constitution does not contain any definitions or indication when these criteria are met. It is, however, important to emphasise that ratification by parliament does not replace the need for implementing legislation to guarantee the international treaty's domestic applicability.[108] Therefore, Section 231(4) of the Constitution provides for the enactment of additional national legislation to transform the international treaty provisions into municipal law, unless the particular agreement contains a self-executing provision. The legislature seems to use three different methods to incorporate international agreements into South African national law.[109] Firstly, the provisions of the particular agreement may be embodied in the text of an act; secondly, the agreement may be included as a schedule to a statute and thus be incorporated by reference; and, lastly, the legislation may authorise the executive to bring the agreement into effect as domestic law by publishing it in the *Government Gazette*. Once an international agreement is incorporated into national legislation its provisions enjoy the same legal status as the implementing legislation itself.[110] Ultimately, Section 39(1)(b) of the Constitution provides that international law must be considered when a court interprets the Bill of Rights. Although Section 39 provides that international law must be considered, it does not require that international law must be applied.[111] However, as stipulated in Section 233, "when interpreting any legislation, every court must prefer any reasonable interpretation of the legislation that is consistent with international law over any alternative interpretation that is inconsistent with international law".

At national level, South Africa has previously promulgated legislation that was aimed at controlling or reducing soil loss. This legislation included the Forest and Veld Conservation Act, No. 13 of 1941, the Soil Conservation Act, No. 76 of 1969, the Conservation of Agricultural Resources Act, No. 43 of 1983, and the Environment Conservation Act, No. 73 of 1989. This legislation, however, was predominantly applied to white-owned areas, while soils protection legislation in black areas fell under the Native Administration Act, No. 38 of 1927, the Bantu Homelands Constitution Act, No. 21 of 1971, legislation formulated by individual homelands governments, and proclamations by the State President, such as Proclamation 116 of 1949, and the

106 Sections 231(2) & (4) Constitution of the Republic of South Africa of 1996.

107 Section 231(3) Constitution of the Republic of South Africa of 1996.

108 Sucker (2014: 426).

109 Dugard (2018: 61).

110 *Glenister v President of the Republic of South Africa and Others* Case *(CCT 48/10) [2011] ZACC 6* (para. 100).

111 Rautenbach (2018: 75).

Betterment Areas Proclamation, R196 of 1967.[112] The Environment Conservation Act, No 73 of 1989 was subsequently replaced by the National Environmental Management Act, No. 107 of 1998 (NEMA), together with the primary legislation aimed at addressing soil conservation, and the Conservation of Agricultural Resources Act, No. 43 of 1983 (CARA), which are complementary frameworks for the safeguarding of soil.[113]

CARA promotes the conservation of soil, water resources and vegetation, with the objects of the Act being to provide for the conservation of the natural agricultural resources of the Republic through the maintenance of the production potential of land, by combating and preventing erosion and weakening or destroying the water resources, and by protecting the vegetation and combating weeds and invader plants.[114] The act provides management plans that guide the eradication of weeds and alien invasive vegetation and promote and protect the integrity of indigenous vegetation, as well as guide the management and protection of soil. CARA provides the Minister of Agriculture with the power to prescribe control measures that need to be complied with and applied by land users which include control measures for the cultivation of virgin soil, and the utilisation and protection of land which is cultivated.[115]

NEMA promotes cooperative environmental governance through the establishment of principles of decision-making in an integrated and cooperative manner for any matters that affect the environment. NEMA further stipulates the procedures, administration and enforcement of environmental management laws, through various management instruments. Furthermore, NEMA Section 24 management principles, requirements, and procedures for environmental authorisation are outlined in order to reduce negative impacts on and degradation of the environment. Section 24 further makes stipulations for actions to be taken in the case of pollution or degradation of the environment by the persons responsible.

The National Action Programme Combating Land Degradation to Alleviate Rural Poverty (2004), set by the Department of Environmental Affairs and Tourism,[116] aims to combat desertification and mitigate the effects of drought in line with the framework of Agenda 21, in order to achieve sustainable development. The Soils Protection Strategy (2005) (yet to be completed)[117] was prompted by the need to identify priority areas for the implementation of integrated soil rehabilitation programmes that have been identified through modelling and mapping land capability and predicted soil erosion. South Africa has been relatively active in dealing with regulatory aspects of climate change.[118] In June 2018, the South African Minister of Environmental Affairs

112 Garland et al. (2000: 69–107).
113 Kidd (2011: 132).
114 Ibid.
115 Kidd (2011: 133).
116 Department of Environment and Tourism (2004).
117 Department of Agriculture (1999).
118 Ruppel et al. (2020: 274).

published the Draft Climate Change Bill (called the Climate Change Bill) in the *Government Gazette*, thus opening the public to submit comments.[119] The Climate Change Bill seeks to "build the Republic's effective climate change response and the long term, just transition to a climate resilient and lower carbon economy and society in the context of an environmentally sustainable development framework; and to provide for matters connected therewith".[120] The bill addresses policy alignment and institutional arrangements; climate change response for provinces and municipalities; national adaptation to impacts of climate change; greenhouse gas emissions and removals; and general matters and transitional arrangements, i.e. public participation, delegation, offences and penalties, etc.[121] The overall objectives of the Climate Change Bill are also relevant to soil protection in that they promote section 24 of the 1996 Constitution, which stipulates that everyone has a right to an environment that is not harmful to their health and well-being; and to have the environment protected for the benefit of present and future generations, through reasonable legislative and other measures that prevent pollution and ecological degradation, promote conservation, secure ecologically sustainable development and use of natural resources, while promoting justifiable economic and social development.[122]

The right to property is found in Section 25 of the Constitution, stating that no person may be deprived of property except in terms of the law of general application and that no law may permit arbitrary deprivation of property.[123] Further, Section 25 provides that property may be expropriated only in terms of the law of general application for the public purpose or in the public interest and subject to compensation.[124] The Constitution allows for the protection of property, but also for the reform of property relations. Common law, precedent and statutory law were traditionally regarded as sources of South African property law but are no longer regarded as exhaustive under the new constitutional dispensation.[125] Public law dealing with landownership and rights before 1996 can be found to be discriminatory. As a result of this, a number of instruments have been introduced in order to right the wrongs of the past. One of the most applicable measures is the 1997 White Paper on Land Policy, which was set up with the purpose if redressing the Apartheid era, nurturing national reconciliation and sustainability to support economic growth, to improve welfare, and to relieve poverty.[126]

119 Government Gazette 41689, 8 June 2018.
120 Climate Change Bill (draft) No. 580 GG 41689 of 8 June 2018.
121 Ibid.
122 Section 24 of the Constitution of the Republic of South Africa of 1996.
123 Constitution of the Republic of South Africa of 1996.
124 Ibid.
125 Mostert & Pope (2010).
126 See https://www.grainsa.co.za/unpacking-the-various-forms-of-land-ownership, accessed 21 February 2020.

In South Africa, as a result of the post-1996 constitutional dispensation, there is a demand for equal consideration be given to (African) customary law and to public law.[127] Customary law is both written and unwritten, having developed from the customs and traditions of communities over time.[128] For customs and traditions to be considered as law, they must be known to the community, followed by the community, and be enforceable. When there is a conflict between public and customary law, both laws are looked at together in order to determine the differences and to ensure that both are in line with the Constitution. A choice of law rule is then made. The purpose of this rule is to select the law that will do justice in the given case – not for one party, but for all.

Planning law is relevant when considering landownership and rights to use and access land. Planning law can be defined as the area of law that provides for the creation of a sustainable land management planning framework, as well as for the management of land development with the purpose of ensuring the health, safety and welfare of society as a whole, while accounting for overarching interests such as the environment.[129] This is an important division of the law in South Africa and is predominantly governed by the Spatial Planning and Land Use Management Act, No. 16 of 2013.

The National Environmental Management: Biodiversity Act, No. 10 of 2004 supports the conservation of plant and animal biodiversity, and the soil and water that it depends on. The Act promotes the management and conservation of South Africa's biodiversity within the framework of NEMA in order to protect species and ecosystems and promote equitable and sustainable use of natural resources.

The National Environmental Management: Protected Areas Act, No. 57 of 2003 makes provision for the protection and conservation of ecologically viable areas that represent South Africa's biological diversity and natural land- and seascapes, and calls for the establishment of national, provincial and local protected areas and their management in accordance with national norms and standards. Amendment 31 of 2004 of the Act supports the conservation of soil, water and biodiversity.

The National Environmental Management: Waste Act, No. 59 of 2008 (NEMWA) stems from NEMA, and is the act which is primarily concerned with waste management in order to protect health and the environment. NEMWA provides reasonable measures for the prevention of pollution and ecological degradation and for securing ecologically sustainable development. Under Section 73(1)(a) of NEMWA, the national norms and standards for "The Remediation of Contaminated Land and Soil Quality" in the Republic of South Africa are stipulated and took effect in 2013. These norms and standards focus on contamination through various land-use activities that have an impact on soil quality, human health and water resources; from this contamination the norms and standards then outline remediation measures that assist with the

127 Mostert & Pope (2010).
128 Ruppel (2008: 23).
129 Van Wyk (2018: 1131).

management of the contaminated site to "prevent, minimise, or mitigate" the damage to human health or the environment.

Further, when addressing public environmental law, the agricultural sector must be addressed because of its relation to and impact on the environment. Agriculture plays an important role in the economy of South Africa and it is therefore necessary to have legislation with provisions dealing with agriculture. CARA aims to provide for the conservation of the natural agricultural resources of South Africa by maintaining the production potential of land – by combating and preventing erosion and halting the weakening or destruction of the water sources, and by protecting vegetation and combating weeds and invader plants.[130]

The Subdivision of Agricultural Land Act, No. 70 of 1970 is another act contributing to the provisions concerning agriculture. This Act provides that agricultural land may not be subdivided unless the Minister of Agriculture, Forestry and Fisheries has consented to the subdivision. The Act was supposed to be replaced by the Subdivision of Agricultural Land Repeal Act, No. 64 of 1998; however, this has not been put into operation yet. Further, the Act has not yet been brought into alignment with the 1996 constitutional framework, leaving much still to be determined. New draft legislation has been developed to replace the Act; however, the finalisation and promulgation is yet to take place.[131]

South African national development imperatives have resulted in calls for radical economic transformation and accelerated land reform. It is therefore clear that Sustainable Development Goal (SDG) 15, which focuses on life on land, and target 15.3, which aims at achieving land degradation neutrality by 2030, will need to come even more to the fore in national development programmes.[132] Therefore, legal measures in relation to soil are conditional, such as legislation and policies that are necessary to enforce and control the protection of soil and to minimise the environmental impact with the accompaniment of social education and sensitisation. Although South Africa has applicable legislation, like that of CARA, there are improvements that need to be made in order to have a legal system that promotes and achieves soil protection. For example, CARA prescribes the creation of soil conservation committees; however, unfortunately, a number of these committees have yet to start functioning, which leaves them purposeless until they begin to do so.

130 Meyer et al. (2018: 335).
131 Ibid.
132 See https://bit.ly/3d1iMUX, accessed 20 May 2020.

8 Africa relevant international regulatory framework on soil[133]

Even though several international conventions recognise the importance of soil conservation, no overarching and transnational framework yet exists. One of the reasons advanced by opponents of an overarching, global and binding framework is that soil is non-moving and has *locally unique* problems, which should be dealt with locally.[134]

The European Soil Charter of 1972 is held to have been the first international document relating to soil.[135] The World Soil Charter and the World Soils Policy were negotiated by the United Nations Environment Programme (UNEP) in coordination with the FAO and were adopted in 1981. Both instruments contain non-binding guidelines and principles relating to soil conservation[136] and were intended to aid states in formulating domestic policies. However, in light of modern environmental practices, these instruments are considered to be outdated.[137]

Yet, 2015 was the International Year of Soils, which has resulted in a wealth of awareness activities across the globe, in addition to putting soils back on the international policy agenda.[138] This has also led to a new international dialogue concerning the protection and rehabilitation of soils and sustainable farming practices in general.[139] The GSP is a body established prior to the International Year of Soils and aided in the implementation and coordination of the roll-out of the year-long activities.[140] The GSP further encourages research, plans conferences and establishes local and regional partnerships.[141] However, criticism has been voiced relating to the felt absence of tangible results and calls for specific actions are mounting.[142]

New scientific knowledge has been gained over the past three decades, "especially with respect to new issues that emerged or were exacerbated during the last decades, like soil pollution and its consequences for the environment, climate change adaptation and mitigation and urban sprawl impacts on soil availability and functions".[143] In this respect, the World Soil Charter has been revised and was unanimously endorsed in June 2015, during the course of the International Year of Soils, by the member states of the FAO during the 39th Session of the FAO Conference.[144] The revised guidelines

133 Cf. Ruppel & von Finckenstein (2016: 309).
134 Montanarella (2015).
135 Alori & Nwapi (2015: 105).
136 Ibid.
137 Ibid.: 106.
138 See http://www.fao.org/soils-2015/news/news-detail/en/c/353737/, accessed 20 January 2021.
139 Ibid.
140 See http://www.fao.org/globalsoilpartnership/iys-2015/en/, accessed 20 January 2021.
141 Montanarella (2015).
142 Ibid.
143 See the revised World Soils Charter at http://www.fao.org/fileadmin/user_upload/GSP/docs/ITPS_Pillars/annexVII_WSC.pdf, accessed 16 January 2021.
144 The revised World Soil Charter is organised into a preamble, nine principles, and guidelines for action.

intend to ensure that "soils are managed sustainably and that degraded soils are rehabilitated or restored".[145] The actions are targeted at individuals and the organised private sector, governments and international organisations, which triggered an international dialogue concerning the protection and rehabilitation of soils and sustainable farming practices.[146] While tools such as FAOLEX and ECOLEX already compile national legislation and policies, and include some legislation on soil protection and soil degradation prevention, the newly established working group on soil legislation will in the time to come contribute to reviewing and updating the SoiLEX database containing all soil-related legal instruments adopted in each country.

While the World Charter on Nature[147] and Agenda 21[148] have been criticised to be inappropriate to aid in soil conservation, as their wording is too broad to establish clear norms,[149] other international law instruments have proved to be more relevant. Particularly for Africa, the UNCCD is the main international legal document to combat desertification and mitigate the effects of drought in affected countries through effective action at all levels supported by international cooperation. This instrument is the only international treaty specifically addressing land-related issues, while the definition of desertification therein clearly relates to soil conservation.[150]

> The UNCCD laid the groundwork for developing and establishing the concept of LDN. After adoption of the SDGs, the CCD claimed leadership for implementation of target 15.3 on LDN. It decided to integrate LDN in its work and has engaged in various activities. Besides a target setting programme this includes elaborating guidance material. In particular, the CCD published a Scientific Conceptual Framework that is intended to apply to all land and guide all parties in implementing LDN. Although the legal and political constraints make the UNCCD's potential difficult to assess, it could continue to pursue a leading role in implementing the LDN target and serve as forum for discussing soil-related issues between developing and developed countries.[151]

So far, however, the tangible effect of the UNCCD remains limited, as the focus is primarily placed on capacity-building, as opposed to creating binding obligations per se.[152]

The 2003 Maputo Convention, which entered into force in 2016 has one article dedicated to land degradation and soil conservation, overlapping with those contained in the UNCCD. Herein, agricultural activities have been identified as one important driver for land degradation in Africa, pointing out conflicts around land tenure that

---

145 See Section 3 of the Revised World Soil Charter.

146 See http://www.fao.org/soils-2015/news/news-detail/en/c/353737/, accessed 20 January 2021.

147 See http://www.un.org/documents/ga/res/37/a37r007.htm, accessed 16 January 2021.

148 United Nations Conference on the Environment and Development, Agenda 21, UN Doc a/ CONE151/4 (1992).

149 Alori & Nwapi (2015: 106).

150 Land degradation in arid, semi-arid and dry sub-humid areas resulting from various factors including climatic variations and human activities.

151 See with further references, Bodle et al. (2020: 14).

152 Alori & Nwapi (2015: 107).

require parties to develop and implement land tenure policies that are able to facilitate the measures to prevent land degradation and to conserve and improve the soil.[153]

It has been stated in recent studies that there is an overlap and potential competition and conflict between the UNCCD and the FAO, which also claims leadership regarding international soil. Both regimes are major international actors with high participation and political legitimacy in this field. Moreover, there seems to be an overlap with the CBD in terms of legal scope and mandate regarding soil biodiversity. Here the CBD is probably the more relevant international instrument, as the diversity within species and ecosystems is closely linked and reliant upon the conservation of soils and ecosystems. It aims at conserving biological diversity, promoting the sustainable use of its components, and encouraging equitable sharing of the benefits arising out of the utilisation of genetic resources.[154]

The 1992 UNFCCC was adopted to regulate levels of greenhouse gas concentration in the atmosphere, so as to, for instance, avoid the occurrence of climate change on a level that would compromise initiatives in food production. In this regard the convention is relevant together with a variety of other multilateral environmental agreements and international legal instruments that (directly or indirectly) deal with climate change.[155]

The 2015 Paris Agreement is part of the UNFCCC regime as it binds all its parties regarding activities on their respective territories and under their control. As such, the Paris Agreement supplements the UNFCCC and the Kyoto Protocol of 1997 by incorporating existing elements of these regimes.

According to its Article 2, the Paris Agreement's overarching objective is to keep the increase in global temperature well below 2°C, or even 1.5°C. Parties are required to prepare and present individual climate plans (nationally determined contributions) every five years that set out how the party intends to contribute to the collective objectives. Of course, soil as well as land use, land degradation and sustainable land management are closely linked to climate change in terms of carbon capture and storage, on the one hand, and the emissions from deforestation and agriculture, on the other. Yet the Paris Agreement fails to explicitly mention 'soil', 'land' or 'agriculture'. As such, the Paris Agreement only indirectly addresses soil protection in the general context of climate change. And despite the importance of land use and soil management for climate change, the UNFCCC, the Kyoto Protocol and the Paris Agreement have not established a comprehensive regime with regard to land-related climate change measures.[156] At COP 23 in 2017, agriculture first appeared in the ongoing climate negotiations under the Koronivia joint work programme.

---

153 See with further references, Bodle et al. (2020: 19).
154 Bodle et al. (2020: 53–54).
155 Ruppel (2013: 29).
156 Bodle et al. (2020: 53–54).

> The decision officially acknowledges the significance of the agriculture sectors in adapting to and mitigating climate change. Countries agreed to work together to make sure that agricultural development ensures both increased food security in the face of climate change and a reduction in emissions. The joint work is expected to address six topics related to soils, nutrient use, water, livestock, methods for assessing adaptation, and the socio-economic and food security dimensions of climate change across the agricultural sectors.[157]

Lastly, the Sustainable Development Goals (SDGs) were formulated as a successor to the Millennium Development Goals at the UN Conference on Sustainable Development. The SDGs were adopted in 2015 and Goal 15.3 therein pertains to achieving the "[p]rotection and promotion of sustainable use of terrestrial ecosystems, halt desertification, land degradation and biodiversity loss" and further aims to "achieve a LDN world". Although not legally binding, the SDGs, and in particular the LDN target in SDG 15.3, have at least established a political consensus for continued dialogue that guides national policies and governmental action for national land and soil policies.[158]

From the aforementioned it becomes clear, that the international soil governance framework remains highly fragmented, while the displayed international law instruments cover different aspects of soil protection in a relatively unconcerted manner.

9 Conclusion

In terms of this chapter, it can be concluded that soil management is an integral part of land management and many jurisdictions in Africa address soil within land management instruments or within soil-specific legislation. Soil management can be found in sectoral legislation on agriculture, land, environment or even water. While some legislative approaches distinguish between different soil types and characteristics in order to determine the specific interventions warranted to achieve the appropriate quality for the land use selected, others focus on issues such as soil quality, contamination and pollution, soil conservation and soil rehabilitation.[159] The fact is that the maintenance and protection of soil in Africa is vital in order to allow a continued reliance upon it. Soil maintenance and protection needs to be governed by legislation and policy, along with prescribed and practised enforcement measures. Incentives and deterrents for sustainable land use ensure that private land use is in line with social and other policy objectives and promote certain practices, fertilizers, subsidies, etc. No doubt, sustainable agriculture, rural development and the upliftment of poor and marginalised communities require a cross-sectoral involvement of environment, climate change, land rights, gender equality, traditional and indigenous affairs, health, economy and trade, among others.

---

157 See http://www.fao.org/climate-change/our-work/what-we-do/koronivia/en/, accessed 16 July 2020.

158 Bodle et al. (2020: 11–21).

159 FAO & UNEP (2020: 132).

Progression in terms of land tenure rights is also necessary to enable soil protection to obviate the effect that land tenure can have on soil. Human influence on the land and natural resources, such as soil, is accelerating as a result of the growth in population on the African continent and the associated increase of food requirements.[160]

While scarce, land is more than a source of food security, income and shelter. Especially in Africa, it is also related to cultural identity and is thus often a source of tribal tension or political competition.[161] Therefore, reliable land tenure arrangements will serve to reduce poverty, support sustainable livelihoods, enable social stability and housing, and foster environmental protection. Moreover, food security and food availability are highly dependent on secure access to and the productivity of land.[162]

Land-use change is displayed in the change of land-cover, and this change is a key component of global environmental change that is affecting the climate, biodiversity and ecosystems, which in turn has an impact on land-use decisions.[163] Increased compacted areas associated with urban development, for example, increase runoff during rainfall, which accelerates erosion and runoff downstream of the urban catchment. The way land is used plays a considerable role in the quality of soil. Land tenure thus also significantly affects soil conservation. In many countries in Africa, there is still a need for the formalisation of land tenure in respect of both individual and communal land rights and for an integration of different land tenure systems, to achieve a unitary approach that can ensure that all land is administered and regulated. This will ensure land protection and, in particular, soil protection.[164] In order to achieve this, a legal framework is necessary for any registration programme to function and bring about the desired outcomes, such as the administration of land usage and protection of natural resources.[165]

> For most of human history, the natural world has been protected from the most disruptive human influences by relatively humble technology, cultural factors ... [and] land ownership by the ancestors ...[166]

And while customary law, under colonised structures, was seen as inferior to colonial law, the so-called 'repugnancy clause' is no longer valid. Under this clause, customary law was only recognised under the condition that it was "not repugnant to the general principles of humanity recognised throughout the whole civilised world".[167] It was therefore in many African countries after independence that:[168]

160 Kanianska (2016: 4).
161 FAO & UNEP (2020: 93).
162 Sandrey (2019/20: 134).
163 Kanianska (2016: 6).
164 Tlale (2018: 267).
165 Ibid.: 266.
166 Hinz & Ruppel (2008: 5).
167 Zenker (2020).
168 Menski (2011: 143).

> [a]fter generations of missionaries, anthropologists and lawyers, whose first interest was to force African customary law into the procrustean bed of either the bible, civilisation or a western paradigm of rule of law, African customary law begins to breathe again: to breathe the air of Africa.

Legal systems in Africa[169] are made up of a melting pot of cultures, religions and community practices that have culminated in the complexity and all-encompassing nature of the systems.[170] This plurality including customary law and indigenous knowledge in soil-related policies:[171]

> is likely to contribute to the development of more effective adaptation strategies that are cost-effective, participatory and sustainable. After all, indigenous people have always been tasked to develop flexible mechanisms to cope with climatic conditions and their vulnerability.

And although there are still many improvements that can be made to enhance the protection of soil in Africa, education in soil law is also important in order to stress the importance of soil protection measures. The training of lawyers and law students in the subject of soil protection and law can promote the need for any legal system that has secure and effective soil protection measures. This training would see an increase in legal personnel who have the relevant expertise and knowledge to ensure that soil protection law is complied with and improved upon, as well as enforced and monitored.

Moreover, when considering improvements that need to be made to soil legislation in Africa, it can also be said that the legislation relating to foreign investors should not be neglected:[172]

> Investment for sustainable development in Africa requires political commitment to overcome substantial barriers at various levels. To enable new markets for sustainable development requires adequate regulatory frameworks (international, regional and national) in order to give investors, the necessary confidence. The national state has to balance the interest of attracting (and securing) international investment while promoting peace and security for its population. The most appropriate approach for achieving both of the aforementioned is adherence to and promotion of the rule of law while creating incentive structures for investors to act sustainably and to respect national social development goals, empowerment policies, labour standards and human rights.

The aforementioned is particularly true in the context of 'land-grabbing', where there is a need for legislation that clearly sets out how the foreign investor needs to comply with national interests, as well as a need for legislation that prescribes how foreign investors can acquire, possess, own and utilise land in African countries. Such legislation should also highlight and clarify social and environmental responsibilities of the foreign investor, along with the consequences should they fail to comply with these responsibilities.

Lastly, both at national and at international law level, improving soil governance includes options for enhancing coordination and coherence. A clearer division of

169 Ruppel & Ruppel-Schlichting (2011).
170 Du Plessis (2019: 15).
171 Ruppel & Ifejika Speranza (2011: 200).
172 Ruppel & Borgmeyer (2018); Ruppel & Shifotoka (2017: 56).

labour between sectors and institutions addressing soil holds significant potential for improving soil governance. After all, it becomes increasingly clear that the element, soil, is both international and domestic in nature and should therefore be pursued in a complementary[173] manner in order be able to counter soil degradation in the context of climate change in the Anthropocene,[174] global human security[175] and cross-border migration processes.[176]

References

Alori, E. & C. Nwapi, 2015, "The international legal regime for sustainable soil". In: Ako, R. & D. Olawuyi (eds), 2015, *Food and agricultural law: Readings on sustainable agriculture and the law in Nigeria*, Ado-Ekiti: Afe Babalola University Press, 98.

Ayee, J.R.A., 1998, "The formulation and implementation of environmental policy in Ghana". *Africa Development* 23 (2), 99.

Bodle, R., H. Stockhaus, F. Wolff, C.-S. Scherf, & S. Oberthür, 2020, *Improving international soil governance – Analysis and recommendations*. Dessau-Roßlau: German Environment Agency.

Boer, B. & I. Hannam, 2015, "Developing a global soil regime". Soil Governance, Special Edition 1, *International Journal of Rural Law and Policy*, 1.

Chiziane, E.A., 2019, "The design of the political and legal framework on soil conservation in Mozambique: Deeply unfinished". In: Ginzky, H., E. Dooley, I.L. Heuser, E. Kasimbazi, T. Markus & T. Qin (eds), *International yearbook of soil law and policy 2018*. Cham: Springer International Publishing, 331.

Department of Agriculture, 1999, *Implementation framework for the land care programme*. Pretoria: Department of Agriculture, at https://www.gov.za/sites/default/files/gcis_document/201409/landcare.pdf, accessed 20 July 2020.

Department of Environment and Tourism, 2004, *National action programme combating land degradation to alleviate rural poverty*. Pretoria: Department of Environment and Tourism, at https://www.gov.za/sites/default/files/gcis_document/201409/27952.pdf, accessed 20 July 2020.

Department of Environmental Affairs, 2012, *National climate change response white paper*. Pretoria: Department of Environmental Affairs, at https://www.environment.gov.za/sites/default/files/legislations/national_climatechange_response_whitepaper.pdf, accessed 20 July 2020.

Dugard, J., 2018, *Dugard's international law: A South African perspective*. 4th edition, Cape Town: JUTA.

Du Plessis, H., 2019, "Legal pluralism, uBuntu and the use of open norms in the South African common law of contract". *Potchefstroom Electronic Law Journal*, 22, 1.

FAO / Food and Agriculture Organisation of the United Nations & UNEP / United Nations Environment Programme, 2020, *Legislative approaches to sustainable agriculture and natural resources governance*. FAO Legislative Study No. 114, at https://www.unenvironment.org/resources/

173 Bodle et al. (2020: 11–21, 126).
174 Ruppel (2013).
175 Ruppel & Ruppel-Schlichting (2013).
176 Ruppel & Van Wyk (2013).

publication/legislative-approaches-sustainable-agriculture-and-natural-resources, accessed 23 July 2020.

Garland, G.G., D.G. Paterson, T.S. Newby, M.C. Laker & M.T. Hoffman, 2000, "Soil degradation". In: Hoffman, M.T., S. Todd, Z. Ntshona & S. Turner (eds), *A national review of land degradation in South Africa*. Pretoria: South African National Biodiversity Institute, 69.

Government of the Republic of Ghana, 1990, *National environment policy and national environment action plan*. Accra: Republic of Ghana, at http://maps.cersgis.org/nipportal/POLICIES/NATIONAL_ENVIRONMENTAL_POLICY_(MAIN).pdf, accessed 8 August 2020.

Government of the Republic of Ghana, 1992, *Environmental resource management project*. Accra: Republic of Ghana, at http://documents1.worldbank.org/curated/en/602661468249936996/pdf/multi-page.pdf, accessed 10 August 2020.

Government of the Republic of Ghana, 1999a, *Policy formulated purpose authority environmental sanitation policy*. Ministry of Local Government and Rural Development, at https://www.documents.clientearth.org/wp-content/uploads/library/2012-01-01-ghana-forest-and-wildlife-policy-2012-ext-en.pdf, accessed 11 August 2020.

Government of the Republic of Ghana, 1999b, *Environmental assessment regulations*. Accra: Republic of Ghana, at https://www.documents.clientearth.org/wp-content/uploads/library/2012-01-01-ghana-forest-and-wildlife-policy-2012-ext-en.pdf, accessed 11 August 2020.

Government of the Republic of Ghana, 2009, *Treaty manual*. Accra: Republic of Ghana, at https://legal.un.org/avl/documents/scans/GhanaTreatyManual2009.pdf?teil=II&j, accessed 8 August 2020.

Government of the Republic of Ghana, 2012, *Forest and wildlife policy*. Accra: Republic of Ghana, Ministry of Land and Natural Resources, at https://www.documents.clientearth.org/wp-content/uploads/library/2012-01-01-ghana-forest-and-wildlife-policy-2012-ext-en.pdf, accessed 11 August 2020.

Government of the Republic of Namibia, 2014, *Third national action programme for Namibia to Implement the United Nations Convention to Combat Desertification 2014-2024*. Windhoek: Ministry of Environment and Tourism, at http://www.unccd.int/ActionProgrammes/Namibia-2014-2024-eng.pdf, accessed 22 November 2015.

Havenga, P., C. Garbers, M. Havenga, W.G. Schulze, K. van der Linde & T. van der Merwe (eds), 2002, *General principles of commercial law*. 4th edition, Lansdowne: Juta Law.

Higgins, T. & J. Fenrich, 2012, "Legal pluralism, gender, and access to land in Ghana". *Fordham Environmental Law Review* 23 (2), 7.

Hinz, M.O. & O.C. Ruppel, 2008, "Legal protection of biodiversity in Namibia". In: Hinz, M.O. & O.C. Ruppel (eds), 2008, *Biodiversity and the ancestors: Challenges to customary and environmental law – Case Studies from Namibia*, Windhoek: Namibia Scientific Society, 3.

Kanianska, R., 2016, *Agriculture and its impact on land-use, environmental, and ecosystem services*. Slovakia: Matej Bel University.

Kasimbazi, E., 2019, "Soil protection law in Uganda". In: Ginzky, H., E. Dooley, I.L. Heuser, E. Kasimbazi, T. Markus & T. Qin (eds), 2019, *International yearbook of soil law and policy 2018*, Cham: Springer International Publishing, 315.

Kidd, M., 2011, *Environmental law*. Cape Town: Juta.

Maria, R.M. & R. Yost, 2006, "A survey of soil fertility status of four agroecological zones of Mozambique". *Soil Science* 171 (11), 902.

Menski, W., 2011, "Flying kites in Africa: Legal pluralism in a plural world". In: Ruppel, O.C., & G. Winter (eds), *Legal pluralism in africa and beyond. Liber amicorum Manfred O. Hinz in celebration of his 75th birthday; Recht von innen: Rechtspluralismus in Afrika und anderswo. Festschrift Manfred O. Hinz anlässlich seines 75. Geburtstages*. Budapest: Dr. Kovac Law Publishers, 141.

Meyer, T., E. Verster, A. Hattingh, N. Olivier, W. du Plessis & T. Snow, 2018, "Soil, land and agriculture". In: King, N.D., H.A. Strydom & F.P. Retief (eds), 2018, *Fuggle & Rabie's environmental management in South Africa.* 3rd edition, Cape Town: Juta, 283.

Montanarella, L, 2015, "Agricultural policy: Govern our soils". *Nature* 528 (7480), 32.

Mostert, H. & A. Pope (eds), 2010, *The principles of the law of property in South Africa.* Cape Town: Oxford University Press South Africa.

Orubebe, B.B., 2020, "Soil governance and sustainable land use system in Nigeria: The paradox of inequalities, natural resource conflict and ecological diversity in a federal system". In: Yahyah, H., H. Ginzky, E. Kasimbazi, R. Kibugi & O.C. Ruppel (eds), *Legal instruments for sustainable soil management in Africa.* Cham: Springer International Publishing, 157.

Rautenbach, C., 2010, "Deep legal pluralism in South Africa: Judicial accommodation of non-state law". *Journal of Legal Pluralism and Unofficial Law* 42 (60), 143.

Rautenbach, C., 2018, *Introduction to legal pluralism in South Africa.* 5th edition, Cape Town: LexisNexis South Africa.

Rees, W.E., 2018, "North American soils and world food". In: Ginzky, H., E. Dooley, I.L. Heuser, E. Kasimbazi, T. Markus & T. Qin (eds), *International yearbook of soil law and policy.* Cham: Springer International Publishing, 21.

República de Moçambique, Ministério da Agricultura, 2007, *Potencialidades das zonas agroecologicas para intensificação e diversificação da agro-pecuaria em Moçambique.* Maputo: Ministério da Agricultura.

Ruppel, O.C. (ed.), 2008, *Women and custom in Namibia: Cultural practice versus gender equality.* Windhoek: MacMillan Education Namibia.

Ruppel, O.C. & C. Ifejika Speranza, 2011, "The international, African and regional institutional, legal and policy framework of climate change". In: AU and AMCEN, 2011, *Addressing climate change challenges in Africa.* Nairobi: African Union, AMCEN and United Nations Environment Programme, 170.

Ruppel, O.C. & K. Ruppel-Schlichting, 2011, "Legal and judicial pluralism in Namibia and beyond: A modern approach to African legal architecture?". *Journal of Legal Pluralism and Unofficial Law* 64, 33.

Ruppel, O.C., 2013, "Intersections of law and cooperative global climate governance – challenges in the Anthropocene". In: Ruppel, O.C., C. Roschmann & K. Ruppel-Schlichting (eds), 2013, *Climate change: International law and global governance, Volume I: Legal responses and global responsibility.* Baden-Baden: Nomos, 29.

Ruppel, O.C. & S. Van Wyk, 2013, "Climate-change induced movement of persons in Africa: Human rights responses to aspects of human security". In: Ruppel, O.C., C. Roschmann & K. Ruppel-Schlichting (eds), *Climate change: International law and global governance*, Volume 2, Baden-Baden: Nomos Law Publishers, 799.

Ruppel, O.C., 2016a, "Environmental law in Namibia: An overview". In: Ruppel, O.C. & K. Ruppel-Schlichting (eds), *Environmental law and policy in Namibia – towards making Africa the tree of life.* Windhoek: Hanns-Seidel-Foundation, 29.

Ruppel, O.C. 2016b, "Introduction to international environmental law". In: Ruppel, O.C. & K. Ruppel-Schlichting (eds), *Environmental law and policy in Namibia – towards making Africa the tree of life.* Windhoek: Hanns-Seidel-Foundation, 55.

Ruppel, O.C. & A. von Finckenstein, 2016, "The protection of soil under Namibian Law". In: Ginzky, H., I. Heuser, T. Qin, O.C. Ruppel & P. Wegerdt (eds), *International yearbook of soil law and policy.* Cham: Springer International Publishing, 309.

Ruppel, O.C. & F. Shifotoka, 2017, "Foreign direct investment protection in Africa – Contemporary legal aspects between BITS and BRICS". In: Yusf, A.A. (ed.), *African yearbook of international law*. Vol. 21, Issue 1, Leiden: Brill | Nijhoff, 5.

Ruppel, O.C. & K. Ruppel-Schlichting, 2012, "Legal and judicial pluralism in Namibia and beyond". *Journal of Legal Pluralism and Unofficial Law* 64 (11), 33.

Ruppel, O.C. & K. Ruppel-Schlichting, 2013, "Climate change, human security and regional integration: The example of the Southern African Development Community". In: Ruppel, O.C., C. Roschmann & K. Ruppel-Schlichting (eds), *Climate Change: International Law and Global Governance Volume I: Legal Responses and Global Responsibility*. Baden-Baden: Nomos Law Publishers, 505.

Ruppel, O.C. & K. Ruppel-Schlichting, 2016, "Namibia and its legal setup". In: Ruppel, O.C. & K. Ruppel-Schlichting (eds), *Environmental law and policy in Namibia – towards making Africa the tree of life*. Windhoek: Hanns-Seidel-Foundation, 1.

Ruppel, O.C. & T. Borgmeyer, 2018, "The BRICS partnership from a South African perspective: Sustainable development space in a new global governance". In: Ndulo, M. & S. Kayizzi-Mugerwa (eds), *Financing innovation and sustainable development in Africa*. Newcastle: Cambridge Scholars Publishing, 282.

Ruppel, O.C., K.M. Knutton & R.A. Marivate, forthcoming 2021, "Soil protection legislation and policy in South Africa: An overview". In: Ginzky, H., B. Desai, E. Dooley, I. Heuser, R. Kibugi, T. Markus, P. Mbote & O.C. Ruppel (eds), *International yearbook of soil law and policy*. Vol. 5, Cham: Springer International Publishing.

Ruppel, O.C., G.W. Junger & K.M. Knutton, 2020, "Der Klimawandel in der Governance, Gesetzgebung und Rechtsprechung Südafrikas: Ein Überblick über die jüngsten Entwicklungen". *Zeitschrift für Umweltrecht (ZUR)* 5, 274.

Sandrey, R., 2019/2020, "African agricultural land: Past, present and future". In: Chidede, T., F. Mbakhwa, M. Moobi, L. Phaleng, R. Sandrey, N. Wagner, W. Viljoen & K. Zosuliwe (eds), 2019/2020, *Agricultural and food security in Africa*. Stellenbosch: Trade Law Centre, South Africa, 133.

Sucker, F., 2014, "Approval of an international treaty in Parliament: How does section 231(2) 'bind the Republic'?". *Constitutional Court Review* 5, 417.

Tlale, M.T., 2018, *A critical evaluation of the South African land tenure policy: A comparison with selected aspects of the Kenyan and Tanzanian law*. PhD Thesis, North-West University.

Tumuhairwe, J.Y., C. Nkwiine, G. Eilu, C. Gumisiriza & F. Tumuhairwe, 2003, "Agro-biodiversity potential of smallholder farms in a dissected highland plateau of western Uganda". In: Kaihura, F. & M. Stocking (eds), *Agricultural Biodiversity in Smallholder Farms of East Africa*. New York: United Nations University Press, 34.

UNEP / United Nations Environment Programme, 2019, *Environmental rule of law: First global report*. Nairobi: United Nations Environment Programme, at https://www.unenvironment.org/resources/assessment/environmental-rule-law-first-global-report, accessed 23 July 2020.

Van Wyk, J., 2018, "The law on planning and the environment". In: King, N.D., H.A. Strydom & F.P. Retief (eds), 2018, *Fuggle & Rabie's environmental management in South Africa*. 3rd edition, Cape Town: Juta, 1131.

Yawson, O.D., M. Osei Adu, B. Ason, F. Ato Armah & G. Tambang Yengoh, 2016, "Putting soil security on the policy agenda: Need for a familiar framework". *Challenges* 7 (2), 1.

Zenker, O., 2020, "Mind the gaps: renegotiating South African legal pluralism with the post-apartheid state". In: Seidel, K. & H. Elliesie (eds), *Normative spaces and legal dynamics in Africa*. Abingdon: Routledge.

The Pan-African Parliament of the African Union: Composition, mandate and partnerships, and its quest for sustainable development

Oliver C. Ruppel & Larissa-Jane Houston

1 Introduction

As initially envisioned under the Organisation of African Unity (OAU) to be established by the African Economic Community (AEC), the Pan-African Parliament (PAP) was successfully established when the African Union (AU) replaced the OAU and called for the speedy establishment of the institutions provided for in the AEC Treaty (Abuja Treaty).[1]

The OAU, predecessor of the AU, was established on 25 May 1963 in Addis Ababa, Ethiopia.[2] Twenty years after the establishment of the OAU Charter Review Committee, the OAU's Assembly of African Heads of State and Government met at Sirte, Libya, on 9 September 1999, for its Fourth Extraordinary Summit where it adopted the Sirte Declaration proposing an Inter-African Union, or African Union, as it would later be known.[3] The meeting of the Fourth Extraordinary Summit sought to:

> discuss ways and means of making the OAU effective so as to keep pace with political and economic developments taking place in the world and the preparation required of Africa within the context of globalization so as to preserve its socio-economic and political potentials.[4]

Article 8 of the Sirte Declaration provided the following:

> Having discussed frankly and extensively on how to proceed with the strengthening of the unity of our continent and its peoples, in the light of those proposals, and bearing in mind the current situation on the Continent, we decide to: (i) Establish an African Union, in conformity with the ultimate objectives of the Charter of our Continental Organization and the provisions of the Treaty establishing the African Economic Community.[5]

---

1 PAP (2020); Magliveras & Naldi (2003).

2 Charter of the Organization of African Unity (adopted 25 May 1963, entered into force 13 September 1963).

3 Murray (2004: 22).

4 OAU (1999).

5 Organisation of African Unity (Assembly of Heads of State and Government) *Sirte Declaration* (Sirte 1999) EAHG/Draft/Decl. (IV) Rev.1.

The legal basis of the PAP is provided for within the Abuja Treaty.[6] According to Article 5(1)(c) of the Constitutive Act of the AU,[7] the PAP is considered to be an organ of the AU. Article 5 of the AU Constitutive Act provides for the establishment of the following institutions: The Assembly; the Executive Council; the Specialised Technical Committees; the Pan-African Parliament; the African Court of Justice (and Human Rights);[8] the financial institutions; the Commission; the Permanent Representatives Committee; the Economic, Social and Cultural Council; and other organs that the Assembly may decide to establish. Each of these has its own mandate and focus areas within the African Union.

Article 17 of the Constitutive Act of the AU pertains specifically to the PAP and provides that, in order to ensure the full participation of African peoples in the development and economic integration of the continent, a Pan-African Parliament will be established. The composition, powers, functions, and organisation of the Pan-African Parliament will be defined in a protocol relating thereto.

Article 17(1) of the Constitutive Act provides the purpose of the PAP in the AU context. According to the PAP, "the Parliament is intended as a platform for people from all African states to be involved in discussions and decision-making on the problems and challenges facing the continent."[9] A joint reading of the purposes as provided by the AU and the PAP indicate an expectation that the PAP will provide a shared platform for African peoples that includes involvement from grassroots organisations.[10]

The Protocol to the Constitutive Act of the African Union Relating to the Pan-African Parliament (PAP Protocol) assists with directing the objectives and functions of the PAP.[11] According to the PAP:[12]

> the mission of the Pan-African Parliament is to provide a common platform for African peoples to represent, and to act as a voice of the people of Africa presenting their opinions, their concerns and aspirations, and thus effectively hold the governing institutions of the AU accountable in the implementation of policies and programmes as well as in the allocation and use of public resources for promoting just, equitable and sustainable development for all the peoples of Africa. The ultimate aim of the Pan-African Parliament is to evolve into an institution with full legislative powers, whose members are elected by universal adult suffrage.

---

6 Dinokopila (2013); Organisation of African Unity (Assembly of Heads of State and Government) Treaty Establishing the African Economic Community (*Abuja Treaty*) entered into force 12 May 1994, Article 14.

7 OAU Doc. CAB/LEG/23.15.

8 See also Protocol on the Statute of the African Court of Justice and Human Rights (Single Protocol) Article 3 (adopted July 2008).

9 PAP (2020).

10 Magliveras & Naldi (2003).

11 Adopted 27 June 2014.

12 PAP (2020).

2 Composition

According to Article 2(3) of the PAP Protocol, the PAP represents all the peoples of Africa. It is at present composed of 229 members of parliament representing 52 of 55 African countries and as such receives its mandate from each member state.[13] PAP membership includes five members elected by each member state, of which at least two are women.[14] The national parliaments or other legislative bodies of each member state elect or designate members to the PAP to represent the interests of each member state.[15] The expectations and qualifications that should be considered during the election process are provided for under Article 5 of the PAP Protocol. The PAP Protocol provides that:

> In addition to the condition on women's representation, the membership of each Member State must reflect the diversity of political opinions in each National Parliament or other deliberative organ. The term of Members of the Pan-African Parliament starts from the day they are sworn into office or make a solemn declaration during a plenary session. While exercising their functions, Members of the Pan-African Parliament shall enjoy immunities and privileges in the territory of each Member State.[16]

As provided under Article 2(2) of the PAP Protocol, the organs of the PAP will be the plenary; the bureau; the secretariat, committees and regional groups. According to Article 12(3) of the PAP Protocol, the Bureau is responsible for the development of policies for the management and administration of the affairs and property of the PAP, which must be submitted to the plenary for approval. The Rules of Procedure, as established under Article 11 of the PAP Protocol, will provide the specific functions of the President and Vice-President of the PAP. The PAP's Secretary-General is the head of the Secretariat and thus responsible for the day-to-day management and administration of the affairs and property of the PAP and is accountable to the PAP through the Bureau, as outlined in Article 13(4) of the PAP Protocol.

Article 9 of the PAP Protocol stipulates privileges and immunities of the PAP parliamentarians, which relate to diplomatic relations and parliamentary immunity in each member state. The PAP consists of 11 permanent committees to assist with issues that are placed before Parliament – in particular the Committee on Rural Economy, Agriculture, Natural Resources and Environment; the Committee on Monetary and Financial Affairs; the Committee on Trade, Customs and Immigration Matters; the Committee on Cooperation, International Relations and Conflict Resolutions; the Committee on Transport, Industry, Communication, Energy, Science and Technology; the Committee on Health, Labour and Social Affairs; the Committee on Education, Culture, Tourism and Human Resources; the Committee on Gender, Family, Youth

13 Article 4 PAP Protocol.
14 Article 4(3) PAP Protocol.
15 PAP (2020); Article 5 PAP Protocol.
16 PAP (2020).

and People with Disabilities; the Committee on Justice and Human Rights; the Committee on Rules, Privileges and Discipline; and the Committee on Audit and Public Accounts. [17]

General functions of these permanent committees are set out under Rule 22(11) of the PAP Rules of Procedure, which provide at the outset that "the President shall, on the advice of the Bureau, determine the business to be handled by the Committees" and that Parliament may allocate any other matter to any committee it deems appropriate, in accordance with Rule 25(3) of the PAP Rules of Procedure.[18]

3 Mandate

Upon its establishment, the broad mandate of the PAP was to "enable all the peoples of Africa to get involved in discussions and decision-making on the problems and challenges which beset Africa".[19] The understanding was that the PAP would represent a common continental (African) vision that would "strengthen the African Union".[20] The specific mandate of the PAP is set out as objectives, functions and powers provided by the PAP Protocol.

The specific objectives of the Pan-African Parliament are to give a voice to the African peoples and the diaspora; facilitate the effective implementation of the policies and objectives of the African Union; promote the principle of human rights and democracy in Africa; encourage good governance, transparency and accountability in member states; familiarise the peoples of Africa with the objectives and policies on the political and socioeconomic integration of the continent; promote peace, security and stability; contribute to a more prosperous future for the peoples of Africa by promoting collective self-reliance and economic recovery; facilitate cooperation and development in Africa; strengthen continental solidarity and build a sense of common destiny among the peoples of Africa; facilitate cooperation among regional economic communities,[21] and their parliamentary forums; encourage national and regional parliaments to ratify and integrate treaties adopted by the AU into their legal systems; cooperate with national and regional parliaments and similar bodies within and outside

17 Dinokopila (2013); PAP (2020).

18 Pan-African Parliament (Ad Hoc Rules Committee) *Rules of Procedure* adopted on 21 November 2004.

19 Mngomezulu (2018).

20 Ibid.: 50.

21 The AU recognises eight RECs: the Arab Maghreb Union (UMA); the Common Market for Eastern and Southern Africa (COMESA); the Community of Sahel–Saharan States (CEN–SAD); the East African Community (EAC); the Economic Community of Central African States (ECCAS); the Economic Community of West African States (ECOWAS); the Intergovernmental Authority on Development (IGAD); and the Southern African Development Community (SADC).

Africa, as well as civil societies, community-based organisations and grassroots organisations; and invite and encourage the full participation of the African diaspora as an important part of the African peoples in the building of the African Union in accordance with modalities approved by the Assembly.[22] A key objective of the PAP is to encourage good governance and to promote the principles of human rights and democracy in Africa.[23]

4 Functions and powers

According to Article 8 of the PAP Protocol, the PAP is the legislative organ of the AU and is responsible for carrying out the functions and wielding the powers of the AU. Article 8 of the PAP Protocol specifically states that:[24]

> The Assembly shall determine the subjects/areas on which the PAP may propose draft model laws; The PAP may on its own make proposals on the subjects/areas on which it may submit or recommend draft Model Laws to the Assembly for its consideration and approval; The PAP shall also: receive and consider reports of other organs of the AU as may be referred to it by the Council or the Assembly, including audit and other reports and make recommendations thereon, debate and discuss its own budget and the budget of the Union and make recommendations thereon to the relevant policy organs, establish any Parliamentary Committee and determine its functions, mandate, composition and term of office, discuss any matter relevant to the AU and make recommendations to the Council or the Assembly as it may deem appropriate, make proposals to the Council on the structure of the Secretariat of the Parliament taking into account its needs, request the attendance of officials of the other organs of the AU at its sessions to offer assistance to the Parliament in the discharge of its duties, promote the programmes and objectives of AU in Member states, receive, consider and submit opinions on draft legal instruments, treaties and other international agreements as may be referred to it by the Council or Assembly, liaise with National Parliaments or other deliberative bodies and the Parliaments of the Regional Economic Communities on all matters relating to the AU and regional integration in Africa, and carry out such other activities as it deems appropriate to achieve the objectives set out in Article 3 of the PAP Protocol.

Moreover, the PAP has powers to:

> discuss and make recommendations on issues relating to human rights, democracy and good governance, to harmonise the laws of member states, make recommendations contributing to the objectives of the AU/AEC, promote the AU/AEC in the member states, and to harmonise the policies and programmes of regional economic communities.[25]

---

22 Article 3 PAP Protocol.

23 Dinokopila (2013).

24 African Union Protocol to the Constitutive Act of the African Union relating to the Pan-African Parliament, at https://au.int/en/treaties/protocol-constitutive-act-african-union-relating-pan-african-parliament, accessed 27 May 2020.

25 Magliveras & Naldi (2003).

5 Partnerships

Given that the PAP is responsible, under Article 3 of the PAP Protocol, for cooperation among regional economic communities (RECs), as well as member states and specialised organisations across the continent, there are a number of partnerships established and supported by the PAP.

Article 19(1) of the PAP Protocol provides that the PAP is required to "work in close co-operation with the Parliaments of the RECs and the National Parliaments or other Organs of Member States."

Article 20 of the PAP Protocol regulates the relations between the PAP and other organs of the AU. These provisions underpin the partnerships between the PAP and member states and the AU. The meaning of 'close cooperation' as provided in the PAP Protocol has not been entirely clarified and is interpreted as the possibility that Parliament will convene annual consultative meetings with the other entities to discuss matters of common interest.[26]

The communication with the relevant RECs is through the East African Legislative Assembly operating in the East African Community; the Southern African Development Community (SADC) Parliamentary Forum; the Economic Community of West African States (ECOWAS) Parliament; and the Economic and Monetary Community of Central Africa (CEMAC) Parliament.[27]

Despite shortcomings faced by the PAP, there have been a number of successfully executed projects and initiatives by the PAP that have been crucial to the achievement of its mandate. The PAP has sought to address challenges through the passing of a number of resolutions, for example those passed at the 3rd Ordinary Session, namely the resolutions on signing of adherence to the African Peer Review Mechanism (PAP_Res.001/05); on the development of a continental code of conduct on the use and exploitation of National Resources and Environmental Protection (PAP_Res.002/05); on the appreciation of the intervention of the Chairperson of the African Union in the Togo crisis (PAP_Res.003/05); on the appreciation of the work of Mr Kofi Annan, the Secretary-General to the United Nations (PAP_Res.004/05); relating to the presidential elections in Togo on 24 April 2005 (PAP_Res.005/05); on the dispatch of the Pan-African Parliament Peace Mission to Cote d'Ivoire at the beginning of May 2005 (PAP_Res.006/05); and on congratulating His Excellency Thabo Mbeki, President of the Republic of South Africa, on his success in achieving a peace agreement between the warring parties in Cote d'Ivoire (PAP_Res.007/05).[28]

26 Ibid.
27 Ibid.
28 Amadi (2016: 5).

The PAP has also looked to strengthen its legislative arm in countries across Africa, in general, through the African Peer Review Mechanism (APRM):[29]

The APRM is a mutually agreed instrument voluntarily acceded to by AU Member States as an African self-monitoring mechanism. The APRM is often described as Africa's unique and innovative approach to governance with the objective of improving governance dynamics at the local, national and continental levels.[30]

The APRM conducts individual governance reviews in specific countries and, once the review is completed, writes a country review report and presents it before the PAP.[31] This is in compliance with the APRM base document which provides that six months after each country review report has been considered by the Heads of State and Government of the participating member countries, it should be formally and publicly tabled in key regional and sub-regional structures such as the PAP.[32]

Another such partnership occurs between the Chairperson of the African Union Peace and Security Council, who routinely attends the PAP sessions and presents reports to the plenary on the prevailing security situation in Africa and the activities of the council in response to such situations. For instance, Sierra Leone's Ambassador to the Federal Democratic Republic of Ethiopia and Permanent Representative to the African Union, Mr Osman Keh Kamara, made a presentation on behalf of the African Union Peace and Security Council at the 3rd Ordinary Session of the 4th sitting of the Pan-African Parliament which took place on 13 October 2016 in Sharm-el Sheikh, Egypt.[33] These reports are debated and recommendations are made, where necessary, on how more effectively to address some of the security challenges.[34]

In connection with the oversight functions of the PAP, it is instructive to recall that the leaders of 27 European and 54 African states, as well as the presidents of the continental institutions launched the Joint Africa-EU Strategy (JAES) at the Africa-EU Summit in Lisbon in 2007, setting out the intention of both continents to move beyond a donor–recipient relationship towards long-term cooperation on jointly identified, mutual and complementary interests.[35]

The PAP and the European Parliament, national and regional parliaments, as well as civil societies on both continents should be fully involved in decision-making at their respective levels in order to ensure that there is proper transparency and accountability to all citizens involved in the process.[36] In particular, the role of the PAP and the European Parliament is to carry out joint monitoring and evaluation on the

29 Ibid.: 7.
30 See https://www.aprm-au.org/page-about/, accessed 21 May 2020.
31 ECA (2011: 1, 6–8).
32 NEPAD (2003: para 25).
33 Kabs Kanu (2016).
34 Nwebo (2019: 134).
35 European Commission (2020).
36 Nwebo (2019: 135).

implementation of the JAES. The two parliaments also issued a joint declaration which they presented to the Summit of the African Heads of State and Government of two unions to guide their discussions.[37]

The PAP has various memoranda of understanding (MoUs) for cooperation and collaboration with organisations and international institutions especially in the promotion of constitutionalism and good governance, for instance.[38] These include the Africa Capacity Building Foundation which, through an agreement with the AUC, supports the advocacy campaigns and capacity-building for the PAP; the European Commission which supports capacity-building efforts of the PAP through provision of resources for staff of the PAP in the finance unit, and in addition supports the advocacy campaign and monitoring and evaluation at the PAP; the Deutsche Gesellschaft für Internationale Zusammenarbeit (GIZ) which supported the recruitment process of the PAP and currently supports the African Governance Architecture programme in which the PAP spearheads the advocacy for the ratification and domestication of AU legal instruments; and the European Parliament which jointly monitors the implementation of the JAES and supports the capacity development of the PAP.

On 10 October 2019 a further and innovative cooperation agreement was signed between Stellenbosch University (through its Development and Rule of Law Programme, DROP),[39] the PAP, and the German Environment Agency, Umweltbundesamt.[40] With this MoU, Stellenbosch University enters the realm of academic diplomacy and policy development. On behalf of the PAP, the MoU was signed by its President the Rt Hon. Roger Nkodo Dang. As the PAP is an organ of the African Union established to ensure the full participation of African peoples in the development and economic integration of the continent, its objectives include the promotion peace, security and stability; good governance; and the principles of human rights and democracy in Africa. In support of this mandate, Stellenbosch University's Development and Rule of Law Programme (DROP), which was founded in 2012, is now tasked to cooperate with the PAP in the context of the implementation of the Sustainable Development Goals (SDGs) with regard to policy development projects. The aim is to reconcile tensions between environmental sustainability, economic development, and human welfare, with a focus on burning legal, political, economic and social developments in Africa. Strategic activities at DROP are transdisciplinary in nature, with a strong legal and socio-political focus on climate change, justice, sustainability and transformation. The partners, PAP and DROP have teamed up with the German Environment Agency (UBA), which is Germany's central federal authority on environmental matters under the supervision of the German Federal Ministry for the Environment, Nature

37 European Union (2019).
38 Nwebo (2019: 185).
39 Cf. https://drop.sun.ac.za/, accessed 20 May 2020.
40 Cf. Academic diplomacy fostering SDG implementation, at https://bit.ly/3jQpn69, accessed 20 May 2020.

Conservation and Nuclear Safety (BMU). UBA′s main task is to provide science-based policy advice on environmental and sustainable development matters, primarily to Germany′s environmental ministry – taking an inter- and transdisciplinary perspective based on about 1,700 employees.

The main objective of the new partnership is to implement the SDGs of the United Nations 2030 sustainability agenda effectively. As a first project, the partners teamed up on the issue of land degradation neutrality (SDG target 15.3) and sustainable soil management on the continent (Article I of the MoU). Another objective of the MoU is to strengthen the parties' shared interest in and commitment to sustainable soil management, which is essential to achieving land degradation neutrality, which needs to be seen in its wider context.

The publication of this book is a direct outcome of the aforementioned partnership and project. The book was financially supported by the German Ministry for Development Cooperation (BMZ), through the Deutsche Gesellschaft für Internationale Zusammenarbeit (GIZ), and ultimately aims at developing model legislation for sustainable soil management in Africa.

6 Quest for Sustainable Development

Since the establishment of the SDGs in 2015, there has been a global movement to attain the SDGs – a movement that has been further invigorated by the Coronavirus global pandemic.[41] Governments, institutions and civil society have all come to the realisation that in order to achieve the SDGs there must be greater collaboration, especially in view of the global social and economic crisis that Covid-19 leaves in its wake.[42]

In the 2020 report on progress towards achieving the SDGs, the Secretary-General, in cooperation with the United Nations system under the United Nations Social and Economic Council, provided an overview of the current situation in terms of the SDGs.[43] Based on 2019 data, it was acknowledged that there is:[44]

> continued unevenness of progress and the many areas where significant improvement is required … In other areas, however, progress had either stalled or been reversed.

The report pointed out how Covid-19 has had impacts on and implications for all 17 SDGs and "what began as a health crisis has quickly become the worst human and economic crisis of our lifetimes".[45] Covid-19 has affected operations and institutions across the entire globe, resulting in unplanned delays in the achievement of the SDGs;

41 UN (2020).
42 Gallagher et al. (2020).
43 United Nations Economic and Social Council (2020).
44 Ibid.
45 Ibid.

however, "[w]hile this crisis is imperilling progress, it also makes [the SDGs'] achievement all the more urgent and necessary".[46] Although there have been improvements in development across the African continent, a closer look at the continent indicates that there is still a way to go in respect of the SDGs. Economic growth and human development levels have shown a rather bleak situation in statistical terms, with dwindling global trade; depressed commodity prices and a Human Capital Index of less than 0.4; a persistent gap in data, where data are not collected at all or, when they are collected, they are not comprehensive or consistent; governance frameworks to achieve the SDGs are still inadequate; and financing SDG achievement in Africa remains a challenge, which may even be intensifying.[47]

The PAP and its members have committed to a specific role and mandate of African parliaments during the ongoing SDG process.[48] One recommendation in this regard is to ensure harmonisation with the African Union's Agenda 2063 through integration of the SDG indicators.[49] African parliamentarians from across the continent have a responsibility – when executing their representative, oversight and legislative roles in terms of the 2030 Agenda implementation – to understand and raise awareness of the SDG framework among constituents; to assess readiness and ensure political neutrality in domesticating the SDG process; and to provide oversight to enhance people's participation.[50] Parliaments also have an important role to play in facilitating domestic resource mobilisation; in outlining and monitoring budgetary allocations for implementing and reaching targets; in scrutinising national plans to ensure harmonisation and domestication of the SDGs; and in making and reviewing laws to facilitate implementation at the local, national, regional and continental levels.[51]

With this in mind, the PAP serves as a platform for sharing best practices, lessons and challenges in parliamentary engagement on the SDGs.[52] These include:[53]

> developing common strategies for effective parliamentary engagement, as well as promoting partnerships and collaboration between parliamentarians and key development stakeholders.

To achieve this, the respective committees within the PAP can be expected increasingly to monitor progress on the SDGs assigned within their relevant mandate.[54]

46 Ibid: 7.
47 Begashaw (2019).
48 Independent Research Forum (2018: 1, 31).
49 *The Independent* (2017).
50 Together 2030 (2016).
51 Ibid.
52 Independent Research Forum (2018: 32).
53 Sustainable Development Goals Action Campaign (2016).
54 See https://bit.ly/3c4PEeE, accessed 20 May 2020.

As a first step, parliamentarians have been undertaking self-assessments in order to gauge whether the work ahead is ensuring that the domestication of the SDGs in their respective countries is people-centred, inclusive and accountable.[55] Such as –[56]

> the leader of Uganda's five-member delegation to the Pan African Parliament, Hon. Jacquilline Amongin, has unanimously been elected chairperson of the Alliance for the Sustainable Development Goals (SDGs) of the PAP. This was during an extraordinary meeting of MPs who subscribe to the alliance from different permanent committees on Wednesday, 16 October 2019 at the side-lines of the 3rd Ordinary Session of the 5th Parliament ongoing in South Africa.

Hon. Amongin, who wrote the Foreword of this book, has been committed to making the PAP a vehicle for achieving sustainable development across the continent.

Moreover, in March 2020, the Permanent Committee on Rural Economy, Agriculture, Natural Resources and Environment gathered during the last day of the Sitting of the Permanent PAP Committees in Midrand, South Africa, to establish the way forward with the development of a soil management model law for the African continent under Committee Chair Hon. Kone Dognon, who said at the commencement:

> We are highly encouraged by the dedication to the movement aimed to improve the legal protection mechanisms related to sustainable soil management and give more prominence to land degradation in Africa. Issues of climate change, food security and land use are closely integrated and are cross-cutting in the realisation of the SDGs.

This assignment was undertaken just one year after the successful establishment of the PAP Alliance on the Sustainable Development Goals (ASDGs).[57] This assignment seems fully in line with Aspiration 1 of the African Union's Vision 2063 (The Future we want), namely a prosperous Africa based on inclusive growth and sustainable development:

> By 2063, African countries shall be amongst the best performers in global quality of life measures. This will be attained through strategies of inclusive growth, job creation, increasing agricultural production; investments in science, technology, research and innovation; gender equality, youth empowerment and the provision of basic services including health, nutrition, education, shelter, water and sanitation.

References

Amadi, E., 2016, "The Pan-African Parliament (PAP): Issues, challenges and prospects". *International Journal of Social Sciences and Management Research* 2 (1), 5.

Begashaw, B., 2019, "Africa and the sustainable development goals: A long way to go". *Africa in focus, at* https://www.brookings.edu/blog/africa-in-focus/2019/07/29/africa-and-the-sustainable-development-goals-a-long-way-to-go/, accessed 27 May 2020.

55 Independent Research Forum (2018: 32).

56 Parliament of Uganda (2019).

57 Cf. PAP maps first steps for model legislation on sustainable soil management in Africa, at http://www.panafricanparliament.org/index.php/news-and-events/181-pap-maps-first-steps-for-model-legislation-on-sustainable-soil-management-in-africa, accessed 20 May 2020.

Dinokopila, B.R., 2013, "The Pan-African Parliament and African Union human rights actors, civil society and national human rights institutions: The importance of collaboration". *African Human Rights Law Journal* 13, 302.

ECA / Economic Commission for Africa, 2011, *The role of parliament in APRM: Information on how Parliamentarians can participate in APRM.* Addis Ababa: ECA, at https://www.uneca.org/archive/sites/default/files/PublicationFiles/5-pamphlet_the_role-of-parliament-in-aprm.pdf, accessed 12 February 2021.

European Commission, 2020, "Africa-EU Cooperation". *International cooperation and development*, at https://ec.europa.eu/international-partnerships/africa-eu-cooperation_en, accessed 20 May 2020.

European Union, 2019, *Declaration of the EP-PAP Parliamentary Summit to the IVth Africa-EU Summit.* At https://www.africa-eu-partnership.org/sites/default/files/userfiles/final_en.pdf, accessed 13 January 2021.

Gallagher, K.P., W.R. King & J.A. Ocampo, 2020, "Calibrating the COVID-19 crisis response to the SDGs". *Blog*, at https://bit.ly/37jDMlV, accessed 27 May 2020.

Independent Research Forum, 2018, *Africa's Agenda 2030: Channelling the SDGs toward inclusive, resilient and accountable development.* London: IIED, at https://pubs.iied.org/pdfs/G04378.pdf, accessed 13 January 2021.

Kabs Kanu, L.W., 2016, "Ambassador Kamara addresses the Pan-African Parliament on behalf of the African Union Peace and Security Council". *News Extra*, at http://cocorioko.net/ambassador-kamara-addresses-the-pan-african-parliament-on-behalf-of-the-african-union-peace-and-security-council/, accessed 20 May 2020.

Magliveras, K.D. & G.J. Naldi, 2003, "The Pan-African Parliament of the African Union: An Overview". *African Human Rights Law Journal* 3 (2), 222.

Mngomezulu, B.R., 2018, "Reflecting on the Pan-African Parliament: Prospects and challenges" *Journal of African Union Studies* 7 (2), 45.

Murray, R., 2004, *Human rights in Africa: From the OAU to the African Union.* Cambridge: Cambridge University Press.

NEPAD / The New Partnership for Africa's Development, 2003, *The African peer review mechanism: Base document.* NEPAD/HSGIC/03-2003/APRM/MOU/Annex II, at https://www.un.org/en/africa/osaa/pdf/aprm-basedoc.pdf, accessed 13 January 2021.

Nwebo, O.E., 2019, *The role of the Pan African Parliament in promoting constitutionalism and democratic governance in Africa: Lessons from other supranational parliaments.* LLD thesis, University of Pretoria.

OAU / Organization of African Unity (Assembly of Heads of State and Government), 1999, *Decision on the convening of an extraordinary session of the OAU Assembly of Heads of State and Government in accordance with Article 33(5) of its Rules of Procedure.* (Algiers 1999) AHG/Dec. 140 (XXXV).

PAP / Pan African Parliament, 2020, "Background". *About Us*, at http://www.panafricanparliament.org/index.php/background, accessed 20 May 2020.

Parliament of Uganda, 2019, "Uganda takes leadership of PAP Alliance on SDGs", at https://www.parliament.go.ug/news/3808/uganda-takes-leadership-pap-alliance-sdgs, accessed 20 May 2020.

Sustainable Development Goals Action Campaign, 2016, "African Parliamentary Conference on the SDGS". *Field story in Africa*, at https://sdgactioncampaign.org/2016/03/15/AFRICAN-PARLIAMENTARY-CONFERENCE-ON-THE-SDGS/, accessed 20 May 2020.

The Independent, 2017, "Pan African Parliament MPs call for review of SDGs". *Africa*, at https://www.independent.co.ug/pan-african-parliament-mps-call-review-sdgs/, accessed 20 May 2020.

Together 2030, 2016, "The role of parliamentarians in the implementation of the 2030 Agenda for Sustainable Development". *4th implementation series webinar*, at https://www.together2030.org/wp-content/uploads/2016/12/FINAL-Closed-Captioning-May-17-Webinar-Role-of-Parliamentarians.pdf, accessed 20 May 2020.

UN / United Nations, 2020, "Dispatches from the field: Scientists, experts and policy makers addressing the Covid-19 crisis around the world". *Covid-19: Dispatches from the field*, at https://sustainabledevelopment.un.org/blog/covid19, accessed 27 May 2020.

United Nations Economic and Social Council, 2020, *Progress towards the sustainable development goals*. Report of the Secretary-General, at https://bit.ly/2MZ9M81, accessed 27 May 2020.

Soil protection and the right to food: Sustainability implications for global climate governance and world agricultural trade?

Oliver C. Ruppel

1 Introduction

Especially in Africa we know that scarce land is more than a source of food security, income and shelter. It is also subject to distributive inequalities, often related to cultural identity. It is thus often a source of political and economic competition, tribal and social tension as well as historical, feudal, imperial, missionary or colonial injustices.[1]

Indeed, the most significant natural capital asset is productive land and fertile soils. For those communities that rely heavily on land as their main source, especially the rural poor, human well-being and sustainable livelihoods are completely dependent upon and intricately linked to the health and productivity of the land.

> Land is territory, property, a resource, our heritage, and much more. Land has economic, social and environmental value and, even when privately owned, it provides many benefits to society.[2]

While Africa's population is expected to double by 2050 the global population is projected to increase by a further 25% by the same year, approaching 10 billion people, which will substantially increase the demand for food and other agricultural products. Access to food is the right of every person, individually or in community with others. This right involves having physical and economic access at all times to sufficient, adequate and culturally acceptable food that is produced and consumed sustainably, so as to preserve access to food for future generations. The normative content of the right to food is linked to availability, accessibility, adequacy and sustainability – all of which must be built into legal entitlements and secured through accountability mechanisms.[3]

Soils are essential ecosystems that deliver valuable services such as the provision of food and carbon sequestration, among others. Therefore, soil is crucial for fighting climate change, protecting human health, safeguarding biodiversity and ecosystems and ensuring food security.[4]

Conventional food and agricultural trade, as well as global value chains, may need to be reconsidered to ameliorate the concerns. Changes in global food systems and the

---

1 FAO (2020a).
2 Larbodière et al. (2020: 8).
3 Cf. with further references, De Schutter (2014: para. 2).
4 European Commission (2020).

increased globalisation of the food supply means that populations worldwide are at risk of exposure to various food safety hazards. This can, among other things affect food security, national economies and international trade.[5]

2 Soil and the right to food

Soils are essential in ensuring food security and thus also the right to food.[6] Strategies in support of the progressive realisation of the right to food seem to be very much in line with the recommendations of the Committee on Economic, Social and Cultural Rights in its general comment No. 12 on the right to adequate food (para. 21).[7]

According to Article 25(1) of the Universal Declaration of Human Rights (UDHR), everyone has the right to a standard of living adequate for the health and well-being of himself and of his family, including food, while Article 11 of International Covenant on Economic, Social and Cultural Rights (ICESCR) recognises the right of everyone to an adequate standard of living for himself and his family, including adequate food; as a fundamental right of everyone to be free from hunger.

Article 11(2) ICESCR in recognising the fundamental right of everyone to be free from hunger, compels Parties to take measures to (a) improve methods of production, conservation and distribution of food by making full use of technical and scientific knowledge, by disseminating knowledge of the principles of nutrition and by developing or reforming agrarian systems in such a way as to achieve the most efficient development and utilization of natural resources; (b) taking into account the problems of both food-importing and food-exporting countries, to ensure an equitable distribution of world food supplies in relation to need.

Similarly, Article 24(2)(c) of the Convention on the Rights of the Child (CRC) obliges Parties to take appropriate measures to combat disease and malnutrition, including within the framework of primary health care, through, inter alia, the provision of adequate nutritious foods, taking into consideration the dangers and risks of environmental pollution.

In addition to the international human rights framework, regional human rights treaties have been developed, such as the African Charter for Human and People's Rights (Banjul Charter). It has been ratified by most African states and is considered to provide implicit recognition to the right to food in its Articles 4 (right to life), 16 (right to health) and 22 (right to economic and social development), as interpreted by the African Commission on Human and People's Rights Principles and Guidelines on the implementation of Economic, Social and Cultural rights in the African Charter on Human

5 FAO (2020b).
6 European Commission (2020).
7 Cf. with further references De Schutter (2014: para. 40).

and People's Rights and in the case law of the African Commission. The right to food is further expressly recognised in relation to women in Article 15 of the Protocol to the Banjul Charter on the Rights of Women in Africa. The vast majority of African countries have ratified these regional and relevant international human rights treaties.[8]

While states have the obligation to respect, protect and fulfill the human right to food, this obligation is complemented by the following principal non-legally binding instruments relating to the right to adequate food, namely the 1974 Universal Declaration on the Eradication of Hunger and Malnutrition; the 1996 Rome Declaration on World Food Security; and the 2004 Voluntary Guidelines to support the progressive realization of the right to adequate food in the context of national food security.

In addition, the 2015 Sustainable Development Goals (SDGs), provide a universally accepted framework to foster global collaboration with a strong emphasis on the rule of law and human rights. While Agenda 2030 is aimed at fostering and renewing multilateralism and international cooperation on the global but common challenges, the SDGs include economic and social development goals that potentially involve trade-offs with environmental sustainability. One of society's most urgent challenges is to satisfy the rights of people to a 'good life', including adequate food and nutrition, while remaining within the planetary boundaries. In other words, we need to reconcile agriculture and the environment to "end hunger, achieve food security and improved nutrition and promote sustainable agriculture" (Zero Hunger, SDG 2) and also "protect, restore and promote sustainable use of terrestrial ecosystems, sustainably manage forests, combat desertification, and halt and reverse land degradation and halt biodiversity loss" (Life on Land, SDG 15).[9]

In terms of the right to food, the SDGs call for more sustainable production and consumption patterns and agricultural and food systems that protect natural resources (i.e., soil). Possible supply chain approaches, for example, intervene at the point of end consumption of such products, the production of which in distant, politically sovereign states causes sustainability risks.

The 2014 Malabo Declaration of the African Union on Accelerated Agricultural Growth and Transformation for Shared Prosperity and Improved Livelihoods is another set of goals for a targeted approach to achieve the agricultural vision for the continent which is shared prosperity and improved livelihoods. In the Declaration the signatories inter alia commit themselves in the pursuit of agriculture-led growth as a main strategy to achieve targets on food and nutrition security and shared prosperity; and especially to ending hunger in Africa and to halving poverty by the year 2025,

8 FAO (2018a).
9 Larbodière et al. (2020: 8).

through inclusive agricultural growth and transformation and by means of enhancing resilience of livelihoods and production systems to climate variability.[10]

3 Soil and global climate governance

3.1 UNFCCC

The 1992 the United Nations Framework Convention on Climate Change (UNFCCC) was adopted to regulate levels of greenhouse gas concentration in the atmosphere, so as to, inter alia, avoid the occurrence of climate change on a level that would compromise initiatives in food production. Article 2 of the UNFCCC defines the parties' ultimate objective as the stabilisation of greenhouse gas concentrations in the atmosphere at a level that would prevent dangerous anthropogenic interference with the climate system.

So far, international climate policy has mostly focused on emission sources and thus on the avoidance of greenhouse gas emissions, for example from the electricity sector, the production industry, transport, and land-use changes. This will, however, be increasingly complemented by the preservation and enhancement of emission sinks to remove carbon dioxide from the atmosphere. To achieve the global climate targets adopted by the UNFCCC, alternative mitigation methods, as for example through programmes for re- or afforestation and the restoration of ecosystems, become more and more relevant. Despite the fact that the combination of bioenergy and carbon capture and storage, increased carbon sequestration in soils,[11] and the direct capture of CO_2 from ambient air need to be further researched and are not yet at the stage of market maturity, the carbon removal approach has considerable potential, while soils are the world's second largest carbon sink after the oceans.[12]

> The most potentially devastating impacts of industrial modes of agricultural production stem from their contribution to increased greenhouse gas emissions. Together, field-level practices represent approximately 15 per cent of total human-made greenhouse gas emissions, inter alia from the loss of soil organic carbon in croplands.[13]

---

10 Malabo Declaration on Accelerated Agricultural Growth and Transformation for Shared Prosperity and Improved Livelihoods Malabo, Equatorial Guinea, 26 June 2014, at https://au.int/sites/default/files/documents/31247-doc-malabo_declaration_2014_11_26.pdf, accessed 25 November 2020.

11 Soil carbon sequestration is the process of capturing atmospheric CO_2 through changing land management practices to increase soil carbon content. Various land management practices promote soil carbon sequestration.

12 Geden & Schenuit (2020: 5).

13 De Schutter (2014: para. 7).

3.2 Paris Agreement

The 2015 Paris Agreement, as part of the UNFCCC regime, in its Preamble includes the explicit acknowledgement "that climate change is a common concern of humankind" and that "Parties should, when taking action to address climate change, respect, promote and consider their respective obligations on human rights". As such the agreement binds its parties regarding activities on their respective territories and under their control.

The Paris Agreement supplements the UNFCCC and the Kyoto Protocol of 1997 by incorporating existing elements of this regime. Both the UNFCCC and Kyoto Protocol adopted rules on reporting and accounting for emissions from land use, land use change and forestry (LULUCF). These rules determine how parties have to report LULUCF in their regular emission inventories, which under the Kyoto Protocol is also relevant for accounting whether parties meet their emission reduction targets.[14]

According to Article 2, the Paris Agreement's overarching objective is to keep the increase in global temperature well below 2°C, or even 1.5°C. Parties are required to prepare and present individual climate plans (Nationally Determined Contributions - NDCs) every five years that set out how the party intends to contribute to the collective objectives. Under the Paris Agreement, the Principle of Common but Differentiated Responsibilities (CBDR) is an obligation for all parties when formulating their NDCs. This is the result of protracted negotiations about the role and impact of historic and present, and of relative and absolute, GHG producers. Although the Paris Agreement does not specify how to take the CBDR principle into account, principles of justice and equity help to improve the understanding of the normative implications of climate law under the Paris Agreement. While equity as a normative concept has a sense of fairness, justice plays an important role in legal-political decisions in relation to climate policy in particular and through differentiation in obligations.[15] GHG emissions have global, not merely national, effects, which on the basis of the need to contain the potential proliferation of trade distortions due to climate policies in terms of equity, may justify sanctioning the inaction by large GHG emitters, which can have a serious impact on local food production affected by global warming.[16]

Through the sustainable development mechanism in Article 6, the Paris Agreement allows the space to harness the lowest cost mitigation options worldwide. This may incentivise policymakers to enhance mitigation ambition by speeding up climate action.[17] This implies that global climate policy development and the future of the carbon market also relate to mechanisms which support and encourage sustainable climate

---

14 Bodle et al. (2020: 17).

15 Lawrence & Reder (2019).

16 Häberli (2018: 34).

17 Tänzler et al. (2019).

policies in host countries as production-based accounting does not necessarily reflect a country's contribution to global emissions because globalisation and consumption can prompt emissions beyond borders.

By signing the Paris Agreement (and in particular Article 14 therein), parties agreed on long-term goals backed by national plans that are collectively reviewed in the global stocktake, which is key to increasing ambition. While the first planned stocktake is scheduled for 2023, it has already become apparent today that the improved accuracy of carbon stock estimates would allow for more targeted interventions and better monitoring of the NDCs – which has equal significance for the protection of soil in the context of agricultural production.[18] Whereas the UNFCCC does not explicitly provide for specific trade measures, the Kyoto Protocol contains more detailed obligations related to the reduction of greenhouse gases and provides for trade-affecting techniques such as tax impositions on carbon dioxide emissions and the elimination of subsidies adversely affecting the objective of the UNFCCC.[19] In addition, the parties to the Paris Agreement explicitly recognise –

> [...] the fundamental priority of safeguarding food security and ending hunger, and the particular vulnerabilities of food production systems to the adverse impacts of climate change;

while Article 2(1)(b) of the Paris Agreement provides for –

> [in]creasing the ability to adapt to the adverse impacts of climate change and foster climate resilience and low greenhouse gas emissions development, in a manner that does not threaten food production [...].

Notwithstanding the legally neutral wording of Article 2(1) when read in isolation, achieving its purpose –[20]

> [...] is mandatory not for any one state or group of states, of course; it is mandatory for the state parties collectively. This straightforward logical implication of the Paris Agreement does not seem to have been noticed before, despite its potentially profound consequences.

The Paris Agreement further requires parties to engage in adaptation planning and implementation that takes into account "vulnerable people, places and ecosystems" and builds "the resilience of socio-economic and ecological systems, including through economic diversification and sustainable management of natural resources". Of course, soil as well as land use, land degradation and sustainable land management are closely linked to climate change in terms of carbon capture and storage and the emissions from deforestation and agriculture. This is underlined by Article 4 of the Paris Agreement, which explicitly includes the target "to achieve a balance between anthropogenic emissions by sources and removals by sinks of greenhouse gases in the second

---

18 Interestingly, in its NDCs, the Republic of South Africa, states that policy instruments under development include regulatory standards and controls for specifically identified GHG pollutants and emitters; see https://www4.unfccc.int/sites/ndcstaging/PublishedDocuments/South%20Africa%20First/South%20Africa.pdf, accessed 12 February 2021.

19 Ruppel (2018).

20 Zahar (2020).

half of this century", although the Paris Agreement fails to explicitly mention 'soil', 'land' or 'agriculture'. As such, the Paris Agreement only indirectly addresses soil protection in the general context of climate change. And despite the importance of land use and soil management for climate change, the UNFCCC, the Kyoto Protocol and the Paris Agreement have not established a comprehensive regime with regard to land-related climate change measures.[21] Article 5(1) of the Paris Agreement obliges parties to take action to conserve and enhance, as appropriate, sinks and reservoirs of greenhouse gases as referred to in Article 4(1)(d) of the Convention. Yet, in fact, agriculture first appeared in the ongoing climate negotiations under the Koronivia joint work on agriculture programme at COP 23 in 2017:[22]

> The decision officially acknowledges the significance of the agriculture sectors in adapting to and mitigating climate change. Countries agreed to work together to make sure that agricultural development ensures both increased food security in the face of climate change and a reduction in emissions. The joint work is expected to address six topics related to soils, nutrient use, water, livestock, methods for assessing adaptation, and the socio-economic and food security dimensions of climate change across the agricultural sectors.

In order to achieve the aforementioned, countries should take all appropriate measures according to their capabilities to progressively achieve the protection of the interests of all concerned. And when speaking of 'all concerned' in the context of global food security, this phrase is by no means an exaggeration. Much of the work to translate the Paris Agreement and the NDCs into concrete climate interventions in agriculture is in progress.

> Food systems are responsible for 21-37% of global greenhouse gas emissions and a major driver of deforestation and land degradation, yet there is still widespread food insecurity and malnutrition. Managing the land sector (agriculture, forestry, wetlands, bioenergy) sustainably and holistically could contribute up to 30% of the global climate mitigation effort.[23]

In 2018, the Paris Agreement adopted a transparency framework which, inter alia, included rules for reporting on and accounting for land use and land-use change, which is expected to eventually replace the existing UNFCCC framework. This may open opportunities also to shape new rules complementing the UNFCCC's Koronivia joint work on agriculture.

A wide range of policy instruments is needed to strengthen the mutually supportive role of the Paris Agreement and other international agreements when it comes to the protection of soil. The AFOLU (agriculture, forestry, and other land use) sector plays an important role in the 1.5°C pathways and is, inter alia, responsible for food production. Changes in the AFOLU sector are driven by demand changes, efficiency of production, and policy assumptions. While demand for agricultural products and other land-based commodities is influenced by consumption patterns, including dietary

---

21 Bodle at al. (2020: 53).

22 See http://www.fao.org/climate-change/our-work/what-we-do/koronivia/en/, accessed 12 February 2021.

23 Palahí et al. (2020).

preferences and food waste (affecting demand for food), policy assumptions relate to the level of land protection, the treatment of food waste, policy choices about the timing of mitigation action, the choice and preference of land-based mitigation options, and interactions with other sectors and trade.[24]

In the soil-land-climate interface, effective policy responses must include carbon pricing, emissions trading schemes (including net CO_2 emissions from agriculture), carbon taxes,[25] regulations limiting GHG emissions and air pollution, forest conservation (mix of land-sharing and land-sparing) through participation, incentives for ecosystem services and secure tenure, protecting the environment, microfinance, crop and livelihood insurance, agriculture extension services, agricultural production subsidies, low export tax and import tariff rates on agricultural goods, dietary awareness campaigns, taxes on and regulations to reduce food waste, improved shelf life, sugar/fat taxes, and instruments supporting sustainable land management (including payment for ecosystem services, land-use zoning, REDD+, standards and certification for sustainable biomass production practices, legal reforms on land ownership and access, legal aid, and legal education), as well as reframing these policies as entitlements for women and small agricultural producers.[26] Similarly, border carbon adjustments can help level the playing field and prevent emissions leakage,[27] which occurs when climate action in one region merely shifts emissions elsewhere.[28]

Such is, for instance, European Union (EU) soil policy action, based on Article 191 of the Treaty on the Functioning of the EU (TFEU), which requires Union policy to aim at preserving, protecting and improving the quality of the environment, protecting human health, a prudent and rational utilisation of natural resources, promoting measures at international level to deal with regional or worldwide environmental problems, and in particular combating climate change.

The EU considers improved soil protection fundamentally important due to (1) the transboundary impacts of soil degradation, such as CO_2 emissions from soil organic

---

24 Rogelj et al. (2018).

25 Such was for example the Carbon Tax Act 15 of 2019, a relatively new addition to South Africa's legislative record, aiming to provide for the imposition of a tax on the carbon dioxide (CO_2) equivalent of greenhouse gas emissions; and to provide for matters connected therewith. This aim is expected to be achieved by the deployment of a range of measures to support the system of desired emissions reduction outcomes, including the appropriate pricing of carbon, the use of emissions offsets and economic incentives for rewarding the efficient use of energy to provide appropriate price signals to help nudge the economy towards a more sustainable growth path. Such tax phased in over time allows for learning, while the tax revenue can for example finance additional climate change mitigation efforts. Whether a carbon tax yields a better result, for global food security, than carbon sequestration, depends on many different factors. Taxation for climate change mitigation could be included under any broad (NDC) commitment to reduce emissions or in the promotion of green technologies.

26 Rogelj et al. (2018).

27 Peters et al. (2011).

28 Kasturi et al. (2019).

carbon and loss of biodiversity, hampering EU food security through reduced production of food commodities traded in the internal market, hampering water quality across borders through contaminants and sediments in river basins, food safety concerns from soil contaminants; (2) the absence of a level playing field for economic operators subject to very different national soil protection regimes, leading to a distortion of the internal market; and (3) the risk that the EU and its Member States will fail to fulfil international and European commitments in the field of environment, sustainable development and climate.[29]

EU Member States have to ensure that greenhouse gas emissions from land use, land use change or forestry are offset by at least an equivalent removal of CO_2 from the atmosphere in the period 2021 to 2030. The Regulation on the inclusion of greenhouse gas emissions and removals from land use, land use change and forestry (LULUCF) into the 2030 climate and energy framework was adopted by the Council on 14 May 2018, following the European Parliament vote on 17 April 2018. It is also in line with the Paris Agreement, which points to the critical role of the land use sector in reaching long-term climate mitigation objectives.[30]

Moreover, the EU Biodiversity Strategy for 2030 announced the update of the 2006 EU Soil Thematic Strategy to address soil and land degradation in a comprehensive way and to help achieve land degradation neutrality by 2030. The Biodiversity Strategy for 2030 highlights that it is essential to step up efforts to protect soil fertility, reduce erosion and increase soil organic matter. The European Court of Auditors recommended to the European Commission to aim at a better understanding of land degradation and desertification in the EU, to assess the need to enhance the EU legal framework for soil, and to step up actions towards delivering EU and international commitments, and particularly land degradation neutrality by 2030. The European Parliament called on the EU and the Member States to make strong commitments towards sustainable food systems, agriculture and forestry, including requirements and strategies for the protection of soils. The European Environment Agency called for a comprehensive and coherent policy framework to protect land and soil. The strong political will and momentum guides the new EU soil strategy, which is already underway to consolidate, complement and steer action in the different policy areas that affect and depend on soil and guide the implementation of sustainable soil and land management practices. It is expected to cover key horizontal aspects from funding instruments to developing knowledge, research, communication and international cooperation. This will be done in close coordination and complementarity with other European Green Deal initiatives, including the upcoming Zero Pollution Action Plan, and other initiatives resulting from the EU Biodiversity Strategy for 2030 and the Farm to Fork Strategy. This also includes the legally binding EU nature restoration targets that the

29 European Commission (2020).
30 Cf. https://ec.europa.eu/clima/policies/forests/lulucf_en, accessed 12 February 2021.

Commission will propose in 2021 and which should contribute to the achievement of the objectives of the new Soil Strategy and the restoration of degraded soils.[31]

In addition, the European Commission aims to enshrine the so-called 'no-debit rule' in EU law by incorporating land use into the EU's emission-reduction efforts. The actions of farmers to secure carbon stored in soils will thus contribute to achieving the EU's commitment under the Paris Agreement on climate change to reduce greenhouse gas emissions by at least 40% by 2030 compared to 1990 levels.[32] This example is worthwhile viewing, as African countries have enormous opportunities to contribute to the global efforts in combatting climate change. However, most NDCs submitted by African countries do not (yet) truly reflect national needs and potential to fully contribute to global targets of achieving a low-carbon and climate-resilient pathway by 2050.

4 Soil agronomy, circular bioeconomy and supply chain management

Driven by a global population projected to rise to over 10 billion people by 2050 (from 7.6 billion today) and an increase in the 'consuming class' with the purchasing power to demand more food per capita (including food with a higher environmental footprint), the world could require a doubling in agricultural production from 2005 levels in order to meet demand. Such a trajectory is unsustainable.[33]

A more circular bioeconomy should be based on healthy, biodiverse and resilient ecosystems that provide the basis of sustainable well-being for society at large. This can be achieved by means of functioning ecosystem services and sustainable management of biological resources, leading to the circular transformation in food, feed, energy and biomaterials within the ecological boundaries of the ecosystem that it relies on.[34]

An alignment of the food and agricultural sector with the SDGs and the Paris Climate Agreement can enhance the interplay between environmental, nutritional, social and governance-related factors that need to be tackled while examining how business indicators might be developed in support of greenhouse gas (GHGs) emissions reductions.[35]

The food and land-use system could significantly benefit from a fundamental shift towards productive and regenerative agriculture. Transforming agricultural landscapes and farming practices for both food and non-food agriculture through a combination

31 See https://ec.europa.eu/environment/news/commission-consults-new-eu-soil-strategy-2021-02-02_en, accessed 10 February 2021.
32 See https://ec.europa.eu/clima/policies/strategies/progress_en, accessed 10 February 2021.
33 World Economic Forum (2020).
34 Lawrence & Reder (2019: 15).
35 Sachs et al. (2020).

of traditional farming techniques, advanced precision technologies, and bio-based inputs can increase biodiversity, enrich soils, improve water management and enhance ecosystem services while improving yields. This transition, however, requires greater understanding and adoption of the appropriate agronomic solutions, including re-alignment of agricultural subsidies, while navigating trade-offs between improving yields and strengthening biodiversity outcomes.[36]

> Long-term scenarios of adoption of agroecological approaches and provision of ecosystems services will help evaluate the benefits and potential trade-offs for society and provide desirable pathways for policy makers. Agriculture and conservation actors should seek consensus over indicators of sustainability and farmers should be supported to improve their performance against those indicators developing scientifically established agroecological approaches.[37]

In the context of end-use and market integration, this, inter alia, involves exploiting economies of scope across products, supply chains, land-use, transportation, city planning, and climate mitigation.[38] It is, for instance, possible to design cities in a way that reduces the amount of soil lost. Designing greener cities with commercial areas scattered throughout the city avoids paving over large areas, shortens transport distances, and leaves room for open landscapes and gardens.[39]

Agricultural policy is influenced by more than just political forces. An understanding of food supply chains is important in the context of soil management practices. Improving soil management is important to the food and farming supply chain, increasing the performance of soil to produce higher yields that are more resilient to physical and financial shocks as well as the effects of climate change. The increased number of regulatory policies can be seen as the result of higher standards of living, which have boosted consumers' demand for safe and high-quality products, and of growing problems with water, air and soil pollution. Economic growth is a driver of poverty reduction but is also responsible for environmental destruction. In a world already confronted with climate change, diminishing exhaustible natural resources, and other threats to the environment, international trade contributes further to these harmful developments through the production of agricultural goods and global transportation as part of the supply chain. Moreover, "the modernisation of food supply chains, together with the implementation of agricultural policies focused more on the production of commodities than on food, has led to the marginalisation of local food systems, which is a trend that must be reversed".[40]

The value and protection of soil is interrelated with production and supply chain management. The environmental effects of production differ widely across countries owing to differences in climate, land availability, soil fertility, use of technology,

36 World Economic Forum (2020).
37 Larbodière (2020: 79).
38 Rogelj et al. (2018).
39 Heinrich Böll Foundation & IASS (2015).
40 De Schutter (2014: para. 36).

energy sources, laws and institutions, and other factors.[41] This indicates that it can also be preferable to produce agricultural goods where this is most environmentally efficient. By promoting specialisation, competition, economies of scale, innovation and technology transfer at a global level, trade can both help to lower the production costs and help to achieve better environmental outcomes.

Supply chain management regulation is a relatively new attempt to address the economic and ethics problem of negative externalities in international trade by legal rule. It has become necessary because of a failure of the first-best solution of global rules and the failure of states to address the issue.

> Subsidies, norms and standards in particular can block as well as encourage the desired transformation. Industry concentration or business strategies can be incompatible with the necessary rediversification of crop rotations and agricultural landscapes. Supply chain arrangements often lead to the concentration of value capture and decision-making power in the downstream part of the supply chain, preventing farmers from transitioning to more sustainable practices.[42]

Global financial flows should be increasingly redirected towards sustainable value chains and healthy landscapes, which would also benefit soil protection. Science can help to develop indicators and standards that can guide those investments towards more sustainable practices, products and processes along the food supply chain.[43] An early identification of emerging risks lies at the heart of protecting public health and the environment and, by identifying such risks, for example in the food supply chain, can assure effective and timely measures to protect consumers.

As supply chain regulation also has inherent effects on international trade, it is crucial for its legality to also meet the requirement of world trade law. There is more leeway for individually agreed tariff preferences in compliance with regulations than at the World Trade Organisation (WTO) level. For this reason, various actors, including those from the supplier regions, should urgently be involved in the formulation of the details.

The African Continental Free Trade Agreement (AfCFTA) is expected to also develop and deepen supply chain trade across the African continent. The Agreement Establishing the African Continental Free Trade Agreement (AfCFTA) entered into force on 30 May 2019 and – after delays due to Covid-19 – was set to begin on 1 January 2021. The AfCFTA can develop new supply chain opportunities by eliminating existing obstacles, such as high tariffs on intermediate inputs to stimulate production of final goods and raise productivity. Moreover, the rules-of-origin (RoO) need to be harmonised and designed in a manner to make them easier to apply.

Through development policy measures more sustainability can be achieved by regulating supply chains to become flexible to react. In principle, the current direction of supply chains can be reversed in the future. Today's suppliers could become processors

41 UNEP & WTO (2018).
42 Larbodière et al. (2020: 68).
43 Ibid.: 81.

at the end of supply chains with greater added value – which could have positive development impacts for currently supplying developing countries.[44]

5 World agricultural trade

Agricultural commodities trade is subject to changes, reflecting the uneven and disproportionate impact of climate change on agricultural sectors across the globe. There is widespread agreement that, for instance coupled subsidy payments, export refunds, and direct market interventions have made a major contribution to increasing agricultural production in the EU and have led to the EU's increased export surplus. Low-priced food imports have weakened the agricultural sectors of African countries in the long-term and hindered the development of competitive agricultural production. However, the more targeted linking of agricultural subsidies to environmental and climate regulations increases the costs of agricultural production in the EU and could be expected to reduce the EU's production and export surpluses. This would create local agricultural investment incentives in Africa.[45]

The fact that the WTO Agreement on the Application of Sanitary and Phytosanitary Measures (SPS Agreement) makes reference to Codex food safety standards, means that the Codex Alimentarius for international food standards also has far reaching implications for international food trade. WTO members that wish to apply stricter food safety measures than those set by Codex may be required to justify these measures scientifically. The Codex standards are based on the assumptions and decisions of the Codex Alimentarius Commission, a joint body of the Food and Agriculture Organisation (FAO) and the World Health Organisation (WHO) of the United Nations and serve in many cases as a basis for national legislation.[46]

International food trade has existed for thousands of years but traditionally food was mainly produced, sold and consumed locally. Over the last century the amount of food traded internationally has grown exponentially, and a quantity and variety of food never before possible, with billions of tonnes of food produced, marketed and transported globally.[47] By for instance moving food from surplus to deficit areas, trade can not only provide a mechanism to address production shortfalls due to extreme weather but can also contribute towards reducing greenhouse gas (GHG) emissions and adjusting agricultural production in a more efficient and local manner. This, in turn, could also be in the interest of soil protection.

---

44 Rudloff & Wieck (2020).

45 Kornher & von Braun (2020).

46 Cf. http://www.fao.org/fao-who-codexalimentarius/en/, accessed 10 February 2021.

47 Ibid.

While the work to translate the Paris Agreement and the NDCs into concrete climate interventions in agriculture is in progress, a wide range of policy instruments is available, from investments in innovative technologies to subsidies that provide incentives to farmers to adopt climate-smart agricultural practices, and regulations to reduce emissions of agricultural activities to carbon taxes.[48] Most of these policy instruments are covered by agreements under the WTO, which is the forum for governments where international trade agreements are negotiated.

5.1 World Trade Organisation

The World Trade Organisation (WTO) provides a system of trade rules covering goods, services and intellectual property, as well as a legal and institutional framework for the implementation and monitoring of these agreements, and a venue for settling disputes arising from the interpretation and application of WTO agreements. Administering WTO trade agreements, monitoring national trade policies, providing technical assistance and training for developing countries, and cooperating with other international organisations are further functions of the WTO.[49]

The WTO's founding and guiding principles remain the pursuit of open borders, the guarantee of the most-favoured-nation principle and non-discriminatory treatment by and among members, and a commitment to transparency in the conduct of its activities. The opening of national markets to international trade, with justifiable exceptions or with adequate flexibilities, can encourage and contribute to sustainable development, raise people's welfare, reduce poverty, and foster peace and stability. At the same time, the liberalisation of markets must be accompanied by sound domestic and international policies which contribute to economic growth and development according to each member's needs and aspirations.[50]

Although the WTO is primarily concerned with reducing trade barriers and eliminating discriminatory treatment in international trade, world trade law is increasingly framed by the concept of sustainable development. The agreement establishing the WTO (unlike the General Agreement on Tariffs and Trade (GATT)) has anchored the objective of sustainable development and the need to protect and preserve the environment within its Preamble:

> Recognizing that their relations in the field of trade and economic endeavour should be conducted with a view to raising standards of living, ensuring full employment and a large and steadily growing volume of real income and effective demand, and expanding the production of and trade in goods and services, while allowing for the optimal use of the world's resources in accordance with the objective of sustainable development, seeking both to protect and preserve the

---

48 FAO (2018b).
49 See Article III of the Agreement Establishing the WTO.
50 Ibid.

> environment and to enhance the means for doing so in a manner consistent with their respective needs and concerns at different levels of economic development.

Although this statement in the Preamble is more of a policy goal than a binding principle, it should have significant weight in decision-making and dispute resolution and can make an important difference to the agreement's operation in practice. Yet, the WTO is, of course, not an environmental protection agency. So far, its competence in the field of trade and environment is limited to trade policies and to the trade-related aspects of environmental policies that have a significant effect on trade. In addressing the link between trade and environment, the two fields should increasingly complement each other.[51]

How can the WTO trading system help with the implementation of the Paris Climate Agreement, mitigate climate change, enhance soil protection and contribute to food security?[52] The WTO has tremendous potential to contribute to decarbonisation and, relatedly, has significant potential to help mitigate climate change.[53] This hypothesis raises the question: How can progressive trade liberalisation be reconciled with the protection of non-economic interests where the trading system can contribute to mitigating climate change, shifting from trade as a major cause of environmental harm to trade as a tool for environmental protection?[54] And what does this mean for the protection of soil and the promotion of food security in the context of climate change, which is likely to affect agricultural production more and more across various sectors?

5.2 Trade in agriculture under the WTO

In the decades following the Second World War, both the United States and nations of Western Europe provided generous subsidies to their agricultural producers and imposed both tariff and non-tariff import barriers to protect these producers from foreign competition.

5.2.1 The 1947 General Agreement on Tariffs and Trade (GATT)

The 1947 General Agreement on Tariffs and Trade (GATT) generally exempted agriculture from the GATT's trade liberalisation obligations:[55]

> Trade in agriculture has been distorted by subsidies and protectionism to the detriment of both producers and consumers. Trade in agricultural products at the same time contributes to global

51 Ruppel (2018).
52 Leal-Arcas & Morelli (2018: 32).
53 Ibid.: 6.
54 Ibid.: 29.
55 Gonzalez (2014).

> food security by helping countries to obtain food supplies from world markets. Agricultural imports can be risky if they crowd out more expensive local production. This can have negative income effects for producers and thereby continuously weaken local agriculture. In the case of acute supply bottlenecks, such effects can often only be quickly remedied by imports, provided that enough food is available on the world market at affordable prices.[56]

Since the start of the *Brexit* negotiations, the agri-food sector suffered under a lack of certainty regarding the future relationship between the European Union (EU) and the United Kingdom (UK). Existing supply chains and trade flows for agricultural goods and food products, within the EU but also with respect to imports from and export to third countries, suggest a significant challenge for farmers and food businesses in the UK, in Ireland, across the EU and around the world. Issues of relevance range from market access to plant protection, food safety, and food and quality labelling.[57]

International trade of food commodities induces a virtual transfer of embodied land, carbon, and other land-based resources, while most of the environmental impacts of agricultural production remain in the producing countries the role of trade in food security is expected to increase due to climate change, population growth and changing diets.[58] The causes of, and contributing factors to, global food insecurity are numerous and complex. It is clear, however, that the WTO and international trading rules play an important role in the pursuit of global food security.[59]

GATT Article XXI forms a controversial WTO provision recognising certain flexibilities for states in the international trading system, permitting ordinarily trade-restrictive measures for the purpose of national security. Article XXI(b)(iii) on "security exceptions" states that nothing in the GATT must be construed to prevent any WTO Member "from taking any action which it considers necessary for the protection of its essential security interests" in times of "emergency in international relations". This provision can justify certain trade restrictions introduced in pursuit of certain political objectives.

In 2019 in the case of *Russia – Measures Concerning Traffic in Transit* the WTO Dispute Settlement Panel found that "essential security interests" could be generally understood as referring to those interests relating to the quintessential functions of the state. The Panel observed that the specific interests at issue will depend on the particular situation and perceptions of the state in question and can be expected to vary with changing circumstances. For these reasons, the Panel held that it is left in general to every Member to define what it considers to be its essential security interests.[60]

According to Article XI of the GATT, supply risks explicitly justify otherwise prohibited trade restrictions and bans for food. Since trigger criteria and deadlines are not regulated, export bans are implemented rapidly, which in principle drives prices up

---

56 Rudloff & Wieck (2020).
57 Fratini Vergano (2018).
58 See Zhou et al. (2020).
59 Stewart & Manaker Bell (2015).
60 Cf. https://bit.ly/2NlydMZ, accessed 10 February 2021.

and results in supply risks for other import-dependent countries. On the import side, protective tariffs can seal off sectors in particularly threatening situations, as is often the case for reasons of supply to stimulate production. In bilateral agreements, the weaker partners often condemn this protection option as too restrictive. At the same time, caution should be given against premature isolation, as it often makes sense to secure supplies through less expensive imports. In principle, the WTO complicates such incentives for specifications on production processes that do not lead to physical product differences, as is usually the case when considering sustainability.[61]

Article XI GATT has been violated in the context of a number of environmental disputes in which countries have imposed bans on the importation of certain products; it therefore has relevance for trade and environment discussions. Article XX grants general exceptions from the aforementioned GATT rules. Article XX(b) lists measures necessary to protect human, animal or plant life and health; Article XX(g) lists measures relating to the conservation of exhaustible natural resources. WTO members may be exempted from GATT rules in specific instances. However, measures must be necessary (necessity-test). If the conditions set by Article XX are fulfilled, they must still pass the test of the introductory clause (Chapeau) of Article XX. According to the Chapeau, measures may not be pronounced as arbitrary and unjustifiable discrimination between countries where the same conditions prevail, and they may not constitute a disguised restriction on international trade. GATT rules provide significant scope for members to adopt national environmental protection policies.[62] GATT rules impose only one requirement in this respect – that of non-discrimination. WTO members are free to adopt national environmental protection policies provided that they do not discriminate between imported and domestically produced like products (NT principle), or between like products imported from different trading partners (MFN clause). Non-discrimination is one of the main principles on which the multilateral trading system is founded. It secures predictable access to markets, protects the economically weak from the more powerful, and guarantees consumer choice.[63]

Certification and appropriate, non-deceptive labelling in line with WTO rules, in particular the Agreement on Technical Barriers to Trade (TBT), can enable consumers to make sustainable food choices avoiding unjustified barriers to trade. International food-safety as well as plant and animal health standards, based on the SPS Agreement, are essential for reaping the benefits of agricultural trade and for avoiding potential risks to human, animal and plant health, while unjustified sanitary and phytosanitary restrictions on food trade can exacerbate food insecurity.[64]

61 Rudloff & Wieck (2020).
62 Ruppel (2018).
63 On the trade and environment negotiations see https://www.wto.org/english/tratop_e/envir_e/envir_negotiations_e.htm, accessed 10 February 2021.
64 Cf. https://bit.ly/3plgHG0, accessed 10 February 2021.

In 2011, the World Health Organization (WHO) reported that several European countries have experienced outbreaks caused by a dangerous strain of Escherichia coli (E. coli) bacteria, while some countries have also reported deaths related to the outbreaks. These E. coli are strains of the bacterium Escherichia coli that produce either Shiga or Shiga-like toxin while only a minority of these cause illness in humans. The ones that do are collectively known as enterohemorrhagic E. coli (EHEC) and are major causes of foodborne illness. Responses then have involved actions that implement and affect international legal regimes on public health and international trade imposing restrictions on international trade in terms of the Agreement on the Application of Sanitary and Phytosanitary Measures (SPS Agreement).[65] Following the detection of EHEC bacteria on Spanish cucumbers on 26 May 2011 (which, however, later proved to be of a different type than the E. coli associated with the outbreak), the competent ministries in various German federal states adopted regulations requiring traders to provide proof of safety for Spanish cucumbers, which was tantamount to a de facto import ban, leading the Spanish government to assert that it would seek compensation for its farmers, who lost sales costing millions of euros. On 1 June 2011, the EU Commission removed the warning label on Spanish cucumbers from the European rapid alert system, citing the latest investigation results. German courts then had to decide on the compensation for the damage suffered by Spanish cucumber suppliers. In turn, outside the EU, Russia imposed an import ban on 2 June 2011, on raw vegetables from all EU countries, prompting complaints from EU members that such a ban was not justified and was disproportionate. The EHEC outbreaks have triggered various trade responses internationally, under EU law and the SPS Agreement. Ultimately, they also underscored a problem with international legal obligations under the WHO and WTO regimes that seek to regulate trade-related responses to disease outbreaks.[66]

Article XX of the GATT 1994 states that measures "necessary to protect human, animal or plant life or health" (b) and those "relating to the conservation of exhaustible natural resources [...]" (g) can be interpreted as a legally accepted exception. While this could be most relevant for the protection of soil, a typical measure that can fall under this exception may be requiring export countries to comply with certain policies prescribed by the importing country.[67]

Further exceptions in accordance with Article XX of the GATT could possibly also be used to justify border carbon adjustment (BCA) measures as a tool for addressing carbon leakage. Such measures could, for instance, be the inclusion of certain imported goods in a Carbon Emissions Trading Scheme (ETS), a customs duty, or a border tax.

> To adhere to WTO principles of non-discrimination, countries cannot ask for more or different compliance from importers than they ask of their own firms producing comparable products.

65 Fidler (2011).
66 Ibid.
67 Van den Bossche & Zdouc (2017).

> That means that only price-based climate policies can be associated with a price at the border. A domestic carbon tax can be complemented by a border tax.[68]

The Paris Agreement does not explicitly state but implies counteracting like products and services with a higher footprint, which can take place in a number of different ways, and not necessarily through discrimination against only foreign goods (MFN/NT).[69] The Paris Agreement does not prescribe border carbon adjustment measures. Whether a carbon tax yields a better result for global food security than carbon sequestration remains open for discussion beyond the scope of this article. Yet, the rapidly increasing food import volumes or price decreases may legitimise safeguarding action by countries which have had to transform their non-tariff barriers (NTBs) into tariffs. Basically, however, rules and limits apply to four categories of protection and support policies. Border protection should be limited to tariffs. The maximum rates (bound/scheduled) should not be increased without compensation as per Article XXVIII of the GATT. Import quotas are prohibited under Article XI of the GATT. A time-limited border protection is available against imports threatening or jeopardising local production, which are generally available safeguards under Article XIX of the GATT.[70] In addition, in Article XXIV(5) of the GATT, WTO members may exclude customs unions and bilateral or regional free-trade areas from compliance with WTO disciplines in certain circumstances. These regional agreements are important, as they establish disciplines which might affect both the adoption of domestic and international carbon rules and measures to promote sustainable development and environmental cooperation.[71]

5.2.2 The WTO agreements on agriculture, subsidies and countervailing measures

The Agreement on Agriculture (AoA) entered into force at the time of the inception of the WTO on 1 January 1995. In principle, all WTO rules on trade in goods apply to agriculture. These rules include, inter alia, the GATT and pacts such as those dealing with sanitary and phytosanitary measures, customs valuation, import licensing, preshipment inspection, safeguarding measures, subsidies in general, and various standards, regulations and labelling requirements that imports have to meet (known as "technical barriers to trade"). The AoA was negotiated in the Uruguay Round (1986–1994) and was a significant step towards fairer competition and a less distorted sector. WTO member governments agreed to improve market access and reduce trade-distorting subsidies in agriculture. The AoA seeks to reform trade in agricultural products and provides the basis for market-oriented policies. In its Preamble, the Agreement

68 Droege & Fischer (2020).
69 Häberli (2018: 20).
70 Ibid.: 8.
71 See with further references Gehring & Hepburn (2013).

reiterates the commitment of members to reform agriculture in a manner which protects the environment. Under the Agreement, domestic support measures with minimal impact on trade (known as green box policies) are excluded from reduction commitments (contained in Annex 2 of the Agreement).[72]

The AoA primarily covers three aspects which need to be adapted to improve international agricultural trade, namely market access, export competition and domestic support. Market access is set out in Articles 4 and 5 of the AoA, and requires member states to convert their non-tariff barriers into tariffs and then to reduce those tariffs to improve agricultural trade market transparency and to strengthen the connection between domestic and international agricultural markets. The AoA also highlights the need for stricter regulation of domestic support measures under Articles 3, 6 and 7 to avoid their use for protectionist strategies which promote unfair competition, and categorises domestic agricultural support measures into 3 boxes according to the level of their trade-distorting effect, namely amber box, blue box and green box measures. Exemptions for reductions in support measures include green box subsidies which are considered minimal or non-trade distorting and include support for public stockholding for food security purposes and domestic food aid, as well as development measures which assist support of agricultural and rural development objectives. Export competition, as set out in articles 9 and 10 of the Agreement on Agriculture, required member states to make reduction commitments on their export subsidies. Article 20 recognises the importance of taking into account non-trade concerns and special and differential treatment for developing country members, resulting in many developing countries, through negotiating groups bringing forward proposed amendments to the AoA on the elimination of export subsidies, the use of public stockholding in the context of food security purposes and trade remedies such as special safeguard mechanisms.

The AoA in Article 21(1) stipulates that the GATT and all other WTO agreements on trade in goods (officially Annex 1A of the Marrakesh Agreement establishing the WTO) apply but if there is a conflict, then the rules in the Agriculture Agreement prevail.[73] While the "AoA professed to ameliorate the double standards in global agricultural trade", it has been said that it –[74]

> was riddled with ambiguities that enabled wealthy countries to continue to subsidize their agricultural producers while requiring market openness in developing countries. Since most developing countries had already liberalised their markets pursuant to structural adjustment programs, the impact of the AoA was to preclude these countries from adopting these subsidies in the future beyond de minimis levels. Agricultural subsidies in the United States and European Union, however, actually increased in the aftermath of the AoA.

---

72 Ruppel (2018).
73 World Trade Organization (2015).
74 Gonzales (2014: 106).

In terms of agricultural product subsidies there is no outright prohibition, but because they are considered to distort trade, they are limited for all WTO members. The conditions for unlimited governmental programmes are narrowly defined. The Developing Country Green Box (Article 6(2) AoA) allows, for instance, certain credit schemes and subsidies, for example for irrigation construction, and even for the running costs of low-income and resource-poor producers. Article 6(2) provides in relevant parts that measures which are "an integral part of the development programmes of developing countries [...] shall be exempt from domestic support reduction commitments that would otherwise be applicable to such measures". These are "*investment subsidies* which are generally available to agriculture in developing country Members and *agricultural input subsidies* generally available to low-income or resource-poor producers in developing country Members".[75]

Nevertheless, there is still a need to update global trade rules to reflect market and policy shifts that have occurred in recent years and to address contemporary agricultural and food challenges in reducing trade-distorting agricultural support of the past.[76] This does not come as a surprise, as the AoA has given rise to a relatively large number of disputes reflecting the fact that agriculture is a sensitive sector in many member countries. In its 2019 recent panel report DS511 on China – Domestic Support for Agricultural Producers the DSB found that China was not in compliance with its domestic support commitments pursuant to Articles 3(2) and 6(3) of the Agreement on Agriculture after the United States contended that China has provided market price support to its agricultural producers of wheat and rice in excess of its commitments under the AoA.[77]

The agriculture, forestry, and other land use (AFOLU) sector is an important sector that services national food requirements and export earnings for many developing countries around the world. It is unique in the sense that it is the only sector within which both sources and sinks for greenhouse gases can be found. AFOLU plays a central role in food security, sustainable development and climate change mitigation and adaptation and could also be considered as a valid motive under Article 6(2) AoA through measures that do not distort trade. Effective climate-smart support to farmers can also improve the comparative advantage of agriculture in countries that will be negatively affected by changing climate, allowing them to become competitive and achieve a better balance in export and import performance.[78]

Further relevant provisions for trade in agricultural products are found in the WTO Agreement on Subsidies and Countervailing Measures (SCM). SCM exerts discipline over the use of subsidies and regulates the actions that countries can take to counter

75 Häberli (2018: 9).
76 Cf. https://bit.ly/3qfnlic, accessed 10 February 2021.
77 Cf. https://bit.ly/3qeGiS7, accessed 10 February 2021.
78 Deutz et al. (2020).

the effects of subsidies. Under the agreement, a country may use the WTO's dispute-settlement procedure to seek the withdrawal of the subsidy or the removal of its adverse effects. Alternatively, a country can launch its own investigation and ultimately charge extra duty (countervailing duty) on subsidised imports found to be detrimental to domestic producers.[79] In line with Article 13 AoA, the SCM agreement now also applies to agricultural export (and import displacement) measures. Although export subsidies – a long-term concern of many competitive agricultural product exporters – were finally prohibited in 2015, there still is no agreement on the implementation details (eg schedule changes) nor on the rules tightening mandated for all export competition measures under the Doha Development Agenda (DDA). This failure is also reflected in the stalling reform process under Article 20 of the AoA to agree on additional disciplines making trade patterns more sustainable, more resilient under a climate change perspective.

> The key for an economic impact assessment of agricultural subsidies in a climate perspective would probably be the contribution of a differentiating subsidy under the Paris Agreement. Here again, not all countries are equal. Some temperate climate countries may actually benefit from global warming, with little or no justification for a subsidy. For countries located closer to the Equator, adaptation subsidies and Official Development Assistance (ODA) might find economic justification especially for farmers without meaningful support from their governments.[80]

This could contribute to global efforts to control atmospheric greenhouse gas concentrations, foster AFOLU-related mitigation pathways and at the same time lead to improved soil conditions. In this regard, trade could become more central in climate change mitigation efforts and this would also benefit soil protection. If trade could provide the necessary signals to farmers to produce low carbon footprint products, emissions could be reduced globally. In practice, this would necessitate the imposition of a carbon tax (or an equivalent mitigation measure) on agricultural products domestically, combined with a corresponding tariff adjustment at the border to discriminate against high carbon footprint imports.

WTO provisions offer flexibility for waivers or exemptions from complying with the non-discrimination principle. While sufficient space for policy discussions needs to be pursued at the intersection of the WTO and the Paris Agreement, the principle of differentiated responsibilities, respective capabilities, and the special and differential treatment of developing countries remain ever relevant when discussing and implementing transformative policies for climate change adaptation and mitigation to make agriculture meet contemporary challenges.[81]

Moreover, regional trade agreements such as the AfCFTA also have high potential to boost intra-African trade and to restore certain imbalances in the world agricultural trade markets, which – for instance – also provides an opportunity to revisit EU-Africa

---

79 See http://www.wto.org/english/tratop_e/scm_e/scm_e.htm, accessed 10 November 2017.

80 Leal-Arcas (2018: 25).

81 FAO (2018b: 97).

trade policy relations in the fields of food and agriculture, where greater emphasis should be laid on African development, including environmental, climate, health and distributional aspects.[82] This was explicitly reflected in 2014 Malabo Declaration of the African Union on Accelerated Agricultural Growth and Transformation for Shared Prosperity and Improved Livelihoods where it was declared to boost intra-African trade in agricultural commodities and services, especially through the establishment of the AfCFTA and to enhance resilience of livelihoods and production systems to climate variability.[83]

6 Conclusion

The fact, that the Norwegian Nobel Committee has decided to award the 2020 Nobel Peace Prize to the World Food Programme (WFP) for its efforts to combat hunger is a clear reflection of the growing significance of food security in our time. The WFP is the world's largest humanitarian organisation addressing hunger and promoting food security and the primary instrument of the United Nations for realising this goal. The Norwegian Nobel Committee emphasised that providing assistance to increase food security not only prevents hunger but can also help to improve prospects for stability and peace in the world.[84]

Ending hunger and achieving food security is at the heart of the SDGs. At the same time, climate change is affecting agriculture and food security and will make the challenge even more difficult. In fact, food insecurity and climate change already undermine basic human rights of entire populations – especially in Africa.

Food security as a primary justice concern connected with climate change must therefore also be viewed in the context of food production and distribution, where producers and consumers are located on different continents. In fact, a better understanding of food security must go beyond a developmental or humanitarian understanding thereof, it must even include linkages with geopolitics.[85]

As the historical impact of global supply chains on nature has been largely negative, characterised by unsustainable practices in agriculture and other sectors. What must, however, be prevented is an increasing securitisation of trade where countries put up trade barriers on just about everything under the pretext of security.[86] Instead of

82 Kornher & von Braun (2020: 5).

83 Malabo Declaration on Accelerated Agricultural Growth and Transformation for Shared Prosperity and Improved Livelihoods Malabo, Equatorial Guinea, 26 June 2014, https://au.int/sites/default/files/documents/31247-doc-malabo_declaration_2014_11_26.pdf, accessed 25 November 2020.

84 See https://www.nobelprize.org/prizes/peace/2020/press-release/, accessed 10 February 2021.

85 Zhou et al. (2020).

86 Narlikar (2020).

disrupting global value chains, a shift toward more responsible supply chain management practices offers an opportunity to avoid harm and even positively impact nature.[87]

Whereas misguided aid, trade and development policies, as well as large-scale land acquisitions that benefit wealthy nations and transnational corporations are often conducted at the expense of the poor,[88] they are also most vulnerable and threatened by climate change, which depresses food production and increases food prices.[89]

International trade, while essential for food security, also creates vulnerabilities through supply disruptions, growing unilateralism and competition over agricultural resources that can be both a cause and a consequence of geopolitical rivalry.[90] The WTO is a crucial institution for the governance of international trade, yet it has been characterised by frequent deadlocks in the past and has suffered from credibility loss due to the persistent failure of the Doha Development Agenda. The WTO is now subject to ongoing trade war dynamics and a dysfunctional appellate body, all of which further exacerbates the need for reforms.[91]

Moreover, some countries have been hoarding food items to ensure supplies for their population in light of the Covid-19 pandemic. Such grain exporters, including Russia, the Ukraine and Kazakhstan, have been said to take a nationalist turn by restricting or planning to restrict exports to ensure enough supplies for their own populations. The is an alarming example on how food availability can easily be threatened in a trade system that encourages import dependence and export-oriented agriculture, but cannot require countries to export food, which could be detrimental to countries that depend on imported food.[92] Trade wars are a huge threat to food security.[93] Further examples are Russia's ban on Western food imports since 2014 and the ongoing trade war between China and the USA that began in 2018 disrupting normal agricultural flows. These geopolitical frictions hamper reform consensus to revive multilateral institutions, including the WTO,[94] which should be empowered beyond the trade effects of trade.[95]

Countries should increase efforts through the international architecture, specifically the WTO, to develop green trade agreements that facilitate and incentivise increased trade in commodities produced without conversion of natural habitats. While subsidies are, for the most part, deployed within the country granting the subsidies and can only be reformed through the actions of domestic governments, reforming harmful

87 Deutz et al. (2020: 66).
88 Gonzales (2014: 104).
89 Niang et al. (2014: 1218).
90 Zhou et al. (2020).
91 Narlikar (2020).
92 Pandey (2020).
93 Cf. https://unctad.org/news/trade-wars-are-huge-threats-food-security, accessed 10 February 2021).
94 Zhou et al. (2020).
95 Messenger (2017).

subsidies still requires an international effort. International organisations can facilitate changing the status quo on subsidies reform and encourage governments to cooperate on ways to implement change.[96]

While every country must have the right to develop its own agricultural model to feed its population, respect for the needs of other countries and international obligations remains key. Policies must therefore assure that trade can meet global challenges, facilitates the sustainable and efficient use of land, protects biodiversity and prevents overexploitation and degradation of land and natural resources. In particular, nationally appropriate measures to conserve natural resources and combat climate change that are respectful of international commitments related to sustainable development, e.g., the Paris Agreement on Climate Change, the Rio Declaration on Environment and Development and the Convention on Biological Diversity.

WTO reform to better accommodate climate change measures is an increasingly urgent issue. Such reform could entail legal changes, namely amending the WTO agreements to accommodate climate change measures; introducing a waiver that temporarily relieves WTO members from their legal obligations under the WTO agreements when pursuing climate action; adopting an authoritative interpretation clarifying the scope of WTO rules in relation to climate policies; and introducing a time-limited peace clause pursuant to which WTO members will not challenge the climate policies of other members. Such changes would, however, involve complex political processes that – for a variety of reasons – would be difficult to implement in practice.

In the meantime, existing flexibilities under current WTO law should be utilised to advance climate action, while it is not unlikely that conflicts between the trade and climate regimes will sooner or later surface in the WTO's dispute settlement system. It has been rightfully stated that international courts and tribunals must become the new environmental sentinels in international law.[97] In the interest of global soil protection and for the sake of sustainable food security, the challenge will be to bridge the gap where measures claiming to implement the Paris mitigation commitments collide with present trade rules. This will require commitment to overcome substantial barriers at various institutional (and conceptual) levels as well as adequate and corresponding regulatory frameworks. With more ambitious NDCs expected in the future, countries can take trade-related climate measures that are likely to assume increasing importance.[98]

The fact is that the climate protection goals of the Paris Agreement can only be reached if, in addition to the decarbonisation of the global economy, more areas of land are used to extract carbon dioxide (CO_2) from the atmosphere.[99] And soil as a

96 Deutz et al. (2020: 66).
97 Desai & Sidhu (2020).
98 Kasturi et al. (2018: 6).
99 WBGU (2020).

natural system is essentially a capital stock (similar to financial, built, and human capital) that provides a flow of services to people. These 'ecosystem services', which include fertile soil must be considered in the context of regenerative or conservation agriculture, yielding a public good. In this light, greater efforts are needed to combine economic and environmental performance in determining soil as a natural capital and a valuable asset that needs a price tag (despite the fact that it is actually priceless). Soil organic carbon is a fundamental ecosystem health indicator.[100] Moreover, when it comes to the protection of soil, the right to private property as a secondary natural right needs to be linked to the principle of the universal destination of the earth's goods, which may require higher consideration in the workings of any future society.[101]

Policymakers who turn to science will discover that it can guide the formulation of laws that actually bring about efficient change consistent with the laws of nature,[102] towards a transformational shift in the way markets, and the discipline of economics more broadly, value nature. The role of science has also become more important in determining parties' rights and in the adjudication of international trade disputes. Science can assist in the process of risk identification and more importantly, risk assessment and the management of such an identified risk.[103] In fact, certain vulnerability situations may even lead to a new realisation that global stability and systemic relevance (e.g., food supply) are not only a matter of economic optimisation.[104]

Unlike the climate, soil protection has so far too often been neglected in international agreements. Despite this oversight, the climate goals cannot be reached without soil protection and conservation. The same applies when it comes to ensuring the right to food. In fact, soil protection should perhaps be viewed in light of the public trust doctrine, which has its origins in the Roman law property concept of *res communis*.[105] These are things which, by their nature, are part of the commons that all humankind has a right or at least a common interest in the protection thereof. Notwithstanding this, the legalisation of guiding principles and cooperation between sectors and institutions addressing soil holds significant potential for improving soil governance and thus enhancing resilience against food insecurity, which must be pursued in a complementary manner in order to be able to counter soil degradation and mitigate climate change.[106]

---

100 Chotte et al. (2019).

101 Pope Francis (2020).

102 Laitos (2019).

103 This is prevalent in both the WTO Appellate Body Report, *European Communities – Measures Concerning Meat and Meat Products (EC – Hormones),* WT/DS48/AB/R, 16 January 1998 and WTO Panel Report, *European Communities – Measures Affecting the Approval and Marketing of Biotech Products (EC – Biotech Products*), WT/DS291/R, 29 September 2006. Science has become a major role in determination of WTO cases. Cf. Du (2018).

104 Ginzky et al. (2020).

105 Preston (2018).

106 Ruppel (2013).

Lastly, due to the vulnerability of African countries there is an increased need for boosting intra-African trade, particularly in agricultural products, to address issues of poverty and hunger, and to guard against food insecurity as a result of competition in trade from the international community, as well as decreased agricultural production as a result of the increasing impact of environmental threats and the degradation of soil. In this light, any transition to climate neutrality and decarbonisation should be guided by the *leitmotiv* to place soil protection and sustainable food security at the centre of economic agricultural trade policy.

References

Bodle, R., H. Stockhaus, F. Wolff, C.-S. Scherf, & S. Oberthür, 2020, *Improving international soil governance – Analysis and recommendations*. Dessau-Roßlau: German Environment Agency.

Chotte, J.L., E. Aynekulu, A. Cowie, E. Campbell, P. Vlek, R. Lal, M. Kapović-Solomun, G. von Maltitz, G. Kust, N. Barger, R. Vargas & S. Gastrow, 2019, *Realising the carbon benefits of sustainable land management practices: Guidelines for estimation of soil organic carbon in the context of land degradation neutrality planning and monitoring*. A report of the science–policy interface. Bonn: UNCCD.

De Schutter, O., 2014, *The transformative potential of the right to food*. 24 January 2014, United Nations General Assembly, A/HRC/25/57, Human Rights Council, twenty-fifth session, Agenda item 3, Promotion and protection of all human rights, civil, political, economic, social and cultural rights, including the right to development, at http://www.srfood.org/images/stories/pdf/officialreports/20140310_finalreport_en.pdf, accessed 12 January 2021.

Desai, B.H. & B.K. Sidhu, 2020, "International courts and tribunals – The new environmental sentinels in International Law". *Environmental Policy and Law* 50, 17.

Deutz, A., G.M. Heal, R. Niu, E. Swanson, T. Townshend, L. Zhu, A. Delmar, A. Meghji, S.A. Sethi, & J. Tobin de la Puente, 2020, *Financing nature: Closing the global biodiversity financing gap*. Chicago: The Paulson Institute, The Nature Conservancy, and the Cornell Atkinson Center for Sustainability.

Droege, S. & C. Fischer, 2020, "Pricing carbon at the border: Key questions for the EU". *ifo DICE Report* 18, 30.

Du, M., 2018, "Re-conceptualizing the role of science in international trade disputes". *Journal of World Trade* 52 (5), 697.

European Commission, 2020, *European Commission Roadmap: New soil strategy - healthy soil for a healthy life*. Ref. Ares (2020) 6391319 - 05/11/2020, at https://ec.europa.eu/info/law/better-regulation/have-your-say/initiatives/12634-New-EU-Soil-Strategy-healthy-soil-for-a-healthy-life, accessed 12 November 2020.

FAO / Food and Agriculture Organization of the United Nations, 2018a, *Right to adequate food in constitutions*. Legal brief for Parliamentarians in Africa, No. 1. Rome: FAO.

FAO / Food and Agriculture Organization of the United Nations, 2018b, *The state of agricultural commodity markets 2018. Agricultural trade, climate change and food security*. Rome: FAO.

FAO / Food and Agriculture Organization of the United Nations, 2020a, *Legislative approaches to sustainable agriculture and natural resources governance*. FAO Legislative Study No. 114. Rome: FAO, at https://www.unenvironment.org/resources/publication/legislative-approaches-sustainable-agriculture-and-natural-resources, accessed 12 January 2021.

FAO / Food and Agriculture Organization of the United Nations, 2020b, *Climate change: Unpacking the burden on food safety*. Food safety and quality series No. 8. Rome: FAO, at http://www.fao.org/3/ca8185en/CA8185EN.pdf, accessed 12 November 2020.

Fidler, D.P., 2011, "International Law and the E. coli outbreaks in Europe". *Insights* 15 (14), American Society of International Law (ASIL), at https://www.asil.org/insights/volume/15/issue/14/international-law-and-e-coli-outbreaks-europe, accessed 12 January 2021.

Fratini Vergano, European Lawyers, 2018, *Trade Perspectives*, Issue No. 18 of 5 October 2018, at http://www.fratinivergano.eu/static/upload/1/1/18.10_.05_TP_Issue_18-2018_.pdf, accessed 12 January 2021.

Geden, O. & F. Schenuit, F, 2020, *Unconventional mitigation carbon dioxide removal as a new approach in EU climate policy*. SWP Research Paper No. 8. Berlin: German Institute for International and Security Affairs.

Gehring, M.W. & J. Hepburn, 2013, "Climate, trade and investment law in the global green economy". In: Ruppel, O.C., C. Roschmann & K. Ruppel-Schlichting (eds), 2013, *Climate change: International Law and Global Governance - Volume I: Legal responses and global responsibility*. Baden-Baden: Nomos.

Ginzky, H., Löwe, C. and Neßhöver, C. 2020. "Lessons from the Corona Crisis: New Guiding Principles Required for Environmental and Sustainability Policy? – A Discussion Paper". German Environment Agency, at https://bit.ly/378d2oC, accessed 30 October 2020.

Gonzalez, C.G. 2014. "World poverty and food insecurity". *Pennsylvania State Journal of Law and International Affairs* 3 (2), 100.

Häberli, C., 2018, *Potential conflicts between agricultural trade rules and climate change treaty commitments. The state of agricultural commodity markets (SOCO) 2018*. Background Paper. Rome: FAO.

Heinrich Böll Foundation & IASS / Institute for Advanced Sustainability Studies. 2015. *Soil Atlas 2015, Facts and Figures about Earth, Land and Fields*. Berlin: Heinrich Böll Foundation and the Institute for Advanced Sustainability Studies, at https://www.boell.de/sites/default/files/soilatlas2015_ii.pdf, accessed 10 February 2021.

Kasturi, D., H. van Asselt, S. Droege & M. Mehling, 2018, *Making the international trade system work for climate change: Assessing the options*. London: Climate Strategies.

Kasturi, D., H. van Asselt, S. Droege & M. Mehling, 2019, "Towards a trade regime that works for the Paris Agreement". *Economic and Political Weekly* December 21, 25.

Kornher, L. & J. von Braun, 2020, *EU common agricultural policy - Impacts on trade with Africa and African agricultural development*. ZEF Discussion Papers on Development Policy No. 294. Bonn: Center for Development Research.

Laitos, J.G., 2019, "How science has influenced, but should now determine, environmental policy". *William and Mary Environmental Law and Policy Review* 43, 759.

Larbodière, L., J. Davies, R. Schmidt, C. Magero, A. Vidal, A. Schnell, P. Bucher, S. Maginnis, N. Cox, O. Hasinger, P.C. Abhilash, N. Conner, V. Westerburg & L. Costa, 2020, *Common Ground: Restoring land health for sustainable agriculture*. Gland: IUCN.

Lawrence, P. & M. Reder, 2019, "Equity and the Paris Agreement: Legal and philosophical perspectives". *Journal for Environmental Law* 31 (3), 511.

Leal-Arcas, R. & A. Morelli, 2018, "The resilience of the Paris Agreement: Negotiating and implementing the climate regime". *The Georgetown Environmental Law Review* 31 (1), 1.

Messenger, G., 2017, "Substantial development and the commodities challenge: The eventual greening of the World Trade Organisation". *Trade Law and Development* 54, 54.

Narlikar, A., 2020, "Reforming the World Trade Organization". Heinrich Böll Stiftung, 17 January 2020, at https://www.boell.de/en/2020/01/17/reforming-world-trade-organization, accessed 12 January 2021.

Niang, I., O.C. Ruppel, M.A. Abdrabo, A. Essel, C. Lennard, J. Padgham & P. Urquhart, 2014, "Africa". In: *Climate change 2014: Impacts, adaptation, and vulnerability. Part B: Regional aspects.* Contribution of Working Group II to the Fifth Assessment Report of the Intergovernmental Panel on Climate Change. Cambridge: Cambridge University Press.

Palahí, M., M. Pantsar, R. Costanza, I. Kubiszewski, J. Potočnik, M. Stuchtey, R. Nasi, H. Lovins, E. Giovannini, L. Fioramonti, S. Dixson-Declève, J. McGlade, K. Pickett, R. Wilkinson, J. Holmgren, K. Trebeck, S. Wallis, M. Ramage, G. Berndes, F.K. Akinnifesi, K.V. Ragnarsdóttir, B. Muys, G. Safonov, A.D. Nobre, D. Ibañez, A. Wijkman, J. Snape & L. Bas, 2020, *Investing in nature as the true engine of our economy: A 10-point action plan for a circular bioeconomy of wellbeing.* Knowledge to Action 02. Joensuu: European Forest Institute.

Pandey, A. 2020. "Will Coronavirus spark a wave of food nationalism?", at https://bit.ly/3c94XTH, accessed 12 January 2021.

Peters, G. P., J.C. Minx, C.L. Weber & O. Edenhofer, 2011, "Growth in emissions transfers via international trade from 1990 to 2008". *Proceedings of the National Academies of Science* 108 (21), 8903.

Pope Francis, 2020, *Fratelli Tutti*. Encyclical Letter of the Holy Father Francis on fraternity and social friendship, at http://www.vatican.va/content/francesco/en/encyclicals/documents/papa-francesco_20201003_enciclica-fratelli-tutti.html, accessed 12 January 2021.

Preston, B.J. 2018. "The evolving role of environmental rights in climate change litigation". *Chinese Journal of Environmental Law* 2, 131.

Rogelj, J., D. Shindell, K. Jiang, S. Fifita, P. Forster, V. Ginzburg, C. Handa, H. Kheshgi, S. Kobayashi, E. Kriegler, L. Mundaca, R. Séférian & M.V. Vilariño, 2018, "Mitigation pathways compatible with 1.5°C in the context of sustainable development". In: IPCC, *Global warming of 1.5°C. An IPCC Special Report on the impacts of global warming of 1.5°C above pre-industrial levels and related global greenhouse gas emission pathways, in the context of strengthening the global response to the threat of climate change, sustainable development, and efforts to eradicate poverty.* Cambridge: Cambridge University Press.

Rudloff, B. & C. Wieck, 2020, "Nachhaltige Lieferketten im Agrarsektor: Wert schöpfen statt Zuliefern. Unternehmerpflichten politikfeldübergreifend in eine EU-Strategie einbinden". *SWP-Aktuell* 2020/A 70, September 2020.

Ruppel, O.C., 2013, "Intersections of law and cooperative global climate governance – challenges in the anthropocene". In: Ruppel, O.C., C. Roschmann & K. Ruppel-Schlichting, (eds), *Climate change: International Law and global governance Volume I: Legal responses and global responsibility*. Baden-Baden: Nomos.

Ruppel, O.C., 2018, "International trade, environment and sustainable development". In: Ruppel, O.C. & E.D. Kam Yogo, (eds) *Environmental law and policy in Cameroon – Towards making Africa the tree of life*. Law and Constitution in Africa, Bd. 37. Baden-Baden: Nomos.

Sachs J., M. Al Khatib, M. Antonelli, K.Y. Cordes, S. Cresti, G. Espinosa, C. Ocampo-Maya, Riccaboni, A. Rossi, L.E. Sachs, G. Schmidt-Traub, E. Sofra & C. Tozzi, 2020, *Fixing the business of food. How to align the agrifood sector with the SDGs*. Parma: Barilla Foundation, at https://www.fixing-food.com/wp-content/uploads/2020/09/Executive_Summary_2020.pdf, accessed 12 January 2021.

Stewart, T.P. & S. Manaker Bell, 2015, "Global hunger and the World Trade Organization: How the international trade rules address food security". *Pennsylvania State Journal of Law and International Affairs* 3 (2), 113.

Tänzler, D., J. Groß, L. Li, C. Warnecke, M.J. Kurdziel, R. Tewari, M. Cames, & S. Healy, 2019, *Analysing the interactions between new market mechanisms and emissions trading schemes: Opportunities and prospects for countries to use Article 6 of the Paris Agreement.* Dessau-Roßlau: German Environment Agency.

UNEP / United Nations Environment Programme & WTO / World Trade Organization, 2018, *Making trade work for the environment, prosperity and resilience*. Nairobi: UNEP.

Van den Bossche, P. & W. Zdouc, 2017, *The law and policy of the World Trade Organization.* 3rd edition. Cambridge: Cambridge University Press.

WBGU / German Advisory Council on Global Change, 2020, *Rethinking land in the Anthropocene: From separation to integration*. Berlin: WBGU.

World Economic Forum, 2020, *The Future of Nature and Business*. Geneva: World Economic Forum, at http://www3.weforum.org/docs/WEF_The_Future_Of_Nature_And_Business_2020.pdf, accessed 12 January 2021.

WTO / World Trade Organization, 2015, *The WTO Agreements Series: Agriculture*, at https://bit.ly/3tIBrd1, accessed 12 January 2021.

Zahar, A., 2020, "Collective obligation and individual ambition in the Paris Agreement". *Transnational Environmental Law* 9 (1), 165.

Zhou, J., L.M. Dellmuth, K.M. Adams, T.S. Neset & N. von Uexkull, 2020, *The geopolitics of food security: Barriers to the sustainable development goal of zero hunger*. Insights on Peace and Security, No. 11. Stockholm: Stockholm International Peace Research Institute (SIPRI).